THE
TOP
100

THE FASTEST-GROWING CAREERS
FOR THE 21ST CENTURY

Fifth Edition

THE
TOP
100

THE FASTEST-GROWING CAREERS
FOR THE 21ST CENTURY

Fifth Edition

☑ Checkmark Books®
An Infobase Learning Company

The Top 100: The Fastest-Growing Careers for the 21st Century, Fifth Edition

Checkmark Books
An imprint of Infobase Learning
132 West 31st Street
New York NY 10001

Library of Congress Cataloging-in-Publication Data

The top 100 : the fastest growing careers for the 21st century. — 5th ed.
   p. cm.
 Includes index.
 ISBN-13: 978-0-8160-8367-1 (hardcover : alk. paper)
 ISBN-10: 0-8160-8367-3 (hardcover : alk. paper)
 ISBN-13: 978-0-8160-8359-6 (pbk. : alk. paper)
 ISBN-10: 0-8160-8359-2 (pbk. : alk. paper) 1. Occupations—United States—Handbooks, manuals,
etc. 2. Vocational guidance—United States—Handbooks, manuals, etc. I. Ferguson Publishing. II.
Title: Top one hundred.
 HF5382.T59 2011
 331.7020973—dc22
                     2011004455

Checkmark Books are available at special discounts when purchased in bulk quantities for businesses, associations, institutions, or sales promotions. Please call our Special Sales Department in New York at (212) 967-8800 or (800) 322-8755.

You can find Ferguson's on the World Wide Web at http://www.infobaselearning.com

Text design by Mary Susan Ryan-Flynn
Composition by Kerry Casey
Cover printed by Sheridan Books, Ann Arbor, MI
Book printed and bound by Sheridan Books, Ann Arbor, MI
Date printed: June 2011
Printed in the United States of America

10 9 8 7 6 5 4 3 2 1

This book is printed on acid-free paper.

CONTENTS

INTRODUCTION

The world of work today is a fast-changing environment very different from what it was even only a few years ago. New technology of all types, especially computer and Internet technology, has become an important part of nearly every industry. Careers have become more specialized and so has the training and education you will need to get a job and move ahead in your career. Continuing education and training is now a fact of life for those who want to be successful in most occupations. In order to stay competitive, you will need to expand and update your skills continuously through after-work reading, on-the-job training, online courses, and even formal college and vocational courses.

The Top 100: The Fastest Growing Careers for the 21st Century, 5th Edition, presents 100 careers that are projected by the U.S. Department of Labor and a variety of other sources to be the fastest growing careers through 2018. Many of these careers, such as Physician Assistants and Software Engineers, are part of rapidly growing fields such as Health Care Services and Computer Technology. Many other careers—for example, Service Industry careers such as Customer Service Representatives—are "fast growing" because of the sheer number of job openings being created.

You'll discover, as you look at the careers profiled in this book, that we discuss far more than 100 careers. Many of the top 100 careers are further broken down into subspecialties. By knowing about these subspecialties, you will also know how to transfer skills or train for positions in entirely different fields. Because not every fast-growing job can be covered in a single book, the jobs presented here were selected from among the fastest-growing occupations to represent a range of earnings, education, industries, interests, skills, and other requirements.

TRENDS IN THE WORKPLACE

Three trends in the future workplace are important to note: the importance of continuing education, the relationship between years of education and earnings, and the increase in number of technician jobs.

TO STAY AHEAD, PURSUE CONTINUING ED

Advances in technology are moving at a speed few ever thought possible, making training and skills quickly obsolete. Many now realize that they will be left behind and lose the chance for promotion and better jobs if they fail to keep their skills and training as up-to-date as possible. To correct this problem, many workers today supplement their knowledge by attending seminars, completing after-work reading, and participating in on-the-job training. Many workers are returning to college or vocational technical schools to receive advanced training and degrees. According to the Bureau of Labor Statistics (BLS), college graduates enjoy significantly lower unemployment rates (5.2 percent in 2009) than those who have not completed high school (14.6 percent in 2009). This continuing education trend has created another appealing benefit for many workers—better positions and higher pay.

HIT THE BOOKS TO EARN MORE

Job growth is expected for workers from all educational backgrounds, but people with a bachelor's degree or higher typically earn better salaries and enjoy greater chances of promotion and career stability. According to the BLS, those with a bachelor's degree earned average annual salaries of $53,300 in 2009, while those with only a high school diploma earned annual salaries of $32,552.

TECH-TASTIC!

A technician is defined as a highly specialized worker who works with scientists, physicians, engineers, and a variety of other professionals, as well as with clients and customers. The technician can be further defined as a type of middleperson, between the scientist in the laboratory and the worker on the floor; between the physician and the patient; between the engineer and the factory worker. In short, the technician's realm is where the

EDUCATION LEVEL AND ANNUAL EARNINGS, 2009	
Doctoral degree:	$79,664
Professional degree:	$79,508
Master's degree:	$65,364
Bachelor's degree:	$53,300
Associate's degree:	$39,572
Some college, no degree:	$36,348
High-school graduate:	$32,552
Less than a high school diploma:	$23,608
Source: U.S. Department of Labor	

U.S. EMPLOYMENT BY MAJOR OCCUPATIONAL GROUP, 2008

Professional and Related:	31 million
Service:	29.6 million
Office and Administrative Support:	24.1 million
Sales and Related:	16 million
Management, Business, and Financial:	15.7 million
Production:	10.1 million
Transportation and Material Moving:	9.8 million
Construction and Extraction:	7.8 million
Installation, Maintenance, and Repair:	5.8 million
Farming, Fishing, and Forestry:	1 million

Source: U.S. Department of Labor

scientific meets the practical application, where theory meets product.

The number and types of technician careers are growing as we increasingly rely on technology to solve problems and help us perform our daily work; in addition, this technology continues to change almost as fast as it is introduced. Skilled technicians design, implement, operate, and repair these highly complex systems and machinery. As you page through *The Top 100: The Fastest Growing Careers for the 21st Century*, you will see the increasing significance of tech jobs in a variety of fields, but especially in Health Services. Biomedical Equipment Technicians, Cardiovascular Technologists, Medical Laboratory Technicians, and Surveying and Mapping Technicians are but a few of the tech jobs featured in this book.

THE HOTTEST GROWTH FIELDS

Four of the fastest growing career fields are Health Services, Computers and Information Services, Green Careers, and the Service Industry.

HEALTH SERVICES

The health services industry is the largest industry in our economy, with approximately 14 million jobs in 2008. More than 30 percent of the jobs in *The Top 100: The Fastest Growing Careers for the 21st Century* relate to health care services. The BLS reports that Health Services will grow by 22 percent—or 3 million jobs—

by 2018. Many factors are responsible for this rapid growth. One reason is that the American population is aging; the U.S. Census Bureau predicts that the number of Americans age 65 and older will double in the first half of the 21st century, increasing from approximately 35 million in 2000 to approximately 82 million in 2050. As the median age of the American population rises, more people will need various types of specialized medical care.

Another reason for job growth is that increasingly, a variety of high tech equipment will be used to diagnose and treat patients. This new technology will improve the survival rates of seriously ill and injured patients and will require trained specialists of all kinds to operate and repair it. The Home Health Care segment of this field will be exceptionally strong as the population ages—growing by 46 percent through 2016. Another factor that has caused the field to expand is the increasing focus on wellness. Health Maintenance Organizations (HMOs) are increasingly focusing on preventative care and will need trained professionals to monitor patients and administer tests and preventative treatments.

When considering a career in the Health Services, you should note that a number of factors may affect employment growth. Continued industry-wide budget cutting, realignment, downsizing, and mergers may affect growth. In terms of the expanding home care subfield, many predict that Medicare programs will be reduced, forcing Medicare patients to pay for some home care costs themselves. This cutback may reduce demand slightly for professionals in this segment of the industry. HMOs will continue to compete with hospitals, as well as Preferred Provider Organizations, for profits. Most experts predict lucrative opportunities for those employed by HMOs, nursing homes, personal care facilities, and home health agencies. The outlook for hospitals is less positive, but will still offer many employment opportunities. While the overall outlook for Health Services is good, you will need to study the market carefully to find the best Health Services concentrations and careers.

COMPUTERS AND INFORMATION SERVICES

Computers and related technology play an integral role in our society. They are used in almost every field, from the computers Architects use to design buildings, sports stadiums, and skate parks; to those used by Paralegals to research legal information on the Internet; to those used by Medical Record Technicians to keep track of your health records. A grasp of the most basic computer—and Internet—skills is a necessity in almost every field.

Employment for computer and mathematical science professionals will grow by 25 percent through 2016, according to the BLS—or twice as fast as the average for all occupations. Businesses need computer professionals of all types to train their staffs in the latest innovations in technology, to address problems, and to repair and upgrade existing equipment. Furthermore, the cost of computers and related hardware and software has decreased, creating many business opportunities within the home. There is an increased demand for people with data processing, word processing, and desktop publishing skills, as well as people who create the actual systems and software that individuals and businesses use.

Finally, the rapid growth of the Internet—more than 215 million people were online in the United States as of November 2007—has created a wide variety of opportunities—and new jobs—for people with flexible and up-to-date training, such as Computer Support Specialists, Software Designers, and Software Engineers.

It is important to note that employment in the computer industry changes almost as continuously as the evolving technology it is based on. Layoffs, mergers, and downsizing occur all of the time, just like in any other fast-growing industry. The key, as always in the new world of work, is education. Workers who continue to upgrade and expand their skills will prosper in any marketplace. There is also an increasing trend toward hiring those with advanced four-year degrees in computer technology.

GREEN CAREERS

One of today's hottest growth fields is green careers—jobs focused on energy conservation, environmental issues, environmentally friendly products and services, and the development of alternative and renewable energy sources. U.S. clean-energy jobs grew nearly two and a half times faster than traditional jobs nationally between 1998 and 2007, according to a June 2009 report by the Pew Foundation. In California, green jobs grew by 3 percent between 2008 and 2009, to a total of 174,000 jobs, according to Next 10, an independent research firm. The U.S. Bureau of Labor Statistics defines green careers as jobs in businesses that produce goods or provide services that benefit the environment or conserve natural resources, or jobs where workers are responsible for making their organization's production processes more environmentally friendly. In-demand green jobs—such as Environmental Engineers, Environmental Scientists, Environmental Technicians, and Wastewater Treatment Plant Operators and Technicians—are found in science, construction, energy, business, engineering, education, communications, and the law.

SERVICE INDUSTRY

Service-producing industries are expected to generate about 14.5 million new jobs from 2008 to 2018, according to the U.S. Department of Labor. The growing U.S. population and the difficulty of automating many job responsibilities in this industry will create strong demand for workers in the service industry. Many service occupations are resistant to offshoring, a workplace trend in which companies move jobs overseas to countries that pay their workers lower wages than are paid to workers in the United States. Some of the service-oriented careers covered in this book include Customer Service Representatives, Firefighters, Home Health Care Aides, Preschool Teachers, and Social Workers.

HOW TO USE THIS BOOK

The following paragraphs describe the major headings used throughout *The Top 100: The Fastest Growing Careers for the 21st Century.*

EMPLOYMENT GROWTH BY EDUCATION AND TRAINING (Projected 2008–2018)	
First professional degree	18%
Doctoral degree	17%
Master's degree	18%
Work experience plus bachelor's or higher degree	18%
Bachelor's degree	17%
Associate's degree	19%
Postsecondary vocational training	13%
Work experience in a related occupation	8%
Long-term on-the-job training	8%
Moderate-term on-the-job training	8%
Short-term on-the-job training	8%
Source: U.S. Department of Labor	

With each article is a sidebar featuring information on recommended School Subjects, Personal Skills, the Minimum Education Level necessary to work in the field, Certification or Licensing requirements, and Work Conditions.

The **Overview** section of a chapter is a brief introductory description of the duties and responsibilities of someone in this career. Oftentimes, a career may have a variety of job titles. When that is the case, alternate career titles are presented in this section. If available, this section also lists the number of workers currently employed in this field.

The **Job** section describes an average day for a worker in this field, including primary and secondary duties; the types of tools, machinery, or equipment used to perform this job; and other types of workers interacted with on a daily basis. Growing subfields or subspecialties of this career are also discussed in detail.

The **Requirements** section describes the formal educational requirements—from high school diploma to advanced college degree—that are necessary to become employed in the field. This section provides information on how students can receive training if a college degree is not required, via on-the-job training, apprenticeships, the armed forces, or other activities. Explained here are certification, licensing, and continuing-education requirements. Finally, the Requirements section recommends personal qualities that will be helpful to someone working in this field.

In the **Exploring** section, you will find a variety of suggestions for exploring the field—such as periodicals to read, Web sites to visit, summer jobs and programs to check out, volunteer opportunities, associations and clubs to join, and hobbies to explore—before you invest time and money in education and training.

The **Employers** section lists major employers of workers in the field.

The **Starting Out** section offers tips on how to land your first job, be it through newspaper ads, the Internet, college career services offices, or personal contacts, This section explains how the average person finds employment in this field.

The **Advancement** section describes the possible career path and the tools or experience you might need—advanced training or outside education—to move up in the career.

The **Earnings** section lists salary ranges for beginning, mid-range, and experienced workers in this field. Average starting salaries by educational achievement are also listed, when available. Fringe benefits, such as paid vacation and sick days, health insurance, pensions, and profit sharing plans, are covered.

In the **Work Environment** section, you will see what a typical day on the job is like. Is indoor or outdoor work required? Are safety measures and equipment such as protective clothing necessary? Is the job in a quiet office or on a noisy assembly line? What are the standard hours of work? Are overtime and weekend work often required? Is travel frequent? If so, to where, and for how long? This is a good place to gauge your true interest in the field.

The **Outlook** section predicts the potential long-term employment outlook for the field: which areas are growing because of technology and which are in decline. Most of this information is obtained from the Bureau of Labor Statistics. Job growth terms follow those used in the *Occupational Outlook Handbook:* growth much faster than the average means an increase of 21 percent or more; growth faster than the average means an increase of 14 to 20 percent; growth about as fast as the average means an increase of 7 to 13 percent.

In the last section, **For More Information**, you'll find the names, street addresses, phone numbers, e-mail, and Web addresses of a variety of associations, government agencies, or unions that can provide further information regarding educational requirements, accreditation and certification, and other general career information.

IN CONCLUSION

We hope this book will expand your knowledge and help you to make informed career choices. But this is only the beginning of your career discovery. If you find a career that catches your interest, find out more. Contact the associations listed at the end of each article. Ask your friends and family if they know someone in this field you can talk to: an expert, a teacher, or someone who is, at least, very experienced in the field. Or, ask your school counselor to arrange a presentation or interview with a worker in this field. Maybe you can take a tour of a job site to see people actually doing the work you're interested in. You'll be surprised at the response you receive. People like to talk about their work, and by listening to someone describe his or her career, likes and dislikes, and career hopes and dreams, you'll find out more about yourself and your future. Only then will you be able to decide if the career is really for you.

No one can be interested in every one of these careers. Browse through these titles, however, and we guarantee that you'll find at least a few careers that match your talents and interests. You may even discover a career that you never knew existed. It's important to note that what is hot today may be only lukewarm tomorrow. That is why your career education must never stop. To survive in this challenging new world of work you will constantly need to analyze the changing marketplace and continue to expand and improve upon your training and skills. That is the only way to guarantee that you will find and keep a good job.

The Editors

ACCOUNTANTS AND AUDITORS

OVERVIEW

Accountants compile, analyze, verify, and prepare financial records, including profit and loss statements, balance sheets, cost studies, and tax reports. Accountants may specialize in areas such as auditing, tax work, cost accounting, budgeting and control, or systems and procedures. Accountants also may specialize in a particular business or field; for example, *agricultural accountants* specialize in drawing up and analyzing financial statements for farmers and for farm equipment companies. *Auditors* examine and verify financial records to ensure that they are accurate, complete, and in compliance with federal laws. There are approximately 1.1 million accountants and auditors employed in the United States.

THE JOB

Accountants' duties depend on the size and nature of the company in which they are employed. The major fields of employment are public, private, and government accounting.

Public accountants work independently on a fee basis or as members of an accounting firm. They perform a variety of tasks for businesses or individuals, including auditing accounts and records, preparing and certifying financial statements, conducting financial investigations and furnishing testimony in legal matters, and assisting in formulating budget policies and procedures.

Private accountants, sometimes called *industrial* or *management accountants,* handle financial records of the firms at which they are employed.

Government accountants work on the financial records of government agencies or, when necessary, they audit the records of private companies. In the federal government, many accountants are employed as *bank examiners, Internal Revenue Service agents and investigators,* as well as in regular accounting positions.

Within these fields, accountants can specialize in a variety of areas.

General accountants supervise, install, and devise general accounting, budget, and cost systems. They maintain records, balance books, and prepare and analyze statements on all financial aspects of business. Administrative officers use this information to make sound business decisions.

SCHOOL SUBJECTS
Business, Economics

PERSONAL SKILLS
Following instructions, Leadership/management

MINIMUM EDUCATION LEVEL
Bachelor's degree

CERTIFICATION OR LICENSING
Recommended

WORK ENVIRONMENT
Primarily indoors, One location with some travel

Budget accountants review expenditures of departments within a firm to make sure expenses allotted are not exceeded. They also aid in drafting budgets and may devise and install budget control systems.

Cost accountants determine unit costs of products or services by analyzing records and depreciation data. They classify and record all operating costs so that management can control expenditures.

Property accountants keep records of equipment, buildings, and other property owned or leased by a company. They prepare mortgage schedules and payments as well as appreciation or depreciation statements, which are used for income tax purposes.

Environmental accountants help utilities, manufacturers, and chemical companies set up preventive systems to ensure environmental compliance and provide assistance in the event that legal issues arise.

Systems accountants design and set up special accounting systems for organizations whose needs cannot be handled by standardized procedures. This may involve installing automated or computerized accounting processes and includes instructing personnel in the new methods.

Forensic accountants and auditors lend their knowledge of accounting principles and law to determine the legality of financial activities, especially in cases of white-collar crime. Forensic accountants and auditors work closely with lawyers and law enforcement officials and may be called upon as witnesses in trials.

Tax accountants prepare federal, state, or local tax returns of an individual, business, or corporation according to prescribed rates, laws, and regulations. They also may conduct research on the effects of taxes on firm operations and recommend changes to reduce taxes. This is one of the most intricate fields of accounting, and many accountants therefore specialize in one area such as corporate, individual income, or property tax.

Assurance accountants help improve the quality of information for clients in assurance services areas such as electronic commerce, risk assessment, and elder care. This information may be financial or nonfinancial in nature.

Auditors ensure that financial records are accurate, complete, and in compliance with federal laws. To do so they review items in original entry books, including purchase orders, tax returns, billing statements, and other important documents. Auditors may also prepare financial statements for clients and suggest ways to improve productivity and profits. *Internal auditors* conduct the same kind of examination and evaluation for one particular company. Because they are salaried employees of that company, their financial audits must be certified by a qualified independent auditor. Internal auditors also review procedures and controls, appraise the efficiency and effectiveness of operations, and make sure their companies comply with corporate policies and government regulations.

Tax auditors review financial records and other information provided by taxpayers to determine the appropriate tax liability. State and federal tax auditors usually work in government offices, but they may perform a field audit in a taxpayer's home or office.

Revenue agents are employed by the federal government to examine selected income tax returns and, when necessary, conduct field audits and investigations to verify the information reported and adjust the tax liability accordingly.

Chief bank examiners enforce good banking practices throughout a state. They schedule bank examinations to ensure that financial institutions comply with state laws and, in certain cases, they take steps to protect a bank's solvency and the interests of its depositors and shareholders.

REQUIREMENTS
High School

If you are interested in an accounting career, take a strong math and business course load in high school. In particular, you must be very proficient in arithmetic and basic algebra. Familiarity with computers and their applications is equally important. Course work in English and communications will also be beneficial.

Postsecondary Training

Postsecondary training in accounting may be obtained in a wide variety of institutions such as private business schools, junior colleges, universities, and correspondence schools. A bachelor's degree with a major in accounting, or a related field such as economics, is highly recommended by professional associations for those entering the field and is required by all states before taking the licensing exam. A four-year college curriculum usually includes about two years of liberal arts courses, a year of general business subjects, and a year of specific accounting work. Although it is possible to become a successful accountant by completing a program at any of the above-mentioned institutions, better positions, particularly in public accounting, require a bachelor's degree with a major in accounting. Large public accounting firms often prefer people with a master's degree in accounting. For beginning positions in accounting, the federal government requires four years of college (including 24 semester hours in accounting or auditing) or an equivalent combination of education and experience.

Certification or Licensing

Certified public accountants (CPAs) must pass a qualifying examination and hold a certificate issued by the state in which they wish to practice. In most states, a college degree is required for admission to the CPA examinations; a few states allow candidates to substitute years of public accounting experience for the college degree requirement. Currently 46 states and the District of Columbia require CPA candidates to have 150 hours of education, which is an additional 30 hours beyond the standard bachelor's degree. These criteria can be met by combining an undergraduate accounting program with graduate study or participating in an integrated five-year professional accounting program. You can obtain information from a state board of accountancy or check out the Web site of the American Institute of Certified Public Accountants (AICPA) to read about new regulations and review last year's exam.

The Uniform CPA Examination administered by the AICPA is used by all states. Nearly all states require at least two years of public accounting experience or its equivalent before a CPA certificate can be earned.

The AICPA offers additional credentialing programs (involving a test and additional requirements) for members with valid CPA certificates. These designations include accredited in business valuation (ABV), certified information technology professional (CITP), and personal financial specialist (PFS). These credentials indicate that a CPA has developed skills in nontraditional areas in which accountants are starting to play larger roles.

Some accountants seek out other credentials. Those who have earned a bachelor's degree, pass a four-part examination, agree to meet continuing education requirements, have at least two years of experience in management accounting, and comply with standards of professional conduct may become a certified management accountant (CMA) through the Institute of Management Accountants.

The Accreditation Council for Accountancy and Taxation confers the following four designations: accredited business accountant (ABA), accredited tax preparer (ATP), accredited tax advisor (ATA), and accredited retirement advisor (ARA).

To become a certified internal auditor (CIA), college graduates with two years of experience in internal auditing must pass a four-part examination given by the Institute of Internal Auditors (IIA). The IIA also offers the specialty certifications certified government auditing professional (CGAP) and certified financial services auditor (CFSA), as well as the certification in control self-assessment (CCSA) to those who pass the exams and meet educational and experience requirements. Visit the IIA Web site for more information.

The designation certified information systems auditor (CISA) is conferred by the Information Systems Audit and Control Association to candidates who pass an examination and who have five years of experience auditing electronic data processing systems.

Other organizations, such as the Bank Administration Institute, confer specialized auditing designations.

Other Requirements

To be a successful accountant you will need strong mathematical, analytical, and problem-solving skills. You need to be able to think logically and to interpret facts and figures accurately. Effective oral and written communication skills are essential in working with both clients and management.

Other important skills are attentiveness to detail, patience, and industriousness. Business acumen and the ability to generate clientele are crucial to service-oriented businesses, as are honesty, dedication, and a respect for the work of others.

EXPLORING

If you think a career as an accountant or auditor might be for you, try working in a retail business, either part time or during the summer. Working at the cash register or even pricing products as a stockperson is good introductory experience. You should also consider working as a treasurer for a student organization requiring financial planning and money management. It may be possible to gain some experience by volunteering with local groups such as churches and small businesses. You should also stay abreast of news in the field by reading trade magazines and checking out the industry Web sites of the AICPA and other accounting associations. The AICPA has numerous free educational publications available.

EMPLOYERS

More than 1.1 million people are employed as accountants and auditors. Accountants and auditors work throughout private industry and government. About one quarter work for accounting, auditing, and bookkeeping firms. Approximately 8 percent are self-employed. A large percentage of all accountants and auditors are certified.

STARTING OUT

Junior public accountants usually start in jobs with routine duties such as counting cash, verifying calculations, and other detailed numerical work. In private accounting, beginners are likely to start as cost accountants and junior internal auditors. They may also enter in clerical positions as cost clerks, ledger clerks, and timekeepers or as trainees in technical or junior executive positions. In the federal government, most beginners are hired as trainees at the GS-5 level after passing the civil service exam.

Some state CPA societies arrange internships for accounting majors, and some offer scholarships and loan programs.

You might also visit the Career Resources section (http://www.aicpa.org/Career/Pages/Career.aspx) of the AICPA Web site. It has detailed information on accounting careers, hiring trends, job search strategies, resumes and cover letters, and job interviews.

ADVANCEMENT

Talented accountants and auditors can advance quickly. Junior public accountants usually advance to senior positions within several years and to managerial positions soon after. Those successful in dealing with top-level management may eventually become supervisors, managers, and partners in larger firms or go into independent practice. Only a small percentage of new hires advance to audit manager, tax manager, or partner.

Private accountants in firms may become audit managers, tax managers, cost accounting managers, or controllers, depending on their specialty. Some become controllers, treasurers, or corporation presidents. Others on the finance side may rise to become managers of financial planning and analysis or treasurers. There are healthy opportunities for mobility among the various parts of this field, but it is more likely for public accountants to move into management accounting or internal auditing than vice versa.

Federal government trainees are usually promoted within a year or two. Advancement to controller and to higher administrative positions is ultimately possible.

Although advancement may be rapid for skilled accountants, especially in public accounting, those with inadequate academic or professional training are often assigned to routine jobs and find it difficult to obtain promotions. All accountants find it necessary to continue their study of accounting and related areas in their spare time. Even those who have already obtained college degrees, gained experience, and earned a CPA certificate may spend many hours studying to keep up with new industry developments. Thousands of practicing accountants enroll in formal courses offered by universities and professional associations to specialize in certain areas of accounting, broaden or update their professional skills, and become eligible for advancement and promotion.

EARNINGS

Beginning salaries for accountants with a bachelor's degree averaged $48,993 a year in 2009; those with a master's degree averaged $49,786 a year, according to the National Association of Colleges and Employers.

According to the U.S. Department of Labor, accountants and auditors had median annual earnings of $60,340 in 2009. The lowest paid 10 percent earned less than $37,690, and the highest paid 10 percent earned more than $104,450. Median annual salaries were highest ($73,920) for accountants and auditors working in accounting, tax preparation, bookkeeping, and payroll services, while those working in state government saw the lowest median annual salaries ($54,040). Although government accountants and auditors make less than those in other areas, they do receive more benefits.

WORK ENVIRONMENT

Accounting is known as a desk job, and a 40-hour (or longer) workweek can be expected in public and private accounting. Although computer work is replacing paperwork, the job can be routine and monotonous,

and concentration and attention to detail are critical. Public accountants experience considerable pressure during the tax period, which runs from November to April, and they may have to work long hours. There is potential for stress aside from tax season, as accountants can be responsible for managing multimillion-dollar finances with no margin for error. Self-employed accountants and those working for a small firm can expect to work longer hours; 40 percent work more than 50 hours per week, compared to 20 percent of public and private accountants.

In smaller firms, most of the public accountant's work is performed in the client's office. A considerable amount of travel is often necessary to service a wide variety of businesses. In a larger firm, however, an accountant may have very little client contact, spending more time interacting with the accounting team.

OUTLOOK

Employment of accountants and auditors is expected to grow much faster than average through 2018, according to the U.S. Department of Labor. This is due to business growth, changing tax and finance laws, and increased scrutiny of financial practices across all businesses. The last decade saw several notable scandals in the accounting industry, and this accounts for much of the increased scrutiny and changing legislation in this industry.

As firms specialize their services, accountants will need to follow suit. Firms will seek out accountants with experience in marketing and proficiency in computer systems to build management consulting practices. As trade increases, so will the demand for CPAs with international specialties and foreign language skills. CPAs with an engineering degree would be well equipped to specialize in environmental accounting. Other accounting specialties that will enjoy good prospects include assurance, forensic, and tax accounting.

This industry is also trending toward international financial reporting standards (IFRS), which uses a judgment-based system to determine the fair-market value of assets and liabilities. This should increase demand for accountants and auditors because of their specialized expertise.

The number of CPAs has dropped off a bit since states have embraced the 150-hour standard for CPA education. Numbers are once again starting to rise, however, as students realize the many opportunities this industry holds, especially in the wake of recent accounting scandals. CPAs with valid licenses should experience favorable job prospects for the foreseeable future. Pursuing advanced degrees and certifications will also greatly increase one's chances of finding employment.

Accounting jobs are more secure than most during economic downswings. Despite fluctuations in the nation's economy, there will always be a need to manage financial information, especially as the number, size, and complexity of business transactions increases. However, competition for jobs will remain, certification requirements will become more rigorous, and accountants and auditors with the highest degrees will be the most competitive.

FOR MORE INFORMATION

For information on accreditation and testing, contact
Accreditation Council for Accountancy and Taxation
1010 North Fairfax Street
Alexandria, VA 22314-1574
Tel: 888-289-7763
E-mail: info@acatcredentials.org
http://www.acatcredentials.org

For information on the Uniform CPA Examination and student membership, contact
American Institute of Certified Public Accountants
1211 Avenue of the Americas
New York, NY 10036-8775
Tel: 212-596-6200
http://www.aicpa.org

For information on accredited programs in accounting, contact
Association to Advance Collegiate Schools of Business
777 South Harbour Island Boulevard, Suite 750
Tampa, FL 33602-5730
Tel: 813-769-6500
http://www.aacsb.edu

For information on certification for bank auditors, contact
Bank Administration Institute
115 South LaSalle Street, Suite 3300
Chicago, IL 60603-3801
Tel: 800-375-5543
E-mail: info@bai.org
http://www.bai.org

For more information on women in accounting, contact
Educational Foundation for Women in Accounting
136 South Keowee Street
Dayton, OH 45402-2241
Tel: 937-424-3391

E-mail: info@efwa.org
http://www.efwa.org

For information on certification, contact
Information Systems Audit and Control Association and Foundation
3701 Algonquin Road, Suite 1010
Rolling Meadows, IL 60008-3124
Tel: 847-253-1545
http://www.isaca.org

For information on internal auditing and certification, contact
Institute of Internal Auditors
247 Maitland Avenue
Altamonte Springs, FL 32701-4201
Tel: 407-937-1100
http://www.theiia.org

For information about management accounting and the CMA designation, as well as student membership, contact
Institute of Management Accountants
10 Paragon Drive, Suite 1
Montvale, NJ 07645-1760
Tel: 800-638-4427
E-mail: ima@imanet.org
http://www.imanet.org

ACTUARIES

OVERVIEW

Actuaries use statistical formulas and techniques to calculate the probability of events such as death, disability, sickness, unemployment, retirement, and property loss. Actuaries develop formulas to predict how much money an insurance company will pay in claims, which determines the overall cost of insuring a group, business, or individual. Increase in risk raises potential cost to the company, which, in turn, raises its rates. Actuaries analyze risk to estimate the number and amount of claims an insurance company will have to pay. They assess the cost of running the business and incorporate the results into the design and evaluation of programs.

Casualty actuaries specialize in property and liability insurance, *life actuaries* in health and life insurance. In recent years, there has been an increase in the number of actuaries—called *pension actuaries*—who deal only with

SCHOOL SUBJECTS

Business, Mathematics

PERSONAL SKILLS

Following instructions, Leadership/management

MINIMUM EDUCATION LEVEL

Bachelor's degree

CERTIFICATION OR LICENSING

Required

WORK ENVIRONMENT

Primarily indoors, One location with some travel

pension plans. The total number of actuaries employed in the United States is approximately 17,940.

THE JOB

Should smokers pay more for their health insurance? Should younger drivers pay higher car insurance premiums? Actuaries answer questions like these to ensure that insurance and pension organizations can pay their claims and maintain a profitable business.

Using their knowledge of mathematics, probability, statistics, and principles of finance and business, actuaries determine premium rates and the various benefits of insurance plans. To accomplish this task, they first assemble and analyze statistics on birth, death, marriage, parenthood, employment, and other pertinent facts and figures. Based on this information, they are able to develop mathematical models of rates of death, accident, sickness, disability, or retirement and then construct tables regarding the probability of such things as property loss from fire, theft, accident, or natural disaster. After calculating all probabilities and the resulting costs to the company, the actuaries can determine the premium rates to allow insurance companies to cover predicted losses, turn a profit, and remain competitive with other businesses.

For example, based on analyses, actuaries are able to determine how many of each 1,000 people 21 years of age are expected to survive to age 65. They can calculate how many of them are expected to die this year or how many are expected to live until age 85. The probability that an insured person may die during the period before reaching 65 is a risk to the company. The actuaries must

figure a price for the premium that will cover all claims and expenses as they occur and still earn a profit for the company assuming the risk. In the same way, actuaries calculate premium rates and determine policy provisions for every type of insurance coverage.

Employment opportunities span across the variety of different types of insurance companies, including life, health, accident, automobile, fire, or workers' compensation organizations. Most actuaries specialize either as casualty actuaries, dealing with property and liability insurance, or as life actuaries, working with life and health insurance. In addition, actuaries may concentrate on pension plan programs sponsored and administered by various levels of government, private business, or fraternal or benevolent associations.

Actuaries work in many departments in insurance companies, including underwriting, group insurance, investment, pension, sales, and service. In addition to their own company's business, they analyze characteristics of the insurance business as a whole. They study general economic and social trends as well as legislative, health, and other developments, all of which may affect insurance practices. With this broad knowledge, some actuaries reach executive positions, where they can influence and help determine company policy and develop new lines of business. *Actuary executives* may communicate with government officials, company executives, policyholders, or the public to explain complex technical matters. They may testify before public agencies regarding proposed legislation that has a bearing on the insurance business, for example, or they may explain proposed changes in premium rates or contract provisions.

Some actuaries are employed in financial services, helping to manage credit and to set a price for corporate securities. In this capacity they may help shape an organization's risk-management policies and serve as advisers to corporate executives, shareholders, and the general public.

Actuaries may also work with a consulting firm, providing advice to clients including insurance companies, corporations, hospitals, labor unions, and government agencies. They develop employee benefits, calculating future benefits and employer contributions, and set up pension and welfare plans. *Consulting actuaries* also advise health care and financial services firms, and they may work with small insurance companies lacking an actuarial department.

Since the government regulates the insurance industry and administers laws on pensions, it also requires the services of actuaries to determine whether companies are complying with the law. A small number of actuaries are employed by the federal government and deal with Social Security, Medicare, disability and life insurance, and pension plans for veterans, members of the armed forces, and federal employees. Those in state governments may supervise and regulate insurance companies, oversee the operations of state retirement or pension systems, and manage problems related to unemployment insurance and workers' compensation.

REQUIREMENTS

High School

If you are interested in this field, you should pursue a traditional college preparatory curriculum including mathematical and computer science classes and also take advantage of advanced courses such as calculus. Introductory business, economics, accounting, and finance courses are important, as is English to develop your oral and written skills.

Postsecondary Training

A bachelor's degree with a major in actuarial science, mathematics, or statistics is highly recommended for entry into the industry. Courses in elementary and advanced algebra, differential and integral calculus, descriptive and analytical statistics, principles of mathematical statistics, probability, and numerical analysis are all important. Computer science is also a vital part of actuarial training. Employers are increasingly hiring graduates with majors in economics, business, and engineering who have a strong math background. College students should broaden their education to include business, economics, and finance, as well as English and communications. Because actuarial work revolves around social and political issues, course work in the humanities and social sciences will also prove useful.

Certification or Licensing

Actuaries must be licensed by either the Society of Actuaries (SOA) or Casualty Actuarial Society (CAS). Full professional status in an actuarial specialty is based on completing a series of nine to 10 examinations, depending on the specialty. SOA certifies actuaries in the fields of life insurance, health benefits systems, retirement systems, and finance and investment. CAS gives a series of examinations in the property and casualty field, which includes automobile, homeowners, medical malpractice, workers compensation, and personal injury liability. Success is based on both formal and on-the-job training.

Actuaries can become associate members of SOA after successfully completing five initial exams; course work in applied statistics, corporate finance, and economics; eight computer modules with two subsequent essays; and a seminar in professionalism. This process generally takes from four to eight years. Similarly, they can reach associate status in the CAS after completing seven exams, attending one course on professionalism, and completing the same course work required by SOA. Actuaries who successfully complete the entire series of exams for either organization are granted full membership and become fellows.

The American Society of Pension Professionals and Actuaries also offers several different designations (both actuarial and nonactuarial) to individuals who pass the required examinations in the pension field and have the appropriate work experience.

Consulting pension actuaries who service private pension plans must be enrolled and licensed by the Joint Board for the Enrollment of Actuaries (http://www.irs.gov/tax pros/actuaries/index.html), a U.S. government agency. Only these actuaries can work with pension plans set up under the Employee Retirement Income Security Act. To be accepted, applicants must meet certain professional and educational requirements stipulated by the Joint Board.

Completion of the entire series of exams may take from five to 10 years. Because the first exams offered by these various boards and societies cover core material (such as calculus, linear algebra, probability and statistics, risk theory, and actuarial math), students generally wait to commit to a specialty until they have taken the initial tests. Students pursuing a career as an actuary should complete the first two or three preliminary examinations while still in college, since these tests cover subjects usually taught in school; the more advanced examinations cover aspects of the profession itself.

Employers prefer to hire individuals who have already passed the first two exams. Once employed, companies generally give employees time during the workday to study. They may also pay exam fees, provide study materials, and award raises upon an employee's successful completion of an exam.

Other Requirements

An aptitude in mathematics, statistics, and computer science is a must to become a successful actuary, as are sound analytical and problem-solving skills. Solid oral and written communication skills are also required in order to be able to explain and interpret complex work to the client, as is skill with programming languages such as Visual Basic for Applications, SAS, and SQL.

Prospective actuaries should also have an inquisitive mind with an interest in historical, social, and political issues and trends. You should have a general feel for the business world and be able to assimilate a wide range of complex information in order to see the "big picture" when planning policies. Actuaries like to solve problems; they are strategists who enjoy and generally excel at games such as chess. Actuaries need to be motivated and self-disciplined to concentrate on detailed work, especially under stress, and to undertake the rigorous study for licensing examinations.

EXPLORING

If you think you are interested in the actuarial field, try pursuing extracurricular opportunities that allow you to practice strategic thinking and problem-solving skills; these may include chess, math, or investment clubs at your school. Other activities that foster leadership and management, such as student council positions, will also be beneficial. Any kind of business or research-oriented summer or part-time experience will be valuable, especially with an accounting or law firm.

There are more than 45 local actuarial clubs and regional affiliates throughout the United States that offer opportunities for informal discussion and networking. Talk with people in the field to better understand the nature of the work, and use associations' resources to learn more about the field. For example, the Society of Actuaries offers free educational publications.

College undergraduates can take advantage of summer internships and employment in insurance companies and consulting firms. Students will have the chance to rotate among jobs to learn various actuarial operations and different phases of insurance work.

EMPLOYERS

There are approximately 17,940 actuaries employed in the United States, and more than 50 percent work in the insurance industry. Other actuaries work for financial service–providing firms including commercial banks, investment banks, and retirement funds. Others are employed by actuarial consulting services and in academia. Some actuaries are self-employed.

STARTING OUT

The best way to enter this field is by taking the necessary beginning examinations while still in college. Once students have graduated and passed these exams, they are in a very good position to apply for entry-level jobs in the field and can command higher starting salaries. Some college students organize interviews and find jobs through their college placement office, while others interview with firms recruiting on campus. Many firms offer summer and year-round actuarial training programs or internships that may result in a full-time job.

Beginning actuaries may prepare calculations for actuarial tables or work with policy settlements or funds. With experience, they may prepare correspondence, reports, and research. Beginners who have already passed the preliminary exams often start with more responsibility and higher pay.

ADVANCEMENT

Advancement within the profession to assistant, associate, or chief actuary greatly depends on the individual's on-the-job performance, competence on the actuarial examinations, and leadership capabilities.

Some actuaries qualify for administrative positions in underwriting, accounting, or investment because of their broad business knowledge and specific insurance experience. Because their judgment is so valuable, actuaries may advance to administrative or executive positions, such as head of a department, vice president or president of a company, manager of an insurance rating bureau, partner in a consulting firm, or, possibly, state insurance commissioner. Actuaries with management skills and a strong business background may move into other areas such as marketing, advertising, and planning.

EARNINGS

Starting salaries for actuaries with bachelor's degrees in actuarial science averaged $56,320 in 2009, according to a survey conducted by the National Association of Colleges and Employers. New college graduates who have not passed any actuarial examinations earn slightly less. Insurance companies and consulting firms offer merit increases or bonuses to those who pass examinations.

The U.S. Department of Labor reports that actuaries earned a median annual salary of $87,210 in 2009. Ten percent earned less than $51,950, while the top 10 percent earned more than $158,240. Actuaries working for insurance companies receive paid vacations, health and life insurance, pension plans, and other fringe benefits.

WORK ENVIRONMENT

Actuaries spend much of their 40-hour workweek behind a desk poring over facts and figures, although some travel to various units of the organization or to other businesses. This is especially true of the consulting actuary, who will most likely work longer hours and travel more. Consulting actuaries tend to have more diverse work and more personal interaction in working with a variety of clients. Though the work can be stressful and demands intense concentration and attention to detail, actuaries find their jobs to be rewarding and satisfying and feel that they make a direct and positive impact on people's lives.

OUTLOOK

The U.S. Department of Labor predicts much faster than average growth for the actuary field through 2018. Growth of the insurance industry—traditionally the leading employer of actuaries—is expected to continue at a stable pace, with many new fields such as annuities and terrorism-related property-risk analysis, compensating for the shrinking life insurance industry. The field's stringent entrance requirements and competition for entry-level jobs will also continue to restrict the number of candidates for jobs.

The insurance industry continues to evolve, and actuaries will be in demand to establish rates in several new areas of coverage, including prepaid legal, dental, and kidnapping insurance. In many cases, actuarial data that have been supplied by rating bureaus are now being developed in new actuarial departments created in companies affected by states' new competitive rating laws. Other new areas of insurance coverage that will involve actuaries include product and pollution liability insurance as well as greater workers' compensation and medical malpractice coverage. Insurers will call on actuaries to help them respond to new state and federal regulations while cutting costs, especially in the areas of pension reform and no-fault automobile insurance. In the future, actuaries will also be employed by noninsurance businesses or will work in business- and investment-related fields. Some are already working in banking and finance.

Actuaries will be needed to assess the financial impact of issues such as AIDS, terrorism, and the changing health care system. As demographics change, people live and work longer, and as medicine advances, actuaries will need to reexamine the probabilities of death, sickness, and retirement.

Casualty actuaries will find more work as companies find themselves held responsible for product liability. In the wake of recent environmental disasters, there will also be a growing need to evaluate environmental risk.

As business goes global, it presents a whole new set of risks and problems as economies develop and new markets emerge. As private enterprise expands in the former Soviet Union, how does a company determine the risk of opening, say, a department store in Moscow?

Actuaries are no longer just mathematical experts. With their unique combination of analytical and business skills, their role is expanding as they become broad-based business professionals solving social as well as financial problems.

FOR MORE INFORMATION

For general information about actuary careers, contact

American Academy of Actuaries
1850 M Street, NW, Suite 300
Washington, DC 20036-5805
Tel: 202-223-8196
http://www.actuary.org

For information about continuing education and professional designations, contact

American Society of Pension Professionals and Actuaries
4245 North Fairfax Drive, Suite 750
Arlington, VA 22203-1648
Tel: 703-516-9300
E-mail: asppa@asppa.org
http://www.asppa.org

The "Be An Actuary" section of the CAS Web site offers comprehensive information on the career of actuary.

Casualty Actuarial Society (CAS)
4350 North Fairfax Drive, Suite 250
Arlington, VA 22203-1695
Tel: 703-276-3100
http://www.casact.org

For information about continuing education and professional designations, contact

Society of Actuaries
475 North Martingale Road, Suite 600
Schaumburg, IL 60173-2252
Tel: 847-706-3500
http://www.soa.org

AEROBICS INSTRUCTORS AND FITNESS TRAINERS

OVERVIEW

Aerobics instructors choreograph and teach aerobics classes of varying types. Classes are geared toward people with general good health as well as to specialized populations, including the elderly and those with specific health

SCHOOL SUBJECTS

Health, Physical Education, Theater/Dance

PERSONAL SKILLS

Helping/teaching, Leadership/management

MINIMUM EDUCATION LEVEL

High school diploma

CERTIFICATION OR LICENSING

Required for certain positions

WORK ENVIRONMENT

Primarily indoors, Primarily one location

problems that affect their ability to exercise. Many people enjoy participating in the lively exercise routines set to music.

Depending on where they are employed, fitness trainers help devise health conditioning programs for clients, from professional athletes to average individuals looking for guidance. Fitness trainers motivate clients to follow prescribed exercise programs and monitor their progress. When injuries occur, either during training or sporting events, fitness trainers determine the extent of the injury and administer first aid for minor problems such as blisters, bruises, and scrapes. Following more serious injury, trainers may work with a physical therapist to help the athlete perform rehabilitative exercises.

There are approximately 228,170 aerobics instructors and fitness trainers employed in the United States.

THE JOB

Three general levels of aerobics classes are recognized today: low impact, moderate, and high intensity. A typical class starts with warm-up exercises (slow stretching movements to loosen up muscles), followed by 35 to 40 minutes of nonstop activity to raise the heart rate, then ends with a cool-down period of stretching and slower movements. Instructors teach class members to monitor their heart rates and listen to their bodies for signs of personal progress.

Aerobics instructors prepare activities prior to their classes. They choose exercises to work different muscles and music to accompany these movements during each phase of the program. Generally, instructors use upbeat music for the more intense exercise portion and more

soothing music for the cool-down period. Instructors demonstrate each step of a sequence until the class can follow along. Additional sequences are added continuously as the class progresses, comprising a longer routine that is set to music. Most classes are structured so that new participants can start any given class. The instructor either faces the rest of the room or faces a mirror in order to observe class progress and ensure that participants do exercises correctly. Many aerobics instructors also lead toning and shaping classes. In these classes, the emphasis is not on aerobic activity but on working particular areas of the body. An instructor begins the class with a brief aerobic period followed by stretching and weight-bearing exercises that loosen and work major muscle groups.

In a health club, fitness trainers evaluate their clients' fitness level with physical examinations and fitness tests. Using various pieces of testing equipment, they determine such things as percentage of body fat and optimal heart and pulse rates. Clients fill out questionnaires about their medical background, general fitness level, and fitness goals. Fitness trainers use this information to design a customized workout plan using weights and other exercise options such as swimming and running to help clients meet these goals. Trainers also advise clients on weight control, diet, and general health. Some fitness trainers also work at the client's home or office. This convenient way of staying physically fit meets the needs of many busy, active adults today.

To start a client's exercise program, the trainer often demonstrates the proper use of weight-lifting equipment to reduce the chance of injury, especially if the client is a beginner. As the client uses the equipment, the trainer observes and corrects any problems before injury occurs. Preventing injury is extremely important. It is good idea for trainers to carry liability insurance to protect themselves should anything beyond their control happen with a client.

Fitness trainers also use exercise tape to wrap weak or injured hands, feet, or other parts of the body. The heavy-duty tape helps strengthen and position the joint to prevent further injury or strain. Fitness trainers also help athletes with therapy or rehabilitation, using special braces or other equipment to support or protect the injured part until it heals. Trainers ensure that the athlete does not overuse a weak joint or muscle, risking further damage.

REQUIREMENTS
High School

Aerobics instructors and fitness trainers should hold a high school diploma. If you are interested in a fitness career, take courses in physical education, biology, and anatomy. In addition, be involved in sports, weight lifting, or dance activities to stay fit and learn to appreciate the value of exercise.

Postsecondary Training

Although it isn't always necessary, a college degree will make you more marketable in the fitness field. Typically, aerobics instructors do not need a college education to qualify for jobs; however, some employers may be more interested in candidates with a balance of ability and education.

Fitness trainers are usually required to have a bachelor's degree from an accredited athletic training program or a related program in physical education or health. These programs often require extensive internships that can range from 500 to 1,800 hours of hands-on experience. Essential college-level courses include anatomy, biomechanics, chemistry, first aid, health, kinesiology, nutrition, physics, physiology, psychology, and safety.

Tony Hinsberger, owner of Summit Fitness Personal Training, highly recommends getting a college degree in physiology, kinesiology, exercise science, or athletic training. "As an owner of a small personal training firm, I hire trainers," he says. "If I had to make a choice between equally experienced and qualified candidates, I would pick the one with a degree." Managers of health clubs often are required to have a bachelor's degree.

Certification or Licensing

Most serious fitness trainers and aerobics instructors become certified. Certification is not required in most states, but most clients and fitness companies expect these professionals to have credentials to prove their worth.

As a current employer of fitness professionals, Hinsberger recommends certification. "I only hire certified trainers," he says. "Most facilities require certification and there are many, many certifying agencies. Certification is also required by most liability insurance plans."

Certifying agencies include the following: Aerobics and Fitness Association of America, American College of Sports Medicine, American Council on Exercise, and National Academy of Sports Medicine. Aerobics instructors should also be certified in cardiopulmonary resuscitation (CPR) before finding a job.

The National Athletic Trainers' Association and the Board of Certification certify fitness trainers who have graduated from accredited college programs or have completed the necessary internship following a degree in a related field. Fitness trainers who seek certification generally also need Red Cross certification in CPR or as an emergency medical technician (EMT).

Whichever career path they follow, aerobics instructors and fitness trainers are expected to keep up-to-date with their fields, becoming thoroughly familiar with the latest knowledge and safety practices. They must take continuing education courses and participate in seminars to keep their certification current.

Other Requirements

Aerobics instructors and fitness trainers are expected to be physically fit, but are not expected to be specimens of human perfection. For example, members of an aerobics class geared to overweight people might feel more comfortable with a heavier instructor; a class geared toward the elderly may benefit from an older instructor.

Anyone who works in this field needs to have strong people skills. Fitness trainers, especially, also need to be talented salespeople, as training sessions are often sold in add-on packages that are not covered by the normal health club fees. A member may receive several free sessions, but it is up to the trainer to convince the member to purchase additional sessions.

EXPLORING

A visit to a health club, park district, or YMCA aerobics class is a good way to observe the work of fitness trainers and aerobics instructors. Part-time or summer jobs are sometimes available for high school students in these facilities. It may also be possible to volunteer in a senior citizen center where aerobics classes are offered.

"To explore this [career] path, I recommend working part time in a gym or fitness facility," Tony Hinsberger suggests. "Some clubs have an orientation position. People in this job take new members on a tour of the facility and show new members how to use the equipment safely. It typically doesn't require a degree, only on-site training."

If possible, enroll in an aerobics class or train with a fitness trainer to experience firsthand what their jobs entail and to see what makes a good instructor. Brett Vicknair agrees: "I would encourage someone wanting to pursue a career as a personal trainer to get involved with working out first, maybe at a local fitness center, and take advantage of any help that is usually offered when someone first becomes a member."

Aerobics instructor workshops are taught to help prospective instructors gain experience. These are usually offered in adult education courses at such places as the YMCA. Unpaid apprenticeships are also a good way for future instructors to obtain supervised experience before teaching classes on their own. The facility may allow prospective aerobics instructors to take their training class for free if there is a possibility that they will work there in the future.

Opportunities for student fitness trainers are available in schools with fitness trainers on staff. This is an excellent way for students to observe and assist a professional fitness trainer on an ongoing basis.

EMPLOYERS

Most aerobics instructors work for fitness centers and gymnasiums. Most employers are for-profit businesses, but some are community based, such as the YMCA or a family center. Other job possibilities can be found in corporate fitness centers, colleges, retirement centers, and resorts. In 2008, nearly 40 percent of aerobics instructors and fitness trainers worked part time.

Some fitness trainers work in more than one facility. Others are self-employed and take clients on an appointment basis, working either in personal homes or in a public gym. Some fitness trainers will work with high-profile athletes on a one-on-one basis to meet specific fitness requirements.

"Trainers work in gyms or fitness centers, in private personal fitness centers where members are seen on an appointment basis only, and in country clubs, just to name some of the opportunities," Brett Vicknair says.

Most medium to large cities have one or more gyms or fitness centers; smaller towns may not have any such facilities. Openings may be limited, however, at retirement homes, schools, and community centers in these small towns.

STARTING OUT

Students should use their schools' placement offices for information on available jobs. Often, facilities that provide training or internships will hire or provide job leads to individuals who have completed programs. Students can also find jobs through classified ads and by applying to health and fitness clubs, YMCAs, YWCAs, Jewish community centers, local schools, park districts, church groups, and other fitness organizations. Because exercise is understood to be a preventive measure for many health and medical problems, insurance companies often reward businesses that offer fitness facilities to their employees with lower insurance rates. As a result, students should consider nearby companies for prospective fitness instructor and trainer positions.

ADVANCEMENT

Experienced aerobics instructors can become instructor trainers, providing tips and insight on how to lead a class and what routines work well.

A bachelor's degree in either sports physiology or exercise physiology is especially beneficial for those who want to advance to the position of health club director or to teach corporate wellness programs.

Fitness trainers working at schools can advance from assistant positions to *head athletic director*, which may involve relocating to another school. Fitness trainers can advance to instruct new fitness trainers in college. They also can work in sports medicine facilities, usually in rehabilitation work. In health clubs, fitness trainers can advance to become health club directors or work in administration. Often, fitness trainers who build up a reputation and a clientele go into business for themselves as personal trainers.

EARNINGS

Aerobics instructors are usually paid by the class and generally start out at about $10 per class. Experienced aerobics instructors can earn up to $50 or $60 per class. The U.S. Department of Labor reports that fitness workers such as aerobics instructors had median annual earnings of $30,670 in 2009. The lowest paid 10 percent earned less than $16,430, and the highest paid 10 percent earned more than $62,120 per year.

Although a sports season lasts only about six months, athletes train year-round to remain in shape and require trainers to guide them. Many personal trainers are paid on a client-by-client basis. Contracts are drawn up and the payment is agreed upon before the training starts. Some trainers get paid more or less depending on the results.

A compensation survey by health and fitness organization IDEA reports that many employers offer health insurance and paid sick and vacation time to full-time employees. They also may provide discounts on products sold in the club (such as shoes, clothes, and equipment) and free memberships to use the facility.

WORK ENVIRONMENT

Most weight training and aerobics classes are held indoors. Depending on the popularity of the class and/or instructor, aerobics classes can get crowded and hectic at times. Instructors need to keep a level head and a positive, outgoing personality in order to motivate people and keep them together. It is important that aerobics instructors make the class enjoyable yet challenging so that members will return class after class. They also need to be unaffected by complaints of class members, some of whom may find the routines too hard, too easy, or who may not like the music selections. Instructors need to realize that these complaints are not personal attacks.

Fitness trainers need to be able to work on a one-on-one basis with amateur and professional athletes and nonathletes. They may work with individuals who are in pain after an injury and must be able to coax them to use muscles they would probably rather not. Trainers must possess patience, especially for beginners or those who are not athletically inclined, and offer encouragement to help them along.

Most trainers find it rewarding to help others achieve fitness goals. "To truly be a great personal fitness trainer, first you must enjoy helping and being around people. I love being able to motivate and give my clients the knowledge to help them meet their fitness goals," Brett Vicknair says.

OUTLOOK

Because of the country's ever-expanding interest in health and fitness, the U.S. Department of Labor predicts that the job outlook for aerobics instructors should remain strong through 2018, with much faster than average growth. The aging baby boomer population is very focused on staying fit and healthy, which will lead to a continued demand for skilled workers in this field. In addition, parents concerned about the implications of childhood obesity—coupled with a reduction in physical education programs in schools—will lead to a greater demand for fitness professionals who work with children, both in health clubs and in private settings.

Currently, some states require high schools to have a fitness trainer on staff. According to Brett Vicknair, home fitness trainers will remain in high demand. The convenience of being able to work out with a personal trainer before work, at lunch, early Saturday morning, or late Friday night makes the use of a personal trainer a flexible option. With the hectic lifestyle of most people today, that aspect alone should keep personal training positions on the rise.

FOR MORE INFORMATION

For information on various certifications, contact the following organizations:

Aerobics and Fitness Association of America
15250 Ventura Boulevard, Suite 200
Sherman Oaks, CA 91403-3215
Tel: 877-968-7263
http://www.afaa.com

Board of Certification Inc.
1415 Harney Street, Suite 200
Omaha, NE 68102-2250
Tel: 877-262-3926
http://www.bocatc.org

National Athletic Trainers' Association
2952 Stemmons Freeway, Suite 200
Dallas, TX 75247-6916
Tel: 800-879-6282
http://www.nata.org

For free information and materials about sports medicine topics, contact
American College of Sports Medicine
PO Box 1440
Indianapolis, IN 46206-1440
Tel: 317-637-9200
http://www.acsm.org

For more information about certification and careers in fitness, contact
American Council on Exercise (ACE)
4851 Paramount Drive
San Diego, CA 92123-1449
Tel: 888-825-3636
http://www.acefitness.org

For fitness facts and articles, visit IDEA's Web site.
IDEA: The Health and Fitness Association
10455 Pacific Center Court
San Diego, CA 92121-4339
Tel: 800-999-4332
E-mail: contact@ideafit.com
http://www.ideafit.com

ALCOHOL AND DRUG ABUSE COUNSELORS

OVERVIEW

Alcohol and drug abuse counselors (sometimes called *substance abuse counselors*) work with people who abuse or are addicted to drugs or alcohol. Through individual and group counseling sessions, they help their clients

SCHOOL SUBJECTS
Health, Psychology, Sociology

PERSONAL SKILLS
Communication/ideas, Helping/teaching

MINIMUM EDUCATION LEVEL
Associate's degree

CERTIFICATION OR LICENSING
Required by certain states

WORK ENVIRONMENT
Primarily indoors, Primarily one location

understand and change their destructive substance abuse behaviors. There are about 78,470 substance abuse and behavioral disorder counselors in the United States.

THE JOB

Alcohol and drug abuse counselors' main goal is to help patients stop their destructive behaviors. Counselors may also work with the families of clients to give them support and guidance in dealing with the problem.

Counselors begin by trying to learn about a patient's general background and history of drug or alcohol use. They may review patient records, including police reports, employment records, medical records, or reports from other counselors.

Counselors also interview the patient to determine the nature and extent of substance abuse. During an interview, the counselor asks questions about what types of substances the patient uses, how often, and for how long. The counselor may also ask patients about previous attempts to stop using the substance and about how the problem has affected their lives in various respects.

Using the information they obtain from the patient and their knowledge of substance abuse patterns, counselors formulate a program for treatment and rehabilitation. A substantial part of the rehabilitation process involves individual, group, or family counseling sessions. During individual sessions, counselors do a great deal of listening, perhaps asking appropriate questions to guide patients to insights about themselves. In group therapy sessions, counselors supervise groups of several patients, helping move their discussion in positive ways. In counseling sessions, counselors also teach patients methods of overcoming their dependencies. For example, they

might help a patient develop a series of goals for behavioral change.

Counselors monitor and assess the progress of their patients. In most cases, counselors deal with several different patients in various stages of recovery—some may need help breaking the pattern of substance abuse; some may already have stopped using but still need support; others may be recovered users who have suffered a relapse. Counselors maintain ongoing relationships with patients to help them adapt to the different recovery stages.

Working with families is another aspect of many alcohol and drug abuse counselors' jobs. They may ask a patient's family for insight into the patient's behavior. They may also teach the patient's family members how to deal with and support the patient through the recovery process.

Counselors may work with other health professionals and social agencies, including physicians, psychiatrists, psychologists, employment services, and court systems. In some cases, the counselor, with the patient's permission, may serve as a spokesperson for the patient, working with corrections officers, social workers, or employers. In other cases, a patient's needs might exceed the counselor's abilities; when this is the case, the counselor refers the patient to an appropriate medical expert, agency, or social program.

There is a substantial amount of paperwork involved in counseling alcohol and drug abusers. Detailed records must be kept on patients in order to follow their progress. For example, a report must be written after each counseling session. Counselors who work in residential treatment settings are required to participate in regular staff meetings to develop treatment plans and review patient progress. They may also meet periodically with family members or social service agency representatives to discuss patient progress and needs.

In some cases, alcohol and drug abuse counselors specialize in working with certain groups of people. Some work only with children or teenagers; others work with businesses to counsel employees who may have problems related to drugs and alcohol. In still other cases, counselors specialize in treating people who are addicted to specific drugs, such as cocaine, heroin, or alcohol. Counselors may need special training in order to work with specific groups.

REQUIREMENTS
High School

High school students who are considering a career in alcohol and drug abuse counseling should choose a curriculum that meets the requirements of the college or university they hope to attend. Typically, four years of English, history, mathematics, a foreign language, and social sciences are necessary. In addition, psychology, sociology, physiology, biology, and anatomy provide a good academic background for potential counselors.

The educational requirements for alcohol and drug abuse counselors vary greatly by state and employer. A high school education may be the minimum requirement for employers who provide on-the-job training, which ranges from six weeks to two years. These jobs, however, are becoming increasingly rare as more states are leaning toward stricter requirements for counselors.

Postsecondary Training

Some employers require an associate's degree in alcohol and drug technology. Most substance abuse counselors, however, have a bachelor's degree in counseling, psychology, health sociology, or social work. Many two- and four-year colleges now offer specific courses for students training to be substance abuse counselors.

Many counselors have a master's degree in counseling with a specialization in substance abuse counseling. Accredited graduate programs in substance abuse counseling are composed of a supervised internship as well as regular class work.

Certification or Licensing

Certification in this field, which is mandatory in some states, is available through state accreditation boards. Currently, 49 states and the District of Columbia have credentialing laws for alcohol and drug abuse counselors. These laws typically require that counselors have a minimum of a master's degree and two to three years of postacademic supervised counseling experience. Candidates must also have passed a written test.

NAADAC, the National Association for Addiction Professionals, also offers a national certified addiction counselor (NCAC) certification.

Other Requirements

In order to be successful in this job, prospective counselors should enjoy working with people. They must have compassion, good communication and listening skills, and a desire to help others. They should also be emotionally stable and able to deal with the frustrations and failures that are often a part of the job.

EXPLORING

Students interested in this career can find a great deal of information on substance abuse and substance abuse counseling at any local library. In addition, by contacting a local hospital, mental health clinic, or treatment center, it might be possible to talk with a counselor about the details of his or her job.

Volunteer work or a part-time job at a residential facility such as a hospital or treatment center is another good way of gaining experience and exploring an aptitude for counseling work. Finally, the professional and government organizations listed at the end of this article can provide information on alcohol and drug abuse counseling.

EMPLOYERS

Counselors are hired by hospitals, private and public treatment centers, government agencies, prisons, public school systems, colleges and universities, health maintenance organizations (HMOs), crisis centers, and mental health centers. More and more frequently, large companies are hiring alcohol and drug abuse counselors as well, to deal with employee substance abuse problems.

STARTING OUT

Counselors who have completed a two- or four-year college degree might start a job search by checking with the career placement office of their college or university. Those who plan to look for a position without first attending college might want to start by getting an entry-level or volunteer position in a treatment center or related agency. In this way, they can obtain practical experience and also make connections that might lead to full-time employment as a counselor.

Job seekers should also watch the classified advertisements in local newspapers. Job openings for counselors are often listed under "alcohol and drug counselor," "substance abuse counselor," or "mental health counselor." Finally, one might consider applying directly to the personnel department of various facilities and agencies that treat alcohol and drug abusers.

ADVANCEMENT

Counselors in this field often advance initially by taking on more responsibilities and earning a higher wage. They may also better themselves by taking a similar position in a more prestigious facility, such as an upscale private treatment center.

As they obtain more experience and perhaps more education, counselors sometimes move into supervisory or administrative positions. They might become directors of substance abuse programs in mental health facilities or executive directors of agencies or clinics.

Career options are more diverse for those counselors who continue their education. They may move into research, consulting, or teaching at the college level.

EARNINGS

Salaries of alcohol and drug abuse counselors depend on education level, amount of experience, and place of employment. Generally, the more education and experience a counselor has, the higher his or her earnings will be. Counselors who work in private treatment centers also tend to earn more than their public sector counterparts.

Alcohol and drug abuse counselors earned a median annual salary of $37,700 in 2009, according to the U.S. Department of Labor. The lowest 10 percent earned less than $24,580. The highest 10 percent earned $60,060 or more. Median annual wages were highest ($45,640) for counselors working in general medical and surgical hospitals. Directors of treatment programs or centers could earn considerably more than the national median salary. Almost all treatment centers provide employee benefits to their full-time counselors. Benefits usually include paid vacations and sick days, insurance, and pension plans.

WORK ENVIRONMENT

The hours that an alcohol and drug abuse counselor works depend upon where he or she is employed. Many residential treatment facilities and mental health centers—and all crisis centers—have counselors on duty during evening and weekend hours. Other employers, such as government agencies and universities, are likely to have more conventional working hours.

Work settings for counselors also vary by employer. Counselors may work in private offices, in the rooms or homes of patients, in classrooms, or in meeting rooms. In some cases, they conduct support group sessions in churches, community centers, or schools. For the most part, however, counselors work at the same work site or sites on a daily basis.

The bulk of a counselor's day is spent dealing with various people—patients, families, social workers, and health care professionals. There may be very little time during a workday for quiet reflection or organization.

Working with alcohol and drug abusers can be an emotionally draining experience. Overcoming addiction is a very hard battle, and patients respond to it in various ways. They may be resentful, angry, discouraged, or profoundly depressed. They may talk candidly with their counselors about tragic and upsetting events in their lives. Counselors spend much of their time listening to and dealing with very strong, usually negative, emotions.

This work can also be discouraging, due to a high failure rate. Many alcoholics and drug addicts do not respond to treatment and return immediately to their addictions. Even after months and sometimes years of recovery, many substance abusers suffer relapses. The counselor must learn to cope with the frustration of having his or her patients fail, perhaps repeatedly.

There is a very positive side to drug and alcohol abuse counseling, however. When it is successful, counselors have the satisfaction of knowing that they had a positive effect on someone's life. They have the reward of seeing some patients return to happy family lives and productive careers.

OUTLOOK

Employment of alcohol and drug abuse counselors is projected to grow much faster than the average for all occupations through 2018, according to the U.S. Department of Labor. There are approximately 17.6 million alcoholics in the United States according to the National Institute on Alcohol Abuse and Alcoholism, and an estimated 8 percent of the U.S. population over the age of 12 used an illicit drug in a given month in 2008, according to the Centers for Disease Control and Prevention. Because no successful method to significantly reduce drug and alcohol abuse has emerged, these numbers are not likely to decrease. As people become more informed about the benefits and options available to them through counseling, this career should be in high demand. Overall population growth will also lead to a need for more substance abuse counselors. Finally, many states are shifting away from criminalizing drug use, seeing it as a mental-health problem that should be treated through the medical system, not the criminal-justice system.

Another reason for the expected growth in counselors' jobs is that an increasing number of employers are offering employee assistance programs that provide counseling services for mental health and alcohol and drug abuse.

Finally, many job openings will arise as a result of job turnover. Because of the stress levels and the emotional demands involved in this career, there is a high burnout rate. As alcohol and drug abuse counselors leave the field, new counselors are needed to replace them.

FOR MORE INFORMATION

For more information on substance abuse and counseling careers, contact the following organizations:

American Counseling Association
5999 Stevenson Avenue
Alexandria, VA 22304-3300
Tel: 800-347-6647
http://www.counseling.org

National Institute on Alcohol Abuse and Alcoholism
National Institutes of Health
5635 Fishers Lane, MSC 9304
Bethesda, MD 20892-9304
http://www.niaaa.nih.gov

National Institute on Drug Abuse
National Institutes of Health
6001 Executive Boulevard, Room 5213
Bethesda, MD 20892-9561
Tel: 301-443-1124
http://www.nida.nih.gov

For information on certification, contact
NAADAC, The National Association for Addiction Professionals
1001 North Fairfax Street, Suite 201
Alexandria, VA 22314-1587
Tel: 800-548-0497
E-mail: naadac2@naadac.org
http://www.naadac.org

ANESTHESIOLOGISTS

OVERVIEW

Anesthesiologists are physicians who specialize in the planning, performance, and maintenance of a patient's anesthesia during surgical, obstetric, or other medical procedures. Using special equipment, monitors, and drugs, the anesthesiologist makes sure the patient feels no pain and remains uninjured during the procedure. There are approximately 37,500 anesthesiologists employed in the United States.

THE JOB

Anesthesiologists make sure that the patient's body is not overstimulated or injured by a medical procedure and that the patient feels no pain while undergoing the procedure. Traditionally, anesthesiologists deal mainly in the area of surgery. They do, however, also oversee the administration of anesthetics during other medical procedures, and if needed, during childbirth.

After reviewing a patient's medical history, the anesthesiologist will determine the best form of anesthesia for the patient. Different medical problems and various kinds of surgery require different kinds of anesthesia. These determinations are based on the anesthesiologist's broad background in medicine, which includes an

SCHOOL SUBJECTS
Biology, Chemistry, Psychology

PERSONAL SKILLS
Leadership/management, Technical/scientific

MINIMUM EDUCATION LEVEL
Medical degree

CERTIFICATION OR LICENSING
Required by all states

WORK ENVIRONMENT
Primarily indoors, Primarily one location

understanding of surgical procedures, physiology, pharmacology, and critical care.

In the operating room, an anesthesiologist gives the patient an anesthetic, making the patient unconscious and numb to pain. This involves administering drugs to put the patient under and maintaining the anesthesia. In some cases, only a regional, or local, anesthesia is required—numbing only the part of the body on which the surgery is being performed. In more complex cases, anesthesiologists may need to prepare special equipment such as blood warming devices. Anesthesiologists use monitoring equipment and insert intravenous lines and breathing tubes. They make sure the mask is secure and allows for a proper airway. In an emergency situation, an anesthesiologist is also part of the cardiopulmonary resuscitation (CPR) team.

An anesthesiologist pays close attention to the patient's well-being by monitoring blood pressure, breathing, heart rate, and body temperature throughout surgery. It is also the anesthesiologist's responsibility to position the patient properly, so that the doctor can perform the surgery and the patient remains uninjured. The anesthesiologist also controls the patient's temperature, cooling or heating different parts of the body during surgery.

Anesthesiologists are not limited to the operating room; they also spend time with patients before and after surgery. When meeting the patient beforehand, an anesthesiologist explains the kind of anesthesia to be used and answers any questions. This interaction helps put the patient at ease and allows the anesthesiologist to get to know the patient before surgery. Unlike other doctors, anesthesiologists do not have the opportunity to work closely for long periods of time with patients.

Anesthesiologists may specialize in different areas, such as pediatric anesthesia, respiratory therapy, critical care, and cardiovascular anesthesia. They often work in teams, consisting of anesthesiology residents, nurse anesthetists, and anesthesiology assistants. The anesthesiologist will delegate responsibilities to other members of the care team.

While emergency cases require anesthesiologists to make quick decisions and act without hesitation, in other cases they have time to carefully plan, to study a patient's medical history, to meet with the surgeons and the patients, and to work by a regular schedule. Most anesthesiologists work in hospitals, though they may actually be part of an individual or group practice. Others direct residents in teaching hospitals or teach at medical schools.

REQUIREMENTS

High School

If you are interested in becoming an anesthesiologist, focus your high school education on college preparatory courses. Mathematics classes and science classes, especially biology and chemistry, should be helpful. In addition, English classes will help you improve your communication and research skills. Also, consider taking a foreign language, since you may be required to show proficiency in another language later on in your schooling.

Postsecondary Training

You must first earn an M.D. degree and pass an examination to become licensed to practice medicine. This requires eight to 10 years of additional education and training after high school. (See the article "Physicians.") Then you must complete a four-year residency. The first year is spent training in an area of clinical medicine other than anesthesia, such as internal or emergency medicine, pediatrics, surgery, obstetrics, or neurology. The final three years of study are then spent in an anesthesiology residency program accredited by the Accreditation Council for Graduate Medical Education. You can find these accredited residency programs listed in the *Graduate Medical Education Directory,* available at your local library or through the American Medical Association.

Certification or Licensing

Anesthesiologists receive certification from the American Board of Anesthesiology. In addition to the license,

the board requires applicants to have completed training in an accredited program and to pass an exam. Applicants must also have a certificate of clinical competence (CCC). This certificate, filed by the residency training program, attests to the applicant's clinical competence.

Other Requirements

Every surgery requires anesthesiologists to pay careful attention and to remain alert. An anesthesiologist sometimes encounters emergency situations, requiring quick, clear-headed responses. The work, however, can also be slower paced and require patience to comfort people preparing for surgery. Not only must anesthesiologists be able to explain the surgery clearly to patients, but they must also be able to direct other members of the anesthesia team.

EXPLORING

One of the best introductions to a career in health care is to volunteer at a local hospital, clinic, or nursing home. In this way it is possible to get a feel for what it is like to work around other health care professionals and patients and possibly determine exactly where your interests lie. As in any career, reading as much as possible about the profession, talking with a high school counselor, and interviewing those working in the field are other important ways to explore your interest.

EMPLOYERS

Anesthesiologists can find employment in a wide variety of settings, including hospitals, nursing homes, managed-care offices, prisons, schools and universities, research laboratories, trauma centers, clinics, and public health centers. Some are self-employed in their own or group practices.

Jobs for anesthesiologists are available all over the world, although licensing requirements may vary. In third world countries, there is great demand for medical professionals of all types. Conditions, supplies, and equipment may be poor and pay is minimal, but there are great rewards in terms of experience. Many doctors fulfill part or all of their residency requirements by practicing in other countries.

Anesthesiologists interested in teaching may find employment at medical schools or university hospitals. There are also positions available in government agencies such as the Centers for Disease Control and Prevention, the National Institutes of Health, and the Food and Drug Administration.

STARTING OUT

There are no shortcuts to entering the medical profession. Requirements are an M.D. degree, a licensing examination, a one- or two-year internship, and a period of residency that may extend as long as five years (and seven years if they are pursuing board certification in a specialty).

Upon completing this program, which may take up to 15 years, physicians are then ready to enter practice. They may choose to open a solo private practice, enter a partnership practice, enter a group practice, or take a salaried job with a managed-care facility or hospital. Salaried positions are also available with federal and state agencies, the military, including the Department of Veterans Affairs, and private companies. Teaching and research jobs are usually obtained after other experience is acquired.

The highest ratio of physicians to patients is in the New England and Middle Atlantic States. The lowest ratio is in the South Central and Mountain States. Most M.D.s practice in urban areas near hospitals and universities.

ADVANCEMENT

Anesthesiologists who work in a managed-care setting or for a large group or corporation can advance by opening a private practice. The average physician in private practice does not advance in the accustomed sense of the word. Their progress consists of advancing in skill and understanding, in numbers of patients, and in income. They may be made a fellow in a professional specialty or elected to an important office in the American Medical Association or American Osteopathic Association. Teaching and research positions may also increase a physician's status.

Some anesthesiologists may become directors of a laboratory, managed-care facility, hospital department, or medical school program. Some may move into hospital administration positions.

Anesthesiologists can achieve recognition by conducting research in new medicines, treatments, and cures, and publishing their findings in medical journals. Participation in professional organizations can also bring prestige.

Anesthesiologists can also advance by pursuing further education in a subspecialty or a second field such as biochemistry or microbiology.

EARNINGS

Salaries for anesthesiologists vary according to the kind of practice (whether the anesthesiologist works individually or as part of a group practice), the amount of overhead required to maintain the business, and geographic location. Though working fewer hours, an anesthesiologist can make as much—or more than—other doctors. The U.S. Department of Labor reports that median annual earnings for primary care physicians were $186,044. In 2009, anesthesiologists had average annual earnings of $166,400, and the lowest paid 10 percent earned $115,470; but they often earn much more, depending on years of experience and the area in which they work. For example, in 2009, anesthesiologists employed in physicians' offices had average salaries of $221,010. Anesthesiologists with many years of experience may earn more than $300,000 a year—one of the highest average salaries in the medical field.

Fringe benefits for physicians typically include health and dental insurance, paid vacations, and retirement plans.

WORK ENVIRONMENT

The offices and examining rooms of most physicians are well equipped, attractive, well lighted, and well ventilated. There is usually at least one nurse-receptionist on the physician's staff, and there may be several nurses, a laboratory technician, one or more secretaries, a bookkeeper, or receptionist.

Physicians usually see patients by appointments that are scheduled according to individual requirements. They may reserve all mornings for hospital visits and surgery. They may see patients in the office only on certain days of the week.

Physicians spend much of their time at the hospital performing surgery, setting fractures, working in the emergency room, or visiting patients.

Physicians in private practice have the advantages of working independently, but 43 percent of all physicians worked an average of 50 hours or more per week in 2008. Also, they may be called from their homes or offices in times of emergency. Telephone calls may come at any hour of the day or night. It is difficult for physicians to plan leisure-time activities, because their plans may change without notice. One of the advantages of group practice is that members of the group rotate emergency duty.

The areas in most need of physicians are rural hospitals and medical centers. Because the physician is normally working alone, and covering a broad territory, the workday can be quite long with little opportunity for vacation. Because placement in rural communities has become so difficult, some towns are providing scholarship money to students who pledge to work in the community for a number of years.

Physicians in academic medicine or in research have regular hours, work under good physical conditions, and often determine their own workload. Teaching and research physicians alike are usually provided with the best and most modern equipment.

OUTLOOK

According to the *Occupational Outlook Handbook,* job opportunities for physicians and surgeons will grow much faster than the average through 2018. This growth can be attributed to the expansion of the health care industry, in addition to the medical needs of the growing elderly population. Most anesthesiologists find work immediately after finishing their residencies. As medical advances allow for different kinds of treatment facilities, anesthesiologists will find more work outside of a traditional hospital setting. The development of more outpatient clinics, freestanding surgical centers, and respiratory therapy clinics has opened up employment opportunities for anesthesiologists.

Managed care organizations have changed the way medicine is practiced and may continue to do so. Because anesthesiology is a hospital-based specialty, anesthesiologists must find ways to work within the guidelines of managed care, sometimes to the detriment of medical treatment. Anesthesiologists and other health care professionals will continue to challenge these organizations in order to practice medicine to the best of their abilities.

FOR MORE INFORMATION

The following organizations can provide information about a career as an anesthesiologist:

American Board of Anesthesiology
4208 Six Forks Road, Suite 900
Raleigh, NC 27609-5735
Tel: 919-881-2570
http://www.theaba.org

American Society of Anesthesiologists
520 North Northwest Highway
Park Ridge, IL 60068-2573
Tel: 847-825-5586
E-mail: communications@asahq.org
http://www.asahq.org

ANIMAL CARETAKERS

OVERVIEW

Animal caretakers, as the name implies, take care of animals. The job ranges from the day-to-day normal activi-

---

SCHOOL SUBJECTS
Biology, Health

PERSONAL SKILLS
Following instructions, Helping/teaching

MINIMUM EDUCATION LEVEL
High school diploma

CERTIFICATION OR LICENSING
None available

WORK ENVIRONMENT
Indoors and outdoors, One location with some travel

---

ties for a healthy animal to caring for sick, injured, or aging animals. Daily animal routine usually involves feeding and providing drinking water for each animal, making sure that their enclosure is clean, safe, appropriately warm, and, if needed, stocked with materials to keep the animal active and engaged. Caretakers may be responsible for creating different enrichment materials so that the animal is challenged by new objects and activities. They may exercise or train the animals. They may assist veterinarians or other trained medical staff in working with animals that require treatment. Animal caretakers may also maintain the written records for each animal. These records can include weight, eating habits, behavior, medicines given, or treatment given. Animal caretakers hold about 132,860 jobs in the United States.

THE JOB

Animal caretakers, also referred to by several other names depending on their specialty, perform the daily duties of animal care, which include feeding, grooming, cleaning, exercising, examining, and nurturing the individuals in their care. These caretakers have titles such as *animal shelter workers, grooms, veterinary assistants, wildlife assistants, animal shelter attendants, laboratory animal technicians, laboratory animal technologists,* and *kennel technicians.*

Animal caretakers are employed in kennels, stables, pet stores, boarding facilities, walking services, shelters, sanctuaries, rescue centers, zoos, aquariums, veterinary facilities, and animal experimentation labs. They may also be employed by the federal government, state or local parks that have educational centers with live animals, the Department of Agriculture in programs such as quarantine centers for animals coming into the United States, and the Centers for Disease Control and Prevention laboratories.

Almost every one of these employers expects the animal caretaker to provide the daily maintenance routine for animals. The caretaker may be responsible for one animal or one species, or may be required to handle many animals and many species. A veterinary assistant is likely to encounter dogs and cats, with the occasional bird or reptile. A wildlife shelter worker works with the local wild population, so for much of the United States that means working with raccoons, skunks, porcupines, hunting birds, songbirds, the occasional predator such as coyote or fox, and perhaps large animals such as bear, elk, moose, or deer.

Caretakers are responsible for some or all of the following tasks: selecting, mixing, and measuring out the appropriate food; providing water; cleaning the animal and the enclosure; changing bedding and groundcover if used; moving the animals from night facilities to day facilities or exercise spaces or different quarters; sterilizing facilities and equipment not in use; recording and filing statistics, medical reports, or lab reports on each animal; and providing general attention and affection to animals that need human contact.

The animal caretaker learns to recognize signs of illness such as lack of appetite, fatigue, skin sores, and changed behavior. They check the animals they can physically approach or handle for lumps, sores, fat, texture of the skin, fur, or feathers, and condition of the mouth. Since most animals do not exhibit signs of illness until they are very ill, it is important that the caretaker who sees the animal most regularly note any small change in the animal's physical or mental state.

The caretaker also maintains the animal's living quarters. For most animals in their care, this will be an enclosure of some type. The enclosure has to be safe and secure. The animal should not be able to injure itself within the enclosure, be able to escape, or have outside animals able to get into the enclosure. Small holes in an enclosure wall would not threaten a coyote, but small holes that a snake can pass through could threaten a rabbit. Horses can injure themselves in their stables, and in addition are vulnerable to a multitude of pasture injuries.

The quarters need to be the right size for the animal. If they are too large, the animal will feel threatened by the amount of open space, feeling it cannot protect the area adequately. Inappropriately small enclosures can be just as damaging. If the animal cannot get sufficient exercise within the enclosure, it will also suffer both psychologically and physically.

Caretakers set up and oversee enrichment activities that provide the animal with something to keep it engaged and occupied while in its home. For even the smallest rodent, enrichment activities are required. Most of us are familiar with enrichment toys for our pets. These are balls and squeaky toys for dogs and cats, bells and different foot surfaces for birds, and tunnels and rolling wheels for hamsters and gerbils. Wild animals require the same stimulation. Animal caretakers hide food in containers that require ingenuity and tools to open (ideal for a raccoon), or ropes and inner tubes for animals such as primates to swing on and play with.

Animals that can be exercised are taken to specially designed areas and worked. For hunting birds this may mean flying on a creance (tether); for dogs it may mean a game of fetch in the yard. Horses may be lunged (run around), or hacked (ridden); they may also simply be turned out in a field to exercise, but some form of training is useful to keep them in optimal riding condition. Domestic animal shelters, vet offices, kennels, boarding facilities, and dog-walking services work predominantly with domesticated dogs and cats, and perhaps horses at boarding centers. Exercise often consists of walks or free runs within an enclosed space. The animal caretaker for these employers often works with a rotating population of animals, some of whom may be in their care only for a few hours or days, although some animals may be cared for over longer periods. Caretakers at sanctuaries, quarantines, laboratories, and such may care for the same animals for months or years.

It is also an unpleasant side of the job that in almost every facility, the caretaker will have to deal with the death of an animal in his or her care. For veterinary offices, shelters, and wildlife facilities of any type, animal deaths are a part of everyone's experience. Shelters may choose to euthanize (kill) animals that are beyond medical treatment, deemed unadoptable, or unmaintainable because of their condition or the facilities' inability to house them. But even for places without a euthanasia policy, any center working with older, injured, sick, or rescued animals is going to lose the battle to save some of them. For the animal caretaker, this may mean losing an animal that just came in that morning, or losing an animal that he or she fed nearly every day for years. It can be as painful as losing one's own pet.

As an animal caretaker gains experience working with the animals, the responsibilities may increase. Caretakers may begin to perform tasks that either senior caretakers were performing or medical specialists were doing. This can include administering drugs; clipping nails, beaks, and wing feathers; banding wild animals with identification tags; and training the animal.

There are numerous clerical tasks that may also be part of the animal caretakers' routine. Beyond the medical reports made on the animals, animal caretakers may be required to screen people looking to take an animal home and write status reports or care plans. The animal caretaker may be responsible for communicating to an animal's owner the status of the animal in his or her care. Other clerical and administrative tasks may be required, depending on the facilities, the specific job, and the employer. But for most animal caretakers, the day is usually spent looking after the well-being of the animals.

REQUIREMENTS

High School

Students preparing for animal caretaker careers need a high school diploma. While in high school, classes in anatomy and physiology, science, and health are recommended. Students can obtain valuable information by taking animal science classes, where available. Any knowledge about animal breeds, behavior, and health is helpful. The basics of human nutrition, disease, reproduction, and aging help to give a background for learning about these topics for different species. A basic grasp of business and computer skills will help with the clerical tasks.

Postsecondary Training

There are two-year college programs in animal health that lead to an associate's degree. This type of program offers courses in anatomy and physiology, chemistry, mathematics, clinical pharmacology, pathology, radiology, animal care and handling, infectious diseases, biology, and current veterinary treatment. Students graduating from these programs go on to work in veterinary practices, shelters, zoos and aquariums, pharmaceutical companies, and laboratory research facilities. Students should look for programs accredited by the American Veterinary Medical Association.

Apprenticing for the handling of wild hunting birds is required by most facilities. This can include having apprentices pursue a falconry license, which means apprenticing to a licensed falconer. Licenses for assistant laboratory animal technician, laboratory animal technician, and laboratory animal technologist are available through the American Association for Laboratory Animal Science and may be required by some employers.

A bachelor's degree is required for many jobs, particularly in zoos and aquariums. Degrees in wildlife management, biology, zoology, animal physiology, or other related fields are most useful.

Other Requirements

Animal caretakers should have great love, empathy, and respect for animals. They should have a strong interest in the environment. Patience, compassion, dependability, and the ability to work on repetitive, physically challenging, or unstimulating tasks without annoyance are essential characteristics for someone to be happy as an animal caretaker.

EXPLORING

Volunteering is the most effective method of experiencing the tasks of an animal caretaker. Most shelters, rescue centers, and sanctuaries, and some zoos, aquariums, and labs rely on volunteers to fill their staff. Opportunities as a volunteer may include the ability to work directly with animals in some or all of the capacities of a paid animal caretaker.

There is always a concern, sometimes justified, that an organization will never pay someone whose services they have gotten for free. You may not be able to get paid employment from the same organization for which you volunteered. But many organizations recognize the benefit of hiring prior volunteers: They get someone who already knows the institution, the system, and the preferred caretaking methods.

Volunteering also provides a line on your resume that demonstrates that you bring experience to your first paying job. It gives you references who can vouch for your skills with animals, your reliability, and your dedication to the field. Thus, you should treat any volunteer position with the same professionalism that you would a paid job.

Other avenues for exploration are interviewing people already in the position, or finding a paid position in a facility where animal caretakers work so you can see them in action. You may also begin by providing a pet walking or sitting service in your neighborhood, but be sure to only take on the number and kinds of animals you know you can handle successfully.

EMPLOYERS

There are about 132,860 animal caretakers in the United States. There are many different types of facilities and businesses that employ animal caretakers, including veterinary offices, kennels, stables, breeding farms, boarding facilities, rescue centers, shelters, sanctuaries, zoos, aquariums, and pet stores. The federal government is also a major employer of animal caretakers, specifically in the U.S. Department of Agriculture. Both federal and state government jobs are available in parks. This field is growing, and increasing job opportunities will be available all over the country for animal caretakers.

Since pet ownership and interest in animals continues to increase, more and more jobs will become available with all kinds of employers, resulting in work in environments ranging from nonprofit organizations to retail stores to laboratories.

STARTING OUT

High school students who volunteer will be able to test the job before committing to it. They will also, as explained earlier, be able to add a job to their resume that demonstrates their experience in the field.

Two- and four-year college programs offer some placement assistance, but familiarity with the regional market for organizations that use animal caretakers will assist you in selecting places to target with your resume. Many animal caretakers work in veterinary offices and boarding facilities or kennels, but animal research laboratories also hire many caretakers. Other employers include the federal government, state governments, pharmaceutical companies, the gaming industry (racetracks, in particular), teaching hospitals, and food production companies.

ADVANCEMENT

Advancement depends on the job setting. There may be promotion opportunities to *senior technician, supervisor, assistant facilities manager,* or *facilities manager.* Some animal caretakers may open their own facilities or services. Services such as dog walking require little in the way of offices or equipment, so these are easy ways for animal caretakers to start on their own, with an established clientele that they bring from a previous position.

Laboratory workers can move from *assistant technician* to *technician* to *technologist* with increased education and experience. For most promotions, however, more education is usually required.

EARNINGS

Salaried employees earned an average salary of $19,550 in 2009, according to the *Occupational Outlook Handbook.* The top 10 percent earned more than $31,660, and the bottom 10 percent earned less than $15,590 a year.

Self-employed animal caretakers who provide dog walking, kennel, sitting, or other cottage industry services do not have salaries that are readily available for review, but in large cities, boarding a dog overnight can cost $25 to $40, with a minimum of three dogs usually at one facility. Dog walkers charge between $5 and $12 a dog. There is little overhead for either service, beyond perhaps providing food.

WORK ENVIRONMENT

Animals may either be kept indoors or outdoors, in any type of weather. Eagles don't come in from the rain, so animal caretakers caring for eagles still have to traipse outside to feed them when it's raining. Horses are turned out in the middle of the winter, so horse grooms still have to carry bales of hay to the pasture in the middle of January snowdrifts. Though currying, saddling, exercising, medicating, and cleaning up after a horse—or horses—may seem like a dream job to some, it is considerably less romantic to clean a stable day in and day out, regardless of weather.

Depending on the facilities, heavy lifting may be part of the job. You may have to lift crates, animals, food, equipment, or other items big enough to accommodate a large animal. The work can sometimes be hard, repetitive, and dirty. Cleaning enclosures and disinfecting spaces can involve hot or cold water and chemicals.

The work can also be dangerous, depending on the animals you work with. The U.S. Department of Labor notes that animal caretakers have a higher incidence of on-the-job injury than most other careers. Although animals that are handled correctly and are treated with the proper respect and distance can be quite safe, situations can arise where the animal is unpredictable, or is frightened or cornered. Although this is more likely with animal caretakers working with wildlife populations, large dogs, horses, and cattle are quite capable of injuring and killing people. There is a certain physical risk involved in working with animals, which may be as minor as scratches from nails or bites, but can be as great as broken or crushed bones, or accidental death.

Many facilities require long workdays, long workweeks, odd hours, weekend work, holiday work, and intermittent schedules. Depending on the hours of the facility, the services provided, and the staffing, there may be several shifts, including a graveyard shift. Animal caretakers should be prepared to work a changing schedule. The needs of animals don't cease for weekends and holidays.

Also, for many facilities, animals that require round-the-clock care have to be taken home with an animal caretaker who is willing to provide whatever service the animal needs, including waking every two hours to bottle-feed a newborn chimp.

OUTLOOK

The animal care field is expected to grow much faster than the average through 2018, according to the U.S. Department of Labor. More people have pets and are more concerned with their pets' care. Since most households have all the adults in full-time employment, animals are left home alone longer than in earlier times. Dog-walking services, pet sitting and in-house care, boarding facilities, kennels, and such that provide assistance with the daily care of an animal for the working or traveling owner are far more prevalent and successful than before.

Veterinary services are also on the rise, with the increased number of pets and the increased awareness on the part of owners that vet services are essential to an animal's well-being.

There is a high turnover in the profession. This is due in part to the seasonal nature of some of the jobs, the low pay, and the lack of advancement opportunities in the field. Wildlife sanctuaries, release and rescue programs, shelters, and zoos and aquariums are heavily dependent on charitable contributions and fund-raising efforts. Staff employment can be tied to the rise and fall of donations. Many of these institutions rely heavily on volunteer labor. As such, the competitiveness for the paid jobs is quite high.

Less favorable job opportunities are predicted for animal caretakers in zoos, aquariums, and rehabilitation and rescue centers, as these are the most sought-after positions, partly because of the ability to work with exotic and wild species. Aspiring animal caretakers will find few openings in these facilities.

Graduates of veterinary technician programs have the best employment prospects. Laboratory animal technicians and technologists also have good opportunities. Increasing concern for animal rights and welfare means that these facilities are staffing more professionals to operate their labs.

FOR MORE INFORMATION
For information about animal laboratory work and certification programs, contact
American Association for Laboratory Animal Science
9190 Crestwyn Hills Drive
Memphis, TN 38125-8538
Tel: 901-754-8620
E-mail: info@aalas.org
http://www.aalas.org

For more information on careers, schools, and resources, contact
American Veterinary Medical Association (AVMA)
1931 North Meacham Road, Suite 100
Schaumburg, IL 60173-4360
Tel: 800-248-2862
http://www.avma.org

For information on available training programs, certification, and industry standards, contact
Pet Care Services Association
401 North Michigan Avenue, Suite 2200
Chicago, IL 60611
Tel: 800-218-9123
http://www.petcareservices.org

For information on the Student Career Experience Program, contact the U.S. Fish and Wildlife Service in your state or visit the following Web site:
U.S. Fish and Wildlife Service
http://www.fws.gov

ARBORISTS

OVERVIEW
Arborists are professionals who practice arboriculture, which is the care of trees and shrubs, especially those found in urban areas. Arborists prune and fertilize trees and other woody plants as well as monitor them for insects and diseases. Arborists are often consulted for various tree-related issues.

THE JOB
Trees and shrubs need more than just sunlight and water. That's where arborists take over. Arborists perform many different tasks for trees and shrubs, some for the sake of maintenance and others for the tree's health and well-being.

SCHOOL SUBJECTS
Biology, Earth science

PERSONAL SKILLS
Technical/scientific

MINIMUM EDUCATION LEVEL
Bachelor's degree

CERTIFICATION OR LICENSING
Recommended

WORK ENVIRONMENT
Primarily outdoors, Primarily multiple locations

Pruning. All trees need some amount of pruning to control their shape; sometimes limbs are trimmed if they interfere with power lines, if they cross property lines, or if they grow too close to houses and other buildings. Arborists may use tools such as pruning shears or hand and power saws to do the actual cutting. If the branches are especially large or cumbersome, arborists may rope them together before the sawing begins. After cutting, the branches can be safely lowered to the ground. Ladders, aerial lifts, and cranes may be used to reach extremely tall trees. Sometimes, arborists need to cable or brace tree limbs weakened by disease or old age or damaged by a storm.

Planting or transplanting. When cities or towns plan a new development, or wish to gentrify an existing one, they often consult with arborists to determine what types of trees to plant. Arborists can suggest trees that will thrive in a certain environment. Young plantings, or immature trees, are more cost effective and are often used, though sometimes larger, more mature trees are transplanted to the desired location.

Diagnosis and treatment. A large part of keeping a tree healthy is the prevention of disease. There are a number of diseases that affect trees, among them anthracnose and Dutch elm disease. Insects pose a potential threat to trees, and have done considerable damage to certain species in the past, by boring into the trunk or spreading disease-causing organisms. Bacteria, fungi, viruses, and disease-causing organisms can also be fatal enemies of trees. Arborists are specially trained to identify the insect or the disease weakening the tree and apply the necessary remedy or medication. Common methods prescribed by arborists include chemical insecticides, or the use of natural insect predators to combat the problem. Arborists closely monitor insect migrations or any other situations that may be harmful to a species of tree.

When a tree is too old or badly diseased, arborists may choose to cut it down. Arborists will carefully cut the tree into pieces to prevent injury to people or damage to surrounding property.

Prevention. Trees, especially young plantings, often need extra nourishment. Arborists are trained to apply fertilizers, both natural and chemical, in a safe and environmentally friendly manner. Arborists are also hired by golf courses and parks to install lightning protection systems for lone trees or mature, valuable trees.

REQUIREMENTS

High School

High school biology classes can provide you with a solid background to be a successful arborist. An inter-est in gardening, conservation, or the outdoors is also helpful.

Postsecondary Training

Take classes in botany, chemistry, horticulture, and plant pathology. Several colleges and universities offer programs in arboriculture and other related fields such as landscape design, nursery stock production, or grounds and turf maintenance. Entry-level positions such as *assistants* or *climbers* do not need a college degree for employment. Advanced education, however, is highly desired if you plan to make this field your career.

Certification or Licensing

The Tree Care Industry Association (TCIA) and the International Society of Arboriculture (ISA) both offer various home study courses and books on arboriculture. Most arborists are certified or licensed. Licensure ensures an arborist meets the state's regulations for working with pesticides and herbicides. Check with your local government—not all states require arborists to be licensed. Certification, given by the ISA after completion of required training and education, is considered by many as a measure of an arborist's skill and experience in the industry. Today's savvy consumers specifically look for certified arborists when it comes to caring for their trees and other precious landscaping plants. Arborists need to apply for recertification every three years and must complete 30 units of continuing education classes and seminars.

EXPLORING

Interested in this field? Surfing the Internet can provide a wealth of information for you to browse. Log onto the Web sites of the TCIA or ISA for industry and career information. If you really want to test the waters, why not find summer work with an arborist? You'll earn extra spending money while learning about the industry firsthand. Check with the TCIA for a complete listing of certified arborists in your area.

EMPLOYERS

Landscaping companies and businesses that offer a host of expert tree services are common employers of arborists. Employment opportunities are also available with municipal governments, botanical gardens, and arboretums. For example, an arborist in the Chicago area may want to seek a position with the Chicago Botanic Garden or the Morton Arboretum; both places are known for their lush gardens and wooded trails. According to the

Department of Labor, there were about 37,830 arborists in the United States in 2009.

STARTING OUT

So you've decided to become an arborist—what's the next step? Start by compiling a list of tree care firms in your area, and then send your resume or fill out an application to the companies that interest you. You should also consider employment with the highway or park department of your city or county—they often hire crews to maintain their trees.

Many colleges and universities offer job placement services, or they at least post employment opportunities in their office. Industry associations and trade magazines are often good sources of job openings.

Don't plan to climb to the top of an American elm your first day on the job. Expect to stay at ground level, at least for a few days. Trainees in this industry start as helpers or ground workers, who load and unload equipment from trucks, gather branches and other debris for disposal, handle ropes, and give assistance to climbers. They also operate the chipper—a machine that cuts large branches into small chips. After some time observing more experienced workers, trainees are allowed to climb smaller trees or the lower limbs of large trees. They are also taught the proper way to operate large machinery and climbing gear. Most companies provide on-the-job training that lasts from one to three months.

ADVANCEMENT

Experienced arborists can advance to supervisory positions such as crew manager or department supervisor. Another option is to become a consultant in the field and work for tree care firms, city or town boards, large nurseries, or gardening groups.

Arborists with a strong entrepreneurial nature can choose to open their own business, but aspiring entrepreneurs must make sure that their business skills are up to par. Even the most talented and hardworking arborists won't stand a chance if they can't balance their accounts or market their services properly.

Advancement to other industries related to arboriculture is another possibility. Some arborists choose to work in landscape design, forestry, or other fields of horticulture.

EARNINGS

The U.S. Department of Labor lists the median yearly salary of arborists as $30,310 in 2009. The bottom 10 percent earned $20,450 a year or less, and the top 10 percent earned $47,650 a year or more.

According to Derek Vannice, ISA's director of certification, entry-level positions, such as grounds workers or trainees, can earn between $7 to $10 an hour; supervisors, with three or more years of experience, earn from $20 to $30 an hour; private consultants with eight to 10 years of experience, or arborists in sales positions, can earn $50,000 to $60,000 or more annually. Salaries vary greatly depending on many factors, among them the size of the company, the region, and the experience of the arborist. Arborists servicing busy urban areas tend to earn more.

Full-time employees receive a benefits package including health insurance, life insurance, paid vacation and sick time, and paid holidays. Most tree companies supply necessary uniforms, tools, equipment, and training.

WORK ENVIRONMENT

Much of an arborist's work is physically demanding, and most of it is done outdoors. Arborists work throughout the year, though their busiest time is in the spring and summer. Tasks done at this time include fertilizing, pruning, and prevention spraying. During the winter months, arborists can expect to care for trees injured or damaged by excess snow, ice storms, or floods.

Equipment such as sharp saws, grinders, chippers, bulldozers, tractors, and other large machinery can be potentially dangerous for arborists. There is also the risk of falling from the top of a tall tree, many of which reach heights of 50 feet or more. Arborists rely on cleated shoes, security belts, and safety hoists to make their job easier as well as safer.

OUTLOOK

The future of arboriculture has never looked so promising. The U.S Department of Labor predicts much faster than average growth for this field through 2018. The public's increasing interest in the planning and the preservation of the environment has increased demand for qualified arborists. Towns across the country are planting large numbers of trees to improve the environment, and arborists will be in demand to care for them. Many homeowners are willing to pay top dollar for professionally designed and maintained landscaping. Increased resistance to pesticides and new species of insects pose constant threats to all trees. While travel abroad is easier and, in a sense, has made our world smaller, it has also placed our environment at risk. For example, Asian longhorned beetles were unknowingly transported to the United States via packing material. By the time the insects were discovered, the beetles had irreversibly damaged hundreds of mature trees throughout New York,

Chicago, and surrounding areas. Arborists, especially those trained to diagnose and treat such cases, will be in demand to work in urban areas.

FOR MORE INFORMATION

For industry and career information, or to receive a copy of Arborist News *or* Careers in Arboriculture, *contact*

International Society of Arboriculture
PO Box 3129
Champaign, IL 61826-3129
Tel: 217-355-9411
E-mail: isa@isa-arbor.com
http://www.isa-arbor.com

For industry information and membership requirements, contact

Society of Municipal Arborists
PO Box 641
Watkinsville, GA 30677
Tel: 706-769-7412
E-mail: urbanforestry@prodigy.net
http://www.urban-forestry.com

For industry and career information, a listing of practicing arborists, or educational programs at the university level, or home study, contact

Tree Care Industry Association
136 Harvey Road, Suite 101
Londonberry, NH 03053-7439
Tel: 800-733-2622
E-mail: membership@tcia.org
http://www.tcia.org

ARCHITECTS

OVERVIEW

Architects plan, design, and observe construction of facilities used for human occupancy and of other structures. They consult with clients, plan layouts of buildings, prepare drawings of proposed buildings, write specifications, and prepare scale and full-sized drawings. Architects also may help clients to obtain bids, select a contractor, and negotiate the construction contract. They visit construction sites to ensure that the work is being completed according to specification. There are approximately 101,630 architects working in the United States.

SCHOOL SUBJECTS
Art, Mathematics

PERSONAL SKILLS
Artistic, Communication/ideas

MINIMUM EDUCATION LEVEL
Bachelor's degree

CERTIFICATION OR LICENSING
Required

WORK ENVIRONMENT
Primarily indoors, Primarily one location

THE JOB

The architect normally has two responsibilities: to design a building that will satisfy the client and to protect the public's health, safety, and welfare. This second responsibility requires architects to be licensed by the state in which they work. Meeting the first responsibility involves many steps. The job begins with learning what the client wants. The architect takes many factors into consideration, including local and state building and design regulations, climate, soil on which the building is to be constructed, zoning laws, fire regulations, and the client's financial limitations.

The architect then prepares a set of plans that, upon the client's approval, will be developed into final design and construction documents. The final design shows the exact dimensions of every portion of the building, including the location and size of columns and beams, electrical outlets and fixtures, plumbing, heating and air-conditioning facilities, windows, and doors. The architect works closely with consulting engineers on the specifics of the plumbing, heating, air-conditioning, and electrical work to be done.

The architect then assists the client in getting bids from general contractors, one of whom will be selected to construct the building to the specifications. The architect helps the client through the completion of the construction and occupancy phases, making certain the correct materials are used and that the drawings and specifications are faithfully followed.

Throughout the process the architect works closely with a design or project team. This team is usually made up of the following: designers, who specialize in design development; a structural designer, who designs the frame of the building in accordance with the work of the architect; the project manager or job superintendent, who sees that the full detail drawings are completed to the satisfaction of the architect; and the specification writer and estimator, who prepare a project manual that describes in more detail the materials to be used in the building, their quality and method of installation, and all details related to the construction of the building.

The architect's job is very complex. He or she is expected to know construction methods, engineering principles and practices, and materials. Architects also must be up-to-date on new design and construction techniques and procedures. Although architects once spent most of their time designing buildings for the wealthy, they are now more often involved in the design of housing developments, individual dwellings, supermarkets, industrial plants, office buildings, shopping centers, air terminals, schools, banks, museums, churches, and dozens of other types of buildings.

Architects may specialize in any one of a number of fields, including building appraisal, city planning, teaching, architectural journalism, furniture design, lighting design, or government service. Regardless of the area of specialization, the architect's major task is that of understanding the client's needs and then reconciling them into a meaningful whole.

REQUIREMENTS
High School

To prepare for this career while in high school, take a college preparatory program that includes courses in English, mathematics, physics, art (especially freehand drawing), social studies, history, and foreign languages. Courses in business and computer science will also be useful.

Postsecondary Training

Because most state architecture registration boards require a professional degree, high school students are advised, early in their senior year, to apply for admission to one of the 117 professional programs accredited by the National Architectural Accrediting Board. Competition to enter these programs is high. Grades, class rank, and aptitude and achievement scores count heavily in determining who will be accepted.

Most schools of architecture offer degrees through either a five-year bachelor's program or a three- or four-year master's program. The majority of architecture students seek out the bachelor's degree in archi-

tecture, going from high school directly into a five-year program. Though this is the fastest route, you should be certain that you want to study architecture. Because the programs are so specialized, it is difficult to transfer to another field of study if you change your mind. The master's degree option allows for more flexibility but takes longer to complete. In this case, students first earn a liberal arts degree then continue their training by completing a master's program in architecture.

A typical college architecture program includes courses in architectural history and theory, the technical and legal aspects of building design, science, and liberal arts.

Certification or Licensing

All states and the District of Columbia require that individuals be licensed before contracting to provide architectural services in that particular state. Though many work in the field without licensure, only licensed architects are required to take legal responsibility for all work. Using a licensed architect for a project is, therefore, less risky than using an unlicensed one. Architects who are licensed usually take on projects with larger responsibilities and have greater chances to advance to managerial or executive positions.

The requirements for registration include graduation from an accredited school of architecture and three years of practical experience through an internship with a licensed architect. After these requirements are met, individuals can take the rigorous four-day Architect Registration Examination. Some states require architects to maintain their licensing through continued education. These individuals may complete a certain number of credits every year or two through seminars, workshops, university classes, self-study courses, or other sources.

In addition to becoming licensed, a growing number of architects choose to obtain certification by the National Council of Architecture Registration Boards. If an architect plans to work in more than one state, obtaining this certification can make it easier to become licensed in different states. In 2009, about one-third of all licensed architects had this certification.

Other Requirements

If you are interested in architecture, you should be intelligent, observant, responsible, and self-disciplined. You should have a concern for detail and accuracy, be able to communicate effectively both orally and in writing, and be able to accept criticism constructively. Although great artistic ability is not necessary, you should be able to visualize spatial relationships and have the capacity to solve technical problems. Mathematical ability is also important, as are strong computer skills, particularly in the use of computer-aided design and drafting (CADD) software. In addition, you should possess organizational skills and leadership qualities and be able to work well with others.

EXPLORING

Most architects will welcome the opportunity to talk with young people interested in entering architecture. You may be able to visit their offices to gain firsthand knowledge of the type of work done by architects. You can also visit a design studio of a school of architecture or work for an architect or building contractor during summer vacations. Also, many architecture schools offer summer programs for high school students. Books and magazines on architecture also can give you a broad understanding of the nature of the work and the values of the profession.

EMPLOYERS

Of the 101,630 architects working in the United States in 2009, most were employed by architectural or engineering firms or other related services. About 21 percent of architects, however, are self-employed—the ultimate dream of many people in the profession. A few develop graphic design, interior design, or product specialties. Still others put their training to work in the theater, film, or television fields, or in museums, display firms, and architectural product and materials manufacturing companies. A small number are employed in government agencies such as the Departments of Defense, Interior, and Housing and Urban Development and the General Services Administration.

STARTING OUT

Students entering architecture following graduation start as interns in an architectural office. As interns, they assist in preparing architectural construction documents. They also handle related details, such as administering contracts, coordinating the work of other professionals on the project, researching building codes and construction materials, and writing specifications. As an alternative to working for an architectural firm, some architecture graduates go into allied fields such as construction, engineering, interior design, landscape architecture, or real estate development.

ADVANCEMENT

Interns and architects alike are given progressively more complex jobs. Architects may advance to supervisory or managerial positions. Some architects become partners in established firms, while others take steps to establish their own practice.

EARNINGS

Architects earned a median annual salary of $72,700 in 2009, according to the U.S. Department of Labor. The lowest paid 10 percent earned less than $42,320 annually, while the highest paid 10 percent earned $122,640 or more.

Well-established architects who are partners in an architectural firm or who have their own businesses generally earn much more than salaried employees. Most employers offer such fringe benefits as health insurance, sick and vacation pay, and retirement plans.

WORK ENVIRONMENT

Architects normally work a 40-hour week. There may be a number of times when they will have to work overtime, especially when under pressure to complete an assignment. Self-employed architects work less regular hours and often meet with clients in their homes or offices during the evening. Architects usually work in comfortable offices, but they may spend a considerable amount of time outside the office visiting clients or viewing the progress of a particular job in the field. Their routines usually vary considerably.

OUTLOOK

Employment in the field is expected to grow faster than the average through 2018, according to the U.S. Department of Labor. As the population of the Sun Belt states in the southern half of the United States continues to grow, architects will be needed to build homes, schools, and businesses in these areas. In addition, the large baby boomer population will create a demand for more retirement communities and health care facilities across the country as it reaches retirement age. The need to replace aging structures of all types will also mean good job prospects for architects throughout the next decade.

Competition for employment will continue to be strong, particularly in prestigious architectural firms. Openings will not be newly created positions but will become available as the workload increases and established architects transfer to other occupations or leave the field.

FOR MORE INFORMATION

For information on education, scholarships, and student membership opportunities, contact the following organizations:

American Institute of Architects
1735 New York Avenue, NW
Washington, DC 20006-5292
Tel: 800-AIA-3837
E-mail: infocentral@aia.org
http://www.aia.org

American Institute of Architecture Students
1735 New York Avenue, NW
Washington, DC 20006-5209
Tel: 202-626-7472
E-mail: mailbox@aias.org
http://www.aias.org

Association of Collegiate Schools of Architecture
1735 New York Avenue, NW, 3rd Floor
Washington, DC 20006-5209
Tel: 202-785-2324
E-mail: info@acsa-arch.org
http://www.acsa-arch.org

BIOCHEMISTS

OVERVIEW

Biochemists explore the tiny world of the cell, study how illnesses develop, and search for ways to improve life on earth. Through studying the chemical makeup of living organisms, biochemists strive to understand the dynamics of life, from the secrets of cell-to-cell communication to the chemical changes in our brains that give us memories. Biochemists examine the chemical combinations and reactions involved in such functions as growth, metabolism, reproduction, and heredity. They also study the effect of environment on living tissue. If cancer is to be cured, the earth's pollution cleaned up, or the aging process slowed, it will be biochemists and molecular biologists who will lead the way. There are approximately 22,860 biochemists and biophysicists employed in the United States. (*Biophysicists* examine the chemical combinations and reactions involved in such functions as metabolism and heredity.)

THE JOB

Depending on a biochemist's education level and area of specialty, this professional can do many types of work for a variety of employers. For instance, a biochemist could have a job doing basic research for a federal government agency or for individual states with laboratories that employ skilled persons to analyze food, drug, air, water,

waste, or animal tissue samples. A biochemist might work for a drug company as part of a basic research team searching for the cause of diseases or conduct applied research to develop drugs to cure disease. A biochemist might work in a biotechnology company focusing on the environment, energy, human health care, agriculture, or animal health. There, he or she might do research or quality control, or work on manufacturing/production or information systems. Another possibility is for the biochemist to specialize in an additional area, such as law, business, or journalism, and use his or her biochemistry or molecular biology background for a career that combines science with regulatory affairs, management, writing, or teaching.

Ph.D. scientists who enter the highest levels of academic life combine teaching and research. In addition to teaching in university classrooms and laboratories, they also do basic research designed to increase biochemistry and molecular biology knowledge. As Ph.D. scientists, these professionals could also work for an industry or government laboratory doing basic research or research and development (R&D). The problems studied, research styles, and type of organization vary widely across different laboratories. The Ph.D. scientist may lead a research group or be part of a small team of Ph.D. researchers. Other Ph.D. scientists might opt for administrative positions. In government, for example, these scientists might lead programs concerned with the safety of new devices, food, drugs, or pesticides and other chemicals. Or they might influence which projects will get federal funding.

Generally, biochemists employed in the United States work in one of three major fields: medicine, nutrition, or agriculture. In medicine, biochemists mass-produce

---

SCHOOL SUBJECTS
Biology, Chemistry

PERSONAL SKILLS
Mechanical/manipulative, Technical/scientific

MINIMUM EDUCATION LEVEL
Bachelor's degree

CERTIFICATION OR LICENSING
Required for certain positions

WORK ENVIRONMENT
Primarily indoors, Primarily one location

life-saving chemicals usually found only in minuscule amounts in the body. Some of these chemicals have been helping diabetics and heart attack victims for years. Biochemists employed in the field of medicine might work to identify chemical changes in organs or cells that signal the development of such diseases as cancer, diabetes, or schizophrenia. Or they may look for chemical explanations for why certain people develop muscular dystrophy or become obese. While studying chemical makeup and changes in these situations, biochemists may work to discover a treatment or a prevention for a disease. For instance, biochemists discovering how certain diseases such as AIDS and cancer escape detection by the immune system are also devising ways to enhance immunity to fight these diseases. Biochemists are also finding out the chemical basis of fertility and how to improve the success of in vitro fertilization to help couples have children or to preserve endangered species.

Biochemists in the pharmaceutical industry design, develop, and evaluate drugs, antibiotics, diagnostic kits, and other medical devices. They may search out ways to produce antibiotics, hormones, enzymes, or other drug components, or they may do quality control on the way in which drugs and dosages are made and determined.

In the field of nutrition, biochemists examine the effects of food on the body. For example, they might study the relationship between diet and diabetes. Biochemists doing this study could look at the nutrition content of certain foods eaten by people with diabetes and study how these foods affect the functioning of the pancreas and other organs. Biochemists in the nutrition field also look at vitamin and mineral deficiencies and how they affect the human body. They examine these deficiencies in relation to body performance, and they may study anything from how the liver is affected by a lack of vitamin B to the effects of poor nutrition on the ability to learn.

Biochemists involved in agriculture undertake studies to discover more efficient methods of crop cultivation, storage, and pest control. For example, they might create genetically engineered crops that are more resistant to frost, drought, spoilage, disease, and pests. They might focus on helping to create fruit trees that produce more fruit by studying the biochemical composition of the plant and determining how to alter or select for this desirable trait. Biochemists may study the chemical composition of insects to determine better and more efficient methods of controlling the pest population and the damage they do to crops. Or they could work on programming bacteria to clean up the environment by "eating" toxic chemicals.

About seven out of 10 biochemists are engaged in basic research, often for a university medical school or nonprofit organization, such as a foundation or research institute. The remaining 30 percent do applied research, using the discoveries of basic research to solve practical problems or develop products. For example, a biochemist working in basic research may make a discovery about how a living organism forms hormones. This discovery will lead to a scientist doing applied research, making hormones in the laboratory, and eventually to mass production. Discoveries made in DNA research have led to techniques for identifying criminals from a single strand of hair or a tiny blood stain left at the scene of a crime. The distinction between basic and applied research is one of degree, however; biochemists often engage in both types of work.

Biochemistry requires skillful use of a wide range of sophisticated analytical equipment and application of newly discovered techniques requiring special instruments or new chemical reagents. Sometimes, biochemists themselves must invent and test new instruments if existing methods and equipment do not meet their needs. Biochemists must also be patient, methodical, and careful in their laboratory procedures.

REQUIREMENTS

Although they usually specialize in one of many areas in the field, biochemists and molecular biologists should also be familiar with several scientific disciplines, including chemistry, physics, mathematics, and computer science. High school can provide the foundation for getting this knowledge, while four years of college expands it, and postgraduate work directs students to explore specific areas more deeply.

High School

If you have an interest in biochemistry as a high school student, you should take at least one year each of biology, chemistry, physics, algebra, geometry, and trigonometry. Introductory calculus is also a good idea. Because scientists must clearly and accurately communicate their results verbally and in writing, English courses that emphasize writing skills are strongly recommended. Many colleges and universities also require several years of a foreign language, a useful skill in this day and age, as scientists frequently exchange information with researchers from other countries.

Postsecondary Training

Some colleges have their own special requirements for admission, so you should do a little research and take any special courses you need for the college that interests you. Also, check the catalogs of colleges and universities to see if they offer a program in biochemistry or related sciences. Some schools award a bachelor's degree in biochemistry, and nearly all colleges and universities offer a major in biology or chemistry.

To best prepare yourself for a career in biochemistry or molecular biology, you should start by earning a bachelor's degree in either of these two areas. Even if your college does not offer a specific program in biochemistry or molecular biology, you can get comparable training by doing one of two things: (1) working toward a bachelor's degree in chemistry and taking courses in biology, molecular genetics, and biochemistry, including a biochemistry laboratory class, or (2) earning a bachelor's degree in biology, but taking more chemistry, mathematics, and physics courses than the biology major may require, and also choosing a biochemistry course that has lab work with it.

It really doesn't matter if you earn a bachelor of science (B.S.) or a bachelor of arts (B.A.) degree; some schools offer both. It is more important to choose your courses thoughtfully and to get advice in your freshman year from a faculty member who knows about the fields of biochemistry and molecular biology.

Many careers in biochemistry, especially those that involve teaching at a college or directing scientific research at a university, a government laboratory, or a commercial company, require at least a master's degree and prefer a doctorate or Ph.D. degree. Most students enter graduate programs with a bachelor's degree in biochemistry, or in chemistry or biology with supplementary courses. Because biochemistry and molecular biology are so broad-based, you can enter their graduate programs from such diverse fields as physics, psychology, nutrition, microbiology, or engineering. Graduate schools prefer students with laboratory or research experience.

However you get there, a graduate education program is intense. A master's degree requires about a year of course work and often a research project as well. For a Ph.D. degree, full-time course work can last up to two years, followed by one or more special test exams. But the most important part of Ph.D. training is the requirement for all students to conduct an extensive research project leading to significant new scientific findings. Most students work under a faculty member's direction. This training is vital, as it will help you develop the skills to frame scientific questions and discover ways to answer them. It will also teach you important laboratory skills useful in tackling other biochemical problems. Most students complete a Ph.D. program in four or five years.

Certification or Licensing

Biochemists who wish to work in a hospital may need certification by a national certifying board such as the American Board of Clinical Chemistry.

Other Requirements

A scientist never stops learning, even when formal education has ended. This is particularly true for biochemists and molecular biologists because constant breakthroughs and technology advances make for a constantly changing work environment. That is why most Ph.D.'s go for more research experience (postdoctoral research) before they enter the workplace. As a "postdoc," you would not take course work, earn a degree, or teach; you would be likely to work full time on a high-level research project in the laboratory of an established scientist. Typically, this postdoctoral period lasts two to three years, during which time you would get a salary or be supported by a fellowship. Though not essential for many industry research jobs, postdoctoral research is generally expected of those wishing to become professors. Also, because biochemistry and medicine are such allies, some Ph.D. recipients also earn their medical degrees, or M.D.s, as a physician does. This is to get the broadest possible base for a career in medical research.

EXPLORING

The analytical, specialized nature of most biochemistry makes it unlikely that you will gain much exposure to it before college. Many high school chemistry and biology courses, however, allow students to work with laboratory tools and techniques that will give them a valuable background before college. In some cases, high school students can take advantage of opportunities to train as laboratory technicians by taking courses at a community college. You might also want to contact local colleges, universities, or laboratories to set up interviews with biochemists to learn as much as you can about the field. In addition, reading science and medical magazines will help you to stay current with recent breakthroughs in the biochemistry field.

EMPLOYERS

There are approximately 22,860 biochemists and biophysicists employed in the United States. Nearly half work in the scientific research and development services industry. Others work for government agencies at the federal, state, and local levels. Some major governmental employers of biochemists include the National Institutes of Health, the Departments of Agriculture and Defense, the National Aeronautics and Space Administration, and national laboratories. At such agencies these scientists may do basic research and analyze food, drug, air, water, waste, or animal tissue samples. Biochemists also work for university medical schools or nonprofit organizations, such as a foundation or research institute, doing basic research. Drug companies employ biochemists to search for the causes of diseases or develop drugs to cure them. Biochemists work in quality control, research, manufacturing/production, or information systems at biotechnology companies that concentrate on the environment, energy, human health care, agriculture, or animal health. Universities hire biochemists to teach in combination with doing research.

STARTING OUT

A bachelor's degree in biochemistry or molecular biology can help you get into medical, dental, veterinary, law, or business school. It can also be a stepping-stone to a career in many different but related fields: biotechnology, toxicology, biomedical engineering, clinical chemistry, plant pathology, animal science, or other fields. Biochemists fresh from a college undergraduate program can take advantage of opportunities to get valuable on-the-job experience in a biochemistry or molecular biology laboratory. The National Science Foundation and the National Institutes of Health, both federal government agencies, sponsor research programs for undergraduates. Groups who can particularly benefit from these programs include women, Hispanics, African Americans, Native Americans, Native Alaskans, and students with disabilities. Your college or university may also offer senior research projects that provide hands-on experience.

Another way to improve your chances of getting a job is to spend an additional year at a university with training programs for specialized laboratory techniques. Researchers and companies like these "certificate programs" because they teach valuable skills related to cell culture, genetic engineering, recombinant DNA technology, biotechnology, in vitro cell biology, protein engineering, or DNA sequencing and synthesis. In some universities, you can work toward a bachelor's degree and a certificate at the same time.

Biochemists with a bachelor's degree usually begin work in industry or government as research assistants doing testing and analysis. In the drug industry, for example, you might analyze the ingredients of a product to verify and maintain its quality. Biochemists with a master's degree may enter the field in management, marketing, or sales positions, whereas those with a doctorate usually go into basic or applied research. Many Ph.D.

graduates work at colleges and universities where the emphasis is on teaching.

ADVANCEMENT

The more education you have, the greater your reward potential. Biochemists with a graduate degree have more opportunities for advancement than those with only an undergraduate degree. It is not uncommon for students to go back to graduate school after working for a while in a job that required a lesser degree. Some graduate students become research or teaching assistants in colleges and universities, qualifying for professorships when they receive their advanced degrees. Having a doctorate allows you to design research initiatives and direct others in carrying out experiments. Experienced biochemists with doctorates can move up to high-level administrative positions and supervise entire research programs. Other highly qualified biochemists who prefer to devote themselves to research often become leaders in a particular aspect of their profession.

EARNINGS

According to a report by the National Association of Colleges and Employers, beginning salaries in July 2009 for graduates with bachelor's degrees in biological and life sciences averaged $33,254 per year.

The U.S. Department of Labor reports that biochemists and biophysicists had average annual incomes of $82,390 in 2009. Salaries ranged from less than $44,990 to more than $138,820 per year.

Colleges and universities also employ many biochemists as professors and researchers. The U.S. Department of Labor reports that in 2009, postsecondary chemistry teachers had median salaries of $68,760, and biological science teachers made $73,980.

Biochemists who work for universities, the government, or industry all tend to receive good benefits packages, such as health and life insurance, pension plans, and paid vacation and sick leave. Those employed as university faculty operate on the academic calendar, which means that they can get summer and winter breaks from teaching classes.

WORK ENVIRONMENT

Biochemists generally work in clean, quiet, and well-lighted laboratories where physical labor is minimal. They must, however, take the proper precautions in handling chemicals and organic substances that could be dangerous or cause illness. They may work with plants and animals; tissues, cells, and products; and with yeast and bacteria.

Biochemists in industry generally work a 40-hour week, although they, like their counterparts in research, often put in many extra hours. They must be ready to spend a considerable amount of time keeping up with current literature, for example. Many biochemists occasionally travel to attend meetings or conferences. Those in research write papers for presentation at meetings or for publication in scientific journals.

Individuals interested in biochemistry must have the patience to work for long periods of time on a project without necessarily getting the desired results. Biochemistry is often a team affair, requiring an ability to work well and cooperate with others. Successful biochemists are continually learning and increasing their skills.

OUTLOOK

Employment for biochemists is expected to grow much faster than the average for all occupations through 2018, according to the U.S. Department of Labor. Biotechnological research and development is fueling job growth. Employment is available in health-related fields, where the emphasis is on finding cures for such diseases as cancer, muscular dystrophy, HIV/AIDS, and Alzheimer's, and in other settings such as agricultural research. Additional jobs will be created to produce genetically engineered drugs and other products in the new and rapidly expanding field of genetic engineering. In this area, the outlook is best for biochemists with advanced degrees who can conduct genetic and cellular research. A caveat exists, however. Competition will be strong for basic research positions, and candidates with more education and the experience it brings will be more likely to find the positions they want. Additionally, employment growth may slow somewhat as the number of new biotechnology firms slows and existing firms merge. Biochemists with bachelor's degrees who have difficulty entering their chosen career field may find openings as technicians or technologists or may choose to transfer their skills to other biological science fields.

FOR MORE INFORMATION

For information about clinical laboratory careers, contact
AACC
1850 K Street, NW, Suite 625
Washington, DC 20006-2215
Tel: 800-892-1400
http://www.aacc.org

For general information about chemistry careers and approved education programs, contact

American Chemical Society
1155 16th Street, NW
Washington, DC 20036-4839
Tel: 800-227-5558
E-mail: help@acs.org
http://www.chemistry.org

For information on careers in the biological sciences, contact
American Institute of Biological Sciences
1900 Campus Commons Drive, Suite 200
Reston, VA 20191-1566
Tel: 703-674-2500
http://www.aibs.org

For information on educational programs, contact
American Society for Biochemistry and Molecular Biology
9650 Rockville Pike
Bethesda, MD 20814-3996
Tel: 301-634-7145
http://www.asbmb.org

For career resources, contact
American Society for Investigative Pathology
9650 Rockville Pike, Suite E133
Bethesda, MD 20814-3999
Tel: 301-634-7130
E-mail: asip@asip.org
http://www.asip.org

For career information, including articles and books, contact
Biotechnology Industry Organization
1201 Maryland Avenue, SW, Suite 900
Washington, DC 20024-2149
Tel: 202-962-9200
E-mail: info@bio.org
http://www.bio.org

BIOMEDICAL ENGINEERS

OVERVIEW

Biomedical engineers are highly trained scientists who use engineering and life science principles to research biological aspects of animal and human life. They develop

SCHOOL SUBJECTS
Biology, Chemistry

PERSONAL SKILLS
Helping/teaching, Technical/scientific

MINIMUM EDUCATION LEVEL
Bachelor's degree

CERTIFICATION OR LICENSING
Required for certain positions

WORK ENVIRONMENT
Primarily indoors, Primarily one location

new theories, and they modify, test, and prove existing theories on life systems. They design health care instruments and devices or apply engineering principles to the study of human systems. There are approximately 14,760 biomedical engineers employed in the United States.

THE JOB
Using engineering principles to solve medical and health-related problems, the biomedical engineer works closely with life scientists, members of the medical profession, and chemists. Most of the work revolves around the laboratory. There are three interrelated work areas: research, design, and teaching.

Biomedical research is multifaceted and broad in scope. It calls upon engineers to apply their knowledge of mechanical, chemical, and electrical engineering as well as anatomy and physiology in the study of living systems. Using computers, biomedical engineers use their knowledge of graphic and related technologies to develop mathematical models that simulate physiological systems.

In biomedical engineering design, medical instruments and devices are developed. Engineers work on artificial organs, ultrasonic imagery devices, cardiac pacemakers, and surgical lasers, for example. They design and build systems that will update hospital, laboratory, and clinical procedures. They also train health care personnel in the proper use of this new equipment.

Biomedical engineering is taught on the university level. Teachers conduct classes, advise students, serve on academic committees, and supervise or conduct research.

Within biomedical engineering, an individual may concentrate on a particular specialty area. Some of the well-established specialties are *biomechanics, biomaterials, bioinstrumentation, systems physiology, orthopedic engineering,* and *rehabilitation engineering*. These specialty areas frequently depend on one another.

Biomechanics is mechanics applied to biological or medical problems. Examples include the artificial heart, the artificial kidney, and the artificial hip. Biomaterials is the study of the optimal materials with which to construct such devices. Bioinstrumentation is the science of measuring physiological functions. Systems physiology uses engineering strategies, techniques, and tools to gain a comprehensive and integrated understanding of living organisms ranging from bacteria to humans. Biomedical engineers in this specialty examine such things as the biochemistry of metabolism and the control of limb movements. Orthopedic engineering is the application of biomedical engineering to diseases and conditions of the musculoskeletal system. Rehabilitation engineering is a new and growing specialty area of biomedical engineering. Its goal is to expand the capabilities and improve the quality of life for individuals with physical impairments. *Rehabilitation engineers* often work directly with the disabled person and modify equipment for individual use.

REQUIREMENTS
High School

You can best prepare for a career as a biomedical engineer by taking courses in biology, chemistry, physics, mathematics, drafting, and computers. Communication and problem-solving skills are necessary, so classes in English, writing, and logic are important. Participating in science clubs and competing in science fairs will give you the opportunity to design and invent systems and products.

Postsecondary Training

Most biomedical engineers have an undergraduate degree in biomedical engineering or a related field and a Ph.D. in some facet of biomedical engineering. Undergraduate study is roughly divided into halves. The first two years are devoted to theoretical subjects, such as abstract physics and differential equations in addition to the core curriculum most undergraduates take. The third and fourth years include more applied science. In the United States, biomedical engineering programs are accredited by the Accreditation Board for Engineering and Technology (http://www.abet.org).

During graduate programs, students work on research or product development projects headed by faculty.

Certification or Licensing

Engineers whose work may affect the life, health, or safety of the public must be registered according to regulations in all 50 states and the District of Columbia. Applicants for registration must have received a degree from an American Board for Engineering and Technology–accredited engineering program and have four years of experience. They must also pass a written examination administered by the state in which they aim to work.

Other Requirements

You should have a strong commitment to learning if you plan on becoming a biomedical engineer. You should be scientifically inclined and be able to apply that knowledge in problem solving. Becoming a biomedical engineer requires long years of schooling because a biomedical engineer needs to be an expert in the fields of engineering and biology. Also, biomedical engineers have to be familiar with chemical, material, and electrical engineering as well as physiology and computers.

EXPLORING

Undergraduate courses offer a great deal of exposure to the field. Working in a hospital where biomedical engineers are employed can also provide you with insight into the field, as can interviews with practicing or retired biomedical engineers. Additionally, you can read *Biomedical Engineering News,* which can be found at the Biomedical Engineering Society's Web site, http://www.bmes.org.

EMPLOYERS

There are approximately 14,760 biomedical engineers working in the United States. About 20 percent are employed in scientific research and development, and nearly 20 percent work in medical equipment and supplies manufacturing. In addition, many biomedical engineers are employed in hospitals and medical institutions, and in research and educational facilities. Employment opportunities also exist in government regulatory agencies.

STARTING OUT

A variety of routes may be taken to gain employment as a biomedical engineer. Recent graduates may use college placement services, or they may apply directly to employers, often to personnel offices in hospitals and industry. A job may be secured by answering an advertisement in the employment section of a newspaper. Information on job openings is also available at state employment offices and the federal Office of Personnel Management (http://usajobs.opm.gov). Additionally, the Biomedical Engineering Society offers job listings at its Web site, http://www.bmes.org.

ADVANCEMENT

Advancement opportunities are tied directly to educational and research background. In a nonteaching capacity, a biomedical engineer with an advanced degree can rise to a supervisory position. In teaching, a doctorate is usually necessary to become a full professor. By demonstrating excellence in research, teaching, and departmental committee involvement, one can move from instructor to assistant professor and then to full professor, department chair, or even dean.

Qualifying for and receiving research grant funding can also be a means of advancing one's career in both the nonteaching and teaching sectors.

EARNINGS

The amount a biomedical engineer earns is dependent upon education, experience, and type of employer. According to the U.S. Department of Labor, biomedical engineers had a median yearly income of $78,860 in 2009. At the low end of the pay scale, 10 percent earned less than $49,480 per year, and at the high end, 10 percent earned more than $123,270 annually.

According to a 2009 survey by the National Association of Colleges and Employers, the average beginning salary for biomedical engineers with bachelor's degrees was $54,158.

Biomedical engineers can expect benefits from employers, including health insurance, paid vacation and sick days, and retirement plans.

WORK ENVIRONMENT

Biomedical engineers who teach in a university will have much student contact in the classroom, the laboratory, and the office. They also will be expected to serve on relevant committees while continuing their teaching, research, and writing responsibilities. As competition for teaching positions increases, the requirement that professors publish papers will increase. Professors usually are responsible for obtaining government or private research grants to support their work.

Those who work in industry and government have much contact with other professionals, including chemists, medical scientists, and doctors. They often work as part of a team, testing and developing new products. All biomedical engineers who do lab work are in clean, well-lighted environments, using sophisticated equipment.

OUTLOOK

There will be great demand for skilled biomedical engineers in the future. Prospects look particularly good in the health care industry, which will continue to grow rapidly, primarily because people are living longer and require better medical devices and equipment. The U.S. Department of Labor predicts that employment for biomedical engineers will increase much faster than the average for all occupations through 2018. New jobs will become available in biomedical research in prosthetics, pharmaceutical manufacturing and related industries (especially in cost-management settings), the development of artificial internal organs, computer applications, and instrumentation and other medical systems. In addition, demand will exist for professors to train the biomedical engineers needed to fill these positions.

Because of the increased demand for biomedical engineers, the number of degrees granted in the field has increased significantly. Graduates with a bachelor's degree will face stiff competition for entry-level jobs. Thus, people entering this field are strongly encouraged to pursue a graduate degree to increase their job prospects.

FOR MORE INFORMATION

For information on medical and biological engineering, contact

American Institute for Medical and Biological Engineering
1701 K Street, NW, Suite 510
Washington, DC 20006-1520
Tel: 202-496-9660
http://www.aimbe.org

For more information on careers in biomedical engineering, contact

American Society for Engineering Education
1818 N Street, NW, Suite 600
Washington, DC 20036-2479
Tel: 202-331-3500
http://www.asee.org

Visit the following Web site for more information on educational programs, job listings, grants, and links to other biomedical engineering sites:

The Biomedical Engineering Network
http://www.bmenet.org

For information on careers, student chapters, and to read the brochure Planning a Career in Biomedical Engineering, *contact or visit the following Web site:*

Biomedical Engineering Society
8401 Corporate Drive, Suite 140
Landover, MD 20785-2224
Tel: 301-459-1999
E-mail: info@bmes.org
http://www.bmes.org

For career information, including articles and books, contact
Biotechnology Industry Organization
1201 Maryland Avenue, SW, Suite 900
Washington, DC 20024-2149
Tel: 202-962-9200
E-mail: info@bio.org
http://www.bio.org

For information on high school programs that provide opportunities to learn about engineering technology, contact JETS.
Junior Engineering Technical Society (JETS)
1420 King Street, Suite 405
Alexandria, VA 22314-2750
Tel: 703-548-5387
E-mail: info@jets.org
http://www.jets.org

For Canadian career information, contact
Canadian Medical and Biological Engineering Society
1485 Laperriere Avenue
Ottawa, ON K1Z 7S8 Canada
http://www.cmbes.ca

BIOMEDICAL EQUIPMENT TECHNICIANS

OVERVIEW

Biomedical equipment technicians, also known as *medical equipment repairers*, handle the complex medical equipment and instruments found in hospitals, clinics, and research facilities. This equipment is used for medical therapy and diagnosis and includes heart-lung machines, artificial kidney machines, patient monitors, chemical analyzers, and other electrical, electronic, mechanical, or pneumatic devices.

Technicians' main duties are to inspect, maintain, repair, and install this equipment. They disassemble

SCHOOL SUBJECTS
Biology, Technical/shop

PERSONAL SKILLS
Mechanical/manipulative, Technical/scientific

MINIMUM EDUCATION LEVEL
Associate's degree

CERTIFICATION OR LICENSING
Recommended

WORK ENVIRONMENT
Primarily indoors, Primarily one location

equipment to locate malfunctioning components, repair or replace defective parts, and reassemble the equipment, adjusting and calibrating it to ensure that it operates according to manufacturers' specifications. Other duties of biomedical equipment technicians include modifying equipment according to the directions of medical or supervisory personnel, arranging with equipment manufacturers for necessary equipment repair, and safety-testing equipment to ensure that patients, equipment operators, and other staff members are safe from electrical or mechanical hazards. Biomedical equipment technicians work with hand tools, power tools, measuring devices, and manufacturers' manuals.

Technicians may work for equipment manufacturers as salespeople or as service technicians, or for a health care facility specializing in the repair or maintenance of specific equipment, such as that used in radiology, nuclear medicine, or patient monitoring. Approximately 34,550 people work as biomedical equipment technicians in the United States.

THE JOB

Biomedical equipment technicians are an important link between technology and medicine. They repair, calibrate, maintain, and operate biomedical equipment working under the supervision of researchers, biomedical engineers, physicians, surgeons, and other professional health care providers.

Biomedical equipment technicians may work with thousands of different kinds of equipment. Some of the most frequently encountered are the following: patient monitors; heart-lung machines; kidney machines; blood-gas analyzers; spectrophotometers; X-ray units; radiation

monitors; defibrillators; anesthesia apparatus; pacemakers; blood pressure transducers; spirometers; sterilizers; diathermy equipment; patient-care computers; defibrillators; voice-controlled operating tables; electric wheelchairs; ultrasound machines; and diagnostic scanning machines, such as the CT (computed tomography) scan machine, PET (positron emission tomography) scanner, and MRI (magnetic resonance imaging) machines. Technicians also work with sophisticated dental, optometric, and ophthalmic equipment. Repairing faulty instruments is one of the chief functions of biomedical equipment technicians. They investigate equipment problems, determine the extent of malfunctions, make repairs on instruments that have had minor breakdowns, and expedite the repair of instruments with major breakdowns, for instance, by writing an analysis of the problem for the factory. In doing this work, technicians rely on manufacturers' diagrams, maintenance manuals, and standard and specialized test instruments, such as oscilloscopes and pressure gauges.

Installing equipment is another important function of biomedical equipment technicians. They inspect and test new equipment to make sure it complies with performance and safety standards as described in the manufacturer's manuals and diagrams, and as noted on the purchase order. Technicians may also check on proper installation of the equipment, or, in some cases, install it themselves. To ensure safe operations, technicians need a thorough knowledge of the regulations related to the proper grounding of equipment, and they need to actively carry out all steps and procedures to ensure safety.

Maintenance is the third major area of responsibility for biomedical equipment technicians. In doing this work, technicians try to catch problems before they become more serious. To this end, they take apart and reassemble devices, test circuits, clean and oil moving parts, and replace worn parts. They also keep complete records of all machine repairs, maintenance checks, and expenses.

In all three of these areas, a large part of technicians' work consists of consulting with physicians, administrators, engineers, and other related professionals. For example, they may be called upon to assist hospital administrators as they make decisions about the repair, replacement, or purchase of new equipment. They consult with medical and research staffs to determine that equipment is functioning safely and properly. They also consult with medical and engineering staffs when called upon to modify or develop equipment. In all of these activities, they use their knowledge of electronics, medical terminology, human anatomy and physiology, chemistry, and physics.

In addition, biomedical equipment technicians are involved in a range of other related duties. Some biomedical equipment technicians maintain inventories of all instruments in the hospital, their condition, location, and operators. They reorder parts and components, assist in providing people with emergency instruments, restore unsafe or defective instruments to working order, and check for safety regulation compliance.

Other biomedical equipment technicians help physicians, surgeons, nurses, and researchers conduct procedures and experiments. In addition, they must be able to explain to staff members how to operate these machines, the conditions under which a certain apparatus may or may not be used, how to solve small operating problems, and how to monitor and maintain equipment.

In many hospitals, technicians are assigned to a particular service, such as pediatrics, surgery, or renal medicine. These technicians become specialists in certain types of equipment. However, unlike electrocardiograph technicians or dialysis technicians, who specialize in one kind of equipment, most biomedical equipment technicians must be thoroughly familiar with a large variety of instruments. They might be called upon to prepare an artificial kidney or to work with a blood-gas analyzer. Biomedical equipment technicians also maintain pulmonary function machines. These machines are used in clinics for ambulatory patients, hospital laboratories, departments of medicine for diagnosis and treatment, and rehabilitation of cardiopulmonary patients.

While most biomedical equipment technicians are trained in electronics technology, there is also a need for technicians trained in plastics to work on the development of artificial organs and for people trained in glass blowing to help make the precision parts for specialized equipment.

Many biomedical equipment technicians work for medical instrument manufacturers. These technicians consult and assist in the construction of new machinery, helping to make decisions concerning materials and construction methods to be used in the manufacture of the equipment.

REQUIREMENTS
High School

There are a number of classes you can take in high school to help you prepare for this work. Science classes, such as chemistry, biology, and physics, will give you the science background you will need for working in a medical environment. Take shop classes that deal with electronics, drafting, or blueprint reading. These classes will give you experience working with your hands, following printed directions, using electricity, and working with machinery. Mathematics classes will help you become comfortable working with numbers and formulas. Don't neglect your English studies. English classes will help you develop your communication skills, which will be important to have when you deal with a variety of different people in your professional life.

Postsecondary Training

To become qualified for this work, you will need to complete postsecondary education that leads either to an associate's degree in biomedical equipment technology, electronics, or engineering from a two-year institution or a bachelor's degree from a four-year college or university. Most biomedical equipment technicians choose to receive an associate's degree. Biomedical equipment technology is a relatively new program in some schools and may also be referred to as *medical electronics technology* or *biomedical engineering technology*. The Association for the Advancement of Medical Instrumentation offers a list of biomedical equipment technology and related educational programs at its Web site, http://www.aami.org/resources/education/ed.map.html.

No matter what the name of the program, however, you should expect to receive instruction in such areas as anatomy, physiology, electrical and electronic fundamentals, chemistry, physics, and biomedical equipment construction and design. In addition, you will study safety methods in health care facilities and medical equipment troubleshooting, as it will be your job to be the problem solver. You should also expect to continue taking communication or English classes since communication skills will be essential to your work. In addition to the classroom work, many programs often provide you with practical experience in repairing and servicing equipment in a clinical or laboratory setting under the supervision of an experienced equipment technician. In this way, you learn about electrical components and circuits, the design and construction of common pieces of machinery, and computer technology as it applies to biomedical equipment.

By studying various pieces of equipment, you learn a problem-solving technique that applies not only to the equipment studied, but also to equipment you have not yet seen, and even to equipment that has not yet been invented. Part of this problem-solving technique includes learning how and where to locate sources of information.

Some biomedical equipment technicians receive their training in the armed forces. During the course of an enlistment period of four years or less, military personnel can receive training that prepares them for entry-level or sometimes advanced-level positions in the civilian workforce.

Certification or Licensing

The Board of Examiners for Biomedical Equipment Technicians, which is affiliated with the Association for the Advancement of Medical Instrumentation (AAMI), maintains certification programs for biomedical equipment technicians. The following categories are available: biomedical equipment technician, radiology equipment specialist, and laboratory equipment specialist. Contact the AAMI for more information. Although certification is not required for employment, it is highly recommended. Technicians with certification have demonstrated that they have attained an overall knowledge of the field and are dedicated to their profession. Many employers prefer to hire technicians who are certified.

Other Requirements

Biomedical equipment technicians need mechanical ability and should enjoy working with tools. Because this job demands quick decision making and prompt repairs, technicians should work well under pressure. You should be extremely precise and accurate in your work and enjoy helping others—an essential quality for anyone working in the health care industry. You should also have good communication skills in order to work well with medical professionals and other technicians, as well as with patients (since you may occasionally be called in to repair a piece of equipment while it is in use).

EXPLORING

The AAMI offers detailed information on the career of biomedical equipment technician at its Web site, http://www.aami.org/student. At the site, you can download a career brochure, watch videos that detail educational training and career options, and ask questions about the field.

You will have difficulty gaining any direct experience in biomedical equipment technology until you are in a training program or working professionally. Your first hands-on opportunities generally come in the clinical and laboratory phases of your education. You can, however, visit school and community libraries to seek out books written about careers in medical technology. You can also join a hobby club devoted to chemistry, biology, radio equipment, or electronics.

Perhaps the best way to learn more about this job is to set up, with the help of teachers or counselors, a visit to a local health care facility or to arrange for a biomedical equipment technician to speak to interested students, either on site or at a career exploration seminar hosted by the school. You may be able to ask the technician about his or her educational background, what a day on the job is like, and what new technologies are on the horizon. Try to visit a school offering a program in biomedical equipment technology and discuss your career plans with an admissions counselor there. The counselor may also be able to provide you with helpful insights about the career and your preparation for it.

Finally, because this work involves the health care field, consider getting a part-time job or volunteering at a local hospital. Naturally, you won't be asked to work with the biomedical equipment, but you will have the opportunity to see professionals on the job and experience being in the medical environment. Even if your duty is only to escort patients to their tests, you may gain a greater understanding of this work.

EMPLOYERS

Approximately 34,550 biomedical equipment technicians are employed in the United States. Nearly one-third work for professional and commercial equipment and supplies merchant wholesalers. Others work for general medical and surgical hospitals. Other places of employment include research institutes, independent service organizations, biological laboratories, and biomedical equipment manufacturers. Government hospitals and the military also employ biomedical equipment technicians.

STARTING OUT

Most schools offering programs in biomedical equipment technology work closely with local hospitals and industries, and career services counselors are usually informed about openings when they become available. In some cases, recruiters may visit a school periodically to conduct interviews. Also, many schools place students in part-time hospital jobs to help them gain practical experience. Students are often able to return to these hospitals for full-time employment after graduation.

Another effective method of finding employment is to communicate directly with hospitals, research institutes, or biomedical equipment manufacturers regarding job openings. Other good sources of leads for job openings include state employment offices, newspaper want ads, and the Web sites of professional associations such as the Medical Equipment and Technology Association (http://www.mymeta.org) and the AAMI (http://www.aami.org/career).

ADVANCEMENT

With experience, biomedical equipment technicians can expect to work with less supervision, and in some cases they may find themselves supervising less-experienced technicians. They may advance to positions in which they serve as instructors, assist in research, or have administrative duties. Although many supervisory positions are open to biomedical equipment technicians, some positions are not available without additional education. In large metropolitan hospitals, for instance, the minimum educational requirement for biomedical engineers, who do much of the supervising of biomedical equipment technicians, is a bachelor's degree; many engineers have a master's degree as well.

EARNINGS

Salaries for biomedical equipment technicians vary in different institutions and localities and according to the experience, training, certification, and type of work done by the technician. According to the U.S. Department of Labor (DOL), the median annual salary for medical equipment repairers was $42,300 in 2009. The top 10 percent in this profession made $67,540 or more a year, while the lowest 10 percent made less than $25,750 per year. The DOL reports the following mean annual salaries for biomedical equipment technicians by specialty: electronic and precision equipment repair and maintenance, $48,510; general medical and surgical hospitals, $47,220; professional and commercial equipment and supplies merchant wholesalers, $44,940; health and personal care stores, $36,220; and consumer goods rental, $35,000. Those in supervisory or senior positions command higher salaries. Benefits, such as health insurance and vacation days, vary with the employer.

WORK ENVIRONMENT

Working conditions for biomedical equipment technicians vary according to employer and type of work done. Hospital employees generally work a 40-hour week; their schedules sometimes include weekends and holidays, and some technicians may be on call for emergencies. Technicians who are employed by equipment manufacturers may have to travel extensively to install or service equipment.

The physical surroundings in which biomedical equipment technicians work may vary from day to day. Technicians may work in a lab or treatment room with patients or consult with engineers, administrators, and other staff members. Other days, technicians may spend most of their time at a workbench repairing equipment.

OUTLOOK

The DOL predicts that employment for biomedical equipment technicians will grow much faster than the average for all careers through 2018. Factors behind this growth include more demand for health care services (especially among those age 65 and older) and the increasing use of electronic medical devices and other sophisticated biomedical equipment.

In hospitals the need for more biomedical equipment technicians exists not only because of the increasing use of biomedical equipment but also because hospital administrators realize that these technicians can help hold down costs. Biomedical equipment technicians do this through their preventive maintenance checks and by taking over some routine activities of engineers and administrators, thus releasing those professionals for activities that only they can perform. Through the coming decades, cost containment will remain a high priority for hospital administrators, and as long as biomedical equipment technicians can contribute to that effort, the demand for them should remain strong.

Job opportunities should continue to grow for the many biomedical equipment technicians who work for companies that build, sell, lease, or service biomedical equipment.

The federal government employs biomedical equipment technicians in its hospitals, research institutes, and the military. Employment in these areas will depend largely on levels of government spending. In the research area, spending levels may vary; however, in health care delivery, spending should remain high for the near future.

Technicians with associate's degrees in biomedical equipment technology or engineering who are willing to relocate to rural areas (where there is a shortage of technicians) will have the best employment prospects.

FOR MORE INFORMATION

For industry information, contact
American Society for Healthcare Engineering
155 North Wacker Drive, Suite 400
Chicago, IL 60606-1719
Tel: 312-422-3800
E-mail: ashe@aha.org
http://www.ashe.org

For information on careers, biomedical technology programs, and certification, contact

Association for the Advancement of Medical
    Instrumentation
4301 North Fairfax Drive, Suite 301
Arlington, VA 22203-1633
Tel: 800-332-2264
http://www.aami.org

For information on careers, contact
Medical Equipment and Technology Association
http://www.mymeta.org

CARDIOVASCULAR TECHNOLOGISTS

OVERVIEW

Cardiovascular technologists assist physicians in diagnosing and treating heart and blood vessel ailments. (See "Physicians.") Depending on their specialties, they operate electrocardiograph machines, perform Holter monitor and stress testing, and assist in cardiac catheterization procedures and ultrasound testing. These tasks help the physicians diagnose heart disease and monitor progress during treatment. Cardiovascular technologists hold approximately 48,070 jobs in the United States.

THE JOB

Technologists who assist physicians in the diagnosis and treatment of heart disease are known as cardiovascular

---

SCHOOL SUBJECTS
Biology, Health

PERSONAL SKILLS
Communication/ideas, Technical/scientific

MINIMUM EDUCATION LEVEL
Some postsecondary training

CERTIFICATION OR LICENSING
Voluntary

WORK ENVIRONMENT
Primarily indoors, Primarily one location

---

technologists. (*Cardio* means heart; *vascular* refers to the blood vessel/circulatory system.) Increasingly, hospitals are centralizing cardiovascular services under one full cardiovascular "service line" overseen by the same administrator. In addition to cardiovascular technologists, the cardiovascular team at a hospital may include radiology (X-ray) technologists, nuclear medicine technologists, nurses, physician assistants, respiratory technicians, and respiratory therapists. (See "Radiologic Technologists," "Registered Nurses," "Nurse Assistants," "Physician Assistants," and "Respiratory Therapists and Technicians.") Cardiovascular technologists contribute by performing one or more of a wide range of procedures in cardiovascular medicine, including invasive (enters a body cavity or interrupts normal body functions), noninvasive, peripheral vascular, or echocardiography (ultrasound) procedures. In most facilities, technologists use equipment that is among the most advanced in the medical field; drug therapies may also be used as part of the diagnostic imaging procedures or in addition to them. Technologists' services may be required when the patient's condition is first being explored, before surgery, during surgery (cardiology technologists primarily), or during rehabilitation of the patient. Some of the work is performed on an outpatient basis.

Depending on their specific areas of skill, some cardiovascular technologists are employed in nonhospital health care facilities. For example, they may work for clinics, mobile medical services, or private doctors' offices. Much of their equipment can go just about anywhere.

Some of the specific duties of cardiovascular technologists are described in the following paragraphs. Exact titles of these technologists often vary from medical facility to medical facility because there is no standardized naming system. *Electrocardiograph technologists,* or *EKG technologists,* use an electrocardiograph machine to detect the electronic impulses that come from a patient's heart. The EKG machine records these signals on a paper graph called an electrocardiogram. The electronic impulses recorded by the EKG machine can tell the physician about the action of the heart during and between the individual heartbeats. This in turn reveals important information about the condition of the heart, including irregular heartbeats or the presence of blocked arteries, which the physician can use to diagnose heart disease, monitor progress during treatment, or check the patient's condition after recovery.

To use an EKG machine, the technologist attaches electrodes (small, disk-like devices about the size of a silver dollar) to the patient's chest. Wires attached to the electrodes lead to the EKG machine. Twelve or more leads may be attached. To get a better reading from the electrodes, the technologist may first apply an adhesive gel to the patient's skin that helps to conduct the electrical impulses. The technologist then operates controls on the EKG machine or (more commonly) enters commands for the machine into a computer. The electrodes pick up the electronic signals from the heart and transmit them to the EKG machine. The machine registers and makes a printout of the signals, with a stylus (pen) recording their pattern on a long roll of graph paper.

During the test, the technologist may move the electrodes in order to get readings of electrical activity in different parts of the heart muscle. Since EKG equipment can be sensitive to electrical impulses from other sources, such as other parts of the patient's body or equipment in the room where the EKG test is being done, the technologist must watch for false readings.

After the test, the EKG technologist takes the electrocardiogram off the machine, edits it or makes notes on it, and sends it to the physician (usually a cardiologist, or heart specialist). Physicians may have computer assistance to help them use and interpret the electrocardiogram; special software is available to assist them with their diagnoses.

EKG technologists do not have to repair EKG machines, but they do have to keep an eye on them and know when they are malfunctioning so they can call someone for repairs. They may also keep the machines stocked with paper. Of all the cardiovascular technical positions, EKG technologist positions are the most numerous.

Holter monitoring and stress testing may be performed by *Holter monitor technologists* or *stress test technologists*, respectively, or they may be additional duties of some EKG technologists. In Holter monitoring, electrodes are fastened to the patient's chest, and a small, portable monitor is strapped to the patient's body, often at the waist. The small monitor contains a magnetic tape or cassette that records the action of the heart during activity—as the patient moves, sits, stands, sleeps, etc. The patient is required to wear the Holter monitor for 24 to 48 hours while he or she goes about normal daily activities. When the patient returns to the hospital, the technologist removes the magnetic tape or cassette from the monitor and puts it in a scanner to produce audio and visual representations of heart activity. (Hearing how the heart sounds during activity helps physicians diagnose a possible heart condition.) The technologist reviews and analyzes the information revealed in the tape. Finally, the technologist may print out the parts of the tape that show abnormal heart patterns or make a full tape for the physician.

Stress tests record the heart's performance during physical activity. In one type of stress test, the technologist connects the patient to the EKG machine, attaching electrodes to the patient's arms, legs, and chest, and obtains a reading of the patient's resting heart activity and blood pressure. Then, the patient is asked to walk on a treadmill for a designated period of time while the technologist and the physician monitor the heart. The treadmill speed is increased so that the technologist and physician can see what happens when the heart is put under higher levels of exertion.

Cardiology technologists specialize in providing support for cardiac catheterization (tubing) procedures. These procedures are classified as invasive because they require the physician and attending technologists to enter a body cavity or interrupt normal body functions. In one cardiac catheterization procedure—an angiogram—a catheter (tube) is inserted into the heart (usually by way of a blood vessel in the leg) in order to see the condition of the heart blood vessels, and whether there is a blockage. In another procedure, known as angioplasty, a catheter with a balloon at the end is inserted into an artery to widen it. According to the American Heart Association's 2010 Heart and Stroke Statistical Update, 1,313,000 percutaneous coronary interventions and 1,115,000 cardiac catherizations were done in the United States in 2006. Cardiology technologists also perform a variety of other procedures.

Unlike some of the other cardiovascular technologists, cardiology technologists actually assist in surgical procedures. They may help secure the patient to the table, set up a 35mm video camera or other imaging device under the instructions of the physician (to produce images that assist the physician in guiding the catheter through the cardiovascular system), enter information about the surgical procedure (as it is taking place) into a computer, and provide other support. After the procedure, the technologist may process the angiographic film for use by the physician. Cardiology technologists may also assist during open-heart surgery by preparing and monitoring the patient and placing or monitoring pacemakers.

Vascular technologists and *echocardiographers* are specialists in noninvasive cardiovascular procedures and use ultrasound equipment to obtain and record information about the condition of the heart. Ultrasound equipment is used to send out sound waves to the area of the body being studied; when the sound waves hit the part being studied, they send echoes to the ultrasound machine. The echoes are "read" by the machine, which creates an image on a monitor, permitting the technologist to get an instant "image" of the part of the body and its condition. Vascular technologists are specialists in the use of ultrasound equipment to study blood flow and circulation problems. Echocardiographers are specialists in the use of ultrasound equipment to evaluate the heart and its structures, such as the valves.

Cardiac monitor technicians are similar to and sometimes perform some of the same duties as EKG technologists. Usually working in the intensive care unit or cardio-care unit of the hospital, cardiac monitor technicians keep watch over the patient, monitoring screens to detect any sign that a patient's heart is not beating as it should. Cardiac monitor technicians begin their shift by reviewing the patient's records to familiarize themselves with what the patient's normal heart rhythms should be, what the current pattern is, and what types of problems have been observed. Throughout the shift, cardiac monitor technicians watch for heart rhythm irregularities that need prompt medical attention. Should there be any, they notify a nurse or doctor immediately so that appropriate care can be given.

In addition to these positions, other cardiovascular technologists specialize in a particular aspect of health care. For example, cardiopulmonary technologists specialize in procedures for diagnosing problems with the heart and lungs. They may conduct electrocardiograph, phonocardiograph (sound recordings of the heart's valves and of the blood passing through them), echocardiograph, stress testing, and respiratory test procedures.

Cardiopulmonary technologists also may assist on cardiac catheterization procedures, measuring and recording information about the patient's cardiovascular and pulmonary systems during the procedure and alerting the cardiac catheterization team to any problems.

REQUIREMENTS

High School

At a minimum, cardiovascular technologists need an associate's degree to enter the field. Although no specific high school classes will directly prepare you to be a technologist, getting a good grounding in basic high school subjects are important to all technologist positions.

During high school, you should take English, health, biology, and typing. You might also consider courses in social sciences to help you understand the social and psychological needs of patients.

Postsecondary Training

In the past, many EKG operators were trained on the job by an EKG supervisor. This still may be true for some EKG technician positions. Increasingly, however, EKG technologists get postsecondary schooling before they are hired. Holter monitoring and stress testing may be

part of your EKG schooling, or may be learned through additional training. Ultrasound and cardiology technologists tend to have the most postsecondary schooling (up to a four-year bachelor's degree) and have the most extensive academic/experience requirements for credentialing purposes.

You can enter these positions without having had previous health care experience. However, some previous exposure to the business side of health care or even training in related areas is helpful. With academic training or professional experience in nursing, radiology science, or respiratory science, for example, you may be able to move into cardiology technology.

As a rule of thumb, medical employers value postsecondary schooling that gives you actual hands-on experience with patients in addition to classroom training. At many of the schools that train cardiovascular technologists, you work with patients in a variety of health care settings and train on more than one brand of equipment.

Some employers still have a physician or EKG department manager train EKG technicians on the job. Training generally lasts from one to six months. Trainees learn how to operate the EKG machine, how to produce and edit the electrocardiogram, and other related tasks.

Some vocational, technical, and junior colleges have one- or two-year training programs in EKG technology, Holter monitoring, stress testing, or all three; otherwise, EKG technologists may obtain training in Holter and stress procedures after they've already started working, either on the job or through an additional six months or more of schooling. Formal academic programs give technologists more preparation in the subject than is available with most on-the-job training and allow them to earn a certificate (one-year programs) or associate's degree (two-year programs). The American Medical Association (AMA)'s Health Care Careers Directory has listings of accredited EKG programs in the "Allied health" section.

Ultrasound technologists usually need a high school diploma or equivalent plus one, two, or four years of postsecondary schooling in a trade school, technical school, or community college. Vascular technologists also may be trained on the job. Again, a list of accredited programs can be found in the AMA's Health Care Careers Directory; also, a directory of training opportunities in sonography is available from the Society of Diagnostic Medical Sonography.

Cardiology technologists tend to have the highest academic requirements of all; for example, a four-year bachelor's degree, a two-year associate's degree, or a certificate of completion from a hospital, trade, or technical cardiovascular program. A two-year program at a junior or community college might include one year of core classes (e.g., mathematics, biology, chemistry, and anatomy) and one year of specialized classes in cardiology procedures.

Cardiac monitor technicians need a high school diploma or equivalent, with additional educational requirements similar to those of EKG technicians.

Certification or Licensing

Right now, certification or licensing for cardiovascular technologists is voluntary, however, it has become the professional standard and most employers require technologist be credentialed. Many credentialing bodies for cardiovascular and pulmonary positions exist, including American Registry of Diagnostic Medical Sonographers (ARDMS), Cardiovascular Credentialing International (CCI), and others, and there are more than a dozen possible credentials for cardiovascular technologists. For example, sonographers can take an exam from ARDMS to receive credentialing in sonography. Their credentials may be as registered diagnostic medical sonographer, registered diagnostic cardiac sonographer, or registered vascular technologist. Credentialing requirements for cardiology technologists or ultrasound technologists may include a test plus formal academic and on-the-job requirements. Professional experience or academic training in a related field, such as nursing, radiology science, and respiratory science, may be acceptable as part of these formal academic and professional requirements. As with continuing education, certification is a sign of interest and dedication to the field and is generally favorably regarded by potential employers.

Cardiology is a cutting-edge area of medicine, with constant advancements, and medical equipment relating to the heart is continually updated. Therefore, keeping up with new developments is vital. In addition, technologists who add to their qualifications through taking part in continuing education tend to earn more money and have more employment opportunities. Major professional societies encourage and provide the opportunities for professionals to continue their education.

Other Requirements

Technicians must be able to put patients at ease about the procedure they are to undergo. Therefore, you should be pleasant, patient, alert, and able to understand and sympathize with the feelings of others. When explaining a procedure to patients, cardiovascular technicians should be able to do so in a calm, reassuring, and confident manner.

Cardiovascular technologists generally work with patients who are ill or who have reason to fear they might be ill. With this in mind, there are opportunities for the technicians to do these people some good, but there is also a chance of causing some unintentional harm as well: A well-conducted test can reduce anxieties or make a physician's job easier; a misplaced electrode or an error in recordkeeping could cause an incorrect diagnosis. Technicians need to be able to cope with these responsibilities and consistently conduct their work in the best interests of their patients.

Part of the technician's job includes putting patients at ease about the procedure they are to undergo. Toward that end, technicians should be pleasant, patient, alert, and able to understand and sympathize with the feelings of others. In explaining the nature of the procedure to patients, cardiovascular technicians should be able to do so in a calm, reassuring, and confident manner.

Inevitably, some patients will try to get information about their medical situation from the technician. In such cases, technicians need to be both tactful and firm in explaining that they are only taking the electrocardiogram; the interpretation is for the physician to make.

Another large part of a technician's job involves getting along well with other members of the hospital staff. This task is sometimes made more difficult by the fact that in most hospitals there is a formal, often rigid, status structure, and cardiovascular technologists may find themselves in a relatively low position in that structure. In emergency situations or at other moments of frustration, cardiovascular technologists may find themselves dealt with brusquely or angrily. Technicians should not take outbursts or rude treatment personally, but instead should respond with stability and maturity.

EXPLORING

Prospective cardiovascular technologists will find it difficult to gain any direct experience on a part-time basis in electrocardiography. The first experience with the work generally comes during on-the-job training sessions. You may, however, be able to gain some exposure to patient-care activities in general by signing up for volunteer work at a local hospital. In addition, you can arrange to visit a hospital, clinic, or physician's office where electrocardiographs are taken. In this way, you may be able to watch a technician at work or at least talk to a technician about what the work is like.

EMPLOYERS

There are approximately 48,070 cardiovascular technologists employed in the United States. Most work in hospitals in cardiology departments, but employment can be found in physicians' offices, clinics, medical and diagnostic laboratories, rehab centers, or anyplace electrocardiographs are taken.

STARTING OUT

Because most cardiovascular technologists receive their initial training on their first job, great care should be taken in finding this first employer. Pay close attention not only to the pay and working conditions, but also to the kind of on-the-job training that is provided for each prospective position. High school vocational counselors may be able to tell you which hospitals have good reputations for EKG training programs. Applying directly to hospitals is a common way of entering the field. Information can also be gained by reading the classified ads in the newspaper and from talking with friends and relatives who work in hospitals.

For students who graduate from one- to two-year training programs, finding a first job should be easier. First, employers are always eager to hire people who are already trained. Second, these graduates can be less concerned about the training programs offered by their employers. Third, they should find that their teachers and guidance counselors can be excellent sources of information about job possibilities in the area. If the training program includes practical experience, graduates may find that the hospital in which they trained or worked before graduation would be willing to hire them after graduation.

ADVANCEMENT

Opportunities for advancement are best for cardiovascular technologists who learn to do or assist with more complex procedures, such as stress testing, Holter monitoring, echocardiography, and cardiac catheterization. With proper training and experience, these technicians may eventually become cardiovascular technologists, echocardiography technologists, cardiopulmonary technicians, cardiology technologists, or other specialty technicians or technologists.

In addition to these kinds of specialty positions, experienced technicians may also be able to advance to various supervisory and training posts.

EARNINGS

The median salary for cardiovascular technologists and technicians was $48,300 in 2009, according to the U.S. Department of Labor. The lowest paid 10 percent earned less than $25,940, and the highest paid 10 percent earned more than $76,220 annually. Earnings

can vary by size and type of employer. For example, technologists working in doctors' offices had the mean annual income $53,000, while those in hospitals had a median salary of $48,830. Those with formal training earn more than those who trained on the job, and those who are able to perform more sophisticated tests, such as Holter monitoring and stress testing, are paid more than those who perform only the basic electrocardiograph tests.

Technologists working in hospitals receive the same fringe benefits as other hospital workers, including medical insurance, paid vacations, and sick leave. In some cases, benefits also include educational assistance, retirement plans, and uniform allowances.

WORK ENVIRONMENT

Cardiovascular technologists usually work in clean, quiet, well-lighted surroundings. They generally work five-day, 40-hour weeks, although technicians working in small hospitals may be on 24-hour call for emergencies, and all technicians in hospitals, large or small, can expect to do occasional evening or weekend work. With the growing emphasis in health care on cost containment, more jobs are likely to develop in outpatient settings, so in the future it is likely that cardiovascular technologists will work more often in clinics, health maintenance organizations, and other nonhospital locations.

OUTLOOK

The overall employment of cardiovascular technologists and technicians should grow much faster than the average through 2018, according to the U.S. Department of Labor. Growth will be primarily due to the increasing numbers of older people, who have a higher incidence of heart problems. The labor department, however, projects employment for EKG technicians to decline during this same period as hospitals train other health care personnel to perform basic EKG procedures.

FOR MORE INFORMATION

For information on careers, contact
Alliance of Cardiovascular Professionals
PO Box 2007
Midlothian, VA 23113-9007
Tel: 804-632-0078
http://www.acp-online.org

For information on the medical field, including listings of accredited medical programs, contact
American Medical Association
515 North State Street

Chicago, IL 60654-4854
Tel: 800-621-8335
http://www.ama-assn.org

For information on certification or licensing, contact
**American Registry of Diagnostic Medical
Sonographers**
51 Monroe Street
Plaza East One
Rockville, MD 20850-2400
Tel: 800-541-9754
http://www.ardms.org

For information on credentials, contact
Cardiovascular Credentialing International
1500 Sunday Drive, Suite 102
Raleigh, NC 27607-5151
Tel: 800-326-0268
http://cci-online.org

For information on sonography programs and other resources, contact
Society of Diagnostic Medical Sonography
2475 Dallas Parkway, Suite 350
Plano, TX 75093-8730
Tel: 800-229-9506
http://www.sdms.org

CHIROPRACTORS

OVERVIEW

Chiropractors, or *doctors of chiropractic*, are health care professionals who emphasize health maintenance and disease prevention through proper nutrition, exercise, posture, stress management, and care of the spine and the nervous system. Approximately 26,310 chiropractors practice in the United States. Most work in solo practice; other work settings include group practices, health care clinics, and teaching institutions.

Because of its emphasis on health maintenance, the whole person, and natural healing, chiropractic is considered an alternative health care approach. At the same time, chiropractic has more of the advantages enjoyed by the medical profession than does any other alternative health care field: Chiropractic has licensure requirements, accredited training institutions, a growing scientific research base, and insurance reimbursement.

SCHOOL SUBJECTS
Biology, Chemistry

PERSONAL SKILLS
Mechanical/manipulative, Technical/scientific

MINIMUM EDUCATION LEVEL
Medical degree

CERTIFICATION OR LICENSING
Required

WORK ENVIRONMENT
Primarily indoors, Primarily one location

THE JOB

Chiropractors are trained primary health care providers, much like medical physicians. Chiropractors focus on the maintenance of health and disease prevention. In addition to symptoms, they consider each patient's nutrition, work, stress levels, exercise habits, posture, and so on. Chiropractors treat people of all ages—from children to senior citizens. They see both women and men. Doctors of chiropractic most frequently treat conditions such as backache, disk problems, sciatica, and whiplash. They also care for people with headaches, respiratory disorders, allergies, digestive disturbances, elevated blood pressure, and many other common ailments. Some specialize in areas such as sports medicine or nutrition. Chiropractors do not use drugs or surgery. If they determine that drugs or surgery are needed, they refer the individual to another professional who can meet those needs.

Doctors of chiropractic look for causes of disorders of the spine. They consider the spine and the nervous system to be vitally important to the health of the individual. Chiropractic teaches that problems in the spinal column (backbone) affect the nervous system and the body's natural defense mechanisms and are the underlying causes of many diseases. Chiropractors use a special procedure called a "spinal adjustment" to try to restore the spine to its natural healthy state. They believe this will also have an effect on the individual's total health and well-being.

On the initial visit, doctors of chiropractic meet with the patient and take a complete medical history before beginning treatment. They ask questions about all aspects of the person's life to help determine the nature of the illness. Events in the individual's past that may seem unrelated or unimportant may be significant to the chiropractor.

After the consultation and the case history, chiropractors perform a careful physical examination, sometimes including laboratory tests. When necessary, they use X-rays to help locate the source of patients' difficulties. Doctors of chiropractic study the X-rays for more than just bone fractures or signs of disease. X-rays are the only means of seeing the outline of the spinal column. Chiropractors are trained to observe whether the structural alignment of the spinal column is normal or abnormal.

Once they have made a diagnosis, chiropractic physicians use a variety of natural approaches to help restore the individual to health. The spinal adjustment is the treatment for which chiropractic is most known. During this procedure, patients usually lie on a specially designed adjusting table. Chiropractic physicians generally use their hands to manipulate the spine. They apply pressure and use specialized techniques of manipulation that are designed to help the affected areas of the spine. Doctors of chiropractic must know many sophisticated techniques of manipulation, and they spend countless hours learning to properly administer spinal adjustments. Chiropractic treatments must often be repeated over the course of several visits. The number of treatments needed varies greatly.

In addition to the spinal adjustment, chiropractic physicians may use "physiologic therapeutics" to relieve symptoms. These are drugless natural therapies, such as light, water, electrical stimulation, massage, heat, ultrasound, and biofeedback. Chiropractors also make suggestions about diet, rest, exercise, and support of the afflicted body part. They may recommend routines for the patient to do at home to maintain and improve the results of the manipulation.

Chiropractors pay special attention to lifestyle factors, such as nutrition and exercise. They believe the body has an innate ability to remain healthy if it has the proper ingredients. Doctors of chiropractic propose that the essential ingredients include clean air, water, proper nutrition, rest, and a properly functioning nervous system. Their goal is to maintain the health and well-being of the whole person. In this respect they have been practicing for many years what has recently become known as "health maintenance."

Chiropractors who are in private practice and some who work as group practitioners also have responsibility for running their businesses. They must promote their practices and develop their patient base. They are responsible for keeping records on their patients and for general bookkeeping. Sometimes they hire and train employees.

In larger practices or clinics, chiropractic assistants or office managers usually perform these duties.

REQUIREMENTS
High School

To become a doctor of chiropractic (DC), you will have to study a minimum of six to seven years after high school. Preparing for this profession is just as demanding as preparing to be a medical doctor, and the types of courses you will need are also similar. Science classes, such as biology, chemistry, physics, and psychology, will prepare you for medical courses in college. English, speech, drama, and debate can sharpen the communication skills that are essential for this profession. Math, business, and computer classes can help you get ready to run a private practice.

Postsecondary Training

Most chiropractic colleges require at least two years of undergraduate study before you can enroll. Some require a bachelor's degree. Currently, 16 institutions in the United States have chiropractic programs that are accredited by the Council on Chiropractic Education (CCE). Find out which chiropractic colleges interest you and learn about their requirements. Selecting chiropractic schools well in advance will allow you to structure your undergraduate study to meet the requirements of the schools of your choice. Some chiropractic colleges provide opportunities for prechiropractic study and bachelor's degree programs. In general, you need course work in biology, communications, English, chemistry, physics, psychology, and social sciences or humanities. Contact the national professional associations listed at the end of this article for information about schools and their requirements.

Upon completing the required undergraduate work and enrolling in a chiropractic college, you can expect to take an array of science and medical courses, such as anatomy, pathology, and microbiology. During the first two years of most chiropractic programs you will spend a majority of your time in the classroom or the laboratory. The last two years generally focus on courses in spinal adjustments. During this time, potential chiropractors also train in outpatient clinics affiliated with the college. Upon successful completion of the six- or seven-year professional degree program, you will receive the DC degree.

Certification or Licensing

All 50 states and the District of Columbia require that chiropractors pass a state board examination to obtain a license to practice. Educational requirements and types of practice for which a chiropractor may be licensed vary from state to state. Most state boards recognize academic training only in chiropractic colleges accredited by the CCE. Most states will accept all or part of the National Board of Chiropractic Examiners' test given to fourth-year chiropractic students in place of a state exam. Most states require that chiropractors take continuing education courses each year to keep their licenses.

Other Requirements

Perhaps the most important personal requirement for any health care professional is the desire to help people and to promote wholeness and health. To be a successful chiropractor, you need good listening skills, empathy, and understanding. As a doctor of chiropractic, you will also need a good business sense and the ability to work independently. Especially sharp observational skills are essential in order for you to recognize physical abnormalities. Good hand dexterity is necessary to perform the spinal adjustments and other manipulations, although you do not need unusual strength.

EXPLORING

If you are interested in becoming a chiropractor, there are many ways to start preparing right now. Join all the science clubs you can, design projects, and participate in science fairs. To develop interviewing and communication skills, you might join the school newspaper staff and ask for interview assignments. Learn to play chess, take up fencing, or study art history to increase your powers of observation. Take up an instrument, such as the piano, guitar, or violin, to improve your manual dexterity. Learning to give massages is another way to increase manual dexterity and learn the human body. Be sure to stay in shape and maintain your own health, and learn all you can about homeopathy, yoga, the Alexander Technique, Rolfing, and other systems of mind/body wholeness.

Contact the chiropractic professional associations and ask about their student programs. Check the Internet for bulletin boards or forums related to chiropractic and other areas of health care. Volunteer at a hospital or nursing home to gain experience working with those in need of medical care.

If there is a doctor of chiropractic or a clinic in your area, ask to visit and talk to a chiropractor. Make an appointment for a chiropractic examination so you can experience what it is like. You may even find a part-time or summer job in a chiropractic office.

EMPLOYERS

There are approximately 26,310 chiropractors employed in the United States. A newly licensed doctor of chiropractic might find a salaried position in a chiropractic clinic or with an experienced chiropractor. Other salaried positions can be found in traditional hospitals, in hospitals that specialize in chiropractic treatment, or in alternative health care centers and clinics. Approximately 44 percent of the doctors of chiropractic in the United States are in private practice. Most maintain offices in a professional building with other specialists or at their own clinics.

Chiropractors practice throughout the United States. Jobs in clinics, hospitals, and alternative health care centers may be easier to find in larger cities that have the population to support them. However, most doctors of chiropractic choose to work in small communities. Chiropractors tend to remain near chiropractic institutions, and this has resulted in higher concentrations of chiropractic practices in those geographical areas.

STARTING OUT

Career services offices of chiropractic colleges have information about job openings, and they may be able to help with job placement. As a newly licensed chiropractor, you might begin working in a clinic or in an established practice with another chiropractor on a salary or income-sharing basis. This would give you a chance to start practicing without the major financial investment of equipping an office. It is sometimes possible to purchase the practice of a chiropractor who is retiring or moving. This is usually easier than starting a new solo practice because the purchased practice will already have patients. Some newly licensed practitioners, however, do go straight into private practice.

National chiropractic associations and professional publications may also list job openings. Attend an association meeting to get to know professionals in the field. Networking is an important way to learn about job openings.

ADVANCEMENT

As with many other professions, advancement in chiropractic usually means building a larger practice. A chiropractor who starts out as a salaried employee in a large practice may eventually become a partner in the practice. Chiropractors also advance their careers by building their clientele and setting up their own group practices. They sometimes buy the practices of retiring practitioners to add to their own practices.

Another avenue for advancement is specialization. Chiropractors specialize in areas such as neurology, sports medicine, or diagnostic imaging (X-ray). As the demand for chiropractors is growing, more are advancing their careers through teaching at chiropractic institutions or conducting research. A few doctors of chiropractic become executives with state or national organizations.

EARNINGS

Self-employed chiropractors usually earn more than salaried chiropractors, such as those working as an associate with another chiropractor or doctor. Chiropractors running their own office, however, must pay such expenses as equipment costs, staff salaries, and health insurance.

According to the U.S. Department of Labor, the median annual income for chiropractors working on a salary basis was $67,650 in 2009. The lowest paid 10 percent earned $32,750 that same year, while the highest paid 10 percent earned more than $150,570 per year. According to a survey conducted by *Chiropractic Economics* magazine, the median net income for chiropractors ranged from $87,000 to $117,600 in 2010.

Self-employed chiropractors must provide for their own benefits. Chiropractors who are salaried employees, such as those working on the staff of another doctor or those working for health clinics, usually receive benefits including health insurance and retirement plans.

WORK ENVIRONMENT

Chiropractic physicians work in clean, quiet, comfortable offices. Most solo practitioners and group practices have an office suite. The suite generally has a reception area. In clinics, several professionals may share this area. The suite also contains examining rooms and treatment rooms. In a clinic where several professionals work, there are sometimes separate offices for the individual professionals. Most chiropractors have chiropractic assistants and a secretary or office manager. Those who are in private practice or partnerships need to have good business skills and self-discipline to be successful.

Doctors of chiropractic who work in clinics, hospitals, universities, or professional associations need to work well in a group environment. They will frequently work under supervision or in a team with other professionals. Chiropractors may have offices of their own, or they may share offices with team members, depending on their work and the facility. In these organizations, the physical work environment varies, but it will generally be clean and comfortable. Because they are larger, these settings may be noisier than the smaller practices.

Most chiropractors work about 42 hours per week, although many put in longer hours. Larger organizations may determine the hours of work, but chiroprac-tors in private practice can set their own hours. Evening and weekend hours are often scheduled to accommodate patients' needs.

OUTLOOK

Employment for doctors of chiropractic is expected to grow much faster than the average through 2018, according to the U.S. Department of Labor. Many areas have a shortage of chiropractors. Public interest in alternative health care is growing. Many health-conscious individuals are attracted to chiropractic because it is natural, drugless, and surgery-free. Because of their holistic, personal approach to health care, chiropractors are increasingly seen as primary physicians, especially in rural areas. The average life span is increasing, and so are the numbers of older people in this country. The elderly frequently have more structural and mechanical difficulties with their bodies, and the growth of this segment of the population will increase the demand for doctors of chiropractic.

More insurance policies and health maintenance organizations (HMOs) now cover chiropractic services, but this still varies according to the insurer. As a result of these developments in HMO and insurance coverage, chiropractors receive more referrals for treatment of injuries that result from accidents.

While the demand for chiropractic is increasing, college enrollments are also growing. New chiropractors may find increasing competition in geographic areas where other practitioners are already located. Because of the high cost of equipment such as X-ray and other diagnostic tools, group practices with other chiropractors or related health care professionals are likely to provide more opportunity for employment or for purchasing a share of a practice.

FOR MORE INFORMATION

For general information, and a career kit, contact
American Chiropractic Association
1701 Clarendon Boulevard
Arlington, VA 22209-2799
Tel: 703-276-8800
E-mail: memberinfo@acatoday.org
http://www.acatoday.org

For information on educational requirements and accredited colleges, contact
Council on Chiropractic Education
8049 North 85th Way
Scottsdale, AZ 85258-4321
Tel: 480-443-8877

E-mail: cce@cce-usa.org

http://www.cce-usa.org

For information on student membership and member chiropractors in your area, contact
International Chiropractors Association
6400 Arlington Boulevard, Suite 800
Falls Church, VA 22042-2346
Tel: 800-423-4690
E-mail: chiro@chiropractic.org
http://www.chiropractic.org

For information on licensure, contact
National Board of Chiropractic Examiners
901 54th Avenue
Greeley, CO 80634-4405
Tel: 800-964-6223
E-mail: nbce@nbce.org
http://www.nbce.org

CIVIL ENGINEERS

SCHOOL SUBJECTS
Mathematics, Physics

PERSONAL SKILLS
Leadership/management, Technical/scientific

MINIMUM EDUCATION LEVEL
Bachelor's degree

CERTIFICATION OR LICENSING
Recommended

WORK ENVIRONMENT
Indoors and outdoors, Primarily multiple locations

OVERVIEW

Civil engineers are involved in the design and construction of the physical structures that make up our surroundings, such as roads, bridges, buildings, and harbors. Civil engineering involves theoretical knowledge applied to the practical planning of the layout of our cities, towns, and other communities. It is concerned with modifying the natural environment and building new environments to better the lifestyles of the general public. Civil engineers are also known as *structural engineers*. There are approximately 259,320 civil engineers in the United States.

THE JOB

Civil engineers use their knowledge of materials science, engineering theory, economics, and demographics to devise, construct, and maintain our physical surroundings. They apply their understanding of other branches of science—such as hydraulics, geology, and physics—to design the optimal blueprint for the project.

Feasibility studies are conducted by *surveying and mapping engineers* to determine the best sites and approaches for construction. They extensively investigate the chosen sites to verify that the ground and other surroundings are amenable to the proposed project. These engineers use sophisticated equipment, such as satellites and other electronic instruments, to measure the area and conduct underground probes for bedrock and groundwater. They determine the optimal places where explosives should be blasted in order to cut through rock.

Many civil engineers work strictly as consultants on projects, advising their clients. These consultants usually specialize in one area of the industry, such as water systems, transportation systems, or housing structures. Clients include individuals, corporations, and the government. Consultants will devise an overall design for the proposed project, perhaps a nuclear power plant commissioned by an electric company. They will estimate the cost of constructing the plant, supervise the feasibility studies and site investigations, and advise the client on whom to hire for the actual labor involved. Consultants are also responsible for such details as accuracy of drawings and quantities of materials to order.

Other civil engineers work mainly as contractors and are responsible for the actual building of the structure; they are known as *construction engineers*. They interpret the consultants' designs and follow through with the best methods for getting the work done, usually working directly at the construction site. Contractors are responsible for scheduling the work, buying the materials, maintaining surveys of the progress of the work, and choosing the machines and other equipment used for construction. During construction, these civil engineers must supervise the labor and make sure the work is completed correctly and efficiently. After the project is finished, they must set up a maintenance schedule and periodically check the structure for a certain length of time. Later, the task of ongoing maintenance and repair is often transferred to local engineers.

Civil engineers may be known by their area of specialization. *Transportation engineers,* for example, are concerned mainly with the construction of highways and mass transit systems, such as subways and commuter rail lines. When devising plans for subways, engineers are responsible for considering the tunneling that is involved. *Pipeline engineers* are specialized civil engineers who are involved with the movement of water, oil, and gas through miles of pipeline.

REQUIREMENTS

High School

Because a bachelor's degree is considered essential in the field, high school students interested in civil engineering must follow a college prep curriculum. Students should focus on mathematics (algebra, trigonometry, geometry, and calculus), the sciences (physics and chemistry), computer science, and English and the humanities (history, economics, and sociology). Students should also aim for honors-level courses.

Postsecondary Training

In addition to completing the core engineering curriculum (including mathematics, science, drafting, and computer applications), students can choose their specialty from the following types of courses: structural analysis; materials design and specification; geology; hydraulics; surveying and design graphics; soil mechanics; and oceanography. Bachelor's degrees can be achieved through a number of programs: a four- or five-year accredited college or university; two years in a community college engineering program plus two or three years in a college or university; or five or six years in a co-op program (attending classes for part of the year and working in an engineering-related job for the rest of the year). About 30 percent of civil engineering students go on to receive a master's degree.

Certification or Licensing

Most civil engineers go on to study and qualify for a professional engineer (PE) license. It is required before one can work on projects affecting property, health, or life. Because many engineering jobs are found in government specialties, most engineers take the necessary steps to obtain the license. Requirements are different for each state—they involve educational, practical, and teaching experience. Applicants must take an examination on a specified date.

Other Requirements

Basic personal characteristics often found in civil engineers are an avid curiosity; a passion for mathematics and science; an aptitude for problem solving, both alone and with a team; and an ability to visualize multidimensional, spatial relationships.

EXPLORING

High school students can become involved in civil engineering by attending a summer camp or study program in the field. For example, the Worcester Polytechnic Institute in Massachusetts has a summer program for high school students who have completed their junior year and will be entering their senior year in the fall. Studies and events focus on science and math and include specialties for those interested in civil engineering.

After high school, another way to learn about civil engineering duties is to work on a construction crew that is involved in the actual building of a project designed and supervised by engineers. Such hands-on experience would provide an opportunity to work near many types of civil workers. Try to work on highway crews or even in housing construction.

EMPLOYERS

Nearly half of all civil engineers work for companies involved in architectural and engineering consulting services. Others work for government agencies at the local, state, or federal level. A small percentage are self-employed, running their own consulting businesses. Approximately 259,320 civil engineers work in the United States.

STARTING OUT

To establish a career as a civil engineer, one must first receive a bachelor's degree in engineering or another appropriate scientific field. College career services offices are often the best sources of employment for beginning engineers. Entry-level jobs usually involve routine work, often as a member of a supervised team. After a year or more (depending on job performance and qualifications), one becomes a junior engineer, then an assistant to perhaps one or more supervising engineers. Establishment as a professional engineer comes after passing the PE exam.

ADVANCEMENT

Professional engineers with many years' experience often join with partners to establish their own firms in design, consulting, or contracting. Some leave long-held positions to be assigned as top executives in industries such as manufacturing and business consulting. Also, there are those who return to academia to teach high school or college students. For all of these potential opportunities, it is necessary to keep abreast of engineering advancements and trends by reading industry journals and taking courses.

EARNINGS

Civil engineers are among the lowest paid in the engineering field; however, their salaries are high when compared to those of many other occupations. The median annual earnings for civil engineers were $76,590 in 2009, according to the U.S. Department of Labor. The lowest paid 10 percent made less than $49,620 per year, and, at the other end of the pay scale, 10 percent earned more than $118,320 annually. Civil engineers working for the federal government had a mean salary of $88,040 in 2009. According to a 2009 survey by the National Association of Colleges and Employers, starting salaries for those with bachelor's degrees in civil engineering were $52,048. As with all occupations, salaries are higher for those with more experience and advanced education. Top civil engineers earn as much as $120,000 or more a year.

Benefits typically include such extras as health insurance, retirement plans, and paid vacation days.

WORK ENVIRONMENT

Many civil engineers work regular 40-hour weeks, often in or near major industrial and commercial areas. Sometimes they are assigned to work in remote areas and foreign countries. Because of the diversity of civil engineering positions, working conditions vary widely. Offices, labs, factories, and actual sites are typical environments for engineers.

A typical work cycle involving various types of civil engineers involves three stages: planning, constructing, and maintaining. Those involved with development of a campus compound, for example, would first need to work in their offices developing plans for a survey. Surveying and mapping engineers would have to visit the proposed site to take measurements and perhaps shoot aerial photographs. The measurements and photos would have to be converted into drawings and blueprints. Geotechnical engineers would dig wells at the site and take core samples from the ground. If toxic waste or unexpected water is found at the site, the contractor determines what should be done.

Actual construction then begins. Very often, a field trailer on the site becomes the engineers' makeshift offices. The campus might take several years to build—it

is not uncommon for engineers to be involved in long-term projects. If contractors anticipate that deadlines will not be met, they often put in weeks of 10- to 15-hour days on the job.

After construction is complete, engineers spend less and less time at the site. Some may be assigned to stay on-site to keep daily surveys of how the structure is holding up and to solve problems when they arise. Eventually, the project engineers finish the job and move on to another long-term assignment.

OUTLOOK

Through 2018, employment for civil engineers is expected to grow much faster than the average for all occupations, according to the U.S. Department of Labor. Employment will come from the need to maintain and repair public works, such as highways, bridges, and water systems. In addition, as the population grows, so does the need for more transportation and pollution control systems, which creates jobs for those who construct these systems. Firms providing management consulting and computer services may also be sources of jobs for civil engineers. Employment is affected by several factors, though, including decisions made by the government to spend further on renewing and adding to the country's basic infrastructure and the health of the economy in general.

FOR MORE INFORMATION

For information on training and scholarships, and to read Career Paths in Civil Engineering, *visit the society's Web site.*

American Society of Civil Engineers
1801 Alexander Bell Drive
Reston, VA 20191-4400
Tel: 800-548-2723
http://www.asce.org

Frontiers is a program for high school seniors that covers science material not traditionally offered in high school. For information, contact

Frontiers at Worcester Polytechnic Institute
100 Institute Road
Worcester, MA 01609-2280
Tel: 508-831-5286
E-mail: frontiers@wpi.edu
http://www.wpi.edu/admissions/undergraduate/
    visit/frontiers.html

For information on careers and colleges and universities with ITE student chapters, contact

Institute of Transportation Engineers (ITE)
1627 Eye Street, NW, Suite 600
Washington, DC 20006-4087
Tel: 202-785-0060
E-mail: ite_staff@ite.org
http://www.ite.org

The JETS offers high school students the opportunity to try engineering through a number of programs and competitions. To find out more about these opportunities or for general career information, contact

Junior Engineering Technical Society (JETS)
1420 King Street, Suite 405
Alexandria, VA 22314-2794
Tel: 703-548-5387
E-mail: info@jets.org
http://www.jets.org

☐ COLLECTION WORKERS

OVERVIEW

Collection workers—sometimes known as *bill collectors, collection correspondents,* or *collection agents*—are employed to persuade people to pay their overdue bills. Some work for collection agencies (that are hired by the business to which the money is owed), while others work for department stores, hospitals, banks, public utilities, and other businesses. Collection workers contact delinquent debtors, inform them of the delinquency, and either secure payment or arrange a new payment schedule. If all else fails, they might be forced to repossess property or turn the account over to an attorney for legal proceedings. There are approximately 403,100 collection workers employed in the United States.

THE JOB

A collection worker's main job is to persuade people to pay bills that are past due. The procedure is generally the same in both collection firms and businesses that employ collection workers. The duties of the various workers may overlap, depending on the size and nature of the company.

When routine billing methods—monthly statements and notice letters—fail to secure payment, the collection worker receives a bad-debt file (usually on a computer tape downloaded to the agency's computer system). This

---

SCHOOL SUBJECTS
Computer science, Psychology, Speech

PERSONAL SKILLS
Communication/ideas, Following instructions

MINIMUM EDUCATION LEVEL
High school diploma

CERTIFICATION OR LICENSING
Voluntary

WORK ENVIRONMENT
Primarily indoors, Primarily one location

---

file contains information about the debtor, the nature and amount of the unpaid bill, the last charge incurred, and the date of the last payment. The collection worker then contacts the debtor by phone or mail to request full or partial payment or, if necessary, to arrange a new payment schedule.

Terrence Sheffert is a collection worker for a collection agency based in Chicago. He describes his typical duties as making phone calls and writing letters. "I am usually in the office, on the phone with clients or the people who owe them," he says. "I never actually go out to make collections, but there are some agents who do."

If the bill has not been paid because the customer believes it is incorrect, the merchandise purchased was faulty, or the service billed for was not performed, the collector takes appropriate steps to settle the matter. If, after investigation, the debt collector finds that the debt is still valid, he or she again tries to secure payment.

In cases where the customer has not paid because of a financial emergency or poor money management, the debt collector may arrange a new payment schedule. In instances where the customer goes to great or fraudulent lengths to avoid payment, the collector may recommend that the file be turned over to an attorney. "Every day, we are protecting the clients' interests and getting the money," Sheffert says. "If we can't get it, then we'll call in legal representation to handle it."

When all efforts to obtain payment fail, a collection worker known as a *repossessor* may be assigned to find the merchandise on which the debtor still owes money and return it to the seller. Such goods as furniture or appliances can be picked up in a truck. To reclaim automobiles and other motor vehicles, the repossessor might be forced to enter and start the vehicle with special tools if the buyer does not surrender the key.

In large agencies, some collection workers specialize as *skip tracers*. Skip tracers are assigned to find debtors who "skip" out on their debts—that is, who move without notifying their creditors so that they don't have to pay their bills. Skip tracers act like detectives, searching telephone directories and street listings and making inquiries at post offices in an effort to locate missing debtors. Increasingly such information can be found through online computer databases (some agencies subscribe to a service to collect this information). Skip tracers also try to find out information about a person's whereabouts by contacting former neighbors and employers, local merchants, friends, relatives, and references listed on the original credit application. They follow every lead and prepare a report of the entire investigation.

In some small offices, collection workers perform clerical duties, such as reading and answering correspondence, filing, or posting amounts paid to people's accounts. They might offer financial advice to customers or contact them to inquire about their satisfaction with the handling of the account. In larger companies, credit and loan collection supervisors might oversee the activities of several other collection workers.

REQUIREMENTS
High School

Most employers prefer to hire high school graduates for collection jobs, but formal education beyond high school is typically not required. High school courses that might prove helpful in this career include those that will help you communicate clearly and properly, such as English and speech. Because collection workers have to talk with people about a very delicate subject, psychology classes might also be beneficial. Finally, computer classes are good choices, since this career, like most others, often requires at least some familiarity with keyboarding and basic computer operation.

Postsecondary Training

Most collection workers learn collection procedures and telephone techniques on the job in a training period spent under the guidance of a supervisor or an experienced collector. The legal restrictions on collection activities, as mandated by the Fair Debt Collection Practices Act and state laws, such as when and how calls can be made, are also covered.

Certification or Licensing

Although it is not required by law, some employers require their employees to become certified by the Association of Credit and Collection Professionals, which offers several certifications, including professional collection specialist, creditor collection specialist, and health care collection specialist. To learn more, visit http://www.acainternational.org.

Other Requirements

Because this is a people-oriented job, you must have a pleasant manner and voice. You may spend much of your time on the telephone speaking with people about overdue payments, which can be a sensitive subject. To succeed as a collector, you must be sympathetic and tactful, yet assertive and persuasive enough to convince debtors to pay their overdue bills. In addition, collectors must be alert, quick-witted, and imaginative to handle the unpredictable and potentially awkward situations that are encountered in this type of work.

Collection work can be emotionally taxing. It involves listening to a bill payer's problems and occasional verbal attacks directed at both the collector and the company. Some people physically threaten repossessors and other collection workers. "The best description of this job would be 'stressful,'" Terrence Sheffert says. "Everything about collecting is very stressful." In the face of these stresses, you must be able to avoid becoming upset, personally involved with, or alarmed by angry or threatening debtors. This requires a cool head and an even temperament.

EXPLORING

The best way to explore collection work is to secure part-time or summer employment in a collection agency or credit office. You might also find it helpful to interview a collection worker to obtain firsthand information about the practical aspects of this occupation. Finally, the associations listed at the end of this article may be able to provide further information about the career.

EMPLOYERS

Of the approximately 403,100 collection workers in the United States, nearly 25 percent work for business support services, 19 percent work for finance and insurance companies, and 18 percent work for health care and social assistance providers. Some work for collection agencies, which are usually independent companies that are hired by various businesses to collect debt that is owed them. Other bill collectors work for a wide range of organizations and businesses that extend credit to customers. Department stores, hospitals, banks, public utilities, and auto financing companies are examples of businesses that frequently hire bill collectors.

The companies that hire collection workers are located throughout the United States, especially in heavily populated urban areas. Companies that have branch offices in rural communities often locate their collection departments in nearby cities.

STARTING OUT

If you are interested in becoming a collection worker, one easy way to start a job search is to apply directly to collection agencies, credit reporting companies, banks, and major retailers that sell large items. To find collection agencies and credit reporting companies, try doing a simple keyword search on one of the Internet's search engines. Another easy way is to look in your local Yellow Pages—or expand your search by going to the library and looking through yellow pages of other cities. Remember that these sorts of jobs are often more plentiful in more urban areas.

You should also check the classified ads of area newspapers for headings such as "Billing" or "Collection." Finally, job openings may be listed at your local employment office.

ADVANCEMENT

Experienced collection workers who have proven to have above-average ability can advance to management positions, such as supervisors or *collection managers.* These workers generally have responsibility for the operations of a specific shift, location, or department of a collection company. They oversee other collection workers. Other avenues of advancement might include becoming a *credit authorizer, credit checker,* or *bank loan officer.* Credit authorizers approve questionable charges against customers' existing accounts by evaluating the customers' computerized credit records and payment histories. Credit checkers in credit bureaus—sometimes also called *credit investigators* or *credit reporters*—search for, update, and verify information for credit reports. Loan officers help borrowers fill out loan applications, verify and analyze applications, and decide whether and how much to loan applicants. Some experienced and successful collections workers might open their own agencies.

EARNINGS

Collection workers might receive a salary plus a bonus or commission on the debt amounts they collect. Others work for a flat salary with no commissions. Since the pay system varies among different companies, incomes vary substantially. In 2009, the median hourly wage for bill collectors working full time was $14.87, according to the U.S. Department of Labor (DOL). This hourly wage translates into a yearly income of approximately $30,940. Earnings for collection workers range from less than $21,250 to a high of more than $46,430 annually.

Depending on their employer, some full-time bill collectors receive a benefits package that may include paid holidays and vacations, sick leave, and health and dental insurance.

WORK ENVIRONMENT

Most collectors work in pleasant offices, sit at a desk, and spend a great deal of time on the telephone. Because they spend so much time on the phone, many collectors use phone headsets and program-operated dialing systems. Because most companies use computers to store information about their accounts, the collection worker frequently works on a computer. He or she may sit in front of a computer terminal, reviewing and entering information about the account while talking to the debtor on the phone.

Rarely does a collector have to make a personal visit to a customer. Repossession proceedings are undertaken only in extreme cases.

Most collection workers work a 40-hour week, from 9:00 a.m. to 5:00 p.m., Monday through Friday. Some collection workers stagger their schedules, however. They might start late in the morning and work into the evening, or they might take a weekday off and work on Saturday. Evening and weekend work is common because debtors are often home during these times.

OUTLOOK

Employment for bill collectors is predicted by the DOL to grow faster than the average through 2018. Demand for cash flow is causing businesses to hire more and more debt collectors. Also, America's debt is growing. Due to the relaxed standards for credit cards, more people, regardless of their financial circumstances, are able to get credit cards, make purchases on credit, and build up large debts they have difficulty repaying. The DOL also notes that the health care industry is one of the fastest growing employers of bill collectors and collection agencies. This is largely because health insurance plans frequently do not adequately cover payment for medical procedures, and patients are often left with large bills that they have difficulty repaying. Economic recessions also increase the amount of personal debt that goes unpaid. Therefore, unlike many occupations, collection workers usually find that their employment and workloads increase during economic slumps.

FOR MORE INFORMATION

For information on collection work and certification, contact

Association of Credit and Collection Professionals
PO Box 390106
Minneapolis, MN 55439-0106
Tel: 952-926-6547
E-mail: aca@acainternational.org
http://www.acainternational.org

For information on careers and certification, contact the NACM.

National Association of Credit Management (NACM)
8840 Columbia 100 Parkway
Columbia, MD 21045-2158
Tel: 410-740-5560
http://www.nacm.org

COLLEGE PROFESSORS

OVERVIEW

College professors instruct undergraduate and graduate students in specific subjects at colleges and universities. They are responsible for lecturing classes, leading small seminar groups, and creating and grading examinations.

SCHOOL SUBJECTS
English, History, Speech

PERSONAL SKILLS
Communication/ideas, Helping/teaching

MINIMUM EDUCATION LEVEL
Master's degree

CERTIFICATION OR LICENSING
None available

WORK ENVIRONMENT
Primarily indoors, Primarily one location

They also may conduct research, write for publication, and aid in administration. Approximately 1.7 million postsecondary teachers are employed in the United States.

THE JOB

College and university faculty members teach at junior colleges or at four-year colleges and universities. At four-year institutions, most faculty members are *assistant professors, associate professors,* or *full professors.* These three types of professorships differ in regard to status, job responsibilities, and salary. Assistant professors are new faculty members who are working to get tenure (status as a permanent professor); they seek to advance to associate and then to full professorships.

College professors perform three main functions: teaching, advising, and research. Their most important responsibility is to teach students. Their role within a college department will determine the level of courses they teach and the number of courses per semester. Most professors work with students at all levels, from college freshmen to graduate students. They may head several classes a semester or only a few a year. Some of their classes will have large enrollment, while graduate seminars may consist of only 12 or fewer students. Though college professors may spend fewer than 10 hours a week in the actual classroom, they spend many hours preparing lectures and lesson plans, grading papers and exams, and preparing grade reports. They also schedule office hours during the week to be available to students outside of the lecture hall, and they meet with students individually throughout the semester. In the classroom, professors lecture, lead discussions, administer exams, and assign textbook reading and other research. In some courses, they rely heavily on laboratories to transmit course material.

Another important responsibility is advising students. Not all faculty members serve as advisers, but those who do must set aside large blocks of time to guide students through the program. College professors who serve as advisers may have any number of students assigned to them, from fewer than 10 to more than 100, depending on the administrative policies of the college. Their responsibility may involve looking over a planned program of studies to make sure the students meet requirements for graduation, or it may involve working intensively with each student on many aspects of college life.

The third responsibility of college and university faculty members is research and publication. Faculty members who are heavily involved in research programs sometimes are assigned a smaller teaching load.

College professors publish their research findings in various scholarly journals. They also write books based on their research or on their own knowledge and experience in the field. Most textbooks are written by college and university teachers. In arts-based programs, such as master's of fine arts programs in painting, writing, and theater, professors practice their craft and exhibit their art work in various ways. For example, a painter or photographer will have gallery showings, while a poet will publish in literary journals.

Publishing a significant amount of work has been the traditional standard by which assistant professors prove themselves worthy of becoming permanent, tenured faculty. Typically, pressure to publish is greatest for assistant professors. Pressure to publish increases again if an associate professor wishes to be considered for a promotion to full professorship.

In recent years, some liberal arts colleges have recognized that the pressure to publish is taking faculty away from their primary duties to the students, and these institutions have begun to place a decreasing emphasis on publishing and more on performance in the classroom. Professors in junior colleges face less pressure to publish than those in four-year institutions.

Some faculty members eventually rise to the position of *department chair,* where they govern the affairs of an entire department, such as English, history, mathematics, or biological sciences. Department chairs, faculty, and other professional staff members are aided in their myriad duties by *graduate assistants,* who may help develop teaching materials, conduct research, give examinations, teach lower level courses, and carry out other activities.

Some college professors may also conduct classes in an extension program. In such a program, they teach evening and weekend courses for the benefit of people who otherwise would not be able to take advantage of the institution's resources. They may travel away from the campus and meet with a group of students at another location. They may work full time for the extension division or may divide their time between on-campus and off-campus teaching.

Distance learning programs, an increasingly popular option for students, give professors the opportunity to use today's technologies to remain in one place while teaching students who are at a variety of locations simultaneously. The professor's duties, like those when teaching correspondence courses conducted by mail, include grading work that students send in at periodic intervals and advising students of their progress. Computers, the Internet, e-mail, and video conferencing, however, are some of the technology tools that allow professors and students to communicate in "real time" in a virtual classroom setting. Meetings may be scheduled during the same time as traditional classes or during evenings and weekends. Professors who do this work are sometimes known as *extension work, correspondence,* or *distance learning instructors.* They may teach online courses in addition to other classes or may have distance learning as their major teaching responsibility.

The *junior college instructor* has many of the same kinds of responsibilities as does the teacher in a four-year college or university. Because junior colleges offer only a two-year program, they teach only undergraduates.

REQUIREMENTS

High School

Your high school's college preparatory program likely includes courses in English, science, foreign language, history, math, and government. In addition, you should take courses in speech to get a sense of what it will be like to lecture to a group of students. Your school's debate team can also help you develop public speaking skills, along with research skills.

Postsecondary Training

At least one advanced degree in your field of study is required to be a professor in a college or university. The master's degree is considered the minimum standard, and graduate work beyond the master's is usually desirable. If you hope to advance in academic rank above instructor, most institutions require a doctorate.

In the last year of your undergraduate program, you'll apply to graduate programs in your area of study. Standards for admission to a graduate program can be high and the competition heavy, depending on the school. Once accepted into a program, your responsibilities will be similar to those of your professors—in addition to attending seminars, you'll research, prepare articles for publication, and teach some undergraduate courses.

You may find employment in a junior college with only a master's degree. Advancement in responsibility and in salary, however, is more likely to come if you have earned a doctorate.

Certification or Licensing

There are no certification or licensing requirements for college professors.

Other Requirements

You should enjoy reading, writing, and researching. Not only will you spend many years studying in school, but your whole career will be based on communicating your thoughts and ideas. People skills are important because you'll be dealing directly with students, administrators, and other faculty members on a daily basis. You should feel comfortable in a role of authority and possess self-confidence. Some versatility with Internet programs and e-mail is also useful, particularly if teaching distance-learning classes. Having a flexible schedule also helps as some classes may be scheduled for evenings and weekends.

EXPLORING

Your high school teachers use many of the same skills as college professors, so talk to your teachers about their careers and their college experiences. You can develop your own teaching experience by volunteering at a community center, working at a day care center, or working at a summer camp. Also, spend some time on a college campus to get a sense of the environment. Write to colleges for their admissions brochures and course catalogs (or check them out online); read about the faculty members and the courses they teach. Before visiting college campuses, make arrangements to speak to professors who teach courses that interest you. These professors may allow you to sit in on their classes and observe. Also, make appointments with college advisers and with people in the admissions and recruitment offices. If your grades are good enough, you might be able to serve as a teaching assistant during your undergraduate years, which can give you experience leading discussions and grading papers.

EMPLOYERS

Employment opportunities vary based on area of study and education. Most universities have many different departments that hire faculty. With a doctorate, a number of publications, and a record of good teaching, professors should find opportunities in universities all across the country. There are more than 4,400 colleges and universities in the United States. Professors teach in undergraduate and graduate programs. The teaching jobs at doctoral institutions are usually better paying and more prestigious. The most sought-after positions are those that offer tenure. Teachers that have only a master's degree will be limited to opportunities with junior colleges, community colleges, and some small private institutions. There are approximately 1.7 million postsecondary teachers employed in the United States.

STARTING OUT

You should start the process of finding a teaching position while you are in graduate school. The process includes developing a curriculum vitae (a detailed, academic resume), writing for publication, assisting with research, attending conferences, and gaining teaching experience and recommendations. Many students begin applying for teaching positions while finishing their graduate program. For most positions at four-year institutions, you must travel to large conferences where interviews can be arranged with representatives from the universities to which you have applied.

Because of the competition for tenure-track positions, you may have to work for a few years in temporary positions, visiting various schools as an adjunct professor. Some professional associations maintain lists of teaching opportunities in their areas. They may also make lists of applicants available to college administrators looking to fill an available position.

ADVANCEMENT

The normal pattern of advancement is from instructor to assistant professor, to associate professor, to full professor. All four academic ranks are concerned primarily with teaching and research. College faculty members who have an interest in and a talent for administration may be advanced to chair of a department or to dean of their college. A few become college or university presidents or other types of administrators.

The instructor is usually an inexperienced college teacher. He or she may hold a doctorate or may have completed all the Ph.D. requirements except for the dissertation. Most colleges look upon the rank of instructor as the period during which the college is trying out the teacher. Instructors usually are advanced to the position of assistant professors within three to four years. Assistant professors are given up to about six years to prove themselves worthy of tenure, and if they do so, they become associate professors. Some professors choose to remain at the associate level. Others strive to become full professors and receive greater status, salary, and responsibilities.

Most colleges have clearly defined promotion policies from rank to rank for faculty members, and many have written statements about the number of years in which instructors and assistant professors may remain in grade. Administrators in many colleges hope to encourage younger faculty members to increase their skills and competencies and thus to qualify for the more responsible positions of associate professor and full professor.

EARNINGS

Earnings vary by the departments professors work in, by the size of the school, by the type of school (public, private, women's only, for example), and by the level of position the professor holds. In its 2009–10 salary survey, the American Association of University Professors (AAUP) reported that professors averaged the following salaries by rank: full professors, $109,843; associate professors, $76,566; assistant professors, $64,433; instructors, $47,592; and lecturers, $53,112. Full professors working in disciplines such as law, business, health professions, computer and information sciences, and engineering usually have the highest salaries. Lower paying disciplines include visual and performing arts, agricultural studies, education, and communications.

According to the U.S. Department of Labor, in 2009, the median salary for all postsecondary instructors was $64,680, with 10 percent earning $128,330 or more and 10 percent earning $32,180 or less. Those with the highest earnings tend to be senior tenured faculty; those with the lowest, graduate assistants. Professors working on the West Coast and the East Coast and those working at doctorate-granting institutions also tend to have the highest salaries. Many professors try to increase their earnings by completing research, publishing in their field, or teaching additional courses.

Benefits for full-time faculty typically include health insurance and retirement funds and, in some cases, stipends for travel related to research, housing allowances, and tuition waivers for dependents.

WORK ENVIRONMENT

A college or university is usually a pleasant place in which to work. Campuses bustle with all types of activities and events, stimulating ideas, and a young, energetic population. Much prestige comes with success as a professor and scholar; professors have the respect of students, colleagues, and others in their community.

Depending on the size of the department, college professors may have their own office, or they may have to share an office with one or more colleagues. Their department may provide them with a computer, Internet access, and research assistants. College professors are also able to do much of their office work at home. They can arrange their schedule around class hours, academic meetings, and the established office hours when they meet with students. Most college teachers work more than 40 hours each week. Although college professors may teach only two or three classes a semester, they spend many hours preparing for lectures, examining student work, and conducting research.

OUTLOOK

The U.S. Department of Labor predicts faster than average employment growth for college and university professors through 2018. College enrollment is projected to grow due to an increased number of 18- to 24-year-olds, and from an increased number of adults returning to college. Opportunities for college teachers will be particularly good in community colleges and for-profit institutions. Retirement of current faculty members will also provide job openings. However, competition for full-time, tenure-track positions at four-year schools will be very strong.

A number of factors threaten to change the way colleges and universities hire faculty. Some university leaders are developing more business-based methods of running their schools, focusing on profits and budgets. This can affect college professors in a number of ways. One of the biggest effects is in the replacement of tenure-track faculty positions with part-time instructors. These part-time instructors include adjunct faculty, visiting professors, and graduate students. Organizations such as the AAUP and the American Federation of Teachers are working to prevent the loss of these full-time jobs, as well as to help part-time instructors receive better pay and benefits. Other issues involve the development of long-distance education departments in many schools. Though these correspondence courses have become very popular in recent years, many professionals believe that students in long-distance education programs receive only a second-rate education. A related concern is about the proliferation of computers in the classroom. Some courses consist only of instruction by computer software and the Internet. The effects of these alternative methods on the teaching profession will be offset somewhat by the expected increases in college enrollment in coming years.

FOR MORE INFORMATION

To read about the issues affecting college professors, contact the following organizations:

American Association of University Professors
1133 19th Street, NW, Suite 200
Washington, DC 20036-3655
Tel: 202-737-5900
E-mail: aaup@aaup.org
http://www.aaup.org

American Federation of Teachers
555 New Jersey Avenue, NW
Washington, DC 20001-2029
Tel: 202-879-4400
http://www.aft.org

COMPUTER NETWORK ADMINISTRATORS

OVERVIEW

Computer network administrators, or *network specialists,* design, install, and support an organization's local area network (LAN), wide area network (WAN), network segment, or Internet system. They maintain network hardware and software, analyze problems, and monitor the network to ensure availability to system users. Administrators might also plan, coordinate, and implement network security measures, including firewalls. Approximately 338,890 computer network and systems administrators work in the United States.

THE JOB

Businesses use computer networks for several reasons One important reason is that networks make it easy for many employees to share hardware and software as well as printers, fax machines, and modems. For example, it would be very expensive to buy individual copies of word-processing programs for each employee in a company. By investing in a network version of the software that all employees can access, companies can often save a lot of money. Also, businesses that rely on databases for daily operations use networks to allow authorized personnel quick and easy access to the most updated version of the database.

Networks vary greatly in size; even just two computers connected together are considered a network. They can also be extremely large and complex, involving hundreds of computer terminals in various geographical locations around the world. A good example of a large network is the Internet, which is a system that allows people from every corner of the globe to access millions of pieces of information about any subject under the sun. Besides varying in size, networks are all at least slightly different in terms of configuration, or what the network is designed to do; businesses customize networks to meet their specific needs. All networks, regardless of size or configuration, experience problems. For example, communications with certain equipment can break down, users might need extra training or forget their passwords, backup files may be lost, or new software might need to be installed and configured. Whatever the crisis, computer network administrators

SCHOOL SUBJECTS

Computer science, Mathematics

PERSONAL SKILLS

Helping/teaching, Leadership/management, Technical/scientific

MINIMUM EDUCATION LEVEL

Bachelor's degree

CERTIFICATION OR LICENSING

Recommended

WORK ENVIRONMENT

Primarily indoors, Primarily one location

must know the network system well enough to diagnose and fix the problem.

Computer network administrators or specialists may hold one or several networking responsibilities. The specific job duties assigned to one person depend on the nature and scope of the employer. For example, in a medium-size company that uses computers only minimally, a computer network specialist might be expected to do everything associated with the office computer system. In larger companies with more sophisticated computing systems, computer network administrators are likely to hold narrower and better-defined responsibilities. The following descriptions highlight the different kinds of computer network administrators.

In the narrowest sense, computer network administrators are responsible for adding and deleting files to the network server, a centralized computer. Among other things, the server stores the software applications used by network users on a daily basis. Administrators update files from the database, electronic mail, and word-processing applications. They are also responsible for making sure that printing jobs run properly. This task entails telling the server where the printer is and establishing a printing queue, or line, designating which print jobs have priority.

Another duty of some network administrators is setting up user access. Since businesses store confidential information on the server, users typically have access to only a limited number of applications. Network administrators tell the computer who can use which programs and when they can use them. They create a series of passwords to secure the system against internal and external spying. They also troubleshoot problems and questions encountered by staff members.

In companies with large computer systems, *network security specialists* concentrate solely on system security. They set up and monitor user access and update security files as needed. For example, it is very important in universities that only certain administrative personnel have the ability to change student grades on the database. Network security specialists must protect the system from unauthorized grade changes. Network security specialists grant new passwords to users who forget them, record all nonauthorized entries, report unauthorized users to appropriate management, and change any files that have been tampered with. They also maintain security files with information about each employee.

Network control operators are in charge of all network communications, most of which operate over telephone lines or fiber optic cables. When users encounter communications problems, they call the network control operator. A typical communications problem is when a user cannot send or receive files from other computers. Since users seldom have a high level of technical expertise on the network, the network control operator knows how to ask appropriate questions in user-friendly language to determine the source of the problem. If it is not a user error, the network control operator checks the accuracy of computer files, verifies that modems are functioning properly, and runs noise tests on the communications lines using special equipment. As with all network specialists, if the problem proves to be too difficult for the network control operator to resolve, he or she seeks help directly from the manufacturer or warranty company.

Network control operators also keep detailed records of the number of communications transactions made, the number and nature of network errors, and the methods used to resolve them. These records help them address problems as they arise in the future.

Network systems administrators who specialize in Internet technology are essential to its success. One of their responsibilities is to prepare servers for use and link them together so others can place things on them. Under the supervision of the *Webmaster,* the systems administrator might set aside areas on a server for particular types of information, such as documents, graphics, or audio. At sites that are set up to handle secure credit card transactions, administrators are responsible for setting up the secure server that handles this job. They also monitor site traffic and take the necessary steps to ensure uninterrupted operation. In some cases, the solution is to provide additional space on the server. In others, the only solution might be to increase bandwidth by upgrading the telephone line linking the site to the Internet.

REQUIREMENTS
High School

In high school, take as many courses as possible in computer science, mathematics, and science, which provide a solid foundation in computer basics and analytical-thinking skills. You should also practice your verbal and written communications skills in English and speech classes. Business courses are valuable in that they can give you an understanding of how important business decisions, especially those concerning investment in computer equipment, are made.

Postsecondary Training

Most network jobs require at least a bachelor's degree in computer science or computer engineering. More specialized positions require an advanced degree. Workers with a college education are more likely to deal with the theoretical aspects of computer networking and are more likely to be promoted to management positions. Opportunities in computer design, systems analysis, and computer programming, for example, are open only to college graduates. If you are interested in this field, you should also pursue postsecondary training in network administration or network engineering.

"I believe that you cannot have enough education and that it should be an ongoing thing," says Nancy Nelson, a network administrator at Baxter Healthcare Corporation in Deerfield, Illinois. "You can learn a lot on your own, but I think you miss out on a lot if you don't get the formal education. Most companies don't even look at a resume that doesn't have a degree. Keeping up with technology can be very rewarding."

Certification or Licensing

Besides the technical/vocational schools that offer courses related to computer networking, several major companies offer professionally taught courses and nationally recognized certification; chief among them are Novell and Microsoft. The certified network professional program supports and complements the aforementioned vendor product certifications. Offered by the Network Professional Association, the program covers fundamental knowledge in client operating systems, microcomputer hardware platforms, network operating system fundamentals, protocols, and topologies.

Commercial postsecondary training programs are flexible. You can complete courses at your own pace, but you must take all parts of the certification test within one year. You may attend classes at any one of many educational sites around the country or you can study on your own. Many students find certification exams difficult.

Other Requirements

Continuing education for any computer profession is crucial to success. Many companies will require you to keep up-to-date on new technological advances by attending classes, workshops, and seminars throughout the year. Also, many companies and professional associations update network specialists through newsletters, other periodicals, and online bulletin boards.

Computer work is complex, detailed, and often very frustrating. In order to succeed in this field, you must be well organized and patient. You should enjoy challenges and problem solving, and you should be a logical thinker. You must also be able to communicate complex ideas in simple terms, as well as be able to work well under pressure and deadlines. As a network specialist, you should be naturally curious about the computing field; you must always be willing to learn more about new and different technologies.

EXPLORING

"One of the greatest learning experiences in this field is just unpacking a new computer, setting it up, and getting connected to the Internet, continually asking yourself how and why as you go," says Dan Creedon, a network administrator at Nesbitt Burns Securities in Chicago.

If you are interested in computer networking, you should join computer clubs at school and community centers and surf the Internet or other online services. Ask your school administration about the possibility of working with the school system's network specialists for a day or longer. Parents' or friends' employers might also be a good place to find this type of opportunity.

Visit the Web sites of professional associations also to learn more about upcoming conferences and networking events. USENIX, the Advanced Computing Systems Network, offers students discounts on memberships and conferences. Learn more by visiting http://www.usenix.org/students/.

If seeking part-time jobs, apply for those that include computer work. Though you will not find networking positions, any experience on computers will increase your general computing knowledge. In addition, once employed, you can actively seek exposure to the other computer functions in the business.

You might also try volunteering at local charities that use computer networks in their office. Because many charities have small budgets, they may offer more opportunities to gain experience with some of the simpler networking tasks. In addition, experiment by creating networks with your own computer, those of your friends, and any printers, modems, and faxes to which you have access.

Basically, you should play around on computers as much as possible. Read and learn from any resource you can, such as magazines, newsletters, and online bulletin boards.

EMPLOYERS

Approximately 338,890 computer network and systems administrators are employed in the United States. Any company or organization that uses computer networks in its business employs network administrators. These include insurance companies, banks, financial institutions, health care organizations, federal and state governments, universities, and other corporations that rely on networking. Also, since smaller companies are moving to client-server models, more opportunities at almost any kind of business are becoming available.

STARTING OUT

There are several ways to obtain a position as a computer network specialist. If you are a student in a technical school or university, take advantage of your campus career services office. Check regularly for internship postings, job listings, and notices of on-campus recruitment. Career services offices are also valuable resources for resume tips and interviewing techniques. Internships and summer jobs with corporations are always beneficial and provide experience that will give you the edge over your competition. General computer job fairs are also held throughout the year in larger cities.

There are many online career sites that post job openings, salary surveys, and current employment trends. The Web also has online publications that deal specifically with computer jobs. You can also obtain information from computer organizations, such as the IEEE Computer Society and the Network Professional Association (see contact information at the end of this article).

When a job opportunity arises, you should send a cover letter and resume to the company promptly. Follow up your mailing with an e-mail or phone call about one week later. If interested, the company recruiter will call you to ask questions and possibly arrange an interview. The commercial sponsors of network certification, such as Novell and Microsoft, also publish newsletters that list current job openings in the field. The same information is distributed through online bulletin boards and on the Internet as well. Otherwise, you can scan the classified ads in local newspapers and computer magazines or work with an employment agency to find such a position.

Individuals already employed but wishing to move into computer networking should investigate the possibility of tuition reimbursement from their employer for network certification. Many large companies have this type of program, which allows employees to train in a field that would benefit company operations. After successfully completing classes or certification, individuals are better qualified for related job openings in their own company and more likely to be hired into them.

ADVANCEMENT

"I would say that as much as a person is willing to learn is really the amount of advancement opportunities that are open to them," notes Dan Creedon. Among the professional options available are promotion to network manager or movement into network engineering. *Network engineers* design, test, and evaluate network systems, such as LAN, WAN, Internet, and other data communications systems. They also perform modeling, analysis, and planning. Network engineers might also research related products and make hardware and software recommendations.

Network specialists also have the option of going into a different area of computing. They can become computer programmers, systems analysts, software engineers, or multimedia professionals. All of these promotions require additional education and solid computer experience.

EARNINGS

Factors such as the size and type of employer, the administrator's experience, and specific job duties influence the earnings of network administrators. The 2011 IT Salary Guide, based on data provided by Robert Half Technology, shows that systems administrators had salaries that ranged from $53,250 to $83,000 in 2010, which was a 3.6 percent increase over the previous year. According to the U.S. Department of Labor, the median yearly income for computer network and systems administrators was $67,710 in 2009. The lowest paid 10 percent made less than $41,940 per year, and the highest paid 10 percent earned more than $105,970 annually.

Most computer network administrators are employed by companies that offer the full range of benefits, includ-

ing health insurance, paid vacation, and sick leave. In addition, many companies have tuition reimbursement programs for employees seeking to pursue education or professional certification.

WORK ENVIRONMENT

Computer network administrators work indoors in a comfortable office environment. Their work is generally fast paced and can be frustrating at times. Some tasks, however, are routine and might get a little boring after a while. But many times, network specialists are required to work under a lot of pressure. If the network goes down, for example, the company is losing money, and it is the network specialist's job to get it up and running as fast as possible. The specialist must be able to remember complicated relationships and many details accurately and quickly. Specialists are also called on to deal effectively with the many complaints from network users.

When working on the installation of a new system, many network specialists are required to work overtime until it is fully operational. This usually includes long and frequent meetings. During initial operations of the system, some network specialists may be on call during other shifts for when problems arise, or they may have to train network users during off hours.

One other potential source of frustration is communications with other employees. Network specialists deal every day with people who usually don't understand the system as well as they do. Network administrators must be able to communicate at different levels of understanding.

OUTLOOK

The U.S. Department of Labor projects that employment for computer network and systems administrators will grow much faster than the average through 2018. Network administrators are in high demand, particularly those with Internet experience. "Technology is constantly changing," Nancy Nelson says. "It is hard to tell where it will lead in the future. I think that the Internet and all of its pieces will be the place to focus on." As more and more companies and organizations discover the economic and convenience advantages linked to using computer networks at all levels of operations, the demand for well-trained network specialists will increase. Companies are also seeking administrators to assist in protecting computer systems from attack. Job opportunities should be best for those with certification and up-to-date training.

FOR MORE INFORMATION

For information on internships, student membership, and the student magazine Crossroads, *contact*

Association for Computing Machinery
2 Penn Plaza, Suite 701
New York, NY 10121-0701
Tel: 800-342-6626
http://www.acm.org

For information on scholarships, student membership, and to read Careers in Computer Science and Computer Engineering, *visit the IEEE's Web site.*
IEEE Computer Society
2000 L Street, NW, Suite 700
Washington, DC 20036-4910
Tel: 202-371-0101
E-mail: help@computer.org
http://www.computer.org

For information on certification, contact
Network Professional Association
1401 Hermes Lane
San Diego, CA 92154-2721
Tel: 888-NPA-NPA0
http://www.npanet.org

For information on certification, contact
System Administrators Guild
2560 9th Street, Suite 215
Berkeley, CA 94710-2565
Tel: 510-528-8649
E-mail: office@sage.org
http://www.sage.org

❑ COMPUTER SUPPORT SERVICE OWNERS

OVERVIEW

The owners of computer support services help businesses and individuals install and maintain computer hardware and software. They offer advice on what computers to purchase; they teach how to operate computers; and they assist with computer problems as they arise. There are approximately 540,560 computer support specialists in the industry, including technicians and entrepreneurs. *Computer consultants* either work out of their homes, or they rent office space. Though some of their assistance is offered over the phone, much of their work is performed on-site.

SCHOOL SUBJECTS
Business, Computer science, Technical/shop

PERSONAL SKILLS
Helping/teaching, Technical/scientific

MINIMUM EDUCATION LEVEL
Associate's degree

CERTIFICATION OR LICENSING
Voluntary

WORK ENVIRONMENT
Primarily indoors, Primarily multiple locations

THE JOB

If your computer is not working, the problem may be simply that you have forgotten to plug in the machine. But it can be much more complicated than that, requiring the assistance of someone with a great deal of computer knowledge. Today's hardware and software are easier to use than in previous years, but can be difficult to install correctly and difficult to learn. Computer support service owners use their computer expertise to help businesses and individuals buy new computers and ready them for daily use.

With their operations based in their home office, computer support service owners take calls from new clients, as well as clients who regularly rely on their services. Clients may have problems with their printers not responding to computer commands; a computer may be locked up; they may have problems performing the particular functions for which their software is designed. In some cases, support service owners are able to diagnose the problem and offer assistance over the phone. But in most cases, they are required to go to the offices and work hands-on with the computer systems. Armed with a cell phone, pager, and laptop, they drive to the offices of businesses small and large and the homes of personal computer owners to help get the computers running again. They will install network systems and new hardware and software. They upgrade existing systems. Computer support service owners also teach the computer operators how to use the new systems, either one on one or in group training sessions. They advise on the purchase of hardware and software, and can prepare backup methods.

Many computer consultants also offer their expertise in Web design and multimedia for uploading a Web page, preparing a presentation, and offering desktop publishing services. They also help to create computer databases. Some computer consultants are involved in issues of programming.

In addition to technical work, the owners of computer support services must handle all the details of running their businesses, managing customer service, bookkeeping, and client records. They must also research new technologies and keep up to date on advanced technical skills. Maintaining connections within the industry is also important; computer support system owners may need to call upon the assistance of other consultants and technicians to help with some projects.

REQUIREMENTS
High School

Of course, you should take any classes that will familiarize you with computers. Computer science classes will help you learn about operating systems and programming. Learn about various software, like word processing and spreadsheet programs, as well as Web page design. A journalism class and working on your school newspaper will involve you with multimedia presentation and teach you about page layout and graphic design. Take courses in business and accounting to prepare for the bookkeeping and administrative details of the work. English composition and communication courses can help you develop teaching skills.

Postsecondary Training

Though a degree is not required for you to start your own computer support service, most service owners and consultants have at least an associate's degree. Some consultants supplement their education with special training offered by computer software companies such as Novell and Microsoft. Many consultants have advanced degrees and highly technical training in such areas as robotics, telecommunications, and nuclear engineering. Community colleges and universities across the country have programs in computer science, computer engineering, and electrical engineering. For a degree in computer science, you will be required to take courses in calculus, English composition, program design, algorithms, computer graphics, and database management. Electrical engineering programs include courses in BASIC programming, industrial electronics, digital integrated circuits, and microprocessor systems. In addition to seminars, you will also attend labs. Some bachelor's programs include research projects in which you will work closely with a faculty member to study new technologies. Some software companies offer training programs.

Very few consultants start their own businesses straight out of college. Some years working full time as part of a computer service staff will give you the firsthand experience you will need. Not only will you develop your computer expertise, but you will learn what is required in operating a business.

Certification or Licensing

There are many different kinds of certifications available to people working in computer support and consulting. No one certification, however, serves all the varying needs of computer professionals. Some consultants get certified in database design and administration. Some consultants have Microsoft certified systems engineer (MCSE) status. Visit http://www.microsoft.com/learning/mcp/mcse for information on the MCSE exam, which tests your understanding of Windows networks, hardware requirements and installations, and system maintenance. This certification should only supplement an extensive computer background, not replace it. The term "paper MCSE" has evolved in the industry to describe those who "look good on paper" with their certification, but do not have the networking and computer science education and experience to back it up.

The Institute for Certification of Computer Professionals offers a certified computer professional exam. More than 50,000 computer professionals hold the certification, having passed an exam that tests knowledge of business information systems, data resource management, software engineering, and other subjects.

Other Requirements

You should have good business and money management skills. Though some months you may have more work than you can handle, with a steady flow of income, other months there may be no work at all. You will have to budget your money to carry you through the lean months. Though computer skills are very important, you will also need good people skills to maintain customer relations. Teaching skills are important as well, because you will be training people in how to use their systems.

EXPLORING

Get to know your own home computer—study the software and its manuals, and familiarize yourself with computer programming languages. Read some of the many magazines devoted to computers, such as *Macworld* and

PC Today. Find out who services the computers in your school, and ask to spend some time with the technicians. But do not just focus on the technical duties of the people who own computer support services; find out how they go about running an office and maintaining a small business. Join your school's business club and you'll have the opportunity to meet small business owners in your area.

EMPLOYERS

Approximately 540,560 computer support specialists are employed in the United States. Computer support service owners work for a variety of different clients, servicing the personal computers in home-based offices, as well as contracting with large companies for long-term assistance. Though many individuals have computers in their homes for their personal use, few of them seek out professional service. The main clients of support service owners will be accounting firms, insurance agencies, government departments—any business or organization that relies upon computers to perform daily operations. Even a company that has its own full-time support staff will occasionally hire outside consultants. Computer support services are in demand all across the country, but are most successful in large cities, as they can draw from a broader client base.

STARTING OUT

As with many start-ups, it's good for you to focus your talents. Decide on a niche, such as networking or package customization, and then promote those specific services. It's also important to use good marketing techniques and a professional image when promoting your business.

ADVANCEMENT

Once they are established in their niche market, support service owners can expand to include other services. Some computer support services are able to offer much more than technical assistance; they also hold training sessions, prepare multimedia reports and presentations, and design Web pages. The more business connections a support service owner can make with support services, computer manufacturers, and other companies, the better they'll be able to build their client base. As their business grows, support service owners can hire staff to deal with administrative duties, as well as technicians to assist with servicing their clients' computers.

EARNINGS

According to the U.S. Department of Labor, median hourly wages for computer support specialists were $21.30 in 2009, which, based on a 40-hour workweek, is a salary of $44,300 a year. Salaries ranged from less than $27,200 to $72,690 or more annually. Those working in large cities like New York and Los Angeles average more than those in the Midwest, the Southwest, and the Northwest. Someone in New York with more than 10 years experience can average more than $90,000 a year, while a consultant with similar experience in the Southwest may make closer to $65,000 a year. Some very experienced, business-minded consultants can make $150,000 a year or more.

WORK ENVIRONMENT

Most computer support businesses are based in a home office or a rented commercial space. Computer support service owners devote a lot of time to sitting at their own computer, managing their accounts and records, but the majority of their time will be in the offices of their clients. In either setting, the work environment will likely be quiet and well lit. The work will be indoors, though support service owners will travel from office to office throughout the day.

When installing and repairing computer hardware, support service owners may have to crawl around behind desks to hook up wires and plug in cords. This work is essentially unsupervised, but some clients may ask to receive instruction and information about the repairs being made. In some cases, support service owners may work as part of a team, particularly if they are brought into a large company with a full-time support staff.

Some consultants work much more than 40 hours a week, though support service owners can avoid this by developing strong business management skills.

OUTLOOK

According to the U.S. Department of Labor, the industry is expected to grow faster than the average for all occupations through 2018, as computer systems become more important to many businesses. Lower prices on computer hardware and software will inspire businesses to expand their systems, and to invest in the services needed to keep them up and running. As computer programs become more sophisticated and are able to perform more complex operations, consultants will be needed to help clients operate these programs. With companies relying more on complex computer systems, they will be less likely to take risks in the installation of hardware and software. To stay at the top of the industry, consultants will have to keep up on technological developments and take continuing education courses.

Computer service specialists will find the best opportunities in such industries as computer systems design and related services; data processing, hosting and related services; software publishing; and management, scientific, and technical consulting.

More consultants may also become involved in broadening computer literacy. Computer resources are generally limited to middle-class students; many nonprofit organizations are forming to bring more computers and support services to inner-city youth, low-income families, and people with disabilities.

FOR MORE INFORMATION

To learn more about membership and career training seminars, contact
Association of Support Professionals
122 Barnard Avenue
Watertown, MA 02472-3414
Tel: 617-924-3944
http://asponline.com

For information on certification programs, contact
Institute for Certification of Computing Professionals
2400 East Devon Avenue, Suite 281
Des Plaines, IL 60018-4629
Tel: 800-843-8227
E-mail: office2@iccp.org
http://www.iccp.org

For resume and cover letter advice, salary statistics, and other career information in information technology, check out the following Web site:
Robert Half Technology
http://www.roberthalftechnology.com

☐ COMPUTER SYSTEMS PROGRAMMER/ ANALYSTS

OVERVIEW

Computer systems programmer/analysts analyze the computing needs of a business and then design a new system or upgrade an old system to meet those needs. The position can be split between two people, the *systems programmer* and the *systems analyst,* but it is frequently held by just one person, who oversees the work from

SCHOOL SUBJECTS
Computer science, Mathematics

PERSONAL SKILLS
Mechanical/manipulative, Technical/scientific

MINIMUM EDUCATION LEVEL
Bachelor's degree

CERTIFICATION OR LICENSING
Voluntary

WORK ENVIRONMENT
Primarily indoors, Primarily one location

beginning to end. There are 512,720 computer systems analysts and 367,880 computer programmers employed in the United Stated.

THE JOB

Businesses invest hundreds of thousands of dollars in computer systems to make their operations more efficient and thus, more profitable. As older systems become obsolete, businesses are also faced with the task of replacing them or upgrading them with new technology. Computer systems programmer/analysts plan and develop new computer systems or upgrade existing systems to meet changing business needs. They also install, modify, and maintain functioning computer systems. The process of choosing and implementing a computer system is similar for programmer analysts who work for very different employers. However, specific decisions in terms of hardware and software differ depending on the industry.

The first stage of the process involves meeting with management and users in order to discuss the problem at hand. For example, a company's accounting system might be slow, unreliable, and generally outdated. During many hours of meetings, systems programmer/analysts and management discuss various options, including commercial software, hardware upgrades, and customizing possibilities that may solve the problems. At the end of the discussions, which may last as long as several weeks or months, the programmer analyst defines the specific system goals as agreed upon by participants.

Next, systems programmer/analysts engage in highly analytic and logical activities. They use tools such as structural analysis, data modeling, mathematics, and cost accounting to determine which computers, including hardware and software and peripherals, will be required to meet the goals of the project. They must consider the trade-offs between extra efficiency and speed and increased costs. Weighing the pros and cons of each additional system feature is an important factor in system planning. Whatever preliminary decisions are made must be supported by mathematical and financial evidence.

As the final stage of the planning process, systems programmer/analysts prepare reports and formal presentations to be delivered to management. Reports must be written in clear, concise language that business professionals, who are not necessarily technical experts, can understand thoroughly. Formal presentations in front of groups of various sizes are often required as part of the system proposal.

If the system or the system upgrades are approved, equipment is purchased and installed. Then, the programmer analysts get down to the real technical work so that all the different computers and peripherals function well together. They prepare specifications, diagrams, and other programming structures and, often using computer-aided systems engineering (CASE) technology, they write the new or upgraded programming code. If they work solely as systems analysts, it is at this point that they hand over all of their information to the systems programmer so that he or she can begin to write the programming code.

Systems design and programming involves defining the files and records to be accessed by the system, outlining the processing steps, and suggesting formats for output that meet the needs of the company. User-friendliness of the front-end applications is extremely important for user productivity. Therefore, programmer analysts must be able to envision how nontechnical system users view their on-screen work. Systems programmer/analysts might also specify security programs that allow only authorized personnel access to certain files or groups of files.

As the programs are written, programmer analysts set up test runs of various parts of the system, making sure each step of the way that major goals are reached. Once the system is up and running, problems, or "bugs," begin to pop up. Programmer analysts are responsible for fixing these last-minute problems. They must isolate the problem and review the hundreds of lines of programming commands to determine where the mistake is located. Then they must enter the correct command or code and recheck the program.

Depending on the employer, some systems programmer/analysts might be involved with computer networking. Network communication programs tell two or more computers or peripherals how to work with each other.

When a system is composed of equipment from various manufacturers, networking is essential for smooth system functioning. For example, shared printers have to know how to order print jobs as they come in from various terminals. Some programmer analysts write the code that establishes printing queues. Others might be involved in user training, since they know the software applications well. They might also customize commercial software programs to meet the needs of their company.

Many programmer analysts become specialized in an area of business, science, or engineering. They seek education and further on-the-job training in these areas to develop expertise. They may therefore attend special seminars, workshops, and classes designed for their needs. This extra knowledge allows them to develop a deeper understanding of the computing problems specific to the business or industry.

REQUIREMENTS

High School

Take a college preparatory program with advanced classes in math, science, and computer science to prepare you for this work. This will provide a foundation of basic concepts and encourage the development of analytic and logical thinking skills. Since programmer analysts do a lot of proposal writing that may or may not be technical in nature, English classes are valuable as well. Speech classes will help prepare you for making formal presentations to management and clients.

Postsecondary Training

A bachelor's degree in computer science, information science, or management information systems is a minimum requirement for systems programmer/analysts. Course work in preparation for this field includes math, computer programming, science, and logic. Several years of related work experience, including knowledge of programming languages, are often necessary as well. For some very high-level positions, an advanced degree in a specific computer subfield may be required. As a result of the rapid growth of electronic commerce, some firms are also seeking analysts with a master's degree in business administration, with a concentration in information systems. Also, depending on the employer, proficiency in business, science, or engineering may be necessary.

Certification or Licensing

Some programmer/analysts pursue certification through the Institute for Certification of Computing

Professionals. In particular, they take classes and exams to become certified computing professionals (CCPs). Certification is voluntary and is an added credential for job hunters. CCPs have achieved a recognized level of knowledge and experience in principles and practices related to systems.

Other Requirements

Successful systems programmer/analysts demonstrate strong analytic skills and enjoy the challenges of problem solving. They are able to understand problems that exist on many levels, from technical to practical to business oriented. They can visualize complicated and abstract relationships between computer hardware and software and are good at matching needs to equipment.

Systems programmer/analysts have to be flexible as well. They routinely deal with many different kinds of people, from management to data entry clerks. Therefore, they must be knowledgeable in a lot of functional areas of the company. They should be able to talk to management about cost-effective solutions, to programmers about detailed coding, and to clerks about user-friendliness of the applications.

As is true for all computer professionals, systems programmer/analysts must be able to learn about new technology quickly. They should be naturally curious about keeping up on cutting-edge developments, which can be time consuming. Furthermore, they are often so busy at their jobs that staying in the know is done largely on their own time.

EXPLORING

You have several options to learn more about what it is like to be a computer systems programmer/analyst. You can spend a day with a working professional in this field in order to experience a typical day firsthand. Career days of this type can usually be arranged through school guidance counselors or the public relations manager of local corporations.

Strategy games, such as chess, played with friends or school clubs are a good way to put your analytic thinking skills to use while having fun. When choosing a game, the key is to make sure it relies on qualities similar to those used by programmer/analysts.

Lastly, you should become a computer hobbyist and learn everything you can about computers by working and playing with them on a daily basis. Surfing the Internet regularly, as well as reading trade magazines, will also be helpful. You might also want to try hooking up a mini-system at home or school, configuring terminals, printers, modems, and other peripherals into a coherent

system. This activity requires a fair amount of knowledge and should be supervised by a professional.

EMPLOYERS

Approximately 512,720 computer systems analysts and 367,880 computer programmers were employed in the United Stated in 2009. Computer systems programmer/analysts work for all types of firms and organizations that do their work on computers. Such companies may include manufacturing companies, data processing service firms, hardware and software companies, banks, insurance companies, credit companies, publishing houses, government agencies, financial institutions, Internet service providers, and colleges and universities. Many programmer analysts are employed by businesses as consultants on a temporary or contractual basis.

STARTING OUT

Since systems programmer/analysts typically have at least some experience in a computer-related job, most are hired into these jobs from lower-level positions within the same company. For example, programmers, software engineering technicians, and network and database administrators all gain valuable computing experience that can be put to good use at a systems job. Alternatively, individuals who acquire expertise in systems programming and analysis while in other jobs may want to work with a headhunter to find the right systems positions for them. Also, trade magazines, newspapers, and employment agencies regularly feature job openings in this field.

Students in four-year degree programs should work closely with their schools' career services offices. Companies regularly work through such offices in order to find the most qualified graduates. Since it may be difficult to find a job as a programmer analyst to begin with, it is important for students to consider their long-term potential within a certain company. The chance for promotion into a systems job can make lower-level jobs more appealing, at least in the short run.

For those individuals already employed in a computer-related job but wanting to get into systems programming and analysis, additional formal education is a good idea. Some employers have educational reimbursement policies that allow employees to take courses inexpensively. If the employee's training could directly benefit the business, companies are more willing to pay for the expense.

ADVANCEMENT

Systems programmer/analysts already occupy a relatively high-level technical job. Promotion, therefore, usually occurs in one of two directions. First, programmer analysts can be put in charge of increasingly larger and more complex systems. Instead of concentrating on a company's local system, for example, an analyst can oversee all company systems and networks. This kind of technically based promotion can also put systems programmer/analysts into other areas of computing. With the proper experience and additional training, they can get into database or network management and design, software engineering, or even quality assurance.

The other direction in which programmer analysts can go is managerial. Depending on the position sought, formal education (either a bachelor's degree in business or a master's in business administration) may be required. As more administrative duties are added, more technical ones are taken away. Therefore, programmer analysts who enjoy the technical aspect of their work more than anything else may not want to pursue this advancement track. Excellent computing managers have both a solid background in various forms of computing and a good grasp of what it takes to run a department. Also, having the vision to see how technology will change in the short and long terms, and how those changes will affect the industry concerned, is a quality of a good manager.

EARNINGS

According to the U.S. Department of Labor, the median annual salary for computer systems analysts was $77,080 in 2009. At the low end of the pay range, 10 percent of systems analysts earned less than $47,130. The top 10 percent earned more than $119,170. Salaries are slightly higher in geographic areas where many computer companies are clustered, such as Silicon Valley in California and Seattle, Washington.

Years of professional experience also affect salary levels. As reported by PayScale.com in January 2011, computer systems analysts with one to four years of work experience earned salaries ranging from $40,312 to $56,964. Those with five to nine years of experience averaged from $48,849 to $70,235, and analysts who had 10 to 19 years experience brought home from $50,677 to $75,602 per year.

Most programmer analysts receive health insurance, paid vacation, and sick leave. Some employers offer tuition reimbursement programs and in-house computer training workshops.

WORK ENVIRONMENT

Computer systems programmer/analysts work in comfortable office environments. If they work as consultants, they may travel frequently. Otherwise, travel is limited to trade shows, seminars, and visitations to vendors for demonstrations. They might also visit other businesses to observe their systems in action.

Programmer analysts usually work 40-hour weeks and enjoy the regular holiday schedule of days off. As deadlines for system installation, upgrades, and spot-checking approach, however, they are often required to work overtime. Extra compensation for overtime hours may come in the form of time-and-a-half pay or compensatory time off, depending on the precise nature of the employee's duties, company policy, and state law. If the employer operates off-shifts, programmer analysts may be on-call to address any problems that might arise at any time of the day or night. This is relatively rare in the service sector but more common in manufacturing, heavy industry, and data processing firms.

Computer systems programming and analysis is very detailed work. The smallest error can cause major system disruptions, which can be a great source of frustration. Systems programmer/analysts must be prepared to deal with this frustration and be able to work well under pressure.

OUTLOOK

Employment for computer systems programmer/analysts will grow much faster than the average for all occupations through 2018. Increases are due mainly to the growing number of businesses that rely extensively on computers. When businesses automate, their daily operations depend on the capacity of their computer systems to perform at desired levels. The continuous development of new technologies means that businesses must also update their old systems to remain competitive in the marketplace. Additionally, the need for businesses to network their information adds to the demand for qualified programmer analysts. Businesses will rely increasingly on systems programmer/analysts to make the right purchasing decisions and to keep systems running smoothly.

Many computer manufacturers are beginning to expand the range of services they offer to business clients. In the years to come, they may hire many systems programmer/analysts to work as consultants on a per-project basis with a potential client. These workers would perform essentially the same duties, with the addition of extensive follow-up maintenance. They would analyze business needs and suggest proper systems to answer them. In addition, more and more independent consulting firms are hiring systems programmer/analysts to perform the same tasks.

In addition, the need for new systems to integrate with the wireless Internet (WiFi) and personal mobile computers has created growth in demand for experienced analysts who are well versed in integration and systems development. Demand for information security specialists, to help protect the transmission of sensitive data, is also expected to grow quickly.

Analysts with advanced degrees in computer science or computer engineering will be in great demand. Individuals with master's degrees in business administration with emphasis in information systems will also be highly desirable.

FOR MORE INFORMATION

For more information about systems programmer/analyst positions, contact

Association of Information Technology Professionals
401 North Michigan Avenue, Suite 2400
Chicago, IL 60611-4267
Tel: 800-224-9371
http://www.aitp.org

For information on certification programs, contact
Institute for Certification of Computing Professionals
2400 East Devon Avenue, Suite 281
Des Plaines, IL 60018-4629
Tel: 800-843-8227
E-mail: office@iccp.org
http://www.iccp.org

CONSTRUCTION LABORERS

OVERVIEW

Construction laborers do a variety of tasks at the construction sites of buildings, highways, bridges, and other public and private building projects. Depending on the type of project, construction laborers may carry materials used by craft workers, clean up debris, operate cement mixers, or lay and seal together lengths of sewer pipe, among other duties. They are also involved in hazardous waste/environmental remediation. Approximately 856,400 construction laborers are employed in the United States.

THE JOB

Construction laborers are employed on all kinds of construction jobs, such as building bridges, viaducts, and piers; office and apartment buildings; highways

SCHOOL SUBJECTS
Mathematics, Technical/shop

PERSONAL SKILLS
Following instructions, Mechanical/manipulative

MINIMUM EDUCATION LEVEL
High school diploma

CERTIFICATION OR LICENSING
Voluntary

WORK ENVIRONMENT
Indoors and outdoors, Primarily multiple locations

and streets; pipelines; railroads; river and harbor projects; and sewers, tunnels, and waterworks. Many laborers are employed by private firms that contract to do these construction jobs. Others work for state or local governments on public works or for utility companies on such activities as road repair. Construction laborers are also involved in remodeling, demolition, and repair work.

At the direction of supervisors or other skilled workers, construction laborers perform a wide variety of tasks, such as loading and unloading materials, erecting and dismantling scaffolding, digging and leveling dirt and gravel, wrecking old buildings, removing rubble, pouring and spreading concrete and asphalt, removing forms from set concrete, and carrying supplies to building craft workers. They use equipment ranging from ordinary picks and shovels to various kinds of machines used in construction, such as air hammers or pile-driving equipment.

On some jobs, laborers are assigned to one type of routine task; on other jobs, they are rotated through different tasks as the job progresses. Some laborers tend to work in one branch of the construction industry, such as laying pipelines or building roads. Others transfer from one area of construction to another, depending on the availability of work.

To do their job well, some construction laborers need to be familiar with the duties of skilled craft workers, as well as with the variety of tools, machines, materials, and methods used at the job site. Some laborers do work that requires a considerable amount of know-how, such as those who work with the explosives used to break up bedrock before excavation work can begin on some construction projects. These workers must know how different kinds of explosives can be used safely, to avoid both injury and property damage.

REQUIREMENTS

High School

Most employers prefer high school graduates. A mix of classes that will help you work in the often technical and exacting environment of a construction site is important. Take advantage of opportunities to strengthen your communication skills. Basic mathematics will also help; advanced courses are even better.

Postsecondary Training

In general, no particular training is necessary for most entry-level construction laborer jobs. As a beginner, you'll learn whatever job skills you need informally as you work under the supervision of more experienced workers. If you must work with potentially dangerous equipment or materials, you'll receive instruction in safety procedures that minimize the chance of accidents.

To become a skilled, productive laborer, training is important, however. In supporting other experienced craftsmen, your work will require that you have a diverse set of skills and are comfortable with the operation of today's increasingly complex and highly technical tools, equipment, and instruments.

Apprenticeship programs are available for those seeking a more structured background in this field. Apprenticeship programs include two to three years of on-the-job and classroom instruction in such areas as site and project preparation and maintenance; tools, equipment, and materials; safety; environmental remediation; building construction; and heavy/highway construction. As an apprentice, you'll receive specific training and instruction in dealing with the removal of asbestos, hazardous waste, lead, radiation, and underground storage tanks, as well as the basics of working with asphalt, concrete, lines and grades, masonry, and pipe-laying, and in reading blueprints. All of these skills and training make you a better all-around worker, and can contribute to your ability to get better jobs.

Certification or Licensing

While not required, certification in certain areas of construction can help laborers hone their skills and enhance employment prospects. Construction laborers may earn certification in welding, scaffolding, and other areas from organizations such as the American Welding Soci-

ety and the Occupational Safety & Health Administration (OSHA).

Other Requirements

Construction work is strenuous, so employers seek workers who are physically fit enough to do the job. Laborers must usually be at least 18 years old and reliable, hardworking, and able to follow oral and written instructions. Though it is not required, many laborers are members of the Laborers' International Union of North America. Among many other services, the union works with employers, seeking to ensure that members receive equitable pay and work in safe conditions. As a construction laborer, you should be prepared to decide whether you want to join the union or not.

EXPLORING

People who are interested in this work can often get summer jobs as laborers on building or construction projects. This is the best kind of experience students can have to help them evaluate their interest and potential in this field. They may also benefit by talking to local contractors or local union officials.

EMPLOYERS

Approximately 856,400 construction laborers are employed throughout the United States. Most work in heavily populated industrial sections and are employed mainly by contractors who complete large projects such as those described earlier. Some rare projects may require travel to foreign countries, though contractors with these jobs often use local workers instead. Increasingly, the industry is making use of temporary workers hired on a project basis to move materials or to clean up a site. Many construction laborers contract their services through temporary help agencies, which hire them out for short-term jobs.

STARTING OUT

The usual first step in getting a job in this field is to apply directly to a construction contractor or to the local office of the Laborers' International Union. Workers who have completed a construction craft worker apprenticeship program are usually considered first for job openings above those applicants who have no prior experience.

ADVANCEMENT

Without additional training, construction laborers have limited opportunities for advancement. Some laborers move into jobs as mechanics or skilled operators of construction equipment. Workers who show responsibility and good judgment may be promoted to supervisory positions. Laborers may also decide to leave the field for training in one of the skilled trades, such as carpentry.

EARNINGS

Construction workers often receive substantial hourly wages, but the hourly rates are often poor indicators of annual earnings. The seasonal nature of construction work and time lost because of other factors can significantly reduce the total income of construction workers. There is also a great difference in the wages paid to construction laborers in different parts of the country. Pay is higher for laborers with certain kinds of special experience or for doing certain kinds of tasks. According to the U.S. Department of Labor, the median hourly wage for construction laborers in 2009 was $14.01. If a laborer making this wage were able to work a 40-hour week year round, his or her annual income would be approximately $29,150. The U.S. Department of Labor also reported that the lowest paid 10 percent of laborers made less than $8.86 per hour (about $18,430 per year), while the highest paid 10 percent earned more than $27.05 per hour (about $56,270 annually). Apprentices or helpers usually make about half the wage paid to fully qualified employees.

Fringe benefits, such as health insurance and paid vacations, are available to most workers in this field and vary with local union contracts. In general, benefits are more likely to be offered on jobs staffed by union workers.

WORK ENVIRONMENT

Construction laborers do demanding physical work that is sometimes dangerous. They may need to lift heavy weights, kneel, crouch, stoop, crawl, or work in awkward positions. Much of the job is outdoors, sometimes in hot or cold weather, in wind or rain, in dust, mud, noise, or other uncomfortable conditions. Laborers may be exposed to fumes, odors, dangerous particles, or irritating chemicals. They need to be constantly aware of danger and must be careful to observe good safety practices at all times. Often they wear gloves, hats, and vision, respiratory, or hearing protection to help avoid injury.

Work schedules, weather conditions, or other factors may require night or weekend shifts, and sometimes hours beyond the standard 40-hour week. Work in the construction industry involves changing from one job location to another, and being laid off from time to time because of poor weather, shortages of materials, or a simple lack of jobs. Laborers must be able to arrange their finances so that they can make it through periods of unemployment.

OUTLOOK

The Department of Labor predicts employment of construction laborers to grow much faster than the average through 2018. While competition for jobs will be keen, laborers with specialized skills and flexibility to relocate for construction projects will have the best chances to secure work.

Construction is a large field, and turnover is high among laborers. For these reasons, every year there will be jobs available, mainly in connection with large projects, because employers need to replace those workers who have changed jobs or left the labor force. In addition, the level of construction activity is always affected by local economic conditions. Regions that are prosperous will offer better job possibilities for construction laborers than areas where the economy is not expanding. Increased funding to repair and reconstruct the country's infrastructure—roads, bridges, public buildings, water lines, etc.—as well as the rapid growth of green construction will create greater demand for construction laborers.

FOR MORE INFORMATION

For information about courses and certification, contact the following organizations:

American Welding Society
550 NW LeJeune Road
Miami, FL 33126-5649
Tel: 800-443-9353
http://awsnow.org

Occupational Safety & Health Administration
200 Constitution Avenue, NW
Washington, DC 20210-0001
Tel: 800-321-6742
http://www.osha.gov

For information about contractor careers, contact
Associated General Contractors of America
2300 Wilson Boulevard, Suite 400
Arlington, VA 22201-5426
Tel: 703-548-3118
E-mail: info@agc.org
http://www.agc.org

For information on the role of union membership in construction jobs, check out this union's Web site.
Laborers' International Union of North America
905 16th Street, NW

Washington, DC 20006-1703
Tel: 202-737-8320
http://www.liuna.org

For information on education programs for construction laborers, contact

National Center for Construction Education and Research
3600 NW 43rd Street, Building G
Gainesville, FL 32606-8137
Tel: 888-622-3720
http://www.nccer.org

COSMETOLOGISTS

SCHOOL SUBJECTS
Art, Business, Speech

PERSONAL SKILLS
Artistic, Mechanical/manipulative

MINIMUM EDUCATION LEVEL
Some postsecondary training

CERTIFICATION OR LICENSING
Required by all states

WORK ENVIRONMENT
Primarily indoors, Primarily one location

OVERVIEW

Cosmetologists practice hair-care skills (including washing, cutting, coloring, perming, and applying various conditioning treatments), esthetics (performing skin care treatments), and nail care (grooming of hands and feet). Barbers are not cosmetologists; they undergo separate training and licensing procedures. There are approximately 349,210 cosmetologists, barbers, and other personal care workers employed in the United States.

THE JOB

Cosmetology uses hair as a medium to sculpt, perm, color, or design to create a fashion attitude. Cosmetologists, also known as hair stylists, perform all of these tasks as well as provide other services, such as deep conditioning treatments, special-occasion long hair designs, and a variety of hair-addition techniques.

A licensed hair stylist can perform the hair services noted above and is also trained and licensed to do the basics of esthetics and nail technology. To specialize in esthetics or nail technology, additional courses are taken in each of these disciplines—or someone can study just esthetics or just nail technology and get a license in either or both of these areas.

Cosmetology schools teach some aspects of human physiology and anatomy, including the bone structure of the head and some elementary facts about the nervous system, in addition to hair skills. Some schools have now added psychology-related courses, dealing with people skills and communications.

Hair stylists may be employed in shops that have as few as one or two employees, or as many as 20 or more. They may work in privately owned salons or in a salon that is part of a large or small chain of beauty shops. They may work in hotels, department stores, hospitals, nursing homes, resort areas, or on cruise ships. In recent years, a number of hair professionals—especially in big cities—have gone to work in larger facilities, sometimes known as spas or institutes, which offer a variety of health and beauty services. One such business, for example, offers complete hair design/treatment/color services; manicures and pedicures; makeup; bridal services; spa services, including different kinds of facials (thermal mask, antiaging, acne treatment), body treatments (exfoliating sea salt glow, herbal body wrap), scalp treatments, hydrotherapy water treatments, massage therapy, eyebrow/eyelash tweezing and tinting, and hair-removal treatments for all parts of the body; a fashion boutique; and even a wellness center staffed with board-certified physicians.

Those who operate their own shops must also take care of the details of business operations. Bills must be paid, orders placed, invoices and supplies checked, equipment serviced, and records and books kept. The selection, hiring, and termination of other workers are also the owner's responsibility. Like other responsible businesspeople, shop and salon owners are likely to be asked to participate in civic and community projects and activities.

Some stylists work for cosmetic/hair product companies. When the company introduces a new product or sells an existing product to a new salon, the company hires hair professionals as "freelance educators" to teach the stylists at the salon how to use the product. These workers travel around the country, teaching color techniques at salons and participating in demonstrations for the company at trade shows.

Cosmetologists must know how to market themselves to build their business. Whether they are self-employed or work for a salon or company, they are in business for themselves. It is the cosmetologist's skills and personality that will attract or fail to attract clients to that particular cosmetologist's chair.

Cosmetologists serving the public must have pleasant, friendly, yet professional attitudes, as well as skill, ability, and an interest in their craft. These qualities are necessary in building a following of steady customers. The nature of their work requires cosmetologists to be aware of the psychological aspects of dealing with all types of personalities. Sometimes this can require diplomacy skills and a high degree of tolerance in dealing with different clients.

REQUIREMENTS
High School

High school students interested in the cosmetology field can help build a good foundation for postsecondary training by taking subjects in the areas of art, science (especially a basic chemistry course), health, business, and communication arts. Psychology and speech courses are also helpful.

Postsecondary Training

To become a licensed cosmetologist, you must have completed an education and training program in a school licensed by the state. Some high schools offer courses in hairstyling, skin care, and other personal appearance services, but high school graduates can also take courses at postsecondary schools and schools that specialize in training for cosmetology and other personal appearance careers. Programs may last up to nine months. Students in some programs can earn an associate's degree. Shorter programs in specialty services, such as manicure, pedicure, or skin care are also available.

Applicants must also pass a written test, and some states also give an oral test, before they receive a license. Most states will allow a cosmetologist to work as an apprentice until the license is received, which is normally a matter of weeks.

Some states offer student internship programs. The program allows a student to experience firsthand the expectations of a salon, to perform salon services to be evaluated by their supervisor, and to experience different types of salon settings. The participating salons have the opportunity to pre-qualify potential employees before they graduate and work with the school regarding the skill levels of the student interns. This will also enhance job placement programs already in place in the school. The state requires that each participating salon be licensed and registered with the appropriate state department and file proof of registration with the school, along with the name and license number of their cosmetologist who is assigned to supervise students, before signing a contract or agreement.

Cosmetologists who want to own and run a business may consider additional education in business management, marketing, and sales.

Certification or Licensing

At the completion of the proper amount of credit hours, students must pass a formal examination before they can be licensed. The exam takes just a few hours. Some states also require a practical (hands-on) test and oral exams. Most, however, just require written tests. State Board Examinations are given at regular intervals. After about a month, test scores are available. Those who have passed then send in a licensure application and a specified fee to the appropriate state department. It takes about four to six weeks for a license to be issued.

Temporary permits are issued in most states, allowing students who have passed the test and applied for a license to practice their profession while they wait to receive the actual license.

Graduate courses on advanced techniques and new methods and styles are also available at many cosmetology schools. Many states require licensed cosmetologists to take a specified number of credit hours, called continuing education units, or CEUs. Illinois, for instance, requires each licensed cosmetologist to complete 10 to 14 CEUs each year. Licenses must be renewed in all states, generally every year or every two years.

In the majority of states, the minimum age for an individual to obtain a cosmetology license is 16. Because standards and requirements vary from state to state, students are urged to contact the licensing board of the state in which they plan to be employed.

Other Requirements

Hairstyles change from season to season. As a cosmetologist, you will need to keep up with current fashion trends and often be learning new procedures to create new looks. You should be able to visualize different styles and make suggestions to your clients about what is best for them. And even if you don't specialize in coloring hair, you should have a good sense of color. One of your most important responsibilities will be to make your clients feel comfortable around you and happy with their looks. To do this, you will need to develop both your talking and listening skills.

EXPLORING

Talk to friends or parents of friends who are working in the industry, or just go to a local salon or cosmetology school and ask questions about the profession. Go to the library and get books on careers in the beauty/hair care industry. Search the Internet for related Web sites. Individuals with an interest in the field might seek after-school or summer employment as a general shop helper in a barbershop or a salon. Some schools may permit potential students to visit and observe classes.

EMPLOYERS

Approximately 349,210 cosmetologists, barbers, and other personal care workers are employed in the United States. The most common employers of hair stylists are, of course, beauty salons. Hair stylists also find work at department stores, hospitals, nursing homes, spas, resorts, cruise ships, and cosmetics companies. Considering that most cosmetology schools have placement services to assist graduates, finding employment usually is not difficult for most cosmetologists. As with most jobs in the cosmetology field, opportunities will be concentrated in highly populated areas; however, there will be jobs available for hair stylists virtually everywhere. Many hair stylists/cosmetologists aspire ultimately to be self-employed. This can be a rewarding avenue if one has plenty of experience and good business sense (not to mention start-up capital or financial backing); it also requires long hours and a great deal of hard work.

STARTING OUT

To be a licensed cosmetologist/hair stylist, you must graduate from an accredited school and pass a state test. Once that is accomplished, you can apply for jobs that are advertised in the newspapers or over the Internet, or apply at an employment agency specializing in these professions. Most schools have placement services to help their graduates find jobs. Some salons have training programs from which they hire new employees.

Scholarships or grants that can help you pay for your schooling are available. One such program is the Access to Cosmetology Education (ACE) Grant. It is sponsored by the American Association of Cosmetology Schools (AACS), the Beauty and Barber Supply Institute Inc., and the Cosmetology Advancement Foundation. Interested students can find out about ACE Grants and obtain applications at participating schools, salons, and distributors or through these institutions. The criteria for receiving an ACE Grant include approval from an AACS member school, recommendations from two salons, and a high school diploma or GED.

ADVANCEMENT

Individuals in the beauty/hair care industry most frequently begin by working at a shop or salon. Many aspire to be self-employed and own their own shop. There are many factors to consider when contemplating going into business on one's own. Usually it is essential to obtain experience and financial capital before seeking to own a shop. The cost of equipping even a one-chair shop can be very high. Owning a large shop or a chain of shops is an aspiration for the very ambitious.

Some pursue advanced educational training in one aspect of beauty culture, such as hair styling or coloring. Others who are more interested in the business aspects can take courses in business management skills and move into shop or salon management, or work for a corporation related to the industry. Manufacturers and distributors frequently have exciting positions available for those with exceptional talent and creativity. Cosmetologists work on the stage as platform artists, or take some additional education courses and teach at a school of cosmetology.

Some schools publish their own texts and other printed materials for students. They want people who have cosmetology knowledge and experience as well as writing skills to write and edit these materials. An artistic director for the publishing venue of one large school has a cosmetology degree in addition to degrees in art. Other cosmetologists might design hairstyles for fashion magazines, industry publications, fashion shows, television presentations, or movies. They might get involved in the regulation of the business, such as working for a state licensing board. There are many and varied career possibilities cosmetologists can explore in the beauty/hair care industry.

EARNINGS

Cosmetologists can make an excellent living in the beauty/hair care industry, but as in most careers, they don't receive very high pay when just starting out. Though their increase in salary may start slowly, the curve quickly escalates. The U.S. Department of Labor reports cosmetologists and hairstylists had a median annual income (including tips) of $23,330 in 2009. The lowest paid 10 percent, which generally included those beginning in the profession, made less than $15,980. The highest paid 10 percent earned more than $43,250. Again, both those salaries include tips. On the extreme upward end of the pay scale, some fashion stylists in New York or Hollywood charge $300 (or more) per haircut! Their annual salary can go into six figures. Salaries in larger cities are greater than those in smaller towns; but then the cost of living is higher in the big cities, too.

Most shops and salons give a new employee a guaranteed income instead of commission. If the employee exceeds the guaranteed amount, then he or she earns a commission. Usually, this guarantee will extend for the first three months of employment, so that the new stylist can focus on building up business before going on straight commission.

In addition, most salon owners grant incentives for product sales; and, of course, there are always tips. True professionals never depend on their tips, however. If a stylist receives a tip, it is a nice surprise for a job well done, but it is good business practice not to expect these bonuses. All tips must be recorded and reported to the Internal Revenue Service.

The benefits a cosmetologist receives, such as health insurance and retirement plans, depend on the place of employment. A small independent salon cannot afford to supply a hefty benefit package, but a large shop or salon or a member of a chain can be more generous. However, some of the professional associations and organizations offer benefit packages at reasonable rates.

WORK ENVIRONMENT

Those employed in the cosmetology industry usually work a five- or six-day week, which averages approximately 40–50 hours. Weekends and days preceding holidays may be especially busy. Cosmetologists are on their feet a lot and are usually working in a small space. Strict sanitation codes must be observed in all shops and salons, and they are comfortably heated, ventilated, and well lighted.

Hazards of the trade include nicks and cuts from scissors and razors, minor burns when care is not used in handling hot towels or instruments, and occasional skin irritations arising from constant use of grooming aids that contain chemicals. Some of the chemicals used in hair dyes or permanent solutions can be very abrasive; plastic gloves are required for handling and contact. Pregnant women are advised to avoid contact with many of those chemicals present in hair products.

Conditions vary depending on the environment in which the stylist is working. Those employed in department store salons will have more of a guaranteed client flow, with more walk-ins from people who are shopping. A freestanding shop or salon might have a more predictable pace, with more scheduled appointments and fewer walk-ins. In a department store salon, for example, stylists have to abide by the rules and regulations of the store. In a private salon, stylists are more like entrepreneurs or freelancers, but they have much more flexibility as to when they come and go and what type of business they want to do.

Some may find it difficult to work constantly in such close, personal contact with the public at large, especially when they strive to satisfy customers who are difficult to please or disagreeable. The work demands an even temperament, pleasant disposition, and patience.

OUTLOOK

The future looks great for cosmetology. According to the U.S. Department of Labor, employment should grow much faster than the average through 2018. Our growing population and changes in hair fashion that are practically seasonal will contribute to the demand for cosmetologists. In addition, turnover in this career is fairly high as cosmetologists move up into management positions, change careers, or leave the field for other reasons. Cosmetologists new to the field will have better chances to find work, whereas competition for more experienced cosmetology positions at higher paying, prestigious salons will be strong.

FOR MORE INFORMATION

For information on cosmetology careers, schools, and the ACE Grant, contact
American Association of Cosmetology Schools
9927 Bell Road, Suite 110
Scottsdale, AZ 85260-2402
Tel: 800-831-1086
http://www.beautyschools.org

For information on accredited cosmetology programs, contact
National Accrediting Commission of Cosmetology Arts and Sciences
4401 Ford Avenue, Suite 1300
Alexandria, VA 22302-1432
Tel: 703-600-7600
http://www.naccas.org

For information on scholarships, contact
Professional Beauty Association/National Cosmetology Association
15825 North 71st Street, Suite 100
Scottsdale, AZ 85254-2187
Tel: 800-468-2274
http://www.probeauty.org

 COST ESTIMATORS

OVERVIEW

Cost estimators use standard estimating techniques to calculate the cost of a construction or manufacturing project. They help contractors, owners, and project planners determine how much a project or product will cost to decide if it is economically viable. There are approximately 197,330 cost estimators employed in the United States.

THE JOB

In the construction industry, the nature of the work is largely determined by the type and size of the project being estimated. For a large building project, for example, the estimator reviews architectural drawings and other bidding documents before any construction begins. The estimator then visits the potential construction site to collect information that may affect the way the structure is built, such as the site's access to transportation, water, electricity, and other needed resources. While out in the field, the estimator also analyzes the topography of the land, taking note of its general characteristics, such as drainage areas and the location of trees and other vegetation. After compiling thorough research, the estimator writes a quantity survey, or takeoff. This is an itemized report of the quantity of materials and labor a firm will need for the proposed project.

Large projects often require several estimators, all specialists in a given area. For example, one estimator may assess the electrical costs of a project, while another concentrates on the transportation or insurance costs. In this case, it is the responsibility of a *chief estimator* to combine the reports and submit one development proposal.

In manufacturing, estimators work with engineers to review blueprints and other designs. They develop a list of the materials and labor needed for production. Aiming to control costs but maintain quality, estimators must weigh the option of producing parts in-house or purchasing them from other vendors. After this research, they write a report on the overall costs of manufacturing, taking into consideration influences such as improved employee learning curves, material waste, overhead, and the need to correct problems as manufacturing proceeds.

To write their reports, estimators must know current prices for labor and materials and other factors that influence costs. They obtain this data through commercial price books, catalogs, and the Internet or by calling vendors directly to obtain quotes.

Estimators should also be able to compute and understand accounting and mathematical formulas in order to make their cost reports. Computer programs are frequently used to do the routine calculations, producing more accurate results and leaving the estimator with more time to analyze data.

REQUIREMENTS

High School

To prepare for a job in cost estimating, you should take courses in accounting, business, economics, and mathematics. Because a large part of this job involves comparing calculations, it is essential that you are comfortable and confident with your math skills. English courses with a heavy concentration in writing are also recommended to develop your communication skills. Cost estimators must be able to write clear and accurate reports of their analyses. Finally, drafting and shop courses are also useful since estimators must be able to review and understand blueprints and other design plans.

Postsecondary Training

Though not required for the job, most employers of cost estimators in both construction and manufacturing prefer applicants with formal education. In construction, cost estimators generally have associate's or bachelor's degrees in construction management, construction science, engineering, or architecture. Those employed with

---

SCHOOL SUBJECTS
Business, Economics, Mathematics

PERSONAL SKILLS
Leadership/management, Technical/scientific

MINIMUM EDUCATION LEVEL
Some postsecondary training

CERTIFICATION OR LICENSING
Recommended

WORK ENVIRONMENT
Indoors and outdoors, Primarily multiple locations

manufacturers often have degrees in physical science, business, mathematics, operations research, statistics, engineering, economics, finance, or accounting.

Many colleges and universities offer courses in cost estimating as part of the curriculum for an associate's, bachelor's, or master's degree. These courses cover subjects such as cost estimating, cost control, project planning and management, and computer applications. The Association for the Advancement of Cost Engineering International offers a list of education programs related to cost engineering. Check out the association's Web site, http://www.aacei.org, for more information.

Certification or Licensing

Although it is not required, many cost estimators find it helpful to become certified to improve their standing within the professional community. Obtaining certification proves that the estimator has obtained adequate job training and education. Information on certification procedures is available from organizations such as the American Society of Professional Estimators, the Association for the Advancement of Cost Engineering International, and the Society of Cost Estimating and Analysis.

Other Requirements

To be a cost estimator, you should have sharp mathematical and analytical skills. Cost estimators must work well with others, and be confident and assertive when presenting findings to engineers, business owners, and design professionals. To work as a cost estimator in the construction industry, you will likely need some experience before you start, which can be gained through an internship or cooperative education program.

EXPLORING

Practical work experience is necessary to become a cost estimator. Consider taking a part-time position with a construction crew or manufacturing firm during your summer vacations. Because of more favorable working conditions, construction companies are the busiest during the summer months and may be looking for additional assistance. Join any business or manufacturing clubs that your school may offer.

Another way to discover more about career opportunities is simply by talking to a professional cost estimator. Ask your school counselor to help arrange an interview with an estimator to ask questions about his or her job demands, work environment, and personal opinion of the job.

EMPLOYERS

Approximately 197,330 cost estimators are employed in the United States: about 59 percent by the construction industry and 15 percent by manufacturing companies. Other employers include engineering and architecture firms, business services, the government, and a wide range of other industries.

Estimators are employed throughout the country, but the largest concentrations are found in cities or rapidly growing suburban areas. More job opportunities exist in or near large commercial or government centers.

STARTING OUT

Cost estimators often start out working in the industry as laborers, such as construction workers. After gaining experience and taking the necessary training courses, a worker may move into the more specialized role of estimator. Another possible route into cost estimating is through a formal training program, either through a professional organization that sponsors educational programs or through technical schools, community colleges, or universities. School placement counselors can be good sources of employment leads for recent graduates. Applying directly to manufacturers, construction firms, and government agencies is another way to find your first job.

Whether employed in construction or manufacturing, most cost estimators are provided with intensive on-the-job training. Generally, new hires work with experienced estimators to become familiar with the work involved. They develop skills in blueprint reading and learn construction specifications before accompanying estimators to the construction site. In time, new hires learn how to determine quantities and specifications from project designs and report appropriate material and labor costs.

ADVANCEMENT

Promotions for cost estimators are dependent on skill and experience. Advancement usually comes in the form of more responsibility and higher wages. A skilled cost estimator at a large construction company may become a chief estimator. Some experienced cost estimators go into consulting work, offering their services to government, construction, and manufacturing firms.

EARNINGS

Salaries vary according to the size of the construction or manufacturing firm and the experience and education of the worker. According to the U.S. Department of Labor, the median annual salary for cost estimators was $57,300 in 2009. The lowest paid 10 percent earned less than

$33,560 and the highest paid 10 percent earned more than $95,190. By industry, the mean annual earnings were as follows: nonresidential building construction, $68,410; building equipment contractors, $64,540; building finishing contractors, $60,740; foundation, structure, and building exterior contractors, $60,270; and residential building construction, $59,430. Starting salaries for graduates of engineering or construction management programs were higher than those with degrees in other fields. A salary survey by the National Association of Colleges and Employers reports that candidates with degrees in construction science/management were offered average starting salaries of $53,199 a year in 2009.

WORK ENVIRONMENT

Much of the cost estimator's work takes place in a typical office setting with access to accounting records and other information. However, estimators must also visit construction sites or manufacturing facilities to inspect production procedures. These sites may be dirty, noisy, and potentially hazardous if the cost estimator is not equipped with proper protective gear such as a hard hat or earplugs. During a site visit, cost estimators consult with engineers, work supervisors, and other professionals involved in the production or manufacturing process.

Estimators usually work a 40-hour week, although longer hours may be required if a project faces a deadline. For construction estimators, overtime hours almost always occur in the summer, when most projects are in full force.

OUTLOOK

Employment for cost estimators is expected to increase much faster than the average through 2018, according to the U.S. Department of Labor. As in most industries, highly trained college graduates and those with the most experience will have the best job prospects.

Many jobs will arise from the need to replace workers leaving the industry, either to retire or change jobs. In addition, growth within the residential and commercial construction industry is a large cause for much of the employment demand for estimators. The fastest growing areas in construction are in special trade and government projects, including the building and repairing of highways, streets, bridges, subway systems, airports, water and sewage systems, and electric power plants and transmission lines. Additionally, opportunities will be good in residential and school construction, as well as in the construction of nursing and extended care facilities. Cost estimators with degrees in construction management or in construction science, engineering, or architecture will

have the best employment prospects. In manufacturing, employment is predicted to remain stable, though growth is not expected to be as strong as in construction. Estimators will be in demand because employers will continue to need their services to control operating costs. Estimators with degrees in engineering, science, mathematics, business administration, or economics will have the best employment prospects in this industry.

FOR MORE INFORMATION

For information on certification and educational programs, contact

American Society of Professional Estimators
2525 Perimeter Place Drive, Suite 103
Nashville, TN 37214-3674
Tel: 888-EST-MATE
http://www.aspenational.org

For information on certification, educational programs, and scholarships, contact

Association for the Advancement of Cost Engineering International
209 Prairie Avenue, Suite 100
Morgantown, WV 26501-5934
Tel: 304-296-8444
E-mail: info@aacei.org
http://www.aacei.org

For information on certification, job listings, and a glossary of cost-estimating terms, visit the SCEA Web site.

Society of Cost Estimating and Analysis (SCEA)
527 Maple Avenue East, Suite 301
Vienna, VA 22180-4753
Tel: 703-938-5090
E-mail: scea@sceaonline.net
http://www.sceaonline.org

COURT REPORTERS

OVERVIEW

Court reporters record every word at hearings, trials, depositions, and other legal proceedings by using a stenotype machine to take shorthand notes. Most court reporters transcribe the notes of the proceedings by using computer-aided transcription systems that print

SCHOOL SUBJECTS

English, Foreign language, Government

PERSONAL SKILLS

Communication/ideas, Following instructions

MINIMUM EDUCATION LEVEL

Some postsecondary training

CERTIFICATION OR LICENSING

Required by certain states

WORK ENVIRONMENT

Primarily indoors, Primarily multiple locations

out regular, legible copies of the proceedings. The court reporter must also edit and proofread the final transcript and create the official transcript of the trial or other legal proceeding. Approximately 18,780 court reporters work in the United States.

THE JOB

Court reporters are best known as the men or women sitting in the courtroom silently typing to record what is said by everyone involved. While that is true, it is only part of the court reporter's job. Much more work is done after the court reporter leaves the trial or hearing.

In the courtroom, court reporters use symbols or shorthand forms of complete words to record what is said as quickly as it is spoken on a stenotype machine that looks like a miniature typewriter. The stenotype machine has 24 keys on its keyboard. Each key prints a single symbol. Unlike a typewriter, however, the court reporter using a stenotype machine can press more than one key at a time to print different combinations of symbols. Each symbol or combination represents a different sound, word, or phrase. As testimony is given, the reporter strikes one or more keys to create a phonetic representation of the testimony on a strip of paper, as well as on a computer disk inside the stenotype machine. The court reporter later uses a computer to translate and transcribe the testimony into legible, full-page documents or stores them for reference. Remember, people in court may speak at a rate of between 250 and 300 words a minute, and court reporters must record this testimony word for word and quickly.

Accurate recording of a trial is vital because the court reporter's record becomes the official transcript for the entire proceeding. In our legal system, court transcripts can be used after the trial for many important purposes. If a legal case is appealed, for example, the court reporter's transcript becomes the foundation for any further legal action. The appellate judge refers to the court reporter's transcript to see what happened in the trial and how the evidence was presented.

Because of the importance of accuracy, a court reporter who misses a word or phrase must interrupt the proceedings to have the words repeated. The court reporter may be asked by the judge to read aloud a portion of recorded testimony during the trial to refresh everyone's memory. Court reporters must pay close attention to all the proceedings and be able to hear and understand everything. Sometimes it may be difficult to understand a particular witness or attorney due to poor diction, a strong accent, or a soft speaking voice. Nevertheless, the court reporter cannot be shy about stopping the trial and asking for clarification.

Court reporters must be adept at recording testimony on a wide range of legal issues, from medical malpractice to income tax evasion. In some cases, court reporters may record testimony at a murder trial or a child-custody case. Witnessing tense situations and following complicated arguments are unavoidable parts of the job. The court reporter must be able to remain detached from the drama that unfolds in court while faithfully recording all that is said.

After the trial or hearing, the court reporter has more work to do. Using a CAT program, the stenotype notes are translated to English. The majority of these translated notes are accurate. This rough translation is then edited either by the court reporter or by a *scopist*—an assistant to the court reporter who edits and cleans up the notes. If a stenotype note did not match a word in the court reporter's CAT dictionary during translation, it shows up still in stenotype form. The court reporter must manually change these entries into words and update the dictionary used in translating. If there are any meanings of words or spellings of names that are unfamiliar to the court reporter, research must be done to verify that the correct term or spelling is used. The court reporter then proofreads the transcript to check for any errors in meaning, such as the word *here* instead of the word *hear*. If necessary or requested by the lawyer or judge, special indexes and concordances are compiled using computer programs. The last step the court reporter must take is printing and binding the transcript to make it an organized and usable document for the lawyers and judge.

In some states, the court reporter is responsible for swearing in the witnesses and documenting items of evidence.

In addition to the traditional method of court reporting discussed above, a number of other methods of reporting have emerged in recent years. In real-time court reporting, the court reporter types the court proceedings on a stenotype machine, which is connected to a computer. The symbols that the court reporter types on the stenotype machine are converted to words that can be read by those involved in the case. This process is known as Communications Access Real-time Translation (CART). In addition to its use in court, CART is used in meetings, educational settings, and for closed captioning for the hearing-impaired on television.

In electronic reporting, the court reporter uses audio equipment to record court proceedings. The court reporter is responsible for overseeing the recording process, taking notes to identify speakers and clarify other issues, and ensuring the quality of the recording. Court reporters who specialize in this method are often asked to create a written transcript of the recorded proceeding.

In voice writing, a court reporter wears a hand-held mask (known as a voice silencer) that is equipped with a microphone, and repeats the testimony of all parties involved in the trial. Some reporters translate the voice recording in real time using computer speech recognition technology. Others wait till after the proceedings to create the translation using voice recognition technology or by doing the translation manually.

REQUIREMENTS
High School

To be a court reporter, you need to have a high school diploma or its equivalent. Take as many high-level classes in English as you can and get a firm handle on grammar and spelling. Take typing classes and computer classes to give you a foundation in using computers and a head start in keyboarding skills. Classes in government and business will be helpful as well. Training in Latin can also be a great benefit because it will help you understand the many medical and legal terms that arise during court proceedings. Knowledge of foreign languages can also be helpful because as a court reporter, you will often transcribe the testimony of non-English speakers with the aid of court-appointed translators.

Postsecondary Training

Court reporters are required to complete a specialized training program in shorthand reporting. These programs usually last between two and four years and include instruction on how to enter at least 225 words a minute on a stenotype machine, which is a requirement for federal government employment. Other topics include computer operations, transcription methods, English grammar, and the principles of law. For court cases involving medical issues, students must also take courses on human anatomy and physiology. Basic medical and legal terms are also explained.

About 100 postsecondary schools and colleges have two- and four-year programs in court reporting; more than 60 of these programs are approved by the National Court Reporters Association (NCRA). Many business colleges offer these programs. As a court reporting student in these programs, you must master machine shorthand, or stenotyping, and real-time reporting. The NCRA states that to graduate from one of these programs, you must be able to type at least 225 words per minute and pass tests that gauge your written knowledge and speed.

Certification or Licensing

The NCRA offers several levels of certification for its members. To receive the registered professional reporter certification, you must pass tests that are administered twice a year at more than 200 sites in the United States and overseas. The registered merit reporter certification means you have passed an exam with speeds up to 260 words per minute. The registered diplomate reporter certification is obtained by passing a knowledge exam. This certification shows that the court reporter has gained valuable professional knowledge and experience through years of reporting. The certified real-time reporter certification is given to reporters who have obtained the specialized skill of converting the spoken word into written word within seconds. Several other specialized certifications are available for the court reporter.

The American Association of Electronic Reporters and Transcribers also offers the following voluntary certifications: certified electronic court reporter, certified electronic court transcriber, and certified electronic court reporter and transcriber. The National Verbatim Reporters Association offers the following voluntary certifications: certified verbatim reporter, certificate of merit, and real-time verbatim reporter. Contact these organizations for information on requirements for each certification.

Some states require reporters to be notary publics or to be certified through a state certification exam. Many states grant licenses in either shorthand reporting or court reporting, although not all of these states require a license to work as a court reporter. Licenses are granted after the court reporter passes state examinations and fulfills any prerequisites (usually an approved shorthand reporting program).

Other Requirements

Because part of a court reporter's work is done within the confines of a courtroom, being able to work under pressure is a must. Court reporters need to be able to meet deadlines with accuracy and attention to detail. As stated previously, a court reporter must be highly skilled at the stenotype machine. A minimum of 225 words per minute is expected from a beginning court reporter.

Court reporters must be familiar with a wide range of medical and legal terms and must be assertive enough to ask for clarification if a term or phrase goes by without the reporter understanding it. Court reporters must be as unbiased as possible and accurately record what is said, not what they believe to be true. Patience and perfectionism are vital characteristics, as is the ability to work closely with judges and other court officials.

EXPLORING

Can you see yourself as a court reporter someday? As with any career, you have much to consider. To get an idea of what a court reporter does—at least the work they do in public—attend some trials at your local courts. Instead of focusing on the main players—witnesses, lawyers, judges—keep an eye on the court reporter. If you can, watch several reporters in different courtrooms under different judges to get a perspective on what the average court reporter does. Try to arrange a one-on-one meeting with a court reporter so you can ask the questions you really want answers for. Maybe you can convince one of your teachers to arrange a field trip to a local court.

EMPLOYERS

Approximately 18,780 court reporters are employed in the United States. Many court reporters are employed by city, county, state, or federal courts. Others work for themselves as freelancers or as employees of freelance reporting agencies. These freelance reporters are hired by attorneys to record the pretrial statements, or depositions, of experts and other witnesses. When people want transcripts of other important discussions, freelance reporters may be called on to record what is said at business meetings, large conventions, or similar events.

Most court reporters work in middle- to large-size cities, although they are needed anywhere a court of law is in session. In smaller cities, a court reporter may only work part time.

A recent application of court-reporting skills and technology is in the field of television captioning. Using specialized computer-aided transcription systems, reporters (also known as *broadcast captioners*) can produce captions for live television events, including sporting events and national and local news, for the benefit of hearing-impaired viewers.

STARTING OUT

After completing the required training, court reporters usually work for a freelance reporting company that provides court reporters for business meetings and courtroom proceedings on a temporary basis. Qualified reporters can also contact these freelance reporting companies on their own. Occasionally a court reporter will be hired directly out of school as a courtroom official, but ordinarily only those with several years of experience are hired for full-time judiciary work. A would-be court reporter may start out working as a medical transcriptionist or other specific transcriptionist to get the necessary experience.

Job placement counselors at community colleges can be helpful in finding that first job. Also, try looking in the Yellow Pages (which can be found online) for the areas that you are interested in working. The Internet is also rich with job boards and employment information for all careers, including court reporting.

ADVANCEMENT

Skilled court reporters may be promoted to a larger court system or to an otherwise more demanding position, with an accompanying increase in pay and prestige. Those working for a freelance company may be hired permanently by a city, county, state, or federal court. Those with experience working in a government position may choose to become a freelance court reporter and thereby have greater job flexibility and perhaps earn more money. Those with the necessary training, experience, and business skills may decide to open their own freelance reporting company.

According to a study funded by the National Court Reporters Foundation, court reporters advance by assuming more responsibility and greater skill levels; that gives the court reporter credibility in the eyes of the professionals in the legal system. Those advanced responsibilities include real-time reporting, coding and cross-referencing the official record, assisting others in finding specific information quickly, and helping the judge and legal counsel with procedural matters.

Court reporters can also follow alternative career paths as captioning experts, legal and medical transcriptionists, and cyber-conference moderators.

EARNINGS

Earnings vary according to the skill, speed, and experience of the court reporter, as well as geographic location. Those who are employed by large court systems generally earn more than their counterparts in smaller communities. The median annual income for all court reporters was $47,810 in 2009, according to the U.S. Department of Labor. Ten percent of reporters were paid less than $25,410 annually, and 10 percent had annual earnings of more than $89,240. Incomes can be even higher depending on the reporter's skill level, length of service, and the amount of time the reporter works. Official court reporters not only earn a salary, but also a per-page fee for transcripts. Freelance court reporters are paid by the job and also per page for transcripts.

Court reporters who work in small communities or as freelancers may not be able to work full time. Successful court reporters with jobs in business environments may earn more than those in courtroom settings, but such positions carry less job security.

Those working for the government or full time for private companies usually receive health insurance and other benefits, such as paid vacations and retirement pensions. Freelancers may receive health insurance or other benefits, depending on the policies of their agencies.

WORK ENVIRONMENT

Offices and courtrooms are usually pleasant places to work. Under normal conditions, a court reporter can expect to work a standard 40 hours per week. During lengthy trials or other complicated proceedings, court reporters often work much longer hours. They must be on hand before and after the court is actually in session and must wait while a jury is deliberating. A court reporter often must be willing to work irregular hours, including some evenings. Court reporters must be able to spend long hours transcribing testimony with complete accuracy. There may be some travel involved, especially for freelance reporters and court reporters who are working for a traveling circuit judge. Normally, a court reporter will experience some down time without any transcript orders and then be hit all at once with several. This uneven workflow can cause the court reporter to have odd hours at times.

Court reporters spend time working with finances as well. Paperwork for record-keeping and tracking invoices, income, and expenses is part of the job.

Long hours of sitting in the same position can be tiring and court reporters may be bothered by eye and neck strain. There is also the risk of repetitive motion injuries, including carpal tunnel syndrome. The constant pressure to keep up and remain accurate can be stressful as well.

OUTLOOK

The U.S. Department of Labor predicts that employment of court reporters should grow faster than the average for all occupations through 2018. The increasing number of criminal court cases and civil lawsuits, coupled with the continuing need for court and pretrial depositions and growth of real-time, broadcast captioning will drive the need for court reporters in both state and federal court systems. Job opportunities should be greatest in and around large metropolitan areas, but qualified court reporters should be able to find work in most parts of the country. Court reporters will also find good work opportunities using their skills to produce captioning for television programs, which is a federal requirement for all television programming, and creating real-time translations for the deaf and hard-of-hearing in legal and academic settings.

As always, job prospects will be best for those with the most training and experience. Because of the reliance on computers in many aspects of this job, computer experience and training are important. Court reporters who are certified—especially with the highest level of certification—will have the most opportunities from which to choose.

As court reporters continue to use cutting-edge technology to make court transcripts more usable and accurate, the field itself should continue to grow.

FOR MORE INFORMATION

For information on digital/electronic court reporting and certification, contact

American Association of Electronic Reporters and Transcribers
PO Box 9826
Wilmington, DE 19809-9826
Tel: 800-233-5306
E-mail: aaert@aaert.org
http://www.aaert.org

For information on certification and court reporting careers, contact

National Court Reporters Association
8224 Old Courthouse Road
Vienna, VA 22182-3808
Tel: 800-272-6272
http://www.ncraonline.org/ncra

For information on scholarships, contact
National Court Reporters Foundation
8224 Old Courthouse Road
Vienna, VA 22182-3808
Tel: 800-272-6272
http://www.ncraonline.org/ncrf

For tips on preparing for certification exams, and for other career information, contact
National Verbatim Reporters Association
629 North Main Street
Hattiesburg, MS 39401-3429
Tel: 601-582-4345
E-mail: nvra@nvra.org
http://www.nvra.org

This organization represents court reporters who are employed at the federal level.
U.S. Court Reporters Association
8430 Gross Point Road, Suite 115
Skokie, IL 60077-2036
Tel: 847-470-9500
E-mail: info.usra@gmail.com
http://www.uscra.org

CUSTOMER SERVICE REPRESENTATIVES

OVERVIEW

Customer service representatives, sometimes called *customer care representatives,* work with customers of one or many companies, assist with customer problems, or answer questions. Customer service representatives work in many different industries to provide "frontline" customer service in a variety of businesses. Most customer service representatives work in an office setting though some may work in the "field" to better meet customer needs. There are approximately 2.2 million customer service representatives employed in the United States.

THE JOB

Customer service representatives work in a variety of fields and business, but one thing is common—the customer. All businesses depend on their customers to keep them in business, so customer service, whether handled

---

SCHOOL SUBJECTS
Business, English, Speech

PERSONAL SKILLS
Communication/ideas, Helping/teaching

MINIMUM EDUCATION LEVEL
High school diploma

CERTIFICATION OR LICENSING
Voluntary

WORK ENVIRONMENT
Primarily indoors, Primarily one location

---

internally or outsourced to a call center, must see that customers' needs are met and that customers are satisfied. Customer service representatives must be able to listen to and understand what customers want and then find solutions to their problems.

The types of inquiries representatives handle may include problems with products, delivery issues, or erroneous charges. Their job is to review the customers' complaints to make sure they are valid, and then take steps, in accordance with company policies, to resolve the problems. They may suggest replacement products, credit customers' accounts, or come up with other solutions. Customer service representatives may also help customers in their decisions about what products to purchase.

Some customer service representatives do most of their work on the telephone. Others may represent companies in the field, where the customer is actually using the product or service. Still other customer service representatives may specialize in Internet service, assisting customers over the Web via e-mail or online chats. Not all customer service representatives work a varied schedule; many work a traditional daytime shift. Customers have problems, complaints, and questions 24 hours a day, though, which is why many companies staff their customer service positions for a longer number of hours, especially to accommodate customers during evenings and weekends.

REQUIREMENTS

High School

A high school diploma is required for most customer service representative positions. High school courses that emphasize communication, such as English and speech, will help you learn to communicate clearly. Any courses that require collaboration with others will also help to teach diplomacy and tact—two important aspects of customer service. Business courses will help you get a good overview of the business world, one that is dependent on customers and customer service. Computer skills are also very important.

Postsecondary Training

While a college degree is not necessary to become a customer service representative, certain areas of postsecondary training are helpful. Courses in business and organizational leadership will help to give you a better feel for the business world. Just as in high school, communication classes are helpful in learning to effectively talk with and meet the needs of other people.

These courses can be taken during a college curriculum or may be offered at a variety of customer service workshops or classes. Bachelor's degrees in business and communications are increasingly required for managerial positions.

Certification or Licensing

Although it is not a requirement, customer service representatives can become certified. The International Customer Service Association offers a manager-level certification program. Upon completion of the program, managers receive the certified customer service professional designation.

Other Requirements

A successful customer service representative will most likely have an outgoing personality and enjoy working with people and assisting them with their questions and problems. Because many customer service representatives work in offices and on the telephone, people with physical disabilities may find this career to be both accessible and enjoyable. Some customers are irate or difficult to deal with, so patience and the ability to maintain professionalism are important in this job.

EXPLORING

Explore your ability for customer service by getting a job that deals with the public on a day-to-day basis. Talk with people who work with customers and customer service every day; find out what they like and dislike about their jobs.

There are other ways that you can prepare for a career in this field while you are still in school. Join your school's business club to get a feel for what goes on in the business world today. Doing volunteer work for a local charity or homeless shelter can help you decide if serving others is something that you'd enjoy doing as a career.

Evaluate the customer service at the businesses you visit. What makes that salesperson at The Gap better than the operator you talked with last week? Volunteer to answer phones at an agency in your town or city. Most receptionists in small companies and agencies are called on to provide customer service to callers. Try a nonprofit organization. They will welcome the help, and you will get a firsthand look at customer service.

EMPLOYERS

Customer service representatives are hired at all types of companies in a variety of areas. Because all businesses rely on customers, customer service is generally a high priority for those businesses. Some companies, like call centers, may employ a large number of customer service representatives to serve a multitude of clients, while small businesses may simply have one or two people who are responsible for customer service.

Approximately 2.2 million workers are employed in the United States as customer service representatives. About 23 percent of all customer service representatives work in the finance and insurance industry, and 15 percent are employed in the administrative and support services industry, including call centers.

STARTING OUT

You can become a customer service representative as an entry-level applicant, although some customer service representatives have first served in other areas of a company. This company experience may provide them with more knowledge and experience to answer customer questions. A college degree is not required, but any postsecondary training will increase your ability to find a job in customer service.

Ads for customer service job openings are readily available in newspapers and on Internet job search sites. With some experience and a positive attitude, it is possible to move into the position of customer service representative from another job within the company.

ADVANCEMENT

Customer service experience is valuable in any business career path. It is also possible to advance to management or marketing jobs or to other areas such as product development after working as a customer service representative. Businesses and their customers are inseparable, so most business professionals are experts at customer relations.

EARNINGS

Earnings vary based on location, level of experience, and size and type of employer. The U.S. Department of Labor reports the median annual income for all customer service representatives as $30,290 in 2009. Salaries ranged from less than $19,410 to more than $49,020. The online employment Web site GlassDoor.com reported the average annual salary for Verizon customer service representatives was $34,342 in 2010.

Other benefits vary widely according to the size and type of company in which representatives are employed. Benefits may include medical, dental, vision, and life insurance, 401(k) plans, or bonus incentives. Full-time customer service representatives can expect to receive vacation and sick pay, while part-time workers may not be offered these benefits.

WORK ENVIRONMENT

Customer service representatives work primarily indoors, although some may work in the field where the customers are using the product or service. Most work in clean, well-lighted environments. Those that work in call centers, however, may be in crowded, noisy spaces. They usually work in a supervised setting and report to a manager. They may spend many hours on the telephone, answering mail, or handling Internet communication. Many of the work hours involve little physical activity.

While most customer service representatives generally work a 40-hour workweek, others work a variety of shifts. Many businesses want customer service hours to coincide with the times that their customers are available to call or contact the business. For many companies, these times are in the evenings and on the weekends, so some customer service representatives work a varied shift and odd hours.

OUTLOOK

The U.S. Department of Labor predicts that employment for customer service representatives will grow faster than the average through 2018. This is a large field of workers and many replacement workers are needed each year as customer service reps leave this job for other positions, retire, or leave for other reasons. In addition, the Internet and e-commerce should increase the need for customer service representatives who will be needed to help customers navigate Web sites, answer questions over the phone, and respond to e-mails.

For customer service representatives with specific knowledge of a product or business, the outlook is very good, as quick, efficient customer service is valuable in any business. Additional training and education will also make finding a job as a customer service representative an easier task.

FOR MORE INFORMATION

For information on customer service and other support positions, contact

Association of Support Professionals
122 Barnard Avenue
Watertown, MA 02472-3414
Tel: 617-924-3944
http://www.asponline.com

For information on jobs, training, workshops, and salaries, contact

Customer Care Institute
17 Dean Overlook, NW
Atlanta, GA 30318-1663
Tel: 404-352-9291
E-mail: info@customercare.com
http://www.customercare.com

For information about the customer service industry, contact

Help Desk Institute
102 South Tejon, Suite 1200
Colorado Springs, CO 80903-2242
Tel: 800-248-5667
E-mail: support@thinkhdi.com
http://www.thinkhdi.com

For information on international customer service careers, contact

International Customer Service Association
24 Wernik Place
Metuchen, NJ 08840-2472
Tel: 732-767-0330
E-mail: info@icsatoday.org
http://www.icsatoday.org

DATABASE SPECIALISTS

OVERVIEW

Database specialists design, install, update, modify, maintain, and repair computer database systems to meet the

SCHOOL SUBJECTS
Computer science, Mathematics

PERSONAL SKILLS
Mechanical/manipulative, Technical/scientific

MINIMUM EDUCATION LEVEL
Bachelor's degree

CERTIFICATION OR LICENSING
Voluntary

WORK ENVIRONMENT
Primarily indoors, Primarily one location

needs of their employers. To do this work they need strong math skills, the ability to work with many variables at once, and a solid understanding of the organization's objectives. They consult with other management officials to discuss computer equipment purchases, determine requirements for various computer programs, and allocate access to the computer system to users. They might also direct training of personnel who use company databases regularly. Database specialists may also be called *database designers, database analysts, database managers,* or *database administrators* in some businesses; at other businesses, these designations represent separate jobs. All of these positions, however, fall under the umbrella category of database specialist. There are approximately 108,080 database specialists working in the United States.

THE JOB

It may be easiest to think of a database as being the computer version of the old-fashioned file cabinet that is filled with folders containing information. The database is the information, and the database specialist is the person who designs or adjusts programs that determine how the information is stored, how separate pieces of information relate and affect one another, and how the overall system should be organized. For example, a specialist may set up a retailer's customer database to have a separate "record" for each customer, in the same way that the retailer may have had a separate file folder in its file cabinet for each customer. In the retailer's sales database, each sale represented by an invoice will have a separate record. Each record contains many "fields" where specific pieces of information are entered. Examples of fields for a customer database might include customer number,

customer name, address, city, state, ZIP code, phone, and contact person. Examples of fields in a sales database might include customer number, item purchased, quantity, price, date of purchase, and total. With information organized in separate fields, the retailer can easily sort customer records or invoices, just like filing folders in a file cabinet. In this way, the retailer could print a list of all its customers in Iowa, for example, or total sales for the month of April.

In the same way that records within a database can be sorted, databases themselves can be related to each other. The customer database can be related to the sales database by the common field: customer number. In this way, a business could print out a list of all purchases by a specific customer, for example, or a list of customers who purchased a specific product.

Database specialists are responsible for the flow of computer information within an organization. They make major decisions concerning computer purchases, system designs, and personnel training. Their duties combine general management ability with a detailed knowledge of computer programming and systems analysis.

The specific responsibilities of a database specialist are determined by the size and type of employer. For example, a database specialist for a telephone company may develop a system for billing customers, while a database specialist for a large store may develop a system for keeping track of in-stock merchandise. To do this work accurately, database specialists need a thorough knowledge and understanding of the company's computer operations.

There are three main areas of the database specialist's work: planning what type of computer system a company needs; implementing and managing the system; and supervising computer room personnel.

To adequately plan a computer system, database specialists must have extensive knowledge of the latest computer technology and the specific needs of their company. They meet with high-ranking company officials and decide how to apply the available technology to the company's needs. Decisions include what type of hardware and software to order and how the data should be stored. Database specialists must be aware of the cost of the proposed computer system as well as the budget within which the company is operating. Long-term planning is also important. Specialists must ensure that the computer system can process not only the existing level of computer information received, but also the anticipated load and type of information the company could receive in the future. Such planning is vitally important since, even for small companies, computer systems can cost several hundred thousand dollars.

Implementing and managing a computer system entails a variety of technical and administrative tasks. Depending on the organization's needs, the specialist may modify a system already in place, develop a whole new system, or tailor a commercial system to meet these needs. To do this type of work, the database specialist must be familiar with accounting principles and mathematical formulas. Scheduling access to the computer is also a key responsibility. Sometimes, database specialists work with representatives from all of a company's departments to create a schedule. The specialist prioritizes needs and monitors usage so that each department can do its work. All computer usage must be documented and stored for future reference.

Safeguarding the computer operations is another important responsibility of database specialists. They must make plans in case a computer system fails or malfunctions so that the information stored in the computer is not lost. A duplication of computer files may be a part of this emergency planning. A backup system must also be employed so that the company can continue to process information. Database specialists must also safeguard a system so that only authorized personnel have access to certain information. Computerized information may be of vital importance to a company, and database specialists ensure that it does not fall into the wrong hands.

Database specialists may also be responsible for supervising the work of personnel in the computer department. They may need to train new computer personnel hires to use the company's database, and they may also need to train all computer personnel when an existing database is modified. At some organizations, specialists are also required to train all employees in the use of an upgraded or a new system. Therefore, specialists need the ability to translate technical concepts into everyday language.

Database specialists may be known by a number of different titles and have a variety of responsibilities, depending on the size and the needs of the organizations that employ them. According to an article in *Computerworld,* the title *database designer* indicates someone who works on database programming. These workers usually have a math or engineering background. The title *database administrator* indicates someone who primarily focuses on the performance of the database, making sure everything is running smoothly. They may also do routine jobs, such as adding new users to the system. The title *database analyst* indicates someone who primarily focuses on the business, its goals, products, and customers. They work on improving the database so that the organization can meet its goals. In large businesses or organizations, the many duties of the database spe-

cialist may be strictly divided among a number of specialists. In smaller organizations there may be only one database specialist, designer, manager, administrator, or analyst who is responsible for carrying out all the tasks mentioned above. No matter what their title is, however, all database specialists work with an operation that processes millions of bits of information at a huge cost. This work demands accuracy and efficiency in decision-making and problem-solving abilities.

REQUIREMENTS
High School

While you are in high school, take as many math, science, and computer classes as you can. These courses will provide you with the basis to develop your logical thinking skills and understanding of computers. Take electronics or other technical courses that will teach you about schematic drawing, working with electricity, and, again, develop logical thinking. You will also benefit from taking accounting courses and English classes, as you will need strong written and verbal communication skills.

Postsecondary Training

A bachelor's degree in computer science, computer information systems, or another computer-related discipline is recommended as the minimum requirement for those wishing to work as database specialists. Some exceptions have been made for people without a degree but who have extensive experience in database administration. Taking this route to become a database specialist, however, is becoming increasingly rare. Most employers will expect you to have at least a four-year degree. Courses in a bachelor's degree program usually include data processing, systems analysis methods, more detailed software and hardware concepts, management principles, and information systems planning. To advance in the field, you will probably need to complete further education. Many businesses today, especially larger companies, prefer database managers to have a master's degree in computer science or business administration. Some companies offer to help with or pay for their employees' advanced education, so you may want to consider this possibility when looking for an entry-level job.

Certification or Licensing

Some database specialists become certified for jobs in the computer field by passing an examination given by the Institute for Certification of Computing Professionals (ICCP). For further information, contact the ICCP at the address given at the end of this article. The ICCP, in cooperation with the Data Management Association (DAMA) International, offers the certified data management professional designation to applicants who pass three examinations. In addition, specialists who want to keep their skills current may take training programs offered by database developers, such as Oracle. These training programs may also lead to certifications.

Other Requirements

Database specialists are strong logical and analytical thinkers. They excel at analyzing massive amounts of information and organizing it into a coherent structure composed of complicated relationships. They are also good at weighing the importance of each element of a system and deciding which ones can be omitted without diminishing the quality of the final project.

Specialists also need strong communication skills. This work requires contact with employees from a wide variety of jobs. Specialists must be able to ask clear, concise, and technical questions of people who are not necessarily familiar with how a database works.

As is true for all computer professionals, specialists should be motivated to keep up with technological advances and able to learn new things quickly. Those who are interested in working almost exclusively in one industry (for example, banking) should be willing to gain as much knowledge as possible about that specific field in addition to their computer training. With an understanding of both fields of knowledge, individuals are more easily able to apply computer technology to the specific needs of the company.

EXPLORING

There are a number of ways to explore your interest in this field while you are still in high school. One good way is to read books. Many books about computer databases are available at bookstores, libraries, and online.

You can also join your high school's computer club to work on computer projects and meet others interested in the field. Learn everything you can about computers by working with them regularly. Online sources can be particularly good for keeping up-to-date with new developments and learning from people who are actively involved in this work. Learn to use a commercial database program, either by teaching yourself or taking a class in it. The Association for Computing Machinery has a Special Interest Group on Management of Data (SIGMOD). The Resources page of SIGMOD's Web site (http://www.sigmod.org/resources) provides an index of free public domain database software that you may want to check out.

You may also want to ask your school guidance counselor or a computer teacher to arrange for a database specialist to speak to your class at school or to arrange for a field trip to a company to see database specialists at work. Another option is to ask your school administrators about databases used by the school and try to interview any database specialists working in or for the school system. Similar attempts could be made with charities in your area that make use of computer databases for membership and client records as well as mailing lists.

Look for direct-experience opportunities, such as part-time work, summer internships, and even summer camps that specialize in computers. If you can't find such a position, you can still put your skills to work by offering to set up small databases, such as address books, recipe databases, or DVD libraries for friends or family members.

EMPLOYERS

Approximately 108,080 database specialists are employed in the United States today. Any business or organization that uses databases as a part of its operations hires database professionals. Database specialists work for investment companies, telecommunications firms, banks, insurance companies, publishing houses, hospitals, school systems, universities, and a host of other large and midsize businesses and nonprofit organizations. There are also many opportunities with federal, state, and city governments.

STARTING OUT

Most graduating college students work closely with their school's career services office to obtain information about job openings and interviews. Local and national employers often recruit college graduates on campus, making it much easier for students to talk with many diverse companies. Another good source of information is through summer internships, which are completed typically between junior and senior year. Many major companies in the computer field, such as Intel (http://www.intel.com/jobs/students) and Oracle (http://www.oracle.com/corporate/employment/college/opportunities/internships.html), have established undergraduate intern programs. This experience is valuable for two reasons. First, it gives students hands-on exposure to computer-related jobs. Second, it allows students to network with working computer professionals who may help them find full-time work after graduation. Interested individuals might also scan the classified ads or work with temporary agencies or headhunters to find entry-level and mid-level positions. Professional organizations, such as SIGMOD, and professional publications are other sources of information about job openings.

ADVANCEMENT

The job of database specialist is in itself a high-level position. Advancement will depend to some extent on the size of the business the specialist works for, with larger companies offering more opportunities for growth at the mid-level and senior levels of management. Further advancement can depend on changing jobs to work at a larger employer or expanding the scope of one's skills.

Another factor influencing advancement is the interests of each individual. Generally, people fall into two categories: those who want to work on the business side and those who prefer to stay in a technical job. For individuals who want to get into the managerial side of the business, formal education in business administration is usually required, usually in the form of a master's degree in business administration. In upper-level management positions, specialists must work on cross-functional teams with professionals in finance, sales, personnel, purchasing, and operations. Superior database specialists at larger companies may also be promoted to executive positions.

Some database specialists prefer to stay on the technical side of the business. For them, the hands-on computer work is the best part of their job. Advancement for these workers will, again, involve further education in terms of learning about new database systems, gaining certification in a variety of database programs, or even moving into another technology area such as software design or networking.

As specialists acquire education and develop solid work experience, advancement will take the form of more responsibilities and higher salaries. One way to achieve this is to move to a better-paying, more challenging database position at a larger company. Some successful database specialists become high-paid consultants or start their own businesses. Whether as a consultant or at a university or community college, teaching is another option for individuals with high levels of experience.

EARNINGS

A fairly wide range of salaries exists for database specialists. Earnings vary with the size, type, and location of the organization as well as a person's experience, education, and job responsibilities. According to the U.S. Department of Labor, median annual earnings for database administrators were $71,550 in 2009. The lowest paid 10 percent earned less than $40,780, while the highest paid 10 percent earned more than $114,200.

Benefits for database professionals depend on the employer; however, they usually include such items as health insurance, retirement or 401(k) plans, and paid vacation days.

WORK ENVIRONMENT

Database specialists work in modern offices, usually located next to the computer room. If they work as consultants, they may travel to client sites as little as once or twice per project or as often as every week. Most duties are performed at a computer at the individual's desk. Travel is occasionally required for conferences and visits to affiliated database locations. Travel requirements vary with employer, client, and level of position held. Database specialists may need to attend numerous meetings, especially during planning stages of a project. They work regular 40-hour weeks but may put in overtime as deadlines approach. During busy periods, the work can be quite stressful since accuracy is very important. Database specialists must therefore be able to work well under pressure and respond quickly to last-minute changes. Emergencies may also require specialists to work overtime or long hours without a break, sometimes through the night.

OUTLOOK

The use of computers and database systems in almost all business settings creates tremendous opportunities for well-qualified database personnel. The U.S. Department of Labor predicts that database specialists and computer support specialists will experience much faster than average job growth through 2018.

Employment opportunities for database specialists should be best in large urban areas because of the many businesses and organizations located there that need employees to work with their databases. Since smaller communities are also rapidly developing significant job opportunities, skilled workers can pick from a wide range of jobs throughout the country. Those with the best education and the most experience in computer systems and personnel management will find the best job prospects. As more databases are connected to, or in some cases created via, the Internet, database specialists with a solid understanding of how to protect databases from online attacks and viruses will be in high demand.

FOR MORE INFORMATION

For information on career opportunities or student chapters, contact

Association of Information Technology Professionals
401 North Michigan Avenue, Suite 2400

Chicago, IL 60611-4267
Tel: 800-224-9371
http://www.aitp.org

For information on certification, contact
DAMA International
19239 North Dale Mabry Highway, No. 132
Lutz, FL 33548-5067
Tel: 813-448-7786
E-mail: info@dama.org
http://www.dama.org

For information about scholarships, student membership, and careers, contact
IEEE Computer Society
2001 L Street NW, Suite 700
Washington, DC 20036-4928
Tel: 202-371-0101
E-mail: help@computer.org
http://www.computer.org

For more information about computer certification, contact
Institute for Certification of Computing Professionals
2400 East Devon Avenue, Suite 281
Des Plaines, IL 60018-4629
Tel: 800-843-8227
E-mail: office@iccp.org
http://www.iccp.org

For more information on the Association for Computing Machinery's special interest group on management of data, visit
Special Interest Group on Management of Data
http://www.sigmod.org

DENTAL ASSISTANTS

OVERVIEW

Dental assistants perform a variety of duties in the dental office, including helping the dentist examine and treat patients and completing laboratory and office work. They assist the dentist by preparing patients for dental exams, handing the dentist the proper instruments, taking and processing X-rays, preparing materials for making impressions and restorations, and instructing patients in

---

SCHOOL SUBJECTS
Business, Health

PERSONAL SKILLS
Helping/teaching, Technical/scientific

MINIMUM EDUCATION LEVEL
High school diploma

CERTIFICATION OR LICENSING
Recommended

WORK ENVIRONMENT
Primarily indoors, Primarily one location

---

oral health care. They also perform administrative and clerical tasks so that the office runs smoothly and the dentist's time is available for working with patients. There are approximately 294,020 dental assistants employed in the United States.

THE JOB

Dental assistants help dentists as they examine and treat patients. They usually greet patients, escort them to the examining room, and prepare them by covering their clothing with paper or cloth bibs. They also adjust the headrest of the examination chair and raise the chair to the proper height. Many dental assistants take X-rays of patients' teeth and process the film for the dentist to examine. They also obtain patients' dental records from the office files, so the dentist can review them before the examination.

During dental examinations and operations, dental assistants hand the dentist instruments as they are needed and use suction devices to keep the patient's mouth dry. When the examination or procedure is completed, assistants may give the patient after-care instructions for the teeth and mouth. They also provide instructions on infection-control procedures, preventing plaque buildup, and keeping teeth and gums clean and healthy between office visits.

Dental assistants also help with a variety of other clinical tasks. When a dentist needs a cast of a patient's teeth or mouth—used for diagnosing and planning the correction of dental problems—assistants may mix the necessary materials. They may also pour, trim, and polish these study casts. Some assistants prepare materials for making dental restorations, and many polish and clean patients' dentures. Some may perform the necessary laboratory work to make temporary dental replacements.

State laws determine which clinical tasks a dental assistant is able to perform. Dental assistants are not the same as *dental hygienists,* who are licensed to perform a wider variety of clinical tasks such as scaling and polishing teeth. Some states allow dental assistants to apply medications to teeth and gums, isolate individual teeth for treatment using rubber dams, and remove excess cement after cavities have been filled. In some states, dental assistants can actually put fillings in patients' mouths. Dental assistants may also check patients' vital signs, update and check medical histories, and help the dentist with any medical emergencies that arise during dental procedures.

Many dental assistants also perform clerical and administrative tasks. These include receptionist duties, scheduling appointments, managing patient records, keeping dental supply inventories, preparing bills for services rendered, collecting payments, and issuing receipts. Dental assistants often act as business managers who perform all nonclinical responsibilities such as hiring and firing auxiliary help, scheduling employees, and overseeing office accounting.

REQUIREMENTS

High School

Most dental assistant positions are entry-level. They usually require little or no experience and no education beyond high school. High school students who wish to work as dental assistants should take courses in general science, biology, health, chemistry, and business management. Typing is also an important skill for dental assistants.

Postsecondary Training

Dental assistants commonly acquire their skills on the job. Many, however, go on to receive training after high school at trade schools, technical institutes, and community and junior colleges that offer dental assisting programs. The armed forces also train some dental assistants. Students who complete two-year college programs receive associate's degrees, while those who complete one-year trade and technical school programs earn a certificate or diploma. Entrance requirements to these programs require a high school diploma and good grades in high school science, typing, and English. Some postsecondary schools require an interview or written examination, and some require that applicants pass physical

and dental examinations. The American Dental Association's Commission on Dental Accreditation accredits about 281 of these programs. Some four- to six-month nonaccredited courses in dental assisting are also available from private vocational schools.

Accredited programs instruct students in dental assisting skills and theory through classes, lectures, and laboratory and preclinical experience. Students take courses in English, speech, and psychology as well as in the biomedical sciences, including anatomy, microbiology, and nutrition. Courses in dental science cover subjects such as oral anatomy and pathology, and dental radiography. Students also gain practical experience in chairside assisting and office management by working in dental schools and local dental clinics that are affiliated with their program.

Graduates of such programs may be assigned a greater variety of tasks initially and may receive higher starting salaries than those with high school diplomas alone.

Certification or Licensing

Dental assistants may wish to obtain certified dental assistant (CDA) certification from the Dental Assisting National Board, but this is usually not required for employment. CDA accreditation shows that an assistant meets certain standards of professional competence. To take the certification examination, assistants must be high school graduates who have taken a course in cardiopulmonary resuscitation and must have either a diploma from a formal training program accredited by the Commission on Dental Accreditation or two years of full-time work experience with a recommendation from the dentist for whom the work was done.

In more than 30 states dental assistants are allowed to take X-rays (under a dentist's direction) only after completing a precise training program and passing a test. Completing the program for CDA certification fulfills this requirement. To keep their CDA credentials, however, assistants must either prove their skills through retesting or acquire further education.

Other Requirements

Dental assistants need a clean, well-groomed appearance and a pleasant personality. Manual dexterity and the ability to follow directions are also important.

EXPLORING

Students in formal training programs receive dental assisting experience as part of their training. High school students can learn more about the field by talking with assistants in local dentists' offices. The American Dental Assistants Association can put students in contact with dental assistants in their areas. Part-time, summer, and temporary clerical work may also be available in dentists' offices.

EMPLOYERS

Approximately 294,020 dental assistants are employed in the United States. More than one-third of all dental assistants work part time. Dental assistants are most likely to find employment in dental offices, whether it be a single dentist or a group practice with several dentists, assistants, and hygienists. Other places dental assistants may find jobs include dental schools, hospitals, public health departments, and U.S. Veterans Affairs and Public Health Service hospitals.

STARTING OUT

High school guidance counselors, family dentists, dental schools, dental placement agencies, and dental associations may provide applicants with leads about job openings. Students in formal training programs often learn of jobs through school career services offices.

ADVANCEMENT

Dental assistants may advance in their field by moving to larger offices or clinics, where they can take on more responsibility and earn more money. In small offices they may receive higher pay by upgrading their skills through education. Specialists in the dental field, who typically earn higher salaries than general dentists, often pay higher salaries to their assistants.

Further educational training is required for advancing to positions in dental assisting education. Dental assistants who wish to become dental hygienists must enroll in a dental hygiene program. Because many of these programs do not allow students to apply dental assisting courses toward graduation, dental assistants who think they would like to move into hygienist positions should plan their training carefully.

In some cases, dental assistants move into sales jobs with companies that sell dental industry supplies and materials. Other areas that are open to dental assistants include office management, placement services, and insurance companies.

EARNINGS

Dental assistants' salaries are determined by specific responsibilities, the type of office they work in, and the geographic location of their employer. The median annual earnings for dental assistants was $33,230 in 2009, according to the U.S. Department of Labor. The highest paid 10 percent earned more than $47,070 a year, while the lowest paid 10 percent earned less than $22,710 a year.

Salaried dental assistants in a private office typically receive paid vacation, health insurance, and other benefits. Part-time assistants in private offices often receive dental coverage, but do not typically receive other benefits.

WORK ENVIRONMENT

Dental assistants work in offices that are generally clean, modern, quiet, and pleasant. They are also well lighted and well ventilated. In small offices, dental assistants may work solely with dentists, while in larger offices and clinics they may work with dentists, other dental assistants, dental hygienists, and laboratory technicians. Although dental assistants may sit at desks to do office work, they spend a large part of the day beside the dentist's chair where they can reach instruments and materials.

About half of all dental assistants work 35- to 40-hour weeks, sometimes including Saturday hours. More than one-third work part time. Some dental assistants work in several dental offices, creating their schedule around different offices' hours of operation.

Taking X-rays poses some risk because regular doses of radiation can be harmful to the body. However, all dental offices must have lead shielding and safety procedures that minimize the risk of exposure to radiation.

OUTLOOK

According to the U.S. Department of Labor, employment for dental assistants is expected to grow much faster than the average through 2018, and is expected to be among the fastest growing occupations. As the population grows, more people will seek dental services for preventive care and cosmetic improvements.

In addition, dentists who earned their dental degrees since the 1970s are more likely than other dentists to hire one or more assistants. Also, as dentists increase their knowledge of innovative techniques such as implantology and periodontal therapy, they generally delegate more routine tasks to assistants so they can make the best use of their time and increase profits.

Job openings will also be created through attrition as assistants leave the field or change jobs.

FOR MORE INFORMATION

For continuing education information and career services, contact
American Dental Assistants Association
35 East Wacker Drive, Suite 1730

Chicago, IL 60601-2211
Tel: 312-541-1550
http://www.dentalassistant.org

For education information, contact
American Dental Association
211 East Chicago Avenue
Chicago, IL 60611-2678
Tel: 312-440-2500
http://www.ada.org

For publications, information on dental schools, and scholarship information, contact
American Dental Education Association
1400 K Street, NW, Suite 1100
Washington, DC 20005-2415
Tel: 202-289-7201
E-mail: adea@adea.org
http://www.adea.org

For information on voluntary certification for dental assistants, contact
Dental Assisting National Board
444 North Michigan Avenue, Suite 900
Chicago, IL 60611-3985
Tel: 800-367-3262
http://www.danb.org

SCHOOL SUBJECTS
Biology, Health

PERSONAL SKILLS
Helping/teaching, Technical/scientific

MINIMUM EDUCATION LEVEL
Associate's degree

CERTIFICATION OR LICENSING
Required by all states

WORK ENVIRONMENT
Primarily indoors, Primarily one location

DENTAL HYGIENISTS

OVERVIEW

Dental hygienists perform clinical tasks, serve as oral health educators in private dental offices, work in public health agencies, and promote good oral health by educating adults and children. Their main responsibility is to perform oral prophylaxis, a process of cleaning teeth by using sharp dental instruments, such as scalers and prophy angles. With these instruments, they remove stains and calcium deposits, polish teeth, and massage gums. There are approximately 173,900 dental hygienists employed in the United States.

THE JOB

In clinical settings, hygienists help prevent gum diseases and cavities by removing deposits from teeth and applying sealants and fluoride to prevent tooth decay. They remove tartar, stains, and plaque from teeth, take X-rays and other diagnostic tests, place and remove temporary fillings, take health histories, remove sutures, polish amalgam restorations, and examine head, neck, and oral regions for disease.

Their tools include hand and rotary instruments to clean teeth, syringes with needles to administer local anesthetic (such as Novocain), teeth models to demonstrate home care procedures, and X-ray machines to take pictures of the oral cavity that the dentist uses to detect signs of decay or oral disease.

A hygienist also provides nutritional counseling and screens patients for oral cancer and high blood pressure. More extensive dental procedures are done by dentists. The hygienist is also trained and licensed to take and develop X-rays. Other responsibilities depend on the employer.

Private dentists might require that the dental hygienist mix compounds for filling cavities, sterilize instruments, assist in surgical work, or even carry out clerical tasks such as making appointments and filling in insurance forms. The hygienist might well fill the duties of receptionist or office manager, functioning in many ways to assist the dentist in carrying out the day's schedule.

Although some of these tasks might also be done by a *dental assistant,* only the dental hygienist is licensed by the state to clean teeth. Licensed hygienists submit charts of each patient's teeth, noting possible decay or disease. The dentist studies these in making further diagnoses.

The *school hygienist* cleans and examines the teeth of students in a number of schools. The hygienist also gives classroom instruction on correct brushing and flossing of teeth, the importance of good dental care, and the effects of good nutrition. They keep dental records of students and notify parents of any need for further treatment.

Dental hygienists may be employed by local, state, or federal public health agencies. These hygienists carry out an educational program for adults and children, in public health clinics, schools, and other public facilities. A few dental hygienists may assist in research projects. For those with further education, teaching in a dental hygiene school may be possible.

Like all dental professionals, hygienists must be aware of federal, state, and local laws that govern hygiene practice. In particular, hygienists must know the types of infection control and protective gear that, by law, must be worn in the dental office to protect workers from infection. Dental hygienists, for example, must wear gloves, protective eyewear, and a mask during examinations. As with most health care workers, hygienists must be immunized against contagious diseases, such as hepatitis.

Dental hygienists are required by their state and encouraged by professional organizations to continue learning about trends in dental care, procedures, and regulations by taking continuing education courses. These may be held at large dental society meetings, colleges and universities, or in more intimate settings, such as a nearby dental office.

REQUIREMENTS

High School

The minimum requirement for admission to a dental hygiene school is graduation from high school. While in high school, you should follow a college preparatory program, which will include courses such as science, mathematics, history, English, and foreign language. It will also be beneficial for you to take health courses.

Postsecondary Training

Two levels of postsecondary training are available in this field. One is a four-year college program offering a bachelor's degree. More common is a two-year program leading to an associate's degree. The bachelor's degree is often preferred by employers, and more schools are likely to require completion of such a degree program in the future. There are about 301 accredited schools in the United States that offer one or both of these courses. Classroom work emphasizes general and dental sciences

and liberal arts. Lectures are usually combined with laboratory work and clinical experience.

Certification or Licensing

After graduating from an accredited school, you must pass state licensing examinations, both written and clinical. The American Dental Association Joint Commission on National Dental Examinations administers the written part of the examination. This test is accepted by all states and the District of Columbia. The clinical part of the examination is administered by state or regional testing agencies.

Other Requirements

Aptitude tests sponsored by the American Dental Hygienists' Association are frequently required by dental hygiene schools to help applicants determine whether they will succeed in this field. Skill in handling delicate instruments, a sensitive touch, and depth perception are important attributes that are tested. To be a successful dental hygienist, you should be neat, clean, and personable.

EXPLORING

Work as a dental assistant can be a stepping-stone to a career as a dental hygienist. As a dental assistant, you could closely observe the work of a dental hygienist. You could then assess your personal aptitude for this work, discuss any questions with other hygienists, and enroll in a dental hygiene school where experience as a dental assistant would certainly be helpful.

You may be able to find part-time or summer work in high school as a dental assistant or clerical worker in a dentist's office. You also may be able to arrange to observe a dental hygienist working in a school or a dentist's office or visit an accredited dental hygiene school. The aptitude testing program required by most dental hygiene schools helps students assess their future abilities as dental hygienists.

EMPLOYERS

Approximately 173,900 dental hygienists are employed in the United States. Dental hygienists can find work in private dentist's offices, school systems, or public health agencies. Hospitals, industrial plants, and the armed forces also employ a small number of dental hygienists.

STARTING OUT

Once you have passed the National Board exams and a licensing exam in a particular state, you must decide on an area of work. Most dental hygiene schools maintain placement services for the assistance of their graduates, and finding a satisfactory position is usually not too difficult.

ADVANCEMENT

Opportunities for advancement, other than increases in salary and benefits that accompany experience in the field, usually require additional study and training. Educational advancement may lead to a position as an administrator, teacher, or director in a dental health program or to a more advanced field of practice. With further education and training, some hygienists may choose to go on to become dentists.

EARNINGS

The dental hygienist's income is influenced by such factors as education, experience, locale, and type of employer. Most dental hygienists who work in private dental offices are salaried employees, although some are paid a commission for work performed or a combination of salary and commission.

According to the U.S. Department of Labor, full-time hygienists earned a median annual salary of $67,340 in 2009. The lowest paid 10 percent of hygienists earned less than $44,900 annually, and the highest paid 10 percent earned $92,860 or more annually. Salaries in large metropolitan areas are generally somewhat higher than in small cities and towns. In addition, dental hygienists in research, education, or administration may earn higher salaries.

A salaried dental hygienist in a private office typically receives a paid two- or three-week vacation. Part-time or commissioned dental hygienists in private offices usually have no paid vacation.

WORK ENVIRONMENT

Working conditions for dental hygienists are pleasant, with well-lighted, modern, and adequately equipped facilities. Hygienists usually sit while working. State and federal regulations require that hygienists wear masks, protective eyewear, and gloves. Most hygienists do not wear any jewelry. They are required by government infection control procedures to leave their work clothes at work, which is why many dentists' offices now have laundry facilities to properly launder work clothes. They must also follow proper sterilizing techniques on equipment and instruments to guard against passing infection or disease.

More than 50 percent of all hygienists work part time, or less than 35 hours a week. It is common prac-

tice among part-time and full-time hygienists to work in more than one office because many dentists schedule a hygienist to come in only two or three days a week. Hygienists frequently piece together part-time positions at several dental offices and substitute for other hygienists who take days off. Many private offices are open on Saturdays. The work hours of government employees are regulated by the particular agency.

OUTLOOK

The U.S. Department of Labor projects that employment of dental hygienists will grow much faster than the average for all occupations through 2018. In fact, the department predicts that dental hygienists will be among the fastest growing occupations. The demand for dental hygienists is expected to grow as younger generations that grew up receiving better dental care keep their teeth longer.

Population growth, increased public awareness of proper oral home care, and the availability of dental insurance should result in the creation of more dental hygiene jobs. Moreover, as the population ages, there will be a special demand for hygienists to work with older people, especially those who live in nursing homes.

FOR MORE INFORMATION

For education information, contact
American Dental Association
211 East Chicago Avenue
Chicago, IL 60611-2678
Tel: 312-440-2500
http://www.ada.org

For publications, information on dental schools, and scholarship information, contact
American Dental Education Association
1400 K Street, NW, Suite 1100
Washington, DC 20005-2415
Tel: 202-289-7201
E-mail: adea@adea.org
http://www.adea.org

For career information and tips for dental hygiene students on finding a job, contact
American Dental Hygienists' Association
444 North Michigan Avenue, Suite 3400
Chicago, IL 60611-3980
Tel: 312-440-8900
E-mail: mail@adha.net
http://www.adha.org

DETECTIVES

OVERVIEW

Detectives are almost always plainclothes investigators who gather difficult-to-obtain information on criminal activity and other subjects. They conduct interviews and surveillance, locate missing persons and criminal suspects, examine records, and write detailed reports. Some make arrests and take part in raids.

THE JOB

The job of a *police detective* begins after a crime has been committed. Uniformed police officers are usually the first to be dispatched to the scene of a crime, however, and it is police officers who are generally required to make out the initial crime report. This report is often the material with which a detective begins an investigation.

Detectives may also receive help early on from other members of the police department. Evidence technicians are sometimes sent immediately to the scene of a crime to comb the area for physical evidence. This step is important because most crime scenes contain physical evidence that could link a suspect to the crime. Fingerprints are the most common physical piece of evidence, but other clues, such as broken locks, broken glass, and footprints, as well as blood, skin, or hair traces, are also useful. If there is a suspect on the scene, torn clothing or any scratches, cuts, and bruises are noted. Physical

SCHOOL SUBJECTS
English, Government, History

PERSONAL SKILLS
Leadership/management, Technical/scientific

MINIMUM EDUCATION LEVEL
High school diploma

CERTIFICATION OR LICENSING
Voluntary (certification),
Required by certain states (licensing)

WORK ENVIRONMENT
Indoors and outdoors,
One location with some travel

evidence may then be tested by specially trained crime lab technicians.

It is after this initial stage that the case is assigned to a police detective. Police detectives may be assigned as many as two or three cases a day, and having 30 cases to handle at one time is not unusual. Because there is only a limited amount of time to devote to each case, an important part of a detective's work is to determine which cases have the greatest chance of being solved. The most serious offenses or those in which there is considerable evidence and obvious leads tend to receive the highest priority. All cases, however, are given at least a routine follow-up investigation.

Police detectives have numerous means of gathering additional information. For example, they contact and interview victims and witnesses, familiarize themselves with the scene of the crime and places where a suspect may spend time, and conduct surveillance operations. Detectives sometimes have informers who provide important leads. Because detectives must often work undercover, they wear ordinary clothes, not police uniforms. Also helpful are existing police files on other crimes, on known criminals, and on people suspected of criminal activity. If sufficient evidence has been collected, the police detective will arrest the suspect, sometimes with the help of uniformed police officers.

Once the suspect is in custody, it is the job of the police detective to conduct an interrogation. Questioning the suspect may reveal new evidence and help determine whether the suspect was involved in other unsolved crimes. Before finishing the case, the detective must prepare a detailed written report. Detectives are sometimes required to present evidence at the trial of the suspect.

Criminal investigation is just one area in which *private investigators* are involved. Some specialize, for example, in finding missing persons, while others may investigate insurance fraud, gather information on the background of persons involved in divorce or child custody cases, administer lie detection tests, debug offices and telephones, or offer security services. Cameras, video equipment, tape recorders, and lock picks are used in compliance with legal restrictions to obtain necessary information. Some private investigators work for themselves, but many others work for detective agencies or businesses. Clients include private individuals, corporations concerned with theft, insurance companies suspicious of fraud, and lawyers who want information for a case. Whomever the client, the private investigator is usually expected to provide a detailed report of the activities and results of the investigation.

REQUIREMENTS

High School

Because detectives work on a wide variety of cases, if you are interested in this field you are encouraged to take a diverse course load. English, American history, business law, government, psychology, sociology, chemistry, and physics are suggested, as are courses in journalism, computers, and a foreign language. The ability to type is often needed. To become a police detective, you must first have experience as a police officer. Hiring requirements for police officers vary, but most departments require at least a high school diploma.

Postsecondary Training

In some police departments a college degree may be necessary for some or all positions. Many colleges and universities offer courses or programs in police science, criminal justice, or law enforcement. Newly hired police officers are generally sent to a police academy for job training.

After gaining substantial experience in the department—usually about three to five years—and demonstrating the skills required for detective work, a police officer may be promoted to detective. In some police departments, candidates must first take a qualifying exam. For new detectives there is usually a training program, which may last from a few weeks to several months.

Private detective agencies usually do not hire individuals without previous experience. A large number of private investigators are former police officers. Those with no law enforcement experience who want to become private investigators can enroll in special private investigation schools, although these do not guarantee qualification for employment. A college degree is an admissions requirement at some private investigation schools. These schools teach skills essential to detective work, such as how to take and develop fingerprints, pick locks, test for the presence of human blood, investigate robberies, identify weapons, and take photographs. The length of these programs and their admissions requirements vary considerably. Some are correspondence programs, while others offer classroom instruction and an internship at a detective agency. Experience can also be gained by taking classes in law enforcement, police science, or criminal justice at a college or university.

Certification or Licensing

The National Association of Legal Investigators awards the certified legal investigator designation to private detectives and investigators who specialize in cases that deal with negligence or criminal defense investigations.

Private detectives and investigators must be licensed in all states except for Alabama, Alaska, Colorado, Idaho, Mississippi, South Dakota, and Wyoming. In general states that have licensing require applicants to pass a written examination and file a bond. Depending on the state, applicants may also need to have a minimum amount of experience, either as a police officer or as an apprentice under a licensed private investigator. An additional license is sometimes required for carrying a gun.

In almost all large cities the hiring of police officers must follow local civil service regulations. In such cases candidates generally must be at least 21 years old, U.S. citizens, and within the locally prescribed height and weight limits. Other requirements include 20/20 corrected vision and good hearing. Background checks are often done.

The civil service board usually gives both a written and physical examination. The written test is intended to measure a candidate's mental aptitude for police work, while the physical examination focuses on strength, dexterity, and agility.

Other Requirements

Among the most important personal characteristics helpful for detectives are an inquisitive mind, good observation skills, a keen memory, and well-developed oral and written communication skills. Being fluent in a second language is also helpful. The large amount of physical activity involved requires that detectives be in good shape. An excellent moral character is especially important.

EXPLORING

There are few means of exploring the field of detective work, and actual experience in the field prior to employment is unlikely. Some police departments, however, do hire teenagers for positions as police trainees and interns. If you are interested in becoming a detective, you should talk with your school guidance counselor, your local police department, local private detective agencies, a private investigation school, or a college or university offering police science, criminal justice, or law enforcement courses. In addition, the FBI operates an Honors Internship Program for undergraduate and graduate students that exposes interns to a variety of investigative techniques.

EMPLOYERS

There are more than 641,590 police and detectives in the United States. A large percentage work for police departments or other government agencies. Approximately 31,250 detectives work as private investigators, employed either for themselves, for a private detective firm, or for a business.

STARTING OUT

If you are interested in becoming a detective, you should contact your local police department, the civil service office or examining board, or private detective agencies in your area to determine hiring practices and any special requirements. Newspapers may list available jobs. If you earn a college degree in police science, criminal justice, or law enforcement, you may benefit from your institution's career services or guidance office. Some police academies accept candidates not sponsored by a police department, and for some people this may be the best way to enter police work.

ADVANCEMENT

Advancement within a police department may depend on several factors, such as job performance, length of service, formal education and training courses, and special examinations. Large city police departments, divided into separate divisions with their own administrations, often provide greater advancement possibilities.

Because of the high dropout rate for private investigators, those who manage to stay in the field for more than five years have an excellent chance for advancement. Supervisory and management positions exist, and some private investigators start their own agencies.

EARNINGS

Median annual earnings of police detectives and criminal investigators were $62,110 in 2009, according to the U.S. Department of Labor. The lowest paid 10 percent earned $37,960 or less, while the highest paid 10 percent earned more than $99,980 annually. Median annual earnings were $75,390 in federal government, $54,940 in state government, and $61,230 in local government. Compensation generally increases considerably with experience. Police departments generally offer better than average benefits, including health insurance, paid vacation, sick days, and pension plans.

Median annual earnings of salaried private detectives and investigators were $42,110 in 2009, according to the U.S. Department of Labor. The lowest paid 10 percent earned less than $24,700, and the highest paid 10 percent earned more than $75,970.

Private investigators who are self-employed have the potential for making much higher salaries. Hourly fees of $50 to $150 and even more, excluding expenses, are possible. Detectives who work for an agency may receive benefits, such as health insurance, but self-employed investigators must provide their own.

WORK ENVIRONMENT

The working conditions of a detective are diverse. Almost all of them work out of an office, where they may consult with colleagues, interview witnesses, read documents, or contact people on the telephone.

Their assignments bring detectives to a wide range of environments. Interviews at homes or businesses may be necessary. Traveling is also common. Rarely do jobs expose a detective to possible physical harm or death, but detectives are more likely than most people to place themselves in a dangerous situation.

Schedules for detectives are often irregular, and overtime, as well as night and weekend hours, may be necessary. At some police departments and detective agencies, overtime is compensated with additional pay or time off.

Although the work of a detective is portrayed as exciting in popular culture, the job has its share of monotonous and discouraging moments. For example, detectives may need to sit in a car for many hours waiting for a suspect to leave a building entrance only to find that the suspect is not there. Even so, the great variety of cases usually makes the work interesting.

OUTLOOK

Employment for police detectives is expected to increase about as fast as the average for all other occupations through 2018, according to the U.S. Department of Labor. Many openings will likely result from police detectives retiring or leaving their departments for other reasons.

Employment for private investigators is predicted to grow much faster than the average through 2018, although it is important to keep in mind that law enforcement or comparable experience is often required for employment. The use of private investigators by insurance firms, hospitals, restaurants, hotels, and other businesses is on the rise. Areas of growth include the investigation of the various forms of identity theft, conducting of employee background checks, and preventing industrial spying and other types of espionage in the financial industry.

FOR MORE INFORMATION

Contact the IACP for information about careers in law enforcement.

International Association of Chiefs of Police (IACP)
515 North Washington Street
Alexandria, VA 22314-2357
Tel: 703-836-6767
http://www.theiacp.org

For more information on private investigation, contact
National Association of Investigative Specialists
PO Box 82148
Austin, TX 78708-2148
Tel: 512-719-3595
http://www.pimall.com/nais/nais.j.html

For information on certification, contact
National Association of Legal Investigators
235 North Pine Street
Lansing, MI 48933-1021
Tel: 866-520-6254
E-mail: info@nalionline.org
http://www.nalionline.org

DIAGNOSTIC MEDICAL SONOGRAPHERS

OVERVIEW

Diagnostic medical sonographers, or *sonographers,* use advanced technology in the form of high-frequency sound waves similar to sonar to produce images of the internal body for analysis by radiologists and other physicians. There are about 51,630 diagnostic medical sonographers employed in the United States.

THE JOB

Sonographers work on the orders of a physician or radiologist. They are responsible for the proper selection and preparation of the ultrasound equipment for each specific exam. They explain the procedure to patients, recording any additional information that may be of later use to the physician. Sonographers instruct patients and assist them into the proper physical position so that the test may begin.

SCHOOL SUBJECTS
Biology, Chemistry

PERSONAL SKILLS
Helping/teaching, Technical/scientific

MINIMUM EDUCATION LEVEL
Associate's degree

CERTIFICATION OR LICENSING
Recommended

WORK ENVIRONMENT
Primarily indoors, Primarily one location

When the patient is properly aligned, the sonographer applies a gel to the skin that improves the diagnostic image. The sonographer selects the transducer, a microphone-shaped device that directs high-frequency sound waves into the area to be imaged, and adjusts equipment controls according to the proper depth of field and specific organ or structure to be examined. The transducer is moved as the sonographer monitors the sound wave display screen in order to ensure that a quality ultrasonic image is being produced. Sonographers must master the location and visualization of human anatomy to be able to clearly differentiate between healthy and pathological areas.

When a clear image is obtained, the sonographer activates equipment that records individual photographic views or sequences as real-time images of the affected area. These images are recorded on computer disk, magnetic tape, strip printout, film, or videotape. The sonographer removes the film after recording and prepares it for analysis by the physician. In order to be able to discuss the procedure with the physician, if asked, the sonographer may also record any further data or observations that occurred during the exam.

Sonographers can be trained in the following specialties: abdomen, breast, echocardiography, neurosonology, obstetrics/gynecology, ophthalmology, and vascular technology.

Other duties include updating patient records, monitoring and adjusting sonographic equipment to maintain accuracy, and, after considerable experience, preparing work schedules and evaluating potential equipment purchases.

REQUIREMENTS

High School

If you are interested in a career in sonography, you should take high school courses in mathematics, biology, physics, anatomy and physiology, and, especially, chemistry. Also, take English and speech classes to improve your communication skills. In this career you will be working with both patients and other medical professionals, and it will be important for you to be able to follow directions as well as explain procedures. Finally, take computer courses to familiarize yourself with using technology.

Postsecondary Training

Instruction in diagnostic medical sonography is offered by hospitals, colleges, universities, technical schools, and the armed forces in the form of hospital certificates and two-year associate's and four-year bachelor's degree programs. Most sonographers enter the field after completing an associate's degree. The Commission on Accreditation of Allied Health Education Programs has accredited more than 150 programs in the United States. Education consists of classroom and laboratory instruction, as well as hands-on experience in the form of internships in a hospital ultrasound department. Areas of study include patient care and medical ethics, general and cross-sectional anatomy, physiology and pathophysiology, applications and limitations of ultrasound, and image evaluation.

Certification or Licensing

After completing their degrees, sonographers may register with the American Registry of Diagnostic Medical Sonography (ARDMS). Registration allows qualified sonographers to take the National Boards to gain certification, which, although optional, is frequently required by employers. Other licensing requirements may exist at the state level but vary greatly. Three registration categories are available to sonographers: registered diagnostic medical sonographer, registered diagnostic cardiac sonographer, and registered vascular technologist.

Students should also be aware of continuing education requirements that exist to keep sonographers at the forefront of current technology and diagnostic theory. They are required to maintain certification through continuing education classes, which vary from state to state. This continuing education, offered by hospitals and ultrasound equipment companies, is usually offered after regular work hours have ended.

Other Requirements

On a personal level, prospective sonographers need to be technically adept, detail-oriented, and precision-minded. You need to enjoy helping others and working with a variety of professionals as part of a team. You must be able to follow physician instructions, while maintaining a creative approach to imaging as you complete each procedure. Sonographers need to cultivate a professional demeanor, while still expressing empathy, patience, and understanding in order to reassure patients. This professionalism is also necessary because, in some instances, tragedy such as cancer, untreatable disease, or fetal death is revealed during imaging procedures. As a result, sonographers must be able to skillfully deflect questions better left to the radiologist or the attending physician. Clear communication, both verbal and written, is a plus for those who are part of a health care team.

EXPLORING

Although it is impossible for you to gain direct experience in sonography without proper education and certification, you can gain insight into duties and responsibilities by speaking directly to an experienced sonographer. You can visit a hospital, health maintenance organization, or other locations to view the equipment and facilities used and to watch professionals at work. You may also consider contacting teachers at schools of diagnostic medical sonography or touring their educational facilities. Guidance counselors or science teachers may also be able to arrange a presentation by a sonographer.

EMPLOYERS

Approximately 51,630 sonographers are employed in the United States. About 60 percent of all sonographers are employed by hospitals. However, increasing employment opportunities exist in nursing homes, HMOs, medical and diagnostic laboratories, imaging centers, private physicians' offices, research laboratories, educational institutions, and industry.

STARTING OUT

Those interested in becoming diagnostic medical sonographers must complete a sonographic educational program such as one offered by teaching hospitals, colleges and universities, technical schools, and the armed forces. You should be sure to enroll in an accredited educational program as those who complete such a program stand the best chances for employment.

Voluntary registration with the American Registry of Diagnostic Medical Sonography (ARDMS) is key to gaining employment. Most employers require registration with ARDMS. Other methods of entering the field include responding to job listings in sonography publications, registering with employment agencies specializing in the health care field, contacting headhunters, or applying to the personnel offices of health care employers. The ARDMS offers a Web site, http://www.ultrasoundjobs. com, to help sonographers locate jobs in the field.

ADVANCEMENT

Many advancement areas are open to sonographers who have considerable experience, and most importantly, advanced education. Sonographers with a bachelor's degree stand the best chance to gain additional duties or responsibilities. Technical programs, teaching hospitals, colleges, universities, and, sometimes, in-house training programs can provide this further training. Highly trained and experienced sonographers can rise to the position of *chief technologist, administrator,* or *clinical supervisor,* overseeing sonography departments, choosing new equipment, and creating work schedules. Others may become *sonography instructors,* teaching ultrasound technology in hospitals, universities, and other educational settings. Other sonographers may gravitate toward marketing, working as *ultrasound equipment sales representatives* and selling ultrasound technology to medical clients. Sonographers involved in sales may market ultrasound technology for nonmedical uses to the plastics, steel, or other industries. Sonographers may also work as *machinery demonstrators,* traveling at the behest of manufacturers to train others in the use of new or updated equipment.

Sonographers may pursue advanced education in conjunction with or in addition to their sonography training. Sonographers may become certified in computer tomography, magnetic resonance imaging, nuclear medicine technology, radiation therapy, and cardiac catheterization. Others may become diagnostic cardiac sonographers or focus on specialty areas such as obstetrics/gynecology, neurosonography, peripheral vascular doppler, and ophthalmology.

EARNINGS

According to the U.S. Department of Labor, diagnostic medical sonographers earned a median annual income of $63,010 in 2009. The lowest paid 10 percent of this group, which included those just beginning in the field, made approximately $43,990. The highest paid 10 percent, which included those with experience and managerial duties, earned more than $85,950 annually. Median earnings for

those who worked in hospitals were $63,770 and for those employed in offices and clinics of medical doctors, $63,820.

Pay scales vary based on experience, educational level, and type and location of employer, with urban employers offering higher compensation than rural areas and small towns. Beyond base salaries, sonographers can expect to enjoy many fringe benefits, including paid vacation, sick and personal days, and health and dental insurance.

WORK ENVIRONMENT

A variety of work settings exist for sonographers, from health maintenance organizations to mobile imaging centers to clinical research labs or industry. In health care settings, diagnostic medical sonographers may work in departments of obstetrics/gynecology, cardiology, neurology, and others.

Sonographers enjoy a workplace that is clean, indoors, well lighted, quiet, and professional. Most sonographers work at one location, although mobile imaging sonographers and sales representatives can expect a considerable amount of travel.

The typical sonographer is constantly busy, seeing as many as 25 patients in the course of an eight-hour day. Overtime may also be required by some employers. The types of examinations vary by institution, but frequent areas include fetal ultrasounds, gynecological (i.e., uterus, ovaries), and abdominal (i.e., gallbladder, liver, and kidney) tests. Prospective sonographers should be aware of the occasionally repetitive nature of the job and the long hours usually spent standing. Daily duties may be both physically and mentally taxing. Although not exposed to harmful radiation, sonographers may nevertheless be exposed to communicable diseases and hazardous materials from invasive procedures. Universal safety standards exist to ensure the safety of the sonographer.

OUTLOOK

According to the U.S. Department of Labor, employment of diagnostic medical sonographers should grow faster than the average for all occupations through 2018. One reason for this growth is that sonography is a safe, nonradioactive imaging process. In addition, sonography has proved successful in detecting life-threatening diseases and in analyzing previously nonimageable internal organs. Sonography will play an increasing role in the fields of obstetrics/gynecology and cardiology. Furthermore, the aging population will create high demand for qualified technologists to operate diagnostic machinery. Demand for qualified diagnostic medical sonographers exceeds the current supply in some areas of the country, especially rural communities, small towns, and some retirement areas. Those flexible about location and compensation will enjoy the best opportunities in current and future job markets.

The health care industry is currently in a state of transition while new laws governing health care are being put into effect following enactment of the Patient Protection and Affordable Care Act in 2010. Also, some procedures may prove too costly for insurance companies or government programs to cover. Hospital sonography departments will also be affected by this debate and continue to downsize. Some procedures will be done only on weekends, weeknights, or on an outpatient basis, possibly affecting employment opportunities, hours, and salaries of future sonographers. Conversely, nursing homes, HMOs, mobile imaging centers, and private physicians' groups will offer new employment opportunities to highly skilled sonographers.

Anyone considering a career in sonography should be aware that there is considerable competition for the most lucrative jobs. Those flexible in regard to hours, salary, and location and who possess advanced education stand to prosper in future job markets. Those complementing their sonographic skills with training in other imaging areas, such as magnetic resonance imaging, computer tomography, nuclear medicine technology, or other specialties, will best be able to meet the changing requirements and rising competition of future job markets.

FOR MORE INFORMATION

For information about available jobs and credentials, contact

American Registry of Diagnostic Medical Sonography
51 Monroe Street, Plaza East One
Rockville, MD 20850-2400
Tel: 800-541-9754
http://www.ardms.org

For information regarding accredited programs of sonography, contact

Commission on Accreditation of Allied Health Education Programs
1361 Park Street
Clearwater, FL 33756-6039
Tel: 727-210-2350
E-mail: mail@caahep.org
http://www.caahep.org

For information regarding a career in sonography or to subscribe to the Journal of Diagnostic Medical Sonography, *contact*

Society of Diagnostic Medical Sonography
2745 Dallas Parkway, Suite 350
Plano, TX 75093-8730
Tel: 800-229-9506
http://www.sdms.org

ENVIRONMENTAL ENGINEERS

OVERVIEW

Environmental engineers design, build, and maintain systems to control waste streams produced by municipalities or private industry. Such waste streams may be wastewater, solid waste, hazardous waste, or contaminated emissions to the atmosphere (air pollution). Environmental engineers typically are employed by the Environmental Protection Agency (EPA), by private industry, or by engineering consulting firms. There are approximately 50,610 environmental engineers employed in the United States.

THE JOB

There is a small pond in Crawford County, Illinois, that provides the habitat and primary food source for several different species of fish, frogs, turtles, insects, and birds, as well as small mammals. About a half-mile away

SCHOOL SUBJECTS
Mathematics, Physics

PERSONAL SKILLS
Leadership/management, Technical/scientific

MINIMUM EDUCATION LEVEL
Bachelor's degree

CERTIFICATION OR LICENSING
Recommended (certification), Required for certain positions (licensing)

WORK ENVIRONMENT
Indoors and outdoors, Primarily multiple locations

is the Jack J. Ryan and Sons Manufacturing Company. For years, this plant has safely treated its wastewater—produced during the manufacturing process—and discharged it into the pond. Then one day, without warning, hundreds of dead fish wash up on the banks of the pond. What's going on? What should be done? It is the job of environmental engineers to investigate and design a system to make the water safe for the flora and fauna that depend on it for survival.

Environmental engineers who work for the federal or state Environmental Protection Agency (EPA) act as police officers or detectives. They investigate problems stemming from systems that aren't functioning properly. They have knowledge about wastewater treatment systems and have the authority to enforce environmental regulations.

The Crawford County pond is in the jurisdiction of the Champaign regional office of the Illinois Environmental Protection Agency (IEPA). There are three divisions: air, land, and water. An environmental engineer in the water division would be alerted to the fish kill at the pond and head out to the site to investigate. The engineer takes photographs and samples of the water and makes notes to document the problem. He or she considers the possibilities: Is it a discharge problem from Jack J. Ryan and Sons? If so, was there an upset in the process? A spill? A flood? Could a storage tank be leaking? Or is the problem farther upstream? The pond is connected to other waterways, so could some other discharger be responsible for killing the fish?

The engineer visits Jack J. Ryan and Sons to talk to the production manager and ask if the plant has been doing anything differently lately. The investigation might include a tour of the plant or an examination of its plans. It might also include questioning other manufacturers farther upstream, to see if they are doing something new that's caused the fish kill.

Once the problem has been identified, the environmental engineer and the plant officials can work together on the solution. For example, the production manager at Jack J. Ryan and Sons reports that they've changed something in the manufacturing process to produce a new kind of die-cast part. They didn't know they were doing something wrong. The EPA engineer informs the company they'll be fined $10,000, and a follow-up investigation will be conducted to make sure it has complied with regulations.

Jack J. Ryan and Sons may have its own environmental engineer on staff. This engineer's job is to help keep the company in compliance with federal and state regulations while balancing the economic concerns of the company. At one time, industries' environmental affairs positions were often filled by employees who also had other positions in the plant. Since the late 1980s, however, these positions are held by environmental experts, including scientists, engineers, lawyers, and communications professionals.

In the Crawford County pond scenario, a Ryan and Sons environmental expert might get a call from an engineer at the IEPA: "There seems to be a fish kill at the pond near your plant. We've determined it's probably from a discharge from your plant." The Ryan and Sons expert looks at the plant's plans, talks to the production manager, and figures out a plan of action to bring the company into compliance.

Some companies rely on environmental engineering consulting firms instead of keeping an engineer on staff. Consulting firms usually provide teams that visit the plant, assess the problem, and design a system to get the plant back into compliance. Consulting firms not only know the technical aspects of waste control, but also have expertise in dealing with the government—filling out the required government forms, for example.

Broadly speaking, environmental engineers may focus on one of three areas: air, land, or water. Those who are concerned with air work on air pollution control, air quality management, and other specialties involved in systems to treat emissions. The private sector tends to have the majority of these jobs. Environmental engineers focused on land include landfill professionals, for whom environmental engineering and public health are key areas. Engineers focused on water work on activities similar to those described above.

A big area for environmental engineers is hazardous waste management. Expertise in designing systems and processes to reduce, recycle, and treat hazardous waste streams is very much in demand. This area tends to be the most technical of all the environmental fields and so demands more professionals with graduate and technical degrees.

Environmental engineers spend a lot of time on paperwork—including writing reports and memos and filling out forms. They also might climb a smokestack, wade in a creek, or go toe-to-toe with a district attorney in a battle over a compliance matter. If they work on company staffs, they may face frustration over not knowing what is going on in their own plants. If they work for the government, they might struggle with bureaucracy. If they work for a consultant, they may have to juggle the needs of the client (including the need to keep costs down) with the demands of the government.

REQUIREMENTS
High School

A bachelor's degree is mandatory to work in environmental engineering. At the high school level, the most important course work is in science and mathematics. It's also good to develop written communication skills. Competition to get into the top engineering schools is tough, so it's important to do well on your ACT or SAT tests.

Postsecondary Training

Environmental degree programs are accredited by the Accreditation Board for Engineering and Technology (http://www.abet.org). Additionally, the American Academy of Environmental Engineers offers the *Environmental Engineering Selection & Career Guide,* which lists accredited environmental engineering programs. It can be accessed by visiting http://www.aaee.net/Website/SelectionGuide.htm. Another possibility is to earn a civil engineering, mechanical engineering, industrial engineering, or other traditional engineering degree with an environmental focus. You could also obtain a traditional engineering degree and learn the environmental knowledge on the job, or obtain a master's degree in environmental engineering.

Certification or Licensing

Certification is voluntary and may be obtained through such organizations as the American Academy of Environmental Engineers, the Institute of Professional Environmental Practice, and the Academy of Board Certified Environmental Professionals.

If your work as an engineer affects public health, safety, or property, you must register with the state. To obtain registration, you must have a degree from an accredited engineering program. Right before you get your degree (or soon after), you must pass an engineer-in-training (EIT) exam covering fundamentals of science and engineering. A few years after you've started your career, you must also pass an exam covering engineering practice. The exams are offered by the National Council of Examiners for Engineering and Surveying (http://www.ncees.org).

Other Requirements

Environmental engineers must like solving problems and have a good background in science and math. They must be able to, in the words of one engineer, "just get in there and figure out what needs to be done." Engineers must be able to communicate verbally and in writing with a variety of people from both technical and nontechnical backgrounds.

EXPLORING

A good way to explore becoming an environmental engineer is to talk to someone in the field. Contact your local EPA office, check the Yellow Pages for environmental consulting firms in your area, or ask a local industrial company if you can visit. The latter is not as far-fetched as you might think: Big industry has learned the value of earning positive community relations, and their outreach efforts may include having an open house for their neighbors in which one can walk through their plants, ask questions, and get a feel for what goes on there.

You cannot work as an environmental engineer without having a bachelor's degree. You can, however, put yourself in situations in which you're around environmental engineers to see what they do and how they work. To do so, you may volunteer for the local chapter of a nonprofit environmental organization, do an internship with an environmental organization, or work first as an environmental technician, a job that requires less education (such as a two-year associate's degree or even a high school diploma).

Another good way to get exposure to environmental engineering is to familiarize yourself with professional journals. Journals that may be available in your library include *Chemical & Engineering News* (http://pubs.acs.org/cen), which regularly features articles on waste management systems, and *Environmental Engineer* (http://www.aaee.net/Website/Magazine.htm) and *Pollution Engineering* (http://www.pollutionengineering.com), which feature articles of interest to environmental engineers.

EMPLOYERS

Approximately 50,610 environmental engineers are employed in the United States. Environmental engineers most often work for the Environmental Protection Agency (EPA), state environmental protection agencies, in private industry, or at engineering consulting firms.

STARTING OUT

The traditional method of entering this field is by obtaining a bachelor's degree and applying directly to companies or to the EPA. School career services offices can assist you in these efforts. Professional associations such as the American Academy of Environmental Engineers also offer job listings at their Web sites. Additionally, the academy offers the *Environmental Engineering Selection & Career Guide,* which lists consulting firms and public and academic institutions that hire certified environmental engineers. It can be accessed by visiting http://www.aaee.net/Website/SelectionGuide.htm.

ADVANCEMENT

After environmental engineers have gained work experience, there are several routes for advancement. Those working for the EPA can become department supervisors or switch to private industry or consulting. In-house environmental staff members may rise to supervisory positions. Engineers with consulting firms may become project managers or specialists in certain areas.

Environmental careers are evolving at a break-neck speed. New specialties are emerging all the time. Advancement may take the form of getting involved at the beginning stages of a new subspecialty that suits an engineer's particular interests, experience, and expertise.

EARNINGS

According to a 2009 salary survey by the National Association of Colleges and Employers, bachelor's degree candidates in environmental health engineering received starting offers of $59,480 a year. The U.S. Department of Labor (DOL) reports that median annual earnings of environmental engineers were $77,040 in 2009. Salaries ranged from less than $47,660 for the lowest paid 10 percent to more than $115,750 for the highest paid 10 percent. The DOL reports the following mean annual earnings by employer: federal government, $96,410; architectural, engineering, and related services, $82,980; management, scientific, and technical consulting services, $81,690; local government, $74,650; and state government, $66,470.

Fringe benefits vary widely depending on the employer. State EPA jobs may include, for example, two weeks of vacation, health insurance, tuition reimbursement, use of company vehicles for work, and similar perks. In-house or consulting positions may add additional benefits to lure top candidates.

WORK ENVIRONMENT

Environmental engineers split their time between working in an office and working out in the field. They may also spend time in courtrooms. Since ongoing education is crucial in most of these positions, engineers must attend training sessions and workshops and study new regulations, techniques, and problems. They usually work as part of a team that may include any of a number of different specialists. Engineers must also give presentations of technical information to those with both technical and nontechnical backgrounds.

OUTLOOK

The *Occupational Outlook Handbook* projects that employment for environmental engineers will grow much faster than the average for all occupations through 2018. Engineers will be needed to clean up existing hazards and help companies comply with government regulations. The shift toward prevention of problems and protecting public health should create job opportunities.

Jobs are available with all three major employers—the EPA, industry, and consulting firms. The EPA has long been a big employer of environmental engineers.

FOR MORE INFORMATION

For information on certification, contact
**Academy of Board Certified Environmental
  Professionals**
PO Box 42564
Towson, MD 21284-2564
Tel: 866-767-8073
E-mail: office@abcep.org
http://www.abcep.org

For information on certification, careers, and salaries or a copy of the Environmental Engineering Selection & Career Guide, *contact*
American Academy of Environmental Engineers
130 Holiday Court, Suite 100
Annapolis, MD 21401-7003
Tel: 410-266-3311
http://www.aaee.net

For information on programs that offer degrees in environmental engineering or sciences, contact
**Association of Environmental Engineering and Science
  Professors**
2303 Naples Court
Champaign, IL 61822-3510
Tel: 217-398-6969
http://www.aeesp.org

For information on certification, contact
Institute of Professional Environmental Practice
600 Forbes Avenue, 339 Fisher Hall
Pittsburgh, PA 15282-0001
Tel: 412-396-1703
E-mail: ipep@duq.edu
http://www.ipep.org

For career guidance information contact
Junior Engineering Technical Society
1420 King Street, Suite 405
Alexandria, VA 22314-2750
Tel: 703-548-5387
E-mail: info@jets.org
http://www.jets.org

The following is a cross-disciplinary environmental association:
National Association of Environmental Professionals
PO Box 460
Collingswood, NJ 08108-0460
Tel: 856-283-7816
http://www.naep.org

For information about the private waste services industry, contact
National Solid Wastes Management Association
4301 Connecticut Avenue, NW, Suite 300
Washington, DC 20008-2304
Tel: 800-424-2869
http://www.environmentalisteveryday.org

Contact SCA for information about programs for high school students.
Student Conservation Association (SCA)
689 River Road
PO Box 550
Charlestown, NH 03603-0550
Tel: 603-543-1700
http://www.thesca.org

☐ ENVIRONMENTAL SCIENTISTS

OVERVIEW

Environmental scientists use physical science (such as biology, chemistry, and geology) and social science (including conservation and resource management) to study and assess the environment in relation to the impact human activity has on it as well as damage incurred through natural interactions. Their work is also used to ensure environmental laws and regulations are being met and to help prevent violations before they occur. Environmental scientists specialize in various areas such as air, soil, and water, and use different tools and software programs to

SCHOOL SUBJECTS
Biology, Chemistry, Earth sciences

PERSONAL SKILLS
Mechanical/manipulative, Technical/scientific

MINIMUM EDUCATION LEVEL
Bachelor's degree

CERTIFICATION OR LICENSING
None required

WORK ENVIRONMENT
Indoors and outdoors, Primarily multiple locations

collect and study samples. They work for federal, state, and local environmental protection agencies, as well as private sector companies, and teach in colleges and universities. There are approximately 83,530 environmental scientists employed in the United States.

THE JOB

Environmental science is interdisciplinary, drawing from many different scientific areas that are needed to have a fuller understanding of environmental issues that have been caused by humans as well as natural activity. It is the study of the interaction between biological, chemical, and physical components of the environment and their effects on all organisms. Environmental scientists use scientific principles, methodologies, and tools to identify and analyze environmental problems and solutions. Because many environmental problems cover multiple scientific areas, environmental scientists often consult with other scientists and may also work in teams that consist of scientists who specialize in different areas.

Environmental scientists are knowledgeable about biology, chemistry, physics, ecology, and earth sciences such as geology. They are also well versed in social science, political science, economics, and environmental legislation and policies. They collect and assess data for governmental agencies, industry, environmental programs, and the general public. Depending on their specialty, they gather soil, water, or air samples to identify, abate, or eliminate sources of pollutants or hazards that affect the environment and or human health. Their work may be used to help design and monitor waste disposal sites, preserve water supplies, and reclaim contaminated land and water so that it complies with federal environmental regulations. Another large part of their job entails identifying and assessing risks, and writing risk assessments based on their findings. In these assessments, they describe risks that may occur from construction and other environmental changes. They also write technical proposals and give presentations to managers and regulators.

The types of issues environmental scientists are called upon to help address may include global warming and other global climate change problems, energy and natural resource depletion, air or water pollution, soil erosion, deforestation, coral reef damage, habitat destruction, the spread of infectious disease, pesticide-resistant bugs, and monitoring and safely disposing of waste. According to the U.S. Department of Labor, environmental scientists are similar to physical and life scientists in the training they receive and work they do, but the difference is that they focus on environmental issues. They specialize in subfields such as environmental biology or chemistry, environmental ecology and conservation, or fisheries science. There are many job titles within the category of environmental science. *Environmental ecologists*, for example, study the interrelationship between organisms and their environments. They examine the effects of population size, pollutants, precipitation, climate, and other factors on both the organisms and environments. *Ecological modelers* use mathematical modeling, systems analysis, thermodynamics, and computer techniques to study ecosystems, pollution control, and resource management. *Environmental chemists* study chemical toxicity, examining the effects these chemicals have on people, animals, and plants. *Geoscientists* are environmental scientists who study the earth. Other aspects of environmental scientists' work include processing and reviewing environmental permits, licenses, and related materials; reviewing and implementing environmental technical standards, guidelines, policies, and formal regulations that meet requirements; and investigating and reporting on accidents that affect the environment.

Environmental scientists use a variety of tools in their work, such as digital mapping, remote sensing, geographic information systems (GIS), and global positioning systems (GPS). They may use air samplers or collectors, radiation detectors, soil core samplers, water samplers and analyzers. Depending on their specialty, the technology they use might include pollution modeling software and emissions tracking software.

Some of the computer programs environmental scientists need to be well versed in are Adobe Illustrator, CorelDRAW, and various map creation software programs.

REQUIREMENTS

High School

Environmental scientists have various educational backgrounds depending on their specialty. A well-rounded education in high school includes classes in biology, chemistry, ecology, geology, physics, algebra, geometry, environmental science, and history. Classes that emphasize writing and public speaking are also useful for future report writing and presentation of findings. Be sure to take English, communications, and speech classes. Course work in computer software programs and foreign language are also beneficial.

Postsecondary Training

Environmental scientists may have degrees in environmental science, or they may have degrees in other specialty areas, such as biology, ecology, chemistry, climatology, geology, or even social science or engineering. A master's degree is generally required, and a doctoral degree is needed for college teaching or research jobs. Securing a bachelor's degree is the first step, and environmental science degree programs offer an interdisciplinary approach to the natural sciences, focusing on biology, chemistry, and geology. Students usually study data analysis and physical geography, which can later be applied to practical work in analyzing pollution abatement or ecosystems protection and management. They may also study atmospheric science, soil science, management or conservation of water resources, hydrology, hazardous waste management, environmental legislation, and geologic logging.

Certification or Licensing

Environmental scientists can pursue voluntary certification from a variety of professional associations such as the Ecological Society of America, Institute of Professional Environmental Practice, and National Association of Environmental Professionals.

Other Requirements

Environmental scientists are avid learners and enjoy puzzling through problems to arrive at solutions. They have a deep appreciation for nature and a strong desire to improve the health and well-being of the environment and people. To thrive in this work, scientists need to have mental flexibility and be open to sharing information with other scientists and specialists when collaborating on projects. The work relies on strong, clear communication skills, both written and verbal. Strong knowledge of computer software programs is essential, and experience with data analysis and integration, and computer modeling is required. Fluency in a foreign language is also useful as more work is being conducted internationally.

EXPLORING

Talk to an environmental scientist about his or her career. Read books, magazines, and journals about environmental science to learn more about the field. Visit Web sites such as e! Science News (http://esciencenews.com) and ScienceDaily (http://www.sciencedaily.com) for the latest news and developments in environmental science. The Environmental Protection Agency's Student Center is another good place to explore environmental science. Visit http://www.epa.gov/students for ideas on ways to explore your neighborhood, start an environmental project, check out environmental careers, and earn environmental awards.

EMPLOYERS

About 83,530 environmental scientists are employed in the United States. Nearly 25 percent work for state and local governments, and approximately 21 percent work for management, scientific, and technical consulting firms. Others work for the federal government (mainly for the Environmental Protection Agency and the Department of Defense); for private companies that provide architectural, engineering, and related services; or as teachers and instructors at colleges and universities. Some environmental scientists run their own businesses and are self-employed.

STARTING OUT

Many environmental scientists get started in their careers as research assistants or technicians in laboratories or offices. While in high school, an internship, volunteer work, or a part-time job with an environmental consulting firm, environmental protection agencies, state departments of conservation or other related state agencies can give you better insight into the field and help you determine which areas of environmental science interest you most. You can explore job, volunteer, and internship listings by visiting organizations' Web sites directly, such as the Careers: Opportunities for Students section of the Environmental Protection Agency's site (http://www.epa.gov/careers/stuopp.html), as well as by checking out environmental employment sites such as eco.ORG (http://www.eco.org) and Environmental Career Opportunities (http://ecojobs.com).

ADVANCEMENT

Environmental scientists can advance by handling more complex projects and managing larger teams of researchers. They can be promoted to project leaders, program managers, or other senior management and research positions. Those who are staff employees of companies may leave their positions to start their own consulting businesses. Advancement for environmental scientists can also come about by gaining knowledge and honing skills in other areas of science by pursuing advanced degrees.

EARNINGS

In 2009, environmental scientists earned median annual incomes of $61,010, with salaries ranging from less than $37,120 to $107,190 or higher, according to the U.S. Department of Labor. Those who worked for management, scientific, and technical consulting services averaged about $73,470 per year, while those who worked for local governments earned $60,030 per year in 2009. The top paying states for environmental scientists were the District of Columbia, Massachusetts, Virginia, Illinois, and California.

In addition to salary, environmental specialists may also receive benefits such as health insurance; paid vacation, holiday, and sick time; employer-paid training; tuition reimbursement; and pension and retirement benefits.

WORK ENVIRONMENT

The work environment for environmental scientists varies: some days they may work indoors in comfortable, clean laboratories, running tests and analyzing data; other days, they may be outside at an industrial site or in a rural area, collecting air, soil, or water samples. Scientists are detail oriented and follow strict procedures and precautions to prevent possible exposure to hazardous conditions. They may need to travel to conduct their studies as well as to attend conferences and seminars. They usually work 40 or more hours per week, depending on the projects and deadlines.

OUTLOOK

The U.S. Department of Labor has a new category for occupations that are seeing a great deal of growth due to the "green economy." Environmental scientists are included in this newly dubbed "Green Increased Demand" section and employment opportunities are expected to be excellent in the years to come. Scientists will find many opportunities, particularly in private-sector consulting firms. Additionally, growth in the world's population is causing greater demand for environmental and water resources, which is spurring increased demand for environmental scientists. Stricter environmental laws—particularly in relation to clean air and clean water—means that business owners and environmental protection agencies will need scientists to make sure operations and procedures are in compliance. An increase in environmental remediation and solution work (particularly focusing on minimizing waste, recovering resources, and preventing and controlling pollution) is also causing job growth for environmental scientists. They will be needed to collect and analyze data, and make recommendations for effective ways to improve environmental health.

FOR MORE INFORMATION

For information on careers and competitions for high school students, contact

Air & Waste Management Association
420 Fort Duquesne Boulevard
One Gateway Center, 3rd Floor
Pittsburgh, PA 15222-1435
Tel: 412-232-3444
E-mail: info@awma.org
http://www.awma.org

For information on geology careers and member societies, visit

American Geological Institute
4220 King Street
Alexandria, VA 22302-1502
Tel: 703-379-2480
http://www.agiweb.org

Find membership information and internship listings at this society's Web site.

American Society for Environmental History
http://www.aseh.net

For information about ecological issues, certification, and publications, contact

Ecological Society of America
1990 M Street, NW, Suite 700
Washington, DC 20036-3415
Tel: 202-833-8773
E-mail: esahq@esa.org
http://esa.org

Learn more about environmental issues and find student employment opportunities by visiting

Environmental Protection Agency
Ariel Rios Building
1200 Pennsylvania Avenue, NW
Washington, DC 20460-0001
Tel: 202-272-0167
http://www.epa.gov

For information on certification, contact

Institute of Professional Environmental Practice
600 Forbes Avenue, 339 Fisher Hall
Pittsburgh, PA 15282-0001
Tel: 412-396-1703
E-mail: ipep@duq.edu
http://www.ipep.org

The following is a cross-disciplinary environmental association:

National Association of Environmental Professionals
PO Box 460
Collingswood, NJ 08108-0460
Tel: 856-283-7816
http://www.naep.org

Contact SCA for information about programs for high school students.

Student Conservation Association (SCA)
689 River Road
PO Box 550
Charlestown, NH 03603-0550
Tel: 603-543-1700
http://www.thesca.org

For information about water quality, water treatment, and conferences and workshops, contact

Water Environment Federation
601 Wythe Street
Alexandria, VA 22314-1994
Tel: 800-666-0206
http://www.wef.org

ENVIRONMENTAL TECHNICIANS

OVERVIEW

Environmental technicians, also known as *pollution control technicians,* conduct tests and field investigations to obtain soil samples and other data. Their research is used by engineers, scientists, and others who help clean up, monitor, control, or prevent pollution. An environmental technician usually specializes in air, water, or soil pollution. Although work differs by employer and specialty, technicians generally collect samples for laboratory analysis with specialized instruments and equipment; monitor pollution control devices and systems, such as smokestack air "scrubbers"; and perform various other tests and investigations to evaluate pollution problems. They follow strict procedures in collecting and recording data in order to meet the requirements of environmental laws.

In general, environmental technicians do not operate the equipment and systems designed to prevent pollution or remove pollutants. Instead, they test environmental conditions. In addition, some analyze and report on their findings.

There are approximately 30,870 environmental science and protection technicians, including health technicians, in the United States.

THE JOB

Environmental technicians usually specialize in one aspect of pollution control, such as water pollution, air pollution, or soil pollution. Sampling, monitoring, and testing are the major activities of the job. No matter what the specialty, environmental technicians work largely for or with government agencies that regulate pollution by industry.

Increasingly, technicians input their data into computers. Instruments used to collect water samples or monitor water sources may be highly sophisticated electronic devices. Technicians usually do not analyze the data they collect, but they may report on what they know to scientists or engineers, either verbally or in writing. The following paragraphs detail specialties in the field.

Water pollution technicians monitor both industrial and residential discharge, such as from wastewater treatment plants. They help to determine the presence and extent of pollutants in water. They collect samples from lakes, streams, rivers, groundwater (the water under the earth), industrial or municipal wastewater, or other sources. Samples are brought to labs, where chemical and other tests are performed. If the samples contain harmful substances, remedial (cleanup) actions will need to be taken. These technicians may also perform various field tests, such as checking the pH, oxygen, and nitrate level of surface waters.

Some water pollution technicians set up monitoring equipment to obtain information on water flow, movement, temperature, or pressure and record readings from these devices. To trace flow patterns, they may inject dyes into the water.

Technicians have to be careful not to contaminate their samples, stray from the specific testing procedure, or otherwise do something to ruin the sample or cause faulty or misleading results.

Depending on the specific job, water pollution technicians may spend a good part of their time outdoors, in good weather and bad, aboard boats, and sometimes near unpleasant smells or potentially hazardous substances. Field sites may be in remote areas. In some cases, the technician may have to fly to a different part of the country, perhaps staying away from home for a long period of time.

Water pollution technicians play a big role in industrial wastewater discharge monitoring, treatment, and control. Nearly every manufacturing process produces wastewater, but U.S. manufacturers today are required to be more careful about what they discharge with their wastewater.

SCHOOL SUBJECTS
Biology, Chemistry

PERSONAL SKILLS
Mechanical/manipulative, Technical/scientific

MINIMUM EDUCATION LEVEL
Some postsecondary training

CERTIFICATION OR LICENSING
Required for certain positions

WORK ENVIRONMENT
Indoors and outdoors, One location with some travel

Some technicians specialize in groundwater, ocean water, or other types of natural waters. *Estuarine resource technicians,* for example, specialize in estuary waters, or coastal areas where fresh water and salt water come together. These bays, salt marshes, inlets, and other tidal water bodies support a wide variety of plant and animal life with ecologically complex relationships. They are vulnerable to destructive pollution from adjoining industries, cities and towns, and other sources. Estuarine resource technicians aid scientists in studying the resulting environmental changes. They may work in laboratories or aboard boats, or may use diving gear to collect samples directly.

Air pollution technicians collect and test air samples (for example, from chimneys of industrial manufacturing plants), record data on atmospheric conditions (such as determining levels of airborne substances from auto or industrial emissions), and supply data to scientists and engineers for further testing and analysis. In labs, air pollution technicians may help test air samples or re-create contaminants. They may use atomic absorption spectrophotometers, flame photometers, gas chromatographs, and other instruments for analyzing samples.

In the field, air pollution technicians may use rooftop sampling devices or operate mobile monitoring units or stationary trailers. The trailers may be equipped with elaborate automatic testing systems, including some of the same devices found in laboratories. Outside air is pumped into various chambers in the trailer where it is analyzed for the presence of pollutants. The results can be recorded by machine on 30-day rolls of graph paper or digitally, or are fed into a computer at regular intervals. Technicians set up and maintain the sampling devices, replenish the chemicals used in tests, replace worn parts, calibrate instruments, and record results. Some air pollution technicians specialize in certain pollutants or pollution sources. For example, *engine emission technicians* focus on exhaust from internal combustion engines.

Soil or *land pollution technicians* collect soil, silt, or mud samples and check them for contamination. Soil can become contaminated when polluted water seeps into the earth, such as when liquid waste leaks from a landfill or other source into surrounding ground. Soil pollution technicians work for federal, state, and local government agencies, for private consulting firms, and elsewhere. (Some soil conservation technicians perform pollution control work.)

A position sometimes grouped with other environmental technicians is that of *noise pollution technician.*

Noise pollution technicians use rooftop devices and mobile units to take readings and collect data on noise levels of factories, highways, airports, and other locations in order to determine noise exposure levels for workers or the public. Some test noise levels of construction equipment, chain saws, snow blowers, lawn mowers, or other equipment.

REQUIREMENTS
High School

In high school, key courses include biology, chemistry, and physics. Conservation or ecology courses will also be useful, if offered at your school. Math classes should include at least algebra and geometry, and taking English and speech classes will help to sharpen your communications skills. In addition, work on developing your computer skills while in high school, either on your own or through a class.

Postsecondary Training

Some technician positions call for a high school diploma plus employer training. As environmental work becomes more technical and complex, more positions are being filled by technicians with at least an associate's degree. To meet this need, many community colleges across the country have developed appropriate programs for environmental technicians. Areas of study include environmental engineering technologies, pollution control technologies, conservation, and ecology. Courses include meteorology, toxicology, source testing, sampling and analysis, air quality management, environmental science, and statistics. Other training requirements vary by employer. Some experts advise attending school in the part of the country where you'd like to begin your career so you can start getting to know local employers before you graduate.

Certification or Licensing

Certification or licensing is required for some positions in pollution control, especially those in which sanitation, public health, a public water supply, or a sewage treatment system is involved. For example, the Institute of Professional Environmental Practice offers the qualified environmental professional and the environmental professional intern certifications. See the end of this article for contact information.

Other Requirements

Environmental technicians should be curious, patient, detail-oriented, and capable of following instructions. Basic manual skills are a must for collecting samples and performing similar tasks. Complex environmental regulations drive technicians' jobs; therefore, it's crucial that they are able to read and understand technical materials and to carefully follow any written guidelines for sampling or other procedures. Computer skills and the ability to read and interpret maps, charts, and diagrams are also necessary.

Technicians must make accurate and objective observations, maintain clear and complete records, and be exact in their computations. In addition, good physical conditioning is a requirement for some activities, for example, climbing up smokestacks to take emission samples. The ability to work well with others and on your own, when necessary, is also important.

EXPLORING

To learn more about environmental jobs, visit your local library and read some technical and general-interest publications in environmental science. This might give you an idea of the technologies being used and issues being discussed in the field today. You can also visit a municipal health department or pollution control agency in your community. Many agencies are pleased to explain their work to visitors.

School science clubs, local community groups, and naturalist clubs may help broaden your understanding of various aspects of the natural world and give you some experience. Most schools have recycling programs that enlist student help.

With the help of a teacher or career counselor, a tour of a local manufacturing plant using an air- or water-pollution abatement system might also be arranged. Many plants offer tours of their operations to the public. This may provide an excellent opportunity to see technicians at work.

As a high school student, it may be difficult to obtain summer or part-time work as a technician due to the extensive operations and safety training required for some of these jobs. However, it is worthwhile to check with a local environmental agency, nonprofit environmental organizations, or private consulting firms to learn of volunteer or paid support opportunities. Any hands-on experience you can get will be of value to a future employer.

EMPLOYERS

Approximately 30,870 environmental science and protection technicians are employed in the United States.

Many jobs for environmental technicians are with the government agencies that monitor the environment, such as the Environmental Protection Agency (EPA), and the U.S. Departments of Agriculture, Energy, and Interior.

Water pollution technicians may be employed by manufacturers that produce wastewater, municipal wastewater treatment facilities, private firms hired to monitor or control pollutants in water or wastewater, and government regulatory agencies responsible for protecting water quality.

Air pollution technicians work for government agencies such as regional EPA offices. They also work for private manufacturers producing airborne pollutants, research facilities, pollution control equipment manufacturers, and other employers.

Soil pollution technicians may work for federal or state departments of agriculture and EPA offices. They also work for private agricultural groups that monitor soil quality for pesticide levels.

Noise pollution technicians are employed by private companies and by government agencies such as OSHA (Occupational Safety and Health Administration).

STARTING OUT

Graduates of two-year environmental programs are often employed during their final term by recruiters who visit their schools. Specific opportunities will vary depending on the part of the country, the segment of the environmental industry, the specialization of the technician (air, water, or land), the economy, and other factors. Many beginning technicians find the greatest number of positions available in state or local government agencies.

Most schools provide job-hunting advice and assistance. Direct application to state or local environmental agencies, employment agencies, or potential employers can also be a productive approach. If you hope to find employment outside your current geographic area, you may get good results by checking with professional organizations or by reading advertisements in technical journals, many of which have searchable job listings on the Internet.

ADVANCEMENT

The typical hierarchy for environmental work is technician (two years of postsecondary education or less), technologist (two years or more of postsecondary training), technician manager (perhaps a technician or technologist with many years of experience), and scientist or engineer (four-year bachelor of science degree or more, up to Ph.D. level).

In some private manufacturing or consulting firms, technician positions are used for training newly recruited professional staff. In such cases, workers with four-year degrees in engineering or physical science are likely to be promoted before those with two-year degrees. Employees of government agencies are usually organized under civil service systems that specify experience, education, and other criteria for advancement. Private industry promotions are structured differently and will depend on a variety of factors.

EARNINGS

Pay for environmental technicians varies widely depending on the nature of the work they do, training and experience required for the work, type of employer, geographic region, and other factors. Public-sector positions tend to pay less than private-sector positions.

Earnings of environmental technicians vary significantly based on the amount of formal training and experience. According to the U.S. Department of Labor, the average annual salary for environmental science and protection technicians was $40,790 in 2009. Salaries ranged from less than $26,570 to more than $65,190. Technicians who work for local government earned mean annual salaries of $46,990 in 2009; those who were employed by state government earned $45,070. Technicians who become managers or supervisors can earn up to $50,000 per year or more. Technicians who work in private industry or who further their education to secure teaching positions can also expect to earn higher than average salaries.

No matter which area they specialize in, environmental technicians generally enjoy fringe benefits such as paid vacation, holidays and sick time, and employer-paid training. Technicians who work full time (and some who work part time) often receive health insurance benefits. Technicians who are employed by the federal government may get additional benefits, such as pension and retirement benefits.

WORK ENVIRONMENT

Conditions range from clean and pleasant indoor offices and laboratories to hot, cold, wet, bad-smelling, noisy, or even hazardous settings outdoors. Anyone planning a career in environmental technology should realize the possibility of exposure to unpleasant or unsafe conditions at least occasionally in his or her career. Employers often can minimize these negatives through special equipment and procedures. Most laboratories and manufacturing companies have safety procedures for potentially dangerous situations.

Some jobs involve vigorous physical activity, such as handling a small boat or climbing a tall ladder. For the most part, technicians need only to be prepared for moderate activity. Travel may be required; technicians go to urban, industrial, or rural settings for sampling.

Because their job can involve a considerable amount of repetitive work, patience and the ability to handle routine are important. Yet, particularly when environmental technicians are working in the field, they also have to be ready to use their resourcefulness and ingenuity to find the best ways of responding to new situations.

OUTLOOK

Demand for environmental technicians is expected to increase much faster than the average for all occupations through 2018, according to the U.S. Department of Labor (DOL). Those trained to handle increasingly complex technical demands will have the best employment prospects. Environmental technicians will be needed to collect soil, water, and air samples to measure the levels of pollutants; to monitor the private industry's compliance with environmental regulations; and to clean up contaminated sites. The DOL predicts that most employment growth will occur in firms that help other companies in environmental monitoring, management, and regulatory compliance.

Demand will be higher in some areas of the country than others depending on specialty; for example, air pollution technicians will be especially in demand in large cities, such as Los Angeles and New York, which face pressure to comply with national air quality standards. Amount of industrialization, stringency of state and local pollution control enforcement, health of local economy, and other factors also will affect demand by region and specialty. Perhaps the greatest factors affecting environmental work are continued mandates for pollution control by the government. As long as federal, state, and local governments support pollution control, environmental technicians will be needed.

FOR MORE INFORMATION

For information on environmental careers and degree programs, contact

Advanced Technology Environmental and Energy Center
500 Belmont Road
Bettendorf, IA 52722-5649
http://www.ateec.org

For information on careers and competitions for high school students, contact

Air & Waste Management Association
420 Fort Duquesne Boulevard
One Gateway Center, 3rd Floor
Pittsburgh, PA 15222-1435
Tel: 412-232-3444
E-mail: info@awma.org
http://www.awma.org

For information on the engineering field and technician certification, contact

American Society of Certified Engineering Technicians
PO Box 1536
Brandon, MS 39043-1536
Tel: 601-824-8991
http://www.ascet.org

For information on environmental careers and student employment opportunities, contact

Environmental Protection Agency
Ariel Rios Building
1200 Pennsylvania Avenue, NW
Washington, DC 20460-0001
Tel: 202-272-0167
http://www.epa.gov

For information on certification, contact

Institute of Professional Environmental Practice
600 Forbes Avenue, 339 Fisher Hall
Pittsburgh, PA 15282-0001
Tel: 412-396-1703
E-mail: ipep@duq.edu
http://www.ipep.org

For information on careers, contact

National Ground Water Association
601 Dempsey Road
Westerville, OH 43081-8978
Tel: 800-551-7379
E-mail: ngwa@ngwa.org
http://www.ngwa.org

For information about water quality, water treatment, and conferences and workshops, contact

Water Environment Federation
601 Wythe Street
Alexandria, VA 22314-1994
Tel: 800-666-0206
http://www.wef.org

EVENT PLANNERS

OVERVIEW

The duties of *event planners* are varied, and may include establishing a site for an event; making travel, hotel, and food arrangements; and planning the program and overseeing the registration. The planner may be responsible for all of the negotiating, planning, and coordinating for a major worldwide convention, or the planner may be involved with a small, in-house meeting involving only a few people. Event planners may also organize virtual conferences. Some professional associations, government agencies, nonprofit organizations, political groups, and educational institutions hire event planners or have employees on staff who have these responsibilities. Many of these organizations and companies outsource their event-planning responsibilities to firms that specialize in these services, such as marketing, public relations, and event planning firms. In addition, many event and meeting planners are independent consultants.

Some event planners' services are also used on a personal level to plan class or family reunions, birthday parties, weddings, or anniversaries. Event planners are also known as *meeting* and *convention planners*. There are approximately 51,530 event planners employed in the United States.

SCHOOL SUBJECTS
Business, English, Foreign language

PERSONAL SKILLS
Communication/ideas, Leadership/management

MINIMUM EDUCATION LEVEL
Some postsecondary training

CERTIFICATION OR LICENSING
Voluntary

WORK ENVIRONMENT
Primarily indoors, One location with some travel

THE JOB

Event planners have a variety of duties depending on their specific title and the firm they work for or the firms they work with. Generally, planners organize and plan an event such as a meeting, a special open house, a convention, or a specific celebration.

Meetings might consist of a small interdepartmental meeting, a board meeting, an all-employee meeting, an in-house training session, a stockholders' meeting, or a meeting with vendors or distributors. When planning these events, meeting planners usually check the calendars of key executives to establish a meeting time that fits into their schedules. Planners reserve meeting rooms, training rooms, or outside facilities for the event. They visit outside sites to make sure they are appropriate for that specific event. Planners notify people of the time, place, and date of the event and set up registration procedures, if necessary. They arrange for food, room layout, audiovisual equipment, instructors, computers, sound equipment, and telephone equipment as required.

In some cases, a company may employ an in-house meeting planner who is responsible for small- to medium-sized events. When a large meeting, trade show, conference, open house, or convention is planned, the in-house event planner may contract with outside meeting planners to assist with specific responsibilities such as registration, catering, and display setup. Some companies have their own trade show or convention managers on staff.

Convention, trade show, or *conference managers* and *coordinators* negotiate and communicate with other enterprises related to the convention or trade show industry such as hotel and catering sales staff, speaker's bureaus, and trade staff such as *electricians* or *laborers* who set up convention display areas. They may also be responsible for contracting the transportation of the equipment and supplies to and from the event site. The manager usually works with an established budget and negotiates fees with these enterprises and enters contracts with them. Additional contracts may also need to be negotiated with professionals to handle registration, marketing, and public relations for the event.

Managers and planners need to be aware of legal aspects of trade show setups such as fire code regulations, floor plan, and space limitations, and make sure they are within these guidelines. They often need to get these arrangements approved in writing. Good record keeping and communication skills are used daily. The convention manager may have staff to handle the sales, registration, marketing, logistics, or other specific aspects of the event, or these duties may be subcontracted to another firm.

Some convention planners are employed specifically by convention and visitors' bureaus, the tourism industry, or by exhibit halls or convention facilities. Their job responsibilities may be specific to one aspect of the show, or they may be required to do any or all of the above-mentioned duties. Some convention and trade show managers may work for the exposition center or association and be responsible for selling booth space at large events.

Special event coordinators are usually employed by large corporations that hold numerous special events or by firms that contract their special event planning services to companies, associations, or religious, political, or educational groups. A special event coordinator is responsible for planning, organizing, and implementing a special event such as an open house, an anniversary, the dedication of a new facility, a special promotion or sale, an ordination, a political rally, or a victory celebration. This coordinator works with the company or organization and determines the purpose of the special event, the type of celebration desired, the site, the budget, the attendees, the food and entertainment preferences, and the anticipated outcome. The special event planner then coordinates the vendors and equipment necessary to successfully hold this event. The coordinator works closely with the client at all times to ensure that the event is being planned as expected. Follow-up assessment of the event is usually part of the services offered by the special event coordinator.

Party planners are often employed by individuals, families, or small companies to help them plan a small party for a special occasion. Many party planners are independent contractors who work out of their homes or are employees of small firms. Party planners may help plan weddings, birthdays, christenings, bar or bat mitzvahs, anniversaries, or other events. They may be responsible for the entire event including the invitations, catering, decorating, entertainment, serving, and cleanup, or planners may simply perform one or two aspects such as contracting with a magician for a children's birthday party, recommending a menu, or greeting and serving guests.

Some event planners specialize in planning virtual events—which are held online using sophisticated computer and telecommunications technology. "Attendees" can view exhibits and speakers online without having to leave the comfort of their office or home. *Virtual event planners* must have specialized computer and information technology skills.

In large organizations, event planners typically have specialized duties. *Database administrators* build and maintain databases of attendees. *Exhibit managers* oversee the exhibit design and layout. *Funds coordinators* handle registration fees and all incoming funds. *Meeting scouts* select the meeting site. *Registration coordinators,* or *registrars,* handle the preregistration and on-site registration. *Education planners* organize the educational content of an event, including speakers and presentations.

REQUIREMENTS
High School

If you are interested in entering the field of event planning, you should take high school classes in business, English, and speech. Because many conferences and meetings are international in scope, you may also want to take foreign language and geography courses. In addition, computer science classes will be beneficial.

Postsecondary Training

Many coordinators and planners must have a four-year college degree to work for a company, corporation, convention, or travel center, but a degree is not always required. Some institutions offer bachelor's degrees in meeting planning; however, degrees in business, English, communications, marketing, public relations, sales, or hotel or hospitality management would also be a good fit for a career as a meetings manager, convention planner, or special event coordinator. Many directors and planners who become company heads have earned graduate degrees.

Some small firms, convention centers, or exhibit facilities may accept persons with associate's degrees or travel industry certification for certain planning positions. Party planners may not always need education beyond high school, but advancement opportunities will be more plentiful with additional education.

Certification or Licensing

There are some professional associations for planners that offer certification programs. For example, Meeting Professionals International offers the certification in meeting management designation. The International Association of Exhibitions and Events offers the certified in exhibition management designation. The Convention Industry Council offers the certified meeting professional designation. The Society of Government Meeting Professionals offers the certified government meeting professional designation. (See "For More Information" at the end of this article for contact information.)

Other Requirements

To be an event planner, you must have excellent organizational skills, the ability to plan projects and events, and the ability to think creatively. You must be able to work well with people and anticipate their needs in advance. You should be willing to pitch in to get a job done even though it may not be part of your duties. In a situation where there is an unforeseen crisis, you need to react quickly and professionally. Planners should have good negotiating and communication skills and be assertive but tactful.

EXPLORING

High school counselors can supply information on event planners or convention coordinators. Public and school librarians may also be able to provide useful books, magazines, and pamphlets. Searching the Internet for companies that provide event-planning services can give you an idea of the types of services that they offer. Professional associations related to the travel, convention, and meeting industries may have career information available to students. Some of these organizations are listed at the end of this article.

Familiarizing yourself with the terminology used by event planners will provide a good introduction to the field. The International Association of Exhibitions and Events offers a glossary of more than 4,000 terms at its Web site, http://www.conventionindustry.org/glossary.

Attending local trade shows and conventions will provide insight into the operations of this industry. Also, some exhibit and convention halls may hire students to assist with various aspects of trade show operations. You can learn more about this profession by subscribing to magazines such as *Meetings & Conventions* (http://www.meetings-conventions.com).

Some party planners may hire assistants to help with children's birthday parties or other special events. Organize and plan a large family event, such as a birthday, anniversary, graduation, or retirement celebration. You will have to find a location, hire caterers or assign family members to bring specific food items, send invitations, purchase and arrange decorations, and organize entertainment, all according to what your budget allows.

You can also gain business experience through school activities. Join the business club, run for student council, or head up the prom committee to learn how to plan and carry out events.

EMPLOYERS

Approximately 51,530 event planners are employed in the United States. About 27 percent work for religious, grantmaking, civic, professional, and similar organizations, and 14 percent are employed in traveler accommodation, including hotels and motels. About 6 percent of event planners are self-employed.

Many large corporations or institutions worldwide hire meeting managers, convention managers, or event planners to handle their specific activities. Although some companies may not have employees with the specific title of event planner or meeting manager, these skills are very marketable and these duties may be part of another job title. In many companies, these duties may be part of a position within the marketing, public relations, or corporate communications department.

Convention facilities, exhibit halls, training and educational institutions, travel companies, and health care facilities also hire event planners. Hotels often hire planners to handle meetings and events held within their facilities. Large associations usually maintain an event planning staff for one or more annual conventions or business meetings for their members.

Job opportunities are also available with companies that contract out event and meeting planning services. Many of these companies have positions that specialize in certain aspects of the planning service, such as travel coordinator, exhibit planner, facilities negotiator, or they have people who perform specific functions such as trade show display setup, registration, and follow-up reporting.

Planners interested in jobs with the convention and trade show industries or hotels may find that larger cities have more demand for planners and offer higher salaries.

Experienced meeting planners or convention managers may choose to establish their own businesses or independently contract out their services. Party planning may also be a good independent business venture.

STARTING OUT

An internship at a visitors and convention bureau, exhibit center, or with a travel agency or meeting planning company is a good way to meet and network with other people in this field. Attending trade shows might offer a chance to speak with people about the field and to discuss any contacts they might have.

Some colleges and universities may offer job placement services for people seeking careers in meeting planning or in the convention and trade show indus-

tries. Professional associations, such as Meeting Professionals International and the Professional Convention Management Association, are also good contacts for someone starting out. Many feature job listings and articles about career planning on their Web sites. Classified ads and trade magazines may also offer some job leads.

ADVANCEMENT

Advancement opportunities for people in the event planning field are good. Experienced planners can expect to move into positions of increased responsibility. They may become senior managers and executive directors of private businesses, hotels, convention facilities, exhibit halls, travel corporations, museums, or other facilities. They can advance within a corporation to a position with more responsibilities or they may go into the planning business for themselves. Planners who have established a good reputation in the industry are often recruited by other firms or facilities and can advance their careers with these opportunities.

EARNINGS

According to the U.S. Department of Labor (DOL), meeting and convention planners earned median annual salaries of $44,780 in 2009. The lowest paid 10 percent earned less than $27,550, and the highest paid 10 percent earned more than $75,160. The DOL reports the following mean annual salaries for meeting and convention planners by industry: business, professional, labor, political, and similar organizations, $51,270; management, scientific, and technical consulting services, $48,840; colleges, universities, and professional schools, $46,110; and traveler accommodation, $44,420.

Benefits may vary depending on the position and the employer but generally include vacation, sick leave, insurance, and other work-related benefits.

WORK ENVIRONMENT

Work environments vary with the planner's title and job responsibilities, but generally planners can expect to work in a business setting as part of a team. Usually, the planner's initial planning work is done in a clean environment with modern equipment prior to the opening of a convention or trade show. Working in convention and trade show environments, however, can be noisy, crowded, and distracting. In addition, the days can be long and may require standing for hours. If the planner is involved with supervising the setup or dismantling of a trade show or convention, the work can be dirty and physically demanding.

Although most facilities have crews that assist with setup, meeting planners occasionally get involved with last-minute changes and may need to do some physical lifting of equipment, tables, or chairs.

Event planners can usually expect to work erratic hours, often putting in long days prior to the event and the day the event is actually held. Travel is often part of the job requirements and may include working and/or traveling nights and on the weekends.

OUTLOOK

Job opportunities for event planners will continue to grow at a faster-than-average rate through 2018, according to the DOL. The introduction of new technology and the growth of international business have enabled more meetings to take place than ever before. Telecommunications technology, which can sometimes take the place of conferences, has been found to also spur growth in this field, as people who initially connect online then meet in person to further their business. Opportunities will be best for those with a bachelor's degree, certification, and experience in the field.

FOR MORE INFORMATION

For information on certification, contact
Convention Industry Council
700 North Fairfax Street, Suite 510
Alexandria, VA 22314-2090
Tel: 571-527-3116
E-mail: cichq@conventionindustry.org
http://www.conventionindustry.org

For information on certification, contact
International Association of Exhibitions and Events
12700 Park Central Drive, Suite 308
Dallas, TX 75251-1526
Tel: 972-458-8002
http://www.iaee.com

For information on postsecondary training programs and certification, contact
Meeting Professionals International
3030 Lyndon B. Johnson Freeway, Suite 1700
Dallas, TX 75234-2759
Tel: 972-702-3000
http://www.mpiweb.org

For information on career development, contact
Professional Convention Management Association
2301 South Lake Shore Drive, Suite 1001

Chicago, IL 60616-1419
Tel: 877-827-7262
http://www.pcma.org

For information on certification, contact
Society of Government Meeting Professionals
908 King Street, Lower Level
Alexandria, VA 22314-3047
Tel: 703-549-0892
E-mail: headquarters@sgmp.org
http://www.sgmp.org

For information on careers in the field of event planning, contact
Society of Independent Show Organizers
2601 Ocean Park Boulevard, Suite 200
Santa Monica, CA 90405-5250
Tel: 877-YES-SISO
E-mail: info@siso.org
http://www.siso.org

FINANCIAL ANALYSTS

OVERVIEW

Financial analysts, also called *security analysts* and *investment analysts,* analyze the financial situation of companies and recommend ways for these companies to manage, spend, and invest their money. The goal of financial analysts is to help their employer or clients make informed, lucrative financial decisions. They assemble and evaluate the company's financial data and assess investment opportunities. They look at the company's financial history, the direction that company wants to take in the future, the company's place in the industry, and current and projected economic conditions. Financial analysts also conduct similar research on companies that might become investment opportunities. They write reports and compile spreadsheets that show the benefits of certain investments or selling certain securities.

Among the businesses employing financial analysts are banks, brokerage firms, government agencies, mutual funds, and insurance and investment companies. There are approximately 235,240 financial analysts employed in the United States.

SCHOOL SUBJECTS
Business, Computer science, Mathematics

PERSONAL SKILLS
Communication/ideas, Leadership/management

MINIMUM EDUCATION LEVEL
Bachelor's degree

CERTIFICATION OR LICENSING
Recommended (certification),
Required for certain positions (licensing)

WORK ENVIRONMENT
Primarily indoors, Primarily one location

THE JOB

The specific types, direction, and scope of analyses performed by financial analysts are many and varied, depending on the industry, the employer or client, and the analyst's training and years of experience, but there are two main types of analysts: *buy-side analysts* and *sell-side analysts*. Buy-side analysts conduct research to track down desirable investments, usually for money management firms (e.g., mutual, hedge, or pension funds; insurance companies; and nonprofit organizations with large endowments). The research is used solely for the firm's purposes in the hopes of turning a profit after purchase. If the firm makes money from the buy-side analyst's investment recommendation, it's likely the analyst will be compensated. Sell-side analysts (also known as *sales analysts* or *Wall Street analysts*) similarly conduct research to track down desirable investments, but do so for brokerage firms. These investment recommendations ("buy," "sell," or "hold") are passed on to a firm's clients and also the public. The firm makes a commission based on customer orders rather than investment performance. The more orders that come in, the more money the firm is likely to pay the analyst.

Financial analysts study their employer's or client's financial status and make financial and investment recommendations. To arrive at these recommendations, financial analysts examine the employer's or client's financial history and objectives, income and expenditures, risk tolerance, and current investments. Once they understand the employer's or client's financial standing and investment goals, financial analysts scout out poten-

tial investment opportunities. They research other companies, perhaps in a single industry, that their employer or client may want to invest in. This in-depth research consists of investigating the business of each company, including history, past and potential earnings, and products. Based on their findings, financial analysts may recommend that their employer or client buy stock in these companies. If the employer or client already holds stock in a particular company, financial analysts' research may indicate that stocks should be held or sold, or that more should be purchased.

Financial analysts work for companies in any number of industries, including banking, transportation, health care, technology, telecommunications, and energy. While investment options and concerns differ among these, financial analysts still apply the same basic analytic tools in devising investment strategies. They try to learn everything they can about the industry in which they are working. They study the markets and make industry comparisons. They also research past performance and future trends of bonds and other investments.

Financial analysts compile many types of reports on their employer or client and on investment opportunities, such as profit-and-loss statements and quarterly outlook statements. They help to develop budgets, analyze and oversee cash flow, and perform cost-benefit analyses. They conduct risk analyses to determine what the employer or client can risk at a given time and/or in future. Another responsibility is to ensure that their employer or client meets any relevant tax or regulatory requirements. Financial analysts compile their work using various software programs, often developing financial models, such as charts or graphs, to display their data.

Companies that want to go public (sell company shares to individual investors for the first time) often ask financial analysts to make projections of future earnings as well as presentations for potential investors. Financial analysts also make sure that all paperwork is in order and compliant with Securities and Exchange Commission rules and regulations.

Entry-level financial analysts, usually working under direct supervision, mainly conduct research and compile statistical data. After a few years of experience, they become more involved in presenting reports. While a financial analyst generally offers recommendations, a senior financial analyst often has the authority to actually decide purchases or sales. Senior financial analysts implement a company's business plan. In larger companies, they also assist different departments in conducting their own financial analyses and business planning.

Those in senior positions become supervisors as well, training junior financial analysts.

Many specialties fall under the job title of financial analyst. These specialties vary from employer to employer, and duties overlap between different types of analysts. In smaller firms a financial analyst may have extensive responsibility, while at larger firms a financial analyst may specialize in one of any number of areas. *Budget analysts*, often *accountants* or *controllers*, look at the operating costs of a company or its individual departments and prepare budget reports. *Credit analysts* examine credit records to determine the potential risk in extending credit or lending money. *Investment analysts* evaluate investment data so they can make suitable investment recommendations. *Mergers and acquisitions analysts* conduct research and make recommendations relating to company mergers and acquisitions. *Money market analysts* assess financial data and investment opportunities, giving advice specifically in the area of money markets. *Ratings analysts* explore a company's financial situation to determine whether or not it will be able to repay debts. *Risk analysts* focus on evaluating the risks of investments. The intent is to identify and then minimize a company's risks and losses. *Security analysts* specialize in studying securities, such as stocks and bonds. *Tax analysts* prepare, file, and examine federal, state, and local tax payments and returns for their employer or client and perhaps also for local affiliates. They analyze tax issues and keep up with tax law changes. *Treasury analysts* manage their company's or client's daily cash position, prepare cash journal entries, initiate wire transfers, and perform bank reconciliations.

Personal financial advisers have many similar responsibilities (assessing finances, projecting income, recommending investments), but these are performed on behalf of individuals rather than companies. (For more information, see the article "Financial Planners.")

REQUIREMENTS
High School

Since financial analysts work with numbers and compile data, you should take as many math classes as are available. Accounting, business, economics, and computer classes will be helpful as well. A good grasp of computer spreadsheet programs such as Excel is vital. Take extra care as you research and write reports in any subject matter or in public speaking, and it will pay off later when you must conduct investment research and write and present investment recommendations.

Postsecondary Training

Most employers require that financial analysts hold a bachelor's degree in accounting, business administration, economics, finance, or statistics. Other possible majors include communications, international business, and public administration. Some companies will hire you if you hold a bachelor's degree in another discipline as long as you can demonstrate mathematical ability. In college, take business, economics, and statistics courses. Since computer technology plays such a big role in a financial analyst's work, computer classes can be helpful as well. English composition classes can prepare you for the writing you will need to do when preparing reports. Some employers require a writing sample prior to an interview.

Financial analysts generally continue to take courses to keep up with the ongoing changes in the world of finance, including international trade, state and federal laws and regulations, and computer technology. Proficiency in certain databases, presentation graphics, spreadsheets, and other software is expected. Some employers require their employees to have a master's degree in business administration or finance.

Many top firms offer summer internship programs. Check company Web sites for the particulars, such as assignments and qualifications. An internship can provide you with helpful contacts and increase your chances of landing a job when you finish with college.

Certification or Licensing

Financial analysts can earn the title chartered financial analyst (CFA). While certification is not required for all financial analyst jobs, it is highly recommended. The CFA program, which is administered by the CFA Institute, consists of three levels of examinations. These rigorous exams deal with such topics as economics, financial statement analysis, corporate finance, and portfolio management. The CFA Institute states that a candidate may need to spend an average of 300 hours studying to prepare for each level. The Motley Fool, a financial education company (http://www.fool.com), reported that about 50 percent of the candidates fail the first level. A candidate can take only one level per year, so a minimum of three years is required to become a CFA charterholder. If a candidate fails a level, it can be taken the next year. Candidates who do not successfully complete all three levels within seven years must reregister.

Before taking the exams, you must already have a bachelor's degree (or four years of professional experience). There is no required course of study. Prior to earning the CFA charter, you must have spent three years in a related field working in the investment decision-making process and you must first apply to become a member of the CFA Institute as well as a local society.

The CFA charter is recognized around the world as a standard in the finance industry. Most employers expect job seekers to be CFA charterholders.

The Association for Financial Professionals (AFP) and American Academy of Financial Management also offer certification.

For certain upper-level positions, some firms require that you have a certified public accountant license. Visit the AFP Web site, http://www.afponline.org, for more information.

The Financial Industry Regulatory Authority is the primary licensing organization for the securities industry. Visit its Web site, http://www.finra.org, for more information on licensing requirements for financial analysts who work as financial services brokers.

Other Requirements

Research, organizational, and communication skills are crucial for this job. Financial analysts conduct in-depth research, often looking for hard-to-find data. Organizational skills are important when it comes to compiling and presenting this data. Once you have explored a company's financial situation, you must communicate complicated ideas through presentations and/or written reports. You should be able to clearly communicate ideas, both verbally when making presentations and on paper when writing reports.

The work requires strong analytic skills, so a knack for numbers and attention to detail are also helpful. An interest in solving problems will go a long way. It is important that a financial analyst be accurate and thorough in preparing financial statements.

You should enjoy reading and be able to retain what you read, since it is important to keep up with what's happening in the industry and take it into account when offering financial solutions to employers or clients. Since many financial analysts must travel at a moment's notice to conduct research or complete a deal, flexibility is another important characteristic.

Financial analysts should be able to work well under pressure, as this line of work often demands long hours and entails strict deadlines. You should have good interpersonal skills and enjoy interacting with others. Deals or important contacts can be made at social functions or business conferences.

EXPLORING

There are many sources of information dealing with the financial services industry. Read publications such as *Barron's* (http://online.barrons.com), *Wall Street Journal* (http://online.wsj.com), *Forbes* (http://www.forbes.com), *Bloomberg Business Week* (http://www.businessweek.com), *Fortune* (http://money.cnn.com/magazines/fortune), and *Financial Times* (http://www.ft.com). In either the print or online versions, you will find a wealth of information on stocks, mutual funds, finance, education, careers, salaries, global business, and more. You can also use these resources to conduct company research. You might have to become a subscriber to access certain sections online.

AnalystForum (http://www.analystforum.com) is a resource for chartered financial analysts and CFA candidates. While this site won't be of much use to you until you've launched your career, you can find links to financial, investment, and security analyst society sites. From within these societies, you can perhaps track down a professional who would be willing to do an information interview with you.

While in high school, you might volunteer to handle the bookkeeping for a school club or student government, or help balance the family checking account to become familiar with simple bookkeeping practices. Your school may have an investment club you can join. If not, ask a parent or teacher to help you research and analyze investment opportunities. Choose a specific industry (e.g., telecommunications, technology, or health care), study companies in that industry, and select and track several stocks that appear to have growth potential.

EMPLOYERS

Approximately 235,240 financial analysts are employed in the United States. Financial analysts work in the public and private sectors. Employers include banks, brokerage and securities firms, corporations, government agencies, manufacturers, mutual and pension funds, and financial management, insurance, investment, trust, and utility companies. Many financial analysts are self-employed. According to the *Occupational Outlook Handbook,* about 47 percent of financial analysts work for security and commodity brokers, banks and credit institutions, and insurance carriers.

Since financial analysts often work in Wall Street companies, many employers are found in New York City. They are also concentrated in other large cities but work in smaller cities as well.

STARTING OUT

Representatives from hiring companies (e.g., banks, brokerage firms, or investment companies) may visit college campuses to meet with students interested in pursuing careers as financial analysts. College career services offices will have details on such visits. Company Web sites may also offer campus recruiting schedules.

Gaining an entry-level position can be difficult. Some companies offer in-house training, but many don't. Beginning as a research assistant might be one way to break into the business. Read member profiles at association sites to see where members have worked as financial analysts. Explore those companies that look appealing.

Make contacts and network with other financial analysts. Your local CFA Institute society or chapter will probably hold regular meetings, affording ample networking opportunities. You can become a CFA Institute member whether or not you are a CFA charterholder, but charterholders enjoy full member benefits, such as access to job postings. (Complete details, including listings for local societies and chapters, can be found at the CFA Institute Web site, http://www.cfainstitute.org.) Also, internships can be an excellent way to make contacts and gain experience in the field.

As an interview tool, the New York Society of Security Analysts suggests that you compile an investment recommendation for potential clients to give them an idea of the kind of research you're capable of and how you present your data.

You can search for job ads online. One resource is the eFinancialCareers.com network (http://www.efinancial careers.com). If you know what companies you'd like to work for, visit their Web sites. Chances are you will find online job listings there.

ADVANCEMENT

Financial analysts who accurately prepare their employer's or client's financial statements and who offer investment advice that results in profits will likely be rewarded for their efforts. Rewards come in the form of promotions and/or bonuses. Successful financial analysts may become senior financial analysts, sometimes in only three or four years. Some become portfolio or financial managers. Rather than simply making recommendations on their company's or client's investment policies, those who advance to a senior position have more decision-making responsibility.

Some financial analysts move on to jobs as investment bankers or advisers. Others become officers in various departments in their company. Positions include chief financial officer and vice president of finance. In time, some cultivate enough contacts to be able to start their own consulting firms.

EARNINGS

The U.S. Department of Labor reports that median annual earnings of financial analysts were $73,670 in 2009. Top earners (the top 10 percent) made more than $139,350, and the lowest salaries (the lowest 10 percent) were less than $44,080. If the investments of financial analysts' employers or clients perform well, it is not uncommon for those financial analysts to receive a bonus in addition to their salary. With bonuses, skilled financial analysts can make much more than their base salary.

Benefits include paid vacation, health, disability, life insurance, and retirement or pension plans. Some employers also offer profit-sharing plans. Tuition reimbursement may also be available.

WORK ENVIRONMENT

Most financial analysts work in an office in a corporate setting. Frequently, they work alone (e.g., when conducting research or talking on the phone to clients). Some may work out of their homes. Much time is spent working on a computer, doing research and compiling data. Travel is frequently required—there are meetings and social functions to attend, clients to meet, and companies to research at their place of business. Because financial analysts spend much of their normal business hours talking or meeting with clients, they often conduct research after hours and generally work long days. It is not uncommon for financial analysts to clock well in excess of 50 hours per week.

OUTLOOK

The state of the economy and the stock market has a direct effect on the employment outlook for financial analysts. When the economy is doing well, companies are more likely to make investments, resulting in a need for financial analysts. When the economy is doing poorly, companies are less likely to make investments, and there will be less need for financial analysts. *The Occupational Outlook Handbook (OOH),* anticipating an increase in business investments, predicts that employment for financial analysts will grow much faster than the average for all careers through 2018. The *OOH* notes, too, that international securities markets, the complexity of financial products, and business mergers and acquisitions demand financial analysts to sort through all the issues involved. Because of the close scrutiny analysts have been under, it might become more desirable for financial analysts to hold the CFA charter. Despite the prediction for excellent growth, competition for positions as financial analysts will be very strong since many people are interested in entering the field. Applicants with strong college grades in finance, accounting, and economics courses, a graduate degree in business or finance, and certification will have the best job prospects.

Individual investing will also affect the need for financial analysts, in that the more people invest in mutual funds (often through 401(k) plans), the greater the need there will be for financial analysts to recommend financial products to the mutual fund companies.

FOR MORE INFORMATION

For information on certification, contact
American Academy of Financial Management
http://www.aafm.us

This organization's Web site offers industry news and certification information.
Association for Financial Professionals
4520 East-West Highway, Suite 750
Bethesda, MD 20814-3574
Tel: 301-907-2862
http://www.afponline.org

For complete CFA Institute information, including lists of institute societies, publications, news, conference details, and certification information, contact
CFA Institute
PO Box 3668
560 Ray C. Hunt Drive
Charlottesville, VA 22903-2981
Tel: 800-247-8132
E-mail: info@cfainstitute.org
http://www.cfainstitute.org

Visit the NYSSA Web site for information on membership for college students, a list of top employers of financial analysts, and scholarships for graduate students.
New York Society of Security Analysts (NYSSA)
1540 Broadway, Suite 1010
New York, NY 10036-2714
Tel: 212-541-4530
http://www.nyssa.org

For information on laws and regulations pertaining to investors and the securities markets, contact
U.S. Securities and Exchange Commission
Office of Investor Education and Advocacy

100 F Street, NE
Washington, DC 20549-2000
Tel: 202-942-8088
E-mail: publicinfo@sec.gov
http://www.sec.gov

This Web site has links to financial, investment, and security analyst societies.
AnalystForum
http://www.analystforum.com

For issues of interest to senior finance executives, see
CFO.com
http://www.cfo.com

FINANCIAL PLANNERS

OVERVIEW

Financial planning is the process of establishing financial goals and creating ways to reach them. Certified *financial planners* examine the assets of their clients and suggest what steps they need to take in the future to meet their goals. They take a broad approach to financial advice, which distinguishes them from other professional advisers, such as insurance agents, stockbrokers, accountants,

SCHOOL SUBJECTS
Business, Mathematics

PERSONAL SKILLS
Helping/teaching, Leadership/management

MINIMUM EDUCATION LEVEL
Bachelor's degree

CERTIFICATION OR LICENSING
Recommended (certification),
Required for certain positions (licensing)

WORK ENVIRONMENT
Primarily indoors, Primarily one location

attorneys, and real estate agents, each of whom typically focuses on only one aspect of a person's finances. Approximately 149,460 personal financial advisers are employed in the United States.

THE JOB

Financial planners advise their clients on many aspects of finance. Although they seem to be jacks-of-all-trades, certified financial planners do not work alone: They meet with their clients' other advisers, such as attorneys, accountants, trust officers, and investment bankers. Financial planners fully research their clients' overall financial picture. After meeting with the clients and their other advisers, certified financial planners analyze the data they have received and generate a written report that includes their recommendations on how the clients can best achieve their goals. This report details the clients' financial objectives, current income, investments, risk tolerance, expenses, tax returns, insurance coverage, retirement programs, estate plans, and other important information.

Financial planning is an ongoing process. The plan must be monitored and reviewed periodically so that adjustments can be made, if necessary, to assure that it continues to meet individual needs.

The plan itself is a set of recommendations and strategies for clients to use or ignore, and financial planners should be ready to answer hard questions about the integrity of the plans they map out. After all, they are dealing with all of the money and investments that people have worked a lifetime accruing.

People need financial planners for different things. Some might want life insurance, college savings plans, or estate planning. Sometimes these needs are triggered by changes in people's lives, such as retirement, death of a spouse, disability, marriage, birth of children, or job changes. Certified financial planners spend the majority of their time on the following topics: investment planning, retirement planning, tax planning, estate planning, and risk management. All of these areas require different types of financial knowledge, and planners are generally expected to be extremely competent in the disciplines of asset management, employee benefits, estate planning, insurance, investments, and retirement, according to the Certified Financial Planner Board of Standards. A financial planner must also have good interpersonal skills, since establishing solid client-planner relationships is essential to the planner's success. It also helps to have good communication skills, since even the best financial plan, if presented poorly to a client, can be rejected.

Clients drive the job of financial planners. The advice planners provide depends on their clients' particular needs, resources, and priorities. Many people think they cannot afford or do not need a comprehensive financial plan. Certified financial planners must have a certain amount of expertise in sales to build their client base.

Certified financial planners use various ways to develop their client lists, including telephone solicitation, giving seminars on financial planning to the general public or specific organizations, and networking with social contacts. Referrals from satisfied customers also help the business grow.

Although certified financial planners are trained in comprehensive financial planning, some specialize in one area, such as asset management, investments, or retirement planning. In most small or self-owned financial planning companies, they are generalists. In some large companies, however, planners might specialize in particular areas, including insurance, real estate, mutual funds, annuities, pensions, or business valuations.

REQUIREMENTS

High School

If financial planning sounds interesting to you, take as many business classes as possible as well as mathematics. Communication courses, such as speech or drama, will help put you at ease when talking in front of a crowd, something financial planners must do occasionally. English courses will help you prepare the written reports planners present to their clients.

Postsecondary Training

Earning a bachelor's degree starts financial planners on the right track, but it will help if your degree indicates a skill with numbers, be it in science or business. A business administration degree with a specialization in financial planning or a liberal arts degree with courses in accounting, business administration, economics, finance, marketing, human behavior, counseling, and public speaking is excellent preparation for this sort of job.

Certification or Licensing

Education alone will not motivate clients to easily turn over their finances to you. Many financial professionals are licensed on the state and federal levels in financial planning specialties, such as stocks and insurance. The U.S. Securities and Exchange Commission and most states have licensing requirements for investment advisers, a category under which most financial planners also fall. However, most of the activities of planners are not regulated by the government. Therefore, to show credibility to clients, most financial planners choose to become certified as either a certified financial planner (CFP) or a chartered financial consultant (ChFC).

To receive the CFP mark of certification, offered by the CFP Board, candidates must meet what the board refers to as the four E's, which comprise the following:

Education: To be eligible to take the certification exam, candidates must meet education requirements in one of the following ways. The first option is to complete a CFP board-registered program in financial planning. The second is to hold a specific degree and professional credentials in one of several areas the board has approved of; these include certified public accountant, licensed attorney, chartered financial consultant, chartered life underwriter, chartered financial analyst, doctor of business administration, and Ph.D. in business or economics. Lastly, applicants may submit transcripts of their undergraduate or graduate education to the board for review. If the board feels the education requirements have been met, the candidate may sit for the exam. Additionally, applicants must have a bachelor's degree in any area of study or program to obtain CFP certification. They do not need to have earned this degree at the time they take the examination, but must show proof of completion of this degree in order to complete the final stage of certification.

Examination: Once candidates have completed the education requirements, they may take the certification exam, which tests knowledge on various key aspects of financial planning.

Experience: Either before or after passing the certification exam, candidates must have three years of work experience.

Ethics: After candidates have completed the education, examination, and experience requirements, they must voluntarily ascribe to the CFP Board's Code of Ethics and Professional Responsibility, Rules of Conduct, and Financial Planning Practice Standards to be allowed to use the CFP mark. This voluntary agreement empowers the board to take action if a CFP licensee violates the code. Such violations could lead to disciplinary action, including permanent revocation of the right to use the CFP mark.

The American College offers the ChFC designation. To receive this designation, candidates must complete certain course work stipulated by The American College, meet experience requirements, and agree to uphold The American College's Code of Ethics and Procedures.

To maintain the CFP and the ChFC designations, professionals will need to meet continuing education and other requirements as determined by the CFP Board and The American College.

Two other organizations offer certification to financial planning professionals. Fi360 offers the accredited investment fiduciary and accredited investment fiduciary analyst designations. The Investment Management Consultants Association offers the following designations: certified investment management analyst and chartered private wealth advisor. Contact these organizations for more information.

Other Requirements

Other factors that contribute to success as a financial planner include keeping up with continuing education, referrals from clients, specialization, people and communication skills, and a strong educational background.

EXPLORING

There is not much that students can do to explore this field, since success as a certified financial planner comes only with training and years on the job. You can, however, check out the financial planning information available on the Internet to familiarize yourself with the terms used in the industry. You should also take as many finance and business classes as possible. Talking to certified financial planners will also help you gather information on the field.

EMPLOYERS

Approximately 149,460 personal financial advisors are employed in the United States. They work for financial planning firms across the country. Many of these firms are small, perhaps employing two to 15 people, and most are located in urban areas. A smaller, but growing, number of financial planners are employed by corporations, banks, credit unions, mutual fund companies, insurance companies, accounting or law firms, colleges and universities, credit counseling organizations, and brokerage firms. In addition, many financial planners are self-employed.

STARTING OUT

Early in their careers, financial planners work for banks, mutual fund companies, or investment firms and usually receive extensive on-the-job training. The job will deal heavily with client-based and research activities. Financial planners may start their own business as they learn personal skills and build their client base. During their first few years, certified financial planners spend many hours analyzing documents, meeting with other advisers, and networking to find new clients.

ADVANCEMENT

Those who have not changed their career track in five years can expect to have established some solid, long-term relationships with clients. Measured success at this point will be the planners' service fees, which will be marked up considerably from when they started their careers.

Those who have worked in the industry for 10 years usually have many clients and a six-figure income. Experienced financial planners can also move into careers in investment banking, financial consulting, and financial analysis. Because people skills are also an integral part of being a financial planner, consulting, on both personal and corporate levels, is also an option. Many planners will find themselves attending business school, either to achieve a higher income or to switch to one of the aforementioned professions.

EARNINGS

There are several methods of compensation for financial planners. Fee-only means that compensation is earned entirely from fees from consultation, plan development, or investment management. These fees may be charged on an hourly or project basis depending on clients' needs or on a percentage of assets under management. Commission-only compensation is received from the sale of financial products that clients agree to purchase to implement financial planning recommendations. There is no charge for advice or preparation of the financial plan. Fee-offset means that compensation received in the form of commission from the sale of financial products is offset against fees charged for the planning process. Combination fee/commission is a fee charged for consultation, advice, and financial plan preparation on an hourly, project, or percentage basis. Planners might also receive commissions from recommended products targeted to achieve goals and objectives. Some planners work on a salary basis for financial services institutions such as banks, credit unions, and other related organizations.

The median annual gross income of certified financial planners was $215,345 in 2009, according to the *2009 Survey of Trends in the Financial Planning Industry,* which was conducted by the College for Financial Plan-

ning. These incomes were earned from financial plan writing, product sales, consulting, and related activities.

The U.S. Department of Labor reports that financial planners earned a median annual salary of $68,200 in 2009. The most experienced financial planners with the highest level of education earned more than $166,400, while the least experienced financial planners earned less than $33,790.

Firms might also provide beginning financial planners with a steady income by paying a draw, which is a minimum salary based on the commission and fees the planner can be expected to earn.

Some financial planners receive vacation days, sick days, and health insurance, but that depends on whether they work for financial institutions or on their own.

WORK ENVIRONMENT

Most financial planners work by themselves in offices or at home. Others work in offices with other financial planners. Established financial planners usually work the same hours as others in the business community. Beginners who are seeking customers probably work longer hours. Many planners accommodate customers by meeting with them in the evenings and on weekends. They might spend a lot of time out of the office, meeting with current and prospective clients, attending civic functions, and participating in trade association meetings.

OUTLOOK

Employment for financial planners is expected to grow much faster than the average for all careers through 2018, according to the U.S. Department of Labor. Strong employment growth is expected for a number of reasons. More funds should be available for investment, as the economy, personal income, and inherited wealth grow. Demographics will also play a role; as increasing numbers of baby boomers turn 50, demand will grow for retirement-related investments. Most people, in general, are likely to turn to financial planners for assistance with retirement planning. Individual saving and investing for retirement are expected to become more important, as many companies reduce pension benefits and switch from defined-benefit retirement plans to defined-contribution plans, which shift the investment responsibility from the company to the individual. Furthermore, a growing number of individual investors are expected to seek advice from financial planners regarding the increasing complexity and array of investment alternatives for assistance with estate planning.

Due to the highly competitive nature of financial planning, many beginners leave the field because they are not able to establish a sufficient clientele. Once established, however, planners have a strong attachment to their occupation because of high earning potential and considerable investment in training. Job opportunities should be best for mature individuals with successful work experience.

FOR MORE INFORMATION

For more information about financial education and the ChFC designation, contact

The American College
270 South Bryn Mawr Avenue
Bryn Mawr, PA 19010-2105
Tel: 888-263-7265
http://www.theamericancollege.edu

To learn more about financial planning and to obtain a copy of the Guide to CFP Certification, *contact*

Certified Financial Planner Board of Standards
1425 K Street, NW, Suite 500
Washington, DC 20005-3686
Tel: 800-487-1497
E-mail: mail@CFPBoard.org
http://www.cfp.net

For information on financial planning, visit the association's Web site.

Financial Planning Association
4100 East Mississippi Avenue, Suite 400
Denver, CO 80246-3053
Tel: 800-322-4237
http://www.fpanet.org

For information about certification, contact

Investment Management Consultants Association
5619 DTC Parkway, Suite 500
Greenwood Village, CO 80111-3044
Tel: 303-770-3377
E-mail: imca@imca.org
http://www.imca.org

For more information on fee-only financial advisers, contact

National Association of Personal Financial Advisors
3250 North Arlington Heights Road, Suite 109
Arlington Heights, IL 60004-1574
Tel: 847-483-5400
E-mail: info@napfa.org
http://www.napfa.org

FIREFIGHTERS

OVERVIEW

Firefighters protect people's lives and property from the hazards of fire and other emergencies. They provide this protection by fighting fires to prevent property damage and by rescuing people trapped or injured by fires or other accidents. Through inspections and safety education, firefighters also work to prevent fires and unsafe conditions that could result in dangerous, life-threatening situations. They assist in many types of emergencies and disasters in everyday life. Although in many rural areas firefighters serve on a volunteer basis, this article is mainly concerned with describing full-time career firefighters. There are approximately 305,500 paid firefighters working in the United States.

THE JOB

The duties of career firefighters vary with the size of the fire department and the population of the city in which they are employed. However, each firefighter's individual responsibilities are well defined and clear-cut. In every fire department there are divisions of labor among firefighters. For example, when their department goes into action, firefighters know whether they are to rescue people caught in fires, raise ladders, connect hoses to water hydrants, or attempt to break down doors, windows, or walls with fire axes so that other firefighters can enter the area with water hoses.

SCHOOL SUBJECTS
Biology, Chemistry

PERSONAL SKILLS
Leadership/management,
Mechanical/manipulative

MINIMUM EDUCATION LEVEL
High school diploma

CERTIFICATION OR LICENSING
Recommended

WORK ENVIRONMENT
Indoors and outdoors, Primarily multiple locations

Firefighters may fight a fire in a massive building giving off intense heat, or they may be called to extinguish nothing more than a small brush fire or a blazing garbage can. Firefighters on duty at fire stations must be prepared to go on an alarm call at any moment. Time wasted may result in more damage or even loss of life. Firefighters wear protective suits to prevent their hands and bodies from injury, including protective gloves, helmets, boots, coats, and self-contained breathing apparatuses. Because of the mass confusion that occurs at the scene of a fire and the dangerous nature of the work, the firefighters are organized into details and units. They work under the supervision of commanding officers, such as fire captains, battalion chiefs, or the fire chief. These officers may reassign the firefighters' duties at any time, depending on the needs of a particular situation.

Once firefighters have extinguished a fire, they often remain at the site for a certain length of time to make sure that the fire is completely out. *Fire investigators* or *fire marshals* may examine the scene to determine the causes of the fire, especially if it resulted in injury or death or may have been set intentionally. They seek clues to the type of fuel or the place where the fire may have started. They may also determine that the fire was the result of arson—that is, it was set deliberately—and they will examine the scene for evidence that will lead them to suspects. These officials may arrest suspected arsonists and testify in court against them.

Firefighters often answer calls requesting emergency medical care, such as help in giving artificial respiration to drowning victims or emergency aid for heart attack victims on public streets. They may also administer emergency medical care. Many fire departments operate emergency medical services. Most firefighters are cross-trained to participate in both fire and emergency activities.

Some firefighters are assigned as *fire inspectors*. Their work is to prevent fires. They inspect buildings for trash, chemicals, and other materials that could easily ignite; for poor, worn-out, or exposed wiring; for inadequate alarm systems, blocked hallways, or impassable exits; and for other conditions that pose fire hazards. These conditions are usually reported to the owners of the property for correction; if not corrected, the owners could be fined and held criminally liable if any fires occur. Fire inspectors also check to see that public buildings are operated in accordance with fire codes and city ordinances and that the building management complies with safety regulations and fire precautions. Often firefighters are called on to give speeches on fire prevention before school and civic groups.

While firefighters are on station duty and between alarm calls, they perform various duties on a regular basis. They must keep all firefighting equipment in first-class condition for immediate use. This includes polishing and lubricating mechanical equipment, keeping water hoses dry and stretched into shape, and keeping their own personal protective gear in good repair. They hold practice drills for improving response times and firefighting techniques to become as efficient and proficient as possible.

Many firefighters study while on duty to improve their skills and knowledge of fire fighting and emergency medical techniques. They also prepare themselves for examinations, which are given regularly and which determine to some extent their opportunities for promotion. They are often required to participate in training programs to hone their skills and learn new techniques.

Since many firefighters must live at the fire station for periods of 24 hours at a time, housekeeping duties and cleaning chores are performed by the on-duty firefighters on a rotation basis. In some small towns, firefighters are only employed on a part-time basis. They are on alarm call from their homes, except perhaps for practice drills. Usually in such situations, only a fire chief and assistant live at the station and are employed full time.

Firefighters work in other settings as well. Many industrial plants employ fire marshals who are in charge of fire-prevention and firefighting efforts and personnel. At airports, potential or actual airplane crashes bring out crash, fire, and rescue workers who prevent or put out fires and save passengers and crewmembers.

The job of firefighters has become more complicated in recent years due to the use of increasingly sophisticated equipment. In addition, many firefighters have assumed additional responsibilities. For example, firefighters work with emergency medical services providing emergency medical treatment, assisting in the rescue and recovery from natural disasters such as earthquakes and tornadoes, as well as manmade disasters, such as the control and cleanup of oil spills and other hazardous chemical incidents, or rescuing victims of bombings. The work of firefighters is very dangerous. The nature of the work demands training, practice, courage, and teamwork. Firefighting is more than a physical activity that requires strength and alertness. It is also a science that demands continual study and learning.

REQUIREMENTS

High School

Most job opportunities open to firefighters today require applicants to have a high school education. "Today's firefighter needs to have a good understanding of the sciences, as much of what line firefighters do revolves around emergency medical services and the extinguishment of fire," says Chief Randy Bruegman, Fresno (California) Fire Department. "Therefore, classes in related sciences such as anatomy, physics, and biology are very helpful."

Postsecondary Training

Once high school is completed, there are a variety of options available in both two- and four-year degree programs that specifically focus on fire science and emergency medical certificates. Both are extremely helpful when competing for a position.

In most cases, applicants are required to pass written intelligence tests. Some municipalities may require a civil service examination. Formal education is an asset to potential firefighters because part of their training involves a continuous education program, and a person's educational progress may affect future opportunities for advancement.

Many junior and community colleges offer two-year fire-technology programs; degrees are also offered by some four-year colleges. Courses involve the study of physics and hydraulics as they apply to pump and nozzle pressures. Fundamentals of chemistry are taught to provide an understanding of chemical methods of extinguishing fires. Skill in communications—both written and spoken—is also emphasized. The International Fire Service Accreditation Congress offers a list of accredited degree programs at its Web site, http://www.ifsac.org.

Beginning firefighters may receive three or more weeks of intensive training, either as on-the-job training or through formal fire department training schools. Training is given both in the classroom and in the field, where new firefighters are taught the fundamentals of fire fighting, fire prevention, ventilation, emergency medical procedures (including first aid and cardiopulmonary resuscitation), hazardous materials control, the use and care of equipment (such as axes, chain saws, and ladders), and general job duties and skills, including search and rescue techniques. Trainees may also be given instruction in local building codes and fire ordinances. Once they complete their training, new firefighters undergo a period of probation.

Firefighter recruits may also train through apprenticeships, which may last up to four years. Apprentice firefighters usually start out on the job as ladder handlers or hose handlers and are given additional responsibilities with training and experience.

Certification or Licensing

Regulations vary by state, but firefighters do not generally need certification before they are hired, and certification is voluntary but recommended. Certification is typically offered through a state's fire academy, fire-service certification board, fire-service training board, or other agency regulating fire and public safety personnel. Certification programs are accredited by the International Fire Service Accreditation Congress (IFSAC), which provides a listing of states offering the Firefighter I and Firefighter II designations. To become certified, candidates must pass written and practical tests. (Contact information for the IFSAC is at the end of this article.)

Other Requirements

Very strict physical examinations are usually required for the job of firefighter. Applicants must also pass rigorous physical performance tests, which may include running, climbing, and jumping. These examinations are clearly defined by local civil service regulations.

In most cases, firefighters must be at least 18 years of age. Generally, the age range for becoming a professional firefighter is between 18 and 35. Candidates must also meet height and weight requirements. Applicants are required to have good vision (20/20 vision is required in some departments), no physical impairments that could keep them from doing their jobs, and great physical stamina. Many cities have residency requirements for their fire department personnel. Most firefighters join the International Association of Fire Fighters (AFL-CIO, CLC) when they are hired.

Usually the individuals who score the highest on their tests have the best chances of getting jobs as firefighters. Those who gained firefighting experience in the military or who have served as volunteer community firefighters may receive preferential consideration on their job applications. Applicants with emergency medical service and training are often in demand as firefighters.

A mechanical aptitude is an asset to a person in this career. Also important are a congenial temperament and the ability to adapt to uncertain situations that call for teamwork. Firefighters must be willing to follow the orders of their superiors. Firefighters need sound judgment, mental alertness, and the ability to reason and think logically in situations demanding courage and bravery. The ability to remain calm and compassionate is a valued asset, as firefighters must cope with the emotions of those they are helping, emotions that range from those of distraught homeowners to burn victims.

"Firefighters must have the willingness to provide service over one's self," says Chief Bruegman. "The qualities that we look for include someone who is willing to work hard, has a commitment to serve others, and is a team player. The shifts that firefighters work are 24 hours on and 48 hours off, and, with a variety of schedules in between, it is crucial that they have personalities that can interact well in that type of environment. We also look for people who can speak well in public, articulate and teach, and can react well in a variety of situations, whether it is in a public education forum or on an emergency scene."

EXPLORING

You can explore this occupation by talking with local firefighters. You may also be able to get permission to sit in on some of the formal training classes for firefighters offered by city fire departments. In some cases, depending on the size and regulations of the town or city department, you may be able to gain experience by working as a volunteer firefighter.

"Many departments offer explorer and cadet programs for high-school age students to become involved in if they are interested in the fire service," notes Chief Bruegman. "There are classes that can be taken at local community colleges even by high school students to begin preparing them for a career in the fire service. Many departments offer programs that allow civilians to ride along. This is a good way for students to spend several hours in a fire station and actually respond to calls to get a feel for whether this is the career that is right for them. Also, any volunteer work, especially in service-related fields such as hospitals and hospices that provide services to people in need, would help prepare students for the jobs that firefighters do every day."

Courses in lifesaving and first aid will offer you experience in these aspects of the firefighter's job. You can explore these areas through community training courses and the training offered by the Boy Scouts of America, Girl Scouts of the United States of America, or the American Red Cross. Individuals serving in the military may request training and assignment to firefighting units to gain experience.

EMPLOYERS

Approximately 305,500 paid firefighters work in the United States. Ninety-one percent of career firefighters work in municipal or county fire departments. Some very large cities have several thousand firefighters, while small towns might only have a few. The remainder work in fire departments on federal and state installations, such as military bases and airports, and for the USDA Forest Service, the National Park Service, and state departments of forestry. Private fire brigades employ a very small number of firefighters. Most volunteers work for departments that protect fewer than 25,000 people. More than half of all volunteer firefighters are located in small, rural departments that protect fewer than 9,999 people, according to the National Volunteer Fire Council. Many industries have their own fire-protection staffs and private fire brigades.

STARTING OUT

You can enter this occupation by applying to take civil service examinations in your municipality. This usually requires passing physical health, physical performance, and written general intelligence examinations.

If you successfully pass all of the required tests and receive a job appointment, you may serve a probationary period during which you receive intensive training. After the completion of this training, you may be assigned to a fire department or engine company for specific duties.

In some small towns and communities, applicants may enter this occupation through on-the-job training as volunteer firefighters or by applying directly to the local government for the position.

ADVANCEMENT

Firefighters are generally promoted from within the department, first to the position of firefighter, first grade. After they demonstrate successful job performance and gain experience, firefighters may be promoted to positions as lieutenants, captains, deputies, battalion chiefs, assistant chiefs, deputy chiefs, and finally fire chief. Firefighters may sometimes work three to five years or more to receive a promotion to lieutenant. Promotions usually depend upon the firefighter's position rating, which is determined by seniority, job performance, and scores made on the periodic written examinations.

EARNINGS

The median hourly pay for firefighters was $21.66 in 2009 (or $45,050 annually based on a 40-hour workweek), according to the U.S. Department of Labor. Ten percent of all firefighters earned less than $11.05 (or $22,990 annually), while the top 10 percent earned more than $35.76 (or $74,390 annually). The department also reports that firefighters employed by local government earned a mean hourly wage of $23.01 (or $47,860 annually); those employed by the federal government earned a mean hourly wage of $23.15 (or $48,150 annually). Many firefighters receive longevity pay for each year they remain in service, which may add as much as $1,000 per year to their salaries. Firefighters also earn overtime pay and are usually given shift, weekend, and holiday pay differentials. In addition, firefighters generally receive a uniform allowance and are eligible to retire after 25 years of service or if disabled in the line of duty. Benefits, including health, life, and disability insurance, vary widely according to the community.

First-line supervisors/managers of fire fighting and prevention workers earned salaries that ranged from less than $41,680 to $109,750 or more in 2009, according to the U.S. Department of Labor, although fire chiefs in larger cities may earn much more. Inspectors and investigators earned an average of $53,720 per year in 2009.

WORK ENVIRONMENT

The work of firefighters can often be exciting; the job, however, is one of grave responsibilities. Someone's life or death often hangs in the balance. The working conditions are frequently dangerous and involve risking one's life in many situations. Floors, walls, or even entire buildings can cave in on firefighters as they work to save lives and property in raging fires. Exposure to smoke, fumes, chemicals, and gases can end a firefighter's life or cause permanent injury.

"A typical day for a firefighter revolves around training, fire inspections, and house duties, including maintaining living quarters and equipment," says Chief Randy Bruegman. "Coupled with the typical day are untypical interruptions. This is what makes the life of a firefighter so interesting. When you place your turnout equipment [system outer protective clothing] on the apparatus you are assigned to, you never know what the day will bring. It can be a day filled with minor responses, typical medical assists, cardiac arrests, or multiple-alarm fires. I think that is what makes the job so challenging, as well as enjoyable. You never really know from one minute to the next what you might be doing."

New equipment that can make the firefighter's job much safer is constantly being developed and tested. For example, a company recently introduced special masks that allow firefighters to see in the dense and smoky environments they enter. These masks display heat sources close in temperature to the human body, allowing firefighters to locate victims in rooms otherwise impenetrable. With developments like these, firefighters will be able to save many more victims and drastically reduce the danger to themselves.

In many fire departments, firefighters may be on duty and live at fire stations for long periods of time. They may work 24-hour shifts followed by either 48 or 72 hours off. Firefighters can also work in split shifts, which require that they work nine-hour days and 15-hour night tours or 10-hour days and 14-hour night tours. After each set of day tours, firefighters receive 72 hours off, and after each set of night tours, they receive 48 hours off. Workweeks can range from 40 to almost 56 hours; across the United States and Canada, firefighters worked an average week of 50 hours.

This occupation requires a great deal of physical strength and stamina, so firefighters must work to keep themselves physically fit and in condition. They must be mentally alert at all times. Firefighters may be called into action at any time of the day or night and be required to work in all types of weather conditions, sometimes for long hours. Firefighters must do their work in a highly organized team effort to be effective, since a great deal of excitement and public confusion is usually present at the site of a fire.

Firefighters know that their work is essential for the public welfare, and they receive a great deal of personal satisfaction, as well as admiration and respect from society. "Fire fighting is probably one of the few careers that taxes people both mentally and physically to their maximum potential on a daily basis," Chief Bruegman adds. "When responding to emergencies, firefighters are charged with taking a chaotic and stressful situation, gaining control of it, and trying to effect a positive outcome. That often happens within just a few minutes and requires an extreme amount of physical exertion and mental readiness."

OUTLOOK

Employment of firefighters is expected to grow faster than the average for all occupations through 2018, according to the U.S. Department of Labor. Despite this prediction, fire fighting is forecasted to remain a very competitive field, and the number of people interested in becoming firefighters will outweigh the number of available positions in most areas. Applicants who are physically fit, have EMT training, have top scores on physical-conditioning and mechanical aptitude exams, and have at least some postsecondary training will have the best employment prospects.

Most new jobs will be created as small communities grow and augment their volunteer staffs with career firefighters. There are also growing numbers of "call" firefighters, who are paid only when responding to fires. Some local governments are expected to contract for firefighting services with private companies. In some fire departments, the hours of each work shift have been shortened, and two people may be employed to cover a shift normally worked by one person. Most job growth will occur as volunteer firefighting departments are converted to paid positions. Layoffs of firefighters are uncommon, given the essential nature of fire protection to communities.

FOR MORE INFORMATION

For news in the firefighting field, visit the association's Web site.

International Association of Fire Chiefs
4025 Fair Ridge Drive, Suite 300
Fairfax, VA 22033-2868
Tel: 703-273-0911
http://www.iafc.org

The IAFF Web site has a Virtual Academy with information on scholarships for postsecondary education.

International Association of Fire Fighters (IAFF)
1750 New York Avenue, NW, Suite 300
Washington, DC 20006-5395
Tel: 202-737-8484
http://www.iaff.org

For information on certification and accredited postsecondary fire science programs, contact

International Fire Service Accreditation Congress
Oklahoma State University
1700 West Tyler
Stillwater, OK 74078-8075
Tel: 405-744-8303
http://www.ifsac.org

For information on fire safety issues, careers in fire protection, and public education, contact

National Fire Protection Association
1 Batterymarch Park
Quincy, MA 02169-7471
Tel: 617-770-3000
E-mail: publicaffairs@nfpa.org
http://www.nfpa.org

FORENSIC EXPERTS

OVERVIEW

Forensic experts apply scientific principles and methods to the analysis, identification, and classification of physical evidence relating to criminal (or suspected criminal) cases. They do much of their work in laboratories, where they subject evidence to tests and then record the results. They may travel to crime scenes to collect evidence and record the physical facts of a site. Forensic experts may also be called upon to testify as expert witnesses and to present scientific findings in court.

THE JOB

Forensic experts, also called *criminalists*, use the instruments of science and engineering to examine physical evidence. They use spectroscopes, microscopes, gas chromatographs, infrared and ultraviolet light, microphotography, and other lab measuring and testing equipment to analyze fibers, fabric, dust, soils, paint chips, glass fragments, fire accelerants, paper and ink, and other substances in order to identify their composition and origin. They analyze poisons, drugs, and other substances found in bodies by examining tissue samples, stomach contents, and blood samples. They analyze and classify blood, blood alcohol, semen, hair, fingernails, teeth, human and animal bones and tissue, and other

SCHOOL SUBJECTS
Biology, Chemistry

PERSONAL SKILLS
Following instructions, Technical/scientific

MINIMUM EDUCATION LEVEL
Bachelor's degree

CERTIFICATION OR LICENSING
Voluntary

WORK ENVIRONMENT
Primarily indoors, Primarily multiple locations

biological specimens. Using samples of the DNA in these materials, they can match a person with a sample of body tissue. They study documents to determine whether they are forged or genuine. They also examine the physical properties of firearms, bullets, and explosives.

At the scene of a crime (whether actual or suspected), forensic experts collect and label evidence. This painstaking task may involve searching for spent bullets or bits of an exploded bomb and other objects scattered by an explosion. They might look for footprints, fingerprints, and tire tracks, which must be recorded or preserved by plaster casting before they are wiped out. Since crime scenes must eventually be cleaned up, forensic experts take notes and photographs to preserve the arrangement of objects, bodies, and debris. They are sometimes called on later to reconstruct the scene of a crime by making a floor plan or map pinpointing the exact location of bodies, weapons, and furniture.

One important discipline within forensic science is identification. *Fingerprint classifiers* catalog and compare fingerprints of suspected criminals with records to determine if the people who left the fingerprints at the scene of a crime were involved in previous crimes. They often try to match the fingerprints of unknown corpses with fingerprint records to establish their identities. They work in laboratories and offices, and travel to other areas such as crime scenes. Retrieving fingerprints outside may be difficult and require specialized processes, such as dusting glassware, windows, or walls with a fine powder. This powder contrasts with many different surfaces and will highlight any fingerprints that remain. Another method of retrieving fingerprints is to lift them off with a flexible tape, which can be brought back to the laboratory for further evaluation and matching.

Fingerprint classifiers compare new prints against those found after the commission of similar crimes. The classifier documents this information and transfers it to the main record-keeping system, often a large mainframe computer system. In the last decade or so, computers have greatly enhanced the possibility of matching new fingerprints to those already on file. A fingerprint classifier may keep individual files on current crimes and note any similarities between them.

Identification technicians work at various jobs related to maintaining police records. In addition to handling fingerprint records, they also work with other kinds of records, such as police reports and eyewitness information about crimes and accidents. They operate equipment used to microfilm police records, as well as store the microfilm and retrieve or copy records upon the request of police or other public officials. *Forensic pathologists* perform autopsies to determine the cause of death; autopsies are almost always performed on victims of crime. *Forensic psychiatrists* also conduct psychiatric evaluations of accused criminals and are often called to testify on whether the accused is mentally fit to stand trial.

Molecular biologists and *geneticists* analyze and review forensic and paternity samples, provide expert testimony in civil and criminal trials, and identify and develop new technologies for use in human identification.

Other job titles within forensic science include *forensic toxicologists,* who are concerned with detecting and identifying the presence of poisons or drugs in a victim's body; *forensic odontologists,* who use dental records and evidence to identify crime victims and to investigate bite marks; and *forensic anthropologists,* who examine and identify bones and skeletal remains.

Forensic experts spend the bulk of their time in the laboratory working with physical evidence. They seldom have direct contact with persons involved in actual or suspected crimes or with police investigators except when collecting evidence and reporting findings. Forensic experts do not interpret their findings relative to the criminal investigation in which they are involved; that is the work of police investigators. The purpose of crime lab work is to provide reliable scientific analysis of evidence that can then be used in criminal investigations and, if needed later, in court proceedings.

REQUIREMENTS

High School

Almost all jobs in this field require at least a bachelor's degree. In high school, you can begin to prepare for a career in forensics by taking a heavy concentration of science courses, including chemistry, biology, physiology, and physics. Computer skills are also important, especially for fingerprint classifiers. A basic grounding in spoken and written communications will be useful because forensic experts must write very detailed reports and are sometimes called on to present their findings in court.

Postsecondary Training

A number of universities and community colleges in the United States offer programs in forensic science, pathology, and various aspects of crime lab work. These courses are often spread throughout the school, in the anatomy, physiology, chemistry, or biology departments, or they may be grouped together as part of the criminal justice department.

Certification or Licensing

Certification may be an advantage for people working in toxicology and document examination. Specialists in these and other disciplines may also be required to take undergraduate and graduate course work in their areas. In a field such as toxicology, advanced chemistry work is important. The American Board of Criminalistics (ABC) offers two levels of certification: diplomate and fellow. Diplomate certification (D-ABC) is designed for laboratory directors, supervisors, and educators. The fellow certification (F-ABC) covers specialty areas, including drug analysis; fire debris analysis and trace evidence; hair, fiber, and trace evidence; and paint and polymers. Visit the ABC Web site (http://www.criminalistics.com) for additional information.

Other Requirements

To be successful in this field, you should have an aptitude for scientific investigation, an inquiring and logical mind, and the ability to make precise measurements and observations. Patience and persistence are important qualities, as is a good memory. Forensic experts must constantly bear in mind that the accuracy of their lab investigations can have great consequences for others.

EXPLORING

A large community police department may have a crime lab of its own with experts who can give you specific information about their work and the preparation that helped them build their careers. Smaller communities often use the lab facilities of a larger city nearby or the state police. A school counselor or a representative of the local police may be able to help you arrange a tour of these labs. Lectures in forensic science given at universities or police conventions may also be open to students. Online services and Internet access may provide entry to forums devoted to forensic science and are good sources of information on the daily and professional experiences of people already active in this field.

EMPLOYERS

Forensic scientists are typically employed by large police departments or state law enforcement agencies nationwide. Individuals in certain disciplines are often self-employed, however, or work in the private sector. For example, forensic engineers—who use mathematical principles to reconstruct accident scenes, determine the origins of explosions and fires, or review the design of chemical or molecular structures—may be employed by large corporations, small firms, or government agencies. Forensic anthropologists—who identify skeletal remains—may work within a university or college, teaching related courses, conducting research, and consulting on cases submitted by law enforcement agencies. They may also be employed by the military or a medical examiner's office. Many forensic science concentrations also offer part-time or consulting opportunities, depending on your level of education and experience.

STARTING OUT

Crime labs are maintained by the federal government and by state and local governments. Applications should be made directly to the personnel department of the government agency supporting the lab. Civil service appointments usually require applicants to take an examination. Such appointments are usually widely advertised well in advance of the application date. Those working for the FBI or other law enforcement agencies usually undergo background checks, which examine their character, background, previous employers, and family and friends.

ADVANCEMENT

In a large crime laboratory, forensic technicians usually advance from an assistant's position to working independently at one or more special types of analysis. From there they may advance to a position as project leader or being in charge of all aspects of one particular investigation. In smaller labs, one technician may have to fill many roles. With experience, such a technician may progress to more responsible work but receive no advancement in title. Fingerprint classifiers who work for police departments may pursue advancement with a different government agency or apply for positions with the FBI.

Further education is crucial to advancement. Forensic experts need to be familiar with scientific procedures such as gas chromatography, ultraviolet and infrared spectrophotometry, mass spectroscopy, electrophoresis, polarizing microscopy, light microscopy, and conventional and isoelectric focusing; knowledge of these analytical techniques and procedures is taught or more fully explored at the master's and doctorate levels. Other, more specific areas of forensics, such as DNA analysis, require advanced degrees in molecular biology and genetics.

EARNINGS

Earnings for forensic analysts vary with the employer, geographic location, and educational and skill levels. The U.S. Department of Labor reports that the median hourly wage for forensic science technicians was $24.75 in 2009. For full-time employment, this means a median salary of approximately $51,480 a year. The lowest paid 10 percent earned $15.59 per hour ($32,420 annually) and the highest paid 10 percent earned $40.51 per hour ($84,260 annually). Those working for the federal government had mean annual earnings of $92,100 in 2009.

WORK ENVIRONMENT

Forensic experts usually perform the analytical portion of their work in clean, quiet, air-conditioned laboratories, but they are frequently required to travel to crime scenes to collect evidence or study the site to understand more fully the evidence collected by detectives. When gathering evidence and analyzing it, forensic experts need to be able to concentrate, sometimes in crowded, noisy situations. For this reason, forensic experts must be adaptable and able to work in a variety of environments, including dangerous or unpleasant places.

Many crime scenes are grisly and may be extremely distressing for beginning workers and even for more seasoned professionals. In addition, forensic experts who work with human remains will regularly view corpses, and, more often than not, these corpses will have been mutilated in some way or be in varying degrees of decomposition. Individuals interested in this field need to develop the detachment and objectivity necessary to view corpses and extract specimens for testing and analysis.

Simulating the precise conditions of a crime site for a full analysis is often crucial, so forensic experts often return to the site so that they can perform tests or functions outside of the controlled environment of their lab. When traveling to the scene of a crime, forensic experts may have to carry cases of tools, cameras, and chemicals. In order not to risk contaminating evidence, they must follow strict procedures (both in and out of the laboratory) for collecting and testing evidence; these procedures can be extremely time-consuming and thus require a great deal of patience. Forensic experts also need to be able to arrive at and present their findings impartially. In large labs, they often work as part of a team under the direction of a senior technologist. They may experience eyestrain and contact with strong chemicals, but little strenuous physical work is involved.

OUTLOOK

The number of forensic experts employed in the United States is expected to grow much faster than the average for all other occupations through 2018, according to the U.S. Department of Labor. Population increases, a rising crime rate, and the greater emphasis on scientific methodology in crime investigation have increased the need for trained experts. Forensic experts who are employed by state public safety departments should experience especially strong employment opportunities, although some government agencies may be under pressure to reduce staff because of budget problems. Forensic experts with a four-year degree in forensic science will enjoy the best employment prospects.

FOR MORE INFORMATION

For information on careers and colleges and universities that offer forensic science programs, contact

American Academy of Forensic Sciences
410 North 21st Street
Colorado Springs, CO 80904-2798
Tel: 719-636-1100
http://www.aafs.org

For information about certification, contact

American Board of Criminalistics
PO Box 1123
Wausau, WI 54402-1123
http://www.criminalistics.com/

To learn more about forensic services at the FBI, visit the FBI Laboratory Division's Web site.

Federal Bureau of Investigation (FBI)
J. Edgar Hoover Building
935 Pennsylvania Avenue, NW
Washington, DC 20535-0001
Tel: 202-324-3000
http://www.fbi.gov and http://www.fbi.gov/hq/lab/labhome.htm

For additional information on forensics and forensics professionals, contact the following organizations:

American Society of Questioned Document Examiners
PO Box 18298
Long Beach, CA 90807-8298
http://www.asqde.org

Society of Forensic Toxicologists Inc.
One MacDonald Center
1 North MacDonald Street, Suite 15

Mesa, AZ 85201-7340
Tel: 888-866-7638
E-mail: office@soft-tox.org
http://www.soft-tox.org

FUNERAL HOME WORKERS

SCHOOL SUBJECTS
Biology, Business, Psychology

PERSONAL SKILLS
Helping/teaching, Leadership/management

MINIMUM EDUCATION LEVEL
Some postsecondary training

CERTIFICATION OR LICENSING
Required

WORK ENVIRONMENT
Primarily indoors, One location with some travel

OVERVIEW

The *funeral director,* also called a *mortician* or *undertaker,* handles all the arrangements for burial and funeral services of the deceased, in accordance with the family's wishes. This includes the removal of the body to the funeral home, securing information and filing for the death certificate, and organizing the service and burial plans. The director also supervises the personnel who prepare bodies for burial. An *embalmer* uses chemical solutions to disinfect, preserve, and restore the body and employs cosmetic aids to simulate a lifelike appearance. A *mortuary science technician* works under the direction of a funeral director to perform embalming and related funeral service tasks. Most are trainees working to become licensed embalmers and funeral directors.

Funeral attendants are responsible for various tasks, including placing the casket in the funeral parlor or chapel before services, organizing flower arrangements and lighting around the casket, escorting mourners during viewings and services, closing the casket, and storing funeral equipment after services are complete.

Funeral home workers are employed throughout the world in small communities as well as large metropolitan areas. Because cultures and religions affect burial customs, funeral home workers must be sensitive and knowledgeable to these differences.

There are approximately 25,820 funeral directors and 8,500 embalmers employed in the United States. Funeral attendants hold another 34,500 jobs.

THE JOB

Funeral directors are responsible for all the details related to the funeral ceremony and burial. The law determines some of their tasks, such as compliance with sanitation and health-related standards. Other responsibilities are administrative and logistical, such as securing information and filing the death certificate. Finally, custom and practice dictate some tasks.

Directors handle all the paperwork that needs to be filed, such as the death certificate, obituary notices, and may even assist the family in applying for the transfer of insurance policies, pensions, or other funds.

They assist the family of the deceased in the choice of casket, type of funeral service, and preparation of the remains, which may be burial, cremation, or entombment. Part of the director's job is to be a caregiver and, at times, a counselor. They must deal respectfully and sympathetically with families of the deceased, guiding them through decisions they may not be prepared to make and taking great care that their wishes are carried out.

First, the funeral director arranges for the body to be transported to the funeral home. The director then makes complete arrangements for the funeral ceremony, determining first the place and time of the service. If there is to be a religious ceremony, it is the director's responsibility to contact the appropriate clergy. Directors oversee the selection and playing of music, notify pallbearers, and arrange the placement of the casket and floral displays in the viewing parlor or chapel. If a service is held in the funeral home, the director arranges seating for guests. After the service, the director organizes the procession of cars to the cemetery, or wherever arrangements have been made for the disposal of remains. Funeral directors may have to make arrangements for transporting a body to another state for burial.

Most directors are also trained, licensed, and practicing embalmers. Embalming is a required sanitary process done to the body within 24 hours of death to preserve the remains for burial services. If a body is not being autopsied, it is brought to a funeral home where it is washed with a germicidal soap. The body is placed in a lifelike position, and an incision is made in a major artery and vein where a tube pumps a preservative and disinfectant solution through the entire circulatory system. Circulation of the chemical solution eventually replaces all blood with the embalming fluid. In addition, embalmers remove all other gases and liquids from the body, replacing it with disinfectant chemicals for preservation.

The preparation of an autopsied body can be much more complex, depending on the condition of the deceased. The embalmer may repair disfigured parts of the body and improve the facial appearance, using wax, cotton, plaster of Paris, and cosmetics. When the embalming process is complete, the body is dressed and put in a casket.

Mortuary science technicians assist directors and embalmers in the funeral home. They are usually involved in a training process that will ultimately lead to a job as a licensed funeral director, embalmer, or both. Technicians may assist in various phases of the embalming process. Since embalming fluids are available in different chemical compositions and color tints, learning the various formulas is one important part of the technician's job. The technician may also be responsible for helping in the application of cosmetics to the body to create a natural, lifelike appearance. It is important that they use the proper products and techniques for applying them, since the result must satisfy and comfort those who view the body. (In some funeral homes, a licensed cosmetologist called a *mortuary cosmetologist* may perform these cosmetic services.) After the cosmetic application is complete, the technician may assist with the dressing and placement of the body for the funeral service. Finally, the technician may be responsible for cleaning the embalming area and equipment in accordance with required standards of sanitation.

Funeral attendants perform duties related to the actual funeral service. They may prepare the casket for the service and transport it to the cemetery. They also assist in receiving and ushering mourners to their seats at the service, organizing and managing the funeral procession, or any other tasks that are necessary for the occasion.

REQUIREMENTS

High School

If you are interested in entering the field of mortuary science, consider taking classes in algebra, chemistry, biology, physics, and any other laboratory courses available. In addition, a psychology class might be helpful since

funeral home workers must deal with distraught families and friends of deceased persons.

Postsecondary Training

Almost all states require funeral service practitioners to have completed postsecondary training in mortuary science varying from nine months to four years. Several colleges and universities now offer two- and four-year programs in funeral service. The American Board of Funeral Service Education accredits 56 mortuary science programs. A typical curriculum at a school of mortuary science would include courses in anatomy, embalming practices, funeral customs, psychology, accounting, and public health laws. Laboratory study is essential in many of the courses and can account for up to a quarter of the program.

After completion of at least a two-year program, the graduate can apply to work as a mortuary science technician. Graduates who want to obtain a license in either embalming or funeral directing must work as an apprentice in an established funeral home for one to three years, depending on the state's requirements. Some schools of mortuary science have arrangements with local area funeral homes to provide students with either a work-study program or a period of school-supervised funeral service work (residency or apprenticeship).

Certification or Licensing

All states require embalmers and funeral directors to be licensed. Some states grant a combination single license covering the activity of both the embalmer and funeral director. In order to maintain licensure, a growing number of states require continuing education classes.

After successfully completing their formal education, including apprenticeship, prospective funeral service practitioners must pass a state board examination that usually consists of written and oral tests and demonstration of skills. Those who wish to practice in another state may have to pass that state's examination as well, although some states have reciprocity arrangements to waive this requirement.

Other Requirements

A strong sense of understanding, empathy, and a genuine desire to help people at a time of great stress are essential qualities for anyone wanting to work at a funeral home. Workers must be tactful and discrete in all contacts with the bereaved family and friends. Funeral service workers must always be compassionate and sympathetic, but also remain strong and confident to accomplish the necessary tasks of the job. Funeral home workers must also be good listeners. For example, when details such as cosmetics and clothing are discussed, they must be especially attentive to the client's wishes.

The work sometimes requires physical strength for lifting the deceased or their caskets. Good coordination is also needed to perform the precise procedures used in embalming, restoration, and cosmetology.

EXPLORING

Ask your high school guidance counselor for information on mortuary science or check out your public and school library for useful books, magazines, and pamphlets. Local funeral homes are the most direct source of information. Arrange a visit with a funeral director and embalming staff to learn about the nature of the work and the importance and intricacies of funeral service. After becoming acquainted with local funeral homes, ask around to see if you can work part time, either handling clerical or custodial duties. Finally, check out the organizations listed at the end of this article for more career information.

EMPLOYERS

Funeral directors are usually employed by a funeral home or are in the business themselves. There are about 25,820 funeral directors in the United States, approximately 13 percent of whom are self-employed. The majority of embalmers, mortuary science technicians, and funeral attendants are also employed by funeral homes, though a small amount work for hospitals and medical schools. Employers for these professions are located worldwide.

STARTING OUT

After attending an accredited school of mortuary science for two to four years, beginning workers start out as mortuary science technicians, working under the supervision of a licensed director or embalmer.

Most mortuary science schools provide placement assistance for graduates. Additionally, since many schools require internship programs, students are often able to obtain permanent jobs where they have trained.

ADVANCEMENT

For many years, most funeral homes were family businesses. Younger members of the family or their husbands or wives were expected to move up into managerial positions when the older members retired. This is changing, however, as the majority are entering the field today having no prior background or family connection. Therefore, the potential for advancement into managerial positions is considerably greater than in the past.

The natural progression in the field is from mortuary science technician to fully licensed embalmer, funeral director, or both. With licensing comes more opportunity for advancement. While many people who enter this field aspire to eventually own their own funeral homes, there are other possibilities as well. One advanced specialty, for example, is that of *trade embalmers,* who embalm under contract for funeral homes. Their work typically includes restorative treatment. Also, an increasing number specialize in selling funeral and burial arrangements in advance. Providing the option to make plans ahead of time can give clients peace of mind. Finally, with sufficient financial backing, funeral service practitioners may establish their own businesses or purchase a portion or all of an existing one.

The percentage of mortuary science graduates who pursue advancement outside the funeral home is small. Opportunities do exist, though. Funeral supply manufacturers employ licensed funeral service personnel because of their familiarity with the products and their ability to handle technical problems. Workers may be employed in customer relations or product sales.

EARNINGS

Salaries of funeral home workers vary depending on experience, services performed, level of formal education, and location. According to the U.S. Department of Labor, the median annual salary for funeral directors was $54,370 in 2009. The lowest paid 10 percent earned less than $30,700 and the highest paid 10 percent earned more than $94,050 a year. The department also reports that embalmers earned a median annual salary of $40,620 in 2009. Funeral attendants earned a median annual salary of $22,530 annually.

According to the American Board of Funeral Service Education, starting salaries for new funeral service licensees often closely approximate those of starting teachers in the same community.

In some metropolitan areas, many funeral home employees are unionized; in these cases, salaries are determined by union contracts and are generally higher than regions in which employees have not organized a union.

Benefits may vary depending on the position and the employer.

WORK ENVIRONMENT

In firms employing two or more licensees, funeral workers generally have a set schedule of eight-hour days, five or six days a week. Because services may be needed at any hour of the day or night, however, shifts are usually arranged so that someone is always available at night and on weekends.

In smaller firms, employees generally work long hours at odd times and often remain on call and within a short distance of the funeral home. Some may work in shifts, such as all days one week and all nights the next. Occasionally, overtime may be necessary.

Employees who transport bodies and accompany the funeral procession to the cemetery are frequently required to lift heavy weights and to be outdoors in inclement weather. Sometimes directors and embalmers must handle the remains of those who have died of contagious diseases, though the risk of infection, given the strict sanitary conditions required in all funeral homes, is minimal.

In this field, much of workers' time is spent trying to help families work through their grief. Because they are exposed daily to such intense emotion, as well as death and sometimes unpleasant or upsetting sights, there is the chance that the work may be depressing or emotionally draining. Employees need to be aware of that possibility and be able to approach situations philosophically and with a clear head.

Many who enter this field find that their occupation can be very rewarding because the work they do may help the family and friends of the deceased adjust at a time when they are greatly stressed by grief. They help provide an essential social service and one that, when well done, brings comfort and satisfaction.

OUTLOOK

Employment for funeral directors should grow about as fast as the average for all occupations through 2018. The need to replace those retiring (more directors are 55 or older than in other occupations) or leaving the profession will spur a demand for newly trained directors. Anticipated growth also reflects the need for services as the population in general ages.

Despite this demand, there are a limited number of employers in any geographical area, and it might be wise for prospective students to check with employers in their area to see what the chances for employment will be. If possible, students should try to arrange postgraduate employment while they are still in school.

Job security in the funeral service industry is relatively unaffected by economic downturns. Despite the flux and

movement in the population, funeral homes are a stable institution. The average firm has been in its community for more than 40 years, and funeral homes with a history of over 100 years are not uncommon.

FOR MORE INFORMATION

For information on careers in the funeral service industry, colleges that offer programs in mortuary science, and scholarships, contact

American Board of Funeral Service Education
3414 Ashland Avenue, Suite G
St. Joseph, MO 64506-1333
Tel: 816-233-3747
E-mail: exdir@abfse.org
http://www.abfse.org

Visit the NFDA's Web site to read Exploring a Career in Funeral Service *or receive the NFDA's continuing education newsletter.*

National Funeral Directors Association (NFDA)
13625 Bishop's Drive
Brookfield, WI 53005-6607
Tel: 800-228-6332
E-mail: nfda@nfda.org
http://www.nfda.org

GAMING OCCUPATIONS

OVERVIEW

The gaming industry supports gambling as a form of recreation in such venues as traditional casinos, riverboats, Native American reservation casinos, racing tracks, and state lotteries. Gaming employees, running the gamut from entry-level service workers to game dealers to casino and track managers, are needed to keep such facilities operating smoothly. The American Gaming Association claims that in 2008, the gaming industry employed approximately 375,000 workers, and that an additional 450,000 workers are employed in related businesses. The U.S. Department of Labor estimates that gaming services' workers hold approximately 178,700 jobs.

THE JOB

The gaming industry relies on a variety of workers for specific customer services and operational tasks. One

SCHOOL SUBJECTS

English, Mathematics

PERSONAL SKILLS

Communication/ideas, Following instructions

MINIMUM EDUCATION LEVEL

High school diploma

CERTIFICATION OR LICENSING

Required by all states

WORK ENVIRONMENT

Primarily indoors, Primarily one location

example of a service position is that of *cashier*. Cashiers may be categorized as either coin cashiers or change persons. Basically, these employees work in a cage or at a station on the gaming floor and make change and sell coins to patrons for slot machines. They may pay off slot machine jackpots and keep records of all transactions. At the end of each shift, they count and balance their money drawers. Cashiers also provide information to guests, call for cocktail servers to visit the slot area, and provide other customer services. The duties performed by cashiers in this capacity are similar to those of a host.

Cage cashiers sell gaming chips to patrons for roulette, card, and dice games. These workers operate the main cashier cage in the casino and act much like a banker. They may provide the *slot cashiers* with additional change. They take in cash, accept checks when appropriate, charge guests' credit cards for currency advances, and check credit references. Likewise, these workers must balance their cash drawers and keep records of their cash transactions.

Slot key persons, or *slot attendants*, coordinate and supervise the operation of slot machines. They must verify and handle payoff for winnings, reset the slot machines, and refill the machines with money. Slot key persons must be able to make minor repairs or adjustments to the machines, as needed.

Dealers conduct the gaming tables for poker, blackjack, baccarat, craps, or roulette. These workers exchange real currency for casino currency, in the form of either chips or coins. They explain the rules of the game and wagering guidelines, ask patrons to place their bets, con-

duct the game, and make appropriate payoffs and collect losing bets. In poker the dealer shuffles and deals the cards to the players, and the casino takes its winnings as a percentage of the pot. *Blackjack dealers* deal themselves a hand of cards and try to win money for the "house," or the casino.

Games such as baccarat, craps, and roulette are conducted by more than one employee. Baccarat requires three dealers, two of whom collect money for bets and the third who calls the game rules. *Craps dealers* also collect money for bets at the game table and exchange money for chips. A manager called a *box person* supervises the exchange of money for chips, and another assistant, called the *stick handler,* collects the dice after they have been thrown, passing them to the next shooter. Because craps is a fast game, there is a greater potential for cheating, so three people work this particular table. *Roulette dealers* sell chips, take bets, spin the roulette wheel, toss the ball in, and announce the winners. In busy games, chips are collected, passed, racked, and sorted by color by the *chip mucker*.

Other game attendants include *keno runners,* who pick up keno tickets, money, and bet orders from patrons who are in the lounge or playing at another gaming table and deliver these to the *keno writer*. The keno writer calls the game, punches the game draw cards, and changes the paper color with each new game. The keno writer also takes players' tickets, makes copies, and checks or calculates payoffs at the request of players. *Runners* take the copies back to the players, check for winning tickets, take winning tickets to the payoff window, and return winnings to the players.

Bingo is another popular form of gambling that is found in many cities across the country. People who work in bingo parlors are *bingo paymasters*, who sell the playing cards and pay money to the winners, and *bingo callers,* who operate the device that chooses the numbers, call out the numbers, check winners' cards, and announce the payouts. Many parlors have *bingo package preparers* who put together packets of bingo cards and special games.

Shift supervisors, floor bosses, and *pit bosses* oversee the performance of the game attendants. Sometimes these workers monitor one or more game tables, while at other times this work is performed by staff dealers. Shift supervisors may be responsible for all the casino games being played during a shift.

The role of *casino hosts* is a visible one. They cover the gaming floor, greet guests, and make sure everyone is enjoying themselves. Some aspects of their job are similar to that of a hotel concierge. Customers may request that dinner or room reservations be made or tickets obtained for special casino functions. Some casinos have *executive casino hosts* designated to care for premium customers, especially high rollers.

"And they're off!" A good *race announcer* adds to the excitement of any race. Besides giving horse, owner, and trainer information prior to the start of the race, an announcer will declare each horse's final odds and racing colors. During the race, the announcer will give a detailed, neck-by-neck account of the race.

REQUIREMENTS

High School

Educational requirements are minimal for many positions in the gaming industry, but a high school education is preferable and personal requirements such as good diction, reliability, a good memory, and personal motivation are necessary. Good mathematical skills for making change and calculating odds are also important. Most casinos have basic math tests that all applicants must pass to be considered for employment. High school math, English, and speech classes will help you develop the skills necessary for this work.

Postsecondary Training

If you are interested in a job with a higher level of responsibility, consider obtaining an associate's or bachelor's degree, emphasizing courses in business management or hospitality. Some colleges and universities—such as Morrisville State College, Northeast Wisconsin Technical College, San Diego State University, and Tulane University—offer certificates or degrees in casino management, tribal gaming, and other areas.

Certification or Licensing

According to the government publication *Occupational Outlook Quarterly,* all gaming workers must be licensed by a regulatory agency such as the state gaming commission or control board. In addition, many schools in resort areas offer training classes that lead to certification for workers in specific games and skills. Other schools may offer certification to students who have learned all the games. This award is called a certificate of professional casino croupier and can prepare an employee for nearly any game table position. In most states, applicants must have a license, or gaming badge, in order to participate in a training session. Most licenses, renewable every two years, cost about $50.

Each casino establishes its own requirements for the training employees, but many casinos now offer in-house training programs to promising employees at no charge. Dealers are taught game rules, shuffling and dealing techniques, and the house regulations and procedures. In the game of blackjack, for example, they learn to control and protect the table. Certain bases, the first and last seats at the table especially, are vulnerable to cheating.

Completion of the training program will not automatically land you a job. Dealers must showcase their skills and training at a casino game audition. Competition for good jobs is usually intense. Though some casinos only require good casino work experience as a prerequisite of their employees, your best bet will be to get certification.

Union representation for gaming workers is very strong in Las Vegas and less strong in Atlantic City. Work permits are required in both locations. The minimum age for receiving work permits is 21. Some casinos require FBI fingerprint clearance for gaming workers, and many require their employees to be bonded. Prospective employees must also have no criminal background.

Other Requirements

People in this industry must be able to work in hectic, stressful environments and enjoy meeting and working with a wide variety of people. Workers should have good communication skills, be pleasant and courteous, and enjoy their work. Quick thinking and calculating skills are necessary in almost all positions in a casino. Workers must also be responsible, alert, and completely trustworthy, since they work around large amounts of money.

Workers should understand the importance of giving good service to guests and be able to handle frustrated, unruly, or angry patrons with tact. They may face the prospect of dealing with people who do not know when to stop gambling. Workers must be able to spot potential problems and notify management without creating a disturbance in the casino.

EXPLORING

Because casino gambling and employment is generally restricted to people who are at least 18 or 21 years old, it is very difficult for high school students to get first-hand experience in this field. Most casino jobs for a high school student will be limited to those in gift shops and eateries. However, part-time and summer jobs in restaurants, hotels, amusement parks, and other areas of the hospitality and entertainment industries will give you a feel for working with the public. Cashier jobs are also good ways to gain experience in handling money. Participating in school fairs, carnivals, state fairs, and other places where skill-type games are played may also offer insight into the gaming industry.

Potential sources for information for this occupation include individual casinos, the departments of tourism in the states that allow gambling, and hotel and motel associations. Don't forget to consult the horse racing industry and the American Gaming Association. Casinos can offer information about the types of jobs available for skilled or unskilled workers. You can also consult your local library for information on the gambling industry.

EMPLOYERS

Approximately 178,700 gaming workers are employed in the United States, according to the Department of Labor. They work for traditional casinos, riverboats, Native American reservation casinos, racing tracks, and state lotteries.

STARTING OUT

Applicants should contact the personnel officers of casinos, hotels, and resorts for information on openings and entry-level requirements. Previous experience may be difficult to obtain if the applicant lives in an area that prohibits gambling. Previous work experience in the hospitality industry, however, is a big advantage for beginners. Applicants may want to contact casinos prior to the heavy vacation season or be willing to accept part-time employment and work their way up. Many casino schools have job placement services for their graduates. Check for this perk before enrolling.

ADVANCEMENT

Advancement often comes to employees who demonstrate professionalism, have self-confidence, and establish good work records. Part-time employees may be offered full-time positions as slot cashiers or keno runners, who may advance to become cage cashiers or keno writers. Dealers generally begin at minimum wager tables and advance to tables featuring higher stakes as they gain experience and sharpen their skills.

Most supervisory positions require additional education and training as well as experience in the casino. Positions such as executive casino host, casino manager, or director of table games, require leadership, managerial skills, and keen perception. Experienced supervisors with advanced education can move into management

positions in other fields such as hospitality or tourism. Another option is to become a casino games trainer.

EARNINGS

Wages for this occupation vary depending on the job. The latest survey conducted by the American Gaming Association found the national salary for gaming employees to be about $26,000, including benefits and tips. Table dealers for such games as blackjack, craps, and poker are paid on an hourly basis, but their wages are greatly supplemented by customers' tips. According to 2009 U.S. Department of Labor data, gaming dealers earned a median salary of $17,030; gaming and sport book writers and runners, $20,350; gaming change persons and booth cashiers, $22,090; slot key workers, $25,900; gaming cage workers, $25,130; gaming supervisors, $47,950; and gaming managers, $67,380.

Unlike most professions, the weekend and evening hours are the prime shift for a gaming worker because these shifts are the busiest playing times and generally bring in the most tips. Tips are usually pooled together and divided evenly among all employees from that shift.

Benefits may include gift shop discounts, health insurance, paid vacations, additional compensation for working holidays, and pension plans. Some casinos provide uniforms, usually a tuxedo or a vest, at a discount or free of charge.

WORK ENVIRONMENT

Some gaming workers may sit while working, but most remain on their feet throughout their shift. Dealers stationed at handicapped tables are able to sit since such tables are positioned lower than others to accommodate wheelchairs. Because many casinos operate 24 hours a day, workers may be assigned to work late at night. Weekend work is common, but these shifts are usually preferred because there are usually more players, and therefore, more tips.

While casinos are usually pleasant, comfortable, and attractive places, the activity inside them may result in considerable noise and potential distraction. This can cause stress in many people, as can the emotions of players who are on a losing streak. Employees must concentrate for long periods of time, work quickly, and often have little opportunity to talk with the gamblers. Many games rely on hand signals or short phrases for communication, so the worker must remain alert at all times. Many casinos have designated smoke-free areas, though most high stakes tables are located in smoking sections.

This is a disadvantage for people sensitive to cigarette smoke. Evening hours are the busiest and may remain busy until early hours of the morning. Numerous breaks are necessary to relieve the stress.

OUTLOOK

The public's interest in gambling, new gaming venues, and the growth of casinos throughout the country will keep this industry growing faster than the average for all occupations through 2018, according to the U.S. Department of Labor. The newer casinos, particularly in Las Vegas, are larger than ever before, and many casinos are open until late in the evening or 24 hours a day. Where employment in the gaming industry was formerly limited to Nevada, and later, Atlantic City, opportunities are now available in almost every region of the country. Casinos are constantly adding new games and prizes, and comps, in the form of free food, drinks, or services, to keep customers coming back for more.

The growing number and size of casinos will increase demand for qualified employees to work service and managerial positions. In addition, many casinos take on additional employees during their busy seasons, and many opportunities are available for part-time as well as full-time employees. Job openings may be more competitive at racetracks. The racing industry has experienced slower than normal growth, partly due to increased competition from casino-type gambling.

Opportunities for cage cashiers will grow about as fast as the average as more casinos incorporate technology that reduces the amount of cash managed by employees. There is a high level of turnover in this particular occupation, which will create some openings as cage cashiers pursue other gaming or leave the field for other opportunities.

FOR MORE INFORMATION

For background information regarding the gaming industry, and salary and industry figures, contact

American Gaming Association
1299 Pennsylvania Avenue, NW, Suite 1175
Washington, DC 20004-2426
Tel: 202-552-2675
E-mail: info@americangaming.org
http://www.americangaming.org

For information regarding vocational training and a list of professional dealing schools, visit

Casino Dealers Schools
http://www.ildado.com/casino_dealer_schools.html

For information on the Native American gambling industry, contact

National Indian Gaming Association
224 Second Street, SE
Washington, DC 20003-1943
Tel: 202-546-7711
E-mail: questions@indiangaming.org
http://www.indiangaming.org

For casino salary information in Nevada, contact

Nevada Department of Employment, Training and Rehabilitation
Information Development and Processing
Research and Analysis Bureau
500 East Third Street
Carson City, NV 89713-0001
Tel: 775-684-3849
http://detr.state.nv.us

 GEOGRAPHERS

OVERVIEW

Geographers study the distribution of physical and cultural phenomena on local, regional, continental, and global scales. There are approximately 1,170 geographers employed in the United States.

THE JOB

Geography can be divided into two broad categories: physical geography and cultural geography. *Physical geographers* study the processes that create the earth's physical characteristics, such as landforms, soils, vegetation, minerals, water resources, oceans, and weather, and the significance of these processes to humans. *Climatologists* analyze climate patterns and how and why they change. *Geomorphologists,* or *physiographers,* study the origin and development of landforms and interpret their arrangement and distribution over the earth. *Mathematical geographers* study the earth's size, shape, and movements, as well as the effects of the sun, moon, and other heavenly bodies.

Other kinds of physical geographers include *plant geographers, soil geographers,* and *animal geographers.* They study the kinds and distributions of the earth's natural vegetation, soils, and animals. *Cartographers* research data necessary for mapmaking and design and draw the maps. *Computer mappers* are cartographers

SCHOOL SUBJECTS
Earth science, Geography

PERSONAL SKILLS
Helping/teaching, Technical/scientific

MINIMUM EDUCATION LEVEL
Bachelor's degree

CERTIFICATION OR LICENSING
None available

WORK ENVIRONMENT
Primarily indoors, One location with some travel

who use computers and graphics software to draw complex maps.

Cultural geography is concerned with political organizations, transportation systems, and a wide variety of other cultural activities. *Cultural geographers* study how aspects of geography relate to different cultures. This subspecialty has much in common with archaeology and anthropology.

Regional geographers study all the geographic aspects of a particular area, such as a river basin, an island, a nation, or even an entire continent. They are concerned with the physical, economic, political, and cultural characteristics of the area, and they are often called upon to advise on special problems of the region.

Economic geographers analyze the regional distribution of resources and economic activities, including manufacturing, mining, farming, trade, marketing, and communications.

Medical geographers study how health is affected by our physical setting, including environmental quality. They are interested in the way vegetation, minerals in the water supply, climate, and air pollution affect our health. They may also analyze access to health care by geographic region or setting.

Urban geographers, or *urban and regional planners*, focus on metropolitan problems of a geographic nature. They assist in planning and developing urban and suburban projects, such as residential developments, shopping centers, parking areas, and traffic control systems. They also advise business and industry on plant locations and other geographic issues.

Political geographers study such factors as national boundaries and the relation of natural resources and physical features to local, state, national, and international affairs. They also consult and advise on problems of a geopolitical nature.

Geographic Information Systems (GIS) is a relatively new but rapidly growing field. Geographers known as *geographic information system specialists* combine computer graphics, artificial intelligence, and high-speed communications in the mapping, manipulation, storage, and selective retrieval of geographic data. In this way, they are able to display and analyze a wide variety of natural, cultural, and economic information in applications as diverse as worldwide weather forecasting, emergency management, crime prevention, and the monitoring of metropolitan land use.

REQUIREMENTS
High School

Plan on continuing your education after high school, and take your school's college prep curriculum. Naturally, you will focus on science classes such as geography and earth sciences. In addition, you will benefit from taking classes in sociology, computer science, English, history, and mathematics.

Postsecondary Training

A bachelor's degree with a major in geography is the basic educational requirement for most positions as a professional geographer. Advanced degrees are usually required for most college teaching positions and for those opportunities involving a considerable amount of research activity.

Many colleges and universities offer undergraduate programs in geography. A good number of these institutions also have a curriculum leading to a master's degree or doctorate in geography.

Courses taken by geography students include general physical geography; political, economic, human, urban, and regional geography; and specialized courses such as meteorology and cartography. Undergraduate study usually includes formal classroom instruction, as well as some field study.

Certification or Licensing

There are no certification or licensing requirements for geographers.

Other Requirements

Prospective geographers need basic skills in statistics and mathematics. They should be able to interpret maps and graphs, express ideas in speech and writing, analyze problems, and make sound judgments.

EXPLORING

There are increasing opportunities to gain experience through college internship programs. A few summer and part-time employment opportunities are available in business or industrial firms. Field experiences, offered as part of the college program, provide the opportunity for potential geographers to test their knowledge and personal qualifications.

You might also want to participate in the National Geography Challenge, which is sponsored by the National Council for Geographic Education. Using a multiple-choice format, you will test your knowledge of geography against students from all over the United States. Ask your geography teacher for more information about the competition.

EMPLOYERS

Many geographers find employment in colleges, universities, and government agencies. Some are employed by business and industrial firms. Most of these positions involve teaching or research responsibilities. A small but growing number of geographers work for map companies, textbook publishers, manufacturers, overseas trading firms, chain stores, market research organizations, real estate developers, environmental consulting firms, travel agencies, banks, and investment firms.

Government agencies that hire geographers include the Central Intelligence Agency, the National Imagery and Mapping Agency, the Bureau of Census, and the U.S. Geological Survey. Some geographers work as business consultants, administrators, or planners.

STARTING OUT

Some beginning jobs are available in teaching geography, mostly in secondary schools. However, high school teaching jobs quite often require study in related fields such as social studies, history, or science. Many beginning geographers find positions connected with mapmaking in either government or private industry. Some obtain positions as research or teaching assistants while working toward advanced degrees. Others enter the planning field. Geographers with advanced degrees can qualify for teaching and research positions at the college level. Many consulting jobs are also available.

Each year the federal government has beginning positions in several geography specialties. Interested students should arrange to take the required civil service examination.

ADVANCEMENT

Advancement is dependent on such factors as amount and type of training, experience, and personal interest and motivation. Promotions to jobs requiring more skill and competency are available in all specialty areas. Such jobs are characterized by more administrative, research, or advisory responsibilities in environmental planning.

EARNINGS

Earnings and other benefits depend on the amount of training, the nature of the employment situation, and the personal interests and attributes of the individual employee. According to the U.S. Department of Labor, median annual earnings for geographers were $71,470 in 2009. Salaries ranged from less than $41,930 annually to more than $99,540. In 2009, the median annual salary for geographers employed by the federal government was $76,170.

There are positions with community colleges for geographers with master's degrees, while four-year colleges and universities generally require a doctorate. In 2009, geographers employed by colleges and universities earned mean annuals salaries of $50,930. In addition to salaried income, experienced geographers often earn supplemental incomes through consulting, research, and writing activities. Ph.D.'s in industry frequently earn more than those in academia.

WORK ENVIRONMENT

Geographers usually enjoy pleasant working conditions. They spend much of their time in an office or classroom under the typical working conditions of a business, school, or federal agency.

The average workweek of most geographers is 40 hours, particularly for those employed in government or business positions. In some jobs, however, there can be unusual work situations. Fieldwork often requires the geographer to spend an extended period of time living in remote areas, often under primitive conditions.

OUTLOOK

Geography is a very small profession. With the increased emphasis on planning and research in U.S. business and government, however, the number of geographers in business has doubled in recent years. According to the *Occupational Outlook Handbook,* employment opportunities for geographers are expected to grow much faster than the average through 2018. The use of GIS technology in traditional and nontraditional settings, such as emergency services, defense, and homeland security, will create many new opportunities for qualified geographers.

Geographers will be needed to analyze or select sites for commercial construction, such as new shopping centers, supermarkets, and industrial parks. There will also be a demand for geographers to work in urban renewal projects, highway programs, real estate development, the telecommunications industry, and environmental planning. Competition for college and university teaching jobs is stiff. Many geographers with graduate degrees seek research and management positions in government and private industry. Others fill nonacademic positions in cartography, health services, climatology, flood management, conservation, and environmental planning.

FOR MORE INFORMATION

For maps, books, journals, and other geography-related materials, contact

American Geographical Society
120 Wall Street, Suite 100
New York, NY 10005-3904
Tel: 212-422-5456
E-mail: AGS@amergeog.org
http://www.amergeog.org

To read the publication Careers in Geography, *visit the AAG's Web site.*

Association of American Geographers (AAG)
1710 16th Street, NW
Washington, DC 20009-3198
Tel: 202-234-1450
http://www.aag.org

For information on how to form a geography club or about the National Geography Challenge, visit the council's Web site.

National Council for Geographic Education
1710 16th Street, NW
Washington, DC 20009-3198
Tel: 202-360-4237
http://www.ncge.org

For information on opportunities for women in geography, contact

Society of Women Geographers
415 East Capitol Street, SE
Washington, DC 20003-3810
Tel: 202-546-9228
E-mail: swghq@verizon.net
http://www.iswg.org

GEOLOGISTS

OVERVIEW

Geologists are geoscientists who study all aspects of the earth, including its origin, history, composition, and structure. Along more practical lines, geologists may, through the use of theoretical knowledge and research data, locate groundwater, oil, minerals, and other natural resources. They play an increasingly important role in studying, preserving, and cleaning up the environment. They advise construction companies and government agencies on the suitability of locations being considered for buildings, highways, and other structures. They also prepare geological reports, maps, and diagrams. According to the U.S. Department of Labor, there are approximately 31,860 geoscientists employed in the United States, which includes geologists, geophysicists, and oceanographers.

SCHOOL SUBJECTS
Earth science, Geography

PERSONAL SKILLS
Helping/teaching, Technical/scientific

MINIMUM EDUCATION LEVEL
Bachelor's degree

CERTIFICATION OR LICENSING
Voluntary (certification),
Required by certain states (licensing)

WORK ENVIRONMENT
Indoors and outdoors,
One location with some travel

THE JOB

The geologist's work includes locating and obtaining physical data and material. This may necessitate the drilling of deep holes to obtain samples, the collection and examination of the materials found on or under the earth's surface, or the use of instruments to measure the earth's gravity and magnetic field. Some geologists may spend three to six months of each year in fieldwork. In laboratory work, geologists carry out studies based on field research. Sometimes working under controlled temperatures or pressures, geologists analyze the chemical and physical properties of geological specimens, such as rock, fossil remains, and soil. Once the data is analyzed and the studies are completed, geologists and geological technicians write reports based on their research.

A wide variety of laboratory instruments are used, including X-ray diffractometers, which determine the crystal structure of minerals, and petrographic microscopes for the study of rock and sediment samples.

Geologists working to protect the environment may design and monitor waste disposal sites, preserve water supplies, and reclaim contaminated land and water to comply with federal environmental regulations.

Geologists often specialize in one of the following disciplines.

Marine geologists study the oceans, including the seabed and subsurface features.

Paleontologists specialize in the study of the earth's rock formations, including remains of plant and animal life, in order to understand the earth's evolution and estimate its age.

Geochronologists are geoscientists who use radioactive dating and other techniques to estimate the age of rock and other samples from an exploration site.

Petroleum geologists attempt to locate natural gas and oil deposits through exploratory testing and study of the data obtained. They recommend the acquisition of new properties and the retention or release of properties already owned by their companies. They also estimate oil reserves and assist petroleum engineers in determining exact production procedures.

Closely related to petroleum geologists are *economic geologists,* who search for new resources of minerals and fuels.

Engineering geologists are responsible for the application of geological knowledge to problems arising in the construction of roads, buildings, bridges, dams, and other structures.

Mineralogists are interested in the classification of minerals composing rocks and mineral deposits. To this end, they examine and analyze the physical and chemi-cal properties of minerals and precious stones to develop data and theories on their origin, occurrence, and possible uses in industry and commerce.

Petrologists study the origin of igneous, metamorphic, and sedimentary rocks.

Stratigraphers study the distribution and relative arrangement of sedimentary rock layers. This enables them to understand evolutionary changes in fossils and plants, which leads to an understanding of successive changes in the distribution of land and sea.

Closely related to stratigraphers are *sedimentologists,* who determine processes and products involved in sedimentary rock formations.

Geohydrologists study the nature and distribution of water within the earth and are often involved in environmental impact studies.

Geomorphologists study the form of the earth's surface and the processes, such as erosion and glaciation, that bring about changes.

Glacial geologists study the physical properties and movement of ice sheets and glaciers.

Volcanologists study volcanoes in an attempt to predict the potential for future eruptions and the impact eruptions may have on the welfare of humans, wildlife, and the environment.

The geologist is far from limited in a choice of work, but a basic knowledge of all sciences is essential in each of these specializations. An increasing number of scientists combine geology with detailed knowledge in another field. *Geochemists,* for example, are concerned with the chemical composition of, and the changes in, minerals and rocks, while planetary geologists apply their knowledge of geology to interpret surface conditions on other planets and the moon.

REQUIREMENTS

High School

Because you will need a college degree in order to find work in this profession, you should take a college preparatory curriculum while in high school. Such a curriculum will include computer science, history, English, and geography classes. Science and math classes are also important to take, particularly earth science, chemistry, and physics. Math classes should include algebra, trigonometry, and statistics.

Postsecondary Training

A bachelor's degree is the minimum requirement for entry into lower-level geology jobs, but a master's degree is usually necessary for beginning positions in research, teaching, and exploration. A person with a strong background in physics, chemistry, mathematics, or computer science may also qualify for some geology jobs. For those wishing to make significant advancements in research and for teaching at the college level, a doctoral degree is required. Those interested in the geological profession should have an aptitude not only for geology but also for physics, chemistry, and mathematics.

A number of colleges, universities, and institutions of technology offer degrees in geology. Programs in geophysical technology, geophysical engineering, geophysical prospecting, and engineering geology also offer related training for beginning geologists.

Traditional geoscience courses emphasize classical geologic methods and concepts. Mineralogy, paleontology, stratigraphy, and structural geology are important courses for undergraduates. Students interested in environmental and regulatory fields should take courses in hydrology, hazardous waste management, environmental legislation, chemistry, fluid mechanics, and geologic logging.

In addition, students should take courses in related sciences, mathematics, English composition, and computer science. Students seeking graduate degrees in geology should concentrate on advanced courses in geology, placing major emphasis on their particular fields.

Certification or Licensing

The American Institute of Professional Geologists (AIPG) grants the certified professional geologist (CPG) designation to geologists who have earned a bachelor's degree or higher in the geological sciences and have eight years of professional experience (applicants with a master's degree need only seven years of professional experience and those with a Ph.D., five years). Candidates must also undergo peer review by three professional geologists (two of whom must be CPGs) and pay an application fee.

The institute also offers the registered member designation to geologists who are registered in various states and are not seeking AIPG certification. Applicants must have at least a bachelor's degree in the geological sciences with at least 30 semester hours of geology, be licensed by the state they wish to work in, undergo peer review, and pay an application fee.

More than 30 states require geologists to be registered or licensed. Most of these states require applicants (who have earned a bachelor's degree in the geological sciences) to pass the Fundamentals of Geology exam, a standardized written exam developed by the Association of State Boards of Geology.

Other Requirements

In addition to academic training and work experience, geologists who work in the field or in administration must have skills in business administration and in working with other people. Computer modeling, data processing, and effective oral and written communication skills are important, as is the ability to think independently and creatively. Experience with geographic information systems and the global positioning system are also important. Physical stamina is needed for those involved in fieldwork.

EXPLORING

If this career sounds interesting, try to read as much as possible about geology and geologists. Your best chance for association with geologists and geological work is to join the clubs or organizations concerned with such things as rock collecting. Amateur geological groups and local museums also offer opportunities for you to gain exposure to the field of geology.

EMPLOYERS

Approximately 31,860 geoscientists (including geologists) are employed in the United States. The majority of geologists are employed in private industry. Some work for oil and gas extraction and mining companies, primarily in exploration. The rest work for business services, environmental and geotechnical consulting firms, or are self-employed as consultants to industry and government. The federal government employs geologists in the Department of the Interior (in the U.S. Geological Survey or the Bureau of Reclamation) and in the Departments of Defense, Agriculture, and Commerce. Geologists also work for state agencies, nonprofit research organizations, and museums. Many geologists hold faculty positions at colleges and universities, and most of these combine their teaching with research.

STARTING OUT

After completing sufficient educational requirements, preferably a master's degree or doctorate, the geologist may look for work in various areas, including private industry and government. For those who wish to teach at the college level, a doctorate is required. College graduates may also take government civil service examinations or possibly find work on state geological surveys, which are sometimes based on civil service competition.

Geologists often begin their careers in field exploration or as research assistants in laboratories. As they gain experience, they are given more difficult assignments and may be promoted to supervisory positions, such as project leader or program manager.

ADVANCEMENT

A geologist with a bachelor's degree has little chance of advancing to higher-level positions. Continued formal training and work experience are necessary, especially as competition for these positions grows more intense. A doctorate is essential for most college or university teaching positions and is preferred for much research work.

EARNINGS

Graduates with a bachelor's degree in the geological sciences earned about $51,778 annually in 2009, according to the National Association of Colleges and Employers.

The U.S. Department of Labor reports that the median annual salary for geoscientists was $81,220 in 2009; the top paid 10 percent earned more than $161,260, while the lowest paid 10 percent earned less than $43,140 a year. In the federal government, the average salary for geologists in managerial, supervisory, and nonsupervisory positions was $94,560 a year in 2009.

Although the petroleum, mineral, and mining industries offer higher salaries, competition for these jobs is stiff and there is less job security than in other areas. In addition, college and university teachers can earn additional income through research, writing, and consulting. Salaries for foreign assignments may be significantly higher than those in the United States.

WORK ENVIRONMENT

Some geologists spend most of their time in a laboratory or office, working a regular 40-hour week in pleasant conditions; others divide their time between fieldwork and office or laboratory work. Those who work in the field often travel to remote sites by helicopter or four-wheel-drive vehicle and cover large areas on foot. They may camp for extended periods of time in primitive conditions with the members of the geological team as their only companions. Exploration geologists often work overseas or in remote areas, and job relocation is not unusual. Marine geologists may spend considerable time at sea.

OUTLOOK

According to the *Occupational Outlook Handbook,* employment of geoscientists, including geologists, is expected to grow faster than the average for all occupations through 2018. Opportunities in the field are expected to be excellent for those with master's degrees, but competition for those with Ph.D.'s wishing to work in research or in university teaching positions will be stiff. Growth should also be strong in the areas of management, scientific, and technical consulting services, increasing the demand for geoscientists who work as consultants.

Additionally, in response to the curtailed petroleum activity in the late 1980s and 1990s, the number of graduates in geology and geophysics, especially petroleum geology, dropped considerably in the last decade. Relative stability has now returned to the petroleum industry, increasing the need for qualified geoscientists. With improved technology and greater demand for energy resources, job opportunities are expected to be good, especially for those with a master's degree and those familiar with computer modeling and the global positioning system. Geologists who are able to speak a foreign language and who are willing to work overseas will also have strong employment prospects. In addition to the oil and gas industries, geologists will be able to find jobs in environmental protection and reclamation.

FOR MORE INFORMATION

For information on geoscience careers, contact
American Geological Institute
4220 King Street
Alexandria, VA 22302-1502
Tel: 703-379-2480
http://www.agiweb.org

For information on careers, certification, and scholarships, contact
American Institute of Professional Geologists
12000 North Washington Street, Suite 285
Thornton, CO 80241-3134
Tel: 303-412-6205
E-mail: aipg@aipg.org
http://www.aipg.org

For career information and profiles of women in geophysics, visit the AWG's Web site.
Association for Women Geoscientists (AWG)
12000 North Washington Street, Suite 285
Thornton, CO 80241-3134

Tel: 303-412-6219
E-mail: office@awg.org
http://www.awg.org

For information on student chapters, contact
**Association of Environmental and Engineering
  Geologists**
PO Box 460518
Denver, CO 80246-0518
Tel: 303-757-2926
E-mail: aeg@aegweb.org
http://aegweb.org

For information on geotechnical engineering, contact
GEOENGINEER
http://www.geoengineer.org

For career information and job listings, contact
Geological Society of America
PO Box 9140
Boulder, CO 80301-9140
Tel: 888-443-4472
E-mail: gsaservice@geosociety.org
http://www.geosociety.org

*For information on the Fundamentals of Geology exam,
contact*
National Association of State Boards of Geology
PO Box 11591
Columbia, SC 29211-1591
Tel: 803-739-5676
http://www.asbog.org

*For career and educational information about the geosci-
ences, visit*
U.S. Geological Survey
http://education.usgs.gov

HEALTH CARE MANAGERS

OVERVIEW

Health care managers, also known as *health services managers* and *health services administrators,* direct the operation of hospitals, nursing homes, and other health care
organizations. They are responsible for facilities, ser-

SCHOOL SUBJECTS
Business, English

PERSONAL SKILLS
Helping/teaching, Leadership/management

MINIMUM EDUCATION LEVEL
Bachelor's degree

CERTIFICATION OR LICENSING
Voluntary (certification),
Required for certain positions (licensing)

WORK ENVIRONMENT
Primarily indoors, One location with some travel

---

vices, programs, staff, budgets, and relations with other
organizations. There are approximately 271,710 health
care managers employed in the United States.

THE JOB

Health care managers of hospitals and health care facilities organize and manage personnel, equipment, and
auxiliary services. They hire and supervise personnel,
handle budgets and fee schedules charged to patients,
and establish billing procedures. In addition, they help
plan space needs, purchase supplies and equipment, oversee building and equipment maintenance, and arrange
mail, phones, laundry, and other services for patients
and staff. In large health care institutions, many of these
duties are delegated to assistants or to various department heads. These assistants may supervise operations in
such clinical areas as surgery, nursing, dietary, or therapy
and in such administrative areas as purchasing, finance,
housekeeping, and maintenance. In smaller health care
institutions, health care managers and administrators are
responsible for managing daily operations.

The health services administrator, or *clinical manager,*
works closely with the institution's governing board in
the development of plans and policies. Following the
board's directions, the administrator may carry out large
projects that expand and develop hospital services. Such
projects include organizing fund-raising campaigns and
planning new research projects. *Health information managers* maintain and secure patient records.

Health services managers meet regularly with their staffs to discuss departmental goals and to address problems. Managers may organize training programs for nurses, interns, and others in cooperation with the medical staff and department heads. Health care executives also represent the health care facility at community or professional meetings.

REQUIREMENTS

High School

Prepare for a career in health management by taking college preparatory classes. Communication skills are important, so be sure to take as many speech and writing classes as possible. Courses in health, business, mathematics, and computer science are also excellent choices.

Postsecondary Training

The training required to qualify for this work depends, to a large extent, on the qualifications established by the individual employer or a facility's governing board. Most employers prefer people with a graduate degree in health services administration. A few require that their chief executives be physicians, while others look for people with formal training in law or general business administration as well as experience in the health care field. The future health care administrator may have a liberal arts foundation with a strong background in the social sciences or business economics.

Specialized training in health services administration is offered at both graduate and undergraduate levels. The graduate program generally takes two years to complete. Graduate students split their time between studying in the classroom and working as an administrative resident in a program-approved health care facility. Successful completion of the course work, the residency, and perhaps a thesis is required to earn the master's degree. An optional third-year fellowship provides additional work experience supervised by a mentor. During this period, the individual may work in various hospital departments as an assistant to department heads.

Certification or Licensing

The American College of Health Care Administrators (ACHCA) offers voluntary certification to nursing home and assisted living administrators who meet educational and work experience requirements and pass an exami-nation. Certification must be renewed every five years. Contact the ACHCA for more information.

Additionally, the American College of Health-care Executives (ACHE) offers the fellow designation (FACHE) to candidates who pass an examination and meet other requirements. Contact the ACHE for more information.

Licensure is not a requirement for health care services executives employed in hospitals. However, all states require nursing home administrators to be licensed. Most states use the licensing exam prepared by the National Association of Long Term Care Administrator Boards. Because requirements vary from state to state, those considering careers in nursing home administration should contact their state's licensing body for specific licensure requirements. Also, it should be noted that continuing education is now a condition of licensure in most states.

Other Requirements

Much of the work of health services managers consists of dealing with people—the hospital's governing board, the medical staff, the department heads and other employees, the patients and their families, and community leaders and businesses. Therefore, health care managers must be tactful and sympathetic.

In addition, administrators must be able to coordinate the health care facility's many related functions. They need to understand, for instance, financial operations, purchasing, organizational development, and public relations. They must also have the ability to make some decisions with speed and others with considerable study. And, of course, health services executives should have a deep interest in the care of sick and injured patients.

Special hospitals, such as mental hospitals, often employ administrators who are physicians in the facility's specialty.

EXPLORING

If you are considering a career as a health services manager, you should take advantage of opportunities in high school to develop some of the skills required in this line of work. Because administrators and other health care executives need strong leadership and communication skills, participation in clubs as a leader or active member and in debate and speech clubs is helpful. Working in your school's health center is also useful. Hospitals, nursing homes, and other health service facilities offer part-time work after school, on weekends, and during

SCHOOL SUBJECTS

Mathematics, Technical/shop

PERSONAL SKILLS

Following instructions, Mechanical/manipulative

MINIMUM EDUCATION LEVEL

High school diploma, Apprenticeship

CERTIFICATION OR LICENSING

Required for certain positions

WORK ENVIRONMENT

Indoors and outdoors, Primarily multiple locations

factories, restaurants, offices, apartment buildings, and private homes. They may work to provide temperature-sensitive products such as computers, foods, medicines, and precision instruments with climate-controlled environments. They may also provide comfortable environments or refrigeration in such modes of transportation as ships, trucks, planes, and trains. There are approximately 244,410 heating and cooling technicians employed in the United States.

THE JOB

Many industries today depend on carefully controlled temperature and humidity conditions while manufacturing, transporting, or storing their products. Many common foods are readily available only because of extensive refrigeration. Less obviously, numerous chemicals, drugs, explosives, oil, and other products our society uses must be produced using refrigeration processes. For example, some room-sized computer systems need to be kept at a certain temperature and humidity; spacecraft must be able to withstand great heat while exposed to the rays of the sun and great cold when the moon or earth blocks the sun, and at the same time maintain a steady internal environment; the air in tractor trailer cabs must be regulated so that truck drivers can spend long hours behind the wheel in maximum comfort and safety. Each of these applications represents a different segment of a large and very diverse industry.

Heating and cooling technicians may work in installation and maintenance (which includes service and repairs), sales, or manufacturing. The majority of technicians who work in installation and maintenance work

for heating and cooling contractors; manufacturers of air-conditioning, refrigeration, and heating equipment; dealers and distributors; or utility companies.

Technicians who assemble and install air-conditioning, refrigeration, and heating systems and equipment work from blueprints. Experienced technicians read blueprints that show them how to assemble components and how the components should be installed into the structure. Because structure sizes and climate-control specifications vary, technicians have to pay close attention to blueprint details. While working from the blueprints, technicians use algebra and geometry to calculate the sizes and contours of duct work as they assemble it.

Heating and cooling technicians work with a variety of hardware, tools, and components. For example, in joining pipes and duct work for an air-conditioning system, technicians may use soldering, welding, or brazing equipment, as well as sleeves, couplings, and elbow joints. Technicians handle and assemble such components as motors, thermometers, burners, compressors, pumps, and fans. They must join these parts together when building climate-control units and then connect this equipment to the duct work, refrigerant lines, and power source.

As a final step in assembly and installation, technicians run tests on equipment to ensure that it functions properly. If the equipment is malfunctioning, technicians must investigate in order to diagnose the problem and determine a solution. At this time, they adjust thermostats, reseal piping, and replace parts as needed. They retest the equipment to determine whether the problem has been remedied, and they continue to modify and test it until everything checks out as functioning properly.

Some technicians may specialize in only one type of cooling, heating, or refrigeration equipment, such as *window air-conditioning unit installers and servicers,* who work on window units only. *Air-conditioning and refrigeration technicians* install and service central air-conditioning systems and a variety of refrigeration equipment. Air-conditioning installations may range from small wall units, either water- or air-cooled, to large central plant systems. Commercial refrigeration equipment may include display cases, walk-in coolers, and frozen-food units such as those in supermarkets, restaurants, and food processing plants.

Other technicians are *furnace installers,* also called *heating-equipment installers.* Following blueprints and other specifications, they install oil, gas, electric, solid fuel (such as coal), and multifuel heating systems. They move the new furnace into place and attach fuel supply lines, air ducts, pumps, and other components. Then they connect the electrical wiring and thermostatic controls and, finally, check the unit for proper operation.

Technicians who work in maintenance perform routine service to keep systems operating efficiently and respond to service calls for repairs. They perform tests and diagnose problems on equipment that has been installed in the past. They calibrate controls, add fluids, change parts, clean components, and test the system for proper operation. For example, in performing a routine service call on a furnace, technicians will adjust blowers and burners, replace filters, clean ducts, and check thermometers and other controls.

Technicians who maintain oil- and gas-burning equipment are called *oil-burner mechanics* and *gas-burner mechanics,* or *gas-appliance servicers.* They usually perform more extensive maintenance work during the warm weather, when the heating system can be shut down. During the summer, technicians replace oil and air filters; vacuum vents, ducts, and other parts that accumulate soot and ash; and adjust the burner so that it achieves maximum operating efficiency. Gas-burner mechanics may also repair other gas appliances such as cooking stoves, clothes dryers, water heaters, outdoor lights, and grills.

Other heating and cooling technicians who specialize in a limited range of equipment include *evaporative cooler installers, hot-air furnace installers-and-repairers, solar-energy system installers and helpers,* and *air and hydronic balancing technicians, radiant heating installers,* and *geothermal heating and cooling technicians.*

In their work on refrigerant lines and air ducts, heating and cooling technicians use a variety of hand and power tools, including hammers, wrenches, metal snips, electric drills, measurement gauges, pipe cutters and benders, and acetylene torches. To check electrical circuits, burners, and other components, technicians work with volt-ohm meters, manometers, and other testing devices.

REQUIREMENTS
High School

In high school, students considering the heating and cooling field should take algebra, geometry, English composition, physics, computer applications and programming, and classes in industrial arts or shop. Helpful shop classes include mechanical drawing and blueprint reading, power and hand tools operations, and metalwork. Shop courses in electricity and electronics provide a strong introduction into understanding circuitry and

wiring and teach students to read electrical diagrams. Classes in computer-aided design are also helpful, as are business courses.

Postsecondary Training

Although postsecondary training is not mandatory to become a heating and cooling technician, employers prefer to hire technicians who have training from a technical school, junior college, or apprenticeship program. Vocational-technical schools, private trade schools, and junior colleges offer both one- and two-year programs. Graduates of two-year programs usually receive an associate's degree in science or in applied science. Certificates, rather than degrees, are awarded to those who complete one-year programs. Although no formal education is required, most employers prefer to hire graduates of two-year applications-oriented training programs. This kind of training includes a strong background in mathematical and engineering theory. The emphasis is on the practical uses of such theories, however, and not on explorations of their origins and development, such as one finds in engineering programs. The following organizations accredit heating and cooling technology programs: HVAC Excellence, the National Center for Construction Education and Research, and the Partnership for Air Conditioning, Heating, Refrigeration Accreditation.

Formal apprenticeship programs typically last three to five years and combine classroom education with on-the-job training. Programs are offered by local chapters of the following organizations: Air Conditioning Contractors of America, Mechanical Contractors Association of America, Plumbing-Heating-Cooling Contractors Association, Sheet Metal Workers International Association, United Association of Journeymen and Apprentices of the Plumbing and Pipe Fitting Industry of the United States and Canada, Associated Builders and Contractors Inc., and National Association of Home Builders.

Certification or Licensing

Voluntary certification for various specialties is available through professional associations. The heating and cooling industry offers a standard certification program for experienced technicians. The program is available to both installation and service technicians and is offered by North American Technician Excellence Inc. Technicians must take and pass a core exam (covering safety, tools, soft skills, principles of heat transfer, and electrical systems) and one specialty exam of their choice (covering installation and service). The specialties available are air-conditioning, air distribution, gas heating, heat pumps, hydronics, oil heating, commercial refrigeration, and HVAC efficiency analyst (senior level). Technicians who become certified as a service technician are automatically certified as an installation technician without additional testing. Certification must be renewed every five years.

The Refrigerating Engineers and Technicians Association offers the certified assistant refrigeration operator and certified industrial refrigeration operator designations to heating and cooling technicians who specialize in industrial plant refrigeration. Contact the association for more information. The Air-Conditioning, Heating, and Refrigeration Institute offers certification to technicians who work for the Environmental Protection Agency. HVAC Excellence offers certification to professionals at a variety of skill levels.

Technicians who handle refrigerants must receive approved refrigerant recovery certification, which is a requirement of the Environmental Protection Agency (EPA) and requires passing a special examination. The following certifications levels are available: Type I (servicing small appliances), Type II (high-pressure refrigerants), and Type III (low-pressure refrigerants). Exams are administered by unions, trade schools, and contractor associations approved by the EPA.

In some areas of the field, such as those who work with design and research engineers, certification is increasingly the norm and viewed as a basic indicator of competence. Even where there are no firm requirements, it generally is better to be qualified for whatever license or certification is available.

Other Requirements

Persons interested in the heating and cooling field need to have an aptitude for working with tools, manual dexterity and manipulation, and the desire to perform challenging work that requires a high level of competence and quality. Students who are interested in how things work, who enjoy taking things apart and putting them back together, and who enjoy troubleshooting for mechanical and electrical problems may enjoy a career in air-conditioning, refrigeration, and heating.

EXPLORING

A student trying to decide on a career in heating and cooling technology may have to base the choice on a variety of indirect evidence. Part-time or summer work is usually not available to high school students because of their lack of the necessary skills and knowledge. It may be possible, however, to arrange field trips to service shops, companies that develop and produce heating and cooling equipment, or other firms concerned with the environmental control field. Such visits can provide a firsthand overview of the day-to-day work. A visit with a local contractor or to a school that conducts a heating and cooling technology training program can also be very helpful.

EMPLOYERS

Approximately 244,410 heating and cooling technicians are employed in the United States. While most heating and cooling technicians work directly with the building, installation, and maintenance of equipment via heating and cooling firms, some technicians work in equipment sales. These technicians are usually employed by manufacturers or dealers and distributors and are hired to explain the equipment and its operation to prospective customers. These technicians must have a thorough knowledge of their products. They may explain newly developed equipment, ideas, and principles, or assist dealers and distributors in the layout and installation of unfamiliar components. Some technicians employed as sales representatives contact prospective buyers and help them plan air-conditioning, refrigeration, and heating systems. They help the client select appropriate equipment and estimate costs.

Other technicians work for manufacturers in engineering or research laboratories, performing many of the same assembling and testing duties as technicians who work for contractors. They perform these operations at the manufacturing site, however, rather than traveling to work sites as most contractors' technicians do. Technicians aid engineers in research, equipment design, and equipment testing. Technicians in a research laboratory may plan the requirements for the various stages of fabricating, installing, and servicing climate-control and refrigeration systems; recommend appropriate equipment to meet specified needs; and calculate heating and cooling capacities of proposed equipment units. They may also conduct operational tests on experimental models and efficiency tests on new units coming off the production lines. They might also investigate the cause of breakdowns reported by customers, and determine the reasons and solutions.

Engineering-oriented technicians employed by manufacturers may perform tests of new equipment, or assist engineers in fundamental research and development, technical report writing, and application engineering.

Other engineering technicians serve as *liaison representatives,* coordinating the design and production engineering for the development and manufacture of new products.

Technicians may also be employed by utility companies to help ensure that their customers' equipment is using energy efficiently and effectively. *Utility technicians,* often called *energy conservation technicians,* may conduct energy evaluations of customers' systems, compile energy surveys, and provide customer information.

Technicians may also work for consulting firms, such as engineering firms or building contractors who hire technicians to estimate costs, determine air-conditioning and heating load requirements, and prepare specifications for climate-control projects.

Large institutions such as hospitals, universities, factories, office complexes, and sports arenas may employ heating and cooling technicians directly, maintaining their own climate-control staffs.

Some technicians also open up their own businesses, either as heating and cooling contractors or consultants specializing in sales, parts supply, service, and installation.

STARTING OUT

Many students in two-year programs work at a job related to their area of training during the summer between the first and second years. Their employers may hire them on a part-time basis during the second year and make offers of full-time employment after graduation. Even if such a job offer cannot be made, the employer may be aware of other companies that are hiring and help the student with suggestions and recommendations, provided the student has a solid work record.

Some schools make work experience part of the curriculum, particularly during the latter part of their program. This is a valuable way for students to gain practical experience in conjunction with classroom work.

It is not unusual for graduates of two-year programs to receive several offers of employment, either from contacts they have made themselves or from companies that routinely recruit new graduates. Representatives of larger companies often schedule interview periods at schools with two-year air-conditioning, refrigeration, and heating technician programs. Other, usually smaller, prospective employers may contact specific faculty advisors who in turn make students aware of opportunities that arise.

In addition to using their schools' career services office, resourceful students can independently explore other leads by applying directly to local heating and cooling contractors; sales, installation, and service shops; or manufacturers of air-conditioning, refrigeration, and heating equipment. State employment offices may also post openings or provide job leads. Finally, student membership in the local chapter of a trade association, such as one of those listed at the end of this article, will often result in good employment contacts.

ADVANCEMENT

There is such a wide range of positions within this field that workers who gain the necessary skills and experience have the flexibility to choose between many different options and types of positions. As employees gain on-the-job work experience, they may decide to specialize in a particular aspect or type of work. They may be able to be promoted into positions requiring more responsibilities and skills through experience and demonstrated proficiency, but in some cases additional training is required.

Many workers continue to take courses throughout their careers to upgrade their skills and to learn new techniques and methods used within the industry. Training can take the form of a class offered by a manufacturer regarding specific equipment or it may be a more extensive program resulting in certification for a specific area or procedure. Skill-improvement programs that offer advanced training in specialized areas are available through vocational-technical institutes and trade associations. Technicians with an interest in the engineering aspect of the industry may go back to school to get a bachelor of science degree in heating and cooling engineering or mechanical engineering.

Technicians increase their value to employers and themselves with continued training. For example, a technician employed by a manufacturer may progress to the position of *sales manager,* who acts as liaison with distributors and dealers, promoting and selling the manufacturer's products, or to a *field service representative,* who solves unusual service problems of dealers and distributors in the area. Technicians working for dealers and distributors or contractors may advance to a *service manager* or supervisory position, overseeing other technicians who install and service equipment. Another possible specialization is mechanical design, which involves designing piping, ductwork, controls, and the distribution systems for consulting engineers, mechanical contractors, manufacturers, and distributors. Technicians who do installation and maintenance may decide to move into sales or work for the research and development department of a manufacturing company.

Some technicians also open up their own businesses, becoming heating and cooling contractors, consultants, self-employed service technicians, or specializing in sales and parts distribution.

EARNINGS

The earnings of heating and cooling technicians vary widely according to the level of training and experience, the nature of their work, type of employer, region of the country, and other factors. Heating and cooling technicians had median hourly earnings of $19.76 (or $41,100 annually) in 2009, according to the U.S. Department of Labor. The lowest paid 10 percent earned less than $12.38 (or $25,750 annually), while the top paid 10 percent earned more than $31.53 (or $65,580 annually).

Heating and cooling apprentices usually earn about 50 percent of the wage rate paid to experienced workers. This percentage rises as apprentices gain experience and skill training in the field.

Many employers offer medical insurance and paid vacation days, holidays, and sick days, although the actual benefits vary from employer to employer. Some companies also offer tuition assistance for additional training.

WORK ENVIRONMENT

Working conditions for heating and cooling technicians vary considerably depending on the area of the industry in which they work. For the most part, the hours are regular, although certain jobs in production may involve shift work, and service technicians may have to be on call some evenings and weekends to handle emergency repairs.

Technicians who work in installation and service may work in a variety of environments ranging from industrial plants to construction sites and can include both indoor and outdoor work. Technicians may encounter extremes in temperature when servicing outdoor and rooftop equipment and cramped quarters when servicing indoor commercial and industrial equipment. They often have to lift heavy objects as well as stoop, crawl, and crouch when making repairs and installations. Working conditions can include dirt, grease, noise, and safety hazards such as falls from rooftops or scaffolds, electric shocks, burns, and handling refrigerants and compressed gases. With proper precautions and safety measures, however, risks can be minimized.

Technicians who work in laboratories usually work in the research and development departments of a manufacturing firm or an industrial plant. Technicians employed by distributors, dealers, and consulting engineers usually work in an office or similar surroundings and are subject to the same benefits and conditions as other office workers. Some technicians, such as sales representatives or service managers, go out periodically to visit customers or installation and service sites.

OUTLOOK

Employment in the heating and cooling field is expected to increase much faster than the average for all occupations through 2018, according to the U.S. Department of Labor. Some openings will occur when experienced workers retire or transfer to other work. Other openings will be generated because of a demand for new climate-control systems for residences and industrial and commercial users. The DOL reports that residential HVACR systems need to be replaced every 10 to 15 years, which means that a large number of homes recently built will need replacement systems by 2018. In addition, many existing systems are being upgraded to provide more efficient use of energy and to provide benefits not originally built into the system. There is a growing emphasis on improving indoor air and making equipment more environmentally friendly. Systems that use chlorofluorocarbons (CFCs) need to be retrofitted or replaced with new equipment, since regulations banning CFC production became effective in 2000. In addition, more people are concerned about improving indoor air quality, which could also lead to more jobs for heating and cooling technicians.

Comfort is only one of the major reasons for environmental control. Conditioned atmosphere is a necessity in any precision industry where temperature and humidity can affect fine tolerances. As products and processes become more complex and more highly automated, the need for closely controlled conditions becomes increasingly important. For example, electronics manufacturers must keep the air bone-dry for many parts of the production processes to prevent damage to parts and to maintain nonconductivity. Pharmaceutical and food manufacturers rely on pure, dirt-free air. High-speed multicolor printing requires temperature control of rollers and moisture control for the paper racing through the presses. There is every reason to expect that these and other sophisticated industries will rely more in the coming years on precision control of room conditions. The actual amount of industry growth for these applications will hinge on the overall health of the nation's economy and the rate of manufacturing.

Technicians who are involved in maintenance and repair are not as affected by the economy as workers in some other jobs. Whereas in bad economic times a consumer may postpone building a new house or installing a new air-conditioning system, hospitals, restaurants, technical industries, and public buildings will still require skilled technicians to maintain their climate-control systems. Technicians who are versed in more than one aspect of the job have greater job flexibility and can count on fairly steady work despite any fluctuations in the economy.

FOR MORE INFORMATION

For information on certification and publications, contact
Air-Conditioning, Heating, and Refrigeration Institute
2111 Wilson Boulevard, Suite 500
Arlington, VA 22201-3001
Tel: 703-524-8800
E-mail: ahri@ahri.org
http://www.ahrinet.org

For information on careers and educational programs, contact
Air Conditioning Contractors of America
2800 Shirlington Road, Suite 300
Arlington, VA 22206-3607
Tel: 703-575-4477
http://www.acca.org

For information on careers, contact
American Society of Heating, Refrigerating and Air-Conditioning Engineers Inc.
1791 Tullie Circle, NE
Atlanta, GA 30329-2305
Tel: 800-527-4723
E-mail: ashrae@ashrae.org
http://www.ashrae.org

For information on accredited programs and certification, contact
HVAC Excellence
PO Box 491
Mt. Prospect, IL 60056-0491
Tel: 800-394-5268
http://www.hvacexcellence.org

For information on certification programs, contact
North American Technician Excellence Inc.
2111 Wilson Boulevard, Suite 510

Arlington, VA 22201-3051
Tel: 877-420-NATE
http://www.natex.org

For information on accredited training programs, contact
Partnership for Air-Conditioning, Heating, Refrigeration Accreditation
2111 Wilson Boulevard, Suite 500
Arlington, VA 22201-3001
http://www.pahrahvacr.org

For information on union membership, contact
Plumbing-Heating-Cooling Contractors Association
PO Box 6808
180 South Washington Street
Falls Church, VA 22046-2900
Tel: 800-533-7694
E-mail: naphcc@naphcc.org
http://www.phccweb.org

For information on industrial plant refrigeration certification, contact
Refrigerating Engineers & Technicians Association
PO Box 1819
Salinas, CA 93902-1819
Tel: 831-455-8783
E-mail: info@reta.com
http://www.reta.com

For information on heating and cooling and the sheet metal industry, contact
Sheet Metal and Air Conditioning Contractors' National Association
4201 Lafayette Center Drive
Chantilly, VA 20151-1209
Tel: 703-803-2980
E-mail: info@smacna.org
http://www.smacna.org

HOME HEALTH CARE AIDES

OVERVIEW

Home health care aides, also known as *home health aides* or *home attendants,* serve elderly and infirm persons by visiting them in their homes and caring for them. Working under the supervision of nurses or social workers, they perform various household chores that clients are unable to perform for themselves as well as attend to patients' personal needs. Although they work primarily with the elderly, home health care aides also attend to clients with disabilities or those needing help with small children. There are approximately 955,220 home health aides employed in the United States.

THE JOB

Home health care aides enable elderly persons to stay in their own homes. For some clients, just a few visits a week are enough to help them look after themselves. Although physically demanding, the work is often emotionally rewarding. Home care aides may not have access to equipment and facilities such as those found in hospitals, but they also don't have the hospital's frantic pace. Home care aides are expected to take the time to get to know their clients and their individual needs. They perform their duties within the client's home environment, which is often a much better atmosphere than the impersonal rooms of a hospital.

In addition to the elderly, home health care aides assist people of any age who are recovering at home following hospitalization. Aides may be trained to supply care to people suffering from specific illnesses such as AIDS, Alzheimer's disease, or cancer, or patients with developmental disabilities who lack sufficient daily living skills.

Clients unable to feed themselves may depend on home care aides to shop for food, prepare their meals, feed them, and clean up after meals. Likewise, home health care aides may assist clients in dressing and grooming, including washing, bathing, cleaning teeth and nails, and fixing the clients' hair.

Massages, alcohol rubs, whirlpool baths, and other therapies and treatments may be a part of a client's required care. Home health care aides may work closely with a physician or home nurse in giving medications and dietary supplements and helping with exercises and other therapies. They may check pulses, temperatures, and respiration rates. Occasionally, they may change nonsterile dressings, use special equipment such as a hydraulic lift, or assist with braces or artificial limbs.

Home health care aides working in home care agencies are supervised by a registered nurse, physical therapist, or social worker who assigns them specific duties. Aides report changes in patients' conditions to the supervisor or case manager.

Household chores are often another aspect of the home health care aide's responsibilities. Light housekeeping, such as changing and washing bed linens, doing the laundry and ironing, and dusting, may be necessary. When a home care aide looks after the children of a parent who is disabled or recently discharged from a hospital, work may include making lunches for the children, helping them with their homework, or providing companionship and adult supervision in the evening.

Personal attention and comfort are important aspects of an aide's care. Home health care aides can provide this support by reading to children, playing checkers or a computer game, or visiting with an elderly client. Often just listening to a client's personal problems will help the client through the day. Because elderly people do not always have the means to venture out alone, a home health care aide may accompany an ambulatory patient to the park for an afternoon stroll or to the physician's office for an appointment.

REQUIREMENTS

High School

Many home health care programs require only a high school diploma for entry-level positions. Previous or additional course work in home economics, cooking, sewing, and meal planning are very helpful, as are courses that focus on family living and home nursing.

Postsecondary Training

Health care agencies usually focus their training on first aid, hygiene, and the principles of health care. Cooking

---

SCHOOL SUBJECTS

Family and consumer science, Health

PERSONAL SKILLS

Following instructions, Helping/teaching

MINIMUM EDUCATION LEVEL

High school diploma

CERTIFICATION OR LICENSING

Required for certain positions

WORK ENVIRONMENT

Primarily indoors, Primarily multiple locations

and nutrition, including meal preparation for patients with specific dietary needs, are often included in the program. Home health care aides may take courses in psychology and child development as well as family living. Because of the need for hands-on work, aides usually learn how to bathe, dress, and feed patients as well as how to help them walk upstairs or get up from bed. The more specific the skill required for certain patients, the more likely an agency is to have comprehensive instruction.

Most agencies will offer free training to prospective employees. Such training may include instruction on how to deal with depressed or reluctant patients, how to prepare easy and nutritious meals, and tips on housekeeping. Specific course work on health and sanitation may also be required.

Certification or Licensing

Home Care University, a subsidiary of the National Association for Home Care and Hospice, offers the home care aide certification to applications who complete educational and skill requirements and pass a written examination. Contact the association for more information.

The federal government has enacted guidelines for home health aides whose employers receive reimbursement from Medicare. Federal law requires home health aides to pass a competency test covering 12 areas: communication skills; observation, reporting, and documentation of patient status and care provided; reading and recording vital signs; basic infection control procedures; basic elements of body functions and changes; maintenance of a clean, safe, and healthy environment; recognition of and procedures for emergency procedures; physical, emotional, and developmental characteristics of patients; personal hygiene and grooming; safe transfer techniques; normal range of motion and positioning; and basic nutrition.

Federal law suggests at least 75 hours of classroom and practical training supervised by a registered nurse. Training and testing programs may be offered by the employing agency, but they must meet the standards of the Centers for Medicare and Medicaid Services. Training programs vary depending upon state regulations.

Other Requirements

Caring for people in their own homes can be physically demanding work. Lifting a client for baths and exercise, helping a client up and down stairs, performing housework, and aiding with physical therapy all require that an aide be in good physical condition. Aides do not have the

equipment and facilities of a hospital to help them with their work, and this requires adaptability and ingenuity. Oftentimes they must make do with the resources available in a typical home.

An even temperament and a willingness to serve others are important characteristics for home health care aides. People in this occupation should be friendly, patient, sensitive to others' needs, and tactful. At times an aide will have to be stern in dealing with uncooperative patients or calm and understanding with those who are angry, confused, despondent, or in pain. Genuine warmth and respect for others are important attributes. Cheerfulness and a sense of humor can go a long way in establishing a good relationship with a client, and a good relationship can make working with the client much easier.

Home health care aides must be willing to follow instructions and abide by the health plan created for each patient. Aides provide an important outreach service, supporting the care administered by the patient's physician, therapist, or social worker. They are not trained medical personnel, however, and must know the limits of their authority.

EXPLORING

Home health care aides are employed in many different areas. Interested students can learn more about the work by contacting local agencies and programs that provide home care services and requesting information on the organization's employment guidelines or training programs. Visiting the county or city health department and contacting the personnel director may provide useful information as well. Often, local organizations sponsor open houses to inform the community about the services they provide. This could serve as an excellent opportunity to meet the staff involved in hiring and program development and to learn about job opportunities. In addition, it may be possible to arrange to accompany a home health care aide on a home visit.

EMPLOYERS

Approximately 955,220 home health aides are employed in the United States. The primary employers of home health care aides are local social service agencies that provide home care services. Such agencies often have training programs for prospective employees. Home health care aides might also find employment with hospitals that operate their own community outreach programs. Most hospitals, however, hire home health care aides through agencies.

STARTING OUT

Some social service agencies enlist the aid of volunteers. By contacting agencies and inquiring about such openings, aspiring home care aides can get an introduction to the type of work this profession requires. Also, many agencies or nursing care facilities offer free training to prospective employees.

Exploring the Internet for agencies that provide health care to the aged and disabled or family service organizations can provide a list of employment prospects. Nursing homes, public and private health care facilities, and local chapters of the Red Cross and United Way are likely to hire entry-level employees. The National Association for Home Care and Hospice can also supply information on reputable agencies and departments that employ home care aides.

ADVANCEMENT

As home health care aides develop their skills and deepen their experience, they may advance to management or supervisory positions. Those who find greater enjoyment working with clients may branch into more specialized care and pursue additional training. Additional experience and education often bring higher pay and increased responsibility.

Aides who wish to work in a clinic or hospital setting may return to school to complete a nursing degree. Other related occupations include social worker, physical or occupational therapist, and dietitian. Along with a desire for advancement, however, must come the willingness to meet additional education and experience requirements.

EARNINGS

Earnings for home health care aides are comparable to the salaries of nursing and psychiatric aides and nurse assistants. Depending on the agency, considerable flexibility exists in working hours and patient load. For many aides who begin as part-time employees, the starting salary is usually the minimum hourly wage. For full-time aides with significant training or experience, earnings may be around $10 to $15 per hour. According to the U.S. Department of Labor, median hourly earnings of home health aides were $9.85 ($20,480 annually) in 2009. Wages ranged from less than $7.67 to more than $14.13 an hour ($15,950 to $29,390 annually).

Aides are usually paid only for the time worked in the home. They normally are not paid for travel time between jobs.

Vacation policies and benefits packages vary with the type and size of the employing agency. Many full-time home health care aides receive one week of paid vacation following their first year of employment, and they often receive two weeks of paid vacation each year thereafter. Full-time aides may also be eligible for health insurance and retirement benefits. Some agencies also offer holiday or overtime compensation.

WORK ENVIRONMENT

Health aides in a hospital or nursing home setting work at a much different pace and in a much different environment than the home health care aide. With home care, aides can take the time to sit with their clients and get to know them. Aides spend a certain amount of time with each client and can perform their responsibilities without the frequent distractions and demands of a hospital. Home surroundings differ from situation to situation. Some homes are neat and pleasant, while others are untidy and depressing. Some patients are angry, abusive, depressed, or otherwise difficult; others are pleasant and cooperative.

Because home health care aides usually have more than one patient, the hours an aide works can fluctuate based on the number of clients and types of services needed. Many clients may be ill or have disabilities. Some may be elderly and have no one else to assist them with light housekeeping or daily errands. These differences can dictate the type of responsibilities a home care aide has for each patient.

Working with the infirm or people with disabilities can be a rewarding experience as aides enhance the quality of their clients' lives with their help and company. However, the personal strains—on the clients as well as the aides—can make the work challenging and occasionally frustrating. There can be difficult emotional demands that aides may find exhausting. Considerable physical activity is involved in this line of work, such as helping patients to walk, dress, or take care of themselves. Traveling from one home to another and running various errands for patients can also be tiring and time-consuming, or it can be a pleasant break.

OUTLOOK

As government and private agencies develop more programs to assist the dependent, the need for home health care aides will continue to grow. Because of the physical and emotional demands of the job, there is high turnover and, therefore, frequent job openings for home health care aides.

Also, the number of people 70 years of age and older is expected to increase substantially in the next decade, and many of them will require at least some home care. Rising health care costs are causing many insurance companies to consider alternatives to hospital treatment, which is why many insurance providers now cover home care services. In addition, hospitals and nursing homes are trying to balance the demand for their services and their limitations in staff and physical facilities. The availability of home health care aides can allow such institutions as hospitals and nursing homes to offer quality care to more people. The U.S. Department of Labor projects that employment of home health aides will grow much faster than the average through 2018.

FOR MORE INFORMATION

For certification information and statistics on the home health care industry, visit

National Association for Home Care and Hospice
228 Seventh Street, SE
Washington, DC 20003-4306
Tel: 202-547-7424
http://www.nahc.org

For information on caring for the elderly, visit
ElderWeb
http://www.elderweb.com

For health care job listings and other resources, visit
Health Care Jobs
http://www.healthcarejobs.org/

HUMAN SERVICES WORKERS

OVERVIEW

Under the supervision of social workers, psychologists, sociologists, and other professionals, *human services workers* offer support to families, the elderly, the poor, and others in need. They teach life and communication skills to people in mental health facilities or substance abuse programs. Employed by agencies, shelters, halfway houses, and hospitals, they work individually with clients or in group counseling. They also direct clients

---

SCHOOL SUBJECTS
Health, Sociology

PERSONAL SKILLS
Communication/ideas, Helping/teaching

MINIMUM EDUCATION LEVEL
Some postsecondary training

CERTIFICATION OR LICENSING
May be required for some positions

WORK ENVIRONMENT
Primarily indoors, Primarily one location

---

to social services and benefits. There are approximately 344,050 human services workers employed in the United States.

THE JOB

A group of teenagers in a large high school are concerned about the violence that threatens them every day. They have seen their friends and classmates hurt in the school's hallways, on the basketball court, and in the parking lot. In a place built for their education, they fear for their safety, and each of them has something to say about it. They have something to say to the administration, to the parents, and, most of all, to the kids who carry guns and knives to school. Human services workers come to their aid. Human services workers step in to support the efforts of social workers, psychologists, and other professional agencies or programs. Human services workers may work in a school, a community center, a housing project, or a hospital. They may work as aides, assistants, technicians, or counselors. In the case of the high school students who want to improve conditions in their school, human services workers serve as group leaders under the supervision of a *school social worker,* meeting with some of the students to discuss their fears and concerns. They also meet with administrators, faculty, and parents. Eventually, they conduct a school-wide series of group discussions—listening, taking notes, offering advice, and most important, empowering people to better their communities and their lives.

The term "human services" covers a wide range of careers, from counseling prison inmates to counseling the families of murder victims; from helping someone with a disability find a job to caring for the child of a teenage mother during the school day. From one-on-one interaction to group interaction, from paperwork to footwork, the human services worker is focused on improving the lives of others.

As society changes, so do the concerns of human services workers. New societal problems (such as the rapid spread of AIDS among teenagers and the threat of gang violence) require special attention, as do changes in the population (such as the increasing number of elderly people living on their own and the increasing number of minimum-wage workers unable to fully provide for their families). New laws and political movements also affect human services workers because many social service programs rely heavily on federal and state aid. Although government policy makers are better educated than the policy makers of years past, social service programs are more threatened than ever before. Despite all these changes in society and the changes in the theories of social work, some things stay the same—human services workers care about the well-being of individuals and communities. They are sensitive to the needs of diverse groups of people, and they are actively involved in meeting the needs of the public.

Human services workers have had many of the same responsibilities throughout the years. They offer their clients counseling, representation, emotional support, and the services they need. Although some human services workers assist professionals with the development and evaluation of social programs, policy analysis, and other administrative duties, most work directly with clients.

This direct work can involve aid to specific populations, such as ethnic groups, women, and the poor. Many human services workers assist poor people in numerous ways. They interview clients to identify needed services. They care for clients' children during job or medical appointments and offer clients emotional support. They determine whether clients are eligible for food stamps, Medicaid, or other welfare programs. In some food stamp programs, aides advise low-income family members how to plan, budget, shop for, and prepare balanced meals, often accompanying or driving clients to the store and offering suggestions on the most nutritious and economical food to purchase.

Some aides serve tenants in public housing projects. They are employed by housing agencies or other groups to help tenants relocate. They inform tenants of the use of facilities and the location of community services, such as recreation centers and clinics. They also explain the management's rules about sanitation and maintenance. They may at times help resolve disagreements between tenants and landlords.

Members of specific populations call on the aid of human services workers for support, information, and representation. The human services worker can provide these clients with counseling and emotional support and direct them to support groups and services. Social workers work with human services workers to reach out to the people; together, they visit individuals, families, and neighborhood groups to publicize the supportive services available.

Other clients of human services workers are those experiencing life-cycle changes. Children, adolescents, and the elderly may require assistance in making transitions. Human services workers help parents find proper day care for their children. They educate young mothers about how to care for an infant. They counsel children struggling with family problems or peer pressure. They offer emotional support to gay, lesbian, and bisexual teenagers and involve them in support groups. Some programs help the elderly stay active and help them prepare meals and clean their homes. They also assist the elderly in getting to and from hospitals and community centers and stay in touch with these clients through home visits and telephone calls.

Some human services workers focus on specific problems, such as drug and alcohol abuse. Human services workers assist in developing, organizing, and conducting programs dealing with the causes of and remedies for substance abuse. Workers may help individuals trying to overcome drug or alcohol addiction to master practical skills, such as cooking and doing laundry, and teach them ways to communicate more effectively with others. Domestic violence is also a problem receiving more attention, as more and more people leave abusive situations. Shelters for victims require counselors, assistants, tutors, and day care personnel for their children. Human services workers may also teach living and communication skills in homeless shelters and mental health facilities.

Record keeping is an important part of the duties of human services workers, because records may affect a client's eligibility for future benefits, the proper assessment of a program's success, and the prospect of future funding. Workers prepare and maintain records and case files of every person with whom they work. They record clients' responses to the various programs and treatment. They must also track costs in group homes in order to stay within budget.

REQUIREMENTS

High School

Some employers hire people with only a high school education, but these employees might find it hard to move beyond clerical positions. Interested high school students should plan to attend a college or university and should take classes in English, mathematics, political science, psychology, and sociology.

Postsecondary Training

Certificate and associate's degree programs in human services or mental health are offered at community and junior colleges, vocational-technical institutes, and other postsecondary institutions. It is also possible to pursue a bachelor's degree in human services. There are 468 bachelor's and 196 master's programs in human services that have been accredited by the Council on Social Work Education; academic programs such as these prepare students for occupations in the human services. Because the educators at these colleges and universities stay in regular contact with the social work employers in their area, the programs are continually revised to meet the changing needs of the field. Students are exposed early and often to the kinds of situations they may encounter on the job.

Undergraduate and graduate programs typically include courses in psychology, sociology, crisis intervention, family dynamics, therapeutic interviewing, rehabilitation, and gerontology.

Certification or Licensing

Certification or licensing may be required for some human services positions, such as social worker. These requirements vary by state.

Other Requirements

Many people perform human services work because they want to make a difference in their community. They may also like connecting on a personal level with other people, offering them emotional support, helping them sort out problems, and teaching them how to care for themselves and their families. A genuine interest in the lives and concerns of others and sensitivity to their situations are important to a human services worker. An artistic background can also be valuable in human services. Some programs in mental health facilities, domestic violence shelters, and other group homes use art therapy. Painting, music, dance, and creative writing are sometimes incorporated into counseling sessions, providing a client with alternative modes of expression.

In addition to the rewarding aspects of the job, a human services worker must be prepared to take on difficult responsibilities. The work can be very stressful. The problems of some populations—such as prison inmates, battered women and children, substance abusers, and the poor—can seem insurmountable. Their stories and day-to-day lives can seem tragic. Even if human services workers are not counseling clients, they are working directly with clients on some level. Just helping a person fill out an application or prepare a household budget requires a good disposition and the ability to be supportive. Clients may not welcome help and may not even care about their own well-being. In these cases, a human services worker must remain firm but supportive and encouraging. Patience is very important, whatever the area of human service.

The workload for a human services worker can also be overwhelming. An agency with limited funding cannot always afford to hire the number of employees it needs. A human services worker employed by an understaffed agency will probably be overworked, which can sometimes result in employee burnout.

EXPLORING

To get an idea of the requirements of human service, volunteer your time to a local human services agency or institution. Church organizations also involve young people in volunteer work, as do the Red Cross, the Boy Scouts, and the Girl Scouts. Volunteer work can include reading to blind or elderly people and visiting nursing homes and halfway homes. You might get involved in organizing group recreation programs at the YMCA or YWCA or performing light clerical duties in an office. You can also encourage any high school organizations to which you belong to become actively involved in charity work.

Some members of high school organizations also perform social services within their own schools, educating classmates on the dangers of gangs, unsafe sex, and substance abuse. By being actively involved in your community, you can gain experience in human services as well as build up a history of volunteer service that will impress future employers.

EMPLOYERS

Approximately 344,050 human services workers are employed in the United States. They are employed in a variety of settings, including agency offices, community centers, group homes, halfway houses, mental health facilities, hospitals, shelters, and the private homes of clients.

STARTING OUT

Students may find jobs through their high school counselors or local and state human services agencies. Sometimes summer jobs and volunteer work can develop into full-time employment upon graduation. Employers try to be selective in their hiring because many human services jobs involve direct contact with people who are impaired and therefore vulnerable to exploitation. Experience with helping others is a definite advantage.

ADVANCEMENT

Job performance has some bearing on pay raises and advancement for human services workers. Career advancement almost always depends on formal education, however, such as a bachelor's or master's degree in social work, counseling, rehabilitation, or some other related field. Many employers encourage their workers to further their education and some may even reimburse part of the costs of school. In addition, many employers provide in-service training such as seminars and workshops.

EARNINGS

Salaries of human services workers depend in part on their employer and amount of experience. According to the U.S. Department of Labor, median annual earnings of social and human service assistants were $27,940 in 2009. Salaries ranged from less than $18,300 to more than $44,760. Salaries for social workers ranged from $28,770 to $75,240 in 2009; the middle 50 percent earned average annual incomes of $49,420. The top paying states for human services workers in 2009 were Alaska, California, Connecticut, Massachusetts, and Hawaii.

WORK ENVIRONMENT

Most human services workers work a standard 40-hour week, spending time both in the office and in the field interviewing clients and performing other support services. Some weekend and evening work may be required, but compensatory time off is usually granted. Workers in residential settings generally work in shifts. Because group homes need 24-hour staffing, workers usually work some evenings and weekends.

Work conditions are affected by the size and location of the town in which the work is found. The societal problems of large, urban areas are different from those of small, rural areas. In a city, human services workers deal with issues of crime, racism, gang warfare, and violence in the schools. These problems can exist in smaller communities as well, but human services workers in rural areas focus more on work with the elderly and the poor. Rural communities typically have an older population, with people living deeper in the country and farther from public and private services. This can require more transportation time. The social services in rural areas, because of lower salaries and poorer facilities, typically have trouble attracting workers.

Offices and facilities may be clean and cheerful, or they may be dismal, cramped, and inadequately equipped. While out in the field with clients, workers may also find themselves in dangerous, squalid areas. In a large city, workers can rely on public transportation, whereas workers in a rural community must often drive long distances.

OUTLOOK

Employment for human services workers will grow much faster than the average through 2018, according to the U.S. Department of Labor. The best opportunities will be in job-training programs, residential care facilities, and private social service agencies, which include such services as adult day care and meal delivery programs. Correctional facilities are also expected to employ many more human services workers. Because counseling inmates and offenders can be undesirable work, there are a number of high-paying jobs available in that area.

New ideas in treating people with disabilities or mental illness also influence employment growth in group homes and residential care facilities. Public concern for the homeless—many of whom are former mental patients who were released under service reductions in the 1980s—as well as for troubled teenagers, and those with substance abuse problems, is likely to bring about new community-based programs and group residences.

Job prospects in public agencies are not as bright as they once were because of fiscal policies that tighten eligibility requirements for federal welfare and other payments. State and local governments are expected to remain major employers, however, as the burden of providing social services such as welfare, child support, and nutrition programs is shifted from the federal government to the state and local level. In larger cities, such as New York or Washington, D.C., jobs in the public sector will be more plentiful than in smaller cities because of the higher demand. There is also a higher burnout rate in the larger cities, resulting in more job opportunities as people vacate their positions for other careers.

FOR MORE INFORMATION

For more information on careers in counseling, contact

American Counseling Association
5999 Stevenson Avenue
Alexandria, VA 22304-3304
Tel: 800-347-6647
http://www.counseling.org

To access the online publication Choices: Careers in Social Work, *visit*

National Association of Social Workers
750 First Street, NE, Suite 700
Washington, DC 20002-4241
http://www.naswdc.org

For information on student memberships, scholarships, and master's degree programs in human services, visit

National Organization for Human Services
5341 Old Highway 5, Suite 206, #214
Woodstock, GA 30188-2494
Tel: 770-924-8899
E-mail: admin@nationalhumanservices.org
http://www.nationalhumanservices.org

For information on employment with government human service agencies, contact

U.S. Department of Health and Human Services
200 Independence Avenue, SW
Washington, DC 20201-0004
Tel: 877-696-6775
http://www.hhs.gov

The following is a job search Web site for social services and social work positions:

SocialService.Com
http://www.socialservice.com

☐ INDUSTRIAL ENGINEERS

OVERVIEW

Industrial engineers use their knowledge of various disciplines—including systems engineering, management

science, operations research, and fields such as ergonomics—to determine the most efficient and cost-effective methods for industrial production. They are responsible for designing systems that integrate materials, equipment, information, and people in the overall production process. Approximately 209,300 industrial engineers are employed in the United States.

THE JOB

Industrial engineers are involved with the development and implementation of the systems and procedures that are utilized by many industries and businesses. In general, they figure out the most effective ways to use the three basic elements of any company: people, facilities, and equipment.

Although industrial engineers work in a variety of businesses, the main focus of the discipline is in manufacturing, also called industrial production. Primarily, industrial engineers are concerned with process technology, which includes the design and layout of machinery and the organization of workers who implement the required tasks.

Industrial engineers have many responsibilities. With regard to facilities and equipment, engineers are involved in selecting machinery and other equipment and then in setting them up in the most efficient production layout. They also develop methods to accomplish production tasks, such as the organization of an assembly line. In addition, they devise systems for quality control, distribution, and inventory.

Industrial engineers are responsible for some organizational issues. For instance, they might study an orga-

---

SCHOOL SUBJECTS
Computer science, Mathematics

PERSONAL SKILLS
Leadership/management, Technical/scientific

MINIMUM EDUCATION LEVEL
Bachelor's degree

CERTIFICATION OR LICENSING
Required by certain states

WORK ENVIRONMENT
Primarily indoors, Primarily one location

nization chart and other information about a project and then determine the functions and responsibilities of workers. They devise and implement job evaluation procedures as well as articulate labor-utilization standards for workers. Engineers often meet with managers to discuss cost analysis, financial planning, job evaluation, and salary administration. Not only do they recommend methods for improving employee efficiency but they may also devise wage and incentive programs.

Industrial engineers evaluate ergonomic issues, the relationship between human capabilities and the physical environment in which they work. For example, they might evaluate whether machines are causing physical harm or discomfort to workers or whether the machines could be designed differently to enable workers to be more productive.

REQUIREMENTS

High School

To prepare for a college engineering program, concentrate on mathematics (algebra, trigonometry, geometry, calculus), physical sciences (physics, chemistry), social sciences (economics, sociology), and English. Engineers often have to convey ideas graphically and may need to visualize processes in three-dimension, so courses in graphics, drafting, or design are also helpful. In addition, round out your education with computer science, history, and foreign language classes. If honor level courses are available to you, be sure to take them.

Postsecondary Training

A bachelor's degree from an accredited institution is usually the minimum requirement for all professional engineering positions. The Accreditation Board for Engineering and Technology (ABET) accredits schools offering engineering programs, including industrial engineering. A listing of accredited colleges and universities is available on the ABET's Web site (http://www.abet.org), and a visit here should be one of your first stops when you are deciding on a school to attend. Colleges and universities offer either four- or five-year engineering programs. Because of the intensity of the curricula, many students take heavy course loads and attend summer sessions in order to finish in four years.

During your junior and senior years of college, you should consider your specific career goals, such as in which industry to work. Third- and fourth-year courses focus on such subjects as facility planning and design, work measurement standards, process design, engineer-

ing economics, manufacturing and automation, and incentive plans.

Many industrial engineers go on to earn a graduate degree. These programs tend to involve more research and independent study. Graduate degrees are usually required for teaching positions.

Certification or Licensing

Licensure as a professional engineer is recommended since an increasing number of employers require it. Even those employers who do not require licensing will view it favorably when considering new hires or when reviewing workers for promotion. Engineers who provide services directly to the public are required by all 50 states and the District of Columbia to be licensed. Licensing requirements vary from state to state. In general, however, they involve having graduated from an accredited school, having four years of work experience, and having passed the eight-hour Fundamentals of Engineering exam and the eight-hour Principles and Practice of Engineering exam. Depending on your state, you can take the Fundamentals exam shortly before your graduation from college or after you have received your bachelor's degree. At that point you will be an engineer-in-training (EIT). Once you have fulfilled all the licensure requirements, you receive the designation of professional engineer (PE).

Other Requirements

Industrial engineers enjoy problem solving and analyzing things as well as being a team member. The ability to communicate is vital since engineers interact with all levels of management and workers. Being organized and detail-minded is important because industrial engineers often handle large projects and must bring them in on time and on budget. Since process design is the cornerstone of the field, an engineer should be creative and inventive.

EXPLORING

Try joining a science or engineering club, such as the Junior Engineering Technical Society (JETS). JETS offers academic competitions in subjects such as computer fundamentals, mathematics, physics, and English. It also conducts design contests in which students learn and apply science and engineering principles. JETS also offers the *JETSNews,* a free newsletter that will be useful if you are interested in engineering. It contains information on engineering specialties, activities, program updates and other resources. Visit http://www.jets.org/newsletter to read the publication. You also might read some engineering books for background on the field or magazines such as *Industrial Engineer, a* magazine published by the Institute of Industrial Engineers (IIE). Selected articles from *Industrial Engineer* can be viewed on the IIE's Web site, http://www.iienet2.org.

EMPLOYERS

Approximately 209,300 industrial engineers are employed in the United States. Although a majority of industrial engineers are employed in the manufacturing industry, related jobs are found in almost all businesses, including aviation, aerospace, transportation, communications, electric, gas and sanitary services, government, finance, insurance, real estate, wholesale and retail trade, construction, mining, agriculture, forestry, and fishing. Also, many work as independent consultants.

STARTING OUT

The main qualification for an entry-level job is a bachelor's degree in industrial engineering. Accredited college programs generally have job openings listed in their career services offices. Entry-level industrial engineers find jobs in various departments, such as computer operations, warehousing, and quality control. As engineers gain on-the-job experience and familiarity with departments, they may decide on a specialty. Some may want to continue to work as process designers or methods engineers, while others may move on to administrative positions.

Some further examples of specialties include work measurement standards, shipping and receiving, cost control, engineering economics, materials handling, management information systems, mathematical models, and operations. Many who choose industrial engineering as a career find its appeal in the diversity of sectors that are available to explore.

ADVANCEMENT

After having worked at least three years in the same job, an industrial engineer may have the basic credentials needed for advancement to a higher position. In general, positions in operations and administration are considered high-level jobs, although this varies from company to company. Engineers who work in these areas tend to earn larger salaries than those who work in warehousing or cost control, for example. If one is interested in moving to a different company, it is considered easier to do so within the same industry.

Industrial engineering jobs are often considered stepping-stones to management positions, even in other fields. Engineers with many years' experience frequently are promoted to higher-level jobs with greater responsibilities. Because of the field's broad exposure, industrial engineering employees are generally considered better prepared for executive roles than are other types of engineers.

EARNINGS

According to the U.S. Department of Labor, the median annual salary for industrial engineers in 2009 was $75,110. The lowest paid 10 percent of all industrial engineers earned less than $48,840 annually. As with most occupations, however, salaries rise as more experience is gained. Very experienced engineers can earn more than $109,220. According to a survey by the National Association of Colleges and Employers, the average starting salary for industrial engineers with a bachelor's degree was $58,358 in 2009.

WORK ENVIRONMENT

Industrial engineers usually work in offices at desks and computers, designing and evaluating plans, statistics, and other documents. Overall, industrial engineering is ranked above other engineering disciplines for factors such as employment outlook, salary, and physical environment. Industrial engineering jobs are considered stressful, though, because they often entail tight deadlines and demanding quotas, and jobs are moderately competitive. Engineers work an average of 46 hours per week.

Industrial engineers generally collaborate with other employees, conferring on designs and procedures, as well as with business managers and consultants. Although they spend most of their time in their offices, they must frequently evaluate conditions at factories and plants, where noise levels are often high.

OUTLOOK

The U.S. Department of Labor anticipates that employment for industrial engineers will grow faster than the average for all occupations through 2018. The demand for industrial engineers will continue as manufacturing and other companies strive to make their production processes more effective and competitive. Engineers who transfer or retire will create the highest percentage of openings in this field.

FOR MORE INFORMATION

For a list of ABET-accredited engineering schools, contact

Accreditation Board for Engineering and Technology (ABET)
111 Market Place, Suite 1050
Baltimore, MD 21202-7116
Tel: 410-347-7700
http://www.abet.org

For comprehensive information about careers in industrial engineering, contact

Institute of Industrial Engineers
3577 Parkway Lane, Suite 200
Norcross, GA 30092-2833
Tel: 800-494-0460
http://www.iienet2.org

Visit the JETS Web site for membership information and to read "JETS News."

Junior Engineering Technical Society (JETS)
1420 King Street, Suite 405
Alexandria, VA 22314-2750
Tel: 703-548-5387
E-mail: info@jets.org
http://www.jets.org

INTERIOR DESIGNERS AND DECORATORS

OVERVIEW

Interior designers and *interior decorators* evaluate, plan, and design the interior areas of residential, commercial, and industrial structures. In addition to helping clients select equipment and fixtures, these professionals supervise the coordination of colors and materials, obtain estimates and costs within the client's budget, and oversee the execution and installation of the project. They also often advise clients on architectural requirements, space planning, and the function and purpose of the environment.

There are currently approximately 46,010 interior designers working in the United States. These specialists are employed by interior design or architectural firms,

SCHOOL SUBJECTS
Art, Business

PERSONAL SKILLS
Artistic, Communication/ideas

MINIMUM EDUCATION LEVEL
Associate's degree

CERTIFICATION OR LICENSING
Required by certain states

WORK ENVIRONMENT
Primarily indoors, Primarily multiple locations

department stores, furniture stores, hotel chains, and large corporations.

THE JOB

The terms "interior designer" and "interior decorator" are sometimes used interchangeably. However, there is an important distinction between the two. Interior designers plan and create the overall design for interior spaces, while interior decorators focus on the decorative aspects of the design and furnishing of interiors. A further distinction concerns the type of interior space on which the design or decorating professional works. Specifically, *residential designers* focus on individual homes, while *contract* or *commercial designers* specialize in office buildings, industrial complexes, hotels, hospitals, restaurants, schools, factories, and other nonresidential environments.

Interior designers and decorators perform a wide variety of services, depending on the type of project and the clients' requirements. A job may range from designing and decorating a single room in a private residence to coordinating the entire interior arrangement of a huge building complex. In addition to planning the interiors of new buildings, interior professionals also redesign existing interiors.

Design and decorating specialists begin by evaluating a project. They first consider how the space will be used. In addition to suiting the project's functional requirements, designs must address the needs, desires, tastes, and budget of the client as well. The designer often works closely with the architect in planning the complete layout of rooms and use of space. The designer's plans must work well with the architect's blueprints and comply with other building requirements. Design work of this kind is usually done in connection with the building or renovation of large structures.

Interior professionals may design the furniture and accessories to be used on a project, or they might work with materials that are already available. They select and plan the arrangement of furniture, draperies, floor coverings, wallpaper, paint, and other decorations. They make their decisions only after considering general style, scale of furnishings, colors, patterns, flow, lighting, safety, communication, and a host of other factors. They must also be familiar with local, state, and federal laws as well as building codes and other related regulations.

Although interior designers and decorators may consult with clients throughout the conceptual phase of the design project, they usually make a formal presentation once the design has been formulated. Such presentations may include sketches, scaled floor plans, drawings, models, color charts, photographs of furnishings, and samples of materials for upholstery, draperies, and wall coverings. Designers and decorators also usually provide a cost estimate of furnishings, materials, labor, transportation, and incidentals required to complete the project.

Once plans have been approved by the client, the interior designer and decorator assembles materials—drapery fabrics, upholstery fabrics, new furniture, paint, and wallpaper—and supervises the work, often acting as agent for the client in contracting the services of craftworkers and specifying custom-made merchandise. Interior professionals must be familiar with many materials used in furnishing. They must know when certain materials are suitable, how they will blend with other materials, and how they will wear. They must also be familiar with historical periods influencing design and have a knack for using and combining the best contributions of these designs of the past. Since designers and decorators supervise the work done from their plans, they should know something about painting, carpet laying, carpentry, cabinet making, and other craft areas. In addition, they must be able to buy materials and services at reasonable prices while producing quality work.

Some designers and decorators specialize in a particular aspect of interior design, such as furniture, carpeting, or artwork. Others concentrate on particular environments, such as offices, hospitals, restaurants, or transportation, including ships, aircraft, and trains. Still others specialize in the renovation of old buildings. In addition to researching the styles in which rooms were originally decorated and furnished, these workers often supervise the manufacture of furniture and accessories to be used.

Considerable paperwork is involved in interior design and decoration, much of it related to budgets and costs. Interior professionals must determine quantities, and make and obtain cost estimates. In addition, designers and decorators write up and administer contracts, obtain permits, place orders, and check deliveries carefully. All of this work requires an ability to attend to detail in the business aspect of interior design.

REQUIREMENTS

High School

Although formal training is not always necessary in the field of interior design, it is becoming increasingly important and is usually essential for advancement. Most architectural firms, department stores, and design firms accept only professionally trained people, even for beginning positions.

If you're considering a career as an interior designer or decorator, classes in home economics, art history, design, fine arts, and drafting will prove to be valuable. Since interior design is both an art and a business, such courses as marketing, advertising, accounting, management, and general business are important as well.

Postsecondary Training

Professional schools offer two- or three-year certificates or diplomas in interior design. Colleges and universities award undergraduate degrees in four-year programs, and graduate study is also available. The Council for Interior Design Accreditation (CIDA) accredits bachelor's degree programs in interior design. There are more than 150 accredited interior design programs offered through art, architecture, and home economics schools in the United States and Canada. The National Association of Schools of Art and Design also accredits approximately 300 colleges and universities with programs in art and design. College students interested in entering the interior design field should take courses in art history, architectural drawing and drafting, fine arts, furniture design, codes and standards of design, and computer-aided design, as well as classes that focus on the types of materials primarily used, such as fibers, wood, metals, and plastics. Knowledge of lighting and electrical equipment, as well as furnishings, art pieces, and antiques, is important.

In addition to art and industry-specific areas of study, courses in business and management are vital to aspiring interior designers and decorators. Learning research methods will help you stay abreast of government regulations and safety standards. You should also have some knowledge of zoning laws, building codes, and other restrictions. Finally, keeping up with product performance and new developments in materials and manufacture is an important part of the ongoing education of the interior designer and decorator.

Art historians, people with architecture or environmental planning experience, and others with qualifications in commercial or industrial design may also qualify for employment in interior design.

Certification or Licensing

A number of states require licensing for interior designers, according to the U.S. Department of Labor. Each state has its own requirements for licensing and regulations for practice, so it's important to contact the specific state in order to find out how one can apply. To become eligible for registration or licensing in these jurisdictions, applicants must satisfy experience and education requirements and take the National Council for Interior Design Qualification (NCIDQ) Examination.

To prepare students for this examination, the NCIDQ offers the Interior Design Experience Program. Program participants are required to complete 3,520 hours of documented interior design experience. According to the council, up to 1,760 hours of qualified work experience can be earned before education is completed.

In addition, the National Kitchen and Bath Association offers several levels of optional certification in residential kitchen and bath design.

Other Requirements

First and foremost, interior designers and decorators need to have artistic talent, including an eye for color, proportion, balance, and detail, and have the ability to visualize. Designers must be able to render an image clearly and carry it out consistently. At the same time, artistic taste and knowledge of current and enduring fashion trends are essential.

In addition, interior designers need to be able to supervise craftworkers and work well with a variety of other people, including clients and suppliers. Designers should be creative, analytical, and ethical. They also need to be able to focus on the needs of clients, develop a global view, and have an appreciation of diversity. Finally, precision, patience, perseverance, enthusiasm, and attention to detail are vital.

EXPLORING

If you're thinking about becoming an interior designer or decorator, there are several ways to learn about the field. Courses in home economics or any of the fine arts, offered either at school or through a local organization, can give you a taste of some of the areas of knowledge needed by interior designers.

To get a sense of the actual work done by design specialists, you may be able to find a part-time or summer job in a department or furniture store. Such experience will enable you to learn more about the materials used in interior design and decorating and to see the store's interior design service in action. Since the business aspects of interior design are just as important as the creative side, any kind of general selling or business experience will prove to be valuable. As a salesperson at any type of store, for example, you'll learn how to talk to customers, write up orders, close sales, and much more.

In addition to learning about interior design itself, knowledge of auxiliary and support industries will be useful as well. To get a firsthand look at associated fields, you may want to arrange a visit to a construction site, examine an architect's blueprints, talk to someone who specializes in lighting, or tour a furniture manufacturing plant.

Ultimately, the best way to learn about interior design or decorating is to talk to a design professional. While interviewing an interior designer or decorator will be interesting and enlightening, finding a mentor who is doing the type of work that you may want to do in the future is ideal. Such a person can suggest other activities that may be of interest to you as you investigate the interior design field, provide you with the names of trade magazines and/or books that can shed some light on the industry, and serve as a resource for questions you might have.

EMPLOYERS

Approximately 46,010 interior designers and decorators are employed in the United States. Interior designers and decorators can be found wherever there is a need to style or beautify the interior environment of a building. The main professional areas in which they work are residential, government, commercial, retail, hospitality, education and research, health care, and facilities management.

In addition to "traditional" interior design and decorating opportunities, some professionals design theater, film, and television settings. A few designers become teachers, lecturers, or consultants, while others work in advertising and journalism.

The majority of interior designers and decorators work either for themselves or for companies employing fewer than five people. Since the industry is not dominated by giant conglomerates or even mid-sized firms, employment opportunities are available all across the United States, as well as abroad, in cities both large and small.

STARTING OUT

Most large department stores and design firms with established reputations hire only trained interior designers and decorators. More often than not, these employers look for prospective employees with a good portfolio and a bachelor of fine arts degree. Many schools, however, offer apprenticeship or internship programs in cooperation with professional studios or offices of interior design. These programs make it possible for students to apply their academic training in an actual work environment prior to graduation.

After graduating from a two- or three-year training program (or a four-year university), the beginning interior professional must be prepared to spend one to three years as an assistant to an experienced designer or decorator before achieving full professional status. This is the usual method of entering the field of interior design and gaining membership in a professional organization.

Finding work as an assistant can often be difficult, so be prepared to take any related job. Becoming a sales clerk for interior furnishings, a shopper for accessories or fabrics, or even a receptionist or stockroom assistant can help you get a foot in the door and provide valuable experience as well.

ADVANCEMENT

While advancement possibilities are available, competition for jobs is intense and interior designers and decorators must possess a combination of talent, personality, and business sense to reach the top. Someone just starting out in the field must take a long-range career view, accept jobs that offer practical experience, and put up with long hours and occasionally difficult clients. It usually takes three to six years of practical, on-the-job

experience in order to become a fully qualified interior designer or decorator.

As interior professionals gain experience, they can move into positions of greater responsibility and may eventually be promoted to such jobs as design department head or interior furnishings coordinator. Professionals who work with furnishings in architectural firms often become more involved in product design and sales. Designers and decorators can also establish their own businesses. Consulting is another common area of work for the established interior professional.

EARNINGS

Interior designers earned median annual salaries of $46,180 in 2009, according to the U.S. Department of Labor. The highest paid 10 percent earned more than $83,620, while the lowest paid 10 percent earned less than $26,980 annually. The U.S. Department of Labor reports the following mean salaries for interior designers by specialty: architectural and engineering services, $56,060; specialized design services, $52,400; furniture stores, $48,510; and building material and supplies dealers, $45,930. In general, interior designers and decorators working in large urban areas make significantly more than those working in smaller cities.

Designers and decorators at interior design firms can earn a straight salary, a salary plus a bonus or commission, or a straight commission. Such firms sometimes pay their employees a percentage of the profits as well. Self-employed professionals may charge an hourly fee, a flat fee, or a combination of the two depending on the project. Some designers and decorators charge a percentage on the cost of materials bought for each project.

The benefits enjoyed by interior designers and decorators, like salaries and bonuses, depend on the particular employer. Benefits may include paid vacations, health and life insurance, paid sick or personal days, employee-sponsored retirement plans, and an employer-sponsored 401(k) program.

WORK ENVIRONMENT

Working conditions for interior designers and decorators vary, depending on where they are employed. While professionals usually have an office or a studio, they may spend the day at a department store, architecture firm, or construction site, working with the decorating materials sold by the firm and the clients who have purchased them. In addition, designers often go on-site to consult with and supervise the projects being completed by various craftworkers.

Whether designers or decorators are employed by a firm or operate their own businesses, much of their time is spent in clients' homes and businesses. While more and more offices are using the services of interior designers and decorators, the larger part of the business still lies in the area of home design. Residential designers and decorators work intimately with customers, planning, selecting materials, receiving instructions, and sometimes subtly guiding the customers' tastes and choices in order to achieve an atmosphere that is both aesthetic and functional.

While designers and decorators employed by department stores, furniture stores, or design firms often work regular 40-hour weeks, self-employed professionals usually work irregular hours—including evenings and weekends—in order to accommodate their clients' schedules. Deadlines must be met, and if there have been problems and delays on the job, the designer or decorator must work hard to complete the project on schedule. In general, the more successful the individual becomes, the longer and more irregular the hours.

The interior professional's main objective is ultimately to please the customer and thus establish a good reputation. Customers may be difficult at times. They may often change their minds, forcing the designer or decorator to revise plans. Despite difficult clients, the work is interesting and provides a variety of activities.

OUTLOOK

Employment opportunities are expected to be excellent for interior designers and decorators through 2018, according to the U.S. Department of Labor. Since the services of design professionals are in many ways a luxury, though, the job outlook is heavily dependent on the economy. In times of prosperity, there is a steady increase in jobs. Conversely, when the economy slows down, opportunities in the field decrease markedly.

According to the International Interior Designers Association's Industry Advisory Council (IAC), a number of trends specific to the industry will also positively influence the employment outlook for interior designers and decorators. Clients in all market areas, for example, will develop an appreciation for the value of interior design work as well as increased respect for the interior professional's expertise. In addition, businesses, ever mindful of their employees' safety, health, and general welfare, will rely more heavily on designers to create interior atmospheres that will positively impact workplace performance.

The IAC also notes the importance of technology in the field of interior design. In addition to affecting the design of homes, technology will impact the production of design materials as well as create the need for multidisciplinary design. Professionals both familiar and comfortable with technology will definitely have an edge in an ever-competitive job market. Finally, the IAC points to the continued importance of education and research in the field of interior design. According to Allison Carll-White, former director of the International Interior Designers Association's Research and Education Forum, design organizations will have to offer programs focusing on basic interior design in order to attract talented students to the profession.

While competition for good designing and decorating positions is expected to be fierce, especially for those lacking experience, there is currently a great need for industrial interior designers in housing developments, offices, restaurants, hospital complexes, senior care facilities, hotels, and other large building projects. Designers with strong knowledge of ergonomics and green design will also enjoy excellent job prospects.

FOR MORE INFORMATION

For industry trends, career guidance, and other resources, contact
American Society of Interior Designers
608 Massachusetts Avenue, NE
Washington, DC 20002-6006
Tel: 202-546-3480
http://www.asid.org

For useful career information, visit the following Web site:
Careers in Interior Design
http://www.careersininteriordesign.com

For a list of accredited interior design programs, contact
Council for Interior Design Accreditation
206 Grandville Avenue, Suite 350
Grand Rapids, MI 49503-4014
Tel: 616-458-0400
E-mail: info@accredit-id.org
http://www.accredit-id.org

For information on continuing education, publications, and a list of accredited graduate programs in interior design, contact
Interior Design Educators Council
9100 Purdue Road, Suite 200
Indianapolis, IN 46268-3165

Tel: 317-328-4437

E-mail: info@idec.org

http://www.idec.org

For information on the industry, contact

International Interior Design Association

222 Merchandise Mart, Suite 567

Chicago, IL 60654-1618

Tel: 888-799-4432

http://www.iida.org

For information on accredited interior design programs, contact

National Association of Schools of Art and Design

11250 Roger Bacon Drive, Suite 21

Reston, VA 20190-5248

Tel: 703-437-0700

E-mail: info@arts-accredit.org

http://nasad.arts-accredit.org

For information on the Interior Design Experience Program, contact

National Council for Interior Design Qualification

1602 L Street, NW, Suite 200

Washington, DC 20036-5684

Tel: 202-721-0220

E-mail: inquiries@ncidq.org

http://ncidq.org

For information about certification, contact

National Kitchen and Bath Association

687 Willow Grove Street

Hackettstown, NJ 07840-1713

Tel: 800-843-6522

http://www.nkba.org

INTERNET DEVELOPERS

OVERVIEW

An *Internet developer,* otherwise known as a *Web developer* or *Web designer,* is responsible for the creation of an Internet site. Most of the time, this is a public Web site, but it can also be a private Internet network. Web developers are employed by a wide range of employers, from small entrepreneurs to large corporate businesses to Internet consulting firms.

SCHOOL SUBJECTS
Computer science, Mathematics

PERSONAL SKILLS
Communication/ideas, Technical/scientific

MINIMUM EDUCATION LEVEL
Bachelor's degree

CERTIFICATION OR LICENSING
Voluntary

WORK ENVIRONMENT
Primarily indoors, Primarily one location

THE JOB

After determining the overall goals, layout, and performance limitations of a client's Web site with input from marketing, sales, advertising, and other departments, an Internet or Web developer designs the site and writes the code necessary to run and navigate it. To make the site, working knowledge of the latest Internet programming languages such as Perl, Visual Basic, Java, C++, HTML, and XML is a must. The developer must also be up-to-date on the latest in graphic file formats and other Web production tools.

The concept of the site must be translated to a general layout. The layout must be turned into a set of pages, which are designed, written, and edited. Those pages are then converted into the proper code so that they can be placed on the server. There are software packages that exist to help the developer create the sites. However, software packages often use templates to create sites that have the same general look to them—which is not a good thing if the site is to stand out and look original. Also, no one software package does it all. Additional scripts or special features, such as banners with the latest advertising slogan, spinning logos, forms that provide data input from users, and easy online ordering, are often needed to add punch to a site.

Perhaps the trickiest part of the job is effectively integrating the needs of the organization with the needs of the customer. For example, the organization might want the content to be visually cutting edge and entertaining, but the targeted customer might not have the Internet connection speed needed to view those highly graphical pages and might prefer to get "just the facts" quickly. The developer must find a happy medium and deliver the information in a practical yet interesting manner.

REQUIREMENTS
High School

In high school, take as many courses as possible in computer science, science, and mathematics. These classes will provide you with a good foundation in computer basics and analytical-thinking skills. You should also take English and speech classes in order to hone your written and verbal communication skills.

Postsecondary Training

There currently is no established educational track for Internet developers. They typically hold bachelor's degrees in computer science or computer programming—although some have degrees in noncomputer areas, such as marketing, graphic design, library and information science, or information systems. Regardless of educational background, you need to have an understanding of computers and computer networks and knowledge of Internet programming languages. Formal college training in these languages may be hard to come by because of the rapid evolution of the Internet. What's hot today might be obsolete tomorrow. Because of this volatility, most of the postsecondary training comes from hands-on experience. This is best achieved through internships or entry-level positions. One year of experience working on a site is invaluable toward landing a job in the field.

Certification or Licensing

Because there is no central governing organization or association for this field, certification is not required. Certifications are available, however, from various vendors of development software applications. These designations are helpful in proving your abilities to an employer. The more certifications you have, the more you have to offer. The Institute for Certification of Computing Professionals also offers certification.

Other Requirements

A good Internet developer balances technological know-how with creativity. You must be able to make a site stand out from the sea of other sites on the Web. For example, if your company is selling a product on the Web, your site needs to "scream" the unique qualities and benefits of the product.

Working with Internet technologies, you must be able to adapt quickly to change. It is not uncommon to learn a new programming language and get comfortable using it, only to have to learn another new language and scrap the old one. If you're a quick study, then you should have an advantage.

EXPLORING

There are many ways to learn more about this career. You can read national news magazines, newspapers, and trade magazines or surf the Web for information about Internet careers. You can also visit a variety of Web sites to study what makes them either interesting or not so appealing. Does your high school have a Web site? If so, get involved in the planning and creation of new content for it. If not, talk to your computer teachers about creating one, or create your own site at home.

EMPLOYERS

Everyone is getting online these days, from the Fortune 500 companies to the smallest of mom-and-pop shops. The smaller companies might have one person in charge of everything Web related: the server, the site, the security, and so on. Larger companies employ a department of many workers, each one taking on specific responsibilities.

An obvious place of employment is Internet consulting firms. Some firms specialize in Web development or Web site management; other firms offer services relating to all aspects of Web site design, creation, management, and maintenance.

The Internet is worldwide; thus, Internet jobs are available worldwide. Wherever there is a business connected to the Internet, people with the right skills can find Web-related jobs.

STARTING OUT

If you are looking for a job as an Internet developer, remember that experience is key. College courses are important, but if you graduate and have lots of book knowledge and no experience, you're going to get a slow start. If at all possible, seek out internships while in school.

Use the Internet to find a job. The search engines of popular Web sites aimed at job seekers (Yahoo! Hot Jobs, http://hotjobs.yahoo.com; Monster, http://www.monster.com; and CareerBuilder.com, http://www.careerbuilder.com) can be useful. While you're online, check out some of the Internet trade magazines for a job bank or classifieds section.

ADVANCEMENT

The next step up the career ladder for Internet developers might be a move to a larger company where the Web site presence consists of more pages. Some Web sites have hundreds and even thousands of pages! Another option is to become a *Webmaster*. Webmasters generally have the responsibility of overseeing all aspects (technical, management, maintenance, marketing, and organization) of a Web site.

EARNINGS

According to GlassDoor.com, salaries for Web developers vary depending upon place of employment and level of experience. In 2010, average salaries ranged from $61,400 (for a Web developer at a university) to $83,250 (for a developer at an Internet company) to more than $112,000 (for a senior Web developer at a computer software development company).

Differences in pay tend to follow the differences found in other careers: the Pacific, Middle-Atlantic, and New England regions of the United States pay more than the North Central, South Atlantic, and South Central regions.

Benefits include paid vacation, paid holidays, paid sick days, health insurance, dental insurance, life insurance, personal days, and bonuses.

WORK ENVIRONMENT

Web developers work at computers in comfortable offices. Most of their work is done alone; however, developers consult frequently with the Webmaster and others write or edit the content of a site.

OUTLOOK

The career of Internet developer, like the Internet itself, is growing at a faster-than-average rate. As more and more companies look to expand their business worldwide, they need technically skilled employees to create the sites to bring their products, services, and corporate images to the Internet. In a survey of information architects by the Argus Center for Information Architecture, respondents predicted that certification and graduate degrees will become increasingly important in this career. Postsecondary training in Internet technology is growing, including graduate degrees in information design, informatics, interactive arts, human-computer interaction, and communication design. Universities that now offer strong programs in computer science, writing, and design will be developing liberal arts programs in information architecture. The Department of Labor predicts that through 2018, demand will be strong for network systems and data communications analysts, including Web developers and Webmasters. Jobs will be plentiful in the next decade for anyone with this specialized training.

FOR MORE INFORMATION

For information on careers, education, and student memberships, contact

IEEE Computer Society
2001 L Street, NW, Suite 700
Washington, DC 20036-4928
Tel: 202-371-0101
E-mail: help@computer.org
http://www.computer.org

For certification information, contact

Institute for Certification of Computing Professionals
2400 East Devon Avenue, Suite 281
Des Plaines, IL 60018-4602
Tel: 800-843-8227
http://iccp.org

INTERNET MARKETING AND ADVERTISING CONSULTANTS

OVERVIEW

Internet marketing and advertising consultants use their business savvy and technological and computer skills to help companies promote their services or products on the Internet. This method is often referred to as e-marketing. Some larger companies may have an in-house staff of Internet professionals, though many smaller or start-up companies often turn to independent consultants or a consulting agency for their needs.

THE JOB

While the work of Internet marketing and advertising consultants can vary depending on their place of employment and the project at hand, they all work toward the same goal: to drive more traffic to a company's Web site and sell more products or services.

SCHOOL SUBJECTS

Business, Computer science, Speech

PERSONAL SKILLS

Communication/ideas, Helping/teaching

MINIMUM EDUCATION LEVEL

Bachelor's degree

CERTIFICATION OR LICENSING

None available

WORK ENVIRONMENT

Primarily indoors, One location with some travel

The first step for many Internet marketing projects is revising or creating a company's Web site. If the Web site already exists, Internet marketing and advertising consultants study it to ensure that it is an effective marketing tool for the company's products or services. They might ask the following questions: Is the site attractive to potential customers? Is it is easy to navigate? Is there enough information available about the products or services? Is purchasing a product easy? Are there any features that may deter customers from completing a purchase? How does the site compare to those of competitors? Once these questions are answered, the consultants revise and revamp the Web site to make it a more effective marketing tool.

Internet marketing and advertising consultants may also be tasked with creating a brand-new Web site for a company that is new to the Web. To do this, they need to consider the company's marketing goals, design elements, user interface, purchasing interface, and the actual products or services that will be marketed. Internet consultants may collaborate with a team of artists, art directors, photographers, graphic designers, stylists, and copywriters to gather images and create merchandise presentations and product descriptions that stay true to the retail's brand.

In addition, marketing and advertising consultants are responsible for implementing an e-commerce strategy that addresses concerns such as retail competition, special promotions, and the overall performance of the site. They must identify the company's potential market (teens, Hispanic males, seniors, etc.), customer's expectations regarding a Web site (state-of-the-art graphics

and vivid colors, quick-loading pages, a straightforward, conservative look, etc.), and customers' buying habits. Customers who shop online typically have very different buying habits than those who purchase products in brick-and-mortar stores. For example, a customer who shops online might like the immediacy of being able to shop at home, but may also be seeking quick delivery options or a large selection of products from which to choose. Others may use the Web site to conduct research, but follow up by purchasing the product on the telephone or by visiting a brick-and-mortar store.

Many Internet marketing and advertising consultants specialize in different areas of the industry. For example, *search engine marketers (SEMs)* are responsible for the day-to-day management of clients' Web sites. They research a client's products or services, and develop advertisements using concise descriptions and keywords that will place their company's Web site high in search rankings. SEMs optimize ad campaigns with the most effective keywords so potential consumers are directed to the client's Web site during a search—the ultimate goal is to be listed as high as possible in a search engine's top 10 results.

Others work as *pay-per-click specialists (PPCs)*. PPCs place, or imbed, a client's advertisement on an existing Web site, often in the form of an image or banner. PPCs research sites, or content providers, that have an interest or relation to their client's business. For example, a PPC representing clients who sell vitamin supplements, health club memberships, or energy drinks may contact the online manager of an exercise Web site to convince him or her to place banner ads or sponsored links at the site. Clicking on these banners or links will direct the user to the advertiser's Web site. PPCs regularly monitor logfiles to determine the number of visits or "clicks," and then pay the content provider accordingly.

REQUIREMENTS

High School

If you are considering a career as an Internet marketing and advertising consultant, you should pursue a general high school curriculum that is college preparatory. Make sure you enroll in advertising, business, computer science, and marketing courses. You should also take courses that develop your analytical and problem-solving skills such as mathematics (including algebra and geometry) and sciences (including chemistry and physics). Take English courses to develop the research and communication skills you'll need for this profession.

Postsecondary Training

While a college degree may not be necessary to gain entry into this field, you will find it easier to get the best jobs and advance if you have one. Some people enter the field with computer- or e-commerce-related degrees; others have traditional liberal arts, advertising, business, or marketing backgrounds that include computer studies. No matter what your major, take plenty of computer classes and spend a lot of time on the Web.

Because consultants are usually responsible for marketing themselves, you should have good business skills and knowledge of marketing and sales, as well as computer knowledge. Therefore, take business and management classes, as well as economics and marketing. The consultant with a broad educational background may have the inside edge in certain situations.

Certification or Licensing

There are no certification or licensing requirements for Internet marketing and advertising consultants.

Other Requirements

Internet marketing and advertising consultants must be lifelong learners. You should have the desire and initiative to keep up on new technology, software, and hardware, as well as new marketing and advertising techniques. You must also have strong communication skills, including good listening skills. Creativity and an eye for graphic design are also desirable. Because marketing and advertising consultants deal with many different people in various lines of work, you must be flexible and have good interpersonal skills. To be a successful consultant, you should be self-motivated and have the ability to work alone as well as with groups. You also need to have the patience and perseverance to see projects through.

EXPLORING

By simply accessing the Internet frequently and observing different Web site designs, marketing techniques, and the increasing number of e-commerce sites, you can gain an insight into the field. Contact advertising and marketing workers, computer consultants, or Web site designers in your area and set up an information interview. At the interview, ask them questions about

their educational background, what they like about the work, how they market their business, what important skills someone wanting to enter the field should have, and any other things you are interested in knowing about this work.

Obtain experience in advertising and marketing by working on your school newspaper or yearbook or by finding a part-time or summer job at an advertising or marketing firm (especially one that specializes in Internet marketing/advertising). You can also create an online advertising or marketing campaign for a real or imaginary product or service.

EMPLOYERS

Many Internet marketing and advertising consultants work independently, running their own consulting businesses. Others may be salaried employees of traditional management consulting firms that have Internet marketing/advertising consulting divisions or departments. And still others may work for traditional brick-and-mortar companies that have a strong presence on the Internet.

Independent consultants have the added responsibility of marketing their services and always looking for new projects. Consultants at a firm are typically assigned to work on certain projects.

Clients that hire marketing and advertising consultants include small businesses, large corporations, and government institutions. Consultants work all across the country (and world), but large cities may offer more job opportunities. Some consultants specialize in working with a certain type of business such as department stores or computer companies.

STARTING OUT

Most consultants enter the field by working for an established consulting firm. This way they can gain experience and develop a portfolio and a list of references before venturing out on their own as an independent consultant or moving to a different firm in a higher position. The Internet is a good resource to use to find employment. Many sites post job openings. Local employment agencies and newspapers and trade magazines also list job opportunities. In addition, your college's career services office should be able to help you.

Networking is a key element to becoming a successful consultant and requires getting in touch with previous business and social associates as well as making new contacts.

ADVANCEMENT

Internet marketing and advertising consultants have several avenues for advancement. As they become known as experts in their field, the demand for their services will increase. This demand can support an increase in fees. They can also specialize in a certain segment of the industry, which can increase their client base and fees. Those working for consulting firms may move into management or partner positions. Consultants who want to work independently can advance by starting their own businesses. Eventually they may be able to hire consultants to work under them. Because of the continuous developments within the information technology industry, advancement possibilities for consultants who continually upgrade their knowledge and skills are practically endless.

EARNINGS

Internet marketing and advertising consultants' earnings vary widely depending on their geographic location, type of company they work for, and their experience and reputation. Beginning consultants may make about $35,000 per year, while many consultants earn around $65,000 annually. PayScale.com reported in January 2011 that the annual average salary for SEM consultants ranged from $34,880 to $67,497. Some consultants have salaries that exceed $100,000 a year.

To receive salaries ranging from mid- to high-$100,000, and up to $200,000, search engine marketers must have at least five or more years of experience, according to the Search Engine Marketing Professional Organization (SEMPO). The average annual salary for SEMs in 2009 was $40,000 to $80,000.

Many independent consultants charge by the hour, with fees ranging from $45 to well above $100 an hour. Consultants who work on contract must estimate the hours needed to complete the project and their rate of pay when determining their contract price. Independent consultants must also realize that not all their work time is "billable," meaning that time spent on general office work, record keeping, billing, maintaining current client contacts, and seeking new business does not generate revenue. This nonbillable time must be factored into contract or hourly rates when determining annual income.

Although independent consultants may generate good contract or hourly fees, they do not receive benefits that may be typical of salaried employees. For example, independent consultants are responsible for their own medical, disability, and life insurance. They do not receive vacation pay, and when they are not working, they are not generating income. Retirement plans must also be self-funded and self-directed.

WORK ENVIRONMENT

Internet marketing and advertising consultants work in a variety of settings. Depending on the project, they may work out of their homes or private offices. At other times, they may be required to work on-site at the client's facilities, which may, for example, be an office building or factory. Consultants employed by a large or small consulting firm or as full-time employees may also spend time working at the organization's office or telecommuting from home.

Internet consultants generally can expect to work in a clean office environment. Consultants may work independently or as part of a team, depending on the project's requirements.

Consulting can be a very intense job that may require long hours to meet a project's deadline. Some settings where employees or consultants are driven by a strict deadline or where a project is not progressing as planned may be stressful. Many people in this field often work more than 40 hours a week and may need to work nights and weekends. In addition, Internet consultants must spend time keeping current with the latest technology and marketing and advertising techniques by reading and researching.

OUTLOOK

There is currently a large demand for Internet marketing and advertising consultants as a result of the rapid growth of Internet sales. Based on its 2009 survey findings, SEMPO predicts there will be "fewer high-level professional jobs and more lower-level openings, so it will present opportunities for entry level professionals to prove their worth." Consultants who keep up to date with technology and industry trends and who are willing to learn and adapt should have plenty of job opportunities.

FOR MORE INFORMATION

For profiles of advertising workers and career information, contact
Advertising Educational Foundation
220 East 42nd Street, Suite 3300
New York, NY 10017-5806
Tel: 212-986-8060
http://www.aef.com

The AAF combines the mutual interests of corporate advertisers, agencies, media companies, suppliers, and academia. Visit its Web site to learn more about internships, scholarships, student chapters, and awards.

American Advertising Federation (AAF)
1101 Vermont Avenue, NW, Suite 500
Washington, DC 20005-6306
Tel: 800-999-2231
E-mail: aaf@aaf.org
http://www.aaf.org

For industry information, contact
American Association of Advertising Agencies
405 Lexington Avenue, 18th Floor
New York, NY 10174-1801
Tel: 212-682-2500
http://www.aaaa.org

For information on the practice, study, and teaching of marketing, contact
American Marketing Association
311 South Wacker Drive, Suite 5800
Chicago, IL 60606-6629
Tel: 800-AMA-1150
http://www.marketingpower.com

For information on search engine marketing, contact
Search Engine Marketing Professional Organization
401 Edgewater Place, Suite 600
Wakefield, MA 01880-6200
http://www.sempo.org

 INTERNET SECURITY SPECIALISTS

OVERVIEW

An *Internet security specialist* is someone who is responsible for protecting a company's network, which can be accessed through the Internet, from intrusion by outsiders. These intruders are referred to as *hackers* (or *crackers*), and the process of breaking into a system is called *hacking* (or *cracking*). Internet security often falls under the jurisdiction of computer systems engineering and network administration within a company.

Any company that has an Internet presence might employ an Internet security specialist. This includes all kinds of companies of all sizes anywhere around the world. Other Internet security specialists work for consulting firms that specialize in Internet security. Internet security specialists are sometimes known as *Internet security administrators, Internet security engineers, information security technicians,* and *network security consultants.*

THE JOB

The duties of an Internet security specialist vary depending on where he or she works, how big the company is, and the degree of sensitivity of the information that is being protected. The duties are also affected by whether the specialist is a consultant or works in-house.

Internet security usually falls under the jurisdiction of a systems engineering or systems administration department. A large company that deals with sensitive information probably has one or two Internet security specialists who devote all of their time and energy to Internet security. Many firms, upon connecting to the Internet, give security duties to the person who is in charge of systems administration. A smaller firm might hire an Internet security specialist to come in and set them up with security systems and software.

A *firewall* is a system set up to act as a barrier of protection between the outside world of the Internet and the company. A specialist can tell the firewall to limit access or permit access to users. The Internet security specialist does this by configuring it to define the kind of access to allow or restrict.

Primarily, Internet security specialists are in charge of monitoring the flow of information through the firewall. Security specialists must be able to write code and configure the software to alert them when certain kinds of activities occur. They can tell the program what activity to allow and what to disallow. They can even program the software to page them or send them an e-mail if some questionable activity occurs. Logs are kept of all access to the network. Security specialists monitor the logs and watch for anything out of the ordinary. If they see something strange, they must make a judgment call as to whether the activity was innocent or malicious. Then they must investigate and do some detective work—perhaps even tracking down the user who initiated the action. In other instances, they might have to create a new program to prevent that action from happening again.

Sometimes the Internet security specialist is in charge of virus protection or encryption and user authentication systems. *Viruses* are programs written with the express purpose of harming a hard drive and can enter a network through e-mail attachments or infected CD-ROMs. Encryption and authentication are used with any network activity that requires transmission of delicate information, such as passwords, user accounts, or even credit card numbers.

Secondary duties can include security administrative work, such as establishing security policies for the company, or security engineering duties, which are more technical in nature. For example, some companies might deal with such sensitive information that the company forbids any of its information to be transmitted over e-mail. Programs can be written to disallow transmission of any company product information or to alert the specialist when this sensitive information is transmitted. The security specialist might also be in charge of educating employees on security policies concerning their network.

Internet security consultants have a different set of duties. Consultants are primarily in charge of designing and implementing solutions to their clients' security problems. They must be able to listen to and detect the needs of the client and then meet their needs. They perform routine assessments to determine if there are attack-prone areas within the clients' network and, if there are, find ways to correct them. A company might employ a consultant as a preventive measure to avoid attacks. Other times, a consultant might be called on after

a security breach has been detected, to find the problem, fix it, and even track down the perpetrator.

Secondary duties of an Internet security consultant include management and administrative duties. He or she manages various accounts and must be able to track them and maintain paperwork and communications. Senior consultants have consultants who report to them and take on supervisory responsibilities in addition to their primary duties.

A benefit of using consultants is bringing new perspectives to an old problem. Often, they can use their many experiences with other clients to help find solutions. The consultant does not work solely with one client but has multiple accounts. He or she spends a lot of time traveling and must be reachable at a moment's notice.

REQUIREMENTS
High School

If you are a high school student and think you want to get into the Internet security industry, first and foremost you need to get involved in computer science/programming classes. Don't just book learn, however. Hands-on experience is key and probably is what will get you your first job. Spend time in the school computer lab, learn how computers work, and dabble with the latest technologies. Most of those employed in the field today began at a young age just playing around with computers. What began as a hobby eventually turned into an enjoyable and challenging career.

If you are interested in management or consulting, a well-rounded educational background is important. You should take classes in mathematics, science, and English. You may also want to take business classes to become familiar with the business world.

Postsecondary Training

College courses show employers that you have what it takes to learn. However, most colleges do not have specific programs in Internet security. Most offer computer science, networking, and programming-related degrees, which are highly recommended. Computer lab courses teach how to work with a team to solve problems and complete assignments—something that you will probably do in this field—especially in the consulting business. Programming requires an understanding of mathematics and algorithms. Law enforcement classes are also beneficial. By learning the mindset of the criminal, you can better protect your client or employer. Being versed in intellectual property law is also important because you will be working with transmitting and protecting sensitive information as it travels to various locations.

Internships are the best way to gain hands-on experience. They offer real-life situations and protected work environments where you can see what Internet security is all about. Internships are not common, however, mostly because of security problems that arise from bringing inexperienced young people into contact with sensitive, confidential information. The majority of exposed hackers are under 20 years of age so it is easy to understand companies' unwillingness to offer internships.

On-the-job training is the best way to break into Internet security. Without experience, you can never land a job in the field.

Certification or Licensing

The International Webmasters Association offers a voluntary certification program for Internet security specialists. Certification is also available from various vendors of Internet security software and other products. Each vendor offers its own training and certification program, which varies from company to company. Some certifications can be completed in a matter of a few days; others take years. The majority of those employed in the field are not certified; however, certification is a trend and is considered an advantage. The more certifications you have, the more you have to offer a company.

The Internet is constantly evolving, and Internet technology changes so rapidly that it is vital for the Internet security specialist to stay on top of current technology. After all, if a hacker has knowledge of cutting-edge technology and can use it to break into a system, the security specialist must be trained to counter those attacks. Security specialists must be well versed in the same cutting-edge technology. Often, the vendor creating the most current technology is the best training source. In the future, the technology is likely to become more complex, and so is the training. Ideally, product certification coupled with a few years of hands-on experience qualifies you for advancement.

Other Requirements

If you like doing the same thing on a daily basis (such as monitoring network activity logs and writing code), a job as Internet security specialist might be a good fit for you. On the other hand, you must be flexible so that you are ready to meet each new challenge with fresh ideas. Some hackers are creative, and it is important that the security specialist be just as creative.

It is not uncommon for those applying for security positions to have background checks or at least have their list of references closely interviewed to make sure the applicants are trustworthy individuals. In fact, many companies prefer to hire individuals who have been recommended to them directly by someone they know and trust.

Consultants must be well organized because they work with many accounts at once. Communication skills are important because consultants often deal with management and try to sell them on the importance of security software. They must also be willing to travel on a regular basis to visit their accounts.

EXPLORING

If Internet security interests you, play around on your computer. Check out programming books from the local library and learn how to write simple code. You might also want to read professional publications such as *Information Security Magazine,* which is published by SearchSecurity (http://searchsecurity.techtarget.com). Another publication to consider is the quarterly magazine *2600* (http://www.2600.com). While *2600* is aimed at hackers, reading the articles will give you an understanding of how some systems are broken into and help you develop your ability to think of defenses.

High school computer clubs and competitions allow you to experiment with computer programming. They are great places to design and implement systems and solutions in a nonthreatening atmosphere. You can also work with other students to get accustomed to working in teams.

The most obvious place to learn about the Internet is on the Internet. Surf the Web and research the many security issues facing users today. Visit the sites of consulting firms where you can get an idea of the services these firms offer.

Online employment sites, national news magazines, newspapers, and trade magazines are good sources of information. You can also find out a lot about current trends and hiring practices. Classified sections reveal what kind of market there is for security specialists and where the jobs are.

EMPLOYERS

Any company with an Internet presence (Web site, FTP site, e-mail service, etc.) has the potential for security breaches and can benefit from the work and advice of an Internet security specialist. Depending on the size of the company and the nature of the company's business, it might use outside consultants or employ one part-time or several full-time employees.

An obvious place of employment is an Internet security consulting firm. Some business consulting firms like Ernst & Young are adding Internet security branches to their current businesses.

Data forensics is another growing business where Internet security specialists are hired to act as detectives to find culprits who break into computer networks. To fight this type of crime, the Federal Bureau of Investigation set up a National Infrastructure Protection Center at its headquarters and Regional Computer Intrusion Squads in selected field offices throughout the United States.

STARTING OUT

It is unlikely that someone fresh out of high school or college will get a job as an Internet security specialist. Although education is important, experience is key in the field. Certifications are beneficial, but again, they do not mean much without experience. An internship in systems administration or engineering might introduce you to the security issues of that company.

Many who are in Internet security began in PC technical support and moved to systems administration or engineering. These jobs often include security responsibilities that then lead to positions focusing primarily on security.

If word-of-mouth does not get you a job, check the classifieds—both in the local newspapers and trade magazines. Many places post job openings on their Web sites.

ADVANCEMENT

Internet security specialists can move into supervisory or management positions and sometimes into executive positions. Those who work for small companies can sometimes advance by moving to larger firms with more sensitive data and more complicated security issues. With experience, an Internet security specialist can become a consultant.

Internet security consultants can become *sneakers* or part of a *tiger team*. Sneakers and tiger teams are the best in the field who are called in to crack a system on purpose in order to find security holes and then patch them.

EARNINGS

The field of Internet security is a lucrative business and the salary potential is growing. Internet security specialists are among the highest paid of all informa-

tion technology professionals. An entry-level specialist can expect to earn $50,000 to $60,000. According to *Computerworld's* 2010 Salary Survey, Internet security specialists had average salaries of $86,965 in 2010. They also received an average bonus of $6,702, which increased their salary to $93,667. Salary.com reported that systems/application security analysts had salaries that ranged from $47,862 or less to $115,805 or higher, as of January 2011.

Salaries increase with the size of the company and the nature of the information specialists are charged with protecting. Specialists working with extremely confidential information in an industry (such as the automotive industry) will receive higher pay than those working at a small family business. The highest paying industries are manufacturing, computers, and communication/utilities companies. Military and government sectors pay the least.

Benefits for full-time employees may include paid vacation, paid sick days, personal days, medical and dental insurance, and bonuses.

WORK ENVIRONMENT

Because Internet security specialists work with computers and computers require a controlled atmosphere, the work environment is typically indoors in a well-lit, climate-controlled office. Security specialists can expect many hours of sitting in front of a computer screen using a keyboard. Work is generally done alone, although a consultant might train an in-house person on how to use certain software.

Most work schedules require 40 to 50 hours a week. Consultants travel frequently, and their work schedules do not necessarily follow typical nine-to-five working hours. There are instances where additional hours are required—for example, if a serious breach of security is detected and time is of the essence to fix it. It is not uncommon for employees to be on call so they can respond quickly to critical situations.

Although this line of work might seem stressful, it generally is not. Most businesses see the value of protecting their information and budget appropriately for the necessary tools, equipment, and staff.

OUTLOOK

Employment for Internet security specialists will grow much faster than the average for all occupations through 2018, according to the Department of Labor. The number of companies with a presence on the Internet is growing rapidly. As these companies connect their private networks to the public Internet, they will need to protect their confidential information. Currently, the demand for Internet security specialists is greater than the supply, and this trend is expected to continue as the number of businesses connecting to the Internet continues to grow.

Until now, most Internet security specialists have gotten by with general skills. In the future, however, they will need more specialized skills and certification. Staying on top of current technologies will be one of the biggest challenges.

Because of the ever-changing new technology, educational institutions will continue to have difficulty in training students for this field. Vendors and on-the-job experience will continue to provide the best training.

FOR MORE INFORMATION

A federally funded organization, the CERT Coordination Center studies, monitors, and publishes security-related activity and research. It also provides an incident response service to those who have been hacked.

CERT Coordination Center
Software Engineering Institute
Carnegie Mellon University
4500 Fifth Avenue
Pittsburgh, PA 15213-2612
Tel: 412-268-7090
E-mail: cert@cert.org
http://www.cert.org

A professional organization for information security professionals, CSI provides education and training for its members.

Computer Security Institute (CSI)
350 Hudson Street, 3rd Floor
New York, NY 10014-4504
http://www.gocsi.com

Information Security is published by SearchSecurity and is a trade magazine for the information security professional.

Information Security
c/o TechTarget
275 Grove Street
Auburndale, MA 02466-2200
Tel: 888-274-4111
http://searchsecurity.techtarget.com

Visit the IWA's Web site for information on its voluntary certification program.

International Webmasters Association (IWA)
119 East Union Street, Suite F
Pasadena, CA 91103-3952
Tel: 626-449-3709
http://www.iwanet.org

INTERPRETERS

OVERVIEW

An *interpreter* translates spoken passages of a foreign language into another specified language. The job is often designated by the language interpreted, such as Spanish or Japanese. In addition, many interpreters specialize according to subject matter. For example, *medical interpreters* have extensive knowledge of and experience in the health care field, while *court* or *judiciary interpreters* speak both a second language and the "language" of law. *Interpreters for the deaf,* also known as *sign language interpreters,* aid in the communication between people who are unable to hear and those who can.

In contrast to interpreters, *translators* focus on written materials, such as books, plays, technical or scientific papers, legal documents, laws, treaties, and decrees. A *sight translator* performs a combination of interpreting and translating by reading printed material in one language while reciting it aloud in another.

There are approximately 40,000 interpreters and translators employed in the United States.

SCHOOL SUBJECTS
English, Foreign language, Speech

PERSONAL SKILLS
Communication/ideas, Helping/teaching

MINIMUM EDUCATION LEVEL
Bachelor's degree

CERTIFICATION OR LICENSING
Recommended

WORK ENVIRONMENT
Primarily indoors, Primarily multiple locations

THE JOB

Although interpreters are needed for a variety of languages and different venues and circumstances, there are only two basic systems of interpretation: simultaneous and consecutive. Spurred in part by the invention and development of electronic sound equipment, simultaneous interpretation has been in use since the charter of the UN.

Simultaneous interpreters are able to convert a spoken sentence instantaneously. Some are so skilled that they are able to complete a sentence in the second language at almost the precise moment that the speaker is conversing in the original language. Such interpreters are usually familiar with the speaking habits of the speaker and can anticipate the way in which the sentence will be completed. The interpreter may also make judgments about the intent of the sentence or phrase from the speaker's gestures, facial expressions, and inflections. While working at a fast pace, the interpreter must be careful not to summarize, edit, or in any way change the meaning of what is being said.

In contrast, *consecutive interpreters* wait until the speaker has paused to convert speech into a second language. In this case, the speaker waits until the interpreter has finished before resuming the speech. Since every sentence is repeated in consecutive interpretation, this method takes longer than simultaneous interpretation.

In both systems, interpreters are placed so that they can clearly see and hear all that is taking place. In formal situations, such as those at the UN and other international conferences, interpreters are often assigned to a glass-enclosed booth. Speeches are transmitted to the booth, and interpreters, in turn, translate the speaker's words into a microphone. Each UN delegate can tune in the voice of the appropriate interpreter. Because of the difficulty of the job, these simultaneous interpreters usually work in pairs, each working 30-minute shifts.

All international *conference interpreters* are simultaneous interpreters. Many interpreters, however, work in situations other than formal diplomatic meetings. For example, interpreters are needed for negotiations of all kinds, as well as for legal, financial, medical, and business purposes. *Court* or *judiciary interpreters,* for example, work in courtrooms and at attorney-client meetings, depositions, and witness preparation sessions.

Other interpreters known as *guide* or *escort interpreters* serve on call, traveling with visitors from foreign countries who are touring the United States. Usually, these language specialists use consecutive interpreta-tion. Their job is to make sure that whatever the visitors say is understood and that they also understand what is being said to them. Still other interpreters accompany groups of U.S. citizens on official tours abroad. On such assignments, they may be sent to any foreign country and might be away from the United States for long periods of time.

Interpreters also work on short-term assignments. Services may be required for only brief intervals, such as for a special conference or single interview with press representatives.

While interpreters focus on the spoken word, translators work with written language. They read and translate novels, plays, essays, nonfiction and technical works, legal documents, records and reports, speeches, and other written material. Translators generally follow a certain set of procedures in their work. They begin by reading the text, taking careful notes on what they do not understand. To translate questionable passages, they look up words and terms in specialized dictionaries and glossaries. They may also do additional reading on the subject to arrive at a better understanding. Finally, they write translated drafts in the target language.

Localization translation is a relatively new specialty. *Localization translators* adapt computer software, Web sites, and other business products for use in a different language or culture.

REQUIREMENTS
High School

If you are interested in becoming an interpreter or translator, you should take a variety of English courses, because most translating work is from a foreign language into English. The study of one or more foreign languages is vital. If you are interested in becoming proficient in one or more of the Romance languages, such as Italian, French, or Spanish, basic courses in Latin will be valuable.

While you should devote as much time as possible to the study of at least one foreign language, other helpful courses include speech, business, cultural studies, humanities, world history, geography, and political science. In fact, any course that emphasizes the written and/or spoken word will be valuable to aspiring interpreters or translators. In addition, knowledge of a particular subject matter in which you may have interest, such as health, law, or science, will give you a professional edge if you want to specialize. Finally, courses in typing and word processing are recommended, especially if you want to pursue a career as a translator.

Postsecondary Training

Because interpreters and translators need to be proficient in grammar, have an excellent vocabulary in the chosen language, and have sound knowledge in a wide variety of subjects, employers generally require that applicants have at least a bachelor's degree. Scientific and professional interpreters are best qualified if they have graduate degrees.

In addition to language and field-specialty skills, you should take college courses that will allow you to develop effective techniques in public speaking, particularly if you're planning to pursue a career as an interpreter. Courses such as speech and debate will improve your diction and confidence as a public speaker.

Hundreds of colleges and universities in the United States offer degrees in languages. In addition, educational institutions now provide programs and degrees specialized for interpreting and translating. Georgetown University (http://linguistics.georgetown.edu) offers both undergraduate and graduate programs in linguistics. Graduate degrees in interpretation and translation may be earned at the University of California at Santa Barbara (http://www.ucsb.edu), University of Puerto Rico (http://www.upr.edu), and Monterey Institute of International Studies (http://www.miis.edu). Many of these programs include both general and specialized courses, such as medical interpretation and legal translation.

Academic programs for the training of interpreters can be found in Europe as well. The University of Geneva's School of Translation and Interpretation (http://www.unige.ch/eti/index_en.html) is highly regarded among professionals in the field.

Certification or Licensing

Although interpreters and translators need not be certified to obtain jobs, employers often show preference to certified applicants. Certification in Spanish, Haitian Creole, and Navajo is also required for interpreters who are employed by federal courts. State and local courts often have their own specific certification requirements. The National Center for State Courts and the National Association of Judiciary Interpreters and Translators have more information on certification for these workers. Interpreters for the deaf who pass an examination may qualify for either comprehensive or legal certification by the National Association of the Deaf and the Registry of Interpreters for the Deaf. The U.S. Department of State has a three-test requirement for interpreters. These include simple consecutive interpreting (escort), simul-taneous interpreting (court/seminar), and conference-level interpreting (international conferences). Applicants must have several years of foreign language practice, advanced education in the language (preferably abroad), and be fluent in vocabulary for a very broad range of subjects.

Foreign language translators may be granted certification by the American Translators Association (ATA) upon successful completion of required exams. ATA certification is available for translators who translate the following languages into English: Arabic, Croatian, Danish, Dutch, French, German, Japanese, Portuguese, Russian, and Spanish. Certification is also available for translators who translate English into the following languages: Chinese, Croatian, Dutch, Finnish, French, German, Hungarian, Italian, Japanese, Polish, Russian, Spanish, and Ukrainian.

Other Requirements

Interpreters should be able to speak at least two languages fluently, without strong accents. They should be knowledgeable of not only the foreign language but also of the culture and social norms of the region or country in which it is spoken. Interpreters and translators should read daily newspapers in the languages in which they work to keep current in both developments and usage.

Interpreters must have good hearing, a sharp mind, and a strong, clear, and pleasant voice. They must be able to be precise and quick in their translation. In addition to being flexible and versatile in their work, both interpreters and translators should have self-discipline and patience. Above all, they should have an interest in and love of language.

Finally, interpreters must be honest and trustworthy, observing any existing codes of confidentiality at all times. The ethical code of interpreters and translators is a rigid one. They must hold private proceedings in strict confidence. Ethics also demands that interpreters and translators not distort the meaning of the sentences that are spoken or written. No matter how much they may agree or disagree with the speaker or writer, interpreters and translators must be objective in their work. In addition, information they obtain in the process of interpretation or translation must never be passed along to unauthorized people or groups.

EXPLORING

If you have an opportunity to visit the United Nations, you can watch the proceedings to get some idea of the techniques and responsibilities of the job of the interpreter. Occasionally, an international conference session is televised, and the work of the interpreters can be observed. You should note, however, that interpreters who work at these conferences are in the top positions of the vocation. Not everyone may aspire to such jobs. The work of interpreters and translators is usually less public, but not necessarily less interesting.

If you have adequate skills in a foreign language, you might consider traveling in a country in which the language is spoken. If you can converse easily and without a strong accent and can interpret to others who may not understand the language well, you may have what it takes to work as an interpreter or translator.

For any international field, it is important that you familiarize yourself with other cultures. You can even arrange to regularly correspond with a pen pal in a foreign country. You may also want to join a school club that focuses on a particular language, such as the French Club or the Spanish Club. If no such clubs exist, consider forming one. Student clubs can allow you to hone your foreign language speaking and writing skills and learn about other cultures.

Finally, participating on a speech or debate team can allow you to practice your public speaking skills, increase your confidence, and polish your overall appearance by working on eye contact, gestures, facial expressions, tone, and other elements used in public speaking.

EMPLOYERS

There are approximately 40,000 interpreters and translators in the United States. Although many interpreters and translators work for government or international agencies, some are employed by private firms. Large import-export companies often have interpreters or translators on their payrolls, although these employees generally perform additional duties for the firm. International banks, companies, organizations, and associations often employ both interpreters and translators to facilitate communication. In addition, translators and interpreters work at publishing houses, schools, bilingual newspapers, radio and television stations, airlines, shipping companies, law firms, and scientific and medical operations.

While translators are employed nationwide, a large number of interpreters find work in New York and Washington, D.C. Among the largest employers of interpreters and translators are the United Nations, World Bank, U.S. Department of State, Bureau of the Census, CIA, FBI, Library of Congress, Red Cross, YMCA, and the armed forces.

Finally, many interpreters and translators work independently in private practice. The Department of Labor reports that 26 percent of interpreters and translators are self-employed. These independent professionals must be disciplined and driven, since they must handle all aspects of the business such as scheduling work and billing clients.

STARTING OUT

Most interpreters and translators begin as part-time freelancers until they gain experience and contacts in the field. Individuals can apply for jobs directly to the hiring firm, agency, or organization. Many of these employers advertise available positions in the classified section of the newspaper or on the Internet. In addition, contact your college career services office and language department to inquire about job leads.

While many opportunities exist, top interpreting and translating jobs are hard to obtain since the competition for these higher-profile positions is fierce. You may be wise to develop supplemental skills that can be attractive to employers while refining your interpreting and translating techniques. The UN, for example, employs administrative assistants who can take shorthand and transcribe notes in two or more languages. The UN also hires tour guides who speak more than one language. Such positions can be initial steps toward your future career goals.

ADVANCEMENT

Competency in language determines the speed of advancement for interpreters and translators. Job opportunities and promotions are plentiful for those who have acquired great proficiency in languages. However, interpreters and translators need to constantly work and study to keep abreast of the changing linguistic trends for a given language. The constant addition of new vocabulary for technological advances, inventions, and processes keeps languages fluid. Those who do not keep up with changes will find that their communication skills become quickly outdated.

Interpreters and translators who work for government agencies advance by clearly defined grade promotions. Those who work for other organizations can aspire to become chief interpreters or chief translators, or reviewers who check the work of others.

Although advancement in the field is generally slow, interpreters and translators will find many opportunities to succeed as freelancers. Some can even establish their own bureaus or agencies.

EARNINGS

Earnings for interpreters and translators vary depending on experience, skills, number of languages used, and employers. In government, trainee interpreters and translators generally begin at the GS-5 rating, earning from $27,431 to $35,657 in 2011 Those with a college degree can start at the higher GS-7 level, earning from $33,979 to $44,176. With an advanced degree, trainees begin at the GS-9 ($41,563 to $54,028), GS-10 ($45,771 to $59,505), or GS-11 level ($50,287 to $65,371).

Interpreters who are employed by the United Nations work under a salary structure called the Common System. In 2010, UN short-term interpreters (workers employed for a duration of 60 days or less in North America) had daily gross pay of $527 (Grade I) or $344 (Grade II). The world rate for short-term interpreters was daily gross pay of $385.50 (Grade II) or $589 (Grade I). The base pay for UN short-term translators ranged from $209 to $404 per day. Local recruits receive slightly higher pay than nonlocal recruits.

Interpreters and translators who work on a freelance basis usually charge by the word, the page, the hour, or the project. Freelance interpreters for international conferences or meetings can earn between $300 and $500 a day from the U.S. government. By the hour, freelance translators usually earn between $20 and $40; however, rates vary depending on the language and the subject matter. Book translators work under contract with publishers. These contracts cover the fees that are to be paid for translating work as well as royalties, advances, penalties for late payments, and other provisions.

Interpreters and translators working in a specialized field have high earning potential. The U.S. federal courts pay $388 per day and $210 per half day for certified and professionally qualified court interpreters. Most work as freelancers, earning annual salaries from $30,000 to $100,000 a year.

Interpreters who work for the deaf also may work on a freelance basis, earning anywhere from $12 to $40 an hour, according to the Registry of Interpreters for the Deaf. Those employed with an agency, government organization, or school system can earn up to $30,000 to start; in urban areas, $40,000 to $50,000 a year.

The U.S. Department of Labor reports that the median salary for interpreters and translators was $40,860 in 2009, with salaries ranging from $22,810 to $74,190 or higher. Interpreters and translators who worked for elementary and secondary schools earned about $37,530 annually. Those who worked for the federal government averaged $72,330 per year ($34.77 per hour). Interpreters and translators who worked for management, scientific, and technical consulting services had higher salaries than those in other industries, averaging about $98,680 per year ($47.44 per hour) in 2009.

Depending on the employer, interpreters and translators often enjoy such benefits as health and life insurance, pension plans, and paid vacation and sick days.

WORK ENVIRONMENT

Interpreters and translators work under a wide variety of circumstances and conditions. As a result, most do not have typical nine-to-five schedules.

Conference interpreters probably have the most comfortable physical facilities in which to work. Their glass-enclosed booths are well lit and temperature controlled. Court or judiciary interpreters work in courtrooms or conference rooms, while interpreters for the deaf work at educational institutions as well as a wide variety of other locations.

Interpreters who work for escort or tour services are often required to travel for long periods of time. Their schedules are dictated by the group or person for whom they are interpreting. A freelance interpreter may work out of one city or be assigned anywhere in the world as needed.

Translators usually work in offices, although many spend considerable time in libraries and research centers. Freelance translators often work at home, using their own personal computers, the Internet, dictionaries, and other resource materials.

While both interpreting and translating require flexibility and versatility, interpreters in particular, especially those who work for international congresses or courts, may experience considerable stress and fatigue. Knowing that a great deal depends upon their absolute accuracy in interpretation can be a weighty responsibility.

OUTLOOK

Employment opportunities for interpreters and translators are expected to grow much faster than the average through 2018, according to the U.S. Department of Labor. However, competition for available positions will be fierce. With the explosion of the Internet, lightning-fast Internet connections, and videoconferencing, global communication has taken great strides. In short, the world has become smaller, so to speak, creating a demand for professionals to aid in the communication between people of different languages and cultural backgrounds.

In addition to new technological advances, demographic factors will fuel demand for translators and interpreters. Although some immigrants who come to the United States assimilate easily with respect to culture and language, many have difficulty learning English. As immigration to the United States continues to increase, interpreters and translators will be needed to help immigrants function in an English-speaking society. According to Ann Macfarlane, past president of the American Translators Association, "community interpreting" for immigrants and refugees is a challenging area requiring qualified language professionals.

Demand will be especially strong for interpreters and translators of Spanish, because of the growing Hispanic population in the United States. Demand should also be strong for translators of Arabic and other Middle Eastern languages.

Another demographic factor influencing the interpreting and translating fields is the growth in overseas travel. Americans on average are spending an increasing amount of money on travel, especially to foreign countries. The resulting growth of the travel industry will create a need for interpreters to lead tours, both at home and abroad.

In addition to leisure travel, business travel is spurring the need for more translators and interpreters. With workers traveling abroad in growing numbers to attend meetings, conferences, and seminars with overseas clients, interpreters and translators will be needed to help bridge both the language and cultural gaps.

While no more than a few thousand interpreters and translators are employed in the largest markets (the federal government and international organizations), other job options exist. The medical field, for example, will provide many jobs for language professionals, translating such products as pharmaceutical inserts, research papers, and medical reports for insurance companies. Interpreters will also be needed to provide non-English speakers with language assistance in health care settings. Opportunities exist for qualified individuals in law, trade and business, health care, tourism, recreation, and the government.

FOR MORE INFORMATION

For information on careers in literary translation, contact

American Literary Translators Association
University of Texas-Dallas
800 West Campbell Road
Mail Station JO51
Richardson, TX 75080-3021
http://www.utdallas.edu/alta/index.html

For more on the translating and interpreting professions, including information on accreditation, contact

American Translators Association
225 Reinekers Lane, Suite 590
Alexandria, VA 22314-2875
Tel: 703-683-6100
E-mail: ata@atanet.org
http://www.atanet.org

For more information on court interpreting and certification, contact

National Association of Judiciary Interpreters and Translators
1707 L Street, NW, Suite 570
Washington, DC 20036-4201
Tel: 206-293-0342
http://www.najit.org

For information on interpreter training programs for working with the deaf and certification, contact

Registry of Interpreters for the Deaf
333 Commerce Street
Alexandria, VA 22314-2801
Tel: 703-838-0030
http://www.rid.org

For information on union membership for freelance interpreters and translators, contact

Translators and Interpreters Guild
PO Box 77624
Washington, DC 20013-8624
Tel: 202-684-3324
E-mail: unionlanguages@aol.com
http://www.unionlanguages.org

LANDSCAPERS AND GROUNDS MANAGERS

OVERVIEW

Landscapers and *grounds managers* plan, design, and maintain gardens, parks, lawns, and other landscaped areas and supervise the care of the trees, plants, and shrubs that are part of these areas. Specific job responsibilities depend on the type of area involved. Landscapers

SCHOOL SUBJECTS
Biology, Chemistry

PERSONAL SKILLS
Helping/teaching, Mechanical/manipulative

MINIMUM EDUCATION LEVEL
Varies by specialty

CERTIFICATION OR LICENSING
Voluntary (certification),
Required for certain positions (licensing)

WORK ENVIRONMENT
Primarily outdoors, Primarily multiple locations

and grounds managers direct projects at private homes, parks, schools, arboretums, office parks, shopping malls, government offices, and botanical gardens. They are responsible for purchasing material and supplies and for training, directing, and supervising employees. Grounds managers maintain the land after the landscaping designs have been implemented. They may work alone or supervise a grounds staff. They may have their own business or be employed by a landscaping firm. There are approximately 1.5 million grounds maintenance workers in the United States; about 103,530 of these workers are in management positions.

THE JOB

There are many different types of landscapers and grounds managers, and their specific job titles depend on the duties involved. One specialist in this field is the *landscape contractor*, who performs landscaping work on a contract basis for homeowners, highway departments, operators of industrial parks, and others. They confer with prospective clients and study the landscape design, drawings, and bills of material to determine the amount of landscape work required. They plan the installation of lighting or sprinkler systems, erection of fences, and the types of trees, shrubs, and ornamental plants required. They inspect the grounds and calculate labor, equipment, and materials costs. They also prepare and submit bids, draw up contracts, and direct and coordinate the activities of landscape laborers who mow lawns, plant shrubbery, dig holes, move topsoil, and perform other related tasks.

Industrial-commercial grounds managers maintain areas in and around industrial or commercial properties by cutting lawns, pruning trees, raking leaves, and shoveling snow. They also plant grass and flowers and are responsible for the upkeep of flower beds and public passageways. These types of groundskeepers may repair and maintain fences and gates and also operate sprinkler systems and other equipment.

Parks-and-grounds managers maintain city, state, or national parks and playgrounds. They plant and prune trees; haul away garbage; repair driveways, walks, swings, and other equipment; and clean comfort stations.

Landscape supervisors supervise and direct the activities of landscape workers who are engaged in pruning trees and shrubs, caring for lawns, and performing related tasks. They coordinate work schedules, prepare job cost estimates, and deal with customer questions and concerns.

Landscapers maintain the grounds of private or business establishments. They care for hedges, gardens, and other landscaped areas. They mow and trim lawns, plant trees and shrubs, apply fertilizers and other chemicals, and repair walks and driveways.

There are many subspecialties in landscaping and grounds management. Below is a listing of a few of the most popular.

Tree surgeons, also known as *arborists,* prune and treat ornamental and shade trees to improve their health and appearance. This may involve climbing with ropes, working in buckets high off the ground, spraying fertilizers and pesticides, or injecting chemicals into the tree trunk or root zone in the ground. *Tree-trimming supervisors* coordinate and direct the activities of workers engaged in cutting away tree limbs or removing trees that interfere with electric power lines. They inspect power lines and direct the placement of removal equipment. Tree-trimming supervisors answer consumer questions when trees are located on private property.

Pest management scouts survey landscapes and nurseries regularly to locate potential pest problems, including insects, diseases, and weeds before they become hard to control, in an effective, safe manner. Scouts may specialize in the treatment of a particular type of infestation, such as gypsy moths or boll weevils.

Lawn-service workers plant and maintain lawns. They remove leaves and dead grass and apply insecticides, fertilizers, and weed killers as necessary. Lawn-service workers also use aerators and other tools to pierce the soil to make holes for the fertilizer and de-thatchers to remove built-up thatch.

A *city forester* advises communities on the selection, planting schedules, and proper care of trees. They also plant, feed, spray, and prune trees and may supervise other workers in these activities. Depending on the situation, landscapers and groundskeepers may perform these functions alone or with city foresters.

Turf grass consultants analyze turf grass problems and recommend solutions. They also determine growing techniques, mowing schedules, and the best type of turf grass to use for specified areas. Depending on the geographic area of the country, lawn-service companies regularly use such consultants.

On golf courses, landscapers and grounds managers are employed as *greenskeepers*. There are two types of greenskeepers: *Greenskeepers I* supervise and coordinate the activities of workers engaged in keeping the grounds and turf of a golf course in good playing condition. They consult with the greens superintendent to plan and review work projects; they determine work assignments, such as fertilizing, irrigating, seeding, mowing, raking, and spraying; and they mix and prepare spraying and dusting solutions. They may also repair and maintain mechanical equipment.

Greenskeepers II follow the instructions of greenskeepers I as they maintain the grounds of golf courses. They cut the turf on green and tee areas; dig and rake grounds to prepare and cultivate new greens; connect hose and sprinkler systems; plant trees and shrubs; and operate tractors as they apply fertilizer, insecticide, and other substances to the fairways or other designated areas.

Greens superintendents, also known as *golf course superintendents,* supervise and coordinate the activities of greenskeepers and other workers engaged in constructing and maintaining golf course areas. They review test results of soil and turf samples, and they direct the application of fertilizer, lime, insecticide, or fungicide. Their other duties include monitoring the course grounds to determine the need for irrigation or better care, keeping and reviewing maintenance records, and interviewing and hiring workers.

REQUIREMENTS
High School

In general, a high school diploma is necessary for most positions, and at least some college training is needed for those with supervisory or specialized responsibilities. High school students interested in this career should take classes in English, mathematics, chemistry, biology, and as many courses as possible in horticulture and botany.

Postsecondary Training

Those interested in college training should enroll in a two- or four-year program in horticulture, landscape management, or agronomy. Classes might include landscape maintenance and design, turf grass management, botany, and plant pathology. Course work should be selected with an area of specialization in mind. Those wishing to have managerial responsibilities should take courses in personnel management, communications, and business-related courses such as accounting and economics.

Many trade and vocational schools offer landscaping, horticulture, and related programs. Several extension programs are also available that allow students to take courses at home.

The minimal educational requirement to become a forester is a bachelor's degree in forestry; however, some foresters combine three years of liberal arts education with two years of professional education in forestry and receive the degrees of Bachelor of Arts and Master of Forestry. Though not required, golf course superintendents typically hold a bachelor's degree in a field related to agronomy or horticulture, or a degree from an intensive, two-year turfgrass management program.

Certification or Licensing

Licensing and certification differ by state and vary according to specific job responsibilities. For example, in most states, landscapers and grounds managers need a certificate to spray insecticides or other chemicals. Landscape contractors must be certified in some states.

Several professional associations offer certification programs for workers in the field. The Professional Landcare Network offers the following certification designations: landscape industry certified manager, landscape industry certified technician–interior, landscape industry certified technician–exterior, landscape industry certified horticultural technician, landscape industry certified lawn care manager, and landscape industry certified lawn care technician. Depending on the certification, applicants must pass a multiple-choice examination or a hands-on field test. The Professional Grounds Management Society offers certification for both grounds managers and workers: the certified grounds manager designation and the certified grounds technician designation. Landscapers and grounds managers who specialize in the care of golf courses and sports fields can receive certification from the Golf Course Superintendents Association of America (GCSAA) or the Sports Turf Managers Association.

Contractors and other self-employed people may also need a license to operate their businesses.

Other Requirements

Aspiring landscapers and grounds managers should have "green thumbs," and an interest in preserving and maintaining natural areas. They should also be reasonably physically fit, have an aptitude for working with machines, and display good manual dexterity.

All managerial personnel must carefully supervise their workers to ensure that they adhere to environmental regulations as specified by the Environmental Protection Agency and other local and national government agencies.

EXPLORING

If you are between the ages of five and 22, you might want to join the National Junior Horticulture Association, which offers horticulture-related projects, contests, and other activities. Visit http://www.njha.org for more information.

Part-time work at a golf course, lawn-service company, greenhouse, botanical garden, or other similar enterprise is an excellent way of learning about this field. Many companies gladly hire part-time help, especially during the busy summer months. In addition, there are numerous opportunities for mowing lawns, growing flowers, and tending gardens. You can also join garden clubs, visit local flower shops, and attend botanical shows.

The American Association of Botanical Gardens and Arboreta (AABGA) has a very strong internship program and offers a directory of internships in more than 100 public gardens throughout the United States. AABGA is a valuable resource to those individuals interested in gaining practical experience. Visit its Web site, http://www.aabga.org, for more information. Finally, a summer job mowing lawns and caring for a neighbor's garden is an easy, simple introduction to the field.

EMPLOYERS

Approximately 1.5 million grounds maintenance workers are employed in the United States. About 103,540 of these workers are in management positions. Landscapers and grounds managers are employed by golf courses, lawn-service companies, greenhouses, nurseries, botanical gardens, and public parks. Many people in this field start their own businesses.

STARTING OUT

Summer or part-time jobs often lead to full-time employment with the same employer. Those who enroll in a college or other training programs can receive help in finding work from the school's career services office. In addition, directly applying to botanical gardens, nurseries, or golf courses is common practice. Jobs may also be listed in newspaper want ads. Most landscaping and related companies provide on-the-job training for entry-level personnel.

ADVANCEMENT

In general, landscapers and grounds managers can expect to advance as they gain experience and additional educational training. For example, a greenskeeper with a high school diploma usually must have at least some college training to become a greens superintendent. It is also possible to go into a related field, such as selling equipment used in maintaining lawns and other natural areas.

Those in managerial positions may wish to advance to a larger establishment or go into consulting work. In some instances, skilled landscapers and grounds managers may start their own consulting or contracting business.

EARNINGS

Salaries depend on the experience and education level of the worker, the type of work being done, and geographic location. Landscaping and groundskeeping workers earned about $11.29 an hour (or $23,480) in 2009, according to the U.S. Department of Labor. Hourly earnings ranged from less than $8.06 (or $16,760 annually) to $17.82 ($37,070 annually) or more. The *Occupational Outlook Handbook* reports the following median hourly earnings for workers in this industry in 2009: tree trimmers and pruners, $14.57 ($30,310 annually); pesticide handlers, sprayers, and applicators, vegetation, $14.39 ($29,940 annually); and grounds maintenance workers, not otherwise classified, $11.49 ($23,890 annually). First-line supervisors/managers of landscaping, lawn service, and groundskeeping workers earned salaries that ranged from less than $26,670 to $67,020 or more in 2009. Median annual earnings for managers were $40,950. Landscape contractors and others who run their own businesses earn between $25,000 and $50,000 per year, with those with a greater ability to locate customers earning even more. According to the Golf Course Superintendents Association of America, the average base salary for golf course superintendents was $78,898 in 2009.

Fringe benefits vary from employer to employer but generally include medical insurance and paid vacation.

WORK ENVIRONMENT

Landscapers and grounds managers spend much of their time outside. Those with administrative or managerial responsibilities spend at least a portion of their workday in an office. Most of the outdoor work is done during daylight hours, but work takes place all year round in all types of weather conditions. Most people in the field work 37 to 40 hours a week, but overtime is especially likely during the summer months when landscapers and grounds managers take advantage of the longer days and warmer weather. Workweeks may be shorter during the winter. Weekend work is highly likely. Managerial personnel should be willing to work overtime updating financial records and making sure the business accounts are in order.

Much of the work can be physically demanding and most of it is performed outdoors in one extreme or another. Workers shovel dirt, trim bushes and trees, constantly bend down to plant flowers and shrubbery, and may have to climb ladders or the tree itself to prune branches or diagnose a problem. There is some risk of injury using planting and pruning machinery and some risk of illness from handling and breathing pesticides, but proper precautions should limit any job-related hazards.

OUTLOOK

Employment for workers in this field is expected to grow faster than the average for all occupations through 2018, according to the *Occupational Outlook Handbook*. Employment of tree trimmers and pruners is expected to grow much faster than the average during the same time span. Landscapers and their services will be in strong demand due to increased construction of buildings, shopping malls, homes, and other structures. Upkeep and renovation of existing landscapes will create jobs as well. There is also a high degree of turnover in this field as many workers transfer to better-paying occupations, retire, or leave the field for other reasons.

Another factor for job growth is the increase in amount of disposable incomes. In order to have more leisure time, people are beginning to contract out for lawn care and maintenance. The popularity of home gardening will create jobs with local nurseries and garden centers. Jobs should be available with government agencies as well as in the private sector.

Nonseasonal work will be more prevalent in states such as California, Arizona, and Florida, where mild climates warrant landscaping and lawn maintenance year-round.

FOR MORE INFORMATION

For information on certification and training programs and to read the online publication Careers in Horticulture, *visit the ASHS Web site.*

American Society for Horticultural Science (ASHS)
1018 Duke Street
Alexandria, VA 22314-3512
Tel: 703-836-4606
http://www.ashs.org

For comprehensive information on golf course management careers, internships, job listings, turfgrass management programs, and certification, contact

Golf Course Superintendents Association of America
1421 Research Park Drive
Lawrence, KS 66049-3859
Tel: 800-472-7878
E-mail: mbrhelp@gcsaa.org
http://www.gcsaa.org

For information on career opportunities and education, contact

Professional Grounds Management Society
720 Light Street
Baltimore, MD 21230-3850
Tel: 410-223-2861
E-mail: pgms@assnhqtrs.com
http://www.pgms.org

For information on certification, careers, internships, and membership for college students, contact

Professional Landcare Network
950 Herndon Parkway, Suite 450
Herndon, VA 20170-5528
Tel: 800-395-2522
E-mail: info@landcarenetwork.org
http://www.landcarenetwork.org

For information on urban forestry, contact

Society of Municipal Arborists
http://www.urban-forestry.com

For certification information, contact

Sports Turf Managers Association
805 New Hampshire, Suite E
Lawrence, KS 66044-2774
Tel: 800-323-3875
http://www.stma.org

For more information on arboriculture, contact

Tree Care Industry Association
136 Harvey Road, Suite 101
Londonderry, NH 03053-7439
Tel: 800-733-2622
http://www.treecareindustry.org

☐ LICENSED PRACTICAL NURSES

OVERVIEW

Licensed practical nurses (LPNs), a specialty of the nursing profession, are sometimes called *licensed vocational nurses.* LPNs are trained to assist in the care and treatment of patients. They may assist registered nurses and physicians or work under various other circumstances. They perform many of the general duties of nursing and may be responsible for some clerical duties. LPNs work in hospitals, public health agencies, nursing homes, or in home health. Approximately 728,670 licensed practical nurses are employed in the United States.

THE JOB

Licensed practical nurses work under the supervision of a registered nurse, or a physician. They are responsible for many general duties of nursing such as administering prescribed drugs and medical treatments to patients, taking patients' vital signs (temperature, blood pressure, pulse, respiration), dressing wounds, assisting in the preparation of medical examination and surgery, giving injections and enemas, and performing routine laboratory tests. LPNs help with therapeutic and rehabilitation sessions; they may also participate in the planning, practice, and evaluation of a patient's nursing care.

A primary duty of an LPN is to ensure that patients are clean and comfortable, and that their needs, both physical and emotional, are met. They sometimes assist patients with daily hygiene such as bathing, brushing teeth, and dressing. Many times they provide emotional comfort by simply talking with the patient.

LPNs working in nursing homes have duties similar to those employed by hospitals. They provide bedside care, administer medications, develop care plans, and

SCHOOL SUBJECTS
Biology, Chemistry

PERSONAL SKILLS
Helping/teaching, Technical/scientific

MINIMUM EDUCATION LEVEL
Some postsecondary training

CERTIFICATION OR LICENSING
Voluntary (certification), Required by all states (licensing)

WORK ENVIRONMENT
Primarily indoors, Primarily multiple locations

supervise nurse assistants. Those working in doctors' offices and clinics are sometimes required to perform clerical duties such as keeping records, maintaining files and paperwork, as well as answering phones and tending the appointment book. Home health LPNs, in addition to their nursing duties, may sometimes prepare and serve meals to their patients. They also teach family members how to provide basic care for their loved ones when medical professionals are unavailable.

REQUIREMENTS
High School

Some LPN programs do not require a high school diploma, but it is highly recommended, particularly if you want to be eligible for advancement opportunities. To prepare for a career as an LPN, you should study biology, chemistry, physics, and science while in high school. English and mathematics courses are also helpful.

Postsecondary Training

Those interested in a career as an LPN usually enroll in a practical nursing program after graduating from high school. There are about 1,200 state-approved programs in the United States that provide practical nursing training. According to the U.S. Department of Labor, 60 percent of all LPNs graduate from a technical or vocational school and 30 percent from a community or junior college. The remainder are enrolled in colleges, hospital programs, or high schools. Most programs last

12 months, with time spent for both classroom study and supervised clinical care. Courses include basic nursing concepts, anatomy, physiology, pharmacology, medical-surgical nursing, pediatrics, obstetrics, nutrition, and first aid. Clinical practice is most often in a hospital setting.

Certification or Licensing

The National Federation of Licensed Practical Nurses offers voluntary certification for LPNs who specialize in IV therapy and gerontology. The National Association for Practical Nurse Education and Service offers voluntary certification for LPNs who specialize in long-term care or pharmacology. Contact these organizations for more information.

All 50 states require graduates of a state-approved practical nursing program to take the National Council Licensure Examination, which has been developed by the National Council of State Boards of Nursing.

Other Requirements

Stamina, both physical and mental, is a must for this occupation. LPNs may be assigned to care for heavy or immobile patients or patients confused with dementia. Patience and a caring, nurturing attitude are valuable qualities to possess in order to be a successful LPN. As part of a health care team, they must be able to follow orders and work under close supervision. Other important traits include good observational skills, strong decision-making abilities, and the ability to communication well with others.

EXPLORING

High school students can explore an interest in this career by reading books or by checking out Web sites devoted to the nursing field. You should also take advantage of any information available in your school career services center. An excellent way to learn more about this career firsthand is to speak with the school nurse or local public health nurse. Visits to the local hospital can give you a feel for the work environment. Volunteer work at a hospital, community health center, or even the local Red Cross chapter can provide valuable experience. Some high schools offer membership in Future Nurses organizations.

EMPLOYERS

Approximately 728,670 licensed practical nurses are employed in the United States. The U.S. Department of Labor reports that 28 percent of LPNs work in nursing facilities, 25 percent work in hospitals, and 12 percent work in physicians' offices and clinics. Others are employed by home health care agencies, public health agencies, schools, residential care facilities, temp agencies, and government agencies.

STARTING OUT

After they fulfill licensing requirements, LPNs should check with human resource departments of hospitals, nursing homes, and clinics for openings. Employment agencies that specialize in health professions, and state employment agencies are other ways to find employment, as are school career services offices. Newspaper classified ads, nursing associations, and professional journals are great sources of job opportunities.

ADVANCEMENT

Many LPNs use their license and experience as a stepping-stone for other occupations in the health field, many of which offer more responsibility and higher salaries. Some LPNs, for example, with additional training, become medical technicians, surgical attendants, optometric assistants, or psychiatric technicians. Many LPNs return to school to become registered nurses. Hospitals often offer LPNs the opportunity for more training, seminars, workshops, and clinical sessions to sharpen their nursing skills. Some LPNs pursue credentialing in specialties such as gerontology, long-term care, IV therapy, and pharmacology.

EARNINGS

According to the U.S. Department of Labor, LPNs earned median annual salaries of $39,820 annually in 2009. Ten percent earned less than $28,890, and 10 percent earned more than $55,090. Many LPNs are able to supplement their salaries with overtime pay and shift differentials.

Licensed practical nurses who are employed full time also usually receive fringe benefits, such as paid sick, holiday, and vacation time, medical coverage, 401(k) plans, and other perks depending on the employer.

WORK ENVIRONMENT

Most LPNs work 40-hour weeks, less if part time. As with other health professionals, they may be asked to work during nights, weekends, or holidays to provide 24-hour care for their patients. Nurses are usually given pay differentials for these shifts. About 18 percent of LPNs work part time.

LPNs employed in hospitals and nursing homes, as well as in clinics, enjoy clean, well-lighted, and generally comfortable work environments. The nature of their work calls for LPNs to be on their feet for most of the shift—providing patient care, dispensing medication, or assisting other health personnel.

OUTLOOK

Employment for LPNs is expected to grow much faster than the average for all occupations through 2018, according to the U.S. Department of Labor. A growing elderly population requiring long-term health care is the primary factor for the demand of qualified LPNs. Traditionally, hospitals have provided the most job opportunities for LPNs. However, this source will only provide a moderate number of openings in the future. Inpatient population is not expected to increase significantly. Also, in many hospitals, certified nursing attendants are increasingly taking over many of the duties of LPNs.

Employment is expected to be strongest for LPNs who work with the elderly in nursing care facilities, home health care services, and community care facilities. Due to advanced medical technology, people are living longer, though many will require medical assistance. Private medical practices will also be excellent job sources because many medical procedures are now being performed on an outpatient basis in doctors' offices. There will be many jobs in rural areas, where there is a shortage of LPNs and other health care professionals.

FOR MORE INFORMATION

For information on licensing, contact

National Council of State Boards of Nursing
111 East Wacker Drive, Suite 2900
Chicago, IL 60601-4277
Tel: 312-525-3600
E-mail: info@ncsbn.org
http://www.ncsbn.org

For career and certification information, contact the following organizations:

National Association for Practical Nurse Education and Service
1940 Duke Street, Suite 200
Alexandria, VA 22314-3452
Tel: 703-933-1003
http://www.napnes.org

National Federation of Licensed Practical Nurses
605 Poole Drive
Garner, NC 27529-5203

Tel: 919-779-0046
http://www.nflpn.org

Discover Nursing, sponsored by Johnson & Johnson Health Care Services, provides information on nursing careers, nursing schools, and scholarships.
Discover Nursing
http://www.discovernursing.com

MANAGEMENT ANALYSTS AND CONSULTANTS

OVERVIEW

Management analysts and consultants analyze business or operating procedures to devise the most efficient methods of accomplishing work. They gather and organize information about operating problems and procedures and prepare recommendations for implementing new systems or changes. They may update manuals outlining established methods of performing work and train personnel in new applications. There are approximately 552,770 management analysts and consultants employed in the United States.

THE JOB

Management analysts and consultants are called in to solve any of a vast array of organizational problems. They are often needed when a rapidly growing small company needs a better system of control over inventories and expenses.

The role of the consultant is to come into a situation in which a client is unsure or inexpert and to recommend actions or provide assessments. There are many different types of management analysts and consultants. In general, they all require knowledge of general management, operations, marketing, logistics, materials management and physical distribution, finance and accounting, human resources, electronic data processing and systems, and management science.

Management analysts and consultants may be called in when a major manufacturer must reorganize its corporate structure when acquiring a new division. For example, they assist when a company relocates to another state by coordinating the move, planning the new facility, and training new workers.

SCHOOL SUBJECTS
Business, Computer science, Speech

PERSONAL SKILLS
Communication/Ideas, Leadership/management

MINIMUM EDUCATION LEVEL
Bachelor's degree

CERTIFICATION OR LICENSING
Voluntary

WORK ENVIRONMENT
Primarily indoors, Primarily multiple locations

The work of management analysts and consultants is quite flexible—it varies from job to job. In general, management analysts and consultants collect, review, and analyze data, make recommendations, and assist in the implementation of their proposals. Some projects require several consultants to work together, each specializing in a different area. Other jobs require the analysts to work independently.

Public and private organizations use management analysts for a variety of reasons. Some organizations lack the resources necessary to handle a project. Other organizations, before they pursue a particular course of action, will consult an analyst to determine what resources will be required or what problems will be encountered. Some companies seek outside advice on how to resolve organizational problems that have already been identified or to avoid troublesome problems that could arise.

Firms providing consulting practitioners range in size from solo practitioners to large international companies employing hundreds of people. The services are generally provided on a contract basis. A company will choose a consulting firm that specializes in the area that needs assistance, and then the two firms negotiate the conditions of the contract. Contract variables include the proposed cost of the project, staffing requirements, and the deadline.

After getting a contract, the analyst's first job is to define the nature and extent of the project. He or she analyzes statistics, such as annual revenues, employment, or expenditures. He or she may also interview employees and observe the operations of the organization on a day-to-day basis.

The next step for the analyst is to use his or her knowledge of management systems to develop solutions. While preparing recommendations, he or she must take into account the general nature of the business, the relationship of the firm to others in its industry, the firm's internal organization, and the information gained through data collection and analysis.

Once they have decided on a course of action, management analysts and consultants usually write reports of their findings and recommendations and present them to the client. They often make formal oral presentations about their findings as well. Some projects require only reports; others require assistance in implementing the suggestions.

REQUIREMENTS
High School

High school courses that will give you a general preparation for this field include business, mathematics, and computer science. Management analysts and consultants must pass on their findings through written or oral presentations, so be sure to take English and speech classes, too.

Postsecondary Training

Employers generally prefer to hire management analysts and consultants with a master's degree in business or public administration, or at least a bachelor's degree and several years of appropriate work experience. Many college majors provide a suitable education for this occupation because of the diversity of problem areas addressed by management analysts and consultants. These include many areas in the computer and information sciences, accounting, economics, engineering, business and management, education, communications, marketing and distribution, and architecture and environmental design.

When hired directly from school, management analysts and consultants often participate in formal company training programs. These programs may include instruction on policies and procedures, computer systems and software, and management practices and principles. Regardless of their background, most management analysts and consultants routinely attend conferences to keep abreast of current developments in the field.

Certification or Licensing

The Institute of Management Consultants USA offers the certified management consultant designation to those consultants who meet minimum educational and experience criteria, and pass a rigorous examination process. All types of consultants (i.e., internal consultants, technical consultants, strategy consultants, etc.) are eligible for certification; the requirement is that they must consult to management of organizations. Certification is voluntary, but provides an additional advantage to those who are interested in demonstrating their competency, experience, and ethics as measured against globally recognized professional standards. The certification is recognized in 46 countries, which is an advantage to those desiring to start an international consulting practice.

Other Requirements

Management analysts and consultants are often responsible for recommending layoffs of staff, so it is important that they learn to deal with people diplomatically. Their job requires a great deal of tact, enlisting cooperation while exerting leadership, debating their points, and pointing out errors. Consultants must be quick thinkers, able to refute objections with finality. They must also be able to make excellent presentations.

A management analyst must also be unbiased and analytical, with a disposition toward the intellectual side of business and a natural curiosity about the way things work best.

EXPLORING

The reference departments of most libraries include business areas that will have valuable research tools such as encyclopedias of business consultants and "who's who" of business consultants. These books should list management analysis and consulting firms across the country, describing their annual sales and area of specialization, like industrial, high tech, small business, and retail. After doing some research, you can contact these firms and ask for more information.

For more general business exploration, see if your school has a business or young leaders club. If there is nothing of the sort, you may want to explore Junior Achievement, a nationwide association that connects young business-minded students with professionals in the field for mentoring and career advice. Visit http://www.ja.org for more information. You should also consider joining Business Professionals of America, a membership organization for middle school, high school, and college students who plan to or who are currently pursuing careers in business management, office administration, information technology, and other related fields. Visit http://www.bpa.org for more information.

Ask a business teacher to arrange an information interview with a management analyst or consultant. Ask the following questions: What made you want to enter the field? What do you like most and least about your job? How did you train for this career? What advice would you give to someone who is interested in this career?

EMPLOYERS

About 26 percent of the 552,770 management analysts and consultants in the United States are self-employed. Federal, state, and local governments employ many of the others. The U.S. Department of Defense employs the majority of those working for the federal government. The remainder work in the private sector for companies that provide consulting services. Although management analysts and consultants are found throughout the country, the majority are concentrated in major metropolitan areas.

STARTING OUT

Most government agencies offer entry-level analyst and consultant positions to people with bachelor's degrees and no work experience. Many entrants are also career changers who were formerly mid- and upper-level managers. With 26 percent of the practicing management consultants self-employed, career changing is a common route into the field.

Anyone with some degree of business expertise can begin to work as an independent consultant. The number of one- and two-person consulting firms in this country is well over 100,000. Establishing a wide range of appropriate personal contacts is by far the most effective way to get started in this field. Consultants have to sell themselves and their expertise, a task far tougher than selling a tangible product the customer can see and handle. Many consultants get their first clients by advertising in newspapers, magazines, and trade or professional periodicals. After some time in the field, word-of-mouth advertising is often the primary method of attracting new clients.

ADVANCEMENT

A new consultant in a large firm may be referred to as an *associate* for the first couple of years. The next progression is to *senior associate*, a title that indicates three to five years' experience and the ability to supervise others and do more complex and independent work. After about five years, the analyst who is progressing well may become an *engagement manager* with the responsibility to lead a consulting team on a particular client project. The best managers become *senior engagement managers,* leading several study teams or a very large project team. After about seven years, those who excel will be considered for appointment as *junior partners* or *principals.* Partnership involves responsibility for marketing the firm and leading client projects. Some may be promoted to senior partnership or *director,* but few people successfully run this full course. Management analysts and consultants with entrepreneurial ambition may open their own firms.

EARNINGS

Salaries and hourly rates for management analysts and consultants vary widely, according to experience, specialization, education, and employer. In 2009, management analysts and consultants had median annual earnings of $75,250, according to the U.S. Department of Labor. Salaries ranged from less than $42,550 to $134,820 or more.

Many consultants can demand between $400 and $1,000 per day. Their fees are often well over $40 per hour. Self-employed management consultants receive no fringe benefits and generally have to maintain their own office, but their pay is usually much higher than salaried consultants. They can make more than $2,000 per day or $250,000 in one year from consulting just two days per week.

Typical benefits for salaried analysts and consultants include health and life insurance, retirement plans, vacation and sick leave, profit sharing, and bonuses for outstanding work. All travel expenses are generally reimbursed by the employer.

WORK ENVIRONMENT

Management analysts and consultants generally divide their time between their own offices and the client's office or production facility. They can spend a great deal of time on the road.

Most management analysts and consultants work at least 40 hours per week plus overtime, depending on the project. The nature of consulting projects—working on location with a single client toward a specific goal—allows these professionals to totally immerse themselves in their work. They sometimes work 14- to 16-hour days, and six- or seven-day workweeks can be fairly common.

While self-employed, consultants may enjoy the luxury of setting their own hours and doing a great deal of their work at home; the trade-off is sacrificing the benefits provided by the large firms. Their livelihood depends on the additional responsibility of maintaining and expanding their clientele on their own.

Although those in this career usually avoid much of the potential tedium of working for one company all day, every day, they face many pressures resulting from deadlines and client expectations. Because the clients are generally paying generous fees, they want to see dramatic results, and the management analyst can feel the weight of this.

OUTLOOK

Employment of management analysts is expected to grow much faster than the average for all occupations through 2018, according to the U.S. Department of Labor (DOL). Industry and government agencies are expected to rely more and more on the expertise of these professionals to improve and streamline the performance of their organizations. Many job openings will result from the need to replace personnel who transfer to other fields or leave the labor force.

Competition for management consulting jobs will be strong. Employers can choose from a large pool of applicants who have a wide variety of educational backgrounds and experience. The challenging nature of this job, coupled with high salary potential, attracts many. A graduate degree, experience and expertise in the industry, as well as a knack for public relations, are needed to stay competitive.

Trends that have increased the growth of employment in this field include advancements in information technology and e-commerce, the growth of international business, and fluctuations in the economy that have forced businesses to streamline and downsize.

The DOL predicts that opportunities will be best at very large consulting firms that have expertise in international business and in smaller firms that focus on providing consulting services in specific areas such as biotechnology, engineering, information technology, health care, marketing, and human resources. Employment for management analysts and consultants who specialize in "green" consulting services that help companies improve energy efficiency and implement "green" initiatives will also be strong.

FOR MORE INFORMATION

Visit the institute's Web site for publications, job listings, career resources, and information on the Uniform CPA

Examination, educational training, scholarships for high school and college students, and membership for college students.

American Institute of Certified Public Accountants
1211 Avenue of the Americas
New York, NY 10036-8775
Tel: 212-596-6200
http://www.aicpa.org

Visit the association's Web site for information about management trends, job listings, and membership for college students.

American Management Association
1601 Broadway
New York, NY 10019-7434
Tel: 877-566-9441
E-mail: customerservice@amanet.org
http://www.amanet.org

Visit the association's Web site for job listings and general information about the field.

Association of Internal Management Consultants
824 Caribbean Court
Marco Island, FL 34145-3422
Tel: 239-642-0580
E-mail: info@aimc.org
http://www.aimc.org

Contact the association for information about the industry and scholarships for MBA students.

Association of Management Consulting Firms
370 Lexington Avenue, Suite 2209
New York, NY 10017-6573
Tel: 212-262 3055
E-mail: info@amcf.org
http://www.amcf.org

Contact the association for information on business consulting.

Association of Professional Consultants
PO Box 51193
Irvine, CA 92619-1193
Tel: 800-745-5050
E-mail: apc@consultapc.org
http://www.consultapc.org

Visit the institute's Web site for information on certification and scholarships and membership for college students.

Institute of Management Consultants USA
2025 M Street, NW, Suite 800

Washington, DC 20036-3309
Tel: 202-367-1134
http://www.imcusa.org

MARKETING RESEARCH ANALYSTS

OVERVIEW

Marketing research analysts collect, analyze, and interpret data in order to determine potential demand for a product or service. By examining the buying habits, wants, needs, and preferences of consumers, research analysts are able to recommend ways to improve products, increase sales, and expand customer bases. There are approximately 226,410 marketing research analysts employed in the United States.

THE JOB

Marketing researchers collect and analyze all kinds of information in order to help companies improve their products, establish or modify sales and distribution policies, and make decisions regarding future plans and directions. In addition, research analysts monitor both in-house studies and off-site research, interpret results,

SCHOOL SUBJECTS
Business, Mathematics

PERSONAL SKILLS
Following instructions, Technical/scientific

MINIMUM EDUCATION LEVEL
Bachelor's degree

CERTIFICATION OR LICENSING
Voluntary

WORK ENVIRONMENT
Primarily indoors, Primarily one location

provide explanations of compiled data, and develop research tools.

One area of marketing research focuses on company products and services. In order to determine consumer likes and dislikes, research analysts collect data on brand names, trademarks, product design, and packaging for existing products, items being test-marketed, and those in experimental stages. Analysts also study competing products and services that are already on the market to help managers and strategic planners develop new products and create appropriate advertising campaigns.

In the sales methods and policy area of marketing research, analysts examine firms' sales records and conduct a variety of sales-related studies. For example, information on sales in various geographical areas is analyzed and compared to previous sales figures, changes in population, and total and seasonal sales volume. By analyzing this data, marketing researchers can identify peak sales periods and recommend ways to target new customers. Such information helps marketers plan future sales campaigns and establish sales quotas and commissions.

Advertising research is closely related to sales research. Studies on the effectiveness of advertising in different parts of the country are conducted and compared to sales records. This research is helpful in planning future advertising campaigns and in selecting the appropriate media to use.

Marketing research that focuses on consumer demand and preferences solicits opinions of the people who use the products or services being considered. In addition to actually conducting opinion studies, marketing researchers often design the ways to obtain the information. They write scripts for telephone interviews, develop direct-mail questionnaires and field surveys, and design focus group programs.

Through one or a combination of these studies, market researchers are able to gather information on consumer reaction to the need for and style, design, price, and use of a product. The studies attempt to reveal who uses various products or services, identify potential customers, or get suggestions for product or service improvement. This information is helpful for forecasting sales, planning design modifications, and determining changes in features.

Once information has been gathered, marketing researchers analyze the findings. They then detail their findings and recommendations in a written report and often orally present them to management as well.

A number of professionals compose the marketing research team. The *project supervisor* is responsible for overseeing a study from beginning to end. The *statistician* determines the sample size—or the number of people to be surveyed—and compares the number of responses. The project supervisor or statistician, in conjunction with other specialists (such as *demographers* and *psychologists*), often determines the number of interviews to be conducted as well as their locations. *Field interviewers* survey people in various public places, such as shopping malls, office complexes, and popular attractions. *Telemarketers* gather information by placing calls to current or potential customers, to people listed in telephone books, or to those who appear on specialized lists obtained from list houses. Once questionnaires come in from the field, *tabulators* and *coders* examine the data, count the answers, code noncategorical answers, and tally the primary counts. The marketing research analyst then analyzes the returns, writes up the final report, and makes recommendations to the client or to management.

Marketing research analysts must be thoroughly familiar with research techniques and procedures. Sometimes the research problem is clearly defined, and information can be gathered readily. Other times, company executives may know only that a problem exists as evidenced by a decline in sales. In these cases, the market research analyst is expected to collect the facts that will aid in revealing and resolving the problem.

REQUIREMENTS

High School

Most employers require their marketing research analysts to hold at least a bachelor's degree, so a college preparatory program is advised. Classes in English, marketing, economics, mathematics, psychology, and sociology are particularly important. Courses in computer science are especially useful, since a great deal of tabulation and statistical analysis is required in the marketing research field.

Postsecondary Training

A bachelor's degree is essential for careers in marketing research. Majors in marketing, business administration, statistics, computer science, history, or economics provide a good background for most types of research positions. In addition, course work in sociology and psychology is helpful for those who are leaning toward consumer demand and opinion research. Since quantitative skills are important in various types of industrial or analytic research, students interested in these areas should take statistics, econometrics, survey design, sampling theory, and other mathematics courses.

Many employers prefer that a marketing research analyst hold a master's degree as well as a bachelor's degree. A master's of business administration, for example, is frequently required on projects calling for complex statistical and business analysis. Other recommended degrees include those in marketing, statistics, communications, and related fields. Graduate work at the doctorate level is not necessary for most positions, but it is highly desirable for those who plan to become involved in advanced research studies.

Certification or Licensing

The Marketing Research Association and the American Marketing Association offer certification for marketing research analysts. Contact these organizations for more information.

Other Requirements

To work in this career, you should be intelligent, detail oriented, and accurate; have the ability to work easily with words and numbers; and be particularly interested in solving problems through data collection and analysis. In addition, you must be patient and persistent, since long hours are often required when working on complex studies.

As part of the market research team, you must be able to work well with others and have an interest in people. The ability to communicate, both orally and in writing, is also important, since you will be responsible for writing up detailed reports on the findings in various studies and presenting recommendations to management.

EXPLORING

You can find many opportunities in high school to learn more about the necessary skills for the field of marketing research. For example, experiments in science, problems in student government, committee work, and other school activities provide exposure to situations similar to those encountered by marketing research analysts.

You can also seek part-time employment as a survey interviewer at local marketing research firms. Gathering field data for consumer surveys offers valuable experience through actual contact with both the public and marketing research supervisors. In addition, many companies seek a variety of other employees to code, tabulate, and edit surveys; monitor telephone interviews; and validate the information entered on written questionnaires.

You can search for job listings in local newspapers and on the Web or apply directly to research organizations.

EMPLOYERS

Approximately 226,410 marketing research analysts are employed in the United States. Large corporations, industrial firms, advertising agencies, data collection businesses, and private research organizations that handle local surveys for companies on a contract basis employ marketing research analysts. While many marketing research organizations offer a broad range of services, some firms subcontract parts of an overall project out to specialized companies. For example, one research firm may concentrate on product interviews, while another might focus on measuring the effectiveness of product advertising. Similarly, some marketing analysts specialize in one industry or area. For example, agricultural marketing specialists prepare sales forecasts for food businesses, which use the information in their advertising and sales programs.

Although many smaller firms located all across the country outsource studies to marketing research firms, these research firms, along with most large corporations that employ marketing research analysts, are located in such big cities as New York or Chicago. Approximately 90 percent of salaried marketing research analysts are employed in private industry, but opportunities also exist in government and academia, as well as at hospitals, public libraries, and a variety of other types of organizations.

STARTING OUT

Students with a graduate degree in marketing research and experience in quantitative techniques have the best chances of landing jobs as marketing research analysts. Since a bachelor's degree in marketing or business is usually not sufficient to obtain such a position, many employees without postgraduate degrees start out as research assistants, trainees, interviewers, or questionnaire editors. In such positions, those aspiring to the job of research analyst can gain valuable experience conducting interviews, analyzing data, and writing reports.

Use your college career services office, the Web, and help wanted sections of local newspapers to look for job leads. Another way to get into the marketing research field is through personal and professional contacts. Names and telephone numbers of potential employers may come from professors, friends, or relatives. Finally, students who have participated in internships or have held marketing research-related jobs on a part-time basis while in school or during the summer may be able to obtain employment at these firms or at similar organizations.

ADVANCEMENT

Most marketing research professionals begin as *junior analysts* or *research assistants.* In these positions, they help in preparing questionnaires and related materials, training survey interviewers, and tabulating and coding survey results. After gaining sufficient experience in these and other aspects of research project development, employees are often assigned their own research projects, which usually involve supervisory and planning responsibilities. A typical promotion path for those climbing the company ladder might be from assistant researcher to marketing research analyst to assistant manager and then to manager of a branch office for a large private research firm. From there, some professionals become market research executives or research directors for industrial or business firms.

Since marketing research analysts learn about all aspects of marketing on the job, some advance by moving to positions in other departments, such as advertising or sales. Depending on the interests and experience of marketing professionals, other areas of employment to which they can advance include data processing, teaching at the university level, statistics, economics, and industrial research and development.

In general, few employees go from starting positions to executive jobs at one company. Advancement often requires changing employers. Therefore, marketing research analysts who want to move up the ranks frequently go from one company to another, sometimes many times during their careers.

EARNINGS

Beginning salaries in marketing research depend on the qualifications of the employee, the nature of the position, and the size of the firm. Interviewers, coders, tabulators, editors, and a variety of other employees are usually paid minimum wage ($8.25 an hour, or $18,850 annually). The U.S. Department of Labor reports that in 2009, median annual earnings of market research analysts were $61,580. The middle 50 percent earned salaries that ranged from $44,600 to $85,230. Salaries ranged from less than $34,260 to more than $111,900. Experienced analysts working in supervisory positions at large firms can earn even higher earnings. Market research directors earn up to $200,000.

Because business or industrial firms employ most marketing research workers, they receive typical fringe benefit packages, including health and life insurance, pension plans, and paid vacation and sick leave.

WORK ENVIRONMENT

Marketing research analysts usually work a 40-hour week. Occasionally, overtime is necessary in order to meet project deadlines. Although they frequently interact with a variety of marketing research team members, analysts also do a lot of independent work, analyzing data, writing reports, and preparing statistical charts.

While most marketing research analysts work in offices located at the firm's main headquarters, those who supervise interviewers may go into the field to oversee work. In order to attend conferences, meet with clients, or check on the progress of various research studies, many market research analysts find that regular travel is required.

OUTLOOK

The U.S. Department of Labor predicts that employment for marketing research analysts will grow much faster than the average for all careers through 2018. Increasing competition among producers of consumer goods and services and industrial products, combined with a growing awareness of the value of marketing research data, will contribute to opportunities in the field. The increasing globalization of business will also create openings for analysts to study foreign markets and competition. Opportunities will be best for those with graduate degrees who seek employment in marketing research firms, consulting firms, companies that design computer systems and software, financial services organizations, health care institutions, advertising firms, manufacturing firms that produce consumer goods, and insurance companies.

While many new graduates are attracted to the field, creating a competitive situation, the best jobs and the highest pay will go to those individuals who hold a master's degree or doctorate in marketing research, statistics, economics, or computer science.

FOR MORE INFORMATION

For profiles of advertising workers and career information, contact

Advertising Educational Foundation
220 East 42nd Street, Suite 3300
New York, NY 10017-5813
Tel: 212-986-8060
http://www.aded.org

For information on college chapters, internship opportunities, and financial aid opportunities, contact
American Advertising Federation
1101 Vermont Avenue, NW, Suite 500
Washington, DC 20005-6306
Tel: 800-999-2231
E-mail: aaf@aaf.org
http://www.aaf.org

For information on graduate programs, contact
American Association for Public Opinion Research
111 Deer Lake Road, Suite 100
Deerfield, IL 60015-4943
Tel: 847-205-2651
E-mail: info@aapor.org
http://www.aapor.org

For information on advertising agencies, contact
American Association of Advertising Agencies
405 Lexington Avenue, 18th Floor
New York, NY 10174-1801
Tel: 212-682-2500
http://www.aaaa.org

For information on careers and certification, contact
American Marketing Association
311 South Wacker Drive, Suite 5800
Chicago, IL 60606-6629
Tel: 800-262-1150
http://www.marketingpower.com

For information on graduate programs in marketing, contact
Council of American Survey Research Organizations
170 North Country Road, Suite 4
Port Jefferson, NY 11777-2606
Tel: 631-928-6954
E-mail: casro@casro.org
http://www.casro.org

For information on education and training, contact
Marketing Research Association
110 National Drive, 2nd Floor
Glastonbury, CT 06033-4372
Tel: 860-682-1000
E-mail: email@mra-net.org
http://www.mra-net.org

For career information, visit
Careers Outside the Box: Survey Research: A Fun, Exciting, Rewarding Career
http://www.casro.org/careers

MASSAGE THERAPISTS

OVERVIEW

Massage therapy is a broad term referring to a number of health-related practices, including Swedish massage, sports massage, Rolfing, Shiatsu and acupressure, trigger point therapy, and reflexology. Although the techniques, or modalities, vary, most *massage therapists* (or *massotherapists*) press and rub the skin and muscles. Relaxed muscles, improved blood circulation and joint mobility, reduced stress and anxiety, and decreased recovery time for sprains and injured muscles are just a few of the potential benefits of massage therapy. Massage therapists are sometimes called *bodyworkers*. The titles *masseur* and *masseuse,* once common, are now rare among those who use massage for therapy and rehabilitation. There are approximately 55,920 massage therapists employed in the United States.

THE JOB

Massage therapists work to produce physical, mental, and emotional benefits through the manipulation of the body's soft tissue. Auxiliary methods, such as the movement of joints and the application of dry and steam heat, are also used. Among the potential physical benefits are the release of muscle tension and stiff-

SCHOOL SUBJECTS
Health, Physical education

PERSONAL SKILLS
Helping/teaching, Mechanical/manipulative

MINIMUM EDUCATION LEVEL
Some postsecondary training

CERTIFICATION OR LICENSING
Recommended (certification),
Required by certain states (licensing)

WORK ENVIRONMENT
Primarily indoors, Primarily one location

ness, reduced blood pressure, better blood circulation, a shorter healing time for sprains and pulled muscles, increased flexibility and greater range of motion in the joints, and reduced swelling from edema (excess fluid buildup in body tissue). Massage may also improve posture, strengthen the immune system, and reduce the formation of scar tissue.

Mental and emotional benefits include a relaxed state of mind, reduced stress and anxiety, clearer thinking, and a general sense of well-being. Physical, mental, and emotional health are all interconnected: Being physically fit and healthy can improve emotional health, just as a positive mental attitude can bolster the immune system to help the body fight off infection. A release of muscle tension also leads to reduced stress and anxiety, and physical manipulation of sore muscles can help speed the healing process.

There are many different approaches a massage therapist may take. Among the most popular are Swedish massage, sports massage, Rolfing, Shiatsu and acupressure, and trigger point therapy.

In Swedish massage the traditional techniques are effleurage, petrissage, friction, and tapotement. Effleurage (stroking) uses light and hard rhythmic strokes to relax muscles and improve blood circulation. It is often performed at the beginning and end of a massage session. Petrissage (kneading) is the rhythmic squeezing, pressing, and lifting of a muscle. For friction, the fingers, thumb, or palm or heel of the hand are pressed into the skin with a small circular movement. The massage therapist's fingers are sometimes pressed deeply into a joint. Tapotement (tapping), in which the hands strike the skin in rapid succession, is used to improve blood circulation.

During the session the client, covered with sheets, lies undressed on a padded table. Oil or lotion is used to smooth the skin. Some massage therapists use aromatherapy, adding fragrant essences to the oil to relax the client and stimulate circulation. Swedish massage may employ a number of auxiliary techniques, including the use of rollers, belts, and vibrators; steam and dry heat; ultraviolet and infrared light; and saunas, whirlpools, steam baths, and packs of hot water or ice.

Sports massage is essentially Swedish massage used in the context of athletics. A light massage generally is given before an event or game to loosen and warm the muscles. This reduces the chance of injury and may improve performance. After the event the athlete is massaged more deeply to alleviate pain, reduce stiffness, and promote healing.

Rolfing, developed by American Ida Rolf, involves deep, sometimes painful massage. Intense pressure is applied to various parts of the body. Rolfing practitioners believe that emotional disturbances, physical pain, and other problems can occur when the body is out of alignment—for example, as a result of poor posture. This method takes 10 sessions to complete.

Like the ancient Oriental science of acupuncture, Shiatsu and acupressure are based on the concept of meridians, or invisible channels of flowing energy in the body. The massage therapist presses down on particular points along these channels to release blocked energy and untie knots of muscle tension. For this approach the patient wears loosely fitted clothes, lies on the floor or on a futon, and is not given oil or lotion for the skin.

Trigger point therapy, a neuromuscular technique, focuses in on a painful area, or trigger point, in a muscle. A trigger point might be associated with a problem in another part of the body. Using the fingers or an instrument, such as a rounded piece of wood, concentrated pressure is placed on the irritated area in order to "deactivate" the trigger point.

All of these methods of massage can be altered and intermingled depending on the client's needs. Massage therapists can be proficient in one or many of the methods, and usually tailor a session to the individual.

REQUIREMENTS
High School

Since massage therapists need to know more than just technical skills, many practitioners use the basic knowledge learned in high school as a foundation to build a solid career in the field. During your high school years, you should take fundamental science courses, such as chemistry, anatomy, and biology. These classes will give you a basic understanding of the human body and prepare you for the health and anatomy classes you will take while completing your postsecondary education. English, psychology, and other classes relating to communications and human development will also be useful as the successful massage therapist is able to express his or her ideas with clients as well as understand the clients' reactions to the therapy. If you think you might wish to run your own massage therapy business someday, computer and business courses are essential. Finally, do not neglect your own physical well-being. Take physical education and health courses to strengthen your body and your understanding of your own conditioning.

Postsecondary Training

The best way to become a successful massage therapist is to attend an accredited massage therapy school after you have finished high school. There are more than 300 state-accredited massage schools located throughout the United States. Nearly 100 of these schools are accredited or approved by the Commission on Massage Therapy Accreditation (COMTA), a major accrediting agency for massage therapy programs and an affiliate of the American Massage Therapy Association (AMTA). COMTA-accredited and -approved schools must provide at least 500 hours of classroom instruction. (The average massage therapist has 624 hours of initial training, according to the AMTA.) Studies should include such courses as anatomy, physiology, theory and practice of massage therapy, and ethics. In addition, students should receive supervised hands-on experience. Most programs offer students the opportunity to participate at clinics, such as those providing massage services at hospices, hospitals, and shelters, or at school clinics that are open to the general public.

Massage therapy training programs typically take about a year to complete. Students can specialize in particular disciplines, such as infant massage or rehabilitative massage. Basic first aid and cardiopulmonary resuscitation (CPR) must also be learned. When choosing a school, you should pay close attention to the philosophy and curricula of the program, since a wide range of program options exists. Also, keep in mind that licensure requirements for massage therapists vary by state. For example, some state medical boards require students to have completed more than 500 hours of instruction before they can be recognized as massage therapists. Part of your process for choosing a school, therefore, should include making sure that the school's curriculum will allow you to meet your state's requirements.

Certification or Licensing

Currently, 42 states and the District of Columbia regulate the practice of massage therapy, requiring licensure, certification, or registration. Because requirements for licensing, certification, registration, and even local ordinances vary, however, you will need to check with your state's department of regulatory agencies to get specifics for your area. Typically, requirements include completing an accredited program and passing a written test and a demonstration of massage therapy techniques.

The National Certification Board for Therapeutic Massage and Bodywork (NCBTMB) offers two national certification examinations for massage therapists: the National Certification Examination for Therapeutic Massage and Bodywork and the National Certification Examination for Therapeutic Massage. Additionally, the NCBTMB is currently developing an advanced certification examination. To learn more about the exams, visit http://www.ncbtmb.org. Another licensing exam, the Massage & Bodywork Licensing Examination, is offered by the Federation of State Massage Therapy Boards (http://www.fsmtb.org). Certification is highly recommended, since it demonstrates a therapist's high level of education and achievement. Certification may also make a therapist a more desirable candidate for job openings.

Other Requirements

Physical requirements of massage therapists generally include the ability to use their hands and other tools to rub or press on the client's body. Manual dexterity is usually required to administer the treatments, as is the ability to stand for at least an hour at a time. Special modifications or accommodations can often be made for people with different abilities.

If you are interested in becoming a massage therapist, you should be, above all, nurturing and caring. Constance Bickford, a certified massage therapist in Chicago, thinks that it is necessary to be both flexible and creative: easily adaptable to the needs of the client, as well as able to use different techniques to help the client feel better. Listening well and responding to the client is vital, as is focusing all attention on the task at hand. Massage therapists need to tune in to their client rather than zone out, thinking about the grocery list or what to cook for supper. An effective massage is a mindful one, where massage therapist and client work together toward improved health.

To be a successful massage therapist, you should also be trustworthy and sensitive. Someone receiving a massage may feel awkward lying naked on a table in an office, covered by a sheet and listening to music while a stranger kneads his or her muscles. A good massage therapist will make the client feel comfortable in what could potentially be perceived as a vulnerable situation.

Therapists considering opening up their own business should be prepared for busy and slow times. In order to both serve their clients well and stay in business, they should be adequately staffed during rush seasons, and must be financially able to withstand dry spells.

EXPLORING

The best way to become familiar with massage therapy is to get a massage. Look for a certified therapist in your area and make an appointment for a session. If you can afford it, consider going to several different therapists who offer different types of massage. Also, ask if you can set up an information interview with one of the therapists. Explain that you are interested in pursuing this career, and come to the interview prepared to ask questions. What is this massage therapist's educational background? Why was he or she drawn to the job? What is the best part of this work? By talking to a massage therapist, you may also have the chance to develop a mentoring relationship with him or her.

A less costly approach is to find a book on massage instruction at a local public library or bookstore. Massage techniques can then be practiced at home. Books on self-massage are available. Many books discuss in detail the theoretical basis for the techniques. One such book is *Mosby's Fundamentals of Therapeutic Massage,* 4th edition, by Sandy Fritz (St. Louis: Mosby, 2008). DVDs that demonstrate massage techniques are available as well.

Consider volunteering at a hospice, nursing home, or shelter. This work will give you experience in caring for others and help you develop good listening skills. It is important for massage therapists to listen well and respond appropriately to their clients' needs. The massage therapist must make clients feel comfortable, and volunteer work can help foster the skills necessary to achieve this.

EMPLOYERS

Approximately 55,920 massage therapists are employed in the United States. After graduating from an accredited school of massage therapy, there are a number of possibilities for employment. Doctors' offices, hospitals, hotels, clinics, health clubs, resorts, country clubs, cruise ships, community service organizations, and nursing homes, for example, all employ massage therapists. Some chiropractors have a massage therapist on staff to whom they can refer patients. A number of massage therapists run their own businesses. Most opportunities for work will be in larger, urban areas with population growth, although massage therapy is slowly spreading to more rural areas as well.

STARTING OUT

There are a number of resources you can use to locate a job. The AMTA provides job listings and career advice at its Web site, http://www.amtamassage.org. Massage therapy schools have career services offices. Newspapers often list jobs. Some graduates are able to enter the field as self-employed massage therapists, scheduling their own appointments and managing their own offices.

Networking is a valuable tool in maintaining a successful massage therapy enterprise. Many massage therapists get clients through referrals, and often rely on word of mouth to build a solid customer base. Beginning massage therapists might wish to consult businesses about arranging on-site massage sessions for their employees.

Health fairs are also good places to distribute information about massage therapy practices and learn about other services in the industry. Often, organizers of large sporting events will employ massage therapists to give massages to athletes at the finish line. These events may include marathons and runs or bike rides held to raise money for charitable organizations.

ADVANCEMENT

For self-employed massage therapists, advancement is measured by reputation, the ability to attract clients, and the fees charged for services. Health clubs, country clubs, and other institutions have supervisory positions for massage therapists. In a community service organization, massage therapists may be promoted to the position of health service director. Licensed massage therapists often become instructors or advisers at schools for massage therapy. They may also make themselves available to advise individuals or companies on the short- and long-term benefits of massage therapy, and how massage therapy can be introduced into professional work environments.

EARNINGS

The earnings of massage therapists vary greatly with the level of experience and location of practice. Therapists in New York and California, for example, typically charge higher rates than those in other parts of the country. Some entry-level massage therapists earn as little as minimum wage (ending up with a yearly income of around $18,850). Hourly earnings are much higher for experienced therapists. The American Massage Therapy Association reports that massage therapists charge an average of $63 for a one-hour massage. Those with earnings at the high end typically worked in higher paying geographic areas (such as large cities), had years of experience, and had built up a large clientele.

The U.S. Department of Labor reports that massage therapists earned median annual salaries of $35,230 a year in 2009. The lowest paid 10 percent earned $17,270 or less, while the highest paid 10 percent earned $68,670 or more.

Self-employed therapists are not paid for the time spent on bookkeeping, maintaining their offices, waiting for customers to arrive, and looking for new clients. In addition, they must pay a self-employment tax and provide their own benefits. With membership in some national organizations, self-employed massage therapists may be eligible for group life, health, liability, and renter's insurance through the organization's insurance agency.

Massage therapists employed by a health club usually get free or discounted memberships to the club. Those who work for resorts or on cruise ships can get free or discounted travel and accommodations, in addition to full access to facilities when not on duty. Massage therapists employed by a sports team often get to attend the team's sporting events.

WORK ENVIRONMENT

Massage therapists work in clean, comfortable settings. Because a relaxed environment is essential, the massage room may be dim, and soft music, scents, and oils are often used. Since massage therapists may see a number of people per day, it is important to maintain a hygienic working area. This involves changing sheets on the massage table after each client, as well as cleaning and sterilizing any implements used, and washing hands frequently.

Massage therapists employed by businesses may use a portable massage chair—that is, a padded chair that leaves the client in a forward-leaning position, which is ideal for massage of the back and neck. Some massage therapists work out of their homes or travel to the homes of their clients.

The workweek of a massage therapist is typically 35 to 40 hours, which may include evenings and weekends. On average, 20 hours per week are spent with clients, and the other hours are spent making appointments and taking care of other business-related details.

Since the physical work is sometimes demanding, massage therapists need to take measures to prevent repetitive stress disorders, such as carpal tunnel syndrome. Also, for their own personal safety, massage therapists who work out of their homes or have odd office hours need to be particularly careful about scheduling appointments with unknown clients.

OUTLOOK

Employment for massage therapists is expected to grow faster than the average for all careers through 2018, according to the U.S. Department of Labor. The growing acceptance of massage therapy as an important health care discipline has led to the creation of additional jobs for massage therapists in many sectors. Opportunities should be strongest for women, as clients—both male and female—report that they are more comfortable working with female massage therapists. Approximately 85 percent of massage therapists are women.

One certified massage therapist points to sports massage as one of the fastest growing specialties in the field. The increasing popularity of professional sports has given massage therapists new opportunities to work as key members of a team's staff. Their growing presence in sports has made massage therapy more visible to the public, spreading the awareness of the physical benefits of massage. Employment for massage therapists who work with the elderly is also experiencing strong growth.

Massages aren't just for athletes. According to a 2010 survey by the American Massage Therapy Association, 18 percent of Americans surveyed had a massage in the past 12 months. The survey found that people are getting massages not just for medical reasons, but to relax and reduce stress.

There is a growing opportunity for massage therapists in the corporate world. Many employers eager to hold on to good employees offer perks, such as workplace massages. As a result, many massage therapists are working as mobile business consultants.

FOR MORE INFORMATION

For information on careers and education programs, contact

American Massage Therapy Association
500 Davis Street
Evanston, IL 60201-4464
Tel: 877-905-2700
E-mail: info@amtamassage.org
http://www.amtamassage.org

For information on careers in the field (including the brochure, Your Massage & Bodywork Career), *state board requirements, and training programs, contact*

Associated Bodywork and Massage Professionals
25188 Genesee Trail Road, Suite 200
Golden, CO 80401-5702
E-mail: expectmore@abmp.com
http://www.abmp.com
http://www.massagetherapy.com

For information on accreditation and programs, contact
Commission on Massage Therapy Accreditation
5335 Wisconsin Avenue, NW, Suite 440
Washington, DC 20015-2054
Tel: 202-895-1518
E-mail: info@comta.org
http://www.comta.org

For information about certification, contact
Federation of State Massage Therapy Boards
7111 West 151st Street, Suite 356
Overland Park, KS 66223-2231
Tel: 888-70-FSMTB
E-mail: info@fsmtb.org
http://www.fsmtb.org

For information about state certification and education requirements, contact
National Certification Board for Therapeutic Massage and Bodywork
1901 South Meyers Road, Suite 240
Oakbrook Terrace, IL 60181-5243
Tel: 800-296-0664
E-mail: info@ncbtmb.org
http://www.ncbtmb.org

MATHEMATICIANS

OVERVIEW

A *mathematician* solves or directs the solution of problems in higher mathematics, including algebra, geometry, number theory, logic, and topology. *Theoretical mathematicians* work with the relationships among mathematical forms and the underlying principles that can be applied to problems, including electronic data processing and military planning. *Applied mathematicians* develop the techniques and approaches to problem solving in the physical, biological, and social sciences. Approximately 2,770 mathematicians are employed in nonacademic settings in the United States.

THE JOB

There are two broad areas of opportunity in mathematics: theoretical and applied. In addition, mathematicians may choose to pursue a career in teaching. The duties performed, the processes involved, the work situations encountered, and the equipment used vary

SCHOOL SUBJECTS
Computer science, Mathematics

PERSONAL SKILLS
Mechanical/manipulative, Technical/scientific

MINIMUM EDUCATION LEVEL
Doctorate degree

CERTIFICATION OR LICENSING
Required for certain positions

WORK ENVIRONMENT
Primarily indoors, Primarily one location

considerably, depending on the institutional or organizational setting.

Theoretical mathematicians deal with pure and abstract mathematical concepts rather than the practical application of such concepts to everyday problems. They might teach in a college or university or work in the research department of a businesses or government office. They are concerned with the advancement of mathematical knowledge, the logical development of mathematical systems, and the study and analysis of relationships among mathematical forms. "Pure" mathematicians focus their efforts mainly on problems dealing with mathematical principles and reasoning.

Applied mathematicians develop and apply mathematical knowledge to practical and research problems in the social, physical, life, and earth sciences. Business, industry, and government agencies such as the National Aeronautics and Space Administration (NASA) rely heavily on applied mathematicians, particularly for research and development programs. Therefore, it is necessary for these mathematicians to be knowledgeable about their employer's operations and products as well as their own field. Applied mathematicians work on problems ranging from the stability of rockets to the effects of new drugs on disease.

The applied and theoretical aspects of mathematicians' work are not always clearly separated. Some mathematicians, usually those dealing with the application of mathematics, may become involved in both aspects. In addition to having general knowledge about modern computing equipment, mathematicians need some basic experience in computer programming and operation because of the reliance on computers by almost every industry.

Specialists in the field of applied mathematics include the following:

Computer applications engineers formulate mathematical models and develop computer systems to solve scientific and engineering problems.

Engineering analysts apply logical analysis to scientific, engineering, and other technical problems and convert them to mathematical terms to be solved by computers.

Operations research analysts employ mathematics to solve management and operational problems.

Weight analysts are concerned with weight, balance, loading, and operational functions of space vehicles, ships, aircraft, missiles, research instrumentation, and commercial and industrial products and systems. These mathematicians use computers to analyze weight factors and work with design engineers to coordinate their specifications with product development.

Mathematics teachers instruct students at the middle school and high school levels. In high school, they provide instruction in more complex mathematics such as algebra, geometry, trigonometry, precalculus, and calculus.

College mathematics professors provide instruction to future mathematicians and students in other disciplines. They often teach courses at various levels of difficulty. Professors usually spend less time in the classroom than high school teachers, but they may have many other responsibilities, including advising doctoral candidates, serving on university or mathematical organization committees, and reading mathematical books and journals to stay up to date regarding developments in the field. Some professors are also actively involved in research and in contributing to the development of the field; this often includes writing and submitting articles on their research to mathematical journals.

REQUIREMENTS
High School

To pursue a career as a mathematician, take all the math classes that are offered and can fit into your schedule. Meet with teachers to get as much insight as you can about doing well in the math courses offered at your school. These courses should include algebra, geometry, trigonometry, and calculus. If your school offers college prep courses, you may be able to study probability, statistics, and logic. Classes such as English composition and computer science are also important.

Postsecondary Training

Undergraduate mathematical study includes work in algebra, geometry, numerical analysis, topology, and statistics. Typical university courses include differential equations, linear and abstract algebra, mathematical analysis, probability theory and statistics, discrete mathematics, and mathematical logic. In addition to these and other courses from which you may choose as a math major, you should also sample broadly in the humanities and the various social, physical, and life sciences.

With the exception of secondary school teaching and working for the federal government, the educational requirement for this profession is a doctoral degree in mathematics. A doctorate is necessary for most research and development positions as well as for college-level teaching. Approximately 200 colleges and universities offer a master's degree, and over 200 offer a Ph.D. in pure or applied mathematics.

Many colleges and universities require that if you major in math, you must also take classes in another area related to math, such as computer science, engineering, physical science, or economics.

Certification or Licensing

If you're interested in teaching math in a public elementary or high school, you must be licensed. You usually do not need a license to teach in a private school. Requirements vary from state to state, although all states require that you have at least a bachelor's degree and have finished an approved teacher training program.

Government positions usually require that applicants take a civil service examination in addition to meeting certain specified requirements that vary according to the type and level of position.

Other Requirements

To be a mathematician requires abilities in abstract reasoning, analyzing, and interpreting mathematical ideas. Speed and accuracy with numbers are necessary skills, too. Communication skills are also important because you will often need to interact with others, many of whom may not have an extensive knowledge of mathematics.

EXPLORING

While in high school, you may wish to accelerate your studies by enrolling in summer session programs offering regular or elective mathematics courses. Some schools have specialized mathematics honors or advanced placement courses that are part of their regular summer or evening school programs. Ask your math teacher or school counselor if there are any mathematics competitions you can enter. Not only can they be fun, but competitions may also offer college scholarships as awards. You can also participate in math summer camps. Visit http://www.ams.org/programs/students/high-school/emp-mathcamps for a list of camps located throughout the United States.

The American Mathematical Society's Web site, http://www.ams.org, offers information on math careers, competitions, and publications.

Summer and part-time employment with NASA or industrial firms can also provide you with valuable experience and offer the opportunity to test your knowledge, interests, abilities, and personal characteristics in a practical work setting.

EMPLOYERS

Mathematicians hold approximately 2,770 jobs in the federal and state government and in various private industries and business. An additional 48,100 work in mathematical faculty positions in colleges and universities.

In government, the U.S. Department of Defense, NASA, and the National Institute of Standards and Technology are the main employers of mathematicians. Significant employers in industry include management and public relations, research and testing, aerospace, securities and commodities, and drug manufacturing companies. Other positions are held in such businesses as banks, insurance companies, securities and commodity exchanges, and public utilities.

STARTING OUT

Most college career services offices assist students in finding positions in business and industry upon graduation. Teaching positions in high schools are usually obtained by personal contacts through friends, relatives, or college professors or through college career services offices and by application and interviews. College and university assistantships, instructorships, and professorships often are obtained by departmental recommendations.

Positions in federal, state, and local governments are usually announced well in advance of the required civil service examination, and students can check for such notices on bulletin boards in their college career services

offices or other locations, such as post offices and government buildings.

ADVANCEMENT

Numerous opportunities for advancement to higher-level positions or into related areas of employment are available to mathematicians. Promotions of mathematicians are generally made on the basis of advanced preparation, knowledge of a specific application, individual appraisal by a superior, or competitive examination.

Opportunities in related fields, such as statistics, accounting, actuarial work, and computers, allow mathematicians to change their profession, relocate geographically, or advance to better positions with higher salaries.

EARNINGS

Mathematicians' income varies with their level of training and the work setting in which they are employed. According to the U.S. Department of Labor, median annual earnings of mathematicians were $93,580 in 2009. Salaries ranged from less than $50,960 to more than $142,460. In 2009, the average yearly salary for mathematicians (including statisticians) in the federal government was $106,090. *Cryptanalysts* (mathematicians who analyze and decipher coding systems to transmit military, political, financial, or law enforcement information) earned $101,645, according to the *Occupational Outlook Handbook*.

Mathematicians receive traditional benefits such as health insurance, vacation time, and sick leave. Teachers usually have more time off during semester breaks and summer vacations, although they are still occupied with tasks such as grading papers and advising students.

WORK ENVIRONMENT

The mathematician in industrial and government positions usually works a regular 40-hour week. Those who work in educational settings may have varied schedules. For both, the work environment is generally pleasant and typical of the modern, well-equipped office. The work may require long periods of close concentration. Professional mathematicians who work with or near computers usually work in air-conditioned buildings, as computers are extremely sensitive to temperature changes.

OUTLOOK

Overall employment of mathematicians is expected to grow much faster than the average for all careers through 2018, according to the U.S. Department of Labor. Despite this prediction, strong competition is expected for jobs since the field is so small. There will be more jobs in applied mathematics (and related areas such as computer programming, operations research, and engineering design) than in theoretical research. Those who have a background in another field in addition to mathematics (such as computer science and software development, physics, engineering, operations research, financial analysis, or life sciences research) will have especially strong opportunities. The Society for Industrial and Applied Mathematics predicts that opportunities will be good in the following emerging fields: computational biology and genomics, data-mining (including applications in astrophysics), neuroscience, materials science (including applications in aerospace, biology, electronics, and engineering), and computer animation and digital imaging. Individuals with only a bachelor's degree in mathematics are not qualified for most mathematician jobs. However, those with a double major will have more opportunities. Holders of bachelor's or master's degrees in mathematics who also meet state certification requirements can find jobs as high school mathematics teachers or with the federal government. For mathematicians with a master's degree but no doctorate, jobs may be harder to find. Strong competition will exist for jobs in theoretical research. More openings should be available in applied areas, such as computer science and data processing.

FOR MORE INFORMATION

For a variety of useful resources about mathematics, including A Guide to Online Resources for High School Math Students, *visit the AMS Web site.*

American Mathematical Society (AMS)
201 Charles Street
Providence, RI 02904-2294
Tel: 800-321-4AMS
E-mail: ams@ams.org
http://www.ams.org

For information on opportunities for women in mathematics, contact

Association for Women in Mathematics
11240 Waples Mill Road, Suite 200
Fairfax, VA 22030-6078
Tel: 703-934-0163
E-mail: awm@awm-math.org
http://www.awm-math.org

For information on student competitions, contact
Mathematical Association of America
1529 18th Street, NW

Washington, DC 20036-1358
Tel: 800-741-9415
E-mail: maahq@maa.org
http://www.maa.org

For information on teaching careers in mathematics, contact
National Council of Teachers of Mathematics
1906 Association Drive
Reston, VA 20191-1502
Tel: 800-235-7566
E-mail: nctm@nctm.org
http://www.nctm.org

For information on publications (including "Thinking of a Career in Applied Mathematics?"), conferences, activity groups, and programs, contact
Society for Industrial and Applied Mathematics
3600 Market Street, 6th Floor
Philadelphia, PA 19104-2688
Tel: 800-447-SIAM
E-mail: service@siam.org
http://www.siam.org

MEDICAL ASSISTANTS

OVERVIEW

Medical assistants help physicians in offices, hospitals, and clinics. They keep medical records, help examine and treat patients, and perform routine office duties to allow physicians to spend their time working directly with patients. Medical assistants are vitally important to the smooth and efficient operation of medical offices. There are approximately 495,970 medical assistants employed in the United States.

THE JOB

Depending on the size of the office, medical assistants may perform clerical or clinical duties, or both. The larger the office, the greater the chance is that the assistant will specialize in one type of work.

In their clinical duties, medical assistants help physicians by preparing patients for examination or treatment. They may check and record patients' blood pressure, pulse, temperature, height, and weight. Medi-

SCHOOL SUBJECTS
Biology, Mathematics

PERSONAL SKILLS
Following instructions, Helping/teaching, Technical/scientific

MINIMUM EDUCATION LEVEL
High school diploma

CERTIFICATION OR LICENSING
Voluntary

WORK ENVIRONMENT
Primarily indoors, Primarily one location

cal assistants often ask patients questions about their medical histories and record the answers in the patient's file. In the examining room, the medical assistant may be responsible for arranging medical instruments and handing them to the physician as requested during the examination. Medical assistants may prepare patients for X-rays and laboratory examinations, as well as administer electrocardiograms. They may apply dressings, draw blood, and give injections. Medical assistants may also give patients instructions about taking medications, watching their diet, or restricting their activities before laboratory tests or surgery. In addition, medical assistants may collect specimens such as throat cultures for laboratory tests and may be responsible for sterilizing examining room instruments and equipment.

Medical assistants prepare examining rooms for patients and keep examining and waiting rooms clean and orderly. After each examination, they straighten the examining room and dispose of used linens and medical supplies. Sometimes medical assistants keep track of office and medical supply inventories and order necessary supplies. They may deal with pharmaceutical and medical supply company representatives when ordering supplies.

At other times, medical assistants may perform a wide range of administrative tasks. *Medical secretaries* and *medical receptionists* also perform administrative activities in medical offices, but these workers are distinguished from medical assistants by the fact that they

rarely perform clinical functions. The administrative and clerical tasks that medical assistants may complete include typing case histories and operation reports; keeping office files, X-rays, and other medical records up to date; keeping the office's financial records; preparing and sending bills and receiving payments; and transcribing dictation from the physician. Assistants may also answer the telephone, greet patients, fill out insurance forms, schedule appointments, take care of correspondence, and arrange for patients to be admitted to the hospital. Most medical assistants use computers for most record-keeping tasks.

Some medical assistants work in ophthalmologists' offices, where their clinical duties involve helping with eye examinations and treatments. They use special equipment to test and measure patients' eyes and check for disease. They administer eye drops and dressings and teach patients how to insert and care for contact lenses. They may maintain surgical instruments and help physicians during eye surgery. Other medical assistants work as *optometric assistants,* who may be required to prepare patients for examination and assist them in eyewear selection; *chiropractor assistants,* whose duties may include treatment and examination of patients' muscular and skeletal problems; and *podiatric assistants,* who assist podiatrists during examinations and surgery, take and develop X-rays, and make castings of patients' feet.

REQUIREMENTS
High School

Medical assistants usually need a high school diploma, but in many cases receive specific training on the job. High school courses in the sciences, especially biology, are helpful, as are courses in algebra, English, bookkeeping, typing, computers, and office practices.

Postsecondary Training

There are no formal educational requirements for medical assistants, although most have a high school diploma and many earn certificates, diplomas, or associate's degrees. On-the-job training is also provided by some employers. Formal training for medical assistants is available at many trade schools, community and junior colleges, and universities. College programs generally award an associate's degree and take two years to complete. Other programs can last as long as a year and award a diploma or certificate. Prior to enrolling in any school program, you should check its curriculum and verify its accreditation.

Schools for medical assistants may be accredited by either the Commission on Accreditation of Allied Health Education Programs, which has approved nearly 600 medical and ophthalmic programs; the Accrediting Bureau of Health Education Schools, which has accredited approximately 300 medical assisting programs; or the Commission on Accreditation of Ophthalmic Medical Programs, which has accredited approximately 26 ophthalmic medical assisting and ophthalmic clinical assisting programs. Course work includes biology, anatomy, physiology, and medical terminology, as well as typing, transcribing, shorthand, record keeping, and computer skills. Perhaps most importantly, these programs provide supervised, hands-on clinical experience in laboratory techniques, first-aid procedures, proper use of medical equipment, and clinical procedures. You also learn administrative duties and procedures in medical offices and receive training in interpersonal communications and medical ethics.

Certification or Licensing

Voluntarily certification is available from certain professional organizations. The registered medical assistant credential is awarded by American Medical Technologists, and the American Association of Medical Assistants awards a credential for certified medical assistant. The National Healthcareer Association awards several designations, including the certified clinical medical assistant and certified medical administrative assistant designations. Ophthalmic assistants can receive the following designations from the Joint Commission on Allied Health Personnel in Ophthalmology: certified ophthalmic assistant, certified ophthalmic technician, and certified ophthalmic medical technologist. The American Society of Podiatric Medical Assistants offers the podiatric medical assistant, certified designation. Medical assistants generally do not need to be licensed. Some states require medical assistants to pass a test or take a course before they can perform certain tasks like taking X-rays.

Other Requirements

To be a successful medical assistant, you must be able to interact with patients and other medical personnel and be able to follow detailed directions. In addition, you must be dependable and compassionate and have the desire to help people. Medical assistants must also respect patients' privacy by keeping medical information confidential. Overall, medical assistants who help patients feel at ease in the doctor's office and other medical settings and have good communication skills and a desire to serve should do well in this job.

EXPLORING

Students in postsecondary school medical assistant programs will have the chance to explore the field through the supervised clinical experience required by the various programs. Others may wish to gain additional experience by volunteering at hospitals, nursing homes, or clinics to get a feel for the work involved in a medical environment. You may want to talk with the medical assistants in your own or other local physicians' offices to find out more about the work they do.

EMPLOYERS

About 495,970 medical assistants are employed in physicians' offices, clinics, hospitals, health maintenance organizations, and other medical facilities. Approximately 62 percent work in private doctors' offices and 13 percent work in hospitals. Another 11 percent work in offices of other health practitioners such as optometrists and chiropractors. Others work in outpatient care centers and nursing and residential care facilities.

STARTING OUT

Students enrolled in college or other postsecondary school medical assistant programs may learn of available positions through their school career services offices. High school counselors may have information about positions for students about to graduate. Newspaper want ads and state employment offices are other good places to look for leads. You may also wish to call local physicians' offices to find out about unadvertised openings.

ADVANCEMENT

Experienced medical assistants may be able to move into managerial or administrative positions without further education, but moving into a more advanced clinical position, such as nursing, requires more education. As more and more clinics and group practices open, more office managers will be needed, and these are positions that well-qualified, experienced medical assistants may be able to fill. As with most occupations, today's job market gives medical assistants with computer skills more opportunities for advancement.

EARNINGS

The earnings of medical assistants vary widely, depending on experience, skill level, and location. According to the U.S. Department of Labor, median annual earnings of medical assistants were $28,650 in 2009. The lowest paid 10 percent earned less than $20,750, and the highest paid 10 percent earned more than $39,970 a year. Mean annual earnings of medical assistants who worked in offices of physicians were $29,810, and in hospitals they were $30,830.

Medical assistants usually receive six or seven paid holidays a year, as well as annual paid vacation days. They often receive health and life insurance, a retirement plan, sick leave, and uniform allowances.

WORK ENVIRONMENT

Most medical assistants work in pleasant, modern surroundings. The average medical assistant works 40 hours a week, including some Saturday and evening hours. Sterilizing equipment and handling medical instruments require care and attentiveness. As most professionals in the health sciences will attest, working with people who are ill may be upsetting at times, but it can also have many personal rewards.

OUTLOOK

Employment for medical assistants will grow much faster than the average for all occupations through 2018, according to the U.S. Department of Labor. In fact, the career of medical assistant is predicted to be among the fastest-growing professions during this time period. Many openings will occur to replace workers who leave their jobs, but most will be the result of a predicted surge in the number of new physicians' offices, clinics, and other outpatient care facilities. The growing number of elderly Americans who need medical treatment is also a factor for this increased demand for health services. In addition, new and more complex paperwork for medical insurance, malpractice insurance, government programs, and other purposes will create a growing need for assistants in medical offices.

Many physicians prefer experienced and formally trained medical assistants, so these workers will have the best employment outlook. Word-processing skills, computer skills, and formal certification are all definite assets.

FOR MORE INFORMATION

For information on accreditation and testing, contact
Accrediting Bureau of Health Education Schools
7777 Leesburg Pike, Suite 314-North

Falls Church, VA 22043-2411
Tel: 703-917-9503
E-mail: info@abhes.org
http://www.abhes.org

For career and certification information, contact the following organizations:
American Association of Medical Assistants
20 North Wacker Drive, Suite 1575
Chicago, IL 60606-2963
Tel: 312-899-1500
http://www.aama-ntl.org

American Medical Technologists
10700 West Higgins Road, Suite 150
Park Ridge, IL 60018-3722
Tel: 847-823-5169
http://www.amt1.com

For information on podiatric medical assisting careers and certification, contact
American Society of Podiatric Medical Assistants
1616 North 78th Court
Elmwood Park, IL 60707-3548
Tel: 888-882-7762
http://www.aspma.org

For information on ophthalmic medical assisting, contact
Association of Technical Personnel in Ophthalmology
2025 Woodlane Drive
St. Paul, MN 55125-2998
Tel: 800-482-4858
http://www.atpo.org

For information on accredited programs, contact
Commission on Accreditation of Allied Health Education Programs
1361 Park Street
Clearwater, FL 33756-6039
Tel: 727-210-2350
http://www.caahep.org

For information on accredited programs, contact
Commission on Accreditation of Ophthalmic Medical Programs
2025 Woodlane Drive
St. Paul, MN 55125-2987
Tel: 800-284-3937
http://www.jcahpo.org/CoA-OMP/about

For information on certification, contact
Joint Commission on Allied Health Personnel in
   Ophthalmology
2025 Woodlane Drive
St. Paul, MN 55125-2995
Tel: 800-284-3937
E-mail: jcahpo@jcahpo.org
http://www.jcahpo.org

For information on certification, contact
National Healthcareer Association
7500 West 160th Street
Stilwell, KS 66085-8100
Tel: 800-499-9092
http://www.nhanow.com

SCHOOL SUBJECTS
Biology, Chemistry

PERSONAL SKILLS
Following instructions, Technical/scientific

MINIMUM EDUCATION LEVEL
Some postsecondary training

CERTIFICATION OR LICENSING
Required by certain states

WORK ENVIRONMENT
Primarily indoors, Primarily one location

☐ MEDICAL LABORATORY TECHNICIANS

OVERVIEW

Medical laboratory technicians, also known as *clinical laboratory technicians*, perform routine tests in medical laboratories. These tests help physicians and other professional medical personnel diagnose and treat disease. Technicians prepare samples of body tissue; perform laboratory tests, such as urinalysis and blood counts; and make chemical and biological analyses of cells, tissue, blood, or other body specimens. They usually work under the supervision of a medical technologist or a laboratory director. Medical laboratory technicians may work in many fields, or specialize in one specific medical area, such as cytology (the study of cells), hematology (the study of blood, especially on the cellular level), serology (the study and identification of antibodies found in the blood), or histology (the study of body tissue). There are approximately 319,280 medical laboratory technicians and technologists employed in the United States.

THE JOB

Medical laboratory technicians may be generalists in the field of laboratory technology; that is, they may be trained to carry out many different kinds of medical laboratory work. Alternatively, they may specialize in one type of medical laboratory work, such as cytology, hematology, blood bank technology, serology, or histology. The following paragraphs describe the work of generalists and those in the specialty fields of cytology, histology, and blood bank technology.

Medical laboratory technicians who work as generalists perform a wide variety of tests and laboratory procedures in chemistry, hematology, urinalysis, blood banking, serology, and microbiology. By performing these tests and procedures, they help to develop vital data on the blood, tissues, and fluids of the human body. This data is then used by physicians, surgeons, pathologists, and other medical personnel to diagnose and treat patients.

The tests and procedures that these technicians perform are more complex than the routine duties assigned to laboratory assistants, but do not require specialized knowledge like those performed by more highly trained medical technologists. In general, medical laboratory technicians work with only limited supervision. This means that while the tests they perform may have well-established procedures, the technicians themselves must exercise independent judgment. For instance, they must be able to discriminate between very similar colors or shapes, correct their own errors using established strategies, and monitor ongoing quality control measures.

To carry out these responsibilities, medical laboratory technicians need a sound knowledge of specific techniques and instruments and must be able to recognize factors that potentially influence both the procedures they use and the results they obtain.

In their work, medical laboratory technicians frequently handle test tubes and other glassware and use precision equipment, such as microscopes and automated blood analyzers. (Blood analyzers determine the levels of certain blood components like cholesterol, sugar, and hemoglobin.) Technicians are also often responsible for making sure machines are functioning and supplies are adequately stocked.

Medical laboratory technicians who specialize in cytology are usually referred to as *cytotechnicians*. Cytotechnicians prepare and stain body cell samplings using special dyes that accentuate the delicate patterns of the cytoplasm, and structures such as the nucleus. Mounted on slides, the various features of the specimen then stand out brightly under a microscope. Using microscopes that magnify cells perhaps 1,000 times, cytotechnicians screen out normal samplings and set aside those with minute irregularities (in cell size, shape, and color) for further study by a pathologist.

Medical laboratory technicians specializing in histology are usually referred to as *histologic technicians* or *tissue technicians*. Histology is the study of the structure and chemical composition of the tissues, and histologic technicians are mainly concerned with detecting tissue abnormalities and assisting in determining appropriate treatments for the disease conditions associated with the abnormalities.

Medical laboratory technicians who specialize in blood bank technology perform a wide variety of routine tests related to running blood banks, offering transfusion services, and investigating blood diseases and reactions to transfusions. Examples of tasks frequently performed by medical laboratory technicians specializing in this field include donor screening, determining blood types, performing tests of patients' blood counts, and assisting physicians in the care of patients with blood-related problems.

REQUIREMENTS

High School

To be hired as a medical laboratory technician, you must have a high school diploma and one or two years of postsecondary training. No specific kind of high school training is required; however, you must be able to meet the admissions requirements of institutions offering post-high school training. In general, courses in biology, chemistry, mathematics, English, and computer science will be most helpful in a career as a medical laboratory technician.

Postsecondary Training

After high school, prospective technicians enroll in one- or two-year training programs accredited by the Commission on Accreditation of Allied Health Education Programs, the Accrediting Bureau of Health Education Schools, or the National Accrediting Agency for Clinical Laboratory Sciences, which fully accredits 479 programs. One-year programs include both classroom work and practical laboratory training and focus on areas such as medical ethics and conduct, medical terminology, basic laboratory solutions and media, manipulation of cytological and histological specimens, blood collecting techniques, and introductions to basic hematology, serology, blood banking, and urinalysis.

To earn an associate's degree, you must complete a two-year post-high school program. Like certificate programs, associate's degree programs include classroom instruction and practical training. Courses are taught both on campus and in local hospitals. On-campus courses focus on general knowledge and basic skills in laboratory testing associated with hematology, serology, chemistry, microbiology, and other pertinent biological and medical areas. The clinical training program focuses on basic principles and skills required in medical diagnostic laboratory testing.

Certification or Licensing

Students who have earned an associate's degree are eligible for certification from several different agencies, including the Board of Certification of the American Society for Clinical Pathology, the American Medical Technologists, the National Credentialing Agency for Laboratory Personnel, and the Board of Registry of the American Association of Bioanalysts.

Prospective medical laboratory technicians who think they might want to specialize in cytology or blood bank technology should definitely consider the two-year program, which will best prepare them for the additional education they may need later.

In addition to completing the educational programs described above, prospective technicians need to pass an examination after graduation to receive certification. In some states, this certificate is all that is required for employment. In other states, state licensure is also required. School officials are the best source of information regarding state requirements.

Other Requirements

Besides fulfilling the academic requirements, medical laboratory technicians must have good manual dexterity, normal color vision, the ability to follow instructions, and a tolerance for working under pressure.

EXPLORING

It is difficult for people interested in a career in medical laboratory technology to gain any direct experience through part-time employment. There are some other ways, however, to learn more about this career on a first-hand basis. Perhaps the best way is to arrange a visit to a hospital, blood bank, or commercial medical laboratory to see technicians at work at their jobs. Another way to learn about this kind of work in general, and about the training required in particular, is to visit an accredited school of medical laboratory technology to discuss career plans with the admissions counselor at the school. You can also contact the sources listed at the end of this article for more reading material on medical laboratory technology. Finally, you should remember that high school science courses with laboratory sections will give you exposure to some of the kinds of work you might do later in your career.

EMPLOYERS

Medical laboratory technicians are employed where physicians work, such as in hospitals, clinics, offices of physicians, blood blanks, and commercial medical laboratories. Approximately 319,280 medical laboratory technicians and technologists are employed in the United States, with more than half working in hospitals.

STARTING OUT

Graduates of medical laboratory technology schools usually receive assistance from faculty and school placement services to find their first jobs. Hospitals, laboratories, and other facilities employing medical laboratory technicians may notify local schools of job openings. Often the hospital or laboratory at which you receive your practical training will offer full-time employment after graduation. Positions may also be secured using the various registries of certified medical laboratory workers. Newspaper job advertisements and commercial placement agencies are other sources of help in locating employment.

ADVANCEMENT

Medical laboratory technicians often advance by returning to school to earn a bachelor's degree. This can lead to positions as medical technologists, histological technologists, cytotechnologists, or specialists in blood bank technology.

Other technicians advance by gaining more responsibility while retaining the title of technician. For instance, with experience, these workers can advance to supervisory positions or other positions assigning work to be done by other medical laboratory workers. Medical laboratory technicians may also advance by training to do very specialized or complex laboratory or research work.

EARNINGS

Salaries of medical laboratory technicians vary according to employer and geographical area. According to the U.S. Bureau of Labor Statistics, median annual earnings of medical and clinical laboratory technicians were $36,030 in 2009. Salaries ranged from less than $23,850 to more than $55,210. Fifty percent of workers in this field earned between $28,770 and $45,420 annually at the end of 2009. Medical laboratory technicians who go on to earn their bachelor's degrees and certification as medical technologists can expect an increase in annual earnings.

Most medical laboratory technicians receive paid vacations and holidays, sick leave, health insurance, and retirement benefits.

WORK ENVIRONMENT

Medical laboratory technicians work in clean, well-lit, and usually air-conditioned settings. There may, however, be unpleasant odors and some infectious materials involved in the work. In general, there are few hazards associated with these odors and materials as long as proper methods of sterilization and handling of specimens, materials, and equipment are used.

Medical laboratory technicians often spend much of their days standing or sitting on stools. A 40-hour, five-day week is normal, although those working in hospitals can expect some evening and weekend work.

Medical laboratory technicians derive satisfaction from knowing their work is very important to patients and their physicians. Although the work involves new patient samples, it also involves some very repetitive tasks that some people may find trying. Additionally, the work must often be done under time pressure, even though it is often very painstaking.

Another factor that aspiring medical laboratory technicians should keep in mind is that advancement opportunities are limited, although they do exist. To maximize their chances for advancement, medical laboratory technicians must consider getting additional training.

OUTLOOK

The U.S. Department of Labor predicts job growth for medical laboratory technicians to be faster than the average through 2018. Competition for jobs, however, may be strong. One reason for this increased competition is the overall national effort to control health care costs. Hospitals, where most medical laboratory technicians are employed, will seek to control costs in part through cutting down on the amount of laboratory testing they do and, consequently, the personnel they require.

Despite such cutbacks, though, the overall amount of medical laboratory testing will probably increase, as much of medical practice today relies on high-quality laboratory testing. However, because of the increased use of automation, this increase in laboratory testing will probably not lead to an equivalent growth in employment.

One other technological factor that will influence employment in this field is the development of laboratory-testing equipment that is easier to use. This means that some testing that formerly had to be done in hospitals can now be done in physicians' offices and other nonhospital settings. This development will slow growth in hospital laboratory employment; however, it should increase the number of technicians hired by medical groups and clinics, medical and diagnostic laboratories, and other ambulatory health care services such as blood and organ banks. In addition, equipment that is easier to use may also lead to technicians being able to do more kinds of testing, including some tests that used to be done only by medical technologists.

These growth projections should not deter aspiring technicians, though, because medical laboratory testing is an absolutely essential element in today's medicine. For well-trained technicians who are flexible in accepting responsibilities and willing to continue their education throughout their careers, employment opportunities should remain good.

FOR MORE INFORMATION

For information on accreditation and testing, contact
Accrediting Bureau of Health Education Schools
7777 Leesburg Pike, Suite 314-North
Falls Church, VA 22043-2411
Tel: 703-917-9503
E-mail: info@abhes.org
http://www.abhes.org

For information on certification, contact
American Association of Bioanalysts
906 Olive Street, Suite 1200

St. Louis, MO 63101-1434
Tel: 314-241-1445
http://www.aab.org

For career and certification information, contact
American Medical Technologists
10700 West Higgins Road, Suite 150
Rosemont, IL 60018-3722
Tel: 847-823-5169
http://www.amt1.com

For information on clinical laboratory careers and certification, contact
American Society for Clinical Laboratory Science
6701 Democracy Boulevard, Suite 300
Bethesda, MD 20817-1574
Tel: 301-657-2768
http://www.ascls.org

For information on certification, contact
American Society for Clinical Pathology: Board of Certification
33 West Monroe, Suite 1600
Chicago IL 60603-5617
Tel: 312-541-4999
E-mail: info@ascp.org
http://www.ascp.org/boc

For information on accredited programs, contact
Commission on Accreditation of Allied Health Education Programs
1361 Park Street
Clearwater, FL 33756-6039
Tel: 727-210-2350
http://caahep.org

MEDICAL RECORD TECHNICIANS

OVERVIEW

In any hospital, clinic, or other health care facility, permanent records are created and maintained for all the patients treated by the staff. Each patient's medical record describes in detail his or her condition

SCHOOL SUBJECTS
Computer science, Health, English

PERSONAL SKILLS
Following instructions, Technical/scientific

MINIMUM EDUCATION LEVEL
Associate's degree

CERTIFICATION OR LICENSING
Recommended

WORK ENVIRONMENT
Primarily indoors, Primarily one location

over time. Entries include illness and injuries, operations, treatments, outpatient visits, and the progress of hospital stays. *Medical record technicians* compile, code, and maintain these records. They also tabulate and analyze data from groups of records in order to assemble reports. They review records for completeness and accuracy; assign codes to the diseases, operations, diagnoses, and treatments according to detailed standardized classification systems; and post the codes on the medical record. They transcribe medical reports; maintain indices of patients, diseases, operations, and other categories of information; compile patient census data; and file records. In addition, they may direct the day-to-day operations of the medical records department. They maintain the flow of records and reports to and from other departments, and sometimes assist medical staff in special studies or research that draws on information in the records. There are approximately 170,580 medical records and health information technicians employed in the United States.

THE JOB

A patient's medical record consists of all relevant information and observations of any health care workers who have dealt with the patient. It may contain, for example, several diagnoses, X-ray and laboratory reports, electrocardiogram tracings, test results, and drugs prescribed. This summary of the patient's medical history is very important to the physician in making speedy and correct decisions about care. Later, information from the record is often needed in authenticating legal forms and insurance claims. The medical record documents the adequacy and appropriateness of the care received by the patient and is the basis of any investigation when the care is questioned in any way.

Patterns and trends can be traced when data from many records are considered together. These types of statistical reports are used by many different groups. Hospital administrators, scientists, public health agencies, accrediting and licensing bodies, people who evaluate the effectiveness of current programs or plan future ones, and medical reimbursement organizations are examples of some groups that rely on health care statistics. Medical records can provide the data to show whether a new treatment or medication really works, the relative effectiveness of alternative treatments or medications, or patterns that yield clues about the causes or methods of preventing certain kinds of disease.

Medical record technicians are involved in the routine preparation, handling, and safeguarding of individual records as well as the statistical information extracted from groups of records. Their specific tasks and the scope of their responsibilities depend a great deal on the size and type of the employing institution. In large organizations, there may be a number of technicians and other employees working with medical records. The technicians may serve as assistants to the medical record administrator as needed or may regularly specialize in some particular phase of the work done by the department. In small facilities, however, technicians often carry out the whole range of activities and may function fairly independently, perhaps bearing the full responsibility for all day-to-day operations of the department. A technician in a small facility may even be a department director. Sometimes technicians handle medical records and also spend part of their time helping out in the business or admitting office.

Whether they work in hospitals or other settings, medical record technicians must organize, transfer, analyze, preserve, and locate vast quantities of detailed information when needed. The sources of this information include physicians, nurses, laboratory workers, and other members of the health care team.

In a hospital, a patient's cumulative record goes to the medical record department at the end of the hospital stay. A technician checks over the information in the file to be sure that all the essential reports and data are included and appear accurate. Certain specific items must be supplied in any record, such as signatures, dates, the patient's physical and social history, the results of physical examinations, provisional and final diagnoses, periodic progress notes on the patient's condition during the hospital stay, medications prescribed and administered, therapeutic treatments, surgical procedures, and an assessment of the outcome or the condition at the time of discharge. If any item is missing, the technician sends the record to the person who is responsible for supplying the information. After all necessary information has been received and the record has passed the review, it is considered the official document describing the patient's case.

The record is then passed to a *medical record coder*. Coders are responsible for assigning a numeric code to every diagnosis and procedure listed in a patient's file. Most hospitals in the United States use a nationally accepted system for coding. The lists of diseases, procedures, and conditions are published in classification manuals that medical records personnel refer to frequently. By reducing information in different forms to a single consistent coding system, the data contained in the record is rendered much easier to handle, tabulate, and analyze. It can be indexed under any suitable heading, such as by patient, disease, type of surgery, physician attending the case, and so forth. Cross-indexing is likely to be an important part of the medical record technician's job. Because the same coding systems are used nearly everywhere in the United States, the data may be used not only by people working inside the hospital, but may also be submitted to one of the various programs that pool information obtained from many institutions.

After the information on the medical record has been coded, technicians may use a packaged computer program to assign the patient to one of several hundred diagnosis-related groupings, or DRGs. The DRG for the patient's stay determines the amount of money the hospital will receive if the patient is covered by Medicare or one of the other insurance programs that base their reimbursement on DRGs.

Because information in medical records is used to determine how much hospitals are paid for caring for patients, the accuracy of the work done by medical records personnel is vital. A coding error could cause the hospital or patient to lose money.

Another vital part of the job concerns filing. Regardless of how accurately and completely information is gathered and stored, it is worthless unless it can be retrieved promptly. If paper records are kept, technicians are usually responsible for preparing records for storage, filing them, and getting them out of storage when needed. In some organizations, technicians supervise other personnel who carry out these tasks.

In many health care facilities, computers, rather than paper, are used for nearly all the medical record keeping. In such cases, medical and nursing staff make notes on an electronic chart. They enter patient-care information into computer files, and medical record technicians access the information using their own terminals. Computers have greatly simplified many traditional routine tasks of the medical records department, such as generating daily hospital census figures, tabulating data for research purposes, and updating special registries of certain types of health problems, such as cancer and stroke.

In the past, some medical records that were originally on paper were later photographed and stored on microfilm, particularly after they were a year or two old. Medical record technicians may be responsible for retrieving and maintaining those films. It is not unusual for a health care institution to have a combination of paper and microfilm files as well as computerized record storage, reflecting the evolution of technology for storing information.

Confidentiality and privacy laws have a major bearing on the medical records field. The laws vary in different states for different types of data, but in all cases, maintaining the confidentiality of individual records is of major concern to medical records workers. All individual records must be in secure storage but also be available for retrieval and specified kinds of properly authorized use. Technicians may be responsible for retrieving and releasing this information. They may prepare records to be released in response to a patient's written authorization, a subpoena, or a court order. This requires special knowledge of legal statutes and often requires consultation with attorneys, judges, insurance agents, and other parties with legitimate rights to access information about a person's health and medical treatment.

Medical record technicians may participate in the quality assurance, risk management, and utilization review activities of a health care facility. In these cases, they may serve as data abstractors and data analysts, reviewing records against established standards to ensure quality of care. They may also prepare statistical reports for the medical or administrative staff that reviews appropriateness of care.

With more specialized training, medical record technicians may participate in medical research activities by maintaining special records, called registries, related to such areas as cancer, heart disease, transplants, or adverse outcomes of pregnancies. In some cases, they are required to abstract and code information from records of patients with certain medical conditions. For instance, *cancer registrars* maintain facility, regional, and national databases of cancer patients. These technicians may also prepare statistical reports and trend analyses for the use of medical researchers.

REQUIREMENTS

High School

If you are contemplating a career in medical records, you should take as many high school English classes as possible, because technicians need both written and verbal communication skills to prepare reports and communicate with other health care personnel. Basic math or business math is very desirable because statistical skills are important in some job functions. Biology courses will help familiarize you with the terminology that medical record technicians use. Other science courses, computer training, typing, and office procedures are also helpful.

Postsecondary Training

Most employers prefer to hire medical record technicians who have completed a two-year associate's degree program accredited by the American Medical Association's Commission on Accreditation of Allied Health Education Programs and the American Health Information Management Association (AHIMA). There are more than 200 of these accredited programs available throughout the United States, mostly offered in junior and community colleges. They usually include classroom instruction in such subjects as anatomy, physiology, medical terminology, medical record science, word processing, medical aspects of recordkeeping, statistics, computers in health care, personnel supervision, business management, English, and office skills.

In addition to classroom instruction, the student is given supervised clinical experience in the medical records departments of local health care facilities. This provides students with practical experience in performing many of the functions learned in the classroom and the opportunity to interact with health care professionals.

Certification or Licensing

Medical record technicians who have completed an accredited training program are eligible to take a national qualifying examination to earn the credential of registered health information technician (RHIT). Most health care institutions prefer to hire individuals with an RHIT credential as it signifies that they have met the standards established by the AHIMA as the mark of a qualified health professional. AHIMA also offers certification to medical coders and health information administrators.

Medical record technicians may also receive coding credentials from the American Academy of Professional Coders (AAPC), Board of Medical Specialty Coding (BMSC), National Cancer Registrars Association (NCRA) or Professional Association of Healthcare Coding Specialists (PAHCS).

Other Requirements

Medical records are extremely detailed and precise. Sloppy work could have serious consequences in terms of payment to the hospital or physician, validity of the patient records for later use, and validity of research based on data from medical records. Therefore, a prospective technician must have the capacity to do consistently reliable and accurate routine work. Records must be completed and maintained with care and attention to detail. You may be the only person who checks the entire record, and you must understand the responsibility that accompanies this task.

The technician needs to be able to work rapidly as well as accurately. In many medical record departments, the workload is very heavy, and you must be well organized and efficient in order to stay on top of the job. You must be able to complete your work accurately, in spite of interruptions such as phone calls and requests for assistance. You also need to be discreet, as you will deal with records that are private and sometimes sensitive.

Computer skills are also essential, and some experience in transcribing dictated reports may be useful.

EXPLORING

To learn more about this and other medical careers, you may be able to find summer, part-time, or volunteer work in a hospital or other health care facility. Sometimes such jobs are available in the medical records area of an organization. You may also be able to arrange to talk with someone working as a medical record technician or administrator. Faculty and counselors at schools that offer medical record technician training programs may also be good sources of information. Reading journals and other literature available online and at a public library is another good way to learn more about this profession.

EMPLOYERS

Although about 39 percent of the 170,580 medical record technicians employed in the United States work in hospitals, many work in other health care settings, including health maintenance organizations (HMOs), industrial clinics, skilled nursing facilities, rehabilitation centers, large group medical practices, ambulatory care centers, and state and local government health agencies. Technicians also work for computer firms, consulting firms, and government agencies. Records are maintained in all these facilities, although record-keeping procedures vary.

Not all medical record technicians are employed in a single health care facility; some serve as consultants to several small facilities. Other technicians do not work in health care settings at all. They may be employed by health and property liability insurance companies to collect and review information on medical claims. A few are self-employed, providing medical transcription services.

STARTING OUT

Most successful medical record technicians are graduates of two-year accredited programs. Graduates of these programs should check with their schools' placement offices for job leads. Those who have taken the accrediting exam and have become certified can use the AHIMA's resume referral service.

You may also apply directly to the personnel departments of hospitals, nursing homes, outpatient clinics, and surgery centers. Many job openings are also listed in the classified advertising sections of local newspapers and with private and public employment agencies.

ADVANCEMENT

Medical record technicians may be able to achieve some advancement and salary increase without additional training simply by taking on greater responsibility in their job function. With experience, technicians may move to supervisory or department head positions, depending on the type and structure of the employing organization. Another means of advancing is through specialization in a certain area of the job. Some technicians specialize in coding, particularly Medicare coding or tumor registry. With a broad range of experience, a medical record technician may be able to become an independent consultant. Generally, technicians with an associate's degree and the RHIT designation are most likely to advance.

More assured job advancement and salary increase come with the completion of a bachelor's degree in medical record administration. The bachelor's degree, along with AHIMA accreditation, makes the technician eligible for a supervisory position, such as department director. Because of a general shortage of medical record administrators, hospitals often assist technicians who are working toward a bachelor's degree by pro-

viding flexible scheduling and financial aid or tuition reimbursement.

EARNINGS

The salaries of medical record technicians are greatly influenced by the location, size, and type of employing institution, as well as the technician's training and experience. According to a 2008 AHIMA salary survey, coders' salaries varied depending upon their credentials. For example, coders with the CCA (certified coding associate) designation averaged $36,893 per year in 2008. Those with the RHIT designation earned about $52,771 annually, while coders with the CCS-P (certified coding specialist, physician based) designation averaged $55,673 annually, and CCS credentialed coders earned $57,872 per year. AHIMA reported the average annual salary for coding professionals was $43,359 in 2008.

According to the U.S. Department of Labor, the median annual earnings of medical records and health information technicians were $31,290 in 2009. Salaries ranged from less than $20,850 to more than $51,510.

PayScale.com reported the following annual salary ranges for medical records/health information technicians in January 2011: $24,821 to $39,483 (one to four years' experience), and $23,538 to $40,479 (five to nine years' experience).

In general, medical record technicians working in large urban hospitals make the most money, and those in rural areas make the least. Like most hospital employees, medical record technicians usually receive paid vacations and holidays, life and health insurance, and retirement benefits.

WORK ENVIRONMENT

Medical records departments are usually pleasantly clean, well-lit, and air-conditioned areas. Sometimes, however, paper or microfilm records are kept in cramped, out-of-the-way quarters. Although the work requires thorough and careful attention to detail, there may be a constant bustle of activity in the technician's work area, which can be disruptive. The job is likely to involve frequent routine contact with nurses, physicians, hospital administrators, other health care professionals, attorneys, and insurance agents. On occasion, individuals with whom the technicians may interact are demanding or difficult. In such cases, technicians may find that the job carries a high level of frustration.

A 40-hour workweek is the norm, but because hospitals operate on a 24-hour basis, the job may regularly include night or weekend hours. Part-time work is sometimes available.

The work is extremely detailed and may be tedious. Some technicians spend the majority of their day sitting at a desk, working on a computer. Others may spend hours filing paper records or retrieving them from storage.

In many hospital settings, the medical record technician experiences pressure caused by a heavy workload. As the demands for health care cost containment and productivity increase, medical record technicians may be required to produce a significantly greater volume of high-quality work in shorter periods of time.

Nonetheless, the knowledge that their work is significant for patients and medical research can be personally very satisfying for medical record technicians.

OUTLOOK

Employment prospects through 2018 are excellent. The U.S. Department of Labor predicts that employment in this field will grow much faster than the average. The demand for well-trained medical record technicians will grow rapidly and will continue to exceed the supply. This expectation is related to the health care needs of a population that is both growing and aging and the trend toward more technologically sophisticated medicine and greater use of diagnostic procedures. It is also related to the increased requirements of regulatory bodies that scrutinize both costs and quality of care of health care providers. Because of the fear of medical malpractice lawsuits, doctors and other health care providers are documenting their diagnoses and treatments in greater detail. Also, because of the high cost of health care, insurance companies, government agencies, and courts are examining medical records with a more critical eye. These factors combine to ensure a healthy job outlook for medical record technicians.

Opportunities will be best in offices of physicians, particularly in large group practices, nursing care facilities, home health care services, and outpatient care centers.

Technicians with associate's degrees and RHIT status will have the best prospects, and the importance of such qualifications is likely to increase.

FOR MORE INFORMATION

For information on earnings, careers in health information management, and accredited programs, contact
American Health Information Management Association
233 North Michigan Avenue, 21st Floor
Chicago, IL 60601-5809
Tel: 312-233-1100
http://www.ahima.org

For a list of schools offering accredited programs in health information management, contact
Commission on Accreditation of Allied Health Education Programs
1361 Park Street
Clearwater, FL 33756-6039
Tel: 727-210-2350
http://www.caahep.org

For further information on accreditation in medical coding specialties, visit the Web sites of these organizations:
American Academy of Professional Coders (AAPC)
http://www.aapc.com/

Board of Medical Specialty Coding (BMSC)
http://www.medicalspecialtycoding.com

National Cancer Registrars Association (NCRA)
http://www.ncra-usa.org/i4a/pages/index.cfm?pageid=1

Professional Association of Healthcare Coding Specialists (PAHCS)
http://www.pahcs.org

NAIL TECHNICIANS

OVERVIEW

Nail technicians clean, shape, and polish fingernails and toenails. They groom cuticles and apply cream to hands and arms (feet and calves in the case of pedicures). They apply a variety of artificial nails and provide ongoing maintenance. Many nail technicians are skilled in "nail art" and decorate clients' nails with stencils, glitter, and ornaments. Nail technicians may also call themselves *manicurists, pedicurists, nail sculpturists,* or *nail artists.* There are approximately 53,020 nail technicians working in the United States.

THE JOB

Nail technicians generally work at a manicurist table and chair or stool across from their clients. Their work implements include finger bowls, electric heaters, wet sanitizer containers, alcohol, nail sticks and files, cuticle

SCHOOL SUBJECTS
Art, Business, Health

PERSONAL SKILLS
Artistic, Helping/teaching

MINIMUM EDUCATION LEVEL
Some postsecondary training

CERTIFICATION OR LICENSING
Required by certain states

WORK ENVIRONMENT
Primarily indoors, Primarily one location

instruments, emery boards and buffers, tweezers, nail polishes and removers, abrasives, creams and oils, and nail dryers.

Standard manicure procedure involves removing old polish, shaping nails, softening and trimming cuticles and applying cuticle cream, cleansing and drying hands and nails, applying polish and topcoat, and applying hand lotion. As an extra service, lotion is often massaged into the wrists and arms as well as the hands. Technicians should always follow a sanitary cleanup procedure at their stations following each manicure, including sanitizing instruments and table, discarding used materials, and washing and drying their hands.

A man's manicure is a more conservative procedure than a woman's; the process is similar, but most men prefer to have a dry polish or to have their nails buffed.

Pedicuring has become a popular and important salon service, especially when fashion and weather dictate open-toed shoe styles. The procedure for a pedicure is much like that of a manicure, with the setup involving a low stool for the technician and an ottoman for the client's feet.

Nail technicians also provide other services, including the application of artificial nails. A number of techniques are employed, depending on the individual client's preferences and nail characteristics. These include nail wrapping, nail sculpturing, nail tipping, press-on nails, and nail dipping. Technicians also repair broken nails and do "fill-ins" on artificial nails as the real nails grow out.

Nail technicians must take care to use only new or sanitized instruments to prevent the spread of disease. The rapid growth of this industry has been accompanied by an increased awareness of the many ways in which viral, fungal, and bacterial infections can be spread. Many states have passed laws regarding the use of various instruments. Although nail technicians may be exposed to such contagious diseases as athlete's foot and ringworm, the use of gloves is not a practical solution due to the level of precision required in a nail technician's work. For this reason, nail technicians must be able to distinguish between skin or nail conditions that can be treated in the salon and disorders and diseases that require medical attention. In so doing, educated and honest nail technicians can contribute to the confidence, health, and well-being of their customers.

REQUIREMENTS

High School

Many states require that nail technicians be high school graduates, although a few states require only an eighth- or tenth-grade education. If you are interested in becoming a nail technician, consider taking health and anatomy classes in high school. These classes will give you a basis for understanding skin and nail conditions. Since many nail technicians are self-employed, you may benefit from taking business classes that teach you how a successful business is run. Take art classes, such as painting, drawing, or sculpting, which will allow you to work with your hands and develop a sense of color and design. Finally, do not forget to take English or communication classes. These courses will help you hone your speaking and writing skills, skills that you will need when dealing with the public. Some high schools with vocational programs may offer cosmetology courses. Such courses may include the study of bacteriology, sanitation, and mathematics. These specialized courses can be helpful in preparing students for their future work. You will need to check with your high school about the availability of such a vocational program.

Postsecondary Training

Your next step on the road to becoming a nail technician is to attend a cosmetology or nail school. Some states have schools specifically for nail technician training; in other states, the course work must be completed within the context of a full cosmetology program. Nail technology courses generally require between 100 and 500 clock hours of training, but requirements can vary widely from state to state. Because of these variations, make sure the school you choose to attend will allow you to meet the educational requirements of the state in which you hope to work. When the required course work has been completed, the student must pass an examination that usually includes a written test and a practical examination to demonstrate mastery of required skills. A health certificate is sometimes required.

Course work in nail schools (or nail technician programs in cosmetology schools) reflects that students are expected to learn a great deal more than just manicuring; typical courses of study encompass a broad array of subjects, such as bacteriology, sanitation, and aseptic control procedures; diseases and disorders of the nail; anatomy (of the nails, hands, and feet); nail styling and artificial nail techniques; spa manicures and pedicures; aromatherapy; reflexology; state law; advertising and sales; and people skills. Course work also includes working on live models so that each student gains hands-on experience in each service studied.

Certification or Licensing

Most states require nail technicians to be licensed. Usually a fee is charged to take the exam, and another fee is assessed before receiving the license. Exams usually include both written and practical tests. Many states now offer special nail technician licenses (sometimes called limited or specialty certificates), which require anywhere from 100 to 500 hours of schooling in a licensed cosmetology or nail school. In states where no limited certificates are offered, a student must complete cosmetology school (substantially more hours than required for a specialty; for example, to graduate from the Illinois-based cosmetology school Pivot Point, students must complete its 1,500-hour cosmetology program), become licensed as a cosmetologist, and then specialize in nail technology. Some states offer special licenses for manicurist managers and nail technician instructors; these require substantially more hours of schooling than do nail technician licenses. Reciprocity agreements exist in some states that enable a nail technician to work in another state without being retested. Some states require that nail technicians be 16 or 18 years old in order to be licensed. You will need to find out the licensing requirements for the state in which you hope to work. Associations and state boards of health can often supply this information.

Other Requirements

Nail technicians must have good vision and manual dexterity, as their work is very exacting in nature. Creativity and artistic talents are helpful, especially in those technicians who perform nail art, which can include painting designs and applying various decorative items to nails.

A steady hand is important, and nail technicians should also have an eye for form and color.

Since nail technicians provide services to a wide variety of people, the personality and attitude of a nail technician to a large extent ultimately determine his or her success. While some clients are easy to please, others are demanding and even unreasonable; a nail technician who is able to satisfy even the most difficult customers will be positioned to develop a large, loyal following. Nail technicians who are punctual, courteous, respectful, and patient will enjoy a distinct competitive advantage over others in the industry that lack these qualities. Tact, professionalism, and competence are important. Knowledge and practice of proper sanitizing techniques should be clearly visible to clients. Naturally, hygiene and grooming are of paramount importance in this profession, and a nail technician's own hands and nails should be perfectly groomed; this is one's best form of advertisement and can help foster confidence in prospective and new clients.

A confident, outgoing personality can be a great boon to a nail technician's success. Customers may readily accept recommendations for additional nail services from a persuasive, knowledgeable, and competent nail technician who appears genuinely interested in the customer's interests. Nail technicians who can successfully sell their services will enjoy increased business.

Unlike most careers in the cosmetology field, nail technicians are not required to be on their feet all day. Nail technology is a good choice for those interested in the beauty industry who prefer to be able to work in a seated, comfortable position.

EXPLORING

If you are considering a career as a nail technician, a good avenue of exploration is to call a cosmetology or nail school and ask for an opportunity to tour the facilities, observe classes, and question instructors. Another enjoyable option is for you to make an appointment with a nail technician for a manicure or pedicure. By receiving one of these services yourself, you will have the opportunity to visit the place of business, take in the atmosphere, and experience the procedure. In addition, you'll be able to talk to someone who can answer your questions about this line of work. Explain that you are interested in becoming a nail technician, and you may find that you can develop a mentoring relationship with this professional technician. A part-time job in a beauty salon that offers nail services may also help you determine your interest in various aspects of the beauty industry. Part-time positions for nontechnicians in nail salons, though, may prove difficult to find.

EMPLOYERS

As with cosmetologists and other personal appearance workers, approximately half of the nail technicians in the country are self-employed. They may rent a "booth" or chair at a salon; some may own their own nail salons. A growing number of nail technicians are employed by nail salons, which are rapidly increasing in number in many areas of the country. Beauty shops and department store salons also employ nail technicians, but most have only one or two on staff (very large salons have more). Since nail services represent one of the fastest-growing segments of the cosmetology industry, there is good potential for those wishing to open their own businesses in the nail industry.

STARTING OUT

In most states, graduating from an accredited cosmetology or nail school that meets the state's requirements for licensing is the vehicle for entry into this field. Nearly all cosmetology schools assist graduates with the process of finding employment. Want ads and personal visits to salons and shops are also productive means of finding a job.

ADVANCEMENT

Advancement in the nail technology industry most often takes the form of establishing a large, loyal clientele. Other opportunities include owning one's own nail salon. This can be a highly profitable endeavor if one has the proper business skills and savvy; the cost of materials and overhead can be relatively low, and, in addition to the earnings realized from services performed for their customers, the owners typically receive half of their operators' earnings.

Some technicians choose to advance by becoming nail instructors in cosmetology or nail schools or becoming inspectors for state cosmetology boards.

Nail technicians who constantly strive to increase their knowledge and proficiency in a wide array of nail services will have a competitive advantage and will be positioned to secure a large and varied clientele.

EARNINGS

Income for nail technicians can vary widely, depending on the skill, experience, and clientele of the nail technician, the type and location of the shop or salon, the tipping habits of the clientele, and the area of the country. The U.S. Department of Labor reports the median annual income for nail technicians was $19,710 in 2009. (This income includes tips.) The lowest paid 10 percent earned $15,940 or less while the highest paid 10 percent earned $31,940 or more. Salary.com, a provider of compensation information, reports that nationwide manicurists had yearly earnings ranging from approximately $16,860 to $24,196 in January 2011. Those working in large metropolitan areas may have slightly higher earnings, but the cost of living is also higher there. According to findings by *NAILS Magazine*, which surveyed professionals to come up with 2010 statistics on the industry, about 23 percent had between 21 and 30 clients per week, with more than half being regular appointments and nearly a quarter as walk-ins. The average price for a manicure was $18.79; pedicure, $30.99; acrylics, $45.06; gels (full set), $48.66; and acrylic fill, $25.87. The average price for a booth rental in 2010 was $367 per month, with rates ranging from $150 or less to $500 or more per month.

The importance of the talents and personality of the nail technician cannot be underestimated when evaluating potential earnings. Those who hold themselves to the highest levels of professionalism, express a genuine interest in clients' well-being, and provide the highest quality service quickly develop loyal clienteles, and these nail technicians will realize earnings that far exceed the averages.

Those technicians who work in beauty shops are less likely than those in nail salons to have appointments scheduled throughout the day; however, customers in beauty salons often pay more and tip better for these services. Also, there is less competition within the beauty shop setting, as the majority of beauty salons employ only one or two nail technicians.

Owning one's own nail salon can be very profitable, as the cost of equipment is relatively low. In addition to taking home one's own earnings from servicing clients, the owner also generally gets half of the income generated by the shop's other operators. Nail salons are a prime example of a small business with tremendous potential for success.

Except for those nail technicians who work in department stores or large salons, most do not enjoy much in the way of benefits; few nail technicians receive health and life insurance or paid vacations.

WORK ENVIRONMENT

Nail technicians work indoors in bright, well-ventilated, comfortable environments. Unlike most careers in the cosmetology industry that require operators to be on their feet most of the day, nail technicians perform their work seated at a table.

Many nail technicians work five-day weeks including Saturdays, which are a high-volume business day in this industry. Working some evenings may be helpful in building one's clientele, as a large percentage of customers are working professionals. Nail technicians often enjoy some flexibility in their hours, and many enjoy successful part-time careers.

A large number of nail technicians are self-employed; they may rent a space in a beauty or nail salon. Often, nail technicians must provide their own supplies and tools. Nail technicians are exposed to a certain amount of chemicals and dust, but this is generally manageable in well-ventilated work surroundings. Those who work in full-service salons may be exposed to additional chemicals and odors.

Inherent in the nature of a nail technician's work is the constant company of others. A nail technician who is not a "people person" will find this line of work most challenging. But since most people who choose this career enjoy the company of others, they find the opportunity to talk with and get to know people to be one of the most satisfying and enjoyable aspects of their work.

OUTLOOK

The nail business (a multibillion dollar industry) has been growing rapidly for years. *NAILS Magazine* reported that from 1997 to 2007, the number of nail salons in the United States had doubled. Nail salons and day spas offering nail services continue to crop up everywhere, and nail technicians represent the fastest-growing segment of the various specialized service providers in the beauty industry. According to the U.S. Department of Labor, employment for nail technicians should grow much faster than the average through 2018. Once a mark of feminine status, nail services are now sought and enjoyed by a wide variety of people, both male and female. Clearly, there is a market for all kinds of nail services, from the most basic hand and nail care to the most involved procedures and outlandish styles.

FOR MORE INFORMATION

This magazine has information on the latest nail technologies, fashions, safety matters, and industry news.
NAILS Magazine
3520 Challenger Street
Torrance, CA 90503-1640
Tel: 310-533-2413
http://www.nailsmag.com

This organization accredits cosmetology schools nationally and can provide lists of licensed training schools.
National Accrediting Commission of Cosmetology Arts and Sciences
4401 Ford Avenue, Suite 1300
Alexandria, VA 22302-1432
Tel: 703-600-7600
http://naccas.org

This organization of nail technicians, stylists, salon owners, and other professionals can provide industry and education information.
National Cosmetology Association / Professional Beauty Association
15825 North 71st Street, Suite 100
Scottsdale, AZ 85254-2187
Tel: 800-468-2274
E-mail: info@probeauty.org
http://www.probeauty.org

This Web site for beauty professionals has a list of state licensing requirements for nail technicians.
Beauty Tech
http://www.beautytech.com/nailtech

NUCLEAR REACTOR OPERATORS AND TECHNICIANS

OVERVIEW

Licensed *nuclear reactor operators* work in nuclear power plant control rooms, where they monitor instruments that record the performance of every pump, compressor, and other treatment system in the reactor unit. Nuclear power plants must have operators on duty at all times. In addition to monitoring the instruments in the control room, the nuclear reactor operator runs periodic tests on equipment at the station. *Nuclear reactor operator technicians* are in training to become operators; they study nuclear science theory and learn to perform reactor operation and control activities. They work under the supervision of licensed nuclear reactor operators, and later they work as beginning operators.

SCHOOL SUBJECTS
Mathematics, Physics

PERSONAL SKILLS
Following instructions, Technical/scientific

MINIMUM EDUCATION LEVEL
Some postsecondary training

CERTIFICATION OR LICENSING
Required

WORK ENVIRONMENT
Primarily indoors, Primarily one location

Senior operators, or *senior reactor operators*, have further training and experience and oversee the activities of nuclear reactor operators and technicians.

THE JOB

Technicians are trained to learn and perform all the duties expected of licensed operators. Almost all the skills and knowledge, however, are learned outside of the reactor control room.

The nuclear reactor is like an engine providing power, in the form of hot steam, to run the entire nuclear power plant. Nuclear reactor operators are the nuclear station's driver, in the sense that they control all the machines used to generate power at the station. Working under the direction of a plant manager, the nuclear reactor operator is responsible for the continuous and safe operation of a reactor. Although most nuclear power plants contain more than one nuclear reactor unit, each nuclear reactor operator is responsible for only one of the units.

From the standpoint of safety and uninterrupted operation, the nuclear reactor operator holds the most critical job in the plant. The operator's performance is considered so essential that any shutdown of an average 1,000-megawatt plant, whether due to an accident or operating error, can result in a minimum loss of the cost of the operator's salary for 10 years.

Licensed nuclear reactor operators work in the station control room, monitoring meters and gauges. They read and interpret instruments that record the performance of every valve, pump, compressor, switch, and water treatment system in the reactor unit. When necessary, they make adjustments to fission rate, pressure, water temperature, and the flow rate of the various pieces of equipment to ensure safe and efficient operation.

During each 24-hour period, operators make rounds four times. This task involves reviewing the unit's control board and writing down the parameters of the instruments. Each hour, a computer generates a reading indicating the amount of power the unit is generating.

In addition to monitoring the instruments in the control room, the nuclear reactor operator runs periodic tests, including pressure readings, flow readings, and vibration analyses on each piece of equipment. The operator must also perform logic testing on the electrical components in order to check the built-in safeguards.

Every 12 to 18 months, the nuclear reactor operator must also refuel the reactor unit, a procedure that is sometimes called an outage. During the refueling, the turbine is brought offline, or shut down. After it cools and depressurizes, the unit is opened, and any repairs, testing, and preventive maintenance are taken care of. Depleted nuclear fuel is exchanged for new fuel. The unit is then repressurized, reheated, and brought back online, or restarted.

Auxiliary equipment operators normally work at the site of the equipment. Their work can include anything from turning a valve to bringing a piece of equipment in and out of service. All of their requests for action on any of the machines must be approved by the nuclear reactor operator.

Precise operation is required in nuclear power plants to be sure that radiation does not contaminate the equipment, the operating personnel, or the nearby population and environment. The most serious danger is the release of large amounts of atomic radiation into the atmosphere. Operating personnel are directly involved in the prevention of reactor accidents and in the containment of radioactivity in the event of an accident.

Nuclear reactor operators always begin their employment as technicians. In this capacity, they gain plant experience and technical knowledge at a functioning nuclear power plant. The technician trains on a simulator and studies the reactor and control room. A simulator is built and equipped as an operating reactor control station. Technicians can practice operating the reactor and learn what readings the instruments in the simulator give when certain adjustments are made in the reactor control settings. This company-sponsored training is provided to help technicians attain the expertise necessary to obtain an operator's license. Even after obtaining a license, however, beginning operators work under the direction of a shift supervisor, senior operator, or other management personnel.

REQUIREMENTS

Although a college degree is not required, many utilities prefer candidates to have some postsecondary training. More and more nuclear reactor operators have completed at least two years of college, and many have a four-year degree. Lack of college experience, however, does not exclude an applicant from being hired. High school graduates are selected based on subjects studied and aptitude test results.

High School

If you wish to enter nuclear technology programs, you should study algebra, geometry, English composition, blueprint reading, and chemistry and physics with laboratory study. In addition, classes in computer science and beginning electronics will help you prepare for the technology program that follows high school.

Postsecondary Training

In the first year of a nuclear technology program at a technical or community college, you will probably take nuclear technology, radiation physics, applied mathematics, electricity and electronics, technical communications, basic industrial economics, radiation detection and measurement, inorganic chemistry, radiation protection, mathematics, basic mechanics, quality assurance and quality control, principles of process instrumentation, heat transfer and fluid flow, metallurgy, and metal properties.

In the second year, you may be required to take technical writing and reporting, nuclear systems, blueprint reading, mechanical component characteristics and specifications, reactor physics, reactor safety, power plant systems, instrumentation and control of reactors and plant systems, power plant chemistry, reactor operations, reactor auxiliary systems, and industrial organizations and institutions.

Upon completing a technical program, you will continue training once you are employed at a plant. On-the-job training includes learning nuclear science theory; radiation detection; and reactor design, operation, and control. In addition, nuclear reactor operator technicians must learn in detail how the nuclear power plant works. Trainees are assigned to a series of work-learn tasks that take them to all parts of the plant. If trainees have been working in the plant as regular employees, their individual training is planned around what they already know. This kind of training usually takes two to three years and includes simulator practice.

The simulator is an exact replica of the station's real control room. The controls in the simulator are connected to an interactive computer. Working under the supervision of a licensed nuclear reactor operator, trainees experience mock events in the simulator, which teach them how to safely handle emergencies.

During this on-the-job training, technicians learn about nuclear power plant materials, processes, material balances, plant operating equipment, pipe systems, electrical systems, and process control. It is crucial to understand how each activity within the unit affects other instruments or systems. Nuclear reactor operator technicians are given written and oral exams, sometimes as often as once a week. In some companies, technicians are dismissed from their job for failing to pass any one training exam.

Some people in the industry believe that one of the most difficult aspects of becoming a nuclear reactor operator is getting hired. Because electric utilities invest a substantial amount of time and money to train nuclear reactor operators, they are extremely selective when hiring.

The application process entails intensive screening, including identity checks, FBI fingerprint checks, drug and alcohol tests, psychological tests, and credit checks. After passing this initial screening, the applicant takes a range of mathematical and science aptitude tests.

Utility companies recruit most nuclear reactor operator technicians from local high schools and colleges, fossil fuel plants (utilities using non-nuclear sources of energy), and nuclear navy programs. Knowledge of nuclear science and the discipline and professionalism gained from navy experience make veterans excellent candidates. Graduates of two-year programs in nuclear technology also make excellent trainees because they are well versed in nuclear and power plant fundamentals.

The standards and course content for all nuclear training programs are established by the Nuclear Regulatory Commission (NRC). In addition, each nuclear power plant training program must be accredited by the Institute of Nuclear Power Operations, which was founded in 1979 by industry leaders to promote excellence in nuclear plant operations.

Certification or Licensing

Nuclear reactor operators are required to be licensed, based on examinations given by the NRC. The licensing process involves passing several exams, including a physical exam. To qualify for the licensing process, nuclear reactor operators must have three years of nuclear power plant experience. The first written licensing exam (Generic Fundamentals Examination) covers topics such as reactor theory and thermodynamics. Candidates who pass this exam then take a site-specific exam that includes a written section and an operating test on the power plant's simulator. Candidates who pass these tests receive their licenses. A license is valid for six years and only for the specific power plant for which the candidate applied.

To maintain their licenses, operators must pass an annual practical, or operating, exam and a written requalification exam given by their employers. Requirements for license renewal include certification from the employer that the operator has successfully completed requalification and operating exams and passed a physical.

Other Requirements

Nuclear reactor operators are subject to continuous exams and ongoing training. They must be diligent about keeping their skills and knowledge up to date. A desire for lifelong learning, therefore, is necessary for those doing this work.

Because of the dangerous nature of nuclear energy, the nuclear reactor operator's performance is critical to the safety of other employees, the community, and the environment. Operators must perform their job with a high degree of precision and accuracy. They must be able to remain calm under pressure and maintain sound judgment in emergencies.

Although nuclear reactor operators must frequently perform numerous tasks at once, they must also be able to remain alert during quiet times and handle the monotony of routine readings and tests.

Responding to requests from other personnel, such as the auxiliary operators, is a regular part of the nuclear reactor operator's job. The ability to communicate and work well with other team members and plant personnel is essential.

EXPLORING

High school guidance counselors and advisers at community or technical colleges are good sources of information about a career as a nuclear reactor operator. The librarians in these institutions may also be helpful in directing you to introductory literature on nuclear reactors.

Opportunities for exploring a career as a nuclear reactor operator are limited because nuclear power plants are usually located in places relatively far from schools and have strictly limited visiting policies. Very few commercial or research reactors provide tours for the general public. Many utility companies with nuclear power plants, however, have visitors' centers, where tours are scheduled at specified hours. In addition, interested high school students can usually arrange visits to non-nuclear power plants, which allows them to learn about the energy-conversion process common to all steam-powered electric power generation plants.

EMPLOYERS

In 2009, there were 4,840 nuclear power plant reactor operators employed in the United States. There are 104 commercial nuclear power plants operating at more than 64 sites in 31 states in the United States, according to the Nuclear Energy Institute. In addition, the NRC regulates 41 research and test reactors. Nuclear reactor operators, naturally, work at nuclear power plants and are employed by utility or energy companies, universities, and other institutions operating these facilities.

STARTING OUT

In recent years, nuclear technology programs have been the best source for hiring nuclear reactor operator technicians. Students are usually interviewed and hired by the nuclear power plant personnel recruiters toward the end of their technical college program and start working in the power plant as trainees after they graduate.

Navy veterans from nuclear programs and employees from other parts of the nuclear power plant may also be good candidates for entering a nuclear reactor operator training program.

ADVANCEMENT

Many licensed reactor operators progress to the position of senior reactor operator (as they gain experience and undergo further study). To be certified as senior reactor operators (SROs), operators must pass the senior reactor operator exam, which requires a broader and more detailed knowledge of the power plant, plant procedures, and company policies. In some locations, the senior reactor operator may supervise other licensed operators.

SROs may also advance into the positions of field foreman and then control room supervisor or unit supervisor. These are management positions, and supervisors are responsible for an operating crew. Successful supervisors can be promoted to shift engineer or even plant manager.

Licensed nuclear reactor operators and senior reactor operators may also become part of a power plant's education staff or gain employment in a technical or four-year college, company employee training department, or an outside consulting company. Both operators and SROs may work for reactor manufacturers and serve as research and development consultants. They may also teach trainees to use simulators or operating models of the manufacturer's reactors. Finally, operators and SROs may work for the NRC, which administers license examinations.

EARNINGS

The beginning salary rate for nuclear reactor operator technicians depends on the technician's knowledge of nuclear science theory and work experience. Graduates of strong nuclear technology programs or former navy nuclear technicians usually earn more than people without this background or training. Salaries also vary among different electric power companies.

According to the U.S. Department of Labor, in 2008 the lowest paid reactor operator technicians earned less than $40,310 per year, with a median of $67,890. Reactor operators earned an annual median income of $72,650 in 2009, according to the U.S. Department of Labor. Salaries ranged from less than $54,590 to more than $100,310 a year.

In addition to a base salary, some operators are paid a premium for working certain shifts and overtime. Standard benefits include insurance, paid holidays, vacations, and retirement benefits.

Employers also pay for the continued formal and on-the-job training of nuclear reactor operators. Of licensed reactor operator staff members, 10 to 20 percent are in formal retraining programs at any one time to renew their operator's licenses or to obtain a senior operator's license.

WORK ENVIRONMENT

Nuclear reactor operator technicians spend their working hours in classrooms and laboratories, learning about every part of the power plant. Toward the end of their training, they work at a reactor control-room simulator or in the control room of an operational reactor unit under the direction of licensed operators.

Operators work in clean, well-lit, but windowless, control rooms. Because nuclear reactor operators spend most of their time in the control room, employers have made great efforts to make it as comfortable as possible.

Some control rooms are painted in bright, stimulating colors, and some are kept a little cooler than is standard in most offices. Some utilities have even supplied exercise equipment for their nuclear reactor operators to use during quiet times.

Because nuclear reactors must operate continuously, operators usually work an eight-hour shift and rotate through each of three shifts, taking turns as required. This means operators will work weekends as well as nights some of the time. During their shift, most operators are required to remain in the control room, often eating their lunches at their station. Being in the same environment for eight hours at a time with the same crew members can be stressful.

Although nuclear reactor operators may work at one station of control boards for a long time, they are not allowed to personalize their space because each station is used by more than one person as the shifts rotate.

Although most operators do not wear suits to work, they dress in office attire. Technicians, however, will spend part of their training outside the reactor area. In this environment, appropriate clothing is worn, including hard hats and safety shoes, if necessary.

Operators are shielded from radiation by the concrete outside wall of the reactor containment vessel. If leaks should occur, operators are less subject to exposure than plant personnel who are more directly involved in maintenance and inspection. Nonetheless, technicians wear film badges that darken with radiation exposure. In addition, radiation measurement is carried out in all areas of the plant and plant surroundings according to a regular schedule.

The tough scrutiny of the NRC is an added stress for operators. Plant management, the local community, and the national and local press also watch for compliance with regulatory and safety measures.

A career as a nuclear reactor operator offers the opportunity to assume a high degree of responsibility and to be paid while training. People who enjoy using precision instruments and learning about the latest technological developments are likely to find this career appealing. Operators must be able to shoulder a high degree of responsibility and to work well under stressful conditions. They must be emotionally stable and calm at all times, even in emergencies.

OUTLOOK

Questions regarding the safety of nuclear power, the environmental effects of nuclear plants, and the safe disposal of radioactive waste have been of public concern since the occurrence of major accidents at the

Three Mile Island and Chernobyl plants. Nevertheless, the Nuclear Energy Institute reports that approximately 74 percent of Americans surveyed in 2010 support the use of nuclear energy, and 84 percent support new nuclear power plants being constructed in the future. A joint effort between the federal government and private industry, Nuclear Power 2010, was charged with identifying sites for new advanced nuclear power plants by 2005 and to begin construction by 2010 of new facilities.

The U.S. Department of Labor forecasts average employment growth for nuclear technicians, and faster-than-average growth for nuclear reactor operators through 2018. New job openings will occur as a result of retirements or transfers to other jobs. More operators will be needed due to new rules on limiting the length of operators' shifts to prevent fatigue. Also, many sites have applied for permits, and if approved, these sites will need to be staffed.

FOR MORE INFORMATION

For information on publications, scholarships, and seminars, contact

American Nuclear Society
555 North Kensington Avenue
LaGrange Park, IL 60526-5592
Tel: 800-323-3044
http://www.ans.org

This organization advocates the peaceful use of nuclear technologies. For information on certification, publications, and local chapters, contact

American Society for Nondestructive Testing
PO Box 28518
1711 Arlingate Plaza
Columbus, OH 43228-0518
Tel: 800-222-2768
http://www.asnt.org

For information on the nuclear industry and careers, as well as a list of academic programs in nuclear energy, contact

Nuclear Energy Institute
1776 I Street, NW, Suite 400
Washington, DC 20006-3708
Tel: 202-739-8000
http://www.nei.org

For information on licensing, contact
U.S. Nuclear Regulatory Commission
Washington, DC 20555-0001

Tel: 800-368-5642
http://www.nrc.gov

NURSE ASSISTANTS

OVERVIEW

Nurse assistants (also called *nurse aides, orderlies,* or *hospital attendants*) work under the supervision of nurses and handle much of the personal care needs of the patients. This allows the nursing staff to perform their primary duties more effectively and efficiently. Nurse assistants help move patients, assist in patients' exercise and nutrition needs, and oversee patients' personal hygiene. Nurse assistants may also be required to take patients to other areas of the hospital for treatment, therapy, or diagnostic testing. They are required to keep charts of their work with their patients for review by other medical personnel and to comply with required reporting. There are about 1.4 million nurse assistants in the United States, and about 41 percent of them are employed in nursing care facilities.

THE JOB

Nurse assistants generally help nurses care for patients in hospital or nursing home settings. Their duties include tending to the daily care of the patients, includ-

SCHOOL SUBJECTS
Biology, Health

PERSONAL SKILLS
Following instructions, Helping/teaching

MINIMUM EDUCATION LEVEL
High school diploma

CERTIFICATION OR LICENSING
Required for certain positions

WORK ENVIRONMENT
Primarily indoors, Primarily multiple locations

ing bathing them, helping them with their meals, and checking their body temperature and blood pressure. In addition, they often help persons who need assistance with their personal hygiene needs and answer their call lights when they need immediate assistance.

The work can be strenuous, requiring the lifting and moving of patients. Nurse assistants must work with partners or in groups when performing the more strenuous tasks to ensure their safety as well as the patient's. Some requirements of the job can be as routine as changing sheets and helping a patient or resident with phone calls, while other requirements can be as difficult and unattractive as assisting a resident with elimination and cleaning up a resident or patient who has vomited.

Nurse assistants may be called upon to perform the more menial and unappealing tasks of health and personal care, but they also have the opportunity to develop meaningful relationships with patients. In a nursing home, nursing assistants work closely with residents, often gaining their trust and friendship.

REQUIREMENTS

High School

Although a high school diploma is not always required to work as a nurse assistant, there are a number of high school classes that can help you do this work. Communication skills are valuable for a nurse assistant to have, so take English classes. Science courses, such as biology and anatomy, and family and consumer science, health, and nutrition classes are also helpful. Some high schools offer courses directly related to nurse assistant training. These classes may include body mechanics, infection control, and resident/patient rights.

Postsecondary Training

Nurse assistants are not required to have a college degree, but they may have to complete a short training course at a community college or vocational school. These training courses, usually taught by a registered nurse, teach basic nursing skills and prepare students for the state certification exam. Nurse assistants typically begin the training courses after getting their first job as an assistant, and the course work is often incorporated into their on-the-job training.

Many people work as nurse assistants as they pursue other medical professions such as a premedical or nursing program.

Certification or Licensing

Some states require nurse assistants to be certified no matter where they work. The Omnibus Budget Reconciliation Act of 1987 requires nurse assistants working in nursing homes to undergo special training. Nursing homes can hire inexperienced workers as nurse assistants, but they must have at least 75 hours of training and pass a competency evaluation program within four months of being hired. Those who fulfill these requirements are then certified.

Other Requirements

You must care about your patients and you must show a genuine understanding and compassion for the ill, the elderly, and people with disabilities. Because of the rigorous physical demands placed on you, you should be in good health and have good work habits. Along with good physical health, you should have good mental health and a cheerful disposition. The job can be emotionally demanding, requiring patience and stability. You should be able to work as a part of a team and also be able to take orders and follow through on your responsibilities.

EXPLORING

Because a high school diploma is frequently not required of nursing aides, many high school students are hired by nursing homes and hospitals for part-time work. Job opportunities may also exist in a hospital or nursing home kitchen, introducing you to diet and nutrition. These jobs will give you an opportunity to become familiar with the hospital and nursing home environments. Also, volunteer work can familiarize you with the work that nurses and nurse assistants perform, as well as introduce you to basic medical terminology.

EMPLOYERS

Approximately 41 percent of the more than 1.4 million nurse assistants in the United States are employed in nursing care facilities, and another 29 percent worked in hospitals. Others are employed in halfway houses, retirement centers, homes for persons with disabilities, and private homes.

STARTING OUT

Because of the high demand for nurse assistants, you can apply directly to the health facilities in your area, contact your local employment office, or check online employment Web sites and your local newspaper's help wanted ads.

ADVANCEMENT

For the most part, there is not much opportunity for advancement with this job. To advance in a health care facility requires additional training. After becoming familiar with the medical and nursing home environments and gaining some knowledge of medical terminology, some nurse assistants enroll in nursing programs or pursue other medically related careers.

Many facilities are recognizing the need to retain good health care workers and are putting some training and advancement programs in place for their employees.

EARNINGS

Salaries for most health care professionals vary by region, population, and size and kind of institution. The pay for nurse assistants in a hospital is usually more than in a nursing home.

According to the U.S. Department of Labor, nurse assistants earned median hourly wages of $11.56 in 2009. For full-time work at 40 hours per week, this hourly wage translates into a yearly income of approximately $24,040. The lowest paid 10 percent earned less than $8.42 per hour (approximately $17,510 per year), and the highest paid 10 percent earned more than $16.33 per hour (approximately $33,970 annually).

Benefits are usually based on the hours worked, length of employment, and the policies of the facility. Some offer paid vacation and holidays, medical or hospital insurance, and retirement plans. Some also provide free meals to their workers.

WORK ENVIRONMENT

The work environment in a health care or long-term care facility can be hectic at times and very stressful. Some patients may be uncooperative and may actually be combative. Often there are numerous demands that must be met at the same time. Nurse assistants are required to be on their feet most of the time, and they often have to help lift or move patients. Most facilities are clean and well lighted, but nurse assistants do have the possibility of exposure to contagious diseases, although using proper safety procedures minimizes their risk.

Nurse assistants generally work a 40-hour workweek, with some overtime. The hours and weekly schedule may be irregular, depending on the needs of the institution. Nurse assistants are needed around the clock, so work schedules may include night shift or swing-shift work.

OUTLOOK

There will continue to be many job opportunities for nurse assistants; the U.S. Department of Labor predicts that this occupation will grow faster than the average through 2018. Because of the physical and emotional demands of the job, and because of the lack of advancement opportunities, there is a high employee turnover rate. Additional opportunities may be available as different types of care facilities are developed and as facilities try to curb operating costs.

In addition, more nurse assistants will be required as government and private agencies develop more programs to assist people with disabilities, dependent people, and the increasing aging population.

FOR MORE INFORMATION

For additional information on nurse assistant careers and training, contact the following organizations:

National Association of Health Care Assistants
2709 West 13th Street
Joplin, MO 64701-3647
Tel: 800-784-6049
http://www.nahcacares.org

National Network of Career Nursing Assistants
3577 Easton Road
Norton, OH 44203-5661
Tel: 330-825-9342
E-mail: cnajeni@aol.com
http://www.cna-network.org

OCCUPATIONAL THERAPISTS

OVERVIEW

Occupational therapists (OTs) select and direct therapeutic activities designed to develop or restore maximum function to individuals with disabilities. There are approximately 97,840 occupational therapists employed in the United States.

SCHOOL SUBJECTS
Biology, Health

PERSONAL SKILLS
Helping/teaching, Mechanical/manipulative

MINIMUM EDUCATION LEVEL
Master's degree

CERTIFICATION OR LICENSING
Required (licensing), Voluntary (certification)

WORK ENVIRONMENT
Primarily indoors, Primarily one location

THE JOB

Occupational therapists use a wide variety of activities to help clients attain their goals for productive, independent living. These goals include developing maximum self-sufficiency in activities of daily living, such as eating, dressing, writing, using a telephone and other communication resources, as well as functioning in the community and the workplace.

In developing a therapeutic program for a client, the occupational therapist often works as a member of a team that can includes physicians, nurses, psychiatrists, physical therapists, speech therapists, rehabilitation counselors, social workers, and other specialists. OTs use creative, educational, and recreational activities, as well as human ingenuity, in helping people achieve their full potential, regardless of their disabilities. Each therapy program is designed specifically for the individual client.

Occupational therapists help clients explore their likes and dislikes, their abilities, and their creative, educational, and recreational experiences. Therapists help people choose activities that have the most appeal and value for them. For example, an activity may be designed to promote greater dexterity for someone with arthritic fingers. Learning to use an adapted computer might help a young person with a spinal cord injury to succeed in school and career goals. The therapist works with the clients' interests and helps them develop practical skills and functional independence.

The occupational therapist may work with a wide range of clients. They may assist a client in learning to use an artificial limb. Another client may have suffered a stroke or other neurological disability, and the therapist works with the client to redevelop the client's motor functions or re-educate his or her muscle function. Therapists may assist in the growth and development of premature infants, or they may work with disabled children, helping them learn motor skills or develop skills and tools that will aid them in their education and social interaction.

Some therapists also conduct research to develop new types of therapies and activities and to measure the effectiveness of a therapy program. They may also design and make special equipment or splints to help clients perform their activities.

Other duties may include supervision of volunteer workers, student therapists, and occupational therapy assistants who give instruction in a particular skill. Therapists must prepare reports to keep members of the professional team informed.

Chief occupational therapists in a hospital may teach medical and nursing students the principles of occupational therapy. Many occupational therapists have administrative duties such as directing different kinds of occupational therapy programs, coordinating patient activities, and acting as consultants or advisors to local and state health departments, mental health authorities, and the division of vocational rehabilitation.

REQUIREMENTS

High School

Since you will need to get a college degree, taking college preparatory classes in high school is a must. Courses such as biology, chemistry, and health will expose you to the science fields. Other courses, such as art and social sciences, will help give you an understanding of other aspects of your future work. Also important is a strong background in English. Remember, occupational therapy is a career oriented toward helping people. To be able to work with many different people with different needs, you will need excellent communication skills. Also keep in mind that college admission officers will look favorably at any experience you have had working in the health care field, either in volunteer or paid positions.

Postsecondary Training

To become an occupational therapist, you will need to complete an accredited program in occupational therapy. Accreditation is granted by the Accreditation Council for Occupational Therapy Education (ACOTE), which is a part of the American Occupational Therapy Association (AOTA). In 2009, ACOTE accredited 150 master's degree programs or combined bachelor's/master's degree programs, and four Ph.D. programs. Anyone wishing to receive the professional credential, occupational therapist, registered (OTR), from the National Board for Certification in Occupational Therapy (NBCOT) must have completed at least a master's degree in the field.

As an undergraduate, you will need to take courses emphasizing biological and behavioral sciences. Your studies should include classes on anatomy, physiology, neurology, psychology, human growth and development, and sociology. Clinical subjects cover general medical and surgical conditions and interpretation of the principles and practice of occupational therapy in pediatrics, psychiatry, orthopedics, general medicine, and surgery. Many bachelor's degree programs require students to fulfill two years of general study before specializing in occupational therapy during the last two years. Graduate-level programs cover many of the same subject areas but in greater depth. In addition, emphasis is put on research and critical thinking. Management and administration are also areas covered more thoroughly in graduate programs.

In addition to classroom work, you must complete fieldwork requirements. According to the AOTA, students need to complete the equivalent of 24 weeks of supervised experience working with clients. This may be done on a full-time basis or a part-time (but not less than half-time) schedule. This training must be completed in order to qualify for professional certification.

Certification or Licensing

All states and the District of Columbia regulate the practice of occupational therapy through certification and licensing. National certification is granted by the NBCOT. In order to take the NBCOT exam, you must graduate from an accredited program and complete the clinical practice period. Those who pass this written test are given the designation, occupational therapist, registered, and may use the initials OTR after their names. Initial certification is good for five years and must be renewed every five years after that. Many hospitals and other employers require that their occupational therapists have the OTR designation. In addition, the NBCOT offers several specialty certifications, such as board certified in pediatrics. To receive a specialty certification, you must fulfill education and experience requirements as well as pass an exam.

License requirements generally include graduation from an accredited program, passing the NBCOT cer-

tification exam, payment of license fees, and, in some cases, passing an exam covering state statutes and regulations. License renewal requirements vary by state.

Other Requirements

In order to succeed as an occupational therapist, you should enjoy working with people. You should have a patient, calm, and compassionate temperament and have the ability to encourage and inspire your clients. Like your clients, you may encounter frustrating situations as a therapist. For example, it can be difficult and stressful when a client does not respond to treatment as you had hoped. In such situations, occupational therapists need to be persistent, not giving up on the client. Imagination and creativity are also important at such times, because you may need to think of new ways to address the client's problem and create new methods or tools for the client to use.

EXPLORING

While in high school, you should meet with occupational therapists, visit the facilities where they work, and gain an understanding of the types of equipment and skills they use. Many hospitals and occupational therapy facilities and departments also have volunteer opportunities, which will give you strong insight into this career.

EMPLOYERS

There are approximately 97,840 occupational therapists at work in hospitals, schools, nursing homes, home health agencies, mental health centers, adult day care programs, outpatient clinics, and residential care facilities. The profession has seen a growing number of therapists becoming self-employed, in either solo or group practice or in consulting firms.

STARTING OUT

Your school's career services office is usually the best place to start your job search as a newly graduated occupational therapist. You may also apply directly to government agencies (such as the U.S. Public Health Service), private hospitals, and clinics. In addition, the AOTA can provide job seekers with assistance through its employment bulletins.

ADVANCEMENT

Newly graduated occupational therapists usually begin as staff therapists and may qualify as senior therapists after several years on the job. The U.S. Army, Navy, Air

Force, and the U.S. Public Health Service commission occupational therapists; other branches of the federal service give civil service ratings. Experienced therapists may become directors of occupational therapy programs in large hospitals, clinics, or workshops, or they may become teachers. Some positions are available as program coordinators and as consultants with large institutions and agencies.

A few colleges and health agencies offer advanced courses in the treatment of special disabilities, such as those resulting from cerebral palsy. Some institutions provide in-service programs for therapists.

EARNINGS

According to the U.S. Department of Labor, the median salary for occupational therapists was $69,630 in 2009. The lowest paid 10 percent earned $45,340 and the top paid 10 percent earned more than $100,430 annually.

Salaries for occupational therapists often vary according to where they work. In areas where the cost of living is higher, occupational therapists generally receive higher pay. Occupational therapists employed in public schools earn salaries that vary by school district. In some states, they are classified as teachers and are paid accordingly.

Therapists employed at hospitals and government and public agencies generally receive full benefit packages that include vacation and sick pay, health insurance, and retirement benefits. Self-employed therapists and those who run their own businesses must provide their own benefits.

WORK ENVIRONMENT

Occupational therapists work in occupational therapy workshops or clinics. As mentioned earlier, these workshops or clinics can be found at a variety of locations, such as hospitals, long-term care facilities, schools, and adult day care centers. No matter what the location, though, these workshops and clinics are well-lighted, pleasant settings. Generally, therapists work eight-hour days and 40-hour weeks, with some evening work required in a few organizations.

OUTLOOK

Opportunities for occupational therapists are expected to be highly favorable through 2018 and employment will grow much faster than the average for all other careers, according to the *Occupational Outlook Handbook*. This growth will occur as a result of the increasing number of middle-aged and elderly people that require therapeutic services. The demand for occupational therapists is also increasing because of growing public interest in and government support for people with disabilities and for occupational therapy programs helping people attain the fullest possible functional status. The demand for rehabilitative and long-term care services is expected to grow strongly over the next decade. There will be numerous opportunities for work with mental health clients, children, and the elderly, as well as with those with disabling conditions.

As the health care industry continues to be restructured, there should be many more opportunities for occupational therapists in nontraditional settings. This factor and proposed changes in the laws should create an excellent climate for therapists wishing to enter private practice. Home health care may experience the greatest growth in the next decade.

FOR MORE INFORMATION

Visit AOTA's Web site to find out about accredited occupational therapy programs, career information, and news related to the field.

American Occupational Therapy Association (AOTA)
4720 Montgomery Lane
PO Box 31220
Bethesda, MD 20824-1220
Tel: 301-652-2682
http://www.aota.org

For information on certification requirements, contact
National Board for Certification in Occupational Therapy
12 South Summit Avenue, Suite 100
Gaithersburg, MD 20877-4150
Tel: 301-990-7979
http://www.nbcot.org

OCCUPATIONAL THERAPY ASSISTANTS AND AIDES

OVERVIEW

Occupational therapy assistants (also called OTAs) help people with mental, physical, developmental, or emotional limitations using a variety of activities to improve basic motor functions and reasoning abilities. They work under the direct supervision of an occupational therapist, and their duties include helping to plan, implement, and evaluate rehabilitation programs designed to regain patients' self-sufficiency and to restore their physical and mental functions. There are 26,680 occupational therapy assistants employed in the United States. *Occupational therapy aides* help OTAs and occupational therapists by doing such things as clerical work, preparing therapy equipment for a client's use, and keeping track of supplies. Approximately 8,040 occupational therapy aides are employed in the United States.

THE JOB

Occupational therapy is used to help provide rehabilitation services to persons with mental, physical, emotional, or developmental disabilities. The goal of occupational therapy is to improve a patient's quality of life by compensating for limitations caused by age, illness, or injury. It differs from physical therapy because it focuses not only on physical rehabilitation, but also on psychological well-being. Occupational therapy emphasizes improvement of the activities of daily living—including such functions as personal hygiene, dressing, eating, and cooking.

Occupational therapy assistants, under the supervision of the therapist, implement patient care plans and activities. They help patients improve mobility and productivity using a variety of activities and exercises. They may use adaptive techniques and equipment to help patients perform tasks many take for granted. For example, a reacher, which is a long-handled device that pinches and grabs small items, may be used to pick up keys from the floor or a book from the shelf. Therapy assistants may have patients mix ingredients for a cake or flip a grilled cheese sandwich using a special spatula. Activities such as dancing, playing cards, or throwing a ball are fun, yet they help improve mobility and give the patients a sense of self-esteem. Therapists evaluate an activity, minimize the number of steps, and streamline movement so the patient will be less fatigued.

Assistants may also help therapists evaluate a patient's progress, change care plans as needed, make therapy appointments, and complete paperwork.

Occupational therapy aides are responsible for materials and equipment used during therapy. They assemble and clean equipment and make certain the therapists and assistants have what they need for a patient's therapy session. A therapy aide's duties are more clerical in nature. They answer telephones, schedule appointments, order supplies and equipment, and complete insurance forms and other paperwork.

REQUIREMENTS

High School

According to the U.S. Department of Labor, most occupational therapy aides receive on-the-job training, while occupational therapy assistants require further education after high school. For either position, however, a high school diploma is a must. Prepare for these careers by taking classes in biology, health, and social sciences. Anyone interested in doing this work must also be able to communicate clearly, follow directions, and work as part of a team. English or communication classes can help you improve on these skills.

In addition, admissions officers at postsecondary programs are favorably impressed if you have experience in the health care field. If you cannot find a paid job, consider volunteering at a local hospital or nursing home during your high school years.

Postsecondary Training

While occupational therapy aides receive on-the-job training, occupational therapy assistants must have either an associate's degree or certificate from an accredited

---

SCHOOL SUBJECTS
Health, Psychology

PERSONAL SKILLS
Helping/teaching, Mechanical/manipulative

MINIMUM EDUCATION LEVEL
Associate's degree (assistants),
High school diploma (aides)

CERTIFICATION OR LICENSING
Required (assistants), None available (aides)

WORK ENVIRONMENT
Primarily indoors, Primarily one location

OTA program. Programs are accredited by the Accreditation Council for Occupational Therapy Education (ACOTE), which is part of the American Occupational Therapy Association (AOTA). In 2011, there were 277 programs fully accredited by the ACOTE. For further information about ACOTE-accredited programs, visit http://www.aota.org.

Generally, programs take two years to complete. Studies include courses such as human anatomy, psychology of adjustment, biology, human kinesiology, therapeutic media, and techniques. Most schools also require their students to take a number of general classes as well to round out their education. These may be courses such as English, business math, and management. In addition to class work, you will be required to complete a period of supervised fieldwork, which will give you hands-on experience with occupational therapy.

Certification or Licensing

Occupational therapy aides do not require certification or licensing. Occupational therapy assistants must pass the certifying test of the National Board for Certification in Occupational Therapy. After passing this test, assistants receive the designation certified occupational therapy assistant. Licensure requirements for assistants vary by state, so you will need to check with the licensing board of the state in which you want to work for specific information.

Other Requirements

Occupational therapy assistants and aides must be able to take directions. OTAs should have a pleasant disposition, strong people skills, and a desire to help those in need. Assistants must also be patient and responsible. Aides, too, should be responsible. They also need to be detail oriented in order to keep track of paperwork and equipment. It is important for assistants and aides to work well as a team.

EXPLORING

A visit to your local hospital's occupational therapy department is the best way to learn about this field. Speak with occupational therapists, assistants, and aides to gain an understanding of the work they do. Also, the AOTA and other related organizations might be able to provide career information. School guidance and job centers, and the library, are good information sources.

EMPLOYERS

There are approximately 26,680 occupational therapy assistants and 8,040 occupational therapy aides employed in the United States. Approximately 27 percent of all assistants and aides work in a hospital setting, 28 percent are employed by offices of other health practitioners, and 20 percent work in nursing facilities. Others work in community care facilities for the elderly, home health care services, outpatient rehabilitation centers, and state government agencies.

STARTING OUT

The career services office of your local community college or technical school can provide a listing of jobs available in the occupational therapy field. Job openings are usually posted in hospital human resource departments. Professional groups are also a good source of information; for example, AOTA's Web site has an employment page for members.

ADVANCEMENT

After some experience, occupational therapy assistants can be promoted to *lead assistant*. Lead assistants are responsible for making work schedules of other assistants and for the training of occupational therapy students. Since occupational therapy assistants work under the supervision of an occupational therapist, there is little room for advancement. Aides may return to school and train to become occupational therapy assistants. Some assistants and aides return to school to become occupational therapists. Some shift to other health care careers.

EARNINGS

According to the U.S. Department of Labor, the median yearly income of occupational therapy assistants was $50,250 in 2009. Salaries ranged from less than $33,350 to $68,450 or more annually. Naturally, experience, location, and type of employer all factor into the salaries paid.

The importance of education, though, cannot be overlooked, as assistants tend to earn more than aides. Median annual earnings of occupational therapist aides were $25,730 in 2009, according to the U.S. Department of Labor. Salaries ranged from less than $16,280 to $47,590 or more annually.

Benefits for full-time workers depend on the employer. They generally include health and life insurance, paid sick and vacation time, holiday pay, and a retirement plan.

WORK ENVIRONMENT

Most occupational therapy assistants and aides work during the day, although depending on the place of employment, some evening or weekend work may be required. Most therapy is done in a hospital or clinic setting that is clean, well lighted, and generally comfortable.

Occupational therapy assistants often use everyday items, settings, and activities to help rehabilitate their patients. Such props include kitchen settings, card games, dancing, or exercises. Therapy assistants should be in good physical shape, since heavy lifting—of patients as well as equipment—is a daily part of the job. Therapy assistants should also have stamina, since they are on their feet for much of the day.

OUTLOOK

According to the *Occupational Outlook Handbook,* employment for occupational therapy assistants and aides will grow much faster than the average through 2018. Only a small number of new jobs will actually be available, however, due to the size of these occupations. Occupational growth will stem from an increased number of people with disabilities and elderly people. Although more people are living well into their 70s, 80s, and in some cases, 90s, they often need the kinds of services occupational therapy provides. Medical technology has greatly improved, saving many lives that in the past would be lost through accidents, stroke, or other illnesses. Such people need rehabilitation therapy as they recuperate. Hospitals and employers are hiring more therapy assistants to help with the workload and to reduce costs.

FOR MORE INFORMATION

For additional information on careers, education, and news related to the field, contact

American Occupational Therapy Association
4720 Montgomery Lane
PO Box 31220
Bethesda, MD 20824-1220
Tel: 301-652-2682
http://www.aota.org

For information on certification, contact

National Board for Certification in Occupational Therapy
12 South Summit Avenue, Suite 100
Gaithersburg, MD 20877-4150
Tel: 301-990-7979
http://www.nbcot.org

OPTOMETRISTS

OVERVIEW

An *optometrist* is a health care professional who provides primary eye care services, including comprehensive eye health and vision examinations, diagnosis and treatment of eye diseases and vision disorders, prescribing of eyeglasses, contact lenses, vision therapy, and medications, performing minor surgical procedures, and counseling patients regarding their vision needs. While examining a patient's eyes, optometrists may also identify signs of diseases and conditions that affect the entire body. Approximately 26,480 optometrists are licensed to practice in the United States.

THE JOB

Optometrists are primarily concerned with examining eyes and performing other services to safeguard and improve vision. To do this, they use special tests and instruments to identify and evaluate eye health, including visual acuity, depth and color perception, and ability to focus and coordinate the eyes. They prescribe what should be done to correct vision problems, which may include prescriptions for eyeglasses, contact lenses, vision therapy, or therapeutic drugs. They diagnose eye diseases caused by systemic conditions such as diabetes or high blood pressure. Optometrists refer these patients to other specialists.

SCHOOL SUBJECTS
Biology, Physics

PERSONAL SKILLS
Helping/teaching, Technical/scientific

MINIMUM EDUCATION LEVEL
Doctorate degree

CERTIFICATION OR LICENSING
Required

WORK ENVIRONMENT
Primarily indoors, Primarily one location

Optometrists are one of three professional groups involved in treatment of the eyes. *Ophthalmologists* are licensed physicians with specialized training in medical and surgical care of the eyes. They prescribe drugs, perform minor and major surgery, diagnose and treat eye diseases, and prescribe lenses and exercises. *Opticians* use the prescriptions provided by ophthalmologists and optometrists to grind lenses, assemble the eyeglasses, and fit and adjust lenses and frames.

Some optometry specialties include work with the elderly, children, or visually impaired individuals who need specialized vision devices, treatment of workplace injuries, contact lenses, sports vision assistance, or vision therapy. Some optometrists teach optometry, conduct research, or specialize in consultations.

Most optometrists are in general practice. Those who have private practices must also handle the business aspects of running an office, such as developing a patient base, hiring employees, keeping records, and ordering equipment and supplies. Optometrists who operate franchise vision care businesses may also have some of these duties.

REQUIREMENTS
High School

If you are interested in pursuing an optometry career, follow a college preparatory schedule, with an emphasis on math and science. Because optometrists typically run their own businesses, a background in business and accounting is also helpful.

Postsecondary Training

Three years of college plus four years in a school or college of optometry is the minimum requirement for becoming an optometrist. The first three years of college are generally devoted to course work in mathematics, physics, biology, and chemistry, as well as the other general education subjects studied by students in colleges of liberal arts and sciences.

In order to be accepted in optometry school, applicants must pass the Optometry Admission Test, which measures general academic ability and science comprehension. Optometry programs are devoted to laboratory, classroom, and clinical work and are accredited by the American Optometric Association. There are 19 accredited schools in the United States and one in Puerto Rico.

Upon completion of study, graduates receive the Doctor of Optometry (O.D.) degree. Some optometrists pursue further study leading to a master's degree or doctorate in physiological optics or other fields.

Certification or Licensing

Before individuals can practice as optometrists, they must secure a license in the state in which they wish to practice. Licensing applicants must have graduated from an accredited school or college of optometry and pass a written test administered by the National Board of Examiners in Optometry and a separate clinical exam. Examinations generally cover the following subjects: ocular anatomy, ocular pathology (disease), optometric methods, theoretical optometry, psychological optics, physical and geometrical optics, physiological optics, physiology, and optometrical mechanics. Licenses must be renewed every one to three years. In all states as well as the District of Columbia, optometrists must earn continuing education credits in optometry to renew their licenses.

Other Requirements

Prospective optometrists must be able to get along well with people, since growth of their practice often depends on customer referrals. Optometrists must also have mechanical aptitude and good vision and coordination. These characteristics are essential to the training required to become licensed.

EXPLORING
It is difficult for students to gain any direct experience on a part-time basis in optometry. The first opportunities afforded students generally come in the clinical phases of their training program. Interested students, however, can visit an optometrist's office and talk to an experienced optometrist. Part-time or summer work for a vision care business or in an optometrist's practice will also expose you to the work environment and routines.

EMPLOYERS
Currently, there are approximately 26,480 licensed optometrists working in the United States. Most are employed in private practice, but others work in health clinics, hospitals, outpatient care centers, the armed forces, and schools and colleges of optometry.

STARTING OUT
There are several ways of entering the field of optometry once an individual has a license to practice. Most

optometrists set up their own practices or purchase an established practice. Other beginners serve as associates to established optometrists until they gain enough experience and financial resources to establish their own practices. Some work in health maintenance organizations (HMOs). Optometrists can also start their careers at government-supported clinics or in the armed forces. Some students of optometry earn their doctorates and go directly into research and teaching in schools and colleges of optometry.

ADVANCEMENT

Optometrists may advance in their profession by specializing in one area. They can also advance from the position of associate optometrist to establish their own practice.

Optometrists in good standing are eligible for membership in the American Optometric Association, which is the major professional organization for optometrists. Optometrists who meet stringent requirements are also eligible for membership in the American Academy of Optometry. Optometrists also hold membership in state and local optometric societies.

EARNINGS

According to the U.S. Department of Labor, the median annual salary of optometrists was $96,140 in 2009, with earnings ranging from less than $48,240 to more than $166,400. Salaried optometrists working in offices of other health practitioners earned a median salary of $103,050 in 2009. According to Salary.com, in 2011 optometrists reported average salaries ranging from $89,929 or less to $144,989 or more, with a median salary of $103,974. Optometrists who accept salaried positions with clinics and government agencies generally have higher earnings in the first few years than do private practitioners. This situation, however, often changes after the private practitioners have had an opportunity to establish themselves.

WORK ENVIRONMENT

Optometrists generally have excellent working conditions. They usually work in their own offices and are free to set their own hours and arrange their vacations and free time. The optometrist usually works in quiet surroundings and is seldom faced with emergencies. Although most optometrists still have solo practices, some have chosen to work in partnerships or teams to alleviate the rising cost of establishing a business and repayment of school loans.

OUTLOOK

Employment for optometrists is expected to grow much faster than the average through 2018. The demand for eye care services will become greater as people continue to become more health conscious. Also, people are more likely to seek such services because they are better able to pay for them as a result of higher income levels, the growing availability of employee vision care plans, and Medicare coverage for optometry services. Increased use of computers by people of all ages appears to lead to eyestrain and aggravated vision problems, creating more need for vision assistance. In addition, a growing elderly population—the group most likely to need eyeglasses—will also keep demand strong. Some of the needed eye care will be provided by physicians who specialize in the treatment of the eyes (ophthalmologists). But there will be more than ample opportunity for optometrists to supply a substantial amount of service. Employment growth will be offset somewhat by productivity gains (in the form of more support staff assistance) that allow for optometrists to see more patients.

FOR MORE INFORMATION

For information on optometry careers and accredited educational programs, contact

American Optometric Association
243 North Lindbergh Boulevard
St. Louis, MO 63141-7881
Tel: 800-365-2219
http://www.aoa.org

For information on training programs, visit the ASCO Web site.

Association of Schools and Colleges of Optometry (ASCO)
6110 Executive Boulevard, Suite 420
Rockville, MD 20852-3942
Tel: 301-231-5944
http://www.opted.org

For information on optometry careers and educational opportunities in Canada, contact

Canadian Association of Optometrists
234 Argyle Avenue
Ottawa, ON K2P 1B9 Canada
Tel: 888-263-4676
E-mail: info@opto.ca
http://www.opto.ca

For information on the Optometric Admissions Test (OAT), contact

Optometry Admission Testing Program
211 East Chicago Avenue, Suite 600
Chicago, IL 60611-2637
Tel: 800-232-2159
https://www.ada.org/oat/index.html

 # ORTHODONTISTS

OVERVIEW

Orth means "straight" and *odont* means "tooth." *Orthodontists* are dental specialists who diagnose problems with teeth, jaws, and lower facial development and treat malpositioned and misaligned teeth and jaws. According to the U.S. Department of Labor, more than 5,410 orthodontists work in the United States.

THE JOB

Orthodontists straighten teeth that are crooked or crowded or that have gaps between them. People who benefit from orthodontics include those whose facial profile shows an overbite, an underbite, protruding lips, or even a "weak chin." People who have dental and facial irregularities often have what is termed "malocclusion," sometimes called a "bad bite." A malocclusion can be corrected for cosmetic reasons, but in some cases crooked

SCHOOL SUBJECTS
Biology, Chemistry, Mathematics

PERSONAL SKILLS
Helping/teaching, Technical/scientific

MINIMUM EDUCATION LEVEL
Medical degree

CERTIFICATION OR LICENSING
Recommended (certification),
Required (licensing)

WORK ENVIRONMENT
Primarily indoors, Primarily one location

teeth can create speech problems or can be more susceptible to decay because the teeth are more difficult to keep clean.

When a patient first comes to the office, the orthodontist takes a complete medical and dental history to determine what is influencing health in general and teeth in particular. Next, the mouth is examined to look for oral evidence of disease. The health of teeth is carefully evaluated. The orthodontist notes the size and shape of each tooth and the relationship between the teeth and the gums, the lips, and the face. The patient's facial profile is assessed for uniformity, symmetry, and proportion. At this time, a "before" photo of a patient's profile and smile may be taken for the patient's record. After treatment is completed, photos will be taken again to show the results.

To make a diagnosis, orthodontists measure and evaluate relationships. They create casts from plaster by asking the patient to bite into a tray of impression material. The three-dimensional models made from the casts are mounted on hinges to show the biting motion of the patient's teeth. It is difficult for patients to hold their mouths open wide for long periods of time, so these models allow orthodontists to study the dynamics of the bite more easily and to take detailed measurements.

Orthodontists also use X-rays to show the status of tissues that can't be seen by the eye, including problems inside the teeth and with the jaws, facial bones, and tooth roots. X-rays can help an orthodontist determine if crowded teeth would benefit from an orthodntic extraction. In other cases, certain jaw discrepancies are detected with radiographs and need correction with orthodontic appliances such as braces or orthognathic (jaw) surgery.

Once a problem is diagnosed, orthodontists may give a patient an oral or a written treatment plan. This plan includes the diagnosis, the recommended treatment specifics, and a cost estimate of treatment.

There are various types of orthodontic treatment, but almost all involve metal, plastic, or ceramic braces that are banded around, or bonded to, teeth. These braces are made up of brackets and wires that move teeth into, or hold them in, proper position. Moving teeth is a very slow process (although it has gotten faster with improved materials) and requires the adjusting of the braces slightly every few weeks to few months.

Additional orthodontic appliances include headgear, a wire appliance that protrudes from the mouth and is fastened by a strap behind the head. Orthodontists use this approach to orthopedically slow the growth of the upper jaw. Rubber bands are another pulling force that, when changed daily by the patient, help move teeth into position. Another type of orthodontic appliance is the retainer. When orthodontists finish active treatment, which usually takes two to three years, the patient comes in much less often for appointments or not at all. To make sure the corrected teeth or jaw don't move back into a poor position, an orthodontist may make a removable or permanent retainer for a patient to wear at night and sometimes during the day as well. Retainers are removed when the patients eat and brush their teeth.

Most orthodontists are in private practice. Some orthodontists teach full or part time at universities. A number perform research at dental schools or for manufacturers, such as dental product manufacturers. Others are government employees, working in the military or for agencies such as the U.S. Public Health Service.

Orthodontists in private practice may need to assume additional responsibilities, such as paying bills, managing staff members, and doing paperwork. Other nonorthodontic responsibilities include working with insurance companies to obtain payment for procedures and overseeing the billing and collection of fees. To ensure the dental office is a safe place for employees and patients alike, orthodontists conduct regular evaluations of procedures and conditions in the office to be certain everything is in compliance with the federal Occupational Safety and Health Administration standards.

Staff members are in charge of taking inventory and ordering supplies, but orthodontists oversee the process. Bookkeeping and accounting are another part of orthodontists' duties—not only for billing purposes but also for keeping track of the staff members' time cards, benefits, and social security and tax deductions, and for setting salaries and raises as well.

REQUIREMENTS

High School

You should begin preparing for an orthodontics career with a course load that emphasizes, but is not restricted to, math and science subjects. Courses such as algebra, geometry, trigonometry, and calculus are important to take. Biology, chemistry, physics, and health are also necessary. Additionally, you should take computer science, English, history, and other classes recommended by your school as baseline courses for college preparation.

Postsecondary Training

Getting admitted to dental school requires that you first complete three to four years of undergraduate college

education. Because gaining acceptance into a dental school is fiercely competitive, maintaining a strong grade point average while you are in college is necessary. While a bachelor's degree is not strictly required, it is a credential that significantly increases an applicant's chances of being admitted to a dental school.

Recommended college courses are similar to those suggested in high school. A typical degree for someone entering this field is a bachelor of science in biology. Required course work generally involves taking math classes, such as algebra, geometry, trigonometry, and calculus. Science courses include biology, anatomy, physiology, anthropology, zoology, botany, and microbiology.

On the practical side, business classes such as marketing, economics, accounting, management, and finance prepare you for owning and operating a business. Liberal arts courses such as psychology, sociology, and English may also help a future orthodontist become more comfortable in communicating with people.

You must score well on the Dental Admissions Test (DAT) before being admitted into a dental program, which usually takes three to five years to complete. Doing well on the DAT helps dental schools determine whether or not you will succeed in dental school. Dental school courses are made up of advanced science classes, clinical work, and laboratory classes. During the last two years of dental school, clinical treatment is emphasized, and you give supervised treatment to patients at a university dental clinic. Graduates receive a Doctor of Dental Surgery (D.D.S.) or Doctor of Dental Medicine (D.M.D.) degree.

This degree qualifies you to work as a general dentist. To become an orthodontist, however, you will be required to continue in your schooling. Postgraduate programs, which are accredited by the American Dental Association Commission on Dental Accreditation, may last from two to three years. Gaining acceptance to a postgraduate program in orthodontics is also competitive. Therefore, it is critical that you maintain a high grade point average during dental school.

To keep abreast of advancements in orthodontics, orthodontists regularly take continuing education courses. Other educational activities include attending workshops and seminars, reading professional journals, and participating in study clubs. This helps a practicing orthodontist acquire the most up-to-date skills and knowledge of the best materials to use.

Certification or Licensing

Board certification is available through the American Board of Orthodontists (ABO). To achieve ABO diplomate status, orthodontists must file an application with the ABO, be interviewed and approved as a candidate, pass written and oral examinations, and provide written orthodontic case histories. It may take eight to 10 years to gain ABO diplomate status.

Before new dentists are allowed to practice, they must first pass a licensing examination in the state in which they are planning to practice. This test may include working on a patient. In some states, orthodontists must also pass a specialty licensing examination. In order to maintain their licenses, orthodontists, like all dentists, must take continuing education courses.

Other Requirements

Orthodontists who run their own practices should be self-motivated and have management skills. These qualities will help them run their practices efficiently and attain maximized profitability while providing the highest quality results.

Good organizational skills and efficient work habits are essential for all orthodontists because they see so many patients, each having individual treatment issues, in a single day. In fact, several patients might be seated in orthodontic chairs at the same time, waiting for treatment. The orthodontist must move swiftly yet efficiently from one to the next.

Being an effective communicator while under time pressure is critical. One moment an orthodontist may be discussing the need for good tooth brushing with an eight-year-old patient while an adult patient is waiting for a consultation on a new treatment plan and an insurance company representative is on hold about a claim misunderstanding. Because they see a large number of patients in a day, orthodontists often do not have the luxury of spending a lot of time to make their point or explain treatment options. In addition to being good communicators, orthodontists must be good listeners. They must have good people skills. Patients want to know that their orthodontist hears and cares about their concerns.

Orthodontists like to help people. After the braces come off, most patients will feel more self-assured and confident when they speak or smile, which is one of the reasons orthodontists find satisfaction in their jobs.

Being an orthodontist is physically challenging. Manual dexterity and strength are necessary assets. Fingers, hands, wrists, and arms are in controlled motion within a small space throughout the day. There is little room for error. Keen vision and perception in three dimensions are needed to locate tiny openings and

parts of only a few millimeters in size. Excellent eye-hand coordination as well as an artistic eye and the ability to judge symmetry will help when it's time to apply the braces. To prevent the back injuries that can plague orthodontists as they lean over patients all day, it's important that orthodontists take the time to stretch during the day and exercise regularly.

EXPLORING

One way to learn more about the field is to talk to an orthodontist to learn about this work. Ask your dentist, check the phonebook, or contact the American Association of Orthodontists to see if there is an orthodontist in your area who would be willing to speak with you. You can then line up an informational interview with this person. Check with nearby dental schools to see if they offer any kind of student programs about dentistry. If they do not have such a program, see if you can take a tour of the school or talk to teachers or students about the dental school. For some hands-on experience, try to get a part-time job (maybe as a receptionist or clerical assistant) at an orthodontist's office. If that is not possible, look for a part-time job at a general dentist's office. Working in such a setting will give you an idea of what to expect in the broad field of dentistry.

EMPLOYERS

The U.S. Department of Labor reports that there are about 5,410 orthodontists in the United States, and almost all of them are in private practice. Orthodontists may own their own practices or may work as associates or partners with other orthodontists. Some orthodontists work in hospitals and dental clinics.

Other opportunities for orthodontists include teaching at university dental schools, either on a full- or part-time basis. Those who teach part time usually maintain a private practice as well. Often part-time instructors are not paid or are paid only a small salary because the prestige of having a university teaching position is considered enough compensation. Also, orthodontists sometimes volunteer to teach a class to build their careers. Some orthodontists work in dental schools where there are research opportunities. Others perform research while testing new materials and procedures and writing about them for industry. Researchers may test new orthodontic materials or techniques by working on anything from model mouths to animals.

Some orthodontists are employed by government agencies, such as the U.S. Public Health Service, the

Indian Health Service, or the Department of Veterans Affairs. Orthodontists also work in the military and are stationed across the country or around the world with the air force, navy, or army.

STARTING OUT

Dentists often start out by working as associates for established dentists with their own practices. They may work as associates for several years to gain experience and build up their financial resources. Then many buy a dental business or start their own.

Orthodontists may start their careers in a similar manner. A good resource to consult is the scientific journal of the AAO, the *American Journal of Orthodontics and Dentofacial Orthopedics*, which lists practices to rent or buy as well as job opportunities. The *Journal of the American Dental Association* also features classified job ads, some of which are for orthodontists.

As is true with other professions, it is important for orthodontists to make and maintain contacts among their colleagues. One way of doing this is by attending AAO or ADA meetings. Through networking at such events, an orthodontist might hear about current job openings or meet someone who is interested in starting a practice with a partner.

ADVANCEMENT

Orthodontists in private practice can advance by increasing the size of their practices. One way to do this is to build a reputation with the general dentists in the surrounding community who will refer patients to the orthodontist. Orthodontists who can effectively communicate with a patient's general dentist and facilitate easy coordination of treatment are more likely to be trusted by the general dentist and therefore get more patient referrals.

Involvement in orthodontic associations and study clubs may lead orthodontists to active participation in organized dental events. Some orthodontists even become officers and committee chairs of their professional associations. Those in research and teaching often advance by publishing papers on techniques and developments in the field.

EARNINGS

Orthodontists' earnings are influenced by factors such as the size of the practice, the amount of experience the orthodontist has, and the size of the population in which he or she works. Despite such variables, though, ortho-

dontists can generally expect to have high earnings. The AAO says that orthodontists under age 30 often have a starting salary that's double the income of other college graduates.

According to research by Salary.com, a typical orthodontist earned a median base salary of approximately $123,287 in 2011. Half of the people in this job earned from less than $101,286 to more than $149,487. The highest paid 10 percent earned $173,342 or more per year. The U.S. Department of Labor reports that the median annual earnings for orthodontists were $166,400 in 2009, with the lowest paid 10 percent earning $102,150 or less and the highest paid 10 percent earning more than $166,400 or more annually. Orthodontists who worked in the offices of dentists in 2009 earned about $208,910 annually.

The location of an orthodontist's private practice can also play a role in determining income. Orthodontists practicing in Virginia, South Carolina, Nevada, Nebraska, and Minnesota typically have higher incomes than those in other states. Orthodontists in affluent and growing suburbs may have greater income potential than those in all but economically thriving parts of urban or rural areas. Specialists' incomes are also affected by how many other specialists in their area of expertise are working in the community. In an area with few or no other orthodontists, an orthodontic practice may have an edge and find it easier to obtain referrals.

Orthodontists who have their own practice will have to make arrangements for their own health insurance, retirement plan, vacation, time off, and sick leave. They will have to do the same for any staff members as well.

WORK ENVIRONMENT

The patient's area in an orthodontist's office, like a dentist's office, is a sterile environment containing such things as orthodontic chairs, supply cabinets, and assorted orthodontic instruments. Orthodontists also usually have a separate office where they do their paperwork and take care of other office matters. Orthodontists often work regular business hours four or five days a week. To accommodate working patients or parents, they may have night or weekend hours too. On their days off they may still go to the office to take care of the miscellaneous things involved in running a small business.

Orthodontists involved in research typically work regular business hours. They have access to labs, which are clean environments, and a variety of medical equipment. Those who teach at universities may have their own offices. When they are supervising students who are working on patients, they are in settings similar to dental offices with orthodontic chairs, supplies, and medical instruments. While university dental schools may be much larger than a private office, a sterile environment is also maintained there.

OUTLOOK

The U.S. Department of Labor predicts employment for all dentists, including specialists like orthodontists, will grow faster than the average through 2018. Since our society values physical attractiveness, the motivation to receive orthodontic treatment can be cosmetic in nature, and demand for these services should continue to be strong. But because orthodontics is largely an optional procedure, poor economic conditions can reduce the number of people who can afford to get braces. Patients without solid income are not likely to pursue or follow through with orthodontic treatment. However, to make the service more accessible, many offices provide financing, accept credit cards, or refer the patient to financing sources where instant over-the-phone approval may be obtainable.

FOR MORE INFORMATION

For information on orthodontic careers, contact

American Association of Orthodontists
401 North Lindbergh Boulevard
St. Louis, MO 63141-7816
Tel: 800-424-2841
E-mail: info@aaortho.org
http://www.braces.org

For information on board certification, contact

American Board of Orthodontists
401 North Lindbergh Boulevard, Suite 300
St. Louis, MO 63141-7839
Tel: 314-432-6130
E-mail: info@americanboardortho.com
http://www.americanboardortho.com

For information on dental careers, licensure, and educational programs, contact

American Dental Association
211 East Chicago Avenue
Chicago, IL 60611-2678
Tel: 312-440-2500
http://www.ada.org

PARALEGALS

OVERVIEW

Paralegals, also known as *legal assistants*, assist in trial preparations, investigate facts, prepare documents such as affidavits and pleadings, and, in general, do work customarily performed by lawyers. Approximately 246,810 paralegals and legal assistants work in law firms, businesses, and government agencies all over the United States; the majority work with lawyers and legislators.

THE JOB

A paralegal's main duty is to do everything a lawyer needs to do but does not have time to do. Although the lawyer assumes responsibility for the paralegal's work, the paralegal may take on all the duties of the lawyer except for setting fees, appearing in court, accepting cases, and giving legal advice.

Paralegals spend much of their time in law libraries, researching laws and previous cases and compiling facts to help lawyers prepare for trial. Paralegals often interview witnesses as part of their research as well. After analyzing the laws and facts that have been compiled for a particular client, the paralegal often writes a report that the lawyer may use to determine how to proceed with the case. If a case is brought to trial, the paralegal helps prepare legal arguments and draft pleadings to be filed in

SCHOOL SUBJECTS
Computer science, English, Government

PERSONAL SKILLS
Communication/ideas, Following instructions

MINIMUM EDUCATION LEVEL
Some postsecondary training

CERTIFICATION OR LICENSING
Voluntary

WORK ENVIRONMENT
Primarily indoors, Primarily multiple locations

court. They also organize and store files and correspondence related to cases.

Not all paralegal work centers on trials. Many paralegals work for corporations, agencies, schools, and financial institutions. *Corporate paralegals* create and maintain contracts, mortgages, affidavits, and other documents. They assist with corporate matters, such as shareholder agreements, contracts, and employee benefit plans. Another important part of a corporate paralegal's job is to stay on top of new laws and regulations to make sure the company is operating within those parameters.

Some paralegals work for the government. They may prepare complaints or talk to employers to find out why health or safety standards are not being met. They often analyze legal documents, collect evidence for hearings, and prepare explanatory material on various laws for use by the public. For example, a *court administrator paralegal* is in charge of keeping the courthouse functioning; tasks include monitoring personnel, handling the case load for the court, and general administration.

Other paralegals are involved in community or public-service work. They may help specific groups, such as poor or elderly members of the community. They may file forms, research laws, and prepare documents. They may represent clients at hearings, although they may not appear in court on behalf of a client.

Many paralegals work for large law firms, agencies, and corporations and specialize in a particular area of law. Some work for smaller firms and have a general knowledge of many areas of law. Paralegals have varied duties, and an increasing number use computers in their work.

REQUIREMENTS

High School

While in high school, take a broad range of subjects, including English, social studies or government, computer science, and languages, especially Spanish and Latin. Because legal terminology is used constantly, word origins and vocabulary should be a focus.

Postsecondary Training

Requirements for paralegals vary by employer. Some paralegals start out as legal secretaries or clerical workers and are gradually given more training and responsibility. The majority, however, choose formal training and education programs.

Formal training programs usually range from one to three years and are offered in a variety of educational settings: four-year colleges and universities, law schools, community and junior colleges, business schools, proprietary schools, and paralegal associations. Admission requirements vary, but good grades in high school and college are always an asset. There are approximately 1,000 paralegal programs, about 260 of which have been approved by the American Bar Association. The National Federation of Paralegal Associations reports that 84 percent of all paralegals receive formal paralegal education.

Some paralegal programs require a bachelor's degree for admission; others do not require any college education. In either case, those who have a college degree usually have an edge over those who do not.

Certification or Licensing

Paralegals are not required to be licensed or certified. Instead, when lawyers employ paralegals, they often follow guidelines designed to protect the public from the practice of law by unqualified persons.

Paralegals may, however, opt to be certified. To do so, they may take and pass an extensive two-day test conducted by the National Association of Legal Assistants (NALA) Certifying Board. Paralegals who pass the test may use the title certified legal assistant (CLA) after their names. According to the NALA, in 2009 there were 15,652 CLAs in the United States.

In 1994, the National Federation of Paralegal Associations established the Paralegal Advanced Competency Exam (PACE), as a means for paralegals who fill education and experience requirements to acquire professional recognition. Paralegals who pass this exam and maintain the continuing education requirement may use the designation registered paralegal (RP).

The American alliance certified paralegal (AACP) designation is offered by the American Alliance of Paralegals. For certification, applicants must have five years of experience and meet educational requirements. The certification must be renewed every two years; renewal includes completion of 18 hours of continuing education.

Other Requirements

Communication skills, both verbal and written, are vital to working as a paralegal. You must be able to turn research into reports that a lawyer or corporate executive can use. You must also be able to think logically and learn new laws and regulations quickly. Research skills, computer skills, and people skills are other necessities.

EXPLORING

There are several ways you can explore the career of a paralegal before deciding this is the job for you. Colleges, universities, and technical schools have a wealth of information available for the asking.

Look for summer or part-time employment as a secretary or in the mailroom of a law firm to get an idea of the nature of the work. If paid positions are not available, offer yourself as a volunteer to the law offices in town. Ask your guidance counselor to help you set up a volunteer/internship agreement with a lawyer.

Talk to your history or government teacher about organizing a trip to a lawyer's office and a courthouse. Ask your teacher to set aside time for you to talk to paralegals working there and to their supervising attorneys.

Searching the World Wide Web for information on student organizations that are affiliated with the legal profession is another option. You can also contact the organizations listed at the end of this article for general information.

EMPLOYERS

Paralegals and legal assistants hold approximately 246,810 jobs. The majority, about 71 percent, work for lawyers in law offices or in law firms. Other paralegals work for the government, namely for the Federal Trade Commission, Justice Department, Treasury Department, Internal Revenue Service, Department of the Interior, and many other agencies and offices. Paralegals also work in the business community. Anywhere legal matters are part of the day-to-day work, paralegals are usually handling them. Paralegals fit in well in business because many smaller corporations must deal with legal regulations but don't necessarily need an attorney or a team of lawyers. A small number of paralegals are self-employed and work as freelance legal assistants, providing services to attorneys or corporate legal departments.

Paralegals in business can be found all over the country. Larger cities employ more paralegals that focus on the legal side of the profession, and government paralegals will find the most opportunities in state capitals and Washington, D.C.

STARTING OUT

Although some law firms promote legal secretaries to paralegal status, most employers prefer to hire individuals who have completed paralegal programs. To have the best opportunity at getting a quality job in the paralegal field, you should attend a paralegal school. In addition to providing a solid background in paralegal studies, most schools help graduates find jobs, or internships that lead to jobs. Even though the job market for paralegals is expected to grow rapidly over the next 10 years, those with the best credentials will get the best jobs.

The National Federation of Paralegal Associations recommends using job banks that are sponsored by paralegal associations across the country. For paralegal associations that may be able to help, see the addresses listed at the end of this article. Many jobs for paralegals are posted on the Internet as well.

ADVANCEMENT

Although no formal advancement paths for paralegals exist, there are some possibilities for advancement, as large firms are beginning to establish career programs for paralegals.

For example, a person may be promoted from a paralegal to a head legal assistant who supervises others. In addition, a paralegal may specialize in one area of law, such as environmental, real estate, or medical malpractice. Many paralegals also advance by moving from small to large firms.

Expert paralegals that specialize in one area of law may go into business for themselves. Rather than work for one firm, these freelance paralegals often contract their services to many lawyers. Some paralegals with bachelor's degrees enroll in law school to train to become lawyers.

Paralegals can also move horizontally by taking their specialized knowledge of the law into another field, such as insurance, occupational health, or law enforcement.

EARNINGS

Salaries vary greatly for paralegals. The size and location of the firm and the education and experience of the employee are some factors that determine the annual earnings of paralegals.

The U.S. Department of Labor reports that paralegals and legal assistants had median annual earnings of $46,980 in 2009. The highest paid 10 percent earned more than $75,700, while the lowest paid 10 percent earned less than $29,000. Salary.com reports the median annual salary for paralegals was $47,269 in January 2011, with the top paid 10 percent earning

$59,600 or more, and the lowest paid 10 percent earning $35,683 or less.

According to a 2009 survey by *Legal Assistant Today*, an industry publication, paralegals working for law firms reported annual salaries of $53,937; those employed by corporations reported the highest annual average earnings, $62,336; and those working for the government earned $56,615 annually.

WORK ENVIRONMENT

Paralegals often work in pleasant and comfortable offices. Much of their work is performed in a law library. Some paralegals work out of their homes in special employment situations. When investigation is called for, paralegals may travel to gather information. Most paralegals work a 40-hour week, although long hours are sometimes required to meet court-imposed deadlines. Longer hours—sometimes as much as 90 hours per week—are usually the normal routine for paralegals starting out in law offices and firms.

Many of the paralegal's duties involve routine tasks, so they must have a great deal of patience. However, paralegals may be given increasingly difficult assignments over time. Paralegals are often unsupervised, especially as they gain experience and a reputation for quality work.

OUTLOOK

Employment for paralegals is expected to grow much faster than the average through 2018, according to the U.S. Department of Labor. One reason for the expected rapid growth in the profession is the financial benefit of employing paralegals. The paralegal, whose duties fall between those of the legal secretary and those of the attorney, helps make the delivery of legal services more cost effective to clients. The growing need for legal services among the general population and the increasing popularity of prepaid legal plans is creating a tremendous demand for paralegals in private law firms. In the private sector, paralegals can work in banks, insurance companies, real estate and title insurance firms, and corporate legal departments. In the public sector, there is a growing need for paralegals in the courts, community legal service programs, government agencies, and consumer organizations.

The growth of this occupation, to some extent, is dependent on the economy. Businesses are less likely to pursue litigation cases when profit margins are down, thus curbing the need for new hires.

FOR MORE INFORMATION

For information about certification, membership, or to read personal profiles of practicing paralegals, visit
American Alliance of Paralegals Inc.
4001 Kennett Pike, Suite 134-146
Wilmington, DE 19807-2315
E-mail: info@aapipara.org
http://www.aapipara.org/

For information regarding accredited educational facilities, contact
American Association for Paralegal Education
19 Mantua Road
Mt. Royal, NJ 08061-1006
Tel: 856-423-2829
E-mail: info@aafpe.org
http://www.aafpe.org

For general information about careers in the law field, contact
American Bar Association
321 North Clark Street
Chicago, IL 60654-7598
Tel: 800-285-2221
http://www.abanet.org

For career information, contact
Association of Legal Administrators
75 Tri-State International, Suite 222
Lincolnshire, IL 60069-4435
Tel: 847-267-1252
http://www.alanet.org

For information about educational and licensing programs, certification, and paralegal careers, contact
National Association of Legal Assistants
1516 South Boston Avenue, Suite 200
Tulsa, OK 74119-4013
Tel: 918-587-6828
E-mail: nalanet@nala.org
http://www.nala.org

For information about almost every aspect of becoming a paralegal, contact
National Federation of Paralegal Associations
PO Box 2016
Edmonds, WA 98020-9516
Tel: 425-967-0045
E-mail: info@paralegals.org
http://www.paralegals.org

For information about employment networks and school listings, contact

National Paralegal Association
PO Box 406
Solebury, PA 18963-0406
Tel: 215-297-8333
E-mail: admin@nationalparalegal.org
http://www.nationalparalegal.org

PETROLEUM ENGINEERS

SCHOOL SUBJECTS
Mathematics, Physics

PERSONAL SKILLS
Helping/teaching, Technical/scientific

MINIMUM EDUCATION LEVEL
Bachelor's degree

CERTIFICATION OR LICENSING
Required for certain positions

WORK ENVIRONMENT
Indoors and outdoors,
One location with some travel

OVERVIEW

Petroleum engineers apply the principles of geology, physics, and the engineering sciences to the recovery, development, and processing of petroleum. As soon as an exploration team has located an area that could contain oil or gas, petroleum engineers begin their work, which includes determining the best location for drilling new wells, as well as the economic feasibility of developing them. They are also involved in operating oil and gas facilities, monitoring and forecasting reservoir performance, and utilizing enhanced oil recovery techniques that extend the life of wells. There are approximately 25,540 petroleum engineers employed in the United States.

THE JOB

Petroleum engineer is a rather generalized title that encompasses several specialties, each one playing an important role in ensuring the safe and productive recovery of oil and natural gas. In general, petroleum engineers are involved in the entire process of oil recovery, from preliminary steps, such as analyzing cost factors, to the last stages, such as monitoring the production rate and then repacking the well after it has been depleted.

Petroleum engineering is closely related to the separate engineering discipline of geoscience engineering. Before petroleum engineers can begin work on an oil reservoir, prospective sites must be sought by *geological engineers*, along with *geologists* and *geophysicists*. These scientists determine whether a site has potential oil. Petroleum engineers develop plans for drilling. Drilling is usually unsuccessful, with eight out of 10 test wells being "dusters" (dry wells) and only one of the remaining two test wells having enough oil to be commercially producible. When a significant amount of oil is discovered, engineers can begin their work of maximizing oil production at the site. The development company's *engineering manager* oversees the activities of the various petroleum engineering specialties, including *reservoir engineers, drilling engineers,* and *production engineers.*

Reservoir engineers use the data gathered by the previous geoscience studies and estimate the actual amount of oil that will be extracted from the reservoir. It is the reservoir engineers who determine whether the oil will be taken by primary methods (simply pumping the oil from the field) or by enhanced methods (using additional energy such as water pressure to force the oil up). The reservoir engineer is responsible for calculating the cost of the recovery process relative to the expected value of the oil produced and simulates future performance using sophisticated computer models. Besides performing studies of existing company-owned oil fields, reservoir engineers also evaluate fields the company is thinking of buying.

Drilling engineers work with geologists and drilling contractors to design and supervise drilling operations. They are the engineers involved with the actual drilling of the well. They determine the best methods for penetrating the earth. It is the responsibility of these workers to supervise the building of the derrick (a platform, constructed over the well, that holds the hoisting devices), choose the equipment, and plan the drilling methods. Drilling engineers must have a thorough understanding of the geological sciences so that they can know, for instance, how much stress to place on the rock being drilled.

Production engineers determine the most efficient methods and equipment to optimize oil and gas production. For example, they establish the proper pumping unit configuration and perform tests to determine well fluid levels and pumping load. They plan field workovers and well stimulation techniques such as secondary and tertiary recovery (for example, injecting steam, water, or a special recovery fluid) to maximize field production.

Various research personnel are involved in this field; some are more specialized than others. They include the *research chief engineer*, who directs studies related to the design of new drilling and production methods, the *oil-well equipment research engineer*, who directs research to design improvements in oil-well machinery and devices, and the *oil-field equipment test engineer*, who conducts experiments to determine the effectiveness and safety of these improvements.

In addition to all of the above, sales personnel play an important part in the petroleum industry. *Oil-well equipment and services sales engineers* sell various types of equipment and devices used in all stages of oil recovery. They provide technical support and service to their clients, including oil companies and drilling contractors.

REQUIREMENTS

High School

In high school, you can prepare for college engineering programs by taking courses in mathematics, physics, chemistry, geology, and computer science. Economics, history, and English are also highly recommended because these subjects will improve your communication and management skills. Mechanical drawing and foreign languages are also helpful.

Postsecondary Training

A bachelor's degree in engineering is the minimum requirement. In college, you can follow either a specific petroleum engineering curriculum or a program in a closely related field, such as geophysics or mining engineering. In the United States, there are approximately 30 universities and colleges that offer programs that concentrate on petroleum engineering, many of which are located in California and Texas. The first two years working toward the bachelor of science degree

involve the study of many of the same subjects taken in high school, only at an advanced level, as well as basic engineering courses. In the junior and senior years, students take more specialized courses: geology, formation evaluation, properties of reservoir rocks and fluids, well drilling, petroleum production, and reservoir analysis.

Because the technology changes so rapidly, many petroleum engineers continue their education to receive a master's degree and then a doctorate. Petroleum engineers who have earned advanced degrees command higher salaries and often are eligible for better advancement opportunities. Those who work in research and teaching positions are usually required to have these higher credentials.

Students considering an engineering career in the petroleum industry should be aware that the industry uses all kinds of engineers. People with chemical, electrical, geoscience, mechanical, environmental, and other engineering degrees are also employed in this field.

Certification or Licensing

Many jobs, especially public projects, require that the engineer be licensed as a professional engineer. To be licensed, candidates must have a degree from an engineering program accredited by the Accreditation Board for Engineering and Technology. Additional requirements for obtaining the license vary from state to state, but all applicants must take an exam and have several years of related experience on the job or in teaching.

Other Requirements

Students thinking about this career should enjoy science and math. You need to be a creative problem-solver who likes to come up with new ways to get things done and try them out. You need to be curious, wanting to know why and how things are done. You also need to be a logical thinker with a capacity for detail, and you must be a good communicator who can work well with others.

EXPLORING

One of the most satisfying ways to explore this occupation is to participate in Junior Engineering Technical Society (JETS) programs. JETS participants enter engineering design and problem-solving contests and learn team development skills, often with an engineering mentor. Science fairs and clubs also offer fun and challenging ways to learn about engineering.

Certain students are able to attend summer programs held at colleges and universities that focus on material not traditionally offered in high school. Usually these programs include recreational activities such as basketball, swimming, and track and field. For example, Worcester Polytechnic Institute offers the Frontiers program, a two-week residential session for high school seniors. For more information, visit http://www.wpi.edu/admissions/undergraduate/visit/frontiers.html. The American Indian Science and Engineering Society (AISES) also sponsors two- to six-week mathematics and science camps that are open to American Indian students and held at various college campuses.

Talking with someone who has worked as a petroleum engineer would also be a very helpful and inexpensive way of exploring this field. One good way to find an experienced person to talk to is through Internet sites that feature career areas to explore, industry message boards, and mailing lists.

You can also explore this career by touring oil fields or corporate sites (contact the public relations department of oil companies for more information), or you can try to land a temporary or summer job in the petroleum industry on a drilling and production crew. Trade journals, high school guidance counselors, the placement office at technical or community colleges, and the associations listed at the end of this article are other helpful resources that will help you learn more about the career of petroleum engineer.

EMPLOYERS

Petroleum engineers are employed by major oil companies as well as smaller oil companies. They work in oil exploration and production. Some petroleum engineers are employed by consulting companies and equipment suppliers. The federal government is also an employer of engineers. A small number of engineers (3 percent) are self-employed. In the United States, oil or natural gas is produced in 30 states, with most sites located in Texas, Louisiana, California, and Oklahoma, plus two offshore regions, the Federal Gulf and Federal Pacific. Many other engineers work in other oil-producing areas such as the Arctic Circle, China's Tarim Basin, and the Middle East. Approximately 25,540 petroleum engineers are employed in the United States.

STARTING OUT

The most common and perhaps the most successful way to obtain a petroleum engineering job is to apply for positions through the student career services office at the college you attend. Oil companies often have recruiters who seek potential graduates while they are in their last year of engineering school.

Applicants are also advised to simply check the job sections of major newspapers and apply directly to companies seeking employees. They should also keep informed of the general national employment outlook in this industry by reading trade and association journals, such as the Society of Petroleum Engineers' *Journal of Petroleum Technology*.

Engineering internships and co-op programs where students attend classes for a portion of the year and then work in an engineering-related job for the remainder of the year allow students to graduate with valuable work experience sought by employers. Many times these students are employed full time after graduation at the place where they had their internship or co-op job.

As in most engineering professions, entry-level petroleum engineers first work under the supervision of experienced professionals for a number of years. New engineers are usually assigned to a field location where they learn different aspects of field petroleum engineering. Initial responsibilities may include well productivity, reservoir and enhanced recovery studies, production equipment and application design, efficiency analyses, and economic evaluations. Field assignments are followed by other opportunities in regional and headquarters offices.

ADVANCEMENT

After several years of working under professional supervision, engineers can begin to move up to higher levels. Workers often formulate a choice of direction during their first years on the job. In the operations division, petroleum engineers can work their way up from the field to district, division, and then operations manager. Some engineers work through various engineering positions from field engineer to staff, then division, and finally chief engineer on a project. Some engineers may advance into top executive management. In any position, however, continued enrollment in educational courses is usually required to keep abreast of technological progress and changes. After about four years of work experience, engineers usually apply for a P.E. (professional engineer) license so they can be certified to work on a larger number of projects.

Others get their master's or doctoral degree so they can advance to more prestigious research engineering, university-level teaching, or consulting positions. Also, petroleum engineers may transfer to many other occupations, such as economics, environmental management, and groundwater hydrology. Finally, some entrepreneurial-minded workers become independent operators and owners of their own oil companies.

EARNINGS

Petroleum engineers with a bachelor's degree earned average starting salaries of $83,121 in 2009, according to the National Association of Colleges and Employers. A survey by the Society of Petroleum Engineers reports that its worldwide members earned an average salary of $130,800 in 2010. According to the U.S. Department of Labor, in 2009 the median annual salary for petroleum engineers was $108,910. The lowest paid 10 percent earned $58,600 or less while the highest paid 10 percent earned $166,400 or more.

Salary rates tend to reflect the economic health of the petroleum industry as a whole. When the price of oil is high, salaries can be expected to grow; low oil prices often result in stagnant wages.

Fringe benefits for petroleum engineers are good. Most employers provide health and accident insurance, sick pay, retirement plans, profit-sharing plans, and paid vacations. Education benefits are also competitive.

WORK ENVIRONMENT

Petroleum engineers work all over the world: the high seas, remote jungles, vast deserts, plains, and mountain ranges. Petroleum engineers who are assigned to remote, foreign locations may be separated from their families for long periods of time or be required to resettle their families when new job assignments arise. Those working overseas may live in company-supplied housing.

Some petroleum engineers, such as drilling engineers, work primarily out in the field at or near drilling sites in all kinds of weather and environments. The work can be dirty and dangerous. Responsibilities such as making reports, conducting studies of data, and analyzing costs are usually tended to in offices either away from the site or in temporary work trailers.

Other engineers work in offices in cities of varying sizes, with only occasional visits to an oil field. Research engineers work in laboratories much of the time, while those who work as professors spend most of their time on campuses. Workers involved in economics, management, consulting, and government service tend to spend their work time exclusively indoors.

OUTLOOK

Employment for petroleum engineers is expected to increase faster than the average for all occupations through 2018, according to the U.S. Department of Labor. Excellent opportunities for petroleum engineers will exist because the number of degrees granted in petroleum engineering is low, leaving more job openings than there are qualified candidates. (According to the Society of Petroleum Engineers, the average age of its members is 52.) Additionally, employment opportunities will increase due to a need to develop new extraction methods for getting more from existing resources as well as acquiring new resources.

The challenge for petroleum engineers in the past decade has been to develop technology that lets drilling and production be economically feasible even in the face of low oil prices. For example, engineers had to rethink how they worked in deep water. They used to believe deep wells would collapse if too much oil was pumped out at once. But the high costs of working in deep water plus low oil prices made low volumes uneconomical. So, engineers learned how to boost oil flow by slowly increasing the quantities wells pumped by improving valves, pipes, and other equipment used. Engineers have also cut the cost of deep-water oil and gas production in the Gulf of Mexico, predicted to be one of the most significant exploration hot spots in the world for the next decade, by placing wellheads on the ocean floor instead of on above-sea production platforms.

Cost-effective technology that permits new drilling and increases production will continue to be essential in the profitability of the oil industry. Therefore, petroleum engineers will continue to have a vital role to play, even in this age of streamlined operations and company restructurings.

FOR MORE INFORMATION

For information on careers in petroleum geology, contact
American Association of Petroleum Geologists
PO Box 979
Tulsa, OK 74101-0979
Tel: 800-364-2274
http://www.aapg.org

For information on summer programs, contact
American Indian Science and Engineering Society
PO Box 9828
Albuquerque, NM 87119-9828
Tel: 505-765-1052
E-mail: info@aises.org
http://www.aises.org

For general information on the petroleum industry, contact

American Petroleum Institute
1220 L Street, NW
Washington, DC 20005-4070
Tel: 202-682-8000
http://www.api.org

For information about JETS programs, products, and engineering career brochures (all disciplines), contact

Junior Engineering Technical Society (JETS)
1420 King Street, Suite 405
Alexandria, VA 22314-2750
Tel: 703-548-5387
E-mail: info@jets.org
http://www.jets.org

For a petroleum engineering career brochure, a list of petroleum engineering schools, and scholarship information, contact

Society of Petroleum Engineers
222 Palisades Creek Drive
Richardson, TX 75080-2040
Tel: 800-456-6863
E-mail: spedal@spe.org
http://www.spe.org

For a Frontiers program brochure and application, contact

Worcester Polytechnic Institute
100 Institute Road
Worcester, MA 01609-2280
Tel: 508-831-5286
E-mail: admissions@wpi.edu
http://www.wpi.edu/admissions/undergraduate/
    visit/frontiers.html

PHARMACISTS

OVERVIEW

Pharmacists are health professionals responsible for the dispensation of prescription and nonprescription medications. They act as consultants to health practitioners and the general public concerning possible adverse drug reactions and interactions, and may also give advice relating to home medical supplies and durable health care equipment. The role of the pharmacist has evolved into that of consultant and medicinal expert, because of the expanded duties of pharmacy technicians and the increasing time restrictions placed on health maintenance organization physicians. There are more than 267,860 pharmacists practicing in the United States.

THE JOB

Pharmacists need a thorough knowledge of drug products. Most importantly, they need to understand how drugs work for people who are sick, how the drugs interact with a person's body as well as illness, and how different drugs may interact with each other. In addition to dispensing drugs according to orders from physicians, dentists, and other health care practitioners, pharmacists advise these professionals on the appropriate selection and use of medications. They monitor how long patients have been taking a medication and provide information to patients and doctors when a generic brand of a drug is available. Pharmacist Shreen Beshures, who has been involved in the pharmacy business since high school, explains that part of her work includes "print[ing] recommendations to the doctors for a reduction in the number of medications [or] a more cost-effective medication." In addition to advising doctors and other health professionals, pharmacists talk with patients or customers about medications, explaining what the medications are supposed to do and how to use them properly. Pharmacists working in retail locations, such as a neighborhood drugstore, may also find that customers come to them with questions about symptoms. They may recommend nonprescrip-

SCHOOL SUBJECTS
Chemistry, Mathematics

PERSONAL SKILLS
Following instructions, Technical/scientific

MINIMUM EDUCATION LEVEL
Doctorate

CERTIFICATION OR LICENSING
Recommended (certification),
Required by all states (licensing)

WORK ENVIRONMENT
Primarily indoors, Primarily one location

tion products such as headache remedies, vitamins, and cough syrups. All pharmacists keep records of drugs and medications dispensed to each person in order to identify duplicate drugs or combinations of drugs that can cause adverse reactions or side effects.

In conjunction with these duties, pharmacists are required to maintain their licenses through continuing education, though education requirements vary by location. Some states may require this education in the form of correspondence (written responses to educational material), or conferences and seminars. Some states may also require continuing education in particular disease topics and treatment.

Pharmacists' duties vary somewhat depending on where they are employed. About 65 percent of pharmacists work for community retail pharmacies, such as a local drugstore pharmacy, a chain drugstore pharmacy, or a grocery store pharmacy. These pharmacists fill prescription orders, contact doctors and other health care professionals by phone when clarification about a prescription is needed, and have frequent interaction with the public. In addition to pharmaceutical duties, they sell merchandise unrelated to health, hire and supervise other workers, and oversee the general operation of the pharmacy.

About 22 percent of pharmacists work at hospitals or clinics. They prepare sterile solutions or special mixtures, dispense medications on-site, and complete administrative duties. They work closely with the medical staff, suggesting what medications to use, explaining their effects, and sometimes demonstrating how to give medications. They also keep precise records of what type and amount of medications each patient is on, keep track of supplies in the pharmacy, and buy new supplies as necessary. They may also interact with patients, meeting with them before their discharge to discuss what medications they will use at home. At a large hospital or clinic employing a number of pharmacists, a supervising pharmacist may also be responsible for arranging schedules and overseeing the work of others.

Some pharmacists are employed by large pharmaceutical manufacturers. They may work in one of several capacities. Some engage in research to help develop new drugs or to improve or find new uses for old ones. Others supervise the preparation of ingredients that go into the tablets, capsules, ointments, solutions, or other dosage forms produced by the manufacturer. Others test or standardize the raw or refined chemicals that eventually will go into the finished drug. Some may assist with advertising the company's products, to make sure that nothing untruthful or misleading is said about

a product in professional literature. Some pharmacists may prepare literature on new products for pharmaceutical or technical journals. Others write material for package inserts.

Pharmacists employed by government agencies may work in a number of different kinds of positions. They may be inspectors who monitor drug manufacturing firms, hospitals, wholesalers, or community pharmacies. They may work in research with agencies such as the FDA, testing the effectiveness of new drugs, or they may work with agencies involved with narcotics and other controlled substances.

Other opportunities for pharmacists include teaching at schools of pharmacy, working in the armed forces, and working for health maintenance organizations (HMOs) or insurance companies. Some pharmacists write or edit reports for journals, draft technical papers, and staff professional associations. An increasing number of pharmacists—senior care pharmacists— are employed by nursing homes and other long-term care facilities to provide and monitor drug therapy for the elderly. Some pharmacists complete additional education to become patent attorneys or experts in pharmaceutical law.

All pharmacists must be diligent in maintaining clean and ordered work areas. They must be exceedingly precise in their calculations and possess a high degree of concentration in order to reduce the risk of error as they compound and assemble prescriptions. Additionally, pharmacists must be proficient with a variety of technical devices and computer systems. However, more and more drug products are shipped in finished form by the pharmaceutical manufacturer. The actual compounding of prescription medications, therefore, is taking a smaller amount of time.

REQUIREMENTS

High School

If you are thinking of becoming a pharmacist, you should take college preparatory courses in high school and concentrate in the areas of mathematics and science. It is especially important that you take biology, chemistry, and physics to prepare for this work. Additionally, you should take English, speech, and a foreign language, because good communication skills will be important as you progress through college, job interviews, and eventual employment as a pharmacist. If working as a community pharmacist sounds interesting to you, consider taking business and accounting courses to prepare yourself for working in and running a drugstore.

Postsecondary Training

To become a pharmacist, you will need to earn the degree Doctor of Pharmacy (Pharm.D.) from a school accredited by the Accreditation Council on Pharmaceutical Education. The Pharm.D. has replaced the Bachelor of Pharmacy degree (B.Pharm.), which is no longer awarded. The doctorate degree generally takes six years to complete. The first year or two of study does not take place in a school of pharmacy but rather in a general college setting. You will take pre-pharmacy classes such as chemistry, organic chemistry, biology, physics, calculus, statistics, English, and social sciences. After you have completed this work you will need to gain admission to a school of pharmacy. You may apply to a school of pharmacy that is part of the university where you completed your pre-pharmacy work, or you may apply to a school of pharmacy that is not part of your undergraduate school. In addition to completing pre-pharmacy courses, some schools of pharmacy require applicants to take the Pharmacy College Admissions Test (P-CAT).

In pharmacy school, you will take courses such as the principles of pharmacology, biochemistry, pharmacy law and ethics, and pharmaceutical care. In addition, your education should include an internship, sometimes known as a clerkship, in which you work under the supervision of a professional pharmacist. When deciding on a school to attend, you should consult the Accreditation Council for Pharmacy Education's annual Directory of Accredited Professional Programs of Colleges and Schools of Pharmacy for accredited programs. It is available on the council's Web site http://www.acpe-accredit. org/deans/schools.asp.

Certification or Licensing

Pharmacists who specialize in a specific health care discipline can obtain voluntary certification. Currently the Board of Pharmaceutical Specialties recognizes and offers certification in five areas: nuclear pharmacy (involving the use of radioactive drugs), nutrition support pharmacy (involving care of patients with special needs in receiving nutrition), oncology pharmacy (involving care of patients with cancer), pharmacotherapy (involving the safe, economic, and proper use of drug therapies), and psychiatric pharmacy (involving the care of those with psychiatric-related illnesses). Pharmacists who specialize in geriatric health care may receive the certified geriatric pharmacist designation from the Commission for Certification in Geriatric Pharmacy (http://www.ccgp.org).

Practicing pharmacists are required to be licensed in all 50 states, the District of Columbia, and all U.S. territories. Applicants for licensure must have graduated from an accredited pharmacy program, completed an internship under a licensed pharmacist, and passed their state's board examination.

Other Requirements

You will need good people skills to deal with patients, other pharmacy workers, and other health care professionals. A good bedside manner (a kind, comforting approach), like that required of doctors, will help you in a hospital or nursing home setting, particularly as pharmacists' responsibilities expand to include counseling and advising. You should also be very organized, and have an eye for detail—doctors, nurses, and patients will all be relying on you to keep accurate drug records.

EXPLORING

To explore this job, talk to a local pharmacist about his or her work. Volunteer at a hospital or clinic in your area to get hands-on experience working in a medical environment. You can also try to get a paid part-time or summer job at a nutrition and vitamin store where you'll have the opportunity to learn about dietary supplements, vitamins, and herbal remedies.

While in high school, Shreen Beshures got a part-time job as a pharmacy technician in a neighborhood drugstore. She advises those considering this career to "get a part-time job in a drugstore or . . . at a pharmacy in a hospital to see if it's really what you want to do." Of course, if you get a job at a pharmacy, do not expect to be in the back mixing medications with a mortar and pestle. Nevertheless, you can benefit by working in a position such as stock clerk, salesclerk, or delivery person. Any one of these jobs will give you the chance to observe firsthand the kind of work that pharmacists do, see how they interact with customers, and gain experience working with customers yourself. After you have demonstrated responsibility and interest, you may even have the opportunity to assist in the pharmacy—entering data in customer computer records, taking inventory on equipment, bottles, and vials, and preparing labels.

Depending on where you live, it may also be possible for you to get an internship through the National Association of Chain Drug Stores Foundation's chain community pharmacy internship program. For more information, visit http://www.nacdsfoundation.org.

EMPLOYERS

Approximately 65 percent of pharmacists work in community pharmacies—the National Association of Chain Drug Stores reports that there are approximately 39,000 pharmacies operated by chain drugstores, supermarkets, and mass merchants, and there are another 17,000 independent pharmacies. Approximately 22 percent of pharmacists work in hospitals. Pharmacists can also find work at mail order pharmacies, pharmaceutical companies, and agencies of the federal government. Some pharmacists are self-employed and fill-in as "temps" at a number of different community pharmacies. There are approximately 267,860 pharmacists working in the United States.

STARTING OUT

"I had always wanted to go to medical school," Shreen Beshures says, "but wasn't sure. I took pre-med classes in college, which were also pre-pharmacy, and decided to transfer to a pharmacy school in New York." Once you are ready to graduate from pharmacy school, the career placement office of your college or university should be one source of information about job openings. Internships also provide the opportunity to make professional contacts, and you may hear about an open position through these contacts. A number of placement services involved in the health care field work with pharmacists, placing them in the jobs they want. Newspaper advertisements and associations, such as the American Society of Health-System Pharmacists, can also provide information on job openings. Once you have become licensed, you may apply directly to a community, hospital, or clinic pharmacy that interests you. Though the level of work is the same for beginning pharmacists as it is for experienced pharmacists, you may have to work long hours, evenings, and weekends until you've gained some seniority with the pharmacy.

ADVANCEMENT

Community pharmacists may enjoy advancement to supervisory positions. The hospital pharmacist may advance to the position of chief pharmacist or director of pharmacy services after accumulating several years of experience.

Pharmacists who are employed by drug manufacturing firms may anticipate increases in both salary and responsibility as they gain experience and increase their value to their firms.

Pharmacists who acquire advanced degrees and education may become pharmacologists, who study the effects of drugs on the body.

EARNINGS

The earnings of salaried pharmacists are largely determined by the location, size, and type of employer as well as by the duties and responsibilities of the individual pharmacist. Pharmacists who own or manage pharmacies often earn considerably more than other pharmacists. According to the U.S. Department of Labor (DOL), pharmacists earned a median yearly income of $109,180 in 2009. The lowest paid 10 percent earned less than $79,270 per year, while the highest paid 10 percent made more than $134,290 during that same time. The DOL also reports that pharmacists earned the following mean salaries in 2009 by type of employer: health and personal care stores, $107,810; general medical and surgical hospitals, $106,210; grocery stores, $105,640; department stores, $105,120; and other general merchandise stores, $109,420.

Pharmacists, in addition to salary, enjoy fringe benefits such as paid vacation, medical and dental insurance, overtime, and sometimes bonuses and profit sharing, depending on the size and type of employer. Because of the high demand for pharmacists who will work odd hours in community drugstores, temp pharmacists can often negotiate for benefits, as well.

WORK ENVIRONMENT

A pharmacy is usually a pleasant place to work. Pharmacies should be well lighted, well ventilated, and kept in a clean and orderly fashion. Many chain-owned pharmacies now provide 18- or 24-hour operations.

Hospital pharmacies are efficient, orderly, and busy with a variety of important activities. The physicians, nurses, technicians, and other medical personnel with whom the pharmacist works are usually intelligent and concerned people. These pharmacies are also usually in operation 18 or 24 hours a day.

The two most unfavorable conditions of the pharmacist's practice are long hours and the necessity to stay on one's feet. It is not unusual to be on duty at least 48 hours a week. Most state laws covering the practice of pharmacy require that there be a pharmacist on duty at all times when the pharmacy is open. Most pharmacies employ at least two pharmacists because it is customary to remain open at least 12 hours a day. Many pharmacies are also open at least part of the time on Sundays. Despite the requirements of the job, most pharmacists appreciate being involved in health care. "I'm an integral part of the health care system," Shreen Beshures says, "preventing medication errors and aiding nurses and physicians with medications."

Pharmacists who operate their own pharmacies have financial responsibilities. Many pharmacies do better than one to two million dollars in gross sales each year in business. They must hire employees, maintain an adequate inventory, and keep records. They must make rent or mortgage payments and pay insurance premiums and taxes. The growing influence of third-party prescription programs has forced pharmacists to spend considerable amounts of time processing claims, maintaining government records, and explaining benefit plans to customers. Many community pharmacy owners complain of restrictions placed on them by government agencies, insurance companies, and HMOs that they claim hinders their ability to compete with chain competitors.

OUTLOOK

The U.S. Department of Labor (DOL) predicts employment growth for pharmacists to be faster than the average through 2018. Reasons for this increase include the growing middle-aged and senior population (generally the largest consumers of medications), technical and scientific advances that will make more drugs available and affordable, and even the advertising of medications that informs consumers of the variety of medicines available, resulting in their asking for these drugs.

Employment at hospital pharmacies should increase about as fast as the average because many hospitals are forced to reduce patient stay times. However, opportunities will open up in nursing homes, assisted-living facilities, and home care settings. Managed care organizations should also provide opportunities for pharmacists. These organizations use the pharmacist's skills to monitor trends in and costs of medication therapies.

The role of the pharmacist is expected to expand. Pharmacists will be more involved in counseling their patients and in advising physicians on the drugs to prescribe. Pharmacists will make house calls and see patients in doctor's offices. They will also be studying more complex medications and sorting out drug information on the Internet.

The DOL predicts that pharmacists will have good opportunities in managed care settings as they will be increasingly relied on to study trends and patterns in the use of medications and analyze the benefits and costs of various drug treatments. Drug companies will also need pharmacists to work in research and development and sales and marketing.

FOR MORE INFORMATION

For more information about pharmacy education, contact
Accreditation Council for Pharmaceutical Education
20 North Clark Street, Suite 2500
Chicago, IL 60602-5109
Tel: 312-664-3575
http://www.acpe-accredit.org

For information on educational programs, contact
American Association of Colleges of Pharmacy
1727 King Street
Alexandria, VA 22314-2700
Tel: 703-739-2330
E-mail: mail@aacp.org
http://www.aacp.org

For information about student membership and publications, and for news about the industry, visit the APhA Web site, or contact
American Pharmacists Association (APhA)
2215 Constitution Avenue, NW
Washington, DC 20037-2985
Tel: 202-628-4410
http://www.pharmacist.com

For information on different areas of pharmacy practice and career opportunities, contact
American Society of Health-System Pharmacists
7272 Wisconsin Avenue
Bethesda, MD 20814-4836
Tel: 866-279-0681
http://www.ashp.org

For more information about pharmacy specialties, visit the BPS Web site.
Board of Pharmaceutical Specialties (BPS)
2215 Constitution Avenue, NW
Washington, DC 20037-2985
Tel: 202-429-7591
http://www.bpsweb.org

For information on state boards of pharmacy, contact
National Association of Boards of Pharmacy
1600 Feehanville Drive

Mount Prospect, IL 60056-6014
Tel: 847-391-4406
http://www.nabp.net

For information on pharmacy careers and industry facts, contact
National Association of Chain Drug Stores
413 North Lee Street
Alexandria, VA 22313-2301
Tel: 703-549-3001
http://www.nacds.org

For information about careers in independent pharmacy, internships, scholarships, and to read America's Pharmacist *magazine, contact*
National Community Pharmacists Association
100 Daingerfield Road
Alexandria, VA 22314-6302
Tel: 703-683-8200
E-mail: info@ncpanet.org
http://www.ncpanet.org

PHARMACY TECHNICIANS

SCHOOL SUBJECTS
Biology, Chemistry

PERSONAL SKILLS
Following instructions, Technical/scientific

MINIMUM EDUCATION LEVEL
Some postsecondary training

CERTIFICATION OR LICENSING
Voluntary

WORK ENVIRONMENT
Primarily indoors, Primarily one location

OVERVIEW

Pharmacy technicians provide technical assistance for pharmacists and work under their direct supervision. They usually work in chain or independent drug stores, hospitals, community ambulatory care centers, home health care agencies, nursing homes, and the pharmaceutical industry. They perform a wide range of technical support functions and tasks related to the pharmacy profession. They maintain patient records; count, package, and label medication doses; prepare and distribute sterile products; and fill and dispense routine orders for stock supplies such as over-the-counter products. There are approximately 331,890 pharmacy technicians employed in the United States.

THE JOB

The roles of the pharmacist and pharmacy technician expanded greatly in the 1990s. The pharmacist's primary responsibility is to ensure that medications are used safely and effectively through clinical patient counseling and monitoring. In order to provide the highest quality of pharmaceutical care, pharmacists now focus on providing clinical services. As a result, pharmacy technicians' duties have evolved into a more specialized role known as pharmacy technology. Pharmacy technicians perform more of the manipulative functions associated with dispensing prescriptions. Their primary duties are drug-product preparation and distribution, but they are also concerned with the control of drug products. Technicians assemble, prepare, and deliver requested medication. Technicians are responsible for record keeping, and they record drug-related information on specified forms, frequently doing this part of the work on computers. Depending on a technician's experience, he or she may order pharmaceuticals and take inventory of controlled substances, such as Valium and Ritalin.

Technicians who work in hospitals have the most varied responsibilities of all pharmacy technicians. In a hospital, technicians fill total parenteral nutrition preparations and standard and chemotherapy IVs (intravenous solutions) for patients under doctors' orders. Other duties that a hospital pharmacy technician may be required to do include filling "stat," or immediate, orders and delivering them; preparing special emergency carts stocked with medications; and monitoring defibrillators and resuscitation equipment. In an emergency, pharmacy technicians respond with doctors and nurses, rushing the cart and other equipment to the emergency site. They also keep legal records of the events that occur during an emergency. Technicians work in the hospital's outpatient pharmacy, which is similar to a commercial drugstore, and assist the pharmacist in dispensing medication.

As their roles increase, trained technicians have become more specialized. Some specialized types of pharmacy technicians include *narcotics control pharmacy technicians, operating room pharmacy technicians, emergency room pharmacy technicians, nuclear pharmacy technicians,* and *home health care pharmacy technicians.* Specially trained pharmacy technicians are also employed as *data entry technicians, lead technicians, supervisors,* and *technician managers.*

REQUIREMENTS

High School

You should take courses in mathematics and science (especially chemistry and biology), because you will be dealing with patient records and drug dosages. Health classes can help you get a basic understanding of the health care industry and various medical treatments. Take English and speech classes to help you develop your writing and communication skills. You will be using a computer a lot to maintain records and prepare labels, so take courses in computer fundamentals.

Postsecondary Training

In the past, pharmacy technicians received most of their training on the job in hospital and community pharmacy-training programs. Since technician functions and duties have changed greatly in recent years, most pharmacy technicians today receive their education through formal training programs offered through community colleges, vocational/technical schools, hospital community pharmacies, and government programs throughout the United States. Program length usually ranges from six months to two years, and leads to a certificate, diploma, or associate's degree in pharmacy technology. A high school diploma is usually required for entry into a training program. The American Society of Health-System Pharmacists (ASHP) is the national accrediting organization for pharmacy technician training programs. ASHP can provide you with information on approved programs across the country (see contact information at end of this article).

In a pharmacy technician training program, you will receive classroom instruction and participate in supervised clinical apprenticeships in health institutions and community pharmacies. Courses include introduction to pharmacy and health care systems, pharmacy laws and ethics, medical terminology, chemistry, and microbiology. Most pharmacy technicians continue their education even after their formal training ends by reading professional journals and attending training or informational seminars, lectures, review sessions, and audiovisual presentations.

Certification or Licensing

Most states require pharmacy technicians to be registered with the state board of pharmacy. Eligibility requirements will vary by state, but most require applicants to have a high school diploma or equivalent and to pay an application fee.

At least three states license pharmacy technicians and all 50 states have adopted the National Pharmacy Technician Certification Examination, a written, standardized test for voluntary certification of technicians. Those who pass the test can use the certified pharmacy technician designation. Some states, including Texas and Louisiana, require certification of pharmacy technicians. To receive certification from the Pharmacy Technician Certification Board, you will be tested on such subjects as the top 200 drugs in use by the medical profession. After receiving certification, you will be required to complete 20 hours of continuing education every two years as part of the qualifications for recertification. Even though it is not required in every state, certification is recommended to enhance your credentials, demonstrate to employers your commitment to the profession, and possibly qualify you for higher pay.

Other Requirements

You must be precision-minded, honest, and mature as you are depended on for accuracy and high levels of quality control, especially in hospitals. You need good communication skills in order to successfully interact with pharmacists, supervisors, and other technicians. You must be able to follow written and oral instructions precisely because a wide variety of people, including physicians, nurses, pharmacists, and patients, rely on your actions. You also need some computer aptitude in order to effectively record pharmaceutical data.

EXPLORING

Ask your school's guidance or career counselor to help you arrange for a pharmacy technician to talk to a group of students interested in this career. Your counselor may also be able to help you arrange for an information interview with a pharmacy technician. During such an interview you will meet one-on-one with the technician and ask him or her about the work. Volunteer work at a local hospital or nursing home will provide you with an excellent opportunity to be in an environment similar to the one in which many professional technicians work. As a volunteer, you can hone your communication skills and learn about medical settings by interacting with both patients and medical staff. You may even have the opportunity to meet and talk with pharmacy technicians. Finally, look for a part-time or summer job at a local retail pharmacy. Although your duties may be limited to stocking the shelves, working the cash register, or making deliveries, you will still gain valuable experience by working in this environment and interacting with trained pharmacists and technicians. By doing this, you may even be able to find a mentor who is willing to give you advice about education and the pharmacy technician career.

EMPLOYERS

Approximately 331,890 pharmacy technicians are employed in the United States. Most opportunities for pharmacy technicians are in retail. According to the National Association of Chain Drug Stores, there are approximately 39,000 pharmacies operated by traditional chain pharmacy companies and supermarkets, as well as nearly 17,000 independent pharmacies. Technicians also work in hospitals and long-term care facilities as well as in clinics at military bases, prisons, and colleges. Technicians are also finding work with home health care agencies, mail-order and Internet pharmacies, and with the federal government.

STARTING OUT

In some cases you may be able to pursue education and certification while employed as a pharmacy technician. Some chain drugstores pay the certification fees for their techs and also reward certified techs with higher hourly pay. This practice will probably increase—industry experts predict a need for pharmacists and technicians as more chain drugstores open across the country, and more pharmacies offer 24-hour service.

Pharmacy technicians often are hired by the hospital or agency where they interned. If you don't find employment this way, you can use employment agencies or newspaper ads to help locate job openings.

ADVANCEMENT

Depending on where they are employed, technicians may direct or instruct newer pharmacy technicians, make

schedules, or move to purchasing or computer work. Some hospitals have a variety of tech designations, based on experience and responsibility, with a corresponding increase in pay. Some pharmacy techs return to school to pursue a degree in pharmacy.

EARNINGS

According to the U.S. Department of Labor, pharmacy technicians had median annual earnings of $28,070 in 2009. The lowest paid 10 percent of technicians earned less than $19,480, while the highest paid 10 percent made $40,160 or more. Pharmacy technicians earned the following median salaries in 2009 by type of employer: general medical and surgical hospitals, $32,710; grocery stores, $28,610; health and personal care stores, $27,590; other general merchandise stores, $26,310; and department stores, $25,660. Pharmacy technicians working for the federal government and scientific research and development services reported the highest annual mean earnings: $39,040 and $38,870, respectively.

Benefits that technicians receive depend on their employers but generally include medical and dental insurance, retirement savings plans, and paid sick, personal, and vacation days.

WORK ENVIRONMENT

Pharmacy technicians work in clean, well-lit, pleasant, and professional surroundings. They may wear scrubs or other uniforms in hospitals, especially in the IV room. In a retail drugstore, a technician may be allowed to wear casual clothing along with a smock. Most pharmacy settings are extremely busy, especially hospital and retail. The job of pharmacy technician, like any other occupation that demands skill, speed, and accuracy, can be stressful. Because most hospitals, nursing homes, health care centers, and retail pharmacies are open between 16 and 24 hours a day, multiple shifts, weekend, and holiday hours are usually required.

OUTLOOK

The U.S. Department of Labor projects much faster than average employment growth for pharmacy technicians through 2018. As the role of the pharmacist shifts to consultation, more technicians will be needed to assemble and dispense medications. Furthermore, new employment avenues and responsibilities will mirror that of the expanding and evolving role of the pharmacist. A strong demand is emerging for technicians with specialized training to work in specific areas, such as emergency room and nuclear pharmacy. An increasing number of pharmacy technicians will be needed as the number of elderly Americans (who, on average, require more prescription medication than younger generations) continues to rise.

Those who want to work as pharmacy technicians should be aware that, in the future, they may need more education to gain certification because of the growing number of complex medications and new drug therapies on the market. Mechanical advances in the pharmaceutical field, such as robot-picking devices and automatic counting equipment, may eradicate some of the duties pharmacy technicians previously performed, yet there will remain a need for skilled technicians to clean and maintain such devices. Traditionally, pharmacists have been required to check the work of technicians; however, in some states, hospitals are allowing techs to check the work of other techs.

FOR MORE INFORMATION

Contact AAPT for more information on membership and continuing education.

American Association of Pharmacy Technicians (AAPT)
PO Box 1447
Greensboro, NC 27402-1447
Tel: 877-368-4771
E-mail: aapt@pharmacytechnician.com
http://www.pharmacytechnician.com

For more information on accredited pharmacy technician training programs, contact

American Society of Health-System Pharmacists (ASHP)
7272 Wisconsin Avenue
Bethesda, MD 20814-4836
Tel: 866-279-0681
http://www.ashp.org

For industry information and employment opportunities in retail, contact

National Association of Chain Drug Stores
413 North Lee Street
Alexandria, VA 22313-2301
Tel: 703-549-3001
http://www.nacds.org

To learn more about certification and training, contact

Pharmacy Technician Certification Board
2215 Constitution Avenue, NW

Washington, DC 20037-2985
Tel: 800-363-8012
http://www.ptcb.org

Pharmacy Week is a newsletter for professionals and pharmacy students. Check out the Web site for articles, industry news, job listings, and continuing education information.

Pharmacy Week
http://www.pharmacyweek.com

PHYSICAL THERAPISTS

OVERVIEW

Physical therapists, formerly called physiotherapists, are health care specialists who restore mobility, alleviate pain and suffering, and work to prevent permanent disability for their patients. They test and measure the functions of the musculoskeletal, neurological, pulmonary, and cardiovascular systems and treat problems in these systems caused by illness, injury, or birth defect. Physical therapists provide preventive, restorative, and rehabilitative treatment for their patients. Approximately 174,490 physical therapists are licensed to practice in the United States.

THE JOB

To initiate a program of physical therapy, the physical therapist consults the individual's medical history, examines the patient and identifies problems, confers with the physician or other health care professionals involved in the patient's care, establishes objectives and treatment goals that are consistent with the patient's needs, and determines the methods for accomplishing the objectives.

Treatment goals established by the physical therapist include preventing disability, relieving pain, and restoring function. In the presence of illness or injury, the ultimate goal is to assist the patient's physical recovery and reentry into the community, home, and work environment at the highest level of independence and self-sufficiency possible.

To aid and maintain recovery, the physical therapist also provides education to involve patients in their own care. The educational program may include exercises,

SCHOOL SUBJECTS
Biology, Chemistry

PERSONAL SKILLS
Helping/teaching, Mechanical/manipulative

MINIMUM EDUCATION LEVEL
Master's degree

CERTIFICATION OR LICENSING
Required by all states

WORK ENVIRONMENT
Primarily indoors, Primarily one location

posture reeducation, and relaxation practices. In many cases, the patient's family is involved in the educational program to provide emotional support or physical assistance as needed. These activities evolve into a continuum of self-care when the patient is discharged from the physical therapy program.

Physical therapists provide care for many types of patients of all ages. This includes working with burn victims to prevent abnormal scarring and loss of movement, with stroke victims to regain movement and independent living, with cancer patients to relieve discomfort, and with cardiac patients to improve endurance and achieve independence. Physical therapists also provide preventive exercise programs, postural improvement, and physical conditioning to individuals who perceive the need to promote their own health and well-being.

Physical therapists should have a creative approach to their work. No two patients respond the same way to exactly the same kind of treatment. The challenge is to find the right way to encourage the patient to make progress, to respond to treatment, to feel a sense of achievement, and to refuse to become discouraged if progress is slow.

Many physical therapists acquire specialized knowledge through clinical experience and educational preparation in specialty areas of practice, such as cardiopulmonary physical therapy, clinical electrophysiologic physical therapy, neurologic physical therapy, orthopedic physical therapy, pediatric physical therapy, geriatric physical therapy, and sports physical therapy.

REQUIREMENTS

High School

While you are in high school, you can begin to prepare for this career by taking college preparatory classes. These should include biology, chemistry, physics, health, and mathematics. Because so much of this work involves direct contact with clients, you should improve your people skills as well as your communication skills by taking psychology, sociology, and English classes. Also, take computer science courses so that you are computer literate. Statistics, history, and a foreign language are also beneficial.

Postsecondary Training

Physical therapists attain their professional skills through extensive education that takes place both in the classroom and in clinical settings. You should attend a school accredited by the Commission on Accreditation in Physical Therapy Education (CAPTE) to receive the most thorough education. There were 212 physical therapist education programs in 2009, and only 12 awarded master's degrees and 200 awarded doctoral degrees, according to the U.S. Department of Labor. CAPTE now only accredits schools offering postbaccalaureate degrees (master's and doctorate degrees), and you will need one of these degrees to practice physical therapy. Previously, CAPTE had accredited bachelor's degree programs; however, this change was made to give students an appropriate amount of time to study liberal arts as well as a physical therapy curriculum. Course work should include classes in the humanities as well as those geared for the profession, such as anatomy, human growth and development, and therapeutic procedures. Clinical experience is done as supervised fieldwork in such settings as hospitals, home care agencies, and nursing homes. Visit the APTA Web site (http://www.apta.org) for a listing of accredited programs.

Certification or Licensing

Specialist certification of physical therapists, while not a requirement for employment, is a desirable advanced credential. The American Board of Physical Therapy Specialties, an appointed group of the American Physical Therapy Association, certifies physical therapists who demonstrate specialized knowledge and advanced clinical proficiency in a specialty area of physical therapy practice and who pass a certifying examination.

The eight areas of specialization are cardiovascular and pulmonary, clinical electrophysiologic, geriatrics, neurology, orthopedics, pediatrics, sports, and women's health.

Upon graduating from an accredited physical therapy educational program, all physical therapists must successfully complete a national examination. Other licensing requirements vary by state. You will need to check with the licensing board of the state in which you hope to work for specific information.

Other Requirements

Successful physical therapists enjoy working with people and helping others to feel better, both physically and emotionally. They need creativity and patience to determine a treatment plan for each client and to help them achieve treatment goals. Physical therapists must also be committed to lifelong learning because new developments in technology and medicine mean that therapists must continually update their knowledge. It is also a plus to have a positive attitude and an outgoing personality.

EXPLORING

Your first step in exploring this field could be to talk with a physical therapist in your community about the work. Your school guidance counselor should be able to help you arrange for such an informational interview. Hands-on experience is important to get because schools that you apply to will take this into consideration. This experience will also help you decide how well you like working with people who are sometimes in pain or confused. One possibility is to volunteer at a physical therapy program. If such an opening is not available, try volunteering at a local hospital, nursing home, or other care facility to gain experience working in these settings. You can also look for volunteer opportunities or summer jobs at camps for the disabled. Paid part-time positions may also be available as a hospital orderly or aide to a physical therapist.

EMPLOYERS

Hospitals and offices of other health practitioners, such as physicians, employ about 60 percent of physical therapists. According to the U.S. Department of Labor, the rest work in settings such as private physical therapy offices, community health centers, sports facilities, nursing care facilities, outpatient care centers, and schools. Physical therapists may be involved in research or teach at colleges and universities. Veterans Administration hospi-

tals and other government agencies also hire physical therapists. Some physical therapists are self-employed. Approximately 174,490 physical therapists are employed in the United States.

STARTING OUT

Physical therapy graduates may obtain jobs through their college career services offices or by answering ads found on Internet employment sites or in any of a variety of professional journals. They can apply in person or send letters and resumes to hospitals, medical centers, rehabilitation facilities, and other places that hire physical therapists. Some find jobs through the APTA.

ADVANCEMENT

In a hospital or other health care facility, one may rise from being a staff physical therapist to being the chief physical therapist and then director of the department. Administrative responsibilities are usually given to those physical therapists who have had several years of experience plus the personal qualities that prepare them for undertaking this kind of assignment.

After serving in a hospital or other institution for several years, some physical therapists open up their own practices or go into a group practice, with both often paying higher salaries.

EARNINGS

Salaries for physical therapists depend on experience and type of employer. Physical therapists earned an annual average salary of $74,480 in 2009, according to the U.S. Department of Labor. The lowest paid 10 percent earned less than $52,170. Fifty percent averaged between $62,270 and $87,940; the top paid 10 percent earned $105,900 or more a year. In 2009, the top paying industries for physical therapists were:; management, scientific, and technical consulting services, $88,260; home health care services, $83,500; individual and family services, $80,390; office administrative services, $79,170; and nursing care facilities, $78,990.

WORK ENVIRONMENT

The typical physical therapist works approximately 40 hours each week, including Saturdays. About 27 percent worked part time. Patient sessions may be brief or may last an hour or more. Usually, treatment is on an individual basis, but occasionally therapy may be given in groups when the patients' problems are similar. Physical therapists work in hospitals, outpatient clinics, and private offices, all of which have specially equipped facilities. In general, their work environment is clean, well ventilated, and well lighted. They may work in large spaces or at patients' bedsides. The job can be physically demanding at times, as therapists spend much of their day working directly with patients. They often have to stoop, kneel, crouch, lift, and stand for long periods. Physical therapists also move heavy equipment and lift patients or help them stand, turn, or walk.

OUTLOOK

Employment for physical therapists is expected to grow much faster than the average through 2018, according to the U.S. Department of Labor. One reason for this strong growth is the fact that the median age of the American population is rising, and this older demographic group develops a higher number of medical conditions that cause physical pain and disability. Also, advances in medical technology save more people, who then require physical therapy. For example, as more trauma victims and newborns with birth defects survive, the need for physical therapists will rise. Another reason is the public's growing interest in physical fitness, which has resulted in an increasing number of athletic injuries requiring physical therapy. In industry and fitness centers, a growing interest in pain and injury prevention also has created new opportunities for physical therapists.

Employment prospects for physical therapists should continue to be excellent into the next decade. If enrollment in accredited physical therapy programs remains at the current level, there will be more openings for physical therapists than qualified individuals to fill them.

FOR MORE INFORMATION

The APTA offers various publications as well as a directory of accredited schools, certification, and general career information on its Web site.

American Physical Therapy Association (APTA)
1111 North Fairfax Street
Alexandria, VA 22314-1488
Tel: 800-999-2782
http://www.apta.org

For information on accredited programs, contact
Commission on Accreditation in Physical Therapy Education
http://www.apta.org/CAPTE

PHYSICAL THERAPY ASSISTANTS

OVERVIEW

Physical therapy assistants help to restore physical function in people with injury, birth defects, or disease. They assist physical therapists with a variety of techniques, such as exercise, massage, heat, and water therapy.

Physical therapy assistants work directly under the supervision of physical therapists. They teach and help patients improve functional activities required in their daily lives, such as walking, climbing, and moving from one place to another. The assistants observe patients during treatments, record the patients' responses and progress, and report these to the physical therapist, either orally or in writing. They fit patients for and teach them to use braces, artificial limbs, crutches, canes, walkers, wheelchairs, and other devices. They may make physical measurements to assess the effects of treatments or to evaluate patients' range of motion, length and girth of body parts, and vital signs. Physical therapy assistants act as members of a team and regularly confer with other members of the physical therapy staff. There are approximately 63,750 physical therapy assistants employed in the United States.

SCHOOL SUBJECTS
Biology, Health

PERSONAL SKILLS
Helping/teaching, Mechanical/manipulative

MINIMUM EDUCATION LEVEL
Associate's degree

CERTIFICATION OR LICENSING
Required by certain states

WORK ENVIRONMENT
Primarily indoors, Primarily one location

THE JOB

Physical therapy personnel work to prevent, diagnose, and rehabilitate, to restore physical function, prevent permanent disability as much as possible, and help people achieve their maximum attainable performance. For many patients, this objective involves daily living skills, such as eating, grooming, dressing, bathing, and other basic movements that unimpaired people do automatically without thinking.

Physical therapy may alleviate conditions such as muscular pain, spasm, and weakness, joint pain and stiffness, and neuromuscular incoordination. These conditions may be caused by any number of disorders, including fractures, burns, amputations, arthritis, nerve or muscular injuries, trauma, birth defects, stroke, multiple sclerosis, and cerebral palsy. Patients of all ages receive physical therapy services; they may be severely disabled or they may need only minimal therapeutic intervention.

Physical therapy assistants always work under the direction of a qualified physical therapist. Other members of the health team may be a physician or surgeon, nurse, occupational therapist, psychologist, or vocational counselor. Each of these practitioners helps establish and achieve realistic goals consistent with the patient's individual needs. Physical therapy assistants help perform tests to evaluate disabilities and determine the most suitable treatment for the patient; then, as the treatment progresses, they routinely report the patient's condition to the physical therapist. If they observe a patient having serious problems during treatment, the assistants notify the therapist as soon as possible. Physical therapy assistants generally perform complicated therapeutic procedures decided by the physical therapist; however, assistants may initiate routine procedures independently.

These procedures may include physical exercises, which are the most varied and widely used physical treatments. Exercises may be simple or complicated, easy or strenuous, active or passive. Active motions are performed by the patient alone and strengthen or train muscles. Passive exercises involve the assistant moving the body part through the motion, which improves mobility of the joint but does not strengthen muscle. For example, for a patient with a fractured arm, both active and passive exercise may be appropriate. The passive exercises may be designed to maintain or increase the range of motion in the shoulder, elbow, wrist, and finger joints, while active resistive exercises strengthen muscles weakened by disuse. An elderly patient who has suffered a stroke may need guided exercises aimed at keeping the joints mobile, regaining the function of a limb, walking, or climbing stairs. A child with cerebral palsy who would otherwise never walk may be helped to learn coordination exercises that enable crawling, sitting balance, standing balance, and, finally, walking.

Patients sometimes perform exercises in bed or immersed in warm water. Besides its usefulness in alleviating stiffness or paralysis, exercise also helps to improve circulation, relax tense muscles, correct posture, and aid the breathing of patients with lung problems.

Other treatments that physical therapy assistants may administer include massages, traction for patients with neck or back pain, ultrasound and various kinds of heat treatment for diseases such as arthritis that inflame joints or nerves, cold applications to reduce swelling, pain, or hemorrhaging, and ultraviolet light.

Physical therapy assistants train patients to manage devices and equipment that they either need temporarily or permanently. For example, they instruct patients how to walk with canes or crutches using proper gait and maneuver well in a wheelchair. They also teach patients how to apply, remove, care for, and cope with splints, braces, and artificial body parts.

Physical therapy personnel must often work on improving the emotional state of patients, preparing them psychologically for treatments. The overwhelming sense of hopelessness and lack of confidence that afflict many disabled patients can reduce the patients' success in achieving improved functioning. The health team must be attuned to both the physical and nonphysical aspects of patients to assure that treatments are most beneficial. Sometimes physical therapy personnel work with patients' families to educate them on how to provide simple physical treatments and psychological support at home.

In addition, physical therapy assistants may perform office duties: They schedule patients, keep records, handle inventory, and order supplies. *Physical therapy aides* may also handle these duties.

REQUIREMENTS

High School

Does this work sound interesting to you? If so, you can prepare for it while still in high school by taking biology, health, and mathematics classes. Psychology, sociology, and even social studies classes will be helpful, because they will give you an understanding of people. And, since you will be working so closely with clients as well as other professionals, you will need excellent communication skills. Therefore, take English courses and other classes that will improve these skills, such as speech. It is also a good idea to take computer science classes since almost all employers require their employees to have computer communication skills.

Postsecondary Training

In order to do this work, you will need a degree from an accredited physical therapy assistant program. Accreditation is given by the Commission on Accreditation in Physical Therapy Education (CAPTE), which is part of the American Physical Therapy Association (APTA). These programs, leading to an associate's degree, are usually offered at community and junior colleges. Typically lasting two years, the programs combine academic instruction with a period of supervised clinical practice in a physical therapy setting. According to the U.S. Department of Labor, in 2009 there were 223 accredited schools offering assistant programs as well as several programs in development. Information about these programs can be found on APTA's Web site, http://www.apta.org. The first year of study is typically taken up with general course work, while the second year is focused on professional classes. Classes you can expect to take include mathematics, biology, applied physical sciences, psychology, human growth and development, and physical therapist assistant procedures such as massage, therapeutic exercise, and heat and cold therapy.

In recent years, admission to accredited programs has been fairly competitive, with three to five applicants for each available opening.

Some physical therapy assistants begin their careers while in the armed forces, which operate training programs. While these programs are not sufficient for state licensure and do not award degrees, they can serve as an excellent introduction to the field for students who later enter more complete training programs.

Certification or Licensing

Many states require regulation of physical therapy assistants in the form of registration, certification, or licensure. Typically, graduation from an CAPTE-accredited program and passing the National Physical Therapy Exam or state exams are needed for licensing. Because requirements vary by state, you will need to check with your state's licensure board for specific information.

Other Requirements

Physical therapy assistants must have stamina, patience, and determination, but at the same time they must be able to establish personal relationships quickly and successfully. They should genuinely like and understand people, both under normal conditions and under the stress of illness. An outgoing personality is highly desirable as is the ability to instill confidence and enthusiasm in patients. Much of the work of physical retraining and restoring is very repetitive, and assistants may not perceive any progress for long periods of time. At times patients may seem unable or unwilling to cooperate. In such cases, assistants need boundless patience, to appreciate small gains and build on them. When restoration to good health is not attainable, physical therapist assistants must help patients adjust to a different way of life and find ways to cope with their situation. Creativity is an asset to devising methods that help disabled people achieve greater self-sufficiency. Assistants should be flexible and open to suggestions offered by their coworkers and willing and able to follow directions closely.

Because the job can be physically demanding, physical therapy assistants must be reasonably strong and enjoy physical activity. Manual dexterity and good coordination are needed to adjust equipment and assist patients. Assistants should be able to lift, climb, stoop, and kneel.

EXPLORING

While still in high school, you can experience this work by getting summer or part-time employment or by volunteering in the physical therapy department of a hospital or clinic. Also, many schools, both public and private, have volunteer assistance programs for work with disabled students. You can also gain direct experience by working with disabled children in a summer camp.

These opportunities will provide you with direct job experience that will help you determine if you have the personal qualities necessary for this career. If you are unable to get direct experience, you should talk to a physical therapist or physical therapy assistant during career-day programs at your high school. It may also be possible for you to arrange to visit a physical therapy department, watch the staff at work, and ask questions.

EMPLOYERS

Physical therapy assistants are employed in hospitals, rehabilitation centers, schools for the disabled, nursing homes, community and government health agencies, physicians' or physical therapists' offices, and facilities for the mentally disabled. There are approximately 63,750 physical therapy assistants employed in the United States.

STARTING OUT

One good way to find a job is to access the resources available at the career services office of your educational institution. Alternatively, you can apply to the physical therapy departments of local hospitals, rehabilitation centers, extended-care facilities, and other potential employers. Openings are listed in the classified ads of newspapers, professional journals, and with private and public employment agencies. In locales where training programs have produced many physical therapy assistants, competition for jobs may be keen. In such cases, you may want to widen your search to areas where there is less competition, especially suburban and rural areas.

ADVANCEMENT

With experience, physical therapy assistants are often given greater responsibility and better pay. In large health care facilities, supervisory possibilities may open up. In small institutions that employ only one physical therapist, the physical therapist assistant may eventually take care of all the technical tasks that go on in the department, within the limitations of his or her training and education.

Physical therapy assistants with degrees from accredited programs are generally in the best position to gain advancement in any setting. They sometimes decide to earn a postbaccalaureate degree in physical therapy and become fully qualified physical therapists.

EARNINGS

Salaries for physical therapy assistants vary considerably depending on geographical location, employer, and level of experience. Physical therapy assistants earned median annual salaries of $48,290 in 2009, according to the U.S. Department of Labor. The lowest paid 10 percent earned less than $30,400; the highest paid 10 percent earned more than $66,460. According to Salary.com, the national average median salary for licensed physical therapy assistants in 2011 was $45,770, with 50 percent earning between $40,258 and $50,132, annually.

Fringe benefits vary, although they usually include paid holidays and vacations, health insurance, and pension plans.

WORK ENVIRONMENT

Physical therapy is generally administered in pleasant, clean, well-lighted, and well-ventilated surroundings. The space devoted to physical therapy services is often large, in order to accommodate activities such as gait training and exercises and procedures requiring equipment. Some procedures are given at patients' bedsides.

In the physical therapy department, patients come and go all day, many in wheelchairs, on walkers, canes, crutches, or stretchers. The staff tries to maintain a purposeful, harmonious, congenial atmosphere as they and the patients work toward the common goal of restoring physical efficacy.

The work can be exhausting. Physical therapy assistants may be on their feet for hours at a time, and they may have to move heavy equipment, lift patients, and help them to stand and walk. Most assistants work daytime hours, five days a week, although some positions require evening or weekend work. Some assistants work on a part-time basis.

The combined physical and emotional demands of the job can exert a considerable strain. Prospective assistants would be wise to seek out some job experience related to physical therapy so that they have a practical understanding of their psychological and physical capacities. By exploring their suitability for the work, they can make a better commitment to the training program.

Job satisfaction can be great for physical therapy assistants as they can see how their efforts help to make people's lives much more rewarding.

OUTLOOK

Employment prospects are very good for physical therapy assistants; the U.S. Department of Labor predicts that employment will grow much faster than the average through 2018. Many new positions for physical therapy assistants are expected to open up as hospital programs that aid the disabled expand and as long-term facilities seek to offer residents more adequate services. Also, physical therapists can assign many parts of treatment to physical therapy assistants and aides, and thus reduce costs of physical therapy services.

A major contributing factor is the increasing number of Americans aged 65 and over. This group tends to suffer a disproportionate amount of the accidents and chronic illnesses that necessitate physical therapy services. Many from the baby boom generation are reaching the age common for heart attacks, thus creating a need for more cardiac and physical rehabilitation. Legislation that requires appropriate public education for all disabled children also may increase the demand for physical therapy services. As more adults engage in strenuous physical exercise, more musculoskeletal injuries will result, thus increasing demand for physical therapy services. In addition, medical and technological developments should permit a growing number of trauma victims and newborns with birth defects to survive, creating more employment opportunities for therapy and rehabilitative services.

FOR MORE INFORMATION

For additional education and career information, contact

American Physical Therapy Association
1111 North Fairfax Street
Alexandria, VA 22314-1488
Tel: 800-999-2782
http://www.apta.org

For information on accredited programs, contact
Commission on Accreditation in Physical Therapy Education (CAPTE)
http://www.apta.org/CAPTE

PHYSICIAN ASSISTANTS

OVERVIEW

Physician assistants (PAs) practice medicine under the supervision of licensed doctors of medicine or osteopathy, providing various health care services to patients. Much of the work they do was formerly limited to physicians. There are approximately 76,900 physician assistants employed in the United States.

THE JOB

Physician assistants help physicians provide medical care to patients. PAs may be assigned a variety of tasks; they may take medical histories of patients, do complete routine physical examinations, order laboratory tests, draw blood samples, give injections, decide on diagnoses, choose treatments, and assist in surgery. Although the duties of PAs vary by state, they always work under the supervision and direction of a licensed physician. The extent of the PA's duties depends on the specific laws of

the state and the practices of the supervising physician, as well as the experience and abilities of the PA. PAs work in a variety of health care settings, including hospitals, clinics, physician's offices, and federal, state, and local agencies.

Many PAs specialize in general medicine, such as family medicine, internal medicine, general pediatrics, and obstetrics and gynecology. Twenty-four percent of PAs are in general surgery/surgical subspecialties; others specialize in emergency medicine or are in internal medicine subspecialties.

All states allow PAs to prescribe medicine to patients; however, those who prescribe controlled medications must have a DEA (Drug Enforcement Administration) number. Physician assistants may be known by other occupational titles such as *child health associates, MEDEX, physician associates, anesthesiologist's assistants,* or *surgeon's assistants.*

PAs are skilled professionals who assume a great deal of responsibility in their work. By handling various medical tasks for their physician employers, PAs allow physicians more time to diagnose and treat more severely ill patients.

REQUIREMENTS

High School

Since a physician assistant needs to be good with numbers and understand how the human body works, anyone interested in this job can begin preparing in high school by taking math and science classes, such as biology and

---

SCHOOL SUBJECTS
Biology, Health

PERSONAL SKILLS
Helping/teaching, Technical/scientific

MINIMUM EDUCATION LEVEL
Some postsecondary training

CERTIFICATION OR LICENSING
Required by all states

WORK ENVIRONMENT
Primarily indoors, Primarily multiple locations

chemistry, as well as health classes. English and social science classes, such as psychology, will also help you improve your communication skills and give you an understanding of people.

Also, keep in mind that it's not too early to gain some experience in the health care field. Many postsecondary institutions take into consideration an applicant's hands-on experience when deciding whom to accept, so look for paid or volunteer positions in your community.

Postsecondary Training

Most states require that PAs complete an educational program approved by the Accreditation Review Commission on Education for the Physician Assistant. There are approximately 142 fully or provisionally accredited PA programs. Admissions requirements vary, but two years of college courses in science or health, and some health care experience, are usually the minimum requirements. The American Academy of Physician Assistants (AAPA) reports that a majority of all students accepted, however, have their bachelor's or master's degrees. Most PA educational programs last 24 to 32 months, although some last only one year and others may last as many as three years.

The first six to 24 months of most programs involve classroom instruction in human anatomy, physiology, microbiology, clinical pharmacology, applied psychology, clinical medicine, and medical ethics. In the last nine to 15 months of most programs, students engage in supervised clinical work, usually including assignments, or rotations, in various branches of medicine, such as family practice, pediatrics, and emergency medicine.

Graduates of these programs may receive a certificate, an associate's degree, a bachelor's degree, or a master's degree; most programs, however, offer graduates a bachelor's degree. The University of Washington offers the MEDEX certification program with bachelor's or master's degree options, http://www.washington.edu/medicine/som/depts/medex). It is designed for medical corpsmen, registered nurses, and others who have had extensive patient-care experience. Candidates typically have more than the minimum requirement of 4,000 hours of paid work experience in patient care. MEDEX students usually obtain most of their clinical experience by working with a physician who will hire them after graduation.

PA programs are offered in a variety of educational and health care settings, including colleges and universities, medical schools and centers, hospitals, and the armed forces. State laws and regulations dictate the scope of the PA's duties, and, in all but a few states, PAs must be graduates of an approved training program.

Certification or Licensing

Currently, all states and the District of Columbia require that PAs be certified by the National Commission on Certification of Physician Assistants (NCCPA). To become certified, applicants must be graduates of an accredited PA program and pass the Physician Assistant National Certifying Examination (PANCE). The examination consists of three parts: The first part tests general medical knowledge, the second section tests the PA's specialty—either primary care or surgery—and the third part tests for practical clinical knowledge. After successfully completing the examination, physician assistants can use the credential, physician assistant-certified.

Once certified, PAs are required to complete 100 hours of continuing medical education courses every two years, and in addition must pass a recertification examination every six years. Besides NCCPA certification, most states also require that PAs register with the state medical board. State rules and regulations vary greatly concerning the work of PAs, and applicants are advised to study the laws of the state in which they wish to practice.

Licensing for physician assistants varies by state. New graduates should contact their state's licensing board to find out about specific requirements. Some states grant temporary licenses to physician assistants who have applied for the PANCE. For permanent licensure, most states require verification of certification or an official record of their exam scores.

Other Requirements

To be a successful physician assistant, you must be able to work well with many different kinds of people, from the physician who supervises you to the many different patients you see every day. In addition to being a caring individual, you should also have a strong desire to continue learning in order to keep up with the latest medical procedures and recertification requirements. Since ill individuals depend on a physician assistant's decisions, anyone interested in this job should have leadership skills and self-confidence as well as compassion.

EXPLORING

If you are interested in exploring the profession, talk with school guidance counselors, practicing PAs, PA students, and various health care employees at local hospitals and clinics. You can also obtain information by contacting one of the organizations listed at the end of this article. Working as a volunteer in a hospital, clinic, or nursing home is a good way to get exposure to the health care profession. In addition, while in college, you may be able to obtain summer jobs as a hospital orderly, nurse assistant, or medical clerk. Such jobs can help you assess your interest in and suitability for work as a PA before you apply to a PA program.

EMPLOYERS

There are 76,900 physician assistants employed in the United States. PAs work in a variety of health care settings. According to the AAPA, many PAs are employed by single physicians or group practices; others work at hospitals or for some type of government agency, with the Department of Veterans' Affairs being the largest government employer of PAs. They are also employed by clinics, nursing homes, long-term care facilities, and prisons. Many areas lacking quality medical care personnel, such as remote rural areas and the inner city, are hiring PAs to meet their needs. The American Association of Physician Assistants estimated that in early 2009, there were 85,345 people eligible to practice as PAs, and nearly 74,000 people were in clinical practice as physician assistants.

STARTING OUT

PAs must complete their formal training programs before entering the job market. Once they complete their studies, PA students can utilize the placement services of their schools to locate jobs. PAs may also seek employment at hospitals, clinics, medical offices, or other health care settings. Information about jobs with the federal government can be obtained by contacting the Office of Personnel Management's Web site at http://www.usajobs.gov.

ADVANCEMENT

Since the PA profession is still quite new, formal lines of advancement have not yet been established. There are still several ways to advance. Hospitals, for example, do not employ head PAs. Those with experience can assume more responsibility at higher pay, or they move on to employment at larger hospitals and clinics.

Some PAs go back to school for additional education to practice in a specialty area, such as surgery, urology, or ophthalmology.

EARNINGS

Salaries of PAs vary according to experience, specialty, and employer. The U.S. Department of Labor reports that the lowest paid 10 percent of all physician assistants earned less than $55,880 in 2009; the median annual salary was $84,420, and the highest paid 10 percent earned $115,080 or more per year. The department also reports that physician assistants employed in offices of physicians had mean annual earnings of $84,720 in 2009, while those employed in hospitals earned $86,850. PayScale.com reported that physician assistants earned median annual salaries that ranged from $72,173 to $94,132 in early 2011. A report by the American Medical Association listed salaries in 2008 for experienced PAs with good work experience at $119,000 to $200,000 a year; the average salary for PAs was $89,987. PAs are well compensated compared with other occupations that have similar training requirements. Most PAs receive health and life insurance among other benefits.

WORK ENVIRONMENT

Most work settings are comfortable and clean, although, like physicians, PAs spend a good part of their day standing or walking. The workweek varies according to the employment setting. A few emergency room PAs may work 24-hour shifts, twice a week; others work 12-hour shifts, three times a week. PAs who work in physicians' offices, hospitals, or clinics may have to work weekends, nights, and holidays. PAs employed in clinics, however, usually work five-day, 40-hour weeks.

OUTLOOK

Employment for physician assistants, according to the U.S. Department of Labor (DOL), is expected to increase much faster than the average for all occupations through 2018. Opportunities will be best in rural areas and inner city clinics—settings which often have trouble attracting the most qualified candidates.

The role of the PA in delivering health care has also expanded over the past decade. PAs have taken on new duties and responsibilities, and they now work in a variety of health care settings. The DOL reports that physician assistants should have good opportunities in hospitals, academic medical centers, public clinics, and prisons. States that offer PAs a wider scope of practice will also offer more employment opportunities.

FOR MORE INFORMATION

For more information on PA careers, educational programs, and scholarships, contact

American Academy of Physician Assistants (AAPA)
950 North Washington Street
Alexandria, VA 22314-1552
Tel: 703-836-2272
http://www.aapa.org

For information on certification, contact

National Commission on Certification of Physician Assistants
12000 Findley Road, Suite 100
Johns Creek, GA 30097-1484
Tel: 678-417-8100
E-mail: nccpa@nccpa.net
http://www.nccpa.net

For industry information and to subscribe ($35 fee) to the PA Programs Directory, contact

Physician Assistant Education Association
300 North Washington Street, Suite 710
Alexandria, VA 22314-2535
Tel: 703-548-5538
E-mail: info@paeaonline.org
http://www.paeaonline.org

 PHYSICIANS

OVERVIEW

Physicians diagnose, prescribe medicines for, and otherwise treat diseases and disorders of the human body. A physician may also perform surgery and often specializes in one aspect of medical care and treatment. Physicians hold either a doctor of medicine (M.D.) or osteopathic medicine (D.O.) degree. Approximately 575,490 M.D.'s and D.O.'s are employed in the United States.

THE JOB

Most physicians specialize in one of the following areas: anesthesiology, family and general medicine, general internal medicine, general pediatrics, obstetrics and gynecology, psychiatry, and surgery. The greatest number of physicians are in private practice. They see

patients by appointment in their offices and examining rooms, and visit patients who are confined to the hospital. In the hospital, they may perform operations or give other kinds of medical treatment. Some physicians also make calls on patients at home if the patient is not able to get to the physician's office or if the illness is an emergency.

Anesthesiologists focus on surgical patients and pain relief. More than 12 percent of physicians are *general practitioners* or *family practitioners*. They see patients of all ages and both sexes and will diagnose and treat those ailments that are not severe enough or unusual enough to require the services of a specialist. When special problems arise, however, the general practitioner will refer the patient to a specialist.

General internists diagnose and treat patients with problems that affect internal organ systems, such as the digestive tract, stomach, liver, and kidneys. *General pediatricians* focus on the health of infants, children, teenagers, and young adults. *Obstetricians and gynecologists* specialize in women's health. *Psychiatrists* diagnose and treat patients with mental health issues. *Surgeons* treat and operate on patients who are injured, deformed, or diagnosed with a disease.

Not all physicians are engaged in private practice. Some are in academic medicine and teach in medical schools or teaching hospitals. Some are engaged only in research. Some are salaried employees of health maintenance organizations or other prepaid health care plans. Some are salaried hospital employees.

Some physicians, often called *medical officers*, are employed by the federal government, in such positions as

SCHOOL SUBJECTS
Biology, Health

PERSONAL SKILLS
Helping/teaching, Technical/scientific

MINIMUM EDUCATION LEVEL
Medical degree

CERTIFICATION OR LICENSING
Required by all states

WORK ENVIRONMENT
Primarily indoors, Primarily multiple locations

public health, or in the service of the Department of Veterans Affairs. State and local governments also employ physicians for public health agency work. A large number of physicians serve with the armed forces, both in this country and overseas.

Industrial physicians or *occupational physicians* are employed by large industrial firms for two main reasons: to prevent illnesses that may be caused by certain kinds of work and to treat accidents or illnesses of employees. Although most industrial physicians may roughly be classified as general practitioners because of the wide variety of illnesses that they must recognize and treat, their knowledge must also extend to public health techniques and to understanding such relatively new hazards as radiation and the toxic effects of various chemicals, including insecticides.

A specialized type of industrial or occupational physician is the *flight surgeon*. Flight surgeons study the effects of high-altitude flying on the physical condition of flight personnel. They place members of the flight staff in special low-pressure and refrigeration chambers that simulate high-altitude conditions and study the reactions on their blood pressure, pulse and respiration rate, and body temperature.

Another growing specialty is the field of nuclear medicine. Some large hospitals have a nuclear research laboratory, which functions under the direction of a *chief of nuclear medicine*, who coordinates the activities of the lab with other hospital departments and medical personnel. These physicians perform tests using nuclear isotopes and use techniques that let physicians see and understand organs deep within the body.

M.D.'s may become specialists in any of the 40 different medical care specialties.

REQUIREMENTS

High School

The physician is required to devote many years to study before being admitted to practice. Interested high school students should enroll in a college preparatory course, and take courses in English, languages (especially Latin), the humanities, social studies, and mathematics, in addition to courses in biology, chemistry, and physics.

Postsecondary Training

To begin a career as a physician, you need to first enter a liberal arts program in an accredited undergraduate institution. Some colleges offer a premedical course, but a good general education, with as many science courses as possible and a major in biology or chemistry, is considered adequate preparation for the study of medicine. Courses should include physics, biology, inorganic and organic chemistry, English, mathematics, and the social sciences.

College students should begin to apply to medical schools early in their senior year, so it is advisable to begin your research into schools as early as your freshman year. There are 129 accredited schools of medicine and 25 accredited schools of osteopathic medicine in the country. For more information, consult a copy of *Medical School Admission Requirements, United States and Canada*, available from the Association of American Medical Colleges or from your college library. It is an annual publication updated each spring. Read carefully the admissions requirements of the several medical schools to which you hope to apply to avoid making mistakes in choosing a graduate program.

Some students may be admitted to medical school after only three years of study in an undergraduate program. There are a few medical schools that award the bachelor's degree at the end of the first year of medical school study. This practice is becoming less common as more students seek admission to medical schools. Most premedical students plan to spend four years in an undergraduate program and to receive the bachelor's degree before entering the four-year medical school program.

During your second or third year in college, you should arrange with an adviser to take the Medical College Admission Test (MCAT). This test is given at various times during the year at certain selected sites. Your adviser should know the date, place, and time; or you may visit the MCAT section of the Association of American Medical Colleges Web site for further information, https://www.aamc.org/students/applying/mcat/reserving/129222/2011_mcat_exam_schedule.html. All medical colleges in the United States require this test for admission, and a student's MCAT score is one of the factors that is weighed in the decision to accept or reject any applicant. Because the test does not evaluate medical knowledge, most college students who are enrolled in liberal arts programs should not find it to be unduly difficult. The examination covers four areas: verbal facility, quantitative ability, knowledge of the humanities and social sciences, and knowledge of biology, chemistry, and physics.

You are encouraged to apply to at least three institutions to increase your chances of being accepted by one of them. Approximately one out of every two qualified applicants to medical schools is admitted each year. To facilitate this process, the American Medical College Application Service (AMCAS) will check, copy, and submit applications to the medical schools you specify. More information about this service may be obtained from AMCAS, premedical advisers, and medical schools.

In addition to the traditional medical schools, there are several schools of basic medical sciences that enroll medical students for the first two years (preclinical experience) of medical school. They offer a preclinical curriculum to students similar to that which is offered by a regular medical school. At the end of the two-year program, you can then apply to a four-year medical school for the final two years of instruction.

Although high scholarship is a determining factor in admitting a student to a medical school, it is actually only one of the criteria considered. By far the greatest number of successful applicants to medical schools are "B" students. Because admission is also determined by a number of other factors, including a personal interview, other qualities in addition to a high scholastic average are considered desirable for a prospective physician. High on the list of desirable qualities are emotional stability, integrity, reliability, resourcefulness, and a sense of service.

The average student enters medical school at age 21 or 22. Then you begin another four years of formal schooling. During the first two years of medical school, studies include human anatomy, biochemistry, physiology, pharmacology, psychology, microbiology, pathology, medical ethics, and laws governing medicine. Most instruction in the first two years is given through classroom lectures, laboratories, seminars, independent research, and the reading of textbook material and other types of literature. You also learn to take medical histories, examine patients, and recognize symptoms.

During the last two years in medical school, you become actively involved in the treatment process. You spend a large proportion of the time in the hospital as part of a medical team headed by a teaching physician who specializes in a particular area. Others on the team may be interns or residents. You are closely supervised as you learn techniques such as how to take a patient's medical history, how to conduct a physical examination, how to work in the laboratory, how to make a diagnosis, and how to keep all the necessary records.

As you rotate from one medical specialty to another, you obtain a broad understanding of each field. You are assigned to duty in internal medicine, pediatrics, psy-chiatry, obstetrics and gynecology, surgery, and other specialties.

In addition to this hospital work, you continue to take course work. You are responsible for assigned studies and also for some independent study.

Most states require all new M.D.s to complete at least one year of postgraduate training, and a few require an internship plus a one-year residency. If you decide to specialize, you will spend from three to seven years in advanced residency training plus another two or more years of practice in the specialty. Then you must pass a specialty board examination to become a board-certified M.D. The residency years are stressful—residents often work 24-hour shifts and put in up to 80 hours per week.

For a teaching or research career, you may also earn a master's degree or a Ph.D. in a biology or chemistry subfield, such as biochemistry or microbiology.

Certification or Licensing

After receiving the M.D. degree, the new physician is required to take an examination to be licensed to practice. Every state requires such an examination. It is conducted through the board of medical examiners in each state. Some states have reciprocity agreements with other states so that a physician licensed in one state may be automatically licensed in another without being required to pass another examination. This is not true throughout the United States, however, so it is wise to find out about licensing procedures before planning to move.

Other Requirements

You must have some plan for financing your long and costly education. You face a period of at least eight years after college when you will not be self-supporting. While still in school, you may be able to work only during summer vacations, because the necessary laboratory courses of the regular school year are so time consuming that little time is left for activities other than the preparation of daily lessons. Some scholarships and loans are available to qualified students.

If you work directly with patients you need to have great sensitivity to their needs. Interpersonal skills are important, even in isolated research laboratories, since you must work and communicate with other scientists. Since new technology and discoveries happen at such a rapid rate, you must continually pursue further education to keep up with new treatments, tools, and medicines.

EXPLORING

One of the best introductions to a career in health care is to volunteer at a local hospital, clinic, or nursing home. In this way it is possible to get a feel for what it is like to work around other health care professionals and patients and possibly determine exactly where your interests lie. As in any career, reading as much as possible about the profession, talking with a high school counselor, and interviewing those working in the field are other important ways to explore your interest.

EMPLOYERS

There are about 575,490 M.D.s and D.O.s working in the United States. Physicians can find employment in a wide variety of settings, including hospitals, nursing homes, managed-care offices, prisons, schools and universities, research laboratories, trauma centers, clinics, and public health centers. Some are self-employed in their own or group practices. In the past, many physicians went into business for themselves, either by starting their own practice or by becoming a partner in an existing one. Few physicians—about 12 percent—are choosing to follow this path today. There are a number of reasons for this shift. Often, the costs of starting a practice or buying into an existing practice are too high. Most are choosing to take salaried positions with hospitals or groups of physicians.

Jobs for physicians are available all over the world, although licensing requirements may vary. In Third World countries, there is great demand for medical professionals of all types. Conditions, supplies, and equipment may be poor and pay is minimal, but there are great rewards in terms of experience. Many doctors fulfill part or all of their residency requirements by practicing in other countries.

Physicians interested in teaching may find employment at medical schools or university hospitals. There are also positions available in government agencies such as the Centers for Disease Control, the National Institutes of Health, and the Food and Drug Administration.

Pharmaceutical companies and chemical companies hire physicians to research and develop new drugs, instruments, and procedures.

STARTING OUT

There are no shortcuts to entering the medical profession. Requirements are an M.D. degree, a licensing examination, a one- or two-year internship, and a period of residency that may extend as long as five years (and seven years if they are pursuing board certification in a specialty).

Upon completing this program, which may take up to 15 years, physicians are then ready to enter practice. They may choose to open a solo private practice, enter a partnership practice, enter a group practice, or take a salaried job with a managed-care facility or hospital. Salaried positions are also available with federal and state agencies, the military, including the Department of Veterans Affairs, and private companies. Teaching and research jobs are usually obtained after other experience is acquired.

The highest ratio of physicians to patients is in the New England and Middle Atlantic States. The lowest ratio is in the South Central and Mountain States. Most M.D.s practice in urban areas near hospitals and universities.

ADVANCEMENT

Physicians who work in a managed-care setting or for a large group or corporation can advance by opening a private practice. The average physician in private practice does not advance in the accustomed sense of the word. Their progress consists of advancing in skill and understanding, in numbers of patients, and in income. They may be made a fellow in a professional specialty or elected to an important office in the American Medical Association or American Osteopathic Association. Teaching and research positions may also increase a physician's status.

Some physicians may become directors of a laboratory, managed-care facility, hospital department, or medical school program. Some may move into hospital administration positions.

A physician can achieve recognition by conducting research in new medicines, treatments, and cures, and publishing their findings in medical journals. Participation in professional organizations can also bring prestige.

A physician can advance by pursuing further education in a subspecialty or a second field such as biochemistry or microbiology.

EARNINGS

Physicians have among the highest average earnings of any occupational group. The level of income for any individual physician depends on a number of factors, such as region of the country, economic status of the patients, and the physician's specialty, skill, experience, professional reputation, and personality. According to the Medical Group Management Association's Physician Compensation and Production Survey, in 2009 primary care physicians earned median salaries of $191,253, a 2.8 percent increase over the previous year. The U.S. Department of Labor reports that the median income in 2009 for family and general practitioners was $160,530; the lowest paid 10 percent earned $51,750 or less. General surgeons, anesthesiologists, and obstetricians/gynecologists had median annual salaries of $166,400 or higher in 2009. Physicians who work in the federal government earned about $173,400 in 2009. Those who work in offices of physicians earned $202,480 annually.

Salaried doctors usually earn fringe benefits such as health and dental insurance, paid vacations, and the opportunity to participate in retirement plans. Self-employed physicians usually have higher median incomes than salaried doctors, although they are also responsible for covering the costs of their health insurance and retirement.

WORK ENVIRONMENT

The offices and examining rooms of most physicians are well equipped, attractive, well lighted, and well ventilated. There is usually at least one nurse-receptionist on the physician's staff, and there may be several nurses, a laboratory technician, one or more secretaries, a bookkeeper, or receptionist.

Physicians usually see patients by appointments that are scheduled according to individual requirements. They may reserve all mornings for hospital visits and surgery. They may see patients in the office only on certain days of the week.

Physicians spend much of their time at the hospital performing surgery, setting fractures, working in the emergency room, or visiting patients.

Physicians in private practice have the advantages of working independently, but 43 percent of all physicians worked an average of 50 hours or more per week in 2008. Also, they may be called from their homes or offices in times of emergency. Telephone calls may come at any hour of the day or night. It is difficult for physicians to plan leisure-time activities, because their plans may change without notice. One of the advantages of group practice is that members of the group rotate emergency duty.

The areas in most need of physicians are rural hospitals and medical centers. Because the physician is normally working alone, and covering a broad territory, the workday can be quite long with little opportunity for vacation. Because placement in rural communities has become so difficult, some towns are providing scholarship money to students who pledge to work in the community for a number of years.

Physicians in academic medicine or in research have regular hours, work under good physical conditions, and often determine their own workload. Teaching and research physicians alike are usually provided with the best and most modern equipment.

OUTLOOK

The U.S. Department of Labor reports that this field is expected to grow by 22 percent, much faster than the average for all other occupations, through 2018. Population growth, particularly among the elderly, is a factor in the demand for physicians. Another factor contributing to the predicted increase is the widespread availability of medical insurance, through both private plans and public programs. More physicians will also be needed for medical research, public health, rehabilitation, and industrial medicine. New technology will allow physicians to perform more procedures to treat ailments once thought incurable.

Employment opportunities will be good for family practitioners and internists, geriatric and preventive care specialists, as well as general pediatricians. Rural and low-income areas are in need of more physicians, and there is a short supply of general surgeons and psychiatrists.

The shift in health care delivery from hospitals to outpatient centers and other nontraditional settings to contain rising costs may mean that more and more physicians will become salaried employees.

There will be considerable competition among newly trained physicians entering practice, particularly in large cities. Physicians willing to locate to inner cities and rural areas—where physicians are scarce—should encounter little difficulty.

FOR MORE INFORMATION

Visit the AAFP Web site to access career information and for news, journals, and other resources.

American Academy of Family Physicians (AAFP)
PO Box 11210
Shawnee Mission, KS 66207-1210
Tel: 800-274-2237
http://www.aafp.org

For general information on health care careers, contact
American Medical Association
515 North State Street
Chicago, IL 60654-4854

Tel: 800-621-8335
http://www.ama-assn.org

*For a list of accredited U.S. and Canadian medical
schools and other education information, contact*
Association of American Medical Colleges
2450 N Street, NW
Washington, DC 20037-1126
Tel: 202-828-0400
http://www.aamc.org

PRESCHOOL TEACHERS

SCHOOL SUBJECTS
Art, English, Family and consumer science

PERSONAL SKILLS
Communication/ideas, Helping/teaching

MINIMUM EDUCATION LEVEL
Some postsecondary training

CERTIFICATION OR LICENSING
Required for certain positions

WORK ENVIRONMENT
Primarily indoors, Primarily one location

OVERVIEW

Preschool teachers promote the general education of children under the age of five. They help students develop physically, socially, and emotionally, work with them on language and communications skills, and help cultivate their cognitive abilities. They also work with families to support parents in raising their young children and reinforcing skills at home. They plan and lead activities developed in accordance with the specific ages and needs of the children. It is the goal of all preschool teachers to help students develop the skills, interests, and individual creativity that they will use for the rest of their lives. Many schools and districts consider *kindergarten teachers*, who teach students five years of age, to be preschool teachers. For the purposes of this article, kindergarten teachers will be included in this category. There are approximately 389,600 preschool teachers and 181,810 kindergarten teachers in the United States.

THE JOB

Preschool teachers plan and lead activities that build on children's abilities and curiosity and aid them in developing skills and characteristics that help them grow. Because children develop at varying skill levels as well as have different temperaments, preschool teachers need to develop a flexible schedule with time allowed for music, art, playtime, academics, rest, and other activities.

Preschool teachers plan activities that encourage children to develop skills appropriate to their developmental needs. For example, they plan activities based

on the understanding that a three-year-old child has different motor skills and reasoning abilities than a five-year-old child. They work with the youngest students on learning the days of the week and the recognition of colors, seasons, and animal names and characteristics; they help older students with number and letter recognition and even simple writing skills. Preschool teachers help children with such simple, yet important, tasks as tying shoelaces and washing hands before snack time. Attention to the individual needs of each child is vital; preschool teachers need to be aware of these needs and capabilities, and when possible, adapt activities to the specific needs of the individual child. Self-confidence and the development of communication skills are encouraged in preschools. For example, teachers may give children simple art projects, such as finger painting, and have children show and explain their finished projects to the rest of the class. Show and tell, or "sharing time" as it is often called, gives students opportunities to speak and listen to others.

Preschool teachers adopt many parental responsibilities for the children. They greet the children in the morning and supervise them throughout the day. Often these responsibilities can be quite demanding and complicated. In harsh weather, for example, preschool teachers contend not only with boots, hats, coats, and mittens, but with the inevitable sniffles, colds, and generally cranky behavior that can occur in young children. For most children, preschool is their first time away from home and family for an extended period of time. A major portion of a preschool teacher's day is spent helping children adjust to being away from home and encouraging them to play together. This is especially true at the beginning of the school year. They may need to gently reassure children who become frightened or homesick.

In both full-day and half-day programs, preschool teachers supervise snack time, helping children learn how to eat properly and clean up after themselves. Proper hygiene, such as hand washing before meals, is also stressed. Other activities include storytelling, music, and simple arts and crafts projects. Full-day programs involve a lunch period and at least one nap time. Programs usually have exciting activities interspersed with calmer ones. Even though the children get nap time, preschool teachers must be energetic throughout the day, ready to face with good cheer the many challenges and demands of young children.

Preschool teachers also work with the parents of each child. It is not unusual for parents to come to preschool and observe a child or go on a field trip with the class, and preschool teachers often take these opportunities to discuss the progress of each child as well as any specific problems or concerns. Scheduled meetings are available for parents who cannot visit the school during the day. Solutions to fairly serious problems are worked out in tandem with the parents, often with the aid of the director of the preschool, or in the case of an elementary school kindergarten, with the principal or headmaster.

Kindergarten teachers usually have their own classrooms, made up exclusively of five-year-olds. Although these teachers do not have to plan activities for a wide range of ages, they need to consider individual developmental interests, abilities, and backgrounds represented by the students. Kindergarten teachers usually spend more time helping students with academic skills than do other preschool teachers. While a teacher of two-, three-, and four-year-olds may focus more on socializing and building confidence in students through play and activities, kindergarten teachers often develop activities that help five-year-olds acquire the skills they will need in grade school, such as introductory activities on numbers, reading, and writing. They may also use computers in the classroom to help students develop basic computer navigation skills, as well as to share educational games and videos.

REQUIREMENTS

High School

You should take child development, home economics, and other classes that involve you with child care, such as

family and consumer science classes. You will also need a fundamental understanding of the general subjects you will be introducing to preschool students, so take English, science, and math. Also, take classes in art, music, and theater to develop creative skills.

Postsecondary Training

Specific education requirements for preschool and kindergarten teachers vary from state to state and also depend on the specific guidelines of the school or district. Many schools and child care centers require preschool teachers to have a bachelor's degree in early childhood education or a related field, but others accept adults with a high school diploma and some childcare experience. Some preschool facilities offer on-the-job training to their teachers, hiring them as assistants or aides until they are sufficiently trained to work in a classroom alone. A college degree program should include course work in a variety of liberal arts subjects, including English, history, and science as well as nutrition, child development, psychology of the young child, and sociology.

Several groups offer on-the-job training programs for prospective preschool teachers. For example, the American Montessori Society offers a career program for aspiring preschool teachers. This program requires a three-month classroom training period followed by one year of supervised on-the-job training.

Certification or Licensing

In some states, licensure may be required. Many states accept the child development associate credential (awarded by the Council for Professional Recognition) or an associate or bachelor's degree as sufficient requirements for work in a preschool facility. Individual state boards of education can provide specific licensure information. Kindergarten teachers working in public elementary schools almost always need teaching certification similar to that required by other elementary school teachers in the school. Other types of licensure or certification may be required, depending upon the school or district. These may include first-aid or cardiopulmonary resuscitation (CPR) training.

Other Requirements

Because young children look up to adults and learn through example, it is especially important that as a preschool teacher, you be a good role model. Patience and a sense of humor are also a great help.

EXPLORING

Preschools, day care centers, and other child care programs often hire high school students for part-time positions as aides. You may also find many volunteer opportunities to work with children. Check with your library or local literacy program about tutoring children and reading to preschoolers. Summer day camps or religious schools with preschool classes also hire high school students as counselors or counselors-in-training. Discussing the field with preschool teachers and observing in their classes are other good ways to discover specific job information and explore your aptitude for this career.

EMPLOYERS

There are approximately 389,660 preschool teachers employed in the United States, as well as 181,810 kindergarten teachers. Approximately 65 percent of preschool teachers (not including special education) are employed in child day care services, and 15 percent work in public and private educational services. Both government and the private sector are working to fill the enormous need for quality childcare. Preschool teachers will find many job opportunities in private and public preschools, including day care centers, government-funded learning programs, churches, and Montessori schools. They may find work in a small center, or with a large preschool with many students and classrooms. Preschool franchises, like Primrose Schools and Kids 'R' Kids International, are also providing more opportunities for preschool teachers.

STARTING OUT

If you hope to become a preschool teacher, you can contact child care centers, nursery schools, Head Start programs, and other preschool facilities to identify job opportunities. Often jobs for preschool teachers are listed in the classified section of newspapers. In addition, many school districts and state boards of education maintain job listings of available teaching positions. If no permanent positions are available at preschools, you may be able to find opportunities to work as a substitute teacher. Most preschools and kindergartens maintain a substitute list and refer to it frequently.

ADVANCEMENT

Many teachers advance by becoming more skillful in what they do. Skilled preschool teachers, especially those with additional training, usually receive salary increases as they become more experienced. A few preschool teachers with administrative ability and an interest in administrative work advance to the position of director. Administrators need to have at least a master's degree in child development or a related field and have to meet any state or federal licensing regulations. Some become directors of Head Start programs or other government programs. A relatively small number of experienced preschool teachers open their own facilities. This entails not only the ability to be an effective administrator but also the knowledge of how to operate a business. Kindergarten teachers sometimes have the opportunity to earn more money by teaching at a higher grade level in the elementary school. This salary increase is especially true when a teacher moves from a half-day kindergarten program to a full-day grade school classroom.

EARNINGS

Although there have been some attempts to correct the discrepancies in salaries between preschool teachers and other teachers, salaries in this profession tend to be lower than teaching positions in public elementary and high schools. Because some preschool programs are held only in the morning or afternoon, many preschool teachers work only part time. As part-time workers, they often do not receive medical insurance or other benefits and may get paid minimum wage to start.

According to the U.S. Department of Labor, preschool teachers earned a median salary of $24,540 a year in 2009. Annual salaries for these workers ranged from less than $16,420 to $43,570 or more. The department reports that kindergarten teachers (which the department classifies separately from preschool teachers) earned median annual salaries of $47,830 in 2009. The lowest paid 10 percent earned less than $31,320, while the highest paid 10 percent earned $75,210 or more.

WORK ENVIRONMENT

Preschool teachers spend much of their workday on their feet in a classroom or on a playground. Facilities vary from a single room to large buildings. Class sizes also vary; some preschools serve only a handful of children, while others serve several hundred. Classrooms may be crowded and noisy, but anyone who loves children will enjoy all the activity.

Many children do not go to preschool all day, so work may be part time. Part-time employees generally work between 18 and 30 hours a week, while full-time employees work 35 to 40 hours a week. Part-time work gives the employee flexibility, and for many, this is one of the advantages of the job. Some preschool teachers teach both morning and afternoon classes, going through the same schedule and lesson plans with two sets of students.

OUTLOOK

Employment opportunities for preschool teachers are expected to increase faster than the average for all occupations through 2018, according to the U.S. Department of Labor. Specific job opportunities vary from state to state and depend on demographic characteristics and level of government funding. Some states are instituting programs to improve early childhood education, such as offering full day and universal preschool. Jobs should also be available at private child care centers, nursery schools, Head Start facilities, public and private kindergartens, and laboratory schools connected with universities and colleges. In the past, the majority of preschool teachers were female, and although this continues to be the case, more males are becoming involved in early childhood education.

Many child care workers leave their centers each year, often because of the low pay and lack of benefits. This will mean plenty of job openings for preschool teachers and possibly improved benefit plans, as centers attempt to maintain qualified preschool teachers.

Employment for all teachers, including preschool teachers, will vary by region and state. The U.S. Department of Labor predicts that Southern and Western states will have strong increases in enrollments. Also, schools located in urban and rural areas will be in need of qualified teachers.

FOR MORE INFORMATION

For information on training programs, contact

American Montessori Society
281 Park Avenue South
New York, NY 10010-6102
Tel: 212-358-1250
E-mail: ams@amshq.org
http://www.amshq.org

For information about certification, contact

Council for Professional Recognition
2460 16th Street, NW
Washington, DC 20009-3575
Tel: 800-424-4310
http://www.cdacouncil.org

For general information on preschool teaching careers, contact

National Association for the Education of Young Children
1313 L Street, NW, Suite 500
Washington, DC 20005-4110
Tel: 800-424-2460
http://www.naeyc.org

For information about student memberships and training opportunities, contact

National Association of Child Care Professionals
PO Box 90723
Austin, TX 78709-0723
Tel: 512-301-5557
E-mail: admin@naccp.org
http://www.naccp.org

PROFESSIONAL ATHLETES— TEAM SPORTS

OVERVIEW

Professional athletic teams compete against one another to win titles, championships, and series; team members are paid salaries and bonuses for their work. Team sports include football, basketball, hockey, baseball, and soccer. There are approximately 13,620 athletes and sports competitors employed in the United States.

THE JOB

Unlike amateur athletes who play or compete in amateur circles for titles or trophies only, professional athletic teams compete against one another to win titles, championships, and series; team members are paid salaries and bonuses for their work.

The athletic performances of individual teams are evaluated according to the nature and rules of each specific sport: Usually the winning team compiles the highest score, as in football, basketball, and soccer. Competitions are organized by local, regional, national, and international organizations and associations whose primary functions are to promote the sport and sponsor competitive events. Within a professional sport there are usually different levels of competition based on age,

SCHOOL SUBJECTS

Health, Physical education

PERSONAL SKILLS

Following instructions,
Physical and mental stamina

MINIMUM EDUCATION LEVEL

High school diploma

CERTIFICATION OR LICENSING

None available

WORK ENVIRONMENT

Indoors and outdoors, Primarily multiple locations

ability, and gender. There are often different designations and divisions within one sport. Professional baseball, for example, is made up of the two major leagues (American and National) each made up of three divisions, East, Central, and West; and the minor leagues (single-A, double-A, triple-A). All of these teams are considered professional because the players are compensated for their work, but the financial rewards are the greatest in the major leagues.

Whatever the team sport, most team members specialize in a specific area of the game. In gymnastics, for example, the entire six-member team trains on all of the gymnastic apparatuses—balance beam, uneven bars, vault, and floor exercise—but usually each of the six gymnasts excels in only one or two areas. Those gymnasts who do excel in all four events are likely to do well in the individual, all-around title, which is a part of the team competition. Team members in football, basketball, baseball, soccer, and hockey all assume different positions, some of which change depending on whether or not the team is trying to score a goal (offensive positions) or prevent the opposition from scoring one (defensive positions). During team practices, athletes focus on their specific role in a game, whether that is defensive, offensive, or both. For example, a pitcher will spend some time running bases and throwing to other positions, but the majority of his or her time will most likely be spent practicing pitching.

Professional teams train for most of the year, but unlike athletes in individual sports, the athletes who are members of a team usually have more of an off-

season. The training programs of professional athletes differ according to the season. Following an off-season, most team sports have a training season, in which they begin to focus their workouts after a period of relative inactivity to develop or maintain strength, cardiovascular ability, flexibility, endurance, speed, and quickness, as well as to focus on technique and control. During the season, the team coach, physician, trainers, and physical therapists organize specific routines, programs, or exercises to target game skills as well as individual athletic weaknesses, whether skill-related or from injury.

These workouts also vary according to the difficulty of the game schedule. During a playoff or championship series, the coach and athletic staff realize that a rigorous workout in between games might tax the athletes' strength, stamina, or even mental preparedness, jeopardizing the outcome of the next game. Instead, the coach might prescribe a mild workout followed by intensive stretching. In addition to stretching and exercising the specific muscles used in any given sport, athletes concentrate on developing excellent eating and sleeping habits that will help them remain in top condition throughout the year. Abstaining from drinking alcoholic beverages during a season is a practice to which many professional athletes adhere.

The coaching or training staff often films the games and practices so that the team can benefit from watching their individual exploits, as well as their combined play. By watching their performances, team members can learn how to improve their techniques and strategies. It is common for professional teams to also study other teams' moves and strategies in order to determine a method of coping with the other teams' plays during a game.

REQUIREMENTS

High School

Most professional athletes demonstrate tremendous skill and interest in their sport well before high school. High school offers student athletes the opportunity to gain experience in the field in a structured and competitive environment. Under the guidance of a coach, you can begin developing suitable training programs for yourself and learn about health, nutrition, and conditioning issues.

High school also offers you the opportunity to experiment with a variety of sports and a variety of positions within a sport. Most junior varsity and some varsity high school teams allow you to try out different positions and begin to discover whether you have more of an aptitude for the defensive dives of a goalie or for the forwards' front-line action. High school coaches will help you learn to expand upon your strengths and abilities and develop yourself more fully as an athlete. High school is also an excellent time to begin developing the concentration powers, leadership skills, and good sportsmanship necessary for success in the field.

People who hope to become professional athletes should take a full load of high school courses including four years of English, math, and science as well as health and physical education. A solid high school education will help ensure success in college (often the next step in becoming a professional athlete) and may help you in earning a college athletic scholarship. A high school diploma will certainly give you something to fall back on if an injury, a change in career goals, or other circumstance prevents you from earning a living as an athlete.

Postsecondary Training

College is important for future professional athletes for several reasons. It provides the opportunity to gain skill and strength in your sport before you try to succeed in the pros, and it also offers you the chance of being observed by professional scouts.

Perhaps most importantly, however, a college education arms you with a valuable degree that you can use if you do not earn a living as a professional athlete or after your performance career ends. College athletes major in everything from communications to pre-med and enjoy careers as coaches, broadcasters, teachers, doctors, actors, and business people, to name a few. As with high school sports, college athletes must maintain certain academic standards in order to be permitted to compete in intercollegiate play.

Certification or Licensing

There are no certification or licensing requirements for professional athletes in team sports.

Other Requirements

If you want to be a professional athlete, you must be fully committed to succeeding. You must work almost non-stop to improve your conditioning and skills and not give up when you don't succeed as quickly or as easily as you had hoped. And even then, because the competition is so fierce, the goal of earning a living as a professional athlete is still difficult to reach. For this reason, professional athletes must not get discouraged easily. They must have the self-confidence and ambition to keep working and keep trying. Professional athletes must also have a love for their sport that compels them to want to reach their fullest potential.

EXPLORING

Students interested in pursuing a career in professional sports should start playing that sport as much and as early as possible. Most junior high and high schools have well-established programs in the sports that have professional teams.

If a team sport does not exist in your school, it does not mean your chances at playing it have evaporated. Petition your school board to establish it as a school sport and set aside funds for it. In the meantime, organize other students into a club team, scheduling practices and unofficial games. If the sport is a recognized team sport in the United States or Canada, contact the professional organization for the sport for additional information; if anyone would have helpful tips for gaining recognition, the professional organization would. Also, try calling the local or state athletic board to see what other schools in your area recognize it as a team sport. Then make a list of those teams and try scheduling exhibition games with them. Your goal is to show that other students have a definite interest in the game and that other schools recognize it.

To determine if you really want to commit to pursuing a professional career in your team sport, talk to coaches, trainers, and any athletes who are currently pursuing a professional career. You can also contact professional organizations and associations for information on how to best prepare for a career in their sport. Sometimes there are specialized training programs available, and the best way to find out is to get in contact with the people whose job it is to promote the sport.

EMPLOYERS

Approximately 13,620 athletes and sports competitors are employed in the United States, according to the Department of Labor. Professional athletes are employed by private and public ownership groups throughout the United States and Canada. At the highest male professional level, there are 32 National Football League franchises, 30 Major League Baseball franchises, 29 National Basketball Association franchises, 30 National Hockey League franchises, and 10 Major League Soccer franchises. The Women's National Basketball Association has 13 franchises.

STARTING OUT

Most team sports have some official manner of establishing which teams acquire which players; often, this is referred to as a draft, although sometimes members of a professional team are chosen through a competition. Usually, the draft occurs between the college and professional levels of the sport. The National Basketball Association (NBA), for example, has its NBA College Draft. During the draft, the owners and managers of professional basketball teams choose players in an order based on the team's performance in the previous season. This means that the team with the worst record in the previous season has a greater chance of getting to choose first from the list of available players.

Furthermore, professional athletes must meet the requirements established by the organizing bodies of their respective sport. Sometimes this means meeting a physical requirement, such as age, height, and weight; and sometimes this means fulfilling a number of required stunts, or participating in a certain number of competitions. Professional organizations usually arrange it so that athletes can build up their skills and level of play by participating in lower-level competitions. College sports, as mentioned before, are an excellent way to improve one's skills while pursuing an education.

ADVANCEMENT

Professional athletes in team sports advance in three ways: when their team advances, when they are traded to better teams, and when they negotiate better contracts. In all three instances, this is achieved by the individual team member who works and practices hard, and who gives his or her best performance in game after game. Winning teams also receive a deluge of media attention that often creates celebrities out of individual players, which in turn provides these top players with opportunities for financially rewarding commercial endorsements.

Professional athletes are usually represented by sports agents in the behind-the-scenes deals that determine for which teams they will be playing and what they will be paid. These agents may also be involved with other key decisions involving commercial endorsements, personal income taxes, and financial investments of the athlete's revenues.

In the moves from high school athletics to collegiate athletics and from collegiate athletics to the pros, coaches and scouts are continually scouring the ranks of high school and college teams for new talent; they are most interested in the athletes who consistently deliver points

or prevent the opposition from scoring. There is simply no substitute for success.

A college education, however, can prepare all athletes for the day when their bodies can no longer compete at the top level, whether because of age or an unforeseen injury. Every athlete should be prepared to move into another career, related to the world of sports or not.

Professional athletes do have other options, especially those who have graduated from a four-year college or university. Many go into some area of coaching, sports administration, management, or broadcasting. The professional athlete's unique insight and perspective can be a real asset in these careers. Other athletes simultaneously pursue other interests, some completely unrelated to their sport, such as education, business, social welfare, or the arts. Many continue to stay involved with the sport they have loved since childhood, coaching young children or volunteering with local school teams.

EARNINGS

Today, professional athletes who are members of top-level teams earn hundreds of thousands of dollars in prize money at professional competitions; the top players or athletes in each sport earn as much or more in endorsements and advertising, usually for sports-related products and services, but increasingly for products or services completely unrelated to their sport. Such salaries and other incomes are not representative of the whole field of professional athletes, but are only indicative of the fantastic revenues a few rare athletes with extraordinary talent can hope to earn. For example, SportsIllustrated.com reported that the following athletes were among the "Fortunate 50," the 50 highest earning athletes in the United States in 2010: LeBron James, Miami Heat (NBA), $45.8 million; Kobe Bryant, Los Angeles Lakers (NBA), $33 million; Alex Rodriguez, NY Yankees (MLB), $37 million; and Matthew Stafford, Detroit Lions (NFL), $27.7 million.

In 2009, athletes and sports competitors had median annual earnings of $40,210, according to the U.S. Department of Labor. Ten percent earned less than $16,020 while the highest paid 10 percent earned $166,400 or much more.

Perhaps the only caveat to the financial success of an elite athlete is the individual's character or personality. An athlete with a bad temper or prone to unsportsmanlike behavior may still be able to participate in team play, helping to win games and garner trophies, but he or she will not necessarily be able to cash in on the commercial endorsements. Advertisers are notoriously fickle about the spokespeople they choose to endorse products; some athletes have lost million-dollar accounts because of their bad behavior on and off the court.

WORK ENVIRONMENT

Athletes compete in many different conditions, according to the setting of the sport (indoors or outdoors) and the rules of the organizing or governing bodies. Athletes who participate in football or soccer, for example, often compete in hot, rainy, or freezing conditions, but at any point, organizing officials can call off the match, or postpone competition until better weather.

Indoor events are less subject to cancellation. However, since it is in the best interests of an organization not to risk the athletes' health, any condition that might adversely affect the outcome of a competition is usually reason to cancel or postpone it. The coach or team physician, on the other hand, may withdraw an athlete from a game if he or she is injured or ill. Nerves and fear are not good reasons to default on a competition, and part of ascending into the ranks of professional athletes means learning to cope with the anxiety that comes with competition. Some athletes, however, actually thrive on the nervous tension.

In order to reach the elite level of any sport, athletes must begin their careers early. Most professional athletes have been honing their skills since they were quite young. Athletes fit hours of practice time into an already full day; many famous players practiced on their own in the hours before school, as well as for several hours after school during team practice. Competitions are often far from the young athlete's home, which means they must travel on a bus or in a van with the team and coaching staff. Sometimes young athletes are placed in special training programs far from their homes and parents. They live with other athletes training for the same sport or on the same team and only see their parents for holidays and vacations. The separation from a child's parents and family can be difficult; often an athlete's family decides to move to be closer to the child's training facility.

The expenses of a sport can be overwhelming, as is the time an athlete must devote to practice and travel to and from competitions. Although most high school athletic programs pay for many expenses, if the athlete wants additional training or private coaching, the child's parents must come up with the extra money. Sometimes, young athletes can get official sponsors or they might qualify for an athletic scholarship from the training program. In addition to specialized equipment and clothing, the athlete must sometimes pay for a coach, travel expenses, competition fees and, depending on the sport,

time at the facility or gym where he or she practices. Gymnasts, for example, train for years as individuals, and then compete for positions on national or international teams. Up until the time they are accepted (and usually during their participation in the team), these gymnasts must pay for their expenses—from coach to travel to uniforms to room and board away from home.

Even with the years of hard work, practice, and financial sacrifice that most athletes and their families must endure, there is no guarantee that an athlete will achieve the rarest of the rare in the sports world—financial reward. An athlete needs to truly love the sport at which he or she excels, and also have a nearly insatiable ambition and work ethic.

OUTLOOK

Employment of athletes overall, as well as coaches, umpires, and related workers, will grow much faster than the average for all occupations through 2018, according to the Bureau of Labor Statistics. The outlook for professional athletes will vary depending on the sport, its popularity, and the number of positions open with professional teams. On the whole, the outlook for the field of professional sports is healthy, but the number of jobs will not increase dramatically and competition will be keen. Some sports, however, may experience a rise in popularity, which will translate into greater opportunities for higher salaries, prize monies, and commercial endorsements.

FOR MORE INFORMATION

For a free brochure and information on the Junior Olympics and other sports events and programs, contact

Amateur Athletic Union
PO Box 22409
Lake Buena Vista, FL 32830-2409
Tel: 407-934-7200
http://www.aausports.org

Individuals interested in pursuing a career in a professional team sport should speak to their coach and contact the professional organization for that sport to receive further information. For other ideas on how to pursue a career in a professional team sport, contact

American Alliance for Health, Physical Education, Recreation, and Dance
1900 Association Drive
Reston, VA 20191-1598
Tel: 800-213-7193
http://www.aahperd.org

PSYCHIATRISTS

OVERVIEW

Psychiatrists are physicians who attend to patients' mental, emotional, and behavioral symptoms. They try to help people function better in their daily lives. Psychiatrists generally specialize by treatment methods, based on their chosen fields. They may explore a patient's beliefs and history. They may prescribe medicine, including tranquilizers, antipsychotics, and antidepressants. If they specialize in treating children, they may use play therapy. There are 22,210 psychiatrists working in the United States.

THE JOB

Psychiatrists are medical doctors (M.D.s) who treat people suffering from mental and emotional illnesses that make it hard for them to cope with everyday living or to behave in socially acceptable ways. Psychiatrists treat problems ranging from being irritable and feeling frustrated to losing touch with reality. Some people, in addition to having a mental illness, may also engage in destructive behavior such as abusing alcohol or drugs or committing crimes. Others may have physical symptoms that spring from mental or emotional disorders. People with mental illness were once so misunderstood and stigmatized by society that they were kept, chained and shackled, in asylums. Today society recognizes that emotional or mental illnesses need to be diagnosed and treated just like any other medical problem.

Some psychiatrists run general practices, treating patients with a variety of mental disorders. Others may specialize in working with certain types of therapy or kinds of patients, such as the chronically ill. When meeting a client for the first time, psychiatrists conduct an evaluation of the client, which involves talking with the person about his or her current circumstances and getting a medical history. In some cases, the psychiatrist will give the client a physical examination or order laboratory tests if he or she feels the client's problem may have a physical cause. Next, the psychiatrist decides on a treatment plan for the client. This may involve medications, psychotherapy, or a combination of these approaches.

As medical doctors, psychiatrists can prescribe medications that affect a client's mood or behavior, such as tranquilizers or antidepressants. Scientific advancements in both the understanding of how the human

SCHOOL SUBJECTS
Biology, Psychology, Sociology

PERSONAL SKILLS
Helping/teaching, Technical/scientific

MINIMUM EDUCATION LEVEL
Medical degree

CERTIFICATION OR LICENSING
Required by all states

WORK ENVIRONMENT
Primarily indoors, Primarily one location

brain functions and the creation of more effective drugs with fewer side effects have helped make medications an important element in the treatment of mental illness. Some psychiatrists will only supervise the medication aspect of a client's treatment and refer the client to another health professional, such as a psychologist, for the psychotherapy aspect of treatment. These psychiatrists often work in private practices and focus on the chemical aspects of a person's illness to find medication to help that client. Other psychiatrists, often those working in hospitals or in small cities and towns, may be the providers of both medication management and psychotherapy.

Psychotherapy, sometimes called talk therapy, is perhaps the best-known type of treatment for mental illness. By having the client talk about problems he or she faces, the therapist helps the client uncover and understand the feelings and ideas that form the root of his or her problems and, thus, overcome emotional pain. Talk therapy can be used with individuals, groups, couples, or families.

Another therapeutic method that some psychiatrists use is behavior therapy or behavior modification therapy. This therapy focuses on changing a client's behavior and may involve teaching the client to use meditation and relaxation techniques as well as other treatment methods, such as biofeedback, a process in which electronic monitors are used to measure the effects that thoughts and feelings have on bodily functions like muscle tension, heart rate, or brain waves. This method allows the client to learn how to consciously control his or her body through stress reduction.

Free association is a technique in which the client is encouraged to relax and talk freely. The therapist's aim is to help the client uncover troubling subconscious beliefs or conflicts and their causes. Dreams may also be examined for hints about the subconscious mind. Subconscious conflicts are believed to cause neurosis, an emotional disorder in which the patient commonly exhibits anxious behavior.

In addition to those working in general psychiatry, there are psychiatrists who specialize in working with certain groups or in certain areas. These specialists include the following.

Child psychiatrists work with youth and usually their parents as well.

At the opposite end of the age scale are *geriatric psychiatrists,* who specialize in working with older individuals.

Industrial psychiatrists are employed by companies to deal with problems that affect employee performance, such as alcoholism or absenteeism.

Forensic psychiatrists work in the field of law. They evaluate defendants and testify on their mental states. They may help determine whether or not defendants understand the charges against them and if they can contribute to their own defense.

Other health professionals who may work with mentally ill people include *psychologists,* who may see clients but are unable to prescribe medications because they are not physicians, and *neurologists,* physicians specializing in problems of the nervous system. In some cases, a person's disturbed behavior results from disorders of the nervous system, and neurologists diagnose and treat these conditions.

REQUIREMENTS

High School

If working as a psychiatrist sounds interesting to you, you should start preparing yourself for college and medical school while you are still in high school. Do this by taking a college preparatory curriculum and concentrating on math and science classes. Biology, chemistry, and physics as well as algebra, geometry, and calculus will all be helpful. You can also start learning about human behavior by taking psychology, sociology, and history classes. In addition, take English classes to develop your communication skills—much of a psychiatrist's work involves speaking, listening, and record keeping.

Postsecondary Training

When you are deciding what college to attend, keep in mind that you'll want one with a strong science department, excellent laboratory facilities, and a strong humanities department. You may want to check *Medical School Admission Requirements*, a publication by the Association of American Medical Colleges (AAMC), to see what specific college classes you should take in preparation for medical school. Some colleges or universities offer a "pre-med" major; other possible majors include chemistry and biology. No matter what your major, though, you can count on taking biology, chemistry, organic chemistry, physics, and psychology classes. Medical schools look for well-rounded individuals, however, so be sure to take other classes in the humanities and social sciences. The AAMC reports that most people apply to medical school after their junior year of college. Most medical schools require the Medical College Admission Test as part of their application, so you should take this test your junior or even sophomore year.

In medical school, students must complete a four-year program of medical studies and supervised clinical work leading to their M.D. degrees. Students will once again concentrate on studying the sciences during their first two years; in addition, they will learn about taking a person's medical history and how to do an examination. The next two years are devoted to clinical work, which is when students first begin to see patients under supervision.

After receiving an M.D., physicians who plan to specialize in psychiatry must complete a residency. In the first year, they work in several specialties, such as internal medicine and pediatrics. Then they work for three years in a psychiatric hospital or a general hospital's psychiatric ward. Here they learn how to diagnose and treat various mental and emotional disorders or illnesses. Some psychiatrists continue their education beyond this four-year residency. To become a child psychiatrist, for example, a doctor must train for at least three years in general residency and two years in child psychiatry residency. Part of psychiatrists' training involves undergoing therapy themselves.

Certification or Licensing

All physicians must be licensed in order to practice medicine. After completing the M.D., graduates must pass a licensing test given by the board of medical examiners for the state in which they want to work. Following their residency, psychiatrists must take and pass a certifying exam given by the American Board of Psychiatry and Neurology. They then receive the designation of diplomate in psychiatry.

Other Requirements

To complete the required studies and training, students need outstanding mental ability and perseverance. Psychiatrists must be emotionally stable so they can deal with their patients objectively. Psychiatrists must be perceptive, able to listen well, and able to work well with others. They must also be dedicated to a lifetime of learning, as new therapeutic techniques and medications are constantly being developed.

EXPLORING

You can easily explore this job by reading as much as you can about the field and the work. To find out what professionals consider worthwhile resources, you may want to read the *Authoritative Guide to Self-Help Resources in Mental Health* by John Norcross and others (Guilford Publications, 2003), and *Leaving It at the Office: A Guide to Psychotherapist Self-Care,* by John Cross and James Guy Jr. (Guilford Press, 2007). To learn about different types of psychotherapies, you may want to read *Essential Psychotherapies: Theory and Practice*, edited by Alan Gurman and Stanley Messer (Guilford Press, 2005). Talk with your guidance counselor or psychology teacher about helping you arrange an informational interview with a local psychiatrist. If this is not possible, try to get an informational interview with any physician, such as your family doctor, to ask about the medical school experience.

An excellent way to explore this type of work is to do volunteer work in health care settings, such as hospitals, clinics, or nursing homes. While you may not be taking care of people with psychiatric problems, you will be interacting with patients and health care professionals. This experience will benefit you when it's time to apply to medical schools and will give you a feel for working with those who are ill.

As a college student, you may be able to find a summer job as a hospital orderly, nurse's aide, or ward clerk.

EMPLOYERS

Approximately half of practicing psychiatrists work in private practice; many others combine private practice with work in a health care institution. These institutions include private hospitals, state mental hospitals, medical schools, community health centers, and government health agencies. Psychiatrists may also work at correc-

tional facilities, for health maintenance organizations, or in nursing homes. They are employed throughout the country. The U.S. Department of Labor reports that 22,210 psychiatrists are employed in the United States.

STARTING OUT

Psychiatrists in residency can find job leads in professional journals and through professional organizations such as the American Psychiatric Association. Many are offered permanent positions with the same institution where they complete their residency.

ADVANCEMENT

Most psychiatrists advance in their careers by enlarging their knowledge and skills, clientele, and earnings. Those who work in hospitals, clinics, and mental health centers may become administrators. Those who teach or concentrate on research may become department heads.

EARNINGS

Psychiatrists' earnings are determined by the kind of practice they have and its location, their experience, and the number of patients they treat. Like other physicians, their average income is among the highest of any occupation.

The median salary for a general psychiatrist in 2009 was around $160,230, according to the U.S. Department of Labor. Salaries ranged from $65,590 to $166,400 or more. The top-paying industries, and median salaries, for psychiatrists in 2009 were nursing care facilities ($199,910); outpatient care centers ($190,340); state government ($189,450); management of companies and enterprises ($181,490); and local government ($179,920). In January 2011, Salary.com reported that the median annual salary for psychiatrists was $191,442; the lowest paid 10 percent earned $152,118 or less, and the highest paid 10 percent earned $226,440 or more per year.

WORK ENVIRONMENT

Psychiatrists in private practice set their own schedules and usually work regular hours. They may work some evenings or weekends to see patients who cannot take time off during business hours. Most psychiatrists, however, put in long workdays, averaging 52 hours a week, according to American Medical Association statistics. Like other physicians, psychiatrists are always on call.

Psychiatrists in private practice typically work in comfortable office settings. Some private psychiatrists also work as hospital staff members, consultants, lecturers, or teachers.

Salaried psychiatrists work in private hospitals, state hospitals, and community mental health centers. They also work for government agencies, such as the U.S. Department of Health and Human Services, the Department of Defense, and the Department of Veterans Affairs. Psychiatrists who work in public facilities often bear heavy workloads. Changes in treatment have reduced the number of patients in hospitals and have increased the number of patients in community health centers.

OUTLOOK

The U.S. Department of Labor predicts employment for all physicians to grow much faster than the average career through 2018. Opportunities for psychiatrists in private practice and salaried positions are good. Demand is great for child psychiatrists, and other specialties are also in short supply, especially in rural areas and public facilities.

A number of factors contribute to this shortage. Growing population and increasing life span add up to more people who need psychiatric care; rising incomes enable more people to afford treatment; and higher educational levels make more people aware of the importance of mental health care. Medical insurance, although it usually limits the amount of mental health care, may provide some coverage, although the amount of benefits being paid out has been reduced over years.

Psychiatrists are also needed as researchers to explore the causes of mental illness and develop new ways to treat it.

FOR MORE INFORMATION

For information on board certification, contact
American Board of Psychiatry and Neurology Inc.
2150 East Lake Cook Road, Suite 900
Buffalo Grove, IL 60089-1875
Tel: 847-229-6500
http://www.abpn.com

For more information on becoming a doctor as well as current health care news, visit the AMA Web site.
American Medical Association (AMA)
515 North State Street
Chicago, IL 60654-4854
Tel: 800-621-8335
http://www.ama-assn.org

For comprehensive information on careers in psychiatry, contact
American Psychiatric Association
1000 Wilson Boulevard, Suite 1825
Arlington, VA 22209-3901

Tel: 703-907-7300
E-mail: apa@psych.org
http://www.psych.org

To learn more about careers in medicine and how to apply to medical schools, visit the following Web site:
Association of American Medical Colleges
2450 N Street, NW
Washington, DC 20037-1126
Tel: 202-828-0400
http://www.aamc.org

For information on mental health issues, contact
National Institute of Mental Health
Science Writing, Press, and Dissemination Branch
6001 Executive Boulevard, Room 8184, MSC 9663
Bethesda, MD 20892-9663
Tel: 866-615-6464
E-mail: nimhinfo@nih.gov
http://www.nimh.nih.gov

For information on mental health, and to read the newsletter The Bell, *which contains current information about the field, visit the NMHA's Web site.*
National Mental Health Association (NMHA)
2000 North Beauregard Street, 6th Floor
Alexandria, VA 22311-1748
Tel: 800-969-6642
http://www.nmha.org

For information on education, advocacy, and certification for Canadian psychiatrists, contact
Canadian Psychiatric Association
141 Laurier Avenue West, Suite 701
Ottawa, ON K1P 5J3 Canada
Tel: 613-234-2815
E-mail: cpa@cpa-apc.org
http://www.cpa-apc.org

PUBLIC RELATIONS SPECIALISTS

OVERVIEW

Public relations (PR) specialists develop and maintain programs that present a favorable public image for an individual or organization. They provide information to the target audience (generally, the public at large) about the client, its goals and accomplishments, and any further plans or projects that may be of public interest.

PR specialists may be employed by corporations, government agencies, nonprofit organizations, or almost any type of organization. Many PR specialists hold positions in public relations consulting firms or work for advertising agencies. There are approximately 242,670 public relations specialists in the United States.

THE JOB

Public relations specialists are employed to do a variety of tasks. They may be employed primarily as writers, creating reports, news releases, and booklet texts. Others write speeches or create copy for radio, TV, or film sequences. These workers often spend much of their time contacting the press, radio, and TV as well as magazines on behalf of the employer. They also use social media, such as Facebook and Twitter, to convey their client's message to target audiences and the general public. Some PR specialists work more as editors than writers, fact-checking and rewriting employee publications, newsletters, shareholder reports, and other management communications.

Specialists may choose to concentrate in graphic design, using their background knowledge of art and layout for developing brochures, booklets, and photographic communications. Other PR workers handle special events, such as press parties, convention exhibits, open houses, or anniversary celebrations.

SCHOOL SUBJECTS
Business, English, Journalism

PERSONAL SKILLS
Communication/ideas, Leadership/management

MINIMUM EDUCATION LEVEL
Bachelor's degree

CERTIFICATION OR LICENSING
Voluntary

WORK ENVIRONMENT
Primarily indoors, One location with some travel

PR specialists must be alert to any and all company or institutional events that are newsworthy. They prepare news releases and direct them toward the proper media. Specialists working for manufacturers and retailers are concerned with efforts that will promote sales and create goodwill for the firm's products. They work closely with the marketing and sales departments in announcing new products, preparing displays, and attending occasional dealers' conventions.

A large firm may have a director of public relations who is a vice president of the company and in charge of a staff that includes writers, artists, researchers, and other specialists. Publicity for an individual or a small organization may involve many of the same areas of expertise but may be carried out by a few people or possibly even one person.

Many PR workers act as consultants (rather than staff) of a corporation, association, college, hospital, or other institution. These workers have the advantage of being able to operate independently, state opinions objectively, and work with more than one type of business or association.

PR specialists are called upon to work with the public opinion aspects of almost every corporate or institutional problem. These can range from the opening of a new manufacturing plant to a college's dormitory dedication to a merger or sale of a company.

Public relations professionals may specialize. *Lobbyists* try to persuade legislators and other office holders to pass laws favoring the interests of the firms or people they represent. Fund-raising directors develop and direct programs designed to raise funds for social welfare agencies and other nonprofit organizations.

Early in their careers, public relations specialists become accustomed to having others receive credit for their behind-the-scenes work. The speeches they draft will be delivered by company officers, the magazine articles they prepare may be credited to the president of the company, and they may be consulted to prepare the message to stockholders from the chairman of the board that appears in the annual report.

REQUIREMENTS

High School

While in high school, take courses in English, journalism, public speaking, humanities, and languages because public relations is based on effective communication with others. Courses such as these will develop your skills in written and oral communication as well as provide a better understanding of different fields and industries to be publicized.

Postsecondary Training

Most people employed in public relations service have a college degree. Major fields of study most beneficial to developing the proper skills are public relations, English, and journalism. Some employers feel that majoring in the area in which the public relations person will eventually work is the best training. Knowledge of business administration is most helpful as is innate talent for selling. A graduate degree may be required for managerial positions. People with a bachelor's degree in public relations can find staff positions with either an organization or a public relations firm.

Many colleges and graduate schools offer degree programs or special courses in public relations. In addition, many other colleges offer at least courses in the field. Public relations programs are sometimes administered by the journalism or communication departments of schools. In addition to courses in theory and techniques of public relations, interested individuals may study organization, management and administration, and practical applications and often specialize in areas such as business, government, and nonprofit organizations. Other preparation includes courses in creative writing, psychology, communications, advertising, and journalism.

Certification or Licensing

The Public Relations Society of America and the International Association of Business Communicators accredit public relations workers who meet educational and work experience requirements and pass a comprehensive examination. Such accreditation is a sign of competence in this field, although it is not a requirement for employment.

Other Requirements

Today's public relations specialist must be a businessperson first, both to understand how to perform successfully in business and to comprehend the needs and goals of the organization or client. Additionally, the public relations specialist needs to be a strong writer and speaker, with good interpersonal, leadership, and organizational skills.

EXPLORING

Almost any experience in working with other people will help you to develop strong interpersonal skills, which are crucial in public relations. The possibilities are almost endless. Summer work on a newspaper or trade paper or with a radio or television station may give insight into communications media. Working as a volunteer on a political campaign can help you to understand the ways in which people can be persuaded. Being selected as a page for the U.S. Congress or a state legislature will help you grasp the fundamentals of government processes. A job in retail will help you to understand some of the principles of product presentation. A teaching job will develop your organization and presentation skills. These are just some of the jobs that will let you explore areas of public relations.

EMPLOYERS

Public relations specialists hold about 242,670 jobs. Workers may be paid employees of the organization they represent or they may be part of a public relations firm that works for organizations on a contract basis. Others are involved in fund-raising or political campaigning. Public relations may be done for a corporation, retail business, service company, utility, association, nonprofit organization, or educational institution.

Most PR firms are located in large cities that are centers of communications. New York, Chicago, San Francisco, Los Angeles, and Washington, D.C., are good places to start a search for a public relations job. Nevertheless, there are many good opportunities in cities across the United States.

STARTING OUT

There is no clear-cut formula for getting a job in public relations. Individuals often enter the field after gaining preliminary experience in another occupation closely allied to the field, usually some segment of communications, and frequently, in journalism. Coming into public relations from newspaper work is still a recommended route. Another good method is to gain initial employment as a public relations trainee or intern, or as a clerk, secretary, or research assistant in a public relations department or a counseling firm.

ADVANCEMENT

In some large companies, an entry-level public relations specialist may start as a trainee in a formal training program for new employees. In others, new employees may expect to be assigned to work that has a minimum of responsibility. They may assemble clippings or do rewrites on material that has already been accepted.

They may make posters or assist in conducting polls or surveys, or compile reports from data submitted by others.

As workers acquire experience, they are typically given more responsibility. They write news releases, direct polls or surveys, or advance to writing speeches for company officials. Progress may seem to be slow, because some skills take a long time to master.

Some advance in responsibility and salary in the same firm in which they started. Others find that the path to advancement is to accept a more rewarding position in another firm.

The goal of many public relations specialists is to open an independent office or to join an established consulting firm. To start an independent office requires a large outlay of capital and an established reputation in the field. However, those who are successful in operating their own consulting firms probably attain the greatest financial success in the public relations field.

EARNINGS

Public relations specialists had median annual earnings of $51,960 in 2009, according to the U.S. Department of Labor. Salaries ranged from less than $30,520 to more than $96,630. The department reports the following 2009 median salaries for public relations specialists by type of employer: advertising, public relations, and related services, $69,930; business, professional, labor, political, and similar organizations, $62,040; colleges, universities, and professional schools, $52,540; management of companies and enterprises, $62,040; and local government, $54,720.

Many PR workers receive a range of fringe benefits from corporations and agencies employing them, including bonus/incentive compensation, stock options, profit sharing/pension plans/401(k) programs, medical benefits, life insurance, financial planning, maternity/paternity leave, paid vacations, and family college tuition. Bonuses can range from 5 to 100 percent of base compensation and often are based on individual and/or company performance.

WORK ENVIRONMENT

Public relations specialists generally work in offices with adequate administrative support, regular salary increases, and expense accounts. They are expected to make a good appearance in tasteful, conservative clothing. They must have social poise, and their conduct in their personal life is important to their firms or their cli-

ents. The public relations specialist may have to entertain business associates.

The PR specialist seldom works conventional office hours for many weeks at a time; although the workweek may consist of 35 to 40 hours, these hours may be supplemented by evenings and even weekends when meetings must be attended and other special events covered. Time behind the desk may represent only a small part of the total working schedule. Travel is often an important and necessary part of the job.

The life of the PR worker is so greatly determined by the job that many consider this a disadvantage. Because the work is concerned with public opinion, it is often difficult to measure the results of performance and to sell the worth of a public relations program to an employer or client. Competition in the consulting field is keen, and if a firm loses an account, some of its personnel may be affected. The demands it makes for anonymity will be considered by some as one of the profession's less inviting aspects. Public relations involves much more hard work and a great deal less glamour than is popularly supposed.

OUTLOOK

Employment of public relations professionals is expected to grow much faster than the average for all other occupations through 2018, according to the U.S. Department of Labor. Competition will be keen for beginning jobs in public relations because so many job seekers are enticed by the perceived glamour and appeal of the field; those with both education and experience will have an advantage.

Most large companies have some sort of public relations resource, either through their own staff or through the use of a firm of consultants. Most are expected to expand their public relations activities, creating many new jobs. Smaller companies are increasingly hiring public relations specialists, adding to the demand for these workers. Additionally, when corporate scandals surface, public relations specialists will be hired to help improve the images of companies and regain the trust of the public.

FOR MORE INFORMATION

For information on accreditation, contact
International Association of Business Communicators
601 Montgomery Street, Suite 1900
San Francisco, CA 94111-2623
Tel: 415-544-4700
http://www.iabc.com

For statistics, salary surveys, and information on accreditation and student membership, contact

Public Relations Society of America

33 Maiden Lane, 11th Floor

New York, NY 10038-5150

Tel: 212-460-1400

E-mail: membership@prsa.org (student membership)

http://www.prsa.org

This professional association for public relations professionals offers an accreditation program and opportunities for professional development.

Canadian Public Relations Society Inc.

4195 Dundas Street West, Suite 346

Toronto, ON M8X 1Y4 Canada

Tel: 416-239-7034

E-mail: admin@cprs.ca

http://www.cprs.ca

☐ RADIOLOGIC TECHNOLOGISTS

OVERVIEW

Radiologic technologists operate equipment that creates images of a patient's body tissues, organs, and bones for the purpose of medical diagnoses and therapies. These images allow physicians to know the exact nature of a patient's injury or disease, such as the location of a broken bone or the confirmation of an ulcer.

Before an X-ray examination, radiologic technologists may administer drugs or chemical mixtures to the patient to better highlight internal organs. They place the patient in the correct position between the X-ray source and film and protect body areas that are not to be exposed to radiation. After determining the proper duration and intensity of the exposure, they operate the controls to beam X-rays through the patient and expose the photographic film.

They may operate computer-aided imaging equipment that does not involve X-rays and may help to treat diseased or affected areas of the body by exposing the patient to specified concentrations of radiation for prescribed times. Radiologic technologists hold about 213,560 jobs in the United States.

SCHOOL SUBJECTS
Biology, Mathematics

PERSONAL SKILLS
Helping/teaching, Technical/scientific

MINIMUM EDUCATION LEVEL
Some postsecondary training

CERTIFICATION OR LICENSING
Voluntary (certification),
Required by certain states (licensing)

WORK ENVIRONMENT
Primarily indoors, Primarily one location

THE JOB

All radiological work is done at the request of and under the supervision of a physician. Just as a prescription is required for certain drugs to be dispensed or administered, so must a physician's request be issued before a patient can receive any kind of imaging procedure.

There are four primary disciplines in which radiologic technologists may work: radiography (taking X-ray pictures or radiographs), nuclear medicine, radiation therapy, and sonography. In each of these medical imaging methods, the technologist works under the direction of a physician who specializes in interpreting the pictures produced by X-rays, other imaging techniques, or radiation therapy. Technologists can work in more than one of these areas. Some technologists specialize in working with a particular part of the body or a specific condition.

X-ray pictures, or radiographs, are the most familiar use of radiologic technology. They are used to diagnose and determine treatment for a wide variety of afflictions, including ulcers, tumors, and bone fractures. Chest X-ray pictures can determine whether a person has a lung disease. Radiologic technologists who operate X-ray equipment first help the patient prepare for the radiologic examination. After explaining the procedure, they may administer a substance that makes the part of the body being imaged more clearly visible on the film. They make sure that the patient is not wearing jewelry or other metal that would obstruct the X-rays. They position the person sitting, standing, or lying down so that the correct view of the body can be radiographed, and then they cover adjacent areas with lead shielding to prevent unnecessary exposure to radiation.

The technologist positions the X-ray equipment at the proper angle and distance from the part to be radiographed and determines exposure time based on the location of the particular organ or bone and thickness of the body in that area. The controls of the X-ray machine are set to produce pictures of the correct density, contrast, and detail. Placing the photographic film closest to the body part being x-rayed, the technologist takes the requested images, repositioning the patient as needed. Typically, there are standards regarding the number of views to be taken of a given body part. The film is then developed for the radiologist or other physician to interpret.

In a fluoroscopic examination (a more complex imaging procedure that examines the gastrointestinal area), a beam of X-rays passes through the body and onto a fluorescent screen, enabling the physician to see the internal organs in motion. For these, the technologist first prepares a solution of barium sulfate to be administered to the patient, either rectally or orally, depending on the exam. The barium sulfate increases the contrast between the digestive tract and surrounding organs, making the image clearer. The technologist follows the physician's guidance in positioning the patient, monitors the machine's controls, and takes any follow-up radiographs as needed.

Radiologic technologists may learn other imaging procedures such as computed tomography (CT) scanning, which uses X-rays to get detailed cross-sectional images of the body's internal structures, and MRI, which uses radio waves, powerful magnets, and computers to obtain images of body parts. These diagnostic procedures are becoming more common and usually require radiologic technologists to undergo additional on-the-job training.

Other specialties within the radiography discipline include mammography and cardiovascular interventional technology. In addition, some technologists may focus on radiography of joints and bones, or they may be involved in such areas as angiocardiography (visualization of the heart and large blood vessels) or neuroradiology (the use of radiation to diagnose diseases of the nervous system).

Radiologic technologists perform a wide range of duties, from greeting patients and putting them at ease by explaining the procedures to developing the finished film. Their administrative tasks include maintaining patients' records, recording equipment usage and maintenance, organizing work schedules, and managing a radiologist's private practice or hospital's radiology department. Some radiologic technologists teach in programs to educate other technologists.

REQUIREMENTS

High School

If this career interests you, take plenty of math and science classes in high school. Biology, chemistry, and physics classes will be particularly useful to you. Take computer classes to become comfortable working with this technology. English classes will help you improve your communication skills. You will need these skills both when interacting with the patients and when working as part of a health care team. Finally, consider taking photography classes. Photography classes will give you experience with choosing film, framing an image, and developing photographs.

Postsecondary Training

After high school, you will need to complete an education program in radiography. Programs range in length from one to four years. Depending on length, the programs award a certificate, associate's degree, or bachelor's degree. Two-year associate's degree programs are the most popular option.

Educational programs are available in hospitals, medical centers, colleges and universities, and vocational and technical institutes. It is also possible to get radiologic technology training in the armed forces.

In 2009, the Joint Review on Education in Radiologic Technology accredited 213 certificate programs, 397 associate degree programs, and 35 bachelor's degree programs. To enter an accredited program, you must be a high school graduate; some programs require one or two years of higher education. Courses in radiologic technology education programs include anatomy, physiology, patient care, physics, radiation protection, medical ethics, principles of imaging, medical terminology, radiobiology, and pathology. For some supervisory or administrative jobs in this field, a bachelor's or master's degree may be required.

Certification or Licensing

Radiologic technologists can become certified through the American Registry of Radiologic Technologists (ARRT) after graduating from an accredited program in radiography, radiation therapy, or nuclear medicine.

After becoming certified, many technologists choose to register with the ARRT. Registration is an annual procedure required to maintain the certification. Registered technologists meet the following three criteria: They agree to comply with the ARRT rules and regulations, comply with the ARRT standards of ethics, and meet continuing education requirements every two years. Only technologists who are currently registered can designate themselves as ARRT Registered Technologists and use the initials RT after their names. Although registration and certification are voluntary, many jobs are open only to technologists who have acquired these credentials.

In addition to being registered in the various imaging disciplines, radiologic technologists can receive advanced qualifications in each of the four radiography specializations: mammography, CT, MRI, and cardiovascular interventional technology. As the work of radiologic technologists grows increasingly complex and employment opportunities become more competitive, the desirability of registration and certification will also grow.

Most states require practicing radiologic technologists to be licensed. You will need to check with the state in which you hope to work about specific requirements there.

Other Requirements

Radiologic technologists should be responsible individuals with a mature and caring nature. They should be personable and enjoy interacting with all types of people, including those who are very ill. A compassionate attitude is essential to deal with patients who may be frightened or in pain.

EXPLORING

There is no way to gain direct experience in this profession without the appropriate qualifications. However, it is possible to learn about the duties of radiologic technologists by talking with them and observing the facilities and equipment they use. It is also possible to have interviews with teachers of radiologic technology. Ask your guidance counselor or a science teacher to help you contact local hospitals or schools with radiography programs to locate technologists who are willing to talk to an interested student.

As with any career in health care, volunteering at a local hospital, clinic, or nursing home provides an excellent opportunity for you to explore your interest in the field. Most hospitals are eager for volunteers, and working in such a setting will give you a chance to see health care professionals in action as well as to have some patient contact.

EMPLOYERS

There are approximately 213,560 radiologic technologists working in the United States. According to the U.S. Department of Labor, about 61 percent of these technologists work in hospitals. Radiologic technologists also find employment in doctors' offices and clinics, at X-ray labs, and in nursing homes and outpatient care facilities.

STARTING OUT

With more states regulating the practice of radiologic technology, certification by the appropriate accreditation body for a given specialty is quickly becoming a necessity for employment. If you get your training from a school that lacks accreditation or if you learn on the job, you may have difficulty in qualifying for many positions, especially those with a wide range of assignments. If you are enrolled in a hospital educational program, you may be able to get a job with the hospital upon completion of the program. If you are in a degree program, get help in finding a job through your school's career services office.

ADVANCEMENT

Many radiologic technologists are employed in hospitals where there are opportunities for advancement to administrative and supervisory positions such as chief technologist or technical administrator. Other technologists develop special clinical skills in advanced imaging procedures, such as CT scanning or MRI. Some radiologic technologists qualify as instructors. Radiologic technologists who hold bachelor's degrees have more opportunities for advancement. The technologist who wishes to become a teacher or administrator will find that a master's degree and considerable experience are necessary.

EARNINGS

Salaries for radiologic technologists compare favorably with those of similar health care professionals. According to the U.S. Department of Labor, median annual earnings of radiologic technologists and technicians were $53,240 in 2009. The lowest paid 10 percent, which typically includes those just starting out in the field, earned less than $35,700. The highest paid 10 percent, which typically includes those with considerable experience, earned more than $75,440.

Median annual earnings of radiologic technologists and technicians who worked in medical and diagnostic laboratories were $57,250 in 2009. Those who worked in hospitals earned a median of $54,770, and those who worked in offices of medical doctors earned $50,860.

Most technologists take part in their employers' vacation and sick leave provisions. In addition, most employers offer benefits such as health insurance and pensions.

WORK ENVIRONMENT

Full-time technologists generally work eight hours a day, 40 hours a week. In addition, they may be on call for some night emergency duty or weekend hours, which pays in equal time off or additional compensation.

In diagnostic radiologic work, technologists perform most of their tasks while on their feet. They move around a lot and often are called upon to lift patients who need help in moving.

Great care is exercised to protect technologists from radiation exposure. Each technologist wears a badge that measures radiation exposure, and records are kept of total exposure accumulated over time. Other routine precautions include the use of safety devices (such as lead aprons, lead gloves, and other shielding) and the use of disposable gowns, gloves, and masks. Careful attention to safety procedures has greatly reduced or eliminated radiation hazards for the technologist.

Radiologic technology is dedicated to conserving life and health. Technologists derive satisfaction from their work, which helps promote health and alleviate human suffering. Those who specialize in radiation therapy need to be able to handle the close relationships they inevitably develop while working with very sick or dying people over a period of time.

OUTLOOK

Overall, employment for radiologic technologists is expected to grow faster than the average through 2018, according to the U.S. Department of Labor. A major reason for this growth is the increasing elderly population in the United States, which will create a need for radiologic technologists' services. The demand for qualified technologists in some areas of the country far exceeds the supply. This shortage is particularly acute in rural areas and small towns. Those who are willing to relocate to these areas may have increased job prospects. Radiologic technologists who are trained to do more than one type of imaging procedure will also

find that they have increased job opportunities. Those specializing in CT and MR should have better odds of securing work as these are being increasingly used as diagnostic tools.

In the years to come, increasing numbers of radiologic technologists will be employed in settings outside of hospitals, such as physicians' offices, clinics, health maintenance organizations, laboratories, government agencies, and diagnostic imaging centers. This pattern will be part of the overall trend toward lowering health care costs by delivering more care outside of hospitals. Nevertheless, hospitals will remain the major employers of radiologic technologists for the near future. Because of the increasing importance of radiologic technology in the diagnosis and treatment of disease, it is unlikely that hospitals will do fewer radiologic procedures than in the past. Instead, they try to do more on an outpatient basis and on weekends and evenings. This should increase the demand for part-time technologists and thus open more opportunities for flexible work schedules.

FOR MORE INFORMATION

For information on certification and educational programs, contact
American Registry of Radiologic Technologists
1255 Northland Drive
St. Paul, MN 55120-1155
Tel: 651-687-0048
http://www.arrt.org

For information about the field, a catalog of educational products, and to access their job bank, contact
American Society of Radiologic Technologists
15000 Central Avenue, SE
Albuquerque, NM 87123-3909
Tel: 800-444-2778
E-mail: memberservices@asrt.org
https://www.asrt.org

For information about classes, conferences, and other resources, contact
Society of Diagnostic Medical Sonography
2745 Dallas Parkway, Suite 350
Plano, TX 75093-8730
Tel: 800-229-9506
http://www.sdms.org

For career and education information, contact
Canadian Association of Medical Radiation Technologists
1000-85 Albert Street

Ottawa, ON K1P 6A4 Canada
Tel: 613-234-0012
http://www.camrt.ca

REFUSE COLLECTORS

OVERVIEW

Refuse collectors gather garbage and other discarded materials set out by customers along designated routes in urban and rural communities and transport the materials to sanitary landfills or incinerator plants for disposal. Refuse collectors may specialize in collecting certain types of material, such as recyclable glass, newsprint, or aluminum. There are approximately 128,940 refuse and recyclable materials collectors working in the United States.

THE JOB

In general, refuse collection teams of two or three workers drive along established routes and empty household trash containers into garbage trucks. The refuse, which is often mechanically compacted in the truck, is taken to a landfill or other appropriate disposal facility.

Refuse workers may collect all kinds of solid wastes, including food scraps, paper products, and plastics. Depending on local requirements, the refuse may be loose in containers, in packaging such as plastic bags, in preapproved containers that indicate recyclable materials, or, for newspapers and magazines, tied in bundles. When the truck is full, the workers drive with the load to the disposal site and empty the truck. Workers may also pick up cast-off furniture, old appliances, or other large, bulky items, although usually such items are collected only on certain days.

An average day for refuse collectors often begins before dawn with an inspection of the truck that includes checking lights, tires, testing air and oil pressure gauges, and making sure a spill kit is on board. Refuse collectors who work on commercial routes or pickup dumpsters stay in contact with dispatchers via radio or cellular phone to learn where they are needed to pick up. Refuse collectors gas up their trucks as needed and recheck the truck's vital equipment at the end of the day.

SCHOOL SUBJECTS
Physical education, Technical/shop

PERSONAL SKILLS
Following instructions, Mechanical/manipulative

MINIMUM EDUCATION LEVEL
High school diploma

CERTIFICATION OR LICENSING
Required for certain positions

WORK ENVIRONMENT
Primarily outdoors, One location with some travel

As they move along their routes, refuse collectors are constantly getting on and off the truck to lift trash containers onto the truck. The containers are often heavy. Sometimes the different work duties are divided among the workers, with the driver doing only the driving all day long. In other cases, the workers alternate between driving and loading and unloading throughout the day.

Some employers send refuse collectors on routes alone, and they are responsible for driving the truck and loading the refuse. Usually, however, refuse collectors working alone have special routes, such as driving a truck that can lift and empty dumpsters. The refuse collector operates the levers and buttons that lift and dump the dumpster's contents into the truck. This kind of system is particularly useful for apartment buildings, construction sites, and other locations that need containers so large they are too heavy to empty by hand. The use of mechanical hoists on trucks makes refuse pickup much faster and more efficient.

Some trucks are built with multiple bins, so that recyclable items that customers have set out separately, such as aluminum or newspaper, can be kept separate in the truck and later taken to buyers. In some communities, the pickup days and the company responsible for disposal are different for recyclable materials than for other mixed general refuse.

Garbage-collection supervisors direct and coordinate the tasks of the various workers involved in the collecting and transporting of refuse. They make work assignments and monitor and evaluate job performance.

REQUIREMENTS

High School

Employers prefer applicants who are high school graduates. Workers who hope to advance to a supervisory position ought to have at least a high school diploma. High school classes that may be helpful include any shop classes that provide hands-on learning opportunities and physical education classes that teach you how to develop strength and endurance. A good understanding of basic math and English is also necessary to read instructions and operate equipment for the job.

Postsecondary Training

Generally, employers will hire people without work experience or specific training. Most employers, however, do require workers to be at least 18 years old and physically able to perform the work. Workers who drive industrial trucks or other dangerous equipment or handle toxic chemicals receive specialized training in safety awareness and procedures.

Refuse workers need to be physically fit and able to lift heavy objects. Sometimes a health examination is required for employment. Employers look for workers who are reliable and hardworking.

Experience in driving a truck and in loading and unloading heavy material is helpful. Many refuse workers, especially those in metropolitan areas, are members of a union such as the International Brotherhood of Teamsters. Those who work for private firms might not be unionized.

Certification or Licensing

Workers who drive collection trucks need a commercial driver's license (CDL). In some areas, where the workers alternate jobs, a CDL is required even of those who are generally loaders. A clean driving record is often a necessity. Refuse collectors may have to pass a civil service test in order to work for a city or town. Seventeen states and six cities require crane operators to be licensed. Licensing requirements vary by state.

EXPLORING

If you are thinking about getting into this kind of work, you may find it helpful to talk with experienced workers in similar jobs. In some areas, there may be opportunities for summer or part-time work, although workers in these positions generally have to meet the same requirements as full-time employees. Contact local recycling centers to check on availability of volunteer or part-time work. A job as a furniture mover or truck driver is another way to learn about some of the responsibilities of refuse collectors. Any experience you can gain in a related job that requires physical strength and reliability is useful to test your work endurance. Experience as a material handler, equipment cleaner, helper, or laborer would be useful.

EMPLOYERS

In the past, refuse collectors were employed almost exclusively by municipalities. Today, refuse collectors may work for private waste haulers that contract with local governments or even specialized firms, such as recycling haulers. Some local governments still operate their own waste-hauling programs, and in these communities, refuse collectors are city employees. But many have found it more cost-effective to contract with private waste haulers who employ their own refuse collectors. Similar jobs may be found at landfills, where workers are needed to assist drivers in dumping collected refuse, or at material recovery facilities (MRFs), where recyclables are taken. MRFs need workers to separate materials, load and unload trucks, and operate equipment such as balers that condense the recyclables into large, dense bales.

STARTING OUT

To apply for refuse collector jobs, contact your local city government's personnel department or department of sanitation. Employees in these offices may be able to supply information on job openings and local requirements. If you are interested in working for a private disposal firm, contact the firm directly. You can find listings for specific job opportunities through the state employment service, employment Web sites, or newspaper classified ads. Contacting a waste disposal union's local branch and becoming a member may help you land a job when one becomes available in your area.

ADVANCEMENT

Opportunities for advancement are usually limited for refuse collectors. Those who work for municipal governments may be able to transfer to better-paying jobs in another department of city government, such as public works. Sometimes advancement means becoming the driver of a refuse truck, rather than a worker who loads and unloads the truck. In larger organizations, refuse collectors who prove to be reliable employees may be promoted to supervisory positions, where they coordinate and direct the activities of other workers. Others may develop knowledge of recyclables, for example, and help coordinate a waste hauler's recycling business.

EARNINGS

Earnings of refuse collectors vary widely depending on their employer, union status, and other factors. Beginning refuse collectors who work for small, private firms and are not union members are sometimes paid at hourly wages not far above the federal minimum wage. Median annual earnings of refuse and recyclable materials collectors in 2009 were $32,070 a year for full-time work, according to the U.S. Bureau of Labor Statistics. Salaries range from less than $18,580 to more than $52,190. In general, workers employed by large cities under union contracts make more money, and those working for small companies without union contracts make less.

Refuse collectors get overtime pay for working extra hours, during the evenings, or on weekends. They may receive paid time during each shift to shower and change clothes. Union workers receive benefits such as health insurance and paid sick leave and vacation days. Most full-time workers with private companies also receive benefits, although they may not receive as desirable a benefits package.

WORK ENVIRONMENT

Refuse workers must work outdoors in all kinds of weather, including cold, snow, rain, and heat, and they must handle dirty, smelly objects. The work is active and often strenuous, requiring the lifting of heavy refuse containers, hopping on and off the truck constantly, and operating hoists and other equipment. Workers often encounter garbage that is not packed correctly. Because there is a danger of infection from raw garbage, they must wear protective gloves and are sometimes provided with uniforms. Workers must always be aware of the dangers of working around traffic and mechanical compactors. Most workers wear heavy steel-toe boots to help avoid foot injuries from accidentally dropping containers or large objects. New employees receive instruction on safety precautions they will need to take as well as instructions about their responsibilities.

Most refuse collectors work during weekday daylight hours, with regular shifts totaling 35 to 40 hours per week. Many workers put in slightly longer hours. Many workers begin their shifts in the predawn hours, while other workers routinely work in the evenings. In emergencies (for removal of storm-downed tree branches, for instance), weekend hours may be necessary. Workers who drive the trucks must have a CDL, and federal law prohibits CDL drivers from working more than 60 hours per week.

OUTLOOK

There are about 128,940 refuse and recyclable materials collectors employed in the United States. The government predicts employment for material movers of all sorts, including refuse collectors, will show little or no change through 2018. However, job turnover is high in this field. Every year, many positions will become available as workers transfer to other jobs or leave the workforce.

Opportunities will be best in heavily populated regions in and near big cities, where the most waste is generated. In cities, increasing use of mechanized equipment for lifting and emptying large refuse containers may decrease the need for these workers. However, as communities encourage more recycling and more resource recovery technologies, job availability may change somewhat for refuse collectors. More varied pickup services may tend to require more workers, expanding the employment opportunities in both the public and private sector.

A trend that favors use of large, nationally based waste management corporations is eliminating smaller competitors in some areas. This suggests that job security may depend on the size of the employer. As recycling becomes more lucrative, large companies may concentrate on this aspect of waste disposal.

FOR MORE INFORMATION

The Environmental Industry Associations is an umbrella organization that includes organizations of interest to the solid waste management industry. It publishes two magazines that follow trends and news of the waste industry, Waste Age *and* Recycling Times.

Environmental Industry Associations
4301 Connecticut Avenue, NW, Suite 300
Washington, DC 20008-2304
Tel: 800-424-4700
http://www.environmentalistseveryday.org/
    membership-solid-waste-industry-associations/
    about-eia-solid-waste-management

The following is a national union whose members include refuse collectors:

International Brotherhood of Teamsters
25 Louisiana Avenue, NW
Washington, DC 20001-2130
Tel: 202-624-6800
http://www.teamster.org

For information on industry news, publications, and membership, contact
National Solid Wastes Management Association
4301 Connecticut Avenue, NW, Suite 300
Washington, DC 20008-2304
Tel: 800-424-4700
http://www.environmentalistseveryday.org/about-nswma-solid-waste-management

REGISTERED NURSES

SCHOOL SUBJECTS
Biology, Chemistry, Health

PERSONAL SKILLS
Helping/teaching, Technical/scientific

MINIMUM EDUCATION LEVEL
Some postsecondary training

CERTIFICATION OR LICENSING
Licensing required in all states

WORK ENVIRONMENT
Primarily indoors, Primarily multiple locations

OVERVIEW

Registered nurses (RNs) help individuals, families, and groups to improve and maintain health and to prevent disease. They care for the sick and injured in hospitals and other health care facilities, physicians' offices, private homes, public health agencies, schools, camps, and industry. Some registered nurses are employed in private practice. RNs hold about 2.6 million jobs in the United States.

THE JOB

Registered nurses work under the direct supervision of nursing departments and in collaboration with physicians. Nearly two-thirds of all nurses work in hospitals, where they may be assigned to general, operating room, or maternity room duty. They may also care for sick children or be assigned to other hospital units, such as emergency rooms, intensive care units, or outpatient clinics. There are many different kinds of RNs.

General duty nurses work together with other members of the health care team to assess the patient's condition and to develop and implement a plan of health care. These nurses may perform such tasks as taking patients' vital signs, administering medication and injections, recording the symptoms and progress of patients, changing dressings, assisting patients with personal care, conferring with members of the medical staff, helping prepare a patient for surgery, and completing any num-

ber of duties that require skill and understanding of patients' needs.

Surgical nurses oversee the preparation of the operating room and the sterilization of instruments. They assist surgeons during operations and coordinate the flow of patient cases in operating rooms.

Maternity nurses, or *neonatal nurses*, help in the delivery room, take care of newborns in the nursery, and teach mothers how to feed and care for their babies.

The activities of staff nurses are directed and coordinated by *head nurses* and *charge nurses*. Heading up the entire nursing program in the hospital is the *nursing service director*, who administers the nursing program to maintain standards of patient care. The nursing service director advises the medical staff, department heads, and the hospital administrator in matters relating to nursing services and helps prepare the department budget.

Private duty nurses may work in hospitals or in a patient's home. They are employed by the patient they are caring for or by the patient's family. Their service is designed for the individual care of one person and is carried out in cooperation with the patient's physician.

Office nurses usually work in the office of a dentist, physician, or health maintenance organization (HMO). An office nurse may be one of several nurses on the staff or the only staff nurse. If a nurse is the only staff member, this person may have to combine some clerical duties with those of nursing, such as serving as receptionist, making appointments for the doctor, helping maintain patient records, sending out monthly statements, and attending to routine correspondence. If the physician's staff is a large one that includes secretaries and clerks, the office nurse will concentrate on screening patients, assisting with examinations, supervising the examining rooms, sterilizing equipment, providing patient education, and performing other nursing duties.

Occupational health nurses, or *industrial nurses*, are an important part of many large firms. They maintain a clinic at a plant or factory and are usually occupied in rendering preventive, remedial, and educational nursing services. They work under the direction of an industrial physician, nursing director, or nursing supervisor. They may advise on accident prevention, visit employees on the job to check the conditions under which they work, and advise management about the safety of such conditions. At the plant, they render treatment in emergencies. *School nurses* may work in one school or in several, visiting each for a part of the day or week. They may supervise the student clinic, treat minor cuts or injuries, or give advice on good health practices. They may examine students to detect conditions of the eyes or teeth that require attention. They also assist the school physician.

Community health nurses, also called *public health nurses*, require specialized training for their duties. Their job usually requires them to spend part of the time traveling from one assignment to another. Their duties may differ greatly from one case to another. For instance, in one day they may have to instruct a class of expectant mothers, visit new parents to help them plan proper care for the baby, visit an aged patient requiring special care, and conduct a class in nutrition. They usually possess many varied nursing skills and are often called upon to resolve unexpected or unusual situations. Administrators in the community health field include *nursing directors*, *educational directors*, and *nursing supervisors*. Some nurses go into nursing education and work with nursing students to instruct them on theories and skills they will need to enter the profession. *Nursing instructors* may give classroom instruction and demonstrations or supervise nursing students on hospital units. Some instructors eventually become *nursing school directors*, university faculty, or deans of a university degree program. Nurses also have the opportunity to direct staff development and continuing education programs for nursing personnel in hospitals.

Advanced practice nurses are nurses with training beyond that required to have the RN designation. There are four primary categories of nurses included in this category: *nurse-midwives, clinical nurse specialists, nurse anesthetists,* and *nurse practitioners.*

Some nurses are consultants to hospitals, nursing schools, industrial organizations, and public health agencies. They advise clients on such administrative matters as staff organization, nursing techniques, curricula, and education programs. Other administrative specialists include *educational directors* for the state board of nursing, who are concerned with maintaining well-defined educational standards, and *executive directors* of professional nurses' associations, who administer programs developed by the board of directors and the members of the association.

Some nurses choose to enter the armed forces. All types of nurses, except private duty nurses, are represented in the military services. They provide skilled nursing care to active-duty and retired members of the armed forces and their families. In addition to basic nursing skills, *military nurses* are trained to provide care in various environments, including field hospitals, on-air evacuation flights, and onboard ships. Military nurses actively influence the development of health care through nursing research. Advances influenced by military nurses include the development of the artificial kidney (dialysis unit) and the concept of the intensive care unit.

REQUIREMENTS

High School

If you are interested in becoming a registered nurse, you should take high school mathematics and science courses, including biology, chemistry, and physics. Health courses will also be helpful. English and speech courses should not be neglected because you must be able to communicate well with patients.

Postsecondary Training

There are three basic kinds of training programs that you may choose from to become a registered nurse: associate's degree, diploma, and bachelor's degree. Deciding on which of the three training programs to pursue depends on your career goals. A bachelor's degree in nursing is required for most supervisory or administrative positions, for jobs in public health agencies, and for admission to graduate nursing programs. A master's degree is usually necessary to prepare for a nursing specialty or to teach. For some specialties, such as nursing research, a Ph.D. is essential.

There are many bachelor's degree programs in nursing in the United States, which can take up to five years to complete, in some cases. The graduate of this program receives a Bachelor of Science in Nursing (B.S.N.) degree. The Associate Degree in Nursing (A.D.N.) is awarded after completion of a two-year study program that is usually offered in a junior or community college. Nursing students receive hospital training at cooperating hospitals in the general vicinity of the community college. The diploma program, which usually lasts three years, is conducted by hospitals and independent schools, although the number of these programs is declining. At the conclusion of each of these programs, you become a graduate nurse, but not, however, a registered nurse. To obtain the RN designation you must pass a licensing examination required in all states.

Nurses can pursue postgraduate training that allows them to specialize in certain areas, such as emergency room, operating room, premature nursery, or psychiatric nursing. This training is sometimes offered through hospital on-the-job training programs.

Certification or Licensing

All states, the District of Columbia, and U.S. territories require a license to practice nursing. To obtain a license, graduates of approved nursing schools must pass a national examination. Nurses may be licensed by more than one state. In some states, continuing education is a condition for license renewal. Different titles require different education and training levels.

Other Requirements

You should enjoy working with people, and be especially sensitive and effective in working with those who may experience fear or anger because of an illness. Patience, compassion, and calmness are qualities needed by anyone working in this career. In addition, you must be able to give directions as well as follow instructions and work as part of a health care team. Anyone interested in becoming a registered nurse should also have a strong desire to continue learning, because new tests, procedures, and technologies are constantly being developed within medicine.

EXPLORING

You can explore your interest in nursing in a number of ways. Read books on careers in nursing and talk with high school guidance counselors, school nurses, and local public health nurses. Visit hospitals to observe the work and talk with hospital personnel to learn more about the daily activities of nursing staff.

Some hospitals now have extensive volunteer service programs in which high school students may work after school, on weekends, or during vacations in order both to render a valuable service and to explore their interests in nursing. There are other volunteer work experiences available with the Red Cross or community health services. Camp counseling jobs sometimes offer related experiences. Some schools offer participation in Future Nurses programs.

The Internet is full of resources about nursing. Check out Nursing Net (http://www.nursingnet.org), and the American Nurses Association's Nursing World (http://www.nursingworld.org).

EMPLOYERS

Approximately 2.6 million registered nurses are employed in the United States. About 60 percent of registered nurses work in hospitals, 8 percent work in offices of physicians, 5 percent in home health care services, another 5 percent in nursing care facilities, and 3 percent in employment services. The rest work in managed-care facilities, clinics, industry, private homes, schools, camps, and government agencies. Some nurses work part time.

STARTING OUT

The only way to become a registered nurse is through completion of one of the three kinds of educational programs, plus passing the licensing examination. Registered nurses may apply for employment directly to hospitals, nursing homes, home care agencies, temporary nursing agencies, companies, and government agencies that hire nurses. Jobs can also be obtained through school career services offices, by signing up with employment agencies specializing in placement of nursing personnel, or through the state employment office. Other sources of jobs include nurses' associations, professional journals, and newspaper want ads.

ADVANCEMENT

Increasingly, administrative and supervisory positions in the nursing field go to nurses who have earned at least the bachelor of science degree in nursing. Nurses with many years of experience who are graduates of a diploma program may achieve supervisory positions, but requirements for such promotions have become more difficult in recent years and in many cases require at least the B.S.N. degree.

Nurses with bachelor's degrees are usually those who are hired as public health nurses. Nurses with master's degrees are often employed as clinical nurse specialists, faculty, instructors, supervisors, or administrators.

RNs can pursue further education to become advanced practice nurses, who have greater responsibilities and command higher salaries.

EARNINGS

According to the U.S. Department of Labor, registered nurses had median annual earnings of $63,750 in 2009. Salaries ranged from less than $43,970 to more than $92,700. Earnings of RNs vary according to employer. According to the *Occupational Outlook Handbook,* those who worked at hospitals earned $67,740; registered nurses employed in physicians' offices earned $67,290; those working in home health care services earned $63,300; and RNs who worked at nursing care facilities earned $59,320.

Salary is determined by several factors: setting, education, and work experience. Most full-time nurses are given flexible work schedules as well as health and life insurance; some are offered education reimbursement and year-end bonuses. A staff nurse's salary is often limited only by the amount of work he or she is willing to take on. Many nurses take advantage of overtime work and shift differentials. Some nurses hold more than one job.

WORK ENVIRONMENT

Most nurses work in facilities that are clean and well lighted and where the temperature is controlled, although some work in rundown inner-city hospitals in less-than-ideal conditions. Usually, nurses work eight-hour shifts. Those in hospitals generally work any of three shifts: 7:00 A.M. to 3:00 P.M.; 3:00 P.M. to 11:00 P.M.; or 11:00 P.M. to 7:00 A.M.

Nurses spend much of the day on their feet, either walking or standing. Handling patients who are ill or infirm can also be very exhausting. Nurses who come in contact with patients with infectious diseases must be especially careful about cleanliness and sterility. Although many nursing duties are routine, many responsibilities are unpredictable. Sick persons are often very demanding, or they may be depressed or irritable. Despite this, nurses must maintain their composure and should be cheerful to help the patient achieve emotional balance.

Community health nurses may be required to visit homes that are in poor condition or very dirty. They may also come in contact with social problems, such as family violence. The nurse is an important health care provider and in many communities he or she is the sole provider.

Both the office nurse and the industrial nurse work regular business hours and are seldom required to work overtime. In some jobs, such as where nurses are on duty in private homes, they may frequently travel from home to home and work with various cases.

OUTLOOK

The nursing field is the largest of all health care occupations, and employment prospects for nurses are excellent. The U.S. Department of Labor projects that registered nurses will have the largest number of new jobs for all professions through 2018: approximately 581,500 new nursing jobs will be added to the field.

There has been a serious shortage of nurses in recent years. Many nurses are expected to leave the profession in the coming years because of unsatisfactory working conditions, including low pay, severe understaffing, high stress, physical demands, mandatory overtime, and irregular hours. The shortage will also be exacerbated by the increasing numbers of baby-boomer-aged nurses who are expected to retire, creating more open positions than there are graduates of nursing programs.

The much-faster-than-average job growth in this field is also a result of improving medical technology that will allow for treatments of many more diseases and health conditions. Nurses will be in strong demand to work with the rapidly growing population of senior citizens in the United States.

Employment in hospitals does not have a bright forecast, however. Because of administrative cost cutting, increased nurse's workload, and rapid growth of outpatient services, hospital nursing jobs will experience slower than average growth within the nursing profession. Employment in home care and nursing homes is expected to grow rapidly. Though more people are living well into their 80s and 90s, many need the kind of long-term care available at a nursing home. Also, because of financial reasons, patients are being released from hospitals sooner and admitted into nursing homes. Many nursing homes have facilities and staff capable of caring for long-term rehabilitation patients, as well as those afflicted with Alzheimer's. Many nurses will also be needed to help staff the growing number of outpatient facilities, such as HMOs, group medical practices, and ambulatory surgery centers.

Nursing specialties will be in great demand, namely clinical nurse specialists, nurse practitioners, nurse-midwives, and nurse anesthetists. There are, in addition, many part-time employment possibilities in nursing.

FOR MORE INFORMATION

Visit the AACN Web site to access a list of member schools and career information.

American Association of Colleges of Nursing (AACN)
One Dupont Circle, NW, Suite 530
Washington, DC 20036-1110
Tel: 202-463-6930
http://www.aacn.nche.edu

For information about opportunities as an RN, contact

American Nurses Association
8515 Georgia Avenue, Suite 400
Silver Spring, MD 20910-3492
Tel: 800-274-4262
http://www.nursingworld.org

For information about state-approved programs and information on nursing, contact the following organizations:

National League for Nursing
61 Broadway, 33rd Floor
New York, NY 10006-2701
Tel: 212-363-5555
http://www.nln.org

National Organization for Associate Degree Nursing
7794 Grow Drive
Pensacola, FL 32514-7072
Tel: 850-484-6948
E-mail: noadn@dancyamc.com
http://www.noadn.org

Discover Nursing, sponsored by Johnson & Johnson Services Inc., provides information on nursing careers, nursing schools, and scholarships.

Discover Nursing
http://www.discovernursing.com

❏ REHABILITATION COUNSELORS

OVERVIEW

Rehabilitation counselors provide counseling and guidance services to people with disabilities to help them resolve life problems and to train for and locate work that is suitable to their physical and mental abilities, interests, and aptitudes. There are approximately 112,690 rehabilitation counselors working in the United States.

THE JOB

Rehabilitation counselors work with people with disabilities to identify barriers to medical, psychological, personal, social, and vocational functioning and to develop a plan of action to remove or reduce those barriers.

Clients are referred to rehabilitation programs from many sources. Sometimes they seek help on their own initiative; sometimes their families bring them in. They may be referred by a physician, hospital, or social worker, or they may be sent by employment agencies, schools, or accident commissions. A former employer may seek help for the individual.

The counselor's first step is to determine the nature and extent of the disability and evaluate how that disability interferes with work and other life functions. This determination is made from medical and psychological reports as well as from family history, educational background, work experience, and other evaluative information.

The next step is to determine a vocational direction and plan of services to overcome the handicaps to employment or independent living.

The rehabilitation counselor coordinates a comprehensive evaluation of a client's physical function-

SCHOOL SUBJECTS
Psychology, Sociology

PERSONAL SKILLS
Helping/teaching, Technical/scientific

MINIMUM EDUCATION LEVEL
Bachelor's degree

CERTIFICATION OR LICENSING
Requirements vary (licensing),
Recommended (certification)

WORK ENVIRONMENT
Primarily indoors, Primarily one location

ing abilities and vocational interests, aptitudes, and skills. This information is used to develop vocational or independent-living goals for the client and the services necessary to reach those goals. Services that the rehabilitation counselor may coordinate or provide include physical and mental restoration, academic or vocational training, vocational counseling, job analysis, job modification or reasonable accommodation, and job placement. Limited financial assistance in the form of maintenance or transportation assistance may also be provided.

The counselor's relationship with the client may be as brief as a week or as long as several years, depending on the nature of the problem and the needs of the client.

REQUIREMENTS

High School

To prepare for becoming a rehabilitation counselor, take your high school's college prep curriculum. These classes should include several years of mathematics and science, such as biology and chemistry. To begin to gain an understanding of people and societies, take history, psychology, and sociology classes. English classes are important because you will need excellent communication skills for this work. Some of your professional responsibilities will include documenting your work and doing research to provide your clients with helpful information; to do these things you will undoubtedly be working with computers. Therefore, you should take computer science classes so that you are skilled in using them. In addition, you may want to consider taking speech and a foreign language, both of which will enhance your communication skills.

Postsecondary Training

Although some positions are available for people with a bachelor's degree in rehabilitation counseling, these positions are usually as aides and offer limited advancement opportunities. Most employers require the rehabilitation counselors working for them to hold master's degrees. Before receiving your master's, you will need to complete a bachelor's degree with a major in behavioral sciences, social sciences, or a related field. Another option is to complete an undergraduate degree in rehabilitation counseling. The Council for Accreditation of Counseling and Related Educational Programs (CACREP) has accredited institutions in the United States, Canada, and Mexico that offer programs in counselor education. If

you decide on an undergraduate degree in rehabilitation, it is recommended you attend an accredited program. Keep in mind, however, that even if you get an undergraduate degree in rehabilitation, you will still need to attend a graduate program to qualify for most counselor positions. No matter which undergraduate program you decide on, you should concentrate on courses in sociology, psychology, physiology, history, and statistics as well as courses in English and communications. Several universities now offer courses in various aspects of physical therapy and special education training. Courses in sign language, speech therapy, and a foreign language are also beneficial.

Master's programs in rehabilitation counseling include courses in medical aspects of disability, psychosocial aspects of disability, testing techniques, statistics, personality theory, personality development, abnormal psychology, techniques of counseling, occupational information, and vocational training and job placement. A supervised internship is also an important aspect of a program. Students who wish to have a thorough education in rehabilitation counseling can secure a graduate degree through programs accredited by the Council on Rehabilitation Education.

Certification or Licensing

The regulation of counselors is required in 49 states and the District of Columbia. This regulation may be in the form of credentialing, registry, certification, or licensure. Regulations, however, vary by state and sometimes by employer. For example, an employer may require certification even if the state does not. You will need to check with your state's licensing board as well as your employer for specific information about your circumstances.

Across the country, many employers now require their rehabilitation counselors to be certified by the Commission on Rehabilitation Counselor Certification (CRCC). The purpose of certification is to provide assurance that professionals engaged in rehabilitation counseling meet set standards and maintain those standards through continuing education. To become certified, counselors must pass an extensive written examination to demonstrate their knowledge of rehabilitation counseling. The CRCC requires the master's degree as the minimum educational level for certification. Applicants who meet these certification requirements receive the designation of certified rehabilitation counselor (CRC). To maintain certification, counselors must retake and pass the certification exam, or complete 100 credit hours of acceptable continuing education, every five years.

Most state government rehabilitation agencies require future counselors to meet state civil service and merit system regulations. The applicant must take a competitive written examination and may also be interviewed and evaluated by a special board.

Other Requirements

The most important personal attribute required for rehabilitation counseling is the ability to get along well with other people. Rehabilitation counselors work with many different kinds of clients and must be able to see situations and problems from their client's point of view. They must be both patient and persistent. Rehabilitation may be a slow process with many delays and setbacks. The counselor must maintain a calm, positive manner even when no progress is made.

EXPLORING

To explore a career in which you work with people with disabilities, look for opportunities to volunteer or work in this field. One possibility is to be a counselor at a children's camp for disabled youngsters. You can also volunteer with a local vocational rehabilitation agency or a facility such as Easter Seals or Goodwill. Other possibilities include reading for the blind or leading a hobby or craft class at an adult day care center. And don't forget volunteer opportunities at a local hospital or nursing home. Even if your only responsibility is to escort people to the X-ray department or talk to patients to cheer them up, you will gain valuable experience interacting with people who are facing challenging situations.

EMPLOYERS

Rehabilitation counselors work in a variety of settings. The majority of rehabilitation counselors work for state agencies; some also work for local and federal agencies. Employment opportunities are available in rehabilitation centers, mental health agencies, developmental disability agencies, sheltered workshops, training institutions, and special schools.

STARTING OUT

School career services offices are the best places for the new graduate to begin the career search. In addition, the National Rehabilitation Counseling Association and the American Rehabilitation Counseling Association (a division of the American Counseling Association) are sources for employment information. The new counselor may also apply directly to agencies for available positions. Vocational rehabilitation agencies employ nearly 27,990 rehabilitation counselors. The Department of Veterans Affairs employs rehabilitation counselors to assist with the rehabilitation of disabled veterans. Many rehabilitation counselors are employed by private for-profit or nonprofit rehabilitation programs and facilities. Others are employed in industry, schools, hospitals, and other settings, while others are self-employed.

ADVANCEMENT

The rehabilitation counselor usually receives regular salary increases after gaining experience in the job. He or she may move from relatively easy cases to increasingly challenging ones. Counselors may advance into such positions as administrator or supervisor after several years of counseling experience. It is also possible to find related counseling and teaching positions, which may represent advancement in other fields.

EARNINGS

The U.S. Department of Labor reports that median annual earnings of rehabilitation counselors in 2009 were $31,210. Salaries ranged from less than $20,440 to more than $55,580.

Rehabilitation counselors employed by the federal government generally start at the GS-9 or GS-11 level. In 2011, basic GS-9 salary was $41,563. Those with master's degrees generally began at the GS-11 level, with a salary of $50,287 in 2011. Salaries for federal government workers vary according to the region of the country in which they work. Those working in areas with a higher cost of living receive additional locality pay.

Counselors employed by government and private agencies and institutions generally receive health insurance, pension plans, and other benefits, including vacation, sick, and holiday pay. Self-employed counselors must provide their own benefits.

WORK ENVIRONMENT

Rehabilitation counselors work approximately 40 hours each week and do not usually have to work during evenings or weekends. They work both in the office and in the field. Depending on the type of training required, lab space and workout or therapy rooms may be available. Rehabilitation counselors must usually keep detailed accounts of their progress with clients and write reports.

They may spend many hours traveling about the community to visit employed clients, prospective employers, trainees, or training programs.

OUTLOOK

The passage of the Americans with Disabilities Act of 1990 increased the demand for rehabilitation counselors. As more local, state, and federal programs are initiated that are designed to assist people with disabilities, and as private institutions and companies seek to comply with this new legislation, job prospects are promising. Budget pressures may serve to limit the number of new rehabilitation counselors to be hired by government agencies; however, the overall outlook remains excellent.

The U.S. Department of Labor predicts that employment growth for all counselors will be faster than average through 2018. Some of this growth can be attributed to the advances in medical technology that are saving more lives, as well as the elderly population living longer and needing rehabilitation counseling. In addition, more employers are offering employee assistance programs that provide mental health and alcohol and drug abuse services.

FOR MORE INFORMATION

For general information on careers in rehabilitation counseling, contact

American Rehabilitation Counseling Association
5999 Stevenson Avenue
Alexandria, VA 22304-3300
Tel: 800-347-6647
http://www.arcaweb.org

For information on certification, contact

Commission on Rehabilitation Counselor Certification
1699 East Woodfield Road, Suite 300
Schaumburg, IL 60173-4957
Tel: 847-944-1325
E-mail: info@crccertification.com
http://www.crccertification.com

For listings of CORE-approved programs as well as other information, contact

Council on Rehabilitation Education (CORE)
1699 East Woodfield Road, Suite 300
Schaumburg, IL 60173-4957
Tel: 847-944-1345
http://www.core-rehab.org

For information on a variety of resources, contact

National Clearinghouse of Rehabilitation Training Materials
Utah State University
6524 Old Main Hill
Logan, UT 84322-6524
Tel: 866-821-5355
E-mail: ncrtm@usu.edu
http://ncrtm.org

To learn about government legislation, visit NRA's Web site.

National Rehabilitation Association (NRA)
633 South Washington Street
Alexandria, VA 22314-4109
Tel: 703-836-0850
E-mail: info@nationalrehab.org
http://www.nationalrehab.org

For news on legislation, employment, and other information, contact

National Rehabilitation Counseling Association (NRCA)
PO Box 4480
Manassas, VA 20108-4480
Tel: 703-361-2077
E-mail: info@nrca-net.org
http://nrca-net.org

RESPIRATORY THERAPISTS AND TECHNICIANS

OVERVIEW

Respiratory therapists, also known as *respiratory care practitioners,* evaluate, treat, and care for patients with deficiencies or abnormalities of the cardiopulmonary (heart/lung) system by either providing temporary relief from chronic ailments or administering emergency care where life is threatened. They are involved with the supervision of other respiratory care workers in their area of treatment. *Respiratory technicians* have many of the same responsibilities as therapists; however, technicians do not supervise other respiratory care workers.

Working under a physician's direction, these workers set up and operate respirators, mechanical ventilators, and other devices. They monitor the functioning of the equipment and the patients' response to the therapy and maintain the patients' charts. They also assist patients with breathing exercises, and inspect, test, and order repairs for respiratory therapy equipment. They may demonstrate procedures to trainees and other health care personnel. Approximately 107,270 respiratory therapy workers and 15,100 respiratory technicians are employed in the United States.

THE JOB

Respiratory therapists and technicians treat patients with various cardiorespiratory problems. They may provide care that affords temporary relief from chronic illnesses such as asthma or emphysema, or they may administer life-support treatment to victims of heart failure, stroke, drowning, or shock. These specialists often mean the difference between life and death in cases involving acute respiratory conditions, as may result from head injuries or drug poisoning. Adults who stop breathing for longer than three to five minutes rarely survive without serious brain damage, and an absence of respiratory activity for more than nine minutes almost always results in death. Respiratory therapists carry out their duties under a physician's direction and supervision. Technicians typically work under the supervision of a respiratory therapist and physician, following specific instructions. Therapists

and technicians set up and operate special devices to treat patients who need temporary or emergency relief from breathing difficulties. The equipment may include respirators, positive-pressure breathing machines, or environmental control systems. Aerosol inhalants are administered to confine medication to the lungs. Respiratory therapists often treat patients who have undergone surgery because anesthesia depresses normal respiration, thus the patients need some support to restore their full breathing capability and to prevent respiratory illnesses.

In evaluating patients, therapists test the capacity of the lungs and analyze the oxygen and carbon dioxide concentration and potential of hydrogen (pH), a measure of the acidity or alkalinity level of the blood. To measure lung capacity, therapists have patients breathe into an instrument that measures the volume and flow of air during inhalation and exhalation. By comparing the reading with the norm for the patient's age, height, weight, and gender, respiratory therapists can determine whether lung deficiencies exist. To analyze oxygen, carbon dioxide, and pH levels, therapists draw an arterial blood sample, place it in a blood gas analyzer, and relay the results to a physician.

Respiratory therapists watch equipment gauges and maintain prescribed volumes of oxygen or other inhalants. Besides monitoring the equipment to be sure it is operating properly, they observe the patient's physiological response to the therapy and consult with physicians in case of any adverse reactions. They also record pertinent identification and therapy information on each patient's chart and keep records of the cost of materials and the charges to the patients.

Therapists instruct patients and their families on how to use respiratory equipment at home, and they may demonstrate respiratory therapy procedures to trainees and other health care personnel. Their responsibilities include inspecting and testing equipment. If it is faulty, they either make minor repairs themselves or order major repairs.

Respiratory therapy workers include therapists, technicians, and assistants. Differences between respiratory therapists' duties and those of other respiratory care workers' include supervising technicians and assistants, teaching new staff, and bearing primary responsibility for the care given in their areas. At times, the respiratory therapist may need to work independently and make clinical judgments on the type of care to be given to a patient. Although technicians can perform many of the same activities as a therapist (for example, monitoring equipment, checking patient responses, and giving medicine), they do not make independent decisions about what type of care to give. *Respiratory assistants* clean, sterilize, store, and generally take care of the equipment but have very little contact with patients.

REQUIREMENTS

High School

To prepare for a career in this field while you are still in high school, take health and science classes, including biology, chemistry, and physics. Mathematics and statistics classes will also be useful to you since much of this work involves using numbers and making calculations. Take computer science courses to become familiar with using technical and complex equipment and to become familiar with programs you can use to document your work. Since some of your responsibilities may include working directly with patients to teach them therapies, take English classes to improve your communication skills. Studying a foreign language may also be useful.

Postsecondary Training

Formal training is necessary for entry to this field. Training is offered at the postsecondary level by hospitals, medical schools, colleges and universities, trade schools, vocational-technical institutes, and the armed forces. The Commission on Accreditation of Allied Health Education Programs (CAAHEP) reports that 31 entry-level and 346 advanced respiratory therapy programs are accredited in the United States. To be eligible for a respiratory therapy program, you must have graduated from high school.

Accredited respiratory therapy programs combine class work with clinical work. Programs vary in length, depending on the degree awarded. A certificate program generally takes one year to complete, an associate's degree usually takes two years, and a bachelor's degree program typically takes four years. In addition, it is important to note that some advanced-level programs will prepare you for becoming a registered respiratory therapist (RRT), while entry-level programs will prepare you for becoming a certified respiratory therapist (CRT). RRT-prepared graduates will be eligible for jobs as respiratory therapists once they have been certified. CRT-prepared graduates, on the other hand, are only eligible for jobs as respiratory technicians after certification. The areas of study for both therapists and technicians cover human anatomy and physiol-ogy, chemistry, physics, microbiology, and mathematics. Technical studies include courses such as patient evaluation, respiratory care pharmacology, pulmonary diseases, and care procedures.

There are no standard hiring requirements for assistants. Department heads in charge of hiring set the standards and may require only a high school diploma.

Certification or Licensing

The National Board for Respiratory Care (NBRC) offers voluntary RRT and CRT certification to graduates of Committee on Accreditation for Respiratory Care (CoARC)-accredited and CAAHEP programs. You must have at least an associate's degree to be eligible to take the CRT exam. Anyone desiring certification must take the CRT exam first. After successfully completing this exam, those who are eligible can take the RRT exam. CRTs who meet further education and experience requirements can qualify for the RRT credential.

Certification is highly recommended because most employers require this credential. Those who are designated CRT or are eligible to take the exam are qualified for technician jobs that are entry-level or generalist positions. Employers usually require those with supervisory positions or those in intensive care specialties to have the RRT (or RRT eligibility).

A license is required by all states, except Alaska and Hawaii, to practice as a respiratory therapist. Also, most employers require therapists to maintain a cardiopulmonary resuscitation certification. Requirements vary, so you will need to check with your state's regulatory board for specific information. The NBRC Web site provides helpful contact information for state licensure agencies at http://www.nbrc.org/StateLicensure/AgencyDirectory/tabid/54/Default.aspx.

Other Requirements

Respiratory therapists must enjoy working with people. You must be sensitive to your patients' physical and psychological needs because you will be dealing with people who may be in pain or who may be frightened. The work of this occupational group is of great significance. Respiratory therapists are often responsible for the lives and well being of people already in critical condition. You must pay strict attention to detail, be able to follow instructions and work as part of a team, and remain cool in emergencies. Mechanical ability and manual dexterity are necessary to operate much of the respiratory equipment.

EXPLORING

Visit the American Association for Respiratory Care's Web site (http://www.aarc.org) for a list of accredited educational programs in respiratory therapy. Formal training in this field is available in hospitals, vocational-technical institutes, private trade schools, and other non-collegiate settings as well. Local hospitals can provide information on training opportunities. School vocational counselors may be sources of additional information about educational matters and may be able to set up interviews with or lectures by a respiratory therapy practitioner from a local hospital.

Hospitals are excellent places to obtain part-time and summer employment. They have a continuing need for helpers in many departments. Even though the work may not be directly related to respiratory therapy, you will gain knowledge of the operation of a hospital and may be in a position to get acquainted with respiratory therapists and observe them as they carry out their duties. If part-time or temporary work is not available, you may wish to volunteer your services.

EMPLOYERS

Approximately 107,270 respiratory therapists and 15,100 respiratory technicians work in the United States. About 81 percent of respiratory therapy jobs are in hospital departments of respiratory care, anesthesiology, or pulmonary medicine. The rest are employed by oxygen equipment rental companies, ambulance services, nursing homes, home health agencies, and physicians' offices. Many respiratory therapists hold a second job.

STARTING OUT

Graduates of CoARC- and CAAHEP-accredited respiratory therapy training programs may use their school's career services offices to help them find jobs. Otherwise, they may apply directly to the individual local health care facilities.

High school graduates may apply directly to local hospitals for jobs as respiratory therapy assistants. If your goal is to become a therapist or technician, however, you will need to enroll in a formal respiratory therapy educational program.

ADVANCEMENT

Many respiratory therapists start out as assistants or technicians. With appropriate training courses and experience, they advance to the therapist level. Respiratory therapists with sufficient experience may be promoted to assistant chief or chief therapist. With graduate education, they may be qualified to teach respiratory therapy at the college level or move into administrative positions such as director.

EARNINGS

Respiratory therapists earned a median salary of $53,330 in 2009, according to the *Occupational Outlook Handbook*. The lowest paid 10 percent earned less than $39,030, and the highest paid 10 percent earned more than $71,920. Median annual earnings of respiratory therapy technicians were $44,700 in 2009. Salaries ranged from less than $28,740 to more than $65,020.

Hospital workers receive benefits that include health insurance, paid vacations and sick leave, and pension plans. Some institutions provide additional benefits, such as uniforms and parking, and offer free courses or tuition reimbursement for job-related courses.

WORK ENVIRONMENT

Respiratory therapists and technicians generally work in extremely clean, quiet surroundings. They usually work 40 hours a week, which may include nights and weekends because hospitals are in operation 24 hours a day, seven days a week. The work requires long hours of standing and may be very stressful during emergencies.

A possible hazard is that the inhalants these employees work with are highly flammable. The danger of fire is minimized, however, if the workers test equipment regularly and are strict about taking safety precautions. As do workers in many other health occupations, respiratory therapists run a risk of catching infectious diseases. Careful adherence to proper procedures minimizes the risk.

OUTLOOK

Employment growth for respiratory therapists is expected to grow at a much faster than average rate through 2018, according to the Department of Labor, despite the fact that efforts to control rising health care costs have reduced the number of job opportunities in hospitals. The employment outlook for respiratory therapy technicians is not as bright, however, with little or no change expected through 2018. Respiratory therapists are increasingly handling the work of technicians, which is creating keen competition for the few jobs that exist.

The increasing demand for respiratory therapists is the result of other factors also. The fields of neonatal care and gerontology are growing, and there are continuing advances in treatments for victims of heart attacks and accidents and for premature babies.

Employment opportunities for respiratory therapists should be very favorable in the rapidly growing field of home health care, although this area accounts for only a small number of respiratory therapy jobs. In addition to jobs in home health agencies and hospital-based home health programs, there should be numerous openings for respiratory therapists in equipment rental companies and in firms that provide respiratory care on a contract basis. In addition, employment is expected to grow due to respiratory therapists' increasing role in case management, disease prevention, emergency care, and the early detection of pulmonary disorders.

FOR MORE INFORMATION

For information on scholarships, continuing education, job listings, and careers in respiratory therapy, contact

American Association for Respiratory Care
9425 North MacArthur Boulevard, Suite 100
Irving, TX 75063-4706
Tel: 972-243-2272
E-mail: info@aarc.org
http://www.aarc.org

For more information on allied health care careers as well as a listing of accredited programs, contact

Commission on Accreditation of Allied Health Education Programs
1361 Park Street
Clearwater, FL 33756-6039
Tel: 727-210-2350
E-mail: mail@caahep.org
http://www.caahep.org

For a list of CoARC-accredited training programs, contact

Committee on Accreditation for Respiratory Care (CoARC)
1248 Harwood Road
Bedford, TX 76021-4244
Tel: 817-283-2835
http://www.coarc.com

For information on licensing and certification, contact

National Board for Respiratory Care
18000 West 105th Street
Olathe, KS 66061-7543
Tel: 888-341-4811
http://www.nbrc.org

SOCIAL WORKERS

OVERVIEW

Social workers help people and assist communities in solving problems. These problems include poverty, racism, discrimination, physical and mental illness, addiction, and abuse. They counsel individuals and families, they lead group sessions, they research social problems, and they develop policy and programs. Social workers are dedicated to empowering people and helping them to preserve their dignity and worth. Approximately 611,570 social workers are employed in the United States.

THE JOB

After months of physical abuse from her husband, a young woman has taken her children and moved out of her house. With no job and no home, and fearing for her safety, she looks for a temporary shelter for herself and her children. Once there, she can rely on the help of social workers who will provide her with a room, food, and security. The social workers will offer counseling and emotional support to help her address the problems in her life. They will involve her in group sessions with other victims of abuse. They will direct her to job training programs and other employment services. They will set up interviews with managers of low-income housing. As the woman makes efforts to improve her life, the shelter will provide day care for the children. All these resources exist because the social work profession has long been committed to empowering people and improving society.

The social worker's role extends even beyond the shelter. If the woman has trouble getting help from other agencies, the social worker will serve as an advocate, stepping in to ensure that she gets the aid to which she is entitled. The woman may also qualify for long-term assistance from the shelter, such as a second-step program in which a social worker offers counseling and other support over several months. The woman's individual experience will also help in the social worker's research of the problem of domestic violence; with that research, the social worker can help the community come to a better understanding of the problem and can direct society toward solutions. Some of these solutions may include the development of special police procedures for

SCHOOL SUBJECTS
Health, Psychology

PERSONAL SKILLS
Communication/ideas, Helping/teaching

MINIMUM EDUCATION LEVEL
Bachelor's degree

CERTIFICATION OR LICENSING
Required by all states

WORK ENVIRONMENT
Primarily indoors, Primarily multiple locations

domestic disputes, or court-ordered therapy groups for abusive spouses.

Direct social work practice is also known as clinical practice. As the name suggests, direct practice involves working directly with the client by offering counseling, advocacy, information and referral, and education. Indirect practice concerns the structures through which the direct practice is offered. *Indirect practice* (a practice consisting mostly of social workers with Ph.D. degrees) involves program development and evaluation, administration, and policy analysis. The vast majority of the more than 150,000 members of the National Association of Social Workers (NASW) work in direct service roles.

Because of the number of problems facing individuals, families and communities, social workers find jobs in a wide variety of settings and with a variety of client groups. Some of these areas are discussed in the following paragraphs.

Mental health and substance abuse care. Mental health care has become the lead area of social work employment. These jobs are competitive and typically go to more experienced social workers. Settings include community mental health centers, where social workers serve persistently mentally ill people and participate in outreach services; state and county mental hospitals, for long-term, inpatient care; facilities of the Department of Veterans Affairs, involving a variety of mental health care programs for veterans; and private psychiatric hospitals, for patients who can pay directly. Social workers also work with patients who have physical illnesses. They help individuals and their families adjust

to the illness and the changes that illness may bring to their lives. They confer with physicians and with other members of the medical team to make plans about the best way to help the patient. They explain the treatment and its anticipated outcome to both the patient and the family. They help the patient adjust to the possible prospect of long hospitalization and isolation from the family.

Child care/family services. Efforts are being made to offer a more universal system of care that would incorporate child care, family services, and community service. Child care services include day care homes, child care centers, and Head Start centers. Social workers in this setting attempt to address all the problems children face from infancy to late adolescence. They work with families to detect problems early and intervene when necessary. They research the problems confronting children and families, and they establish new services or adapt existing services to address these problems. They provide parenting education to teenage parents, which can involve living with a teenage mother in a foster care situation, teaching parenting skills, and caring for the baby while the mother attends school. Social workers alert employers to employees' needs for daytime child care.

Social workers in this area of service are constantly required to address new issues. In recent years, for example, social workers have developed services for families composed of different cultural backgrounds, services for children with congenital disabilities resulting from the mother's drug use, and disabilities related to HIV or AIDS.

Geriatric social work. Within this field, social workers provide individual and family counseling services in order to assess the older person's needs and strengths. Social workers help older people locate transportation and housing services. They also offer adult day care services, or adult foster care services that match older people with families. Adult protective services protect older people from abuse and neglect, and respite services allow family members time off from the care of an older person. A little-recognized problem is the rising incidence of AIDS among the elderly; 10 percent of all AIDS patients are aged 50 or over.

School social work. In schools, social workers serve students and their families, teachers, administrators, and other school staff members. Education, counseling, and advocacy are important aspects of school social work. With education, social workers attempt to prevent alcohol and drug abuse, teen pregnancy, and the spread of AIDS and other sexually transmitted diseases. They provide multicultural and family life education. They counsel students who are discriminated against because of their sexual orientation or racial, ethnic, or religious background. They also serve as advocates for these students, bringing issues of discrimination before administrators, school boards, and student councils.

A smaller number of social workers are employed in the areas of *social work education* (a field composed of the professors and instructors who teach and train students of social work); *group practice* (in which social workers facilitate treatment and support groups); and *corrections* (providing services to inmates in penal institutions). Social workers also offer counseling, occupational assistance, and advocacy to those with addictions and disabilities, to the homeless, and to women, children, and the elderly who have been in abusive situations.

Client groups expand and change as societal problems change. Social work professionals must remain aware of the problems affecting individuals and communities in order to offer assistance to as many people as possible.

Computers have become important tools for social workers. Client records are maintained on computers, allowing for easier collection and analysis of data. Interactive computer programs are used to train social workers, as well as to analyze case histories (such as for an individual's risk of HIV infection).

REQUIREMENTS

High School

To prepare for a social work career, you should take courses in high school that will improve your communications skills, such as English, speech, and composition. On a debate team, you could further develop your skills in communication as well as research and analysis. History, social studies, and sociology courses are important in understanding the concerns and issues of society. Although limited work is available for those with only an associate's degree (as a social work aide or social services technician), the most opportunities exist for people with more advanced degrees in social work.

Postsecondary Training

There are approximately 468 accredited B.S.W. (bachelor's in social work) programs and 196 accredited M.S.W. (master's in social work) programs accredited by the Council on Social Work Education. The Group for the Advancement of Doctoral Education lists 74 doctoral programs for Ph.D.'s in social work or D.S.W.'s (doctor of social work). The Council on Social Work Education requires that five areas be covered in accredited bachelor's degree social work programs: human behavior and the social environment; social welfare policy and services; social work practice; research; and field practicum. Most programs require two years of liberal arts study followed by two years of study in the social work major. Also, students must complete a field practicum of at least 400 hours. Graduates of these programs can find work in public assistance or they can work with the elderly or with people with mental or developmental disabilities.

Although no clear lines of classification are drawn in the social work profession, most supervisory and administrative positions require at least an M.S.W. degree. Master's programs are organized according to fields of practice (such as mental health care), problem areas (substance abuse), population groups (the elderly), and practice roles (practice with individuals, families, or communities). They are usually two-year programs that require at least 900 hours of field practice. Most positions in mental health care facilities require an M.S.W. Doctoral degrees are also available and prepare students for research and teaching. Most social workers with doctorates go to work in community organizations.

Certification or Licensing

Licensing, certification, or registration of social workers is required by all states. To receive the necessary licensing, a social worker will typically have to gain a certain amount of experience and also pass an exam. Most states require two years of 3,000 hours of supervised clinical experience for licensure of clinical social workers. Five voluntary certification programs help to identify those social workers who have gained the knowledge and experience necessary to meet national standards.

The National Association of Social Workers offers voluntary credentials to social workers with an M.S.W. degree, based on their experience: the academy of certified social workers (ACSW), the qualified clinical social worker (QCSW), or the diplomate in clinical social work (DCSW). These credentials are particularly valuable for social workers in private practice, as some health insurance providers require them for reimbursement purposes.

Other Requirements

Social work requires great dedication. As a social worker, you have the responsibility of helping whole families, groups, and communities, as well as focusing on the needs of individuals. Your efforts will not always be supported by the society at large; sometimes you must work against a community's prejudice, disinterest, and denial. You must also remain sensitive to the problems of your clients, offering support, and not moral judgment or personal bias. The only way to effectively address new social problems and new client groups is to remain open to the thoughts and needs of all human beings. Assessing situations and solving problems requires clarity of vision and a genuine concern for the well-being of others.

With this clarity of vision, your work will be all the more rewarding. Social workers have the satisfaction of making a connection with other people and helping them through difficult times. Along with the rewards, however, the work can cause a great deal of stress. Hearing repeatedly about the deeply troubled lives of prison inmates, the mentally ill, abused women and children, and others can be depressing and defeating. Trying to convince society of the need for changes in laws and services can be a long, hard struggle. You must have perseverance to fight for your clients against all odds.

EXPLORING

As a high school student, you may find openings for summer or part-time work as a receptionist or file clerk with a local social service agency. If there are no opportunities for paid employment, you could work as a volunteer. You can also gain good experience by working as a counselor in a camp for children with physical, mental, or developmental disabilities. Your local YMCA, park district, or other recreational facility may need volunteers for group recreation programs, including programs designed for the prevention of delinquency. By reporting for your high school newspaper, you'll have the opportunity to interview people, conduct surveys, and research social change, all of which are important aspects of the social work profession.

You could also volunteer a few afternoons a week to read to people in retirement homes or to the blind. Work as a tutor in special education programs is sometimes available to high school students.

EMPLOYERS

Social workers can be employed in direct or clinical practice, providing individual and family counseling services, or they may work as administrators for the organizations that provide direct practice. Social workers are employed by community health and mental health centers; hospitals and mental hospitals; child care, family services, and community service organizations, including day care and Head Start programs; elderly care programs, including adult protective services and adult day care and foster care; prisons; shelters and halfway houses; schools; courts; and nursing homes.

STARTING OUT

Most students of social work pursue a master's degree and in the process learn about the variety of jobs available. They also make valuable connections through faculty and other students. Through the university's job placement service or an internship program, a student will learn about job openings and potential employers.

A social work education in an accredited program will provide you with the most opportunities, and the best salaries and chances for promotion, but practical social work experience can also earn you full-time employment. A part-time job or volunteer work will introduce you to social work professionals who can provide you with career guidance and letters of reference. Agencies with limited funding may not be able to afford to hire social workers with M.S.W.'s and therefore will look for applicants with a great deal of experience and lower salary expectations.

ADVANCEMENT

More attractive and better-paying jobs tend to go to those with more years of practical experience. Dedication to your job, an extensive resume, and good references will lead to advancement in the profession. Also, many social work programs offer continuing education workshops, courses, and seminars. These refresher courses help practicing social workers to refine their skills and to learn about new areas of practice and new methods and problems. The courses are intended to supplement your social work education, not substitute for a bachelor's or master's degree. These continuing education courses can lead to job promotions and salary increases.

EARNINGS

The more education a social worker has completed, the more money he or she stands to make in the profession. The area of practice also determines earnings; the areas of mental health, group services, and community organization and planning provide higher salaries, while elderly and disabled care generally provide lower pay. Salaries also vary among regions. Social workers on the East and West Coasts earn higher salaries than those in the Midwest. Earnings in Canada vary from province to province as well. During their first five years of practice, social workers' salaries generally increase faster than in later years.

The median salary range for child, family, and school social workers was $39,960 in 2009, according to the *Occupational Outlook Handbook*. The top paid 10 percent earned more than $67,360, while the lowest paid 10 percent earned less than $26,050. Medical and public health social workers' salaries ranged from less than $28,600 to more than $71,190, with a median salary of $46,300 in 2009; mental health and substance abuse social workers earned between $24,940 and $62,7600, with a median salary of $38,200. All other social workers had median salaries of $49,420, with the lowest paid 10 percent earning $28,770 or less, and the highest paid 10 percent earning $75,240 or more in 2009.

WORK ENVIRONMENT

Social workers do not always work at a desk. When they do, they may be interviewing clients, writing reports, or conferring with other staff members. Depending on the size of the agency, office duties such as typing letters, filing, and answering phones may be performed by an aide or volunteer. Social workers employed at shelters or halfway houses may spend most of their time with clients, tutoring, counseling, or leading groups.

Some social workers have to drive to remote areas to make a home visit. They may go into inner-city neighborhoods, schools, courts, or jails. In larger cities, domestic violence and homeless shelters are sometimes located in rundown or dangerous areas. Most social workers are involved directly with the people they serve and must carefully examine the client's living conditions and family relations. Although some of these living conditions can be pleasant and demonstrate a good home situation, others can be squalid and depressing.

Advocacy involves work in a variety of different environments. Although much of this work may require making phone calls and sending faxes and letters, it also requires meetings with clients' employers, directors of agencies, local legislators, and others. It may sometimes require testifying in court as well.

OUTLOOK

The field of social work is expected to grow faster than the average for all occupations through 2018, according to the U.S. Department of Labor. The greatest factor for this growth is the increased number of older people who are in need of social services. Social workers that specialize in gerontology will find many job opportunities in nursing homes, hospitals, and home health care agencies. The needs of the future elderly population are likely to be different from those of the present elderly. Currently, the elderly appreciate community living, while subsequent generations may demand more individual care.

Schools will also need more social workers to deal with issues such as teenage pregnancies, children from single-parent households, and any adjustment problems recent immigrants may have. The trend to integrate students with disabilities into the general school population will require the expertise of social workers to make the transition smoother. However, job availability in schools will depend on funding given by state and local sources.

To help control costs, hospitals are encouraging early discharge for some of their patients. Social workers will be needed by hospitals to help secure health services for patients in their homes. There are also a growing number of people with physical disabilities or impairments staying in their own homes, requiring home health care workers.

Increased availability of health insurance funding and the growing number of people able to pay for professional help will create opportunities for those in private practice. Many businesses hire social workers to help in employee assistance programs, often on a contractual basis.

Poverty is still a main issue that social workers address. Families are finding it increasingly challenging to make ends meet on wages that are just barely above the minimum. The problem of fathers who do not make their court-ordered child support payments forces single mothers to work more than one job or rely on welfare. An increased awareness of domestic violence has also pointed up the fact that many homeless and unemployed people are women who have left abusive situations. Besides all this, working with the poor is often considered unattractive, leaving many social work positions in this area unfilled.

Competition for jobs in urban areas will remain strong. However, there is still a shortage of social workers in rural areas; these areas usually cannot offer the high salaries or modern facilities that attract large numbers of applicants.

The social work profession is constantly changing. The survival of social service agencies, both private and public, depends on shifting political, economic, and workplace issues.

Social work professionals are worried about the threat of declassification. Because of budget constraints and a need for more workers, some agencies have lowered their job requirements. When unable to afford qualified professionals, they hire those with less education and experience. This downgrading raises questions about quality of care and professional standards. Just as in some situations low salaries push out the qualified social worker, so do high salaries. In the area of corrections, attractive salaries (up to $40,000 for someone with a two-year associate's degree) have resulted in more competition from other service workers.

Liability is another growing concern. If a social worker, for example, tries to prove that a child has been beaten or attempts to remove a child from his or her home, the worker can potentially be sued for libel. At the other extreme, a social worker can face criminal charges for failure to remove a child from an abusive home. More social workers are taking out malpractice insurance.

FOR MORE INFORMATION

For information on social work careers and educational programs, contact

Council on Social Work Education
1701 Duke Street, Suite 200
Alexandria, VA 22314-3457
Tel: 703-683-8080
E-mail: info@cswe.org
http://www.cswe.org

To access the online publication Choices: Careers in Social Work, *contact*

National Association of Social Workers
750 First Street, NE, Suite 700
Washington, DC 20002-4241
Tel: 202-408-6600
http://www.naswdc.org

For information on educational programs in Canada, contact

Canadian Association for Social Work Education
226 Argyle Avenue
Ottawa, ON K2P 1B9
Canada

Tel: 613-792-1953
http://www.caswe-acfts.ca

 SOCIOLOGISTS

OVERVIEW

Sociologists study the behavior and interaction of people in groups. They research the characteristics of families, communities, the workplace, religious and business organizations, and many other segments of society. By studying a group, sociologists can gain insight about individuals; they can develop ideas about the roles of gender, race, age, and other social traits in human interaction. This research helps the government, schools, and other organizations address social problems and understand social patterns. In addition to research, a sociologist may teach, publish, consult, or counsel. There are approximately 4,430 sociologists working in the United States.

THE JOB

Curiosity is the main tool of a successful sociologist. Sociologists are intrigued by questions. For example, why do the members of different high school sports teams interact with each other in certain ways? Or why do some people work better in teams than others? What are the opportunities for promotion for workers with disabilities? Sociologists can even be inspired to question social policies based on their everyday experiences. For example, a sociologist reading a newspaper article about someone on a state's death row may wonder what the effect that the state's death penalty has on its crime level. Or an article on a new casino may cause the sociologist to wonder what effects legalized gambling have on the residents of that area. Such curiosity is one of the driving forces behind a sociologist's work.

With thoughtful questions and desire for knowledge, sociologists investigate the origin, development, and functioning of groups of people. This can involve extensively interviewing people or distributing form questionnaires. It can involve conducting surveys or researching historical records, both public and personal. A sociologist may need to set up an experiment, studying a cross section of people from a given society. The sociologist may choose to watch the interaction from a distance, or to participate as well as observe.

SCHOOL SUBJECTS
Psychology, Sociology

PERSONAL SKILLS
Communication/ideas, Helping/teaching

MINIMUM EDUCATION LEVEL
Master's degree

CERTIFICATION OR LICENSING
None available

WORK ENVIRONMENT
Primarily indoors, Primarily one location

The information sociologists compile from this variety of research methods is then used by administrators, lawmakers, educators, and other officials engaged in solving social problems. By understanding the common needs, thoughts, patterns, and ideas of a group of people, an organization can better provide for the individuals within those groups. With a sociologist's help, a business may be able to create a better training program for its employees; counselors in a domestic violence shelter may better assist clients with new home and job placement; teachers may better educate students with special needs.

Sociologists work closely with many other professionals. One of the closest working relationships is between sociologists and *statisticians* to analyze the significance of data. Sociologists also work with *psychologists*. Psychologists attempt to understand individual human behavior, while sociologists try to discover basic truths about groups. Sociologists also work with *cultural anthropologists*. Anthropologists study whole societies and try to discover what cultural factors have produced certain kinds of patterns in given communities. Sociologists work with *economists*. The ways in which people buy and sell are basic to understanding how groups behave. They also work with political scientists to study systems of government.

Ethnology and ethnography, social sciences that treat the subdivision of humans and their description and classification, are other fields with which sociologists work closely. Problems in racial understanding and cooperation, in failures in communication, and in dif-

ferences in belief and behavior are all concerns of the sociologist who tries to discover underlying reasons for group conduct.

Sociologists and *psychiatrists* have cooperated to discover community patterns of mental illness and mental health. They have attempted to compare such things as socioeconomic status, educational level, residence, and occupation to the incidence and kind of mental illness or health to determine in what ways society may be contributing to or preventing emotional disturbances.

Some sociologists choose to work in a specialized field. *Criminologists* specialize in investigations of causes of crime and methods of prevention, and *penologists* investigate punishment for crime, management of penal institutions, and rehabilitation of criminal offenders. *Social pathologists* specialize in investigation of group behavior that is considered detrimental to the proper functioning of society. *Demographers* are population specialists who collect and analyze vital statistics related to population changes, such as birth, marriages, and death. *Rural sociologists* investigate cultures and institutions of rural communities, while *urban sociologists* investigate origin, growth, structure, composition, and population of cities. *Social welfare research workers* conduct research that is used as a tool for planning and carrying out social welfare programs.

REQUIREMENTS

High School

Since a master's degree is recommended, if not required, in this field, you should take college prep courses while in high school. Take English classes to develop composition skills; you will be expected to present your research findings in reports, articles, and books. In addition to sociology classes, you should take other classes in the social sciences, such as psychology, history, and anthropology. Math and business will prepare you for the analysis of statistics and surveys. Government and history classes will help you to understand some of the basic principles of society, and journalism courses will bring you up to date on current issues.

Postsecondary Training

Most sociologists get their undergraduate degree in sociology, but a major in other areas of the liberal arts is also possible. Courses that you will likely take include statistics, mathematics, psychology, logic, and possibly a foreign language. In addition, keep up your computer skills because the computer is an indispensable research and communication tool.

Keep in mind that only limited entry-level positions will be available to you with only a bachelor's degree. New graduates may be able to start as a *research assistant* or *interviewer*. These workers are needed in research organizations, social service agencies, and corporate marketing departments.

Students who go on to get their master's and doctorate degrees will have a wider variety of employment opportunities. With a master's degree, opportunities are available in the federal government, industrial firms, or research organizations. Individuals with specific training in research methods will have an advantage. Those with a master's degree can also teach at the community or junior college level.

More than half of all sociologists hold doctorates. A large majority of the sociologists at the doctoral level teach in four-year colleges and universities throughout the country. Job candidates fare best if their graduate work includes specialized research and fieldwork.

Certification or Licensing

There are no specific certification or licensing requirements for sociologists.

Other Requirements

In addition to the natural curiosity mentioned above, a good sociologist must also possess an open mind. You must be able to assess situations without bias or prejudice that could affect the results of your studies. Social awareness is also important. As a sociologist, you must pay close attention to the world around you, to the way the world progresses and changes. Because new social issues arise every day, you will be frequently reading newspapers, magazines, and reports to maintain an informed perspective on these issues.

Good communication skills are valuable to the sociologist. In many cases, gathering information will involve interviewing people and interacting within their societies. The better your communication skills, the more information you can get from the people you interview.

EXPLORING

There are books about sociology, and possibly some journals of sociology, in your school and public libraries. By reading recent books and articles you can develop an understanding of the focus and requirements of socio-

logical study. If no specific sociology courses are offered in your high school, courses in psychology, history, or English literature can prepare you for the study of groups and human interaction; within these courses you may be able to write reports or conduct experiments with a sociological slant. A school newspaper, magazine, or journalism course can help you to develop important interview, research, and writing skills, while also heightening your awareness of your community and the communities of others.

EMPLOYERS

There are about 4,430 sociologists employed in the United States. Nearly half of all sociologists work in the scientific research and development services industry, and about 30 percent teach in colleges, universities, and professional schools. Some sociologists work for agencies of the federal government. In such agencies, their work lies largely in research, though they may also serve their agencies in an advisory capacity. Some sociologists are employed by private research organizations, and some work in management consulting firms. Sociologists also work with various medical groups and with physicians. Some sociologists are self-employed, providing counseling, research, or consulting services.

STARTING OUT

Many sociologists find their first jobs through the career services offices of their colleges and universities. Some are placed through the professional contacts of faculty members. A student in a doctorate program will make many connections and learn about fellowships, visiting professorships, grants, and other opportunities.

Those who wish to enter a research organization, industrial firm, or government agency should apply directly to the prospective employer. If you have been in a doctorate program, you should have research experience and publications to list on your resume, as well as assistantships and scholarships.

ADVANCEMENT

Sociologists who become college or university teachers may advance through the academic ranks from instructor to full professor. Those who like administrative work may become a head of a department. Publications of books and articles in journals of sociology will assist in a professor's advancement.

Those who enter research organizations, government agencies, or private business advance to positions of responsibility as they acquire experience. Salary increases usually follow promotions.

EARNINGS

Median annual earnings for sociologists were $69,620 in 2009, according to the U.S. Bureau of Labor Statistics. The lowest paid 10 percent earned less than $41,910, while the highest paid 10 percent earned over $123,410.

According to the U.S. Department of Labor, sociologists working for the federal government earned mean annual salaries of $101,320, in 2009. Those employed with social advocacy organizations earned mean annual salaries of $90,930; with scientific research and development services, $79,850; with colleges, universities, and professional schools, $73,210; with local governments, $63,010; and with state governments, $56,050.

WORK ENVIRONMENT

An academic environment can be ideal for a sociologist intent on writing and conducting research. If required to teach only a few courses a semester, a sociologist can then devote a good deal of time to his or her own work. And having contact with students can create a balance with the research.

The work of a sociologist takes place mostly in the classroom or at a computer writing reports and analyzing data. Some research requires visiting the interview subjects or setting up an experiment within the community of study.

OUTLOOK

Employment for sociologists is expected to grow much faster than the average through 2018, according to the U.S. Department of Labor. Opportunities are best for those with broad training and education in analytical, methodological, conceptual, and qualitative and quantitative analysis and research. Competition will be strong in all areas, however, as many sociology graduates continue to enter the job market.

As the average age of Americans rises, more opportunities of study will develop for those working with the elderly. Sociologists who specialize in gerontology will have opportunities to study the aging population in a variety of environments. Sociologists will find more opportunities in marketing, as companies conduct research on specific populations, such as the children of baby boomers. The Internet is also opening up new areas of sociological research; sociologists, demographers, market researchers, and other profes-

sionals are studying online communities and their impact.

FOR MORE INFORMATION

ASA offers career publications as well as job information.

American Sociological Association (ASA)
1430 K Street, NW, Suite 600
Washington, DC 20005-2529
Tel: 202-383-9005
http://www.asanet.org

To learn about sociologists working outside academia, contact

Association for Applied and Clinical Sociology
Department of Sociology, Anthropology, and
    Criminology
Eastern Michigan University
712 Pray-Harrold, EMU
Ypsilanti, MI 48197-2207
Tel: 734-487-0012
http://www.aacsnet.org

SOFTWARE DESIGNERS

OVERVIEW

Software designers, also known as *software developers*, are responsible for creating new ideas and designing prepackaged and customized computer software. Software designers devise applications such as word processors, front-end database programs, and spreadsheet programs that make it possible for computers to complete given tasks and to solve problems. Once a need in the market has been identified, software designers first conceive of the program on a global level by outlining what the program will do. Then they write the specifications from which programmers code computer commands to perform the given functions.

THE JOB

Without software, computer hardware would have nothing to do. Computers need to be told exactly what to do, and software is the set of codes that gives the computer those instructions. It comes in the form of the familiar prepackaged software that you find in a computer store,

SCHOOL SUBJECTS
Computer science, Mathematics

PERSONAL SKILLS
Communication/ideas, Technical/scientific

MINIMUM EDUCATION LEVEL
Bachelor's degree

CERTIFICATION OR LICENSING
Voluntary

WORK ENVIRONMENT
Primarily indoors, Primarily one location

such as games, word processing, spreadsheet, and desktop publishing programs, and in customized applications designed to fit specific needs of a particular business. Software designers are the initiators of these complex programs. Computer programmers then create the software by writing the code that carries out the directives of the designer.

Software designers must envision every detail of what an application will do, how it will do it, and how it will look (the user interface). A simple example is how a home accounting program is created. The software designer first lays out the overall functionality of the program, specifying what it should be able to do, such as balancing a checkbook, keeping track of incoming and outgoing bills, and maintaining records of expenses. For each of these tasks, the software designer will outline the design details for the specific functions that he or she has mandated, such as what menus and icons will be used, what each screen will look like, and whether there will be help or dialog boxes to assist the user. For example, the designer may specify that the expense record part of the program produce a pie chart that shows the percentage of each household expense in the overall household budget. The designer can specify that the program automatically display the pie chart each time a budget assessment is completed or only after the user clicks on the appropriate icon on the toolbar.

Some software companies specialize in building custom-designed software. This software is highly specialized for specific needs or problems of particular businesses. Some businesses are large enough that they employ in-house software designers who create software applications for their computer systems. A related field is software engineering, which involves writing customized, complex software to solve specific engineering or technical problems of a business or industry.

Whether the designer is working on a mass-market or a custom application, the first step is to define the overall goals for the application. This is typically done in consultation with management if working at a software supply company, or with the client if working on a custom-designed project. Then, the software designer studies the goals and problems of the project. If working on custom-designed software, the designer must also take into consideration the existing computer system of the client. Next, the software designer works on the program strategy and specific design detail that he or she has envisioned. At this point, the designer may need to write a proposal outlining the design and estimating time and cost allocations. Based on this report, management or the client decides if the project should proceed.

Once approval is given, the software designer and the programmers begin working on writing the software program. Typically, the software designer writes the specifications for the program, and the applications programmers write the programming codes.

In addition to the duties involved in design, a software designer may be responsible for writing a user's manual or at least writing a report for what should be included in the user's manual. After testing and debugging the program, the software designer will present it to management or to the client.

REQUIREMENTS
High School

If you are interested in computer science, you should take as many computer, math, and science courses as possible; they provide fundamental math and computer knowledge and teach analytical thinking skills. Classes that focus on schematic drawing and flowcharts are also very valuable. English and speech courses will help you improve your communication skills, which are very important to software designers who must make formal presentations to management and clients. Also, many technical/vocational schools offer programs in software programming and design. The qualities developed by these classes, plus imagination and an ability to work well under pressure, are key to success in software design.

Postsecondary Training

A bachelor's degree in computer science plus one year's experience with a programming language is required for most software designers; however, a master's degree is preferred for some positions.

In the past, the computer industry has tended to be pretty flexible about official credentials; demonstrated computer proficiency and work experience have often been enough to obtain a good position. As more people enter the field, though, competition has increased, and job requirements have become more stringent. Technical knowledge alone does not suffice in the field of software design anymore. In order to be a successful software designer, you should have at least a peripheral knowledge of the field for which you intend to design software, such as business, education, or science. Individuals with degrees in education and subsequent teaching experience are much sought after as designers for educational software. Those with bachelor's degrees in computer science with a minor in business or accounting have an excellent chance for employment in designing business or accounting software.

Certification or Licensing

Certification in software development is offered by companies such as Sun Microsystems, Hewlett-Packard, IBM, Novell, and Oracle. While not required, certification tells employers that your skills meet industry education and training standards.

Other Requirements

Software design is project- and detail-oriented, and therefore, you must be patient and diligent. You must also enjoy problem-solving challenges and be able to work under a deadline with minimal supervision. As a software designer, you should also possess good communication skills for consulting both with management and with clients who will have varying levels of technical expertise.

Software companies are looking for individuals with vision and imagination to help them create new and exciting programs to sell in the ever-competitive software market. Superior technical skills and knowledge combined with motivation, imagination, and exuberance will make you an attractive candidate.

EXPLORING

Spending a day with a professional software designer or applications programmer will allow you to experience firsthand what this work entails. School guidance counselors can often help you organize such a meeting.

If you are interested in computer industry careers in general, you should learn as much as possible about computers. Keep up with new technology by talking to other computer users and by reading related magazines, such as *Computer* (http://www.computer.org/portal/web/computer/home). You will also find it helpful to join computer clubs and use online services and the Internet to find more information about this field.

Advanced students can put their design ideas and programming knowledge to work by designing and programming their own applications, such as simple games and utility programs.

EMPLOYERS

Software designers are employed throughout the United States. Opportunities are best in large cities and suburbs where business and industry are active. Programmers who develop software systems work for software manufacturers, many of which are in Silicon Valley, in northern California. There are also concentrations of software manufacturers in Boston, Chicago, and Atlanta, among other places. Designers who adapt and tailor the software to meet specific needs of end-users work for those end-user companies, many of which are scattered across the country.

STARTING OUT

Software design positions are regarded as some of the most interesting, and therefore the most competitive, in the computer industry. Some software designers are promoted from an entry-level programming position. Software design positions in software supply companies and large custom software companies will be difficult to secure straight out of college or technical/vocational school.

Entry-level programming and design jobs may be listed in the help wanted sections of newspapers. Employment agencies and online job banks are other good sources.

Students in technical schools or universities should take advantage of their school's career services office. They should check regularly for internship postings, job listings, and notices of on-campus recruitment. Career services offices are also valuable resources for resume tips and interviewing techniques. Internships and summer jobs with such corporations are always beneficial and provide experience that will give you the edge over your competition. General computer job fairs are also held throughout the year in larger cities.

There are many online career sites listed on the World Wide Web that post job openings, salary surveys, and current employment trends. The Web also has online publications that deal specifically with computer jobs. You can also obtain information from computer organizations such as the IEEE Computer Society. Because this is such a competitive field, you will need to show initiative and creativity that will set you apart from other applicants.

ADVANCEMENT

In general, *programmers* work between one and five years before being promoted to *software designer*. A programmer can move up by demonstrating an ability to create new software ideas that translate well into marketable applications. Individuals with a knack for spotting trends in the software market are also likely to advance.

Those software designers who demonstrate leadership may be promoted to *project team leader*. Project team leaders are responsible for developing new software projects and overseeing the work done by software designers and applications programmers. With experience as a project team leader, a motivated software designer may be promoted to a position as a *software manager* who runs projects from an even higher level.

EARNINGS

Salaries for software designers vary with the size of the company and by location. Salaries may be slightly higher in areas where there is a large concentration of computer companies, such as the Silicon Valley in northern California and parts of Washington, Oregon, and the East Coast.

The National Association of Colleges and Employers reports that the average starting salary for graduates with a bachelor's degree in computer science averaged $61,407 in 2009.

Median salaries for computer software engineers specializing in systems software were $93,470 in 2009, according to the U.S. Department of Labor. Salaries ranged from less than $59,600 to $139,930 or more annually. Those employed by software publishing companies had median annual earnings of $97,840 in 2009. Glassdoor.com reported that software design engineers earned median annual salaries of $90,859 in early 2011; salaries ranged from $75,000 to $110,000 per year.

Most designers work for large companies, which offer a full benefits package that includes health insurance, vacation and sick time, and a profit sharing or retirement plan.

WORK ENVIRONMENT

Software designers work in comfortable environments. Many computer companies are known for their casual work atmosphere; employees generally do not have to wear suits, except during client meetings. Overall, software designers work standard weeks. However, they may be required to work overtime near a deadline. It is common in software design to share office or cubicle space with two or three coworkers, which is typical of the team approach to working. As a software designer or applications programmer, much of the day is spent in front of the computer, although a software designer will have occasional team meetings or meetings with clients.

Software design can be stressful work for several reasons. First, the market for software is very competitive and companies are pushing to develop more innovative software and to get it on the market before competitors do. For this same reason, software design is also very exciting and creative work. Second, software designers are given a project and a deadline. It is up to the designer and team members to budget their time to finish in the allocated time. Finally, working with programming languages and so many details can be very frustrating, especially when the tiniest glitch means the program will not run. For this reason, software designers must be patient and diligent.

OUTLOOK

Jobs in software design are expected to grow much faster than the average through 2018, according to the *Occupational Outlook Handbook (OOH)*. The expanding integration of Internet technologies by businesses has resulted in a rising demand for a variety of skilled professionals who can develop and support a variety of Internet applications. Concerns about information security have also increased the need for software that protects computer networks and electronic infrastructure. The *OOH* predicts expansion of this technology will continue over the next 10 years, and will increase the need for designers and engineers who can develop secure applications and systems and integrate them into older systems.

On another positive note, software design jobs are less prone to being outsourced to offshore companies that pay lower wages. Employers hire software designers for their innovation, creativity, and technical expertise.

FOR MORE INFORMATION

For information on internships, student membership, and the student magazine Crossroads, *contact*

Association for Computing Machinery
Two Penn Plaza, Suite 701
New York, NY 10121-0701
Tel: 800-342-6626
E-mail: acmhelp@acm.org
http://www.acm.org

For information on scholarships, student membership, and to read articles in Computing Now, contact

IEEE Computer Society
2001 L Street, NW, Suite 700
Washington, DC 20036-4928
Tel: 202-371-0101
E-mail: help@computer.org
http://www.computer.org

For industry information, contact the following organizations:

Software & Information Industry Association
1090 Vermont Ave, NW, 6th Floor
Washington, DC 20005-4095
Tel: 202-289-7442
http://www.siia.net

Software Testing Institute
http://www.softwaretestinginstitute.com

☐ SOFTWARE ENGINEERS

OVERVIEW

Software engineers are responsible for customizing existing software programs to meet the needs and desires of a particular business or industry. First, they spend considerable time researching, defining, and analyzing the problem at hand. Then, they develop software programs to resolve the problem on the computer. There are about 880,700 computer software engineers employed in the United States; 495,500 work with applications software and 385,200 work with systems software.

THE JOB

Every day, businesses, scientists, and government agencies encounter difficult problems that they cannot solve manually, either because the problem is just too complicated or because it would take too much time to calculate the appropriate solutions. For example, astronomers receive thousands of pieces of data every hour from probes and satellites in space as well as from telescopes here on Earth. If they had to process the information themselves, compile careful comparisons with previous years' readings, look for patterns or cycles, and keep accurate records of the origin of the data, it would be so cumbersome and lengthy a project as to make it next to impossible. They can, however, process the data with the extensive help of computers. Computer software engineers define and analyze specific problems in business or science and help develop computer software applications that effectively solve them. The software engineers who work in the field of astronomy are well versed in its concepts, but many other kinds of software engineers exist as well.

Software engineers fall into two basic categories. *Systems software engineers* build and maintain entire computer systems for a company. *Applications software engineers* design, create, and modify general computer applications software or specialized utility programs.

Engineers who work on computer systems research how a company's departments and their respective computer systems are organized. For example, there might be customer service, ordering, inventory, billing, shipping, and payroll recordkeeping departments. Systems software engineers suggest ways to coordinate

SCHOOL SUBJECTS
Computer science, Mathematics

PERSONAL SKILLS
Mechanical/manipulative, Technical/scientific

MINIMUM EDUCATION LEVEL
Bachelor's degree

CERTIFICATION OR LICENSING
Recommended

WORK ENVIRONMENT
Primarily indoors, Primarily one location

all these parts. They might set up intranets or networks that link computers within the organization and ease communication.

Some applications software engineers develop packaged software applications, such as word processing, graphic design, or database programs, for software development companies. Other applications engineers design customized software for individual businesses or organizations. For example, a software engineer might work with an insurance company to develop new ways to reduce paperwork, such as claim forms, applications, and bill processing. Applications engineers write programs using programming languages like C++ and Java.

Software engineers sometimes specialize in a particular industry such as the chemical industry, insurance, or medicine, which requires knowledge of that industry in addition to computer expertise. Some engineers work for consulting firms that complete software projects for different clients on an individual basis. Others work for large companies that hire full-time engineers to develop software customized to their needs.

Software engineering technicians assist engineers in completing projects. They are usually knowledgeable in analog, digital, and microprocessor electronics and programming techniques. Technicians know enough about program design and computer languages to fill in details left out by engineers or programmers, who conceive of the program from a large-scale perspective. Technicians might also test new software applications with special diagnostic equipment.

Both systems and applications software engineering involve extremely detail-oriented work. Since computers do only what they are programmed to do, engineers have to account for every bit of information with a programming command. Software engineers are thus required to be very well organized and precise. In order to achieve this, they generally follow strict procedures in completing an assignment.

First, they interview clients and colleagues to determine exactly what they want the final program to accomplish. Defining the problem by outlining the goal can sometimes be difficult, especially when clients have little technical training. Then, engineers evaluate the software applications already in use by the client to understand how and why they are failing to fulfill the needs of the operation. After this period of fact gathering, the engineers use methods of scientific analysis and mathematical models to develop possible solutions to the problems. These analytical methods help them pre-

dict and measure the outcomes of different proposed designs.

When they have developed a clear idea of what type of program is required to fulfill the client's needs, they draw up a detailed proposal that includes estimates of time and cost allocations. Management must then decide if the project will meet their needs, is a good investment, and whether or not it will be undertaken.

Once a proposal is accepted, both software engineers and technicians begin work on the project. They verify with hardware engineers that the proposed software program can be completed with existing hardware systems. Typically, the engineer writes program specifications and the technician uses his or her knowledge of computer languages to write preliminary programming. Engineers focus most of their effort on program strategies, testing procedures, and reviewing technicians' work.

Software engineers are usually responsible for a significant amount of technical writing, including project proposals, progress reports, and user manuals. They are required to meet regularly with clients to keep project goals clear and learn about any changes as quickly as possible.

When the program is completed, the software engineer organizes a demonstration of the final product to the client. Supervisors, management, and users are generally present. Some software engineers may offer to install the program, train users on it, and make arrangements for ongoing technical support.

REQUIREMENTS

High School

A high school diploma is the minimum requirement for software engineering technicians, but an associate's degree is required for most of these positions. A bachelor's or advanced degree in computer science or engineering is required for most software engineers. Thus, to prepare for college studies while in high school, take as many computer, math, and science courses as possible; they provide fundamental math and computer knowledge and teach analytical thinking skills. Classes that rely on schematic drawing and flowcharts are also very valuable. English and speech courses will help you improve your communication skills, which are very important for software engineers.

Postsecondary Training

There are several ways to enter the field of software engineering, although it is becoming increasingly necessary to pursue formal postsecondary education. If you don't have an associate's degree, you may first be hired in the quality assurance or technical support departments of a company. Many individuals complete associate degrees while working and then are promoted into software engineering technician positions. As more and more well-educated professionals enter the industry, however, it is becoming more important for you to have at least an associate's degree in computer engineering or programming. Many technical and vocational schools offer a variety of programs that will prepare you for a job as a software engineering technician.

If you are interested in this career, you should consider carefully your long-range goals. A bachelor's degree is usually required for promotion from technician to software engineer, and a master's degree is also required for some positions. In the past, the computer industry has tended to be fairly flexible about official credentials; demonstrated computer proficiency and work experience have often been enough to obtain a good position. This may hold true for some in the future. The majority of young computer professionals entering the field for the first time, however, will be college educated. Therefore, if you have no formal education or work experience you will have less chance of gaining employment.

Obtaining a postsecondary degree in computer engineering is usually considered challenging and even difficult. In addition to natural ability, you should be hard working and determined to succeed. If you plan to work in a specific technical field, such as medicine, law, or business, you should receive some formal training in that particular discipline.

Certification or Licensing

Another option if you're interested in software engineering is to pursue commercial certification. These programs are usually run by computer companies that wish to train professionals to work with their products. Classes are challenging and examinations can be rigorous. New programs are introduced every year.

Other Requirements

As a software engineer, you will need strong communication skills in order to be able to make formal business presentations and interact with people having different levels of computer expertise. You must also be detail oriented and work well under pressure.

EXPLORING

Try to spend a day with a working software engineer or technician in order to experience firsthand what their job is like. School guidance counselors can help you arrange such a visit. You can also talk to your high school computer teacher for more information.

In general, you should be intent on learning as much as possible about computers and computer software. You should learn about new developments by reading trade magazines and talking to other computer users. You can also join computer clubs and surf the Internet for information about working in this field.

EMPLOYERS

About 880,700 computer software engineers are employed in the United States. Approximately 495,500 work with applications and 385,200 work with systems software. Software engineering is done in many fields, including medical, industrial, military, communications, aerospace, scientific, and other commercial businesses. Almost 30 percent of software engineers—the largest concentration in the field—work in computer systems design and related services.

STARTING OUT

If you have work experience and perhaps even an associate's degree, you may be promoted to a software engineering technician position from an entry-level job in quality assurance or technical support. Those already employed by computer companies or large corporations should read company job postings to learn about promotion opportunities. If you are already employed and would like to train in software engineering, either on the job or through formal education, you can investigate future career possibilities within your same company and advise management of your wish to change career tracks. Some companies offer tuition reimbursement for employees who train in areas applicable to business operations.

As a technical, vocational, or university student of software engineering, you should work closely with your school's career services office, as many professionals find their first position through on-campus recruiting. Career services office staff are well trained to provide tips on resume writing, interviewing techniques, and locating job leads.

Individuals not working with a school career services office can check the classified ads for job openings. They can also work with a local employment agency that places computer professionals in appropriate jobs.

Many openings in the computer industry are publicized by word of mouth, so you should stay in touch with working computer professionals to learn who is hiring. In addition, these people may be willing to refer you directly to the person in charge of recruiting.

ADVANCEMENT

Software engineers who demonstrate leadership qualities and thorough technical know-how may become project team leaders who are responsible for full-scale software development projects. Project team leaders oversee the work of technicians and engineers. They determine the overall parameters of a project, calculate time schedules and financial budgets, divide the project into smaller tasks, and assign these tasks to engineers. Overall, they do both managerial and technical work.

Software engineers with experience as project team leaders may be promoted to a position as software manager, running a large research and development department. Managers oversee software projects with a more encompassing perspective; they help choose projects to be undertaken, select project team leaders and engineering teams, and assign individual projects. In some cases, they may be required to travel, solicit new business, and contribute to the general marketing strategy of the company.

Many computer professionals find that their interests change over time. As long as individuals are well qualified and keep up-to-date with the latest technology, they are usually able to find positions in other areas of the computer industry.

EARNINGS

Computer software engineers with a bachelor's degree in computer engineering earned starting salaries of $61,407 in 2009, according to the National Association of Colleges and Employers. Computer engineers specializing in applications earned median annual salaries of $87,480 in 2009, according to the U.S. Department of Labor. The lowest paid 10 percent averaged less than $54,840, and the highest paid 10 percent earned $132,080 or more annually. Software engineers specializing in systems software earned median salaries of $93,470 in 2009. The lowest paid 10 percent averaged $59,600 annually, and the highest paid engineers made $139,930 per year. When software engineers are promoted to *project team leader* or *software manager*, they earn even more. Software engineers generally earn more in geographical areas where there are clusters of computer companies, such as the Silicon Valley in northern California.

Most software engineers work for companies that offer extensive benefits, including health insurance, sick leave, and paid vacation. In some smaller computer companies, however, benefits may be limited.

WORK ENVIRONMENT

Software engineers usually work in comfortable office environments. Overall, they usually work 40-hour weeks, but their hours depend on the nature of the employer and expertise of the engineer. In consulting firms, for example, it is typical for software engineers to work long hours and frequently travel to out-of-town assignments.

Software engineers generally receive an assignment and a time frame within which to accomplish it; daily work details are often left up to the individuals. Some engineers work relatively lightly at the beginning of a project, but work a lot of overtime at the end in order to catch up. Most engineers are not compensated for overtime. Software engineering can be stressful, especially when engineers must work to meet deadlines. Working with programming languages and intense details is often frustrating. Therefore, software engineers should be patient, enjoy problem-solving challenges, and work well under pressure.

OUTLOOK

Employment opportunities for software engineers are expected to grow much faster than the average for all occupations through 2018, according to the U.S. Department of Labor. Demands made on computers increase every day and from all industries. Rapid growth in the computer systems design and related industries will account for much of this growth. In addition, businesses will continue to implement new and innovative technology to remain competitive, and they will need software engineers to do this. Software engineers will also be needed to handle ever-growing capabilities of computer networks, e-commerce, and wireless technologies, as well as the security features needed to protect such systems from outside attacks. Outsourcing of jobs in this field to foreign countries will temper growth somewhat, but overall the future of software engineering is very bright.

Since technology changes so rapidly, software engineers are advised to keep up on the latest developments. While the need for software engineers will remain high, computer languages will probably change every few years and software engineers will need to attend seminars and workshops to learn new computer languages and software design. They also should read trade magazines, surf the Internet, and talk with colleagues about the field. These kinds of continuing education techniques help ensure that software engineers are best equipped to meet the needs of the workplace.

FOR MORE INFORMATION

For information on internships, student membership, and the student magazine Crossroads, *contact*

Association for Computing Machinery
Two Penn Plaza, Suite 701
New York, NY 10121-0701
Tel: 800-342-6626
E-mail: acmhelp@acm.org
http://www.acm.org

For information on scholarships, student membership, and to read articles in Computing Now, *contact*

IEEE Computer Society
2001 L Street, NW, Suite 700
Washington, DC 20036-4928
Tel: 202-371-0101
E-mail: help@computer.org
http://www.computer.org

For certification information, contact

Institute for Certification of Computing Professionals
2400 East Devon Avenue, Suite 281
Des Plaines, IL 60018-4629Tel: 800-843-8227
http://www.iccp.org

For more information on careers in computer software, contact

Software & Information Industry Association
1090 Vermont Ave, NW, 6th Floor
Washington, DC 20005-4095
Tel: 202-289-7442
http://www.siia.net

SPECIAL EDUCATION TEACHERS

OVERVIEW

Special education teachers teach students ages three to 21 who have a variety of disabilities. They design indi-

vidualized education plans and work with students one-on-one to help them learn academic subjects and life skills. Approximately 477,310 special education teachers are employed in the United States, mostly in public schools.

THE JOB

Special education teachers instruct students who have a variety of disabilities. Their students may have physical disabilities, such as vision, hearing, or orthopedic impairment. They may also have learning disabilities or serious emotional disturbances. Although less common, special education teachers sometimes work with students who are gifted and talented, children who have limited proficiency in English, children who have communicable diseases, or children who are neglected and abused.

In order to teach special education students, these teachers design and modify instruction so that it is tailored to individual student needs. Teachers collaborate with school psychologists, social workers, parents, and occupational, physical, and speech-language therapists to develop a specially designed Individualized Education Program (IEP) for each of their students. The IEP sets personalized goals for a student based upon his or her learning style and ability, and it outlines specific steps to prepare him or her for employment or postsecondary schooling.

Special education teachers teach at a pace that is dictated by the individual needs and abilities of their students. Unlike most regular classes, special education classes do not have an established curriculum that is taught to all students at the same time. Because student abilities vary widely, instruction is individualized; it is part of the teacher's responsibility to match specific techniques with a student's learning style and abilities. They may spend much time working with students one-on-one or in small groups.

Working with different types of students requires a variety of teaching methods. Some students may need to use special equipment or skills in the classroom in order to overcome their disabilities. For example, a teacher working with a student with a physical disability might use a computer that is operated by touching a screen or by voice commands. To work with hearing-impaired students, the teacher may need to use sign language. With visually impaired students, he or she may use teaching materials that have Braille characters or large, easy-to-see type. Gifted and talented students may need extra-challenging assignments, a faster learn-

SCHOOL SUBJECTS
English, Speech

PERSONAL SKILLS
Communication/ideas, Helping/teaching

MINIMUM EDUCATION LEVEL
Bachelor's degree

CERTIFICATION OR LICENSING
Required by all states

WORK ENVIRONMENT
Primarily indoors, Primarily one location

ing pace, or special attention in one curriculum area, such as art or music.

In addition to teaching academic subjects, special education teachers help students develop both emotionally and socially. They work to make students as independent as possible by teaching them functional skills for daily living. They may help young children learn basic grooming, hygiene, and table manners. Older students might be taught how to balance a checkbook, follow a recipe, or use the public transportation system.

Special education teachers meet regularly with their students' parents to inform them of their child's progress and offer suggestions of how to promote learning at home. They may also meet with school administrators, social workers, psychologists, various types of therapists, and students' general education teachers.

The current trend in education is to integrate students with disabilities into regular classrooms to the extent that it is possible and beneficial to them. This is often called "mainstreaming." As mainstreaming becomes increasingly common, special education teachers frequently work with general education teachers in general education classrooms. They may help adapt curriculum materials and teaching techniques to meet the needs of students with disabilities and offer guidance on dealing with students' emotional and behavioral problems.

In addition to working with students, special education teachers are responsible for a certain amount of paperwork. They document each student's progress and may fill out any forms that are required by the school system or the government.

REQUIREMENTS
High School

If you are considering a career as a special education teacher, you should focus on courses that will prepare you for college. These classes include natural and social sciences, mathematics, and English. Speech classes would also be a good choice for improving your communication skills. Finally, classes in psychology might be useful, to help you understand the students you will eventually teach and prepare you for college-level psychology course work.

Postsecondary Training

All states require that teachers have at least a bachelor's degree and that they complete a prescribed number of subject and education credits. It is increasingly common for special education teachers to complete an additional fifth year of training after they receive their bachelor's degree. Many states require special education teachers to get a master's degree in special education.

There are approximately 800 colleges and universities in the United States that offer programs in special education, including undergraduate, master's, and doctoral programs. These programs include general and specialized courses in special education, including educational psychology, legal issues of special education, child growth and development, and knowledge and skills needed for teaching students with disabilities. The student typically spends the last year of the program student teaching in an actual classroom, under the supervision of a licensed teacher.

Certification or Licensing

All states require that special education teachers be licensed, although the particulars of licensing vary by state. In some states, these teachers must first be certified as elementary or secondary school teachers and then meet specific requirements to teach special education. Some states offer general special education licensure; others license several different subspecialties within special education. Some states allow special education teachers to transfer their license from one state to another, but many still require these teachers to pass licensing requirements for that state.

Other Requirements

To be successful in this field, you need to have many of the same personal characteristics as regular classroom teachers: the ability to communicate, a broad knowledge of the arts, sciences, and history, and a love of children. In addition, you will need a great deal of patience and persistence. You need to be creative, flexible, cooperative, and accepting of differences in others. Finally, you need to be emotionally stable and consistent in your dealings with students.

EXPLORING

There are a number of ways to explore the field of special education. One of the first and easiest is to approach a special education teacher at his or her school and ask to talk about the job. Perhaps the teacher could provide a tour of the special education classroom or allow you to visit while a class is in session.

You might also want to become acquainted with special-needs students at your own school or become involved in a school or community mentoring program for these students. There may also be other opportunities for volunteer work or part-time jobs in schools, community agencies, camps, or residential facilities that will allow you to work with persons with disabilities.

EMPLOYERS

Approximately 477,310 special education teachers are employed in the United States. The majority of special education teachers teach in public and private schools. Others work in state education agencies, individual and social assistance agencies, homebound or hospital environments, or residential facilities. States with the highest concentration of special education teachers are New York, New Jersey, Massachusetts, West Virginia, and New Mexico.

STARTING OUT

Because public school systems are by far the largest employers of special education teachers, this is where you should begin your job search.

You can also use your college's career services office to locate job leads. This may prove a very effective place to begin. You may also write to your state's department of education for information on placement and regulations, or contact state employment offices to inquire about job openings. Applying directly to local school systems can sometimes be effective. Even if a school system does not have an immediate opening, it will usually keep your resume on file should a vacancy occur.

ADVANCEMENT

Advancement opportunities for special education teachers, as well as for regular classroom teachers, are fairly limited. They may take the form of higher wages, better facilities, or more prestige. In some cases, special education teachers advance to become supervisors or administrators, although this may require continued education on the teacher's part. Another option is for special education teachers to earn advanced degrees and become instructors at the college level.

EARNINGS

In some school districts, salaries for special education teachers follow the same scale as general education teachers. In 2009, the median annual salary for special education teachers working in preschools, kindergartens, and elementary schools was $50,950, according to the *Occupational Outlook Handbook*. Special education teachers working in middle schools had median annual earnings of $51,970, and those in secondary schools earned $52,900. The lowest paid 10 percent of all special education teachers made less than $34,010 a year, and the highest paid 10 percent made more than $82,590. Private school teachers usually earn less than their public school counterparts. Teachers can supplement their annual salaries by becoming an activity sponsor, or by summer work. Some school districts pay their special education teachers on a separate scale, which is usually higher than that of general education teachers.

In 2008, almost 64 percent of all special education teachers belonged to unions, which help them secure fair working hours, salaries, and working conditions.

Regardless of the salary scale, special education teachers usually receive a complete benefits package, which includes health and life insurance, paid holidays and vacations, and a pension plan.

WORK ENVIRONMENT

Special education teachers usually work from 7:30 or 8:00 A.M. to 3:00 or 3:30 P.M. Like most teachers, however, they typically spend several hours in the evening grading papers, completing paperwork, or preparing lessons for the next day. Altogether, most special education teachers work more than the standard 40 hours per week.

Although some schools offer year-round classes for students, the majority of special education teachers work the traditional 10-month school year, with a two-month vacation in the summer. Many teachers find this work schedule very appealing, as it gives them the opportunity to pursue personal interests or additional education during the summer break. Teachers typically also get a week off at Christmas and for spring break.

Special education teachers work in a variety of settings in schools, including both ordinary and specially equipped classrooms, resource rooms, and therapy rooms. Some schools have newer and better facilities for special education than others. Although it is less common, some teachers work in residential facilities or tutor students who are homebound or hospitalized.

Working with special education students can be very demanding, due to their physical and emotional needs. Teachers may fight a constant battle to keep certain students, particularly those with behavior disorders, under control. Other students, such as those with mental impairments or learning disabilities, learn so slowly that it may seem as if they are making no progress. The special education teacher must deal daily with frustration, setbacks, and classroom disturbances.

These teachers must also contend with heavy workloads, including a great deal of paperwork to document each student's progress. In addition, they may sometimes be faced with irate parents who feel that their child is not receiving proper treatment or an adequate education.

The positive side of this job is that special education teachers help students overcome their disabilities and learn to be as functional as possible. For a special education teacher, knowing that he or she is making a difference in a child's life can be very rewarding and emotionally fulfilling.

OUTLOOK

The field of special education is expected to grow faster than the average career through 2018, according to the U.S. Department of Labor. This demand is caused partly by the growth in the number of special education students needing services. Medical advances resulting in more survivors of illness and accidents, a rise in birth defects, increased awareness and understanding of learning disabilities, and general population growth are also significant factors for strong demand. Because of the rise in the number of youths with disabilities under the age of 21, the government has given approval for more federally funded programs. Growth of jobs in this field has also been influenced positively by legislation emphasizing training and employment for individuals with disabilities

and a growing public awareness and interest in those with disabilities.

Finally, there is a fairly high turnover rate in this field, as some special education teachers find the work too stressful and switch to mainstream teaching or change jobs altogether. Many job openings will arise out of a need to replace teachers who leave their positions. There is a shortage of qualified teachers in rural areas and in the inner city. Jobs will also be plentiful for teachers who specialize in speech and language impairments, learning disabilities, and early childhood intervention. Bilingual teachers with multicultural experience will be in high demand.

FOR MORE INFORMATION

For general information about special education, contact

Council for Exceptional Children
2900 Crystal Drive, Suite 1000
Arlington, VA 22202-3557
Tel: 888-232-7733
http://www.cec.sped.org

For information on current issues, legal cases, and conferences, contact

Council of Administrators of Special Education
Osigian Office Centre
101 Katelyn Circle, Suite E
Warner Robins, GA 31088-6484
Tel: 478-333-6892
http://www.casecec.org

For information on special education degree programs, visit

eLearners.com
http://www.elearners.com/online-degrees/special-education.htm

For information about careers in special education, contact

National Center to Improve Recruitment and Retention of Qualified Personnel for Children with Disabilities
Personnel Improvement Center
National Association of State Directors of Special Education
1800 Diagonal Road, Suite 320
Alexandria, VA 22314-2862
Tel: 866-BECOME1
http://www.personnelcenter.org

SPEECH-LANGUAGE PATHOLOGISTS AND AUDIOLOGISTS

OVERVIEW

Speech-language pathologists and *audiologists* help people who have speech and hearing defects. They identify the problem and use tests to further evaluate it. Speech-language pathologists try to improve the speech and language skills of clients with communications disorders. Audiologists perform tests to measure the hearing ability of clients, who may range in age from the very young to the very old. Since it is not uncommon for clients to require assistance for both speech and hearing, pathologists and audiologists may frequently work together to help clients. Some professionals decide to combine these jobs into one, working as speech-language pathologists or audiologists. Audiologists and speech-language pathologists may work for school systems, in private practice, and at clinics and other medical facilities. Other employment possibilities for these professionals include teaching at universities, and conducting research on what causes certain speech and hearing defects. There are approximately 111,640 speech-language pathologists and 12,590 audiologists employed in the United States.

THE JOB

Even though the two professions seem to blend together at times, speech-language pathology and audiology are very different from one another. However, because both speech and hearing are related to one another, a person competent in one discipline must have familiarity with the other.

The duties performed by speech-language pathologists and audiologists differ depending on education, experience, and place of employment. Most speech-language pathologists provide direct clinical services to individuals and independently develop and carry out treatment programs. In medical facilities, they may work with physicians, social workers, psychologists, and other therapists to develop and execute treatment plans. In a school environment, they develop individual or group

SCHOOL SUBJECTS
Biology, Health, Speech

PERSONAL SKILLS
Helping/teaching, Technical/scientific

MINIMUM EDUCATION LEVEL
Master's degree (speech-language pathologists), Doctorate (audiologists)

CERTIFICATION OR LICENSING
Required (audiologists),
Required in some states (speech-language pathologists)

WORK ENVIRONMENT
Primarily indoors, Primarily one location

programs, counsel parents, and sometimes help teachers with classroom activities.

Clients of speech-language pathologists include people who cannot make speech sounds, or cannot make them clearly; those with speech rhythm and fluency problems such as stuttering; people with voice quality problems, such as inappropriate pitch or harsh voice; those with problems understanding and producing language; and those with cognitive communication impairments, such as attention, memory, and problem-solving disorders. Speech-language pathologists may also work with people who have oral motor problems that cause eating and swallowing difficulties. Clients' problems may be congenital, developmental, or acquired, and caused by hearing loss, brain injury or deterioration, cerebral palsy, stroke, cleft palate, voice pathology, mental retardation, or emotional problems.

Speech-language pathologists conduct written and oral tests and use special instruments to analyze and diagnose the nature and extent of impairment. They develop an individualized plan of care, which may include automated devices and sign language. They teach clients how to make sounds, improve their voices, or increase their language skills to communicate more effectively. Speech-language pathologists help clients develop, or recover, reliable communication skills.

People who have hearing, balance, and related problems consult audiologists, who use audiometers and other testing devices to discover the nature and extent of hearing loss. Audiologists interpret these results and may coordinate them with medical, educational, and psychological information to make a diagnosis and determine a course of treatment.

Hearing disorders can result from trauma at birth, viral infections, genetic disorders, or exposure to loud noise. Treatment may include examining and cleaning the ear canal, fitting and dispensing a hearing aid or other device, and audiologic rehabilitation (including auditory training or instruction in speech or lip reading). Audiologists provide fitting and tuning of cochlear implants and help those with implants adjust to the implant amplification systems. They also test noise levels in workplaces and conduct hearing protection programs in industrial settings, as well as in schools and communities.

Audiologists provide direct clinical services to clients and sometimes develop and implement individual treatment programs. In some environments, however, they work as members of professional teams in planning and implementing treatment plans.

In a research environment, speech pathologists and audiologists investigate communicative disorders and their causes and ways to improve clinical services. Those teaching in colleges and universities instruct students on the principles and bases of communication, communication disorders, and clinical techniques used in speech and hearing.

Speech-language pathologists and audiologists keep records on the initial evaluation, progress, and discharge of clients to identify problems and track progress. They counsel individuals and their families on how to cope with the stress and misunderstanding that often accompany communication disorders.

REQUIREMENTS

High School

Since a college degree is a must for practicing this profession, make sure your high school classes are geared toward preparing you for higher education. Health and science classes, including biology, are very important. Mathematics classes and English classes will help you develop the math, research, and writing skills you will need in college. Because speech-language pathologists and audiologists work so intensely with language, you may also find it beneficial to study a foreign language, paying special attention to how you learn to make sounds and remember words. Speech classes will also improve your awareness of sounds and language as well as improve your speaking and listening skills.

Postsecondary Training

Most states require a master's degree in speech-language pathology or audiology for a beginning job in either profession. As of 2009, 47 states required speech-language pathologists to be licensed if they work in a health care setting. Typical majors for those going into this field include communication sciences and disorders, speech and hearing, or education.

Regardless of your career goal (speech-language pathologist or audiologist), your undergraduate course work should include classes in anatomy, biology, physiology, physics, and other related areas, such as linguistics, semantics, and phonetics. It is also helpful to have some exposure to child psychology.

Accredited graduate programs in speech-language pathology are available from 240 colleges and universities. Graduate-level work for those in speech-language pathology includes studies in evaluating and treating speech and language disorders, stuttering, pronunciation, and voice modulation. To be eligible for certification, which most employers and states require, you must have at least a master's degree from a program accredited by the accreditation council of the American Speech-Language-Hearing Association (ASHA).

Also as of 2009, all states require audiologists to be licensed to practice and 18 states require audiologists to earn a doctorate in order to be certified. Currently there are 70 Council on Academic Accreditation (CAA) accredited doctoral programs in audiology. Graduate-level course work in audiology includes such studies as hearing and language disorders, normal auditory and speech-language development, balance, and audiology instrumentation.

Students of both disciplines are required to complete supervised clinical fieldwork or practicum. It is in your best interest to contact the ASHA or the CAA for a listing of accredited programs before you decide on a graduate school to attend. Some schools offer graduate degrees only in speech-language pathology or graduate degrees only in audiology. A number of schools offer degrees in both fields.

If you plan to practice in some states or go into research, teaching, or administration, you will need to complete a doctorate degree.

Certification or Licensing

To work as a speech pathologist or audiologist in a public school, you will be required to be a certified teacher and you must meet special state requirements if treating children with disabilities. All states regulate audiology and 47 states regulate speech-language pathology through licensure or title registration, and most of those require continuing education for license renewal. In order to become licensed, you must have completed an advanced degree in the field (generally a master's degree, but a doctorate is becoming the new standard for audiologists), pass a standardized test, and complete 300 to 375 hours of supervised clinical experience and nine months of postgraduate professional clinical experience. Some states permit audiologists to dispense hearing aids under an audiology license. Specific education and experience requirements, type of regulation, and title use vary by state.

Many states base their licensing laws on ASHA or CCA certification. ASHA offers speech-language pathologists the certificate of clinical competence in speech-language pathology and the CCA offers audiologists the certificate of clinical competence in audiology. To be eligible for these certifications, you must meet certain education requirements, such as the supervised clinical fieldwork experience, and have completed a postgraduate clinical fellowship. The fellowship must be no less than 36 weeks of full-time professional employment or its part-time equivalent. You must then pass an examination in the area in which you want certification.

Other Requirements

Naturally, speech-language pathologists and audiologists should have strong communication skills. Note, though, that this means more than being able to speak clearly. You must be able to explain diagnostic test results and treatment plans in an easily understood way for a variety of clients who are already experiencing problems. As a speech-language pathologist or audiologist, you should enjoy working with people, both your clients and other professionals who may be involved in the client's treatment. In addition, you need patience and compassion. A client's progress may be slow, and you should be supportive and encouraging during these times.

EXPLORING

Although the specialized nature of this work makes it difficult for you to get an informal introduction to either profession, there are opportunities to be found. Official training must begin at the college or university level, but it is possible for you to volunteer in clinics and hospitals. As a prospective speech-language pathologist or audiologist, you may also find it helpful to learn sign language or volunteer your time in speech, language, and hearing centers.

EMPLOYERS

According to the *Occupational Outlook Handbook*, about 111,640 speech-language pathologists and 12,590 audiologists were employed in the United States as of 2009. About 48 percent of speech-language pathologists are employed in education, from elementary school to the university level, while 64 percent of audiologists work in physicians' offices and medical facilities. Other professionals in this field work in state and local governments, hearing aid stores (audiologists), and scientific research facilities. A small but growing number of speech-language pathologists and audiologists are in private practice, generally working with patients referred to them by physicians and other health practitioners.

Some speech-language pathologists and audiologists contract to provide services in schools, hospitals, or nursing homes, or work as consultants to industry.

STARTING OUT

If you want to work in the public school systems, the college career services office can help you with interviewing skills. Professors sometimes know of job openings and may even post these openings on a centrally located bulletin board. It may be possible to find employment by contacting a hospital or rehabilitation center. To work in colleges and universities as a specialist in the classroom, clinic, or research center, it is almost mandatory to be working on a graduate degree. Many scholarships, fellowships, and grants for assistants are available in colleges and universities giving courses in speech-language pathology and audiology. Most of these and other assistance programs are offered at the graduate level. The U.S. Rehabilitation Services Administration, the Children's Bureau, the U.S. Department of Education, and the National Institutes of Health allocate funds for teaching and training grants to colleges and universities with graduate study programs. In addition, the Department of Veterans Affairs provides stipends (a fixed allowance) for predoctoral work.

ADVANCEMENT

Advancement in speech-language pathology and audiology is based chiefly on education. Individuals who have completed graduate study will have the best opportunities to enter research and administrative areas, supervising other speech-language pathologists or audiologists either in developmental work or in public school systems.

EARNINGS

The U.S. Department of Labor reports that in 2009, speech-language pathologists earned a median annual salary of $65,090. Salaries ranged from to less than $42,310 to more than $101,820. Also in 2009, audiologists earned a median annual salary of $63,230. The lowest paid 10 percent of these workers earned less than $40,650, while the highest paid 10 percent earned $100,480 or more per year. Geographic location and type of facility are important salary variables. Almost all employment situations provide fringe benefits such as paid vacations, sick leave, and retirement programs.

WORK ENVIRONMENT

Most speech-language pathologists and audiologists work 40 hours a week at a desk or table in clean, comfortable surroundings. Speech-language pathologists and audiologists who focus on research, however, may work longer hours. The job is not physically demanding but does require attention to detail and intense concentration. The emotional needs of clients and their families may be demanding.

OUTLOOK

Population growth, lengthening life spans, and increased public awareness of the problems associated with communicative disorders indicate a highly favorable employment outlook for well-qualified personnel. The U.S. Department of Labor predicts that employment for speech-language pathologists will grow faster than the average and audiologists will grow much faster than the average for all occupations through 2018. Much of this growth depends on economic factors, further budget cutbacks by health care providers and third-party payers, and legal mandates requiring services for people with disabilities.

Many of the new jobs emerging through the end of the decade are expected to be in speech and hearing clinics, physicians' offices, and outpatient care facilities. Speech-language pathologists and audiologists will be needed in these places, for example, to carry out the increasing number of rehabilitation programs for stroke victims and patients with head injuries.

Substantial job growth will continue to occur in elementary and secondary schools because of the Education for All Handicapped Children Act of 1975 and the Individuals with Disabilities Education Act in 1990, 1997, and 2004. Such laws guarantee special education and related services to minors with disabilities.

Many new jobs will be created in hospitals, nursing homes, rehabilitation centers, and home health agencies; most of these openings will probably be filled by private practitioners employed on a contract basis. Opportunities for speech-language pathologists and audiologists in private practice should increase in the future. There should be a greater demand for consultant audiologists in the area of industrial and environmental noise as manufacturing and other companies develop and carry out noise-control programs.

FOR MORE INFORMATION

The American Auditory Society is concerned with hearing disorders, how to prevent them, and the rehabilitation of individuals with hearing and balance dysfunction.

American Auditory Society
19 Mantua Road
Mount Royal, NJ 08061-1006
Tel: 856-423-3118
http://www.amauditorysoc.org

This professional, scientific, and credentialing association offers information about communication disorders and career and membership information.

American Speech-Language-Hearing Association
2200 Research Boulevard
Rockville, MD 20850-3289
Tel: 800-638-8255
E-mail: actioncenter@asha.org
http://www.asha.org

This association is for undergraduate and graduate students studying human communication. For news related to the field and to find out about regional chapters, contact

National Student Speech, Language, Hearing Association
2200 Research Boulevard, #450
Rockville, MD 20850-3289
Tel: 800-498-2071
E-mail: nsslha@asha.org
http://www.nsslha.org

□ SPORTS INSTRUCTORS AND COACHES

OVERVIEW

Sports instructors demonstrate and explain the skills and rules of particular sports, like golf or tennis, to individuals or groups. They help beginners learn basic rules, stances, grips, movements, and techniques of a game. Sports instructors often help experienced athletes to sharpen their skills.

Coaches work with a single, organized team or individual, teaching the skills associated with that sport. A coach prepares her or his team for competition. During the competition, he or she continues to give instruction from a vantage point near the court or playing field.

THE JOB

The specific job requirements of sports instructors and coaches vary according to the type of sport and athletes involved. For example, an instructor teaching advanced skiing at a resort in Utah will have different duties and responsibilities than an instructor teaching beginning swimming at a municipal pool. Nevertheless, all instructors and coaches are teachers. They must be very knowledgeable about rules and strategies for their respective sports. They must also have an effective teaching method that reinforces correct techniques and procedures so their students or players will be able to gain from that valuable knowledge. Also, instructors and coaches need to be aware of and open to new procedures and techniques. Many attend clinics or seminars to learn more about their sport or even how to teach more effectively. Many are also members of professional organizations that deal exclusively with their sport.

Safety is a primary concern for all coaches and instructors. Coaches and instructors make sure their students have the right equipment and know its correct use. A major component of safety is helping students feel comfortable and confident with their abilities. This entails teaching the proper stances, techniques, and movements of a game, instructing students on basic rules, and answering any questions.

While instructors may tutor students individually or in small groups, a coach works with all the members of

> **SCHOOL SUBJECTS**
> English, Physical education
>
> **PERSONAL SKILLS**
> Communication/ideas, Helping/teaching
>
> **MINIMUM EDUCATION LEVEL**
> Some postsecondary training
>
> **CERTIFICATION OR LICENSING**
> Required in certain positions
>
> **WORK ENVIRONMENT**
> Indoors and outdoors, Primarily multiple locations

a team. Both use lectures and demonstrations to show students the proper skills, and both point out students' mistakes or deficiencies.

Motivation is another key element in sports instruction. Almost all sports require stamina, and most coaches will tell you that psychological preparation is every bit as important as physical training.

Coaches and instructors also have administrative responsibilities. College coaches actively recruit new players to join their team. Professional coaches attend team meetings with owners and general managers to determine which players they will draft the next season. Sports instructors at health and athletic clubs schedule classes, lessons, and contests.

REQUIREMENTS

Training and educational requirements vary, depending on the specific sport and the ability level of students being instructed. Most coaches who are associated with schools have bachelor's degrees. Many middle and high school coaches are also teachers within the school. Most instructors need to combine several years of successful experience in a particular sport with some educational background, preferably in teaching. A college degree is becoming more important as part of an instructor's background.

High School

To prepare for college courses, high school students should take courses that teach human physiology. Biology, health, and exercise classes would all be helpful.

Courses in English and speech are also important to improve or develop communication skills.

There is no substitute for developing expertise in a sport. If you can play the sport well and effectively explain to other people how they might play, you will most likely be able to get a job as a sports instructor. The most significant source of training for this occupation is gained while on the job.

Postsecondary Training

Postsecondary training in this field varies greatly. College and professional coaches often attended college as athletes, while others attended college and received their degrees without playing a sport. If you are interested in becoming a high school coach, you will need a college degree because you will most likely be teaching as well as coaching. At the high school level, coaches spend their days teaching everything from physical education to English to mathematics, and so the college courses these coaches take vary greatly. Coaches of some youth league sports may not need a postsecondary degree, but they must have a solid understanding of their sport and of injury prevention.

Certification or Licensing

Many facilities require sports instructors to be certified. Information on certification is available from any organization that deals with the specific sport in which one might be interested.

Since most high school coaches also work as teachers, those interested in this job should plan to obtain teacher certification in their state.

Other Requirements

Coaches have to be experts in their sport. They must have complete knowledge of the rules and strategies of the game, so that they can creatively design effective plays and techniques for their athletes. But the requirements for this job do not end here. Good coaches are able to communicate their extensive knowledge to the athletes in a way that not only instructs the athletes, but also inspires them to perform to their fullest potential. Therefore, coaches are also teachers.

"I think I'm good at my job because I love working with people and because I'm disciplined in everything I do," says Dawn Shannahan, former assistant girls' basketball and track coach at Leyden High School in Franklin Park, Illinois. Discipline is important for athletes, as they must practice plays and techniques over and over again. Coaches who cannot demonstrate and encourage this type of discipline will have difficulty helping their athletes improve. Shannahan adds, "I've seen coaches who are really knowledgeable about their sport but who aren't patient enough to allow for mistakes or for learning." Patience can make all the difference between an effective coach and one who is unsuccessful.

Similarly, Shannahan says, "A coach shouldn't be a pessimist. The team could be losing by a lot, but you have to stay optimistic and encourage the players." Coaches must be able to work under pressure, guiding teams through games and tournaments that carry great personal and possibly financial stakes for everyone involved.

EXPLORING

Try to gain as much experience as possible in all sports and a specific sport in particular. It is never too early to start. High school and college offer great opportunities to participate in sporting events as a player, manager, trainer, or in intramural leagues.

Most communities have sports programs such as Little League baseball or track and field meets sponsored by the recreation commission. Get involved by volunteering as a coach, umpire, or starter.

Talking with sports instructors already working in the field is also a good way to discover specific job information and find out about career opportunities.

EMPLOYERS

Approximately 179,830 sports coaches and scouts, and 228,170 fitness trainers and instructors, are employed in the United States. Besides working in high schools, coaches and instructors are hired by colleges and universities, professional sports teams, individual athletes such as tennis players, and by youth leagues, summer camps, and recreation centers.

STARTING OUT

People with expertise in a particular sport, who are interested in becoming an instructor, should apply directly to the appropriate facility. Sometimes a facility will provide training.

For those interested in coaching, many colleges offer positions to *graduate assistant coaches*. Graduate assistant coaches are recently graduated players who are interested in becoming coaches. They receive a stipend and gain valuable coaching experience.

ADVANCEMENT

Advancement opportunities for both instructors and coaches depend on the individual's skills, willingness to learn, and work ethic. A sports instructor's success can be measured by caliber of play and number of students. Successful instructors may become well known enough to open their own schools or camps, write books, or produce how-to videos.

Some would argue that a high percentage of wins is the only criteria for success for professional coaches. However, coaches in the scholastic ranks have other responsibilities and other factors that measure success; for example, high school and college coaches must make sure their players are getting good grades. All coaches must try to produce a team that competes in a sportsmanlike fashion regardless of whether they win or lose.

Successful coaches are often hired by larger schools. High school coaches may advance to become college coaches, and the most successful college coaches often are given the opportunity to coach professional teams. Former players sometimes land assistant or head coaching positions.

EARNINGS

Earnings for sports instructors and coaches vary considerably depending on the sport and the person or team being coached. The coach of a Wimbledon champion commands much more money per hour than the swimming instructor for the tadpole class at the municipal pool.

The U.S. Department of Labor (DOL) reports that the median earnings for sports coaches and scouts were $28,380 in 2009. The lowest paid 10 percent earned less than $15,910, while the highest paid 10 percent earned more than $62,750. Often, much of the work is part time, and part-time employees generally do not receive paid vacations, sick days, or health insurance.

Instructors who teach group classes for beginners through park districts or at city recreation centers can expect to earn around $6 per hour. An hour-long individual lesson through a golf course or tennis club averages $75. Many times, coaches for children's teams work as volunteers.

Many sports instructors work in camps teaching swimming, archery, sailing and other activities. These instructors generally earn between $1,000 and $2,500, plus room and board, for a summer session.

According to the DOL, full-time fitness and aerobics instructors at gyms or health clubs earned between $16,430 and $62,120 per year, with a median salary of $30,670, in 2009. Instructors with many years of experience and a college degree have the highest earning potential.

Most coaches who work at the high school level or below also teach within the school district. Besides their teaching salary and coaching fee—either a flat rate or a percentage of their annual salary—school coaches receive a benefits package that includes paid vacations and health insurance.

College head football coaches in the NCAA's top-level, 120-school Football Bowl Subdivision earn an average of $1.36 million, although top coaches can earn as much as $5 million or more per year. Head coaches of Division I men's college basketball teams average about $1.7 million annually, while coaches of women's teams at the same level average considerable less at $850,000 a year. Many larger and more successful universities pay more. Coaches for professional teams often earn more than $1 million per year. Many popular coaches augment their salaries with personal appearances and endorsements.

WORK ENVIRONMENT

An instructor or coach may work indoors, in a gym or health club, or outdoors, perhaps at a swimming pool. Much of the work is part time. Full-time sports instructors generally work between 35 and 40 hours per week. During the season when their teams compete, coaches can work 16 hours each day, five or six days each week.

It is not unusual for coaches or instructors to work evenings or weekends. Instructors work then because that is when their adult students are available for instruction. Coaches work nights and weekends because those are the times their teams compete.

One significant drawback to this job is the lack of job security. A club may hire a new instructor on very little notice, or may cancel a scheduled class for lack of interest. Athletic teams routinely fire coaches after losing seasons.

Sports instructors and coaches should enjoy working with a wide variety of people. They should be able to communicate clearly and possess good leadership skills to effectively teach complex skills. They can take pride in the knowledge that they have helped their students or their players reach new heights of achievement and training.

OUTLOOK

Americans' interest in health, physical fitness, and body image continues to send people to gyms and playing fields. This fitness boom has created strong employment opportunities for many people in sports-related occupations.

Health clubs, community centers, parks and recreational facilities, and private business now employ sports instructors who teach everything from tennis and golf to scuba diving.

According to the U.S. Department of Labor, this occupation will grow much faster than the average through 2018. Job opportunities will be best in high schools and in amateur athletic leagues. Health clubs, adult education programs, and private industry will require competent, dedicated instructors. Those with the most training, education, and experience will have the best chance for employment.

The creation of new professional leagues, as well as the expansion of current leagues, will open some new employment opportunities for professional coaches, but competition for these jobs will be very intense. There will also be openings as other coaches retire or are terminated. However, there is very little job security in coaching, unless a coach can consistently produce a winning team.

FOR MORE INFORMATION

For certification information, trade journals, job listings, and a list of graduate schools, visit the AAHPERD Web site.

American Alliance for Health, Physical Education, Recreation and Dance (AAHPERD)
1900 Association Drive
Reston, VA 20191-1598
Tel: 800-213-7193
http://www.aahperd.org

For information on membership and baseball coaching education, coaching Web links, and job listings, visit the ABCA Web site.

American Baseball Coaches Association (ABCA)
108 South University Avenue, Suite 3
Mount Pleasant, MI 48858-2327
Tel: 989-775-3300
E-mail: abca@abca.org
http://www.abca.org

For information on careers in sports and physical education, contact

National Association for Sport and Physical Education
1900 Association Drive

Reston, VA 20191-1598
Tel: 800-213-7193
E-mail: naspe@aahperd.org
http://www.aahperd.org/naspe

For information on high school coaching opportunities, contact

National High School Athletic Coaches Association
PO Box 5921
Rochester, MN 55903-5921
E-mail: jg.NHSACA@charter.net
http://www.hscoaches.org

SURGEONS

OVERVIEW

Surgeons are physicians who make diagnoses and provide preoperative, operative, and postoperative care in surgery affecting almost any part of the body. These doctors also work with trauma victims and the critically ill. Approximately 44,560 surgeons are employed in the United States.

THE JOB

The work of a surgeon will vary according to his or her work environment and specialty. For example, a general surgeon who specializes in trauma care would most likely work in a large, urban hospital where he or she would spend a great deal of time in the operating room performing emergency surgical procedures at a moment's notice. On the other hand, a general surgeon who specializes in hernia repair would probably have a more predictable work schedule and would spend much of his or her time in an ambulatory (also called outpatient) surgery center.

The surgeon is responsible for the diagnosis of the patient, for performing operations, and for providing patients with postoperative surgical care and treatment. In emergency room situations, the patient typically comes with an injury or severe pain. If the patient needs surgery, the on-duty general surgeon will schedule the surgery. Depending on the urgency of the case, surgery may be scheduled for the following day, or the patient will be operated on immediately.

A surgeon sees such cases as gunshot, stabbing, and accident victims. Other cases that often involve emergency surgery include appendectomies and removal

SCHOOL SUBJECTS
Biology, Chemistry, Health

PERSONAL SKILLS
Helping/teaching, Technical/scientific

MINIMUM EDUCATION LEVEL
Medical degree

CERTIFICATION OR LICENSING
Required by all states

WORK ENVIRONMENT
Primarily indoors, Primarily multiple locations

of kidney stones. When certain problems, such as a kidney stone or inflamed appendix, are diagnosed at an early stage, the surgeon can perform nonemergency surgery.

There are several specialties of surgery and four areas of subspecialization of general surgery. For these areas, the surgeon can receive further education and training leading to certification. A few of these specializations include *neurosurgery* (care for disorders of the nervous system), *plastic and reconstructive surgery* (care for defects of the skin and underlying musculoskeletal structure), *orthopaedic surgery* (care for musculoskeletal disorders that are present at birth or develop later), and *thoracic surgery* (care for diseases and conditions of the chest). The subspecializations for general surgery are: *general vascular surgery, pediatric surgery, hand surgery,* and *surgical critical care*.

REQUIREMENTS
High School

Training to become a surgeon or physician is among the most rigorous of any profession, but the pay is also among the highest. To begin preparing for the demands of college, medical school, and an internship and residency in a hospital, be sure to take as many science and mathematics courses as possible. English, communication, and psychology classes will help prepare you for the large amount of reporting and interacting with patients and staff that surgeons do on a daily basis.

Postsecondary Training

Many students who want to become a physician or surgeon enroll in premedical programs at a college or university. Premedical students take classes in biology, organic and inorganic chemistry, physics, mathematics, English, and the humanities. Some students who major in other disciplines go on to pursue a medical degree, but they generally have to complete additional course work in math and science. All students must take the standardized Medical College Admission Test (MCAT) and then apply to medical schools to pursue the M.D. degree. Note that medical school admissions are fiercely competitive, so developing strong study habits, attaining good grades, and pursuing extracurricular activities are all important characteristics for a medical school applicant to have.

Physicians wishing to pursue general surgery must complete a five-year residency in surgery according to the requirements set down by the Accreditation Council for Graduate Medical Education.

Throughout the surgery residency, residents are supervised at all levels of training by assisting on and then performing basic operations, such as the removal of an appendix. As the residency years continue, residents gain responsibility through teaching and supervisory duties. Eventually the residents are allowed to perform complex operations independently.

Subspecialties require from one to three years of additional training.

Certification or Licensing

The American Board of Surgery administers board certification in surgery. While certification is a voluntary procedure, it is highly recommended. Most hospitals will not grant privileges to a surgeon without board certification. HMOs and other insurance groups will not make referrals or payments to a surgeon without board certification. Also, insurance companies are not likely to insure a surgeon for malpractice if he or she is not board certified.

To be eligible to apply for certification in surgery, a candidate must have successfully completed medical school and the requisite residency in surgery. Once a candidate's application has been approved, the candidate may take the written examination. After passing the written exam, the candidate may then take the oral exam.

Certification in surgery is valid for 10 years. To obtain recertification, surgeons must apply to the American Board of Surgery with documentation of their continuing medical education activities and of the operations and procedures they have performed since being certified, and submit to a review by their peers. They must also pass a written exam.

Certification is available in a number of surgical specialties, including plastic surgery, colon and rectal surgery, neurological surgery, orthopaedic surgery, and thoracic surgery. The American Board of Medical Specialties and the American Medical Association (AMA) recognizes 24 specialty boards that certify physicians and surgeons.

All physicians and surgeons must be licensed by the state in which they work.

Other Requirements

To be a successful surgeon, you should be able to think quickly and act decisively in stressful situations, enjoy helping and working with people, have strong organizational skills, be able to give clear instructions, have good hand-eye coordination, and be able to listen and communicate well.

EXPLORING

If you are interested in becoming a surgeon, pay special attention to the work involved in your science laboratory courses. Obviously, working on a living human being is a much weightier prospect than dissecting a lab sample, but what you learn about basic handling and cleaning of tools, making incisions, and identifying and properly referring to the body's structures will prove invaluable in your future career. Also ask your science teacher or guidance counselor to try to get a surgeon to speak to your biology class, so that he or she can help you understand more of what the job involves.

EMPLOYERS

There are approximately 44,560 surgeons employed in the United States. Almost half of all licensed physicians and surgeons in the United States work in private solo or group practices. Others work for hospitals, federal and state government offices, educational services, and outpatient care facilities. The New England and Mid-Atlantic states have the most physicians and surgeons per capita, and the South-Central and Mountain states have the least.

STARTING OUT

Many new physicians and surgeons choose to join existing practices instead of attempting to start their own.

Establishing a new practice is costly, and it may take time to build a patient base. In a clinic, group practice, or partnership, physicians share the costs for medical equipment and staff salaries, and of establishing a wider patient base.

Surgeons who hope to join an existing practice may find leads through their medical school or residency. During these experiences, they work with many members of the medical community, some of whom may be able to recommend them to appropriate practices.

Another approach would be to check the various medical professional journals, which often run ads for physician positions. Aspiring physicians can also hire a medical placement agency to assist them in the job search.

Physicians who hope to work for a managed care organization or government sponsored clinic should contact the source directly for information on position availability and application procedures.

EARNINGS

According to the U.S. Department of Labor, surgeons with over a year of experience made median salaries of $166,400 or more in 2009. Even the lowest paid 10 percent of surgeons earned incomes over $121,830. According to Salary.com, in early 2011, general surgeons reported annual earnings of $230,708 to $411,315, with median annual earnings of $302,072.

Incomes may vary from specialty to specialty. Other factors influencing individual incomes include the type and size of practice, the hours worked per week, the geographic location, and the reputation a surgeon has among both patients and fellow professionals.

WORK ENVIRONMENT

Surgeons work in sterile operating rooms that are well equipped, well lighted, and well ventilated. They meet patients and conduct all regular business in clean, well-lit offices. There are usually several nurses, a laboratory technician, one or more secretaries, a bookkeeper, and a receptionist available to assist the surgeon.

General practitioners usually see patients by appointments that are scheduled according to individual requirements. They may reserve all mornings for hospital visits and minor surgery. They may see patients in the office only on certain days of the week. General practitioners may also visit patients in nursing homes, hospices, and home-care settings.

Most surgeons work 60 or more hours a week.

OUTLOOK

The wide-ranging skills and knowledge of the surgeon will always be in demand, whether or not the surgeon has a subspecialty. According to the *Occupational Outlook Handbook*, physician jobs, including surgeons, are expected to grow much faster than the average for all occupations through 2018. Many industry experts are now predicting a shortage of general surgeons in the next decade as more students enter nonsurgical specialties, such as anesthesiology and radiology, which require less intensive training. Because of the growing and aging population, more surgeons will be required to meet medical needs.

FOR MORE INFORMATION

For information on certification in medical specialties, contact

American Board of Medical Specialties
222 North LaSalle Street, Suite 1500
Chicago, IL 60601-1117
Tel: 312-436-2600
http://www.abms.org

For information on certification for plastic surgeons, contact

American Board of Plastic Surgery Inc.
Seven Penn Center, Suite 400
1635 Market Street
Philadelphia, PA 19103-2204
Tel: 215-587-9322
E-mail: info@abplsurg.org
http://www.abplsurg.org

For information on certification, contact

American Board of Surgery
1617 John F. Kennedy Boulevard, Suite 860
Philadelphia, PA 19103-1847
Tel: 215-568-4000
http://www.absurgery.org

For information on women in surgical careers, contact

Association of Women Surgeons
5204 Fairmont Avenue, Suite 208
Downers Grove, IL 60515-5058
Tel: 630-655-0392
E-mail: info@womensurgeons.org
http://www.womensurgeons.org

For information on surgical specialties, contact the following organizations:

American Academy of Orthopaedic Surgeons
6300 North River Road
Rosemont, IL 60018-4262
Tel: 847-823-7186
http://www.aaos.org

American Association of Neurological Surgeons
5550 Meadowbrook Drive
Rolling Meadows, IL 60008-3852
Tel: 888-566-2267
E-mail: info@aans.org
http://www.aans.org

Society of Thoracic Surgeons
633 North Saint Clair Street, Suite 2320
Chicago, IL 60611-3658
Tel: 312-202-5800
E-mail: sts@sts.org
http://www.sts.org

SURGICAL TECHNOLOGISTS

OVERVIEW

Surgical technologists, also called *surgical technicians* or *operating room technicians*, are members of the surgical team who work in the operating room with surgeons, nurses, anesthesiologists, and other personnel before, during, and after surgery. (See "Surgeons," "Registered Nurses," and "Anesthesiologists.") They ensure a safe and sterile environment. To prepare a patient for surgery, they may wash, shave, and disinfect the area where the incision will be made. They arrange the equipment, instruments, and supplies in the operating room according to the preference of the surgeons and nurses. During the operation, they adjust lights and other equipment as needed. They count sponges, needles, and instruments used during the operation, hand instruments and supplies to the surgeon, and hold retractors and cut sutures as directed. They maintain specified supplies of fluids (for example, saline, plasma, blood, and glucose), and may assist in administering these fluids. Following the operation, they may clean and restock the operating room and wash and sterilize the used equipment using germicides, autoclaves, and sterilizers, although in most larger hospitals these tasks are done by other central service personnel. There are approximately 91,250 surgical technologists employed in the United States.

THE JOB

Surgical technologists are health professionals who work in the surgical suite with surgeons, anesthesiologists, registered nurses, and other surgical personnel delivering surgical patient care.

In general, the work responsibilities of surgical technologists may be divided into three phases: preoperative (before surgery), intraoperative (during surgery), and postoperative (after surgery). Surgical technologists may work as the *scrub person*, *circulator*, or *surgical first assistant*.

In the preoperative phase, surgical technologists prepare the operating room by selecting and opening sterile supplies such as drapes, sutures, sponges, electrosurgical devices, suction tubing, and surgical instruments. They assemble, adjust, and check nonsterile equipment to ensure that it is in proper working order. Surgical technologists also operate sterilizers, lights, suction machines, electrosurgical units, and diagnostic equipment.

When patients arrive in the surgical suite, surgical technologists may assist in preparing them for surgery by providing physical and emotional support, checking charts, and observing vital signs. They properly position the patient on the operating table, assist in connecting and applying surgical equipment and moni-

toring devices, and prepare the incision site by cleansing the skin with an antiseptic solution.

During surgery, surgical technologists have primary responsibility for maintaining the sterile field. They constantly watch that all members of the team adhere to aseptic techniques so the patient does not develop a postoperative infection. As the scrub person, they most often function as the sterile member of the surgical team who passes instruments, sutures, and sponges during surgery. After "scrubbing," which involves the thorough cleansing of the hands and forearms, they put on a sterile gown and gloves and prepare the sterile instruments and supplies that will be needed. After other members of the sterile team have scrubbed, they assist them with gowning and gloving and applying sterile drapes around the operative site.

Surgical technologists must anticipate the needs of surgeons during the procedure, passing instruments and providing sterile items in an efficient manner. Checking, mixing, and dispensing appropriate fluids and drugs in the sterile field are other common tasks. They share with the *circulator* the responsibility for accounting for sponges, needles, and instruments before, during, and after surgery. They may hold retractors or instruments, sponge or suction the operative site, or cut suture material as directed by the surgeon. They connect drains and tubing and receive and prepare specimens for subsequent pathologic analysis.

Surgical technologists most often function as the scrub person, but may function in the nonsterile role of *circulator*. The circulator does not wear a sterile gown and gloves, but is available to assist the surgical team. As a circulator, the surgical technologist obtains additional supplies or equipment, assists the anesthesiologist, keeps a written account of the surgical procedure, and assists the scrub person.

Surgical first assistants, who are technologists with additional education or training, provide aid in retracting tissue, controlling bleeding, and other technical functions that help surgeons during the procedure.

After surgery, surgical technologists are responsible for preparing and applying dressings, including plaster or synthetic casting materials, and for preparing the operating room for the next patient. They may provide staffing in postoperative recovery rooms where patients' responses are carefully monitored in the critical phases following general anesthesia.

Some of these responsibilities vary, depending on the size of the hospital and department in which the surgical technologist works; they also vary based on geographic location and health care needs of the local community.

REQUIREMENTS

High School

During your high school years, you should take courses that develop your basic skills in mathematics, science, and English. You also should take all available courses in health and biology.

Postsecondary Training

Surgical technology education is available through postsecondary programs offered by community and junior colleges, vocational and technical schools, the military, universities, and structured hospital programs in surgical technology. A high school diploma is required for entry into any of these programs.

More than 450 of these programs are accredited by the Commission on Accreditation of Allied Health Education Programs (CAAHEP). The accredited programs vary from nine to 12 months for a diploma or certificate, to two years for an associate's degree. You can expect to take courses in medical terminology, communications, anatomy, physiology, microbiology, pharmacology, medical ethics, and legal responsibilities. You gain a thorough knowledge of patient preparation and care, surgical procedures, surgical instruments and equipment, and principles of asepsis (how to prevent infection). In addition to classroom learning, you receive intensive supervised clinical experience in local hospitals, which is an important component of your education.

Certification or Licensing

Increasing numbers of hospitals are requiring certification as a condition of employment. Surgical technologists may earn a professional credential by passing a nationally administered certifying examination. To take the examination, you must be currently or previously certified or be a graduate of a CAAHEP-accredited program. The Liaison Council on Certification for the Surgical Technologist (LCC-ST), an independent affiliate of the Association of Surgical Technologists, is the certifying agency for the profession. Those who pass the exam and fulfill education and experience requirements are granted the designation of certified surgical technologist (CST). To renew the four-year certificate, the CST must earn continuing education credits or retake the certifying examination. The LCC-ST also offers an advanced credential for surgical first assistants; this exam awards the designation of CST certified first assistant (CST/CFA). Another certification for surgical technologists can be obtained from the National Center for Competency Testing. To take the certification exam, candidates must either complete an accredited training program, attend a two-year hospital on-the-job training program, or have seven years of experience in the field. Upon passing the exam, surgical technologists obtain the designation of Tech in Surgery-Certified, TS-C (NCCT). This certification must be renewed every five years either through reexamination or continuing education.

Other Requirements

Surgical technologists must possess an educational background in the medical sciences, a strong sense of responsibility, a concern for order, and an ability to integrate a number of tasks at the same time. You need good manual dexterity to handle awkward surgical instruments with speed and agility. In addition, you need physical stamina to stand through long surgical procedures.

EXPLORING

It is difficult to gain any direct experience on a part-time basis in surgical technology. The first opportunities for direct experience generally come in the clinical and laboratory phases of your educational programs. However, interested students can explore some aspects of this career in several ways. You or your teachers can arrange a visit to a hospital, clinic, or other surgical setting in order to learn about the work. You can also visit a school with a CAAHEP-accredited program. During such a visit, you can discuss career plans with the admissions counselor. In addition, volunteering at a local hospital or nursing home can give you insight into the health care environment and help you evaluate your aptitude to work in such a setting.

EMPLOYERS

Approximately 91,250 surgical technologists work in the United States. Most surgical technologists are employed in hospital operating rooms, clinics, and surgical centers. They also work in delivery rooms, cast rooms, emergency departments, ambulatory care areas, and central supply departments. Surgical technologists may also be employed directly by surgeons as private scrubs or as surgical first assistants.

STARTING OUT

Graduates of programs are often offered jobs in the same hospital in which they received their clinical training. Programs usually cooperate closely with hospitals in the area, which are usually eager to employ technologists educated in local programs. Available positions are also advertised in newspaper want ads.

ADVANCEMENT

With increased experience, surgical technologists can serve in management roles in surgical services departments and may work as *central service managers, surgery schedulers*, and *materials managers*. The role of *surgical first assistant* on the surgical team requires additional training and experience and is considered an advanced role.

Surgical technologists must function well in a number of diverse areas. Their competency with multiple skills is demonstrated by their employment in organ and tissue procurement/preservation, cardiac catheterization laboratories, medical sales and research, and medical-legal auditing for insurance companies. A number are *instructors* and *directors* of surgical technology programs.

EARNINGS

Salaries vary greatly in different institutions and localities. According to the U.S. Department of Labor, the average salary for surgical technologists was $39,400 in 2009, and ranged from $27,910 to $55,620 a year (excluding overtime). Some technologists with experience earn much more. Most surgical technologists are required to be periodically on call—available to work on short notice in cases of emergency—and can earn overtime from such work. Graduates of educational programs usually receive salaries higher than technologists without formal education. In general, technologists working on the East Coast and West Coast earn more than surgical technologists in other parts of the country. *Surgical first assistants* and *private scrubs* employed directly by surgeons tend to earn more than surgical technologists employed by hospitals.

WORK ENVIRONMENT

Surgical technologists naturally spend most of their time in the operating room. Operating rooms are cool, well lighted, orderly, and extremely clean. Technologists are often required to be on their feet for long intervals, during which their attention must be closely focused on the operation.

Members of the surgical team, including surgical technologists, wear sterile gowns, gloves, caps, masks, and eye protection. This surgical attire is meant not only to protect the patient from infection but also to protect the surgical team from any infection or blood-borne diseases that the patient may have. Surgery is usually performed during the day; however, hospitals, clinics, and other facilities require 24-hour-a-day coverage. Most surgical technologists work regular 40-hour weeks, although many are required to be periodically on call.

Surgical technologists must be able to work under great pressure in stressful situations. The need for surgery is often a matter of life and death, and one can never assume that procedures will go as planned. If operations do not go well, nerves may fray and tempers flare. Technologists must understand that this is the result of stressful conditions and should not take this anger personally.

In addition, surgical technologists should have a strong desire to help others. Surgery is performed on people, not machines. Patients literally entrust their lives to the surgical team, and they rely on them to treat them in a dignified and professional manner. Individuals with these characteristics find surgical technology a rewarding career in which they can make an important contribution to the health and well-being of their community.

OUTLOOK

According to the U.S. Department of Labor, the field of surgical technology is projected to experience rapid job growth through 2018. Population growth, longevity, and improvement in medical and surgical procedures have all contributed to a growing demand for surgical services and hence for surgical technologists. As long as the rate at which people undergo surgery continues to increase, there will continue to be a need for this profession. Also, as surgical methods become increasingly complex, more surgical technologists will likely be needed.

An increasing number of surgical procedures are being performed in the offices of physicians and ambulatory surgical centers, requiring the skills of surgical technologists. As a result, employment for technologists in these non-hospital settings should grow much faster than the average.

FOR MORE INFORMATION

For information on education programs and certification, contact the following organizations:

Association of Surgical Technologists
6 West Dry Creek Circle, Suite 200
Littleton, CO 80120-8031
Tel: 800-637-7433
http://www.ast.org

National Board of Surgical Technology and Surgical Assisting
6 West Dry Creek Circle, Suite 100
Littleton, CO 80120-8031
Tel: 800-707-0057
E-mail: mail@nbstsa.org
http://www.nbstsa.org/

SURVEYING AND MAPPING TECHNICIANS

OVERVIEW

Surveying and mapping technicians help determine, describe, and record geographic areas or features. They are usually the leading assistant to the *professional surveyor, civil engineer,* and *mapmaker.* (See "Surveyors.") They operate modern surveying and mapping instruments and may participate in other operations. Technicians must have a basic knowledge of the current practices and legal implications of surveys to establish and record property size, shape, topography, and boundaries. They often supervise other assistants during routine surveying conducted within the bounds established by a professional surveyor. There are approximately 62,940 surveying and mapping technicians working in the United States.

THE JOB

As essential assistants to civil engineers, surveyors, and mapmakers, surveying and mapping technicians are usually the first to be involved in any job that requires precise plotting. This includes highways, airports, housing developments, mines, dams, bridges, and buildings of all kinds.

The surveying and mapping technician is a key worker in field parties and major surveying projects and is often assigned the position of chief instrument worker under the surveyor's supervision. Technicians use a variety of surveying instruments, including the theodolite, transit, level, and other electronic equipment, to measure distances or locate a position. Technicians may be rod workers, using level rods or range poles to make elevation and distance measurements. They may also be chain workers, measuring shorter distances using a surveying chain or a metal tape. During the survey, it is important to accurately record all readings and keep orderly field notes to check for accuracy.

Surveying and mapping technicians may specialize if they join a firm that focuses on one or more particular types of surveying. In a firm that specializes in land surveying, technicians are highly skilled in technical measuring and tasks related to establishing township, property, and other tract-of-land boundary lines. They help the professional surveyor with maps, notes, and title deeds. They help survey the land, check the accuracy of existing records, and prepare legal documents such as deeds and leases.

Similarly, technicians who work for highway, pipeline, railway, or power line surveying firms help to establish grades, lines, and other points of reference for construction projects. This survey information provides the exact locations for engineering design and construction work.

Technicians who work for geodetic surveyors help take measurements of large masses of land, sea, or space. These measurements must take into account the curvature of Earth and its geophysical characteristics. Their findings set major points of reference for smaller land surveys, determining national boundaries, and preparing maps.

SCHOOL SUBJECTS
Geography, Mathematics

PERSONAL SKILLS
Following instructions, Technical/scientific

MINIMUM EDUCATION LEVEL
Some postsecondary training

CERTIFICATION OR LICENSING
Voluntary

WORK ENVIRONMENT
Primarily outdoors, Primarily multiple locations

Technicians may also specialize in hydrographic surveying, measuring harbors, rivers, and other bodies of water. These surveys are needed to design navigation systems, prepare nautical maps and charts, establish property boundaries, and plan for breakwaters, levees, dams, locks, piers, and bridges.

Mining surveying technicians are usually on the geological staffs of either mining companies or exploration companies. In recent years, costly new surveying instruments have changed the way they do their jobs. Using highly technical machinery, technicians can map underground geology, take samples, locate diamond drill holes, log drill cores, and map geological data derived from boreholes. They also map data on mine plans and diagrams and help the geologist determine ore reserves. In the search for new mines, technicians operate delicate instruments to obtain data on variations in Earth's magnetic field, its conductivity, and gravity. They use their data to map the boundaries of areas for potential further exploration.

Surveying and mapping technicians may find topographical surveys to be interesting and challenging work. These surveys determine the contours of the land and indicate such features as mountains, lakes, rivers, forests, roads, farms, buildings, and other distinguishable landmarks. In topographical surveying, technicians help take aerial or land photographs with photogrammetric equipment, and various sensors such as light-imaging detection and ranging (LIDAR), installed in an airplane or ground station that can take pictures of large areas. This method is widely used to measure farmland planted with certain crops and to verify crop average allotments under government production planning quotas.

A large number of survey technicians are employed in construction work. Technicians are needed from start to finish on any job. They check the construction of a structure for size, height, depth, level, and form specifications. They also use measurements to locate the critical construction points as specified by design plans, such as corners of buildings, foundation points, center points for columns, walls, and other features, floor or ceiling levels, and other features that require precise measurements and location.

Technological advances such as the Global Positioning System (GPS) and Geographic Information Systems (GIS) have revolutionized surveying and mapping work. Using these systems, surveying teams can track points on Earth with radio signals transmitted from satellites and store this information in computer databases.

REQUIREMENTS
High School

If you are interested in becoming a surveying and mapping technician, take mathematics courses, such as algebra, geometry, and trigonometry, as well as mechanical drawing in high school. Physics, chemistry, and biology are other valuable classes that will help you gain laboratory experience. Reading, writing, and comprehension skills as well as knowledge of computers are also vital in surveying and mapping, so English and computer science courses are also highly recommended.

Postsecondary Training

Though not required to enter the field, graduates of accredited postsecondary training programs for surveying, photogrammetry, and mapping are in the best position to become surveying and mapping technicians. Postsecondary training is available from institutional programs and correspondence schools. These demanding technical programs generally last two years, with a possible field study in the summer. First-year courses include English, composition, drafting, applied mathematics, surveying and measurements, construction materials and methods, applied physics, statistics, and computer applications. Second-year courses cover subjects such as technical physics, advanced surveying, photogrammetry and mapping, soils and foundations, technical reporting, legal issues, and transportation and environmental engineering. Contact the American Congress on Surveying and Mapping (ACSM) for a list of accredited programs (see the end of this article for contact information).

With additional experience and study, technicians can specialize in geodesy, topography, hydrography, or photogrammetry. Many graduates of two-year programs later pursue a bachelor's degree in surveying, engineering, or geomatics.

Certification or Licensing

Unlike professional land surveyors, there are no certification or licensing requirements for becoming a surveying and mapping technician. However, technicians who seek government employment must pass a civil service examination.

Many employers prefer certified technicians for promotions into higher positions with more responsibility. ACSM offers the voluntary survey technician certification at four levels. With each level, the technician must have more experience and pass progressively challenging examinations. If the technician hopes one day to work as a surveyor, he or she must be specially certified to work in his or her state.

Other Requirements

To be a successful surveying and mapping technician, you must be patient, orderly, systematic, accurate, and objective in your work. You must be willing to work cooperatively and have the ability to think and plan ahead. Because of the increasingly technical nature of their work, you must have computer skills to be able to use highly complex equipment such as GPS and GIS technology.

EXPLORING

One of the best opportunities for experience is to work part time or during your summer vacation for a construction firm or a company involved in survey work. Even if the job does not involve direct contact with survey crews, you may be able to observe their work and converse with them to discover more about their daily activities. Another possibility is to work for a government agency overseeing land use. The Bureau of Land Management, for example, has employment opportunities for students who qualify, as well as many volunteer positions. The Forest Service also offers temporary positions for students.

EMPLOYERS

There are approximately 62,940 surveying and mapping technicians working in the United States. Almost two-thirds of technicians find work with engineering or architectural service firms. The federal government also employs a number of technicians to work for the U.S. Geological Survey, the Bureau of Land Management, the National Oceanic and Atmospheric Administration, the national Imagery and Mapping Agency, and the Forest Service. State and local governments also hire surveying and mapping technicians to work for highway departments and urban planning agencies. Construction firms and oil, gas, and mining companies also hire technicians.

STARTING OUT

If you plan on entering surveying straight from high school, you may first work as an apprentice. Through on-the-job training and some classroom work, appren-

tices build up their skills and knowledge of the trade to eventually become surveying and mapping technicians.

If you plan to attend a technical institute or four-year college, check out your school's career services office for help in arranging examinations or interviews. Employers of surveying technicians often send recruiters to schools before graduation and arrange to employ promising graduates. Some community or technical colleges have work-study programs that provide cooperative part-time or summer work for pay. Employers involved with these programs often hire students full time after graduation.

Finally, many cities have employment agencies that specialize in placing technical workers in positions in surveying, mapping, construction, mining, and related fields. Check your local newspaper, or surf the Web to see if your town offers these services.

ADVANCEMENT

Possibilities for advancement are linked to levels of formal education and experience. As technicians gain experience and technical knowledge, they can advance to positions of greater responsibility and eventually work as chief surveyor. To advance into this position, technicians will most likely need a two- or four-year degree in surveying and many years of experience. Also, all 50 states require surveyors to be licensed, requiring varying amounts of experience, schooling, and examinations.

Regardless of the level of advancement, all surveying and mapping technicians must continue studying to keep up with the technological developments in their field. Technological advances in computers, lasers, and microcomputers will continue to change job requirements. Studying to keep up with changes combined with progressive experience gained on the job will increase the technician's opportunity for advancement.

EARNINGS

According to the U.S. Department of Labor, the 2009 median hourly salary for all surveying and mapping technicians, regardless of the industry, was $17.88 (amounting to $37,190 for full-time work). The lowest paid 10 percent earned less than $10.90 ($22,680 for full-time work), and the highest paid 10 percent earned over $28.74 an hour ($59,780 for full-time work). Technicians working for the public sector in federal, state, and local governments generally earn more per hour than those working in the private sector for engineering and architectural services. In 2009, surveying and mapping technicians working for the federal government made an average of $46,830 per year.

WORK ENVIRONMENT

Surveying and mapping technicians usually work about 40 hours a week except when overtime is necessary. The peak work period for many kinds of surveying work is during the summer months when weather conditions are most favorable. However, surveying crews are exposed to all types of weather conditions.

Some survey projects involve certain hazards depending upon the region and the climate as well as local plant and animal life. Field survey crews may encounter snakes and poison ivy. They are subject to heat exhaustion, sunburn, and frostbite. Some projects, particularly those being conducted near construction projects or busy highways, impose dangers of injury from cars and flying debris. Unless survey technicians are employed for office assignments, their work location changes from survey to survey. Some assignments may require technicians to be away from home for varying periods of time.

While on the job, technicians who supervise other workers must take special care to observe good safety practices. Construction and mining workplaces usually require hard hats, special clothing, and protective shoes.

OUTLOOK

Surveying and mapping technicians are expected to enjoy strong job prospects if they have skills in the use of new technologies used in digital surveying and mapping such as GPS and GIS. According to the *Occupational Outlook Handbook*, employment is expected to grow faster than the average for all occupations through 2018.

One of the factors that is expected to increase the demand for surveying services, and therefore surveying technicians, is growth in urban and suburban areas. New streets, homes, shopping centers, schools, and gas and water lines will require property and boundary line surveys. Other factors are the continuing state and federal highway improvement programs and the increasing number of urban redevelopment programs. The expansion of industrial and business firms and the relocation of some firms in large undeveloped areas are also expected to create a need for surveying services.

The need to replace workers who have either retired or transferred to other occupations will also provide opportunities. In general, technicians with more education and skill training will have more job options.

FOR MORE INFORMATION

For more information on accredited surveying programs, contact

Accreditation Board for Engineering and Technology Inc.
111 Market Place, Suite 1050
Baltimore, MD 21202-4012
Tel: 410-347-7700
http://www.abet.org

For information on careers, scholarships, certification, and educational programs, contact

American Congress on Surveying and Mapping
6 Montgomery Village Avenue, Suite 403
Gaithersburg, MD 20879-3546
Tel: 240-632-9716
http://www.acsm.net

For information about the Bureau of Land Management and its responsibilities, visit its Web site.

Bureau of Land Management
1849 C Street, Room 5665
Washington, DC 20240-0001
Tel: 202-208-3801
http://www.blm.gov

For more information on Geographic Information Systems (GIS), visit the following Web site:

GIS.com
http://www.gis.com

 SURVEYORS

OVERVIEW

Surveyors mark exact measurements and locations of elevations, points, lines, and contours on or near Earth's surface. They measure distances between points to determine property boundaries and to provide data for mapmaking, construction projects, and other engineering purposes. There are approximately 50,360 *surveyors* and 11,750 *cartographers* and *photogrammetrists* employed in the United States.

THE JOB

On proposed construction projects, such as highways, airstrips, and housing developments, it is the surveyor's responsibility to make necessary measurements through an accurate and detailed survey of the area. The surveyor

---

SCHOOL SUBJECTS
Geography, Mathematics

PERSONAL SKILLS
Communication/ideas, Technical/scientific

MINIMUM EDUCATION LEVEL
Bachelor's degree

CERTIFICATION OR LICENSING
Required

WORK ENVIRONMENT
Primarily outdoors, Primarily multiple locations

---

usually works with a field party consisting of several people. Instrument assistants, called *surveying and mapping technicians*, handle a variety of surveying instruments including the theodolite, transit, level, surveyor's chain, rod, and other electronic equipment. (See "Surveying and Mapping Technicians.") In the course of the survey, it is important that all readings be recorded accurately and field notes maintained so that the survey can be checked for accuracy.

Surveyors may specialize in one or more particular types of surveying.

Land surveyors establish township, property, and other tract-of-land boundary lines. Using maps, notes, or actual land title deeds, they survey the land, checking for the accuracy of existing records. This information is used to prepare legal documents such as deeds and leases. *Land surveying managers* coordinate the work of surveyors, their parties, and legal, engineering, architectural, and other staff involved in a project. In addition, these managers develop policy, prepare budgets, certify work upon completion, and handle numerous other administrative duties.

Highway surveyors establish grades, lines, and other points of reference for highway construction projects. This survey information is essential to the work of the numerous engineers and the construction crews who build the new highway.

Geodetic surveyors measure large masses of land, sea, and space that must take into account the curvature of Earth and its geophysical characteristics. Their work is helpful in establishing points of reference for smaller land surveys, determining national boundaries, and

preparing maps. Geodetic computers calculate latitude, longitude, angles, areas, and other information needed for mapmaking. They work from field notes made by an engineering survey party and also use reference tables and a calculating machine or computer.

Marine surveyors measure harbors, rivers, and other bodies of water. They determine the depth of the water through measuring sound waves in relation to nearby land masses. Their work is essential for planning and constructing navigation projects, such as breakwaters, dams, piers, marinas, and bridges, and for preparing nautical charts and maps.

Mine surveyors make surface and underground surveys, preparing maps of mines and mining operations. Such maps are helpful in examining underground passages within the levels of a mine and assessing the volume and location of raw material available.

Geophysical prospecting surveyors locate and mark sites considered likely to contain petroleum deposits. *Oil-well directional surveyors* use sonic, electronic, and nuclear measuring instruments to gauge the presence and amount of oil- and gas-bearing reservoirs. *Pipeline surveyors* determine rights-of-way for oil construction projects, providing information essential to the preparation for and laying of the lines.

Photogrammetric engineers determine the contour of an area to show elevations and depressions and indicate such features as mountains, lakes, rivers, forests, roads, farms, buildings, and other landmarks. Aerial, land, and water photographs are taken with special equipment able to capture images of very large areas. From these pictures, accurate measurements of the terrain and surface features can be made. These surveys are helpful in construction projects and in the preparation of topographical maps. Photogrammetry is particularly helpful in charting areas that are inaccessible or difficult to travel.

REQUIREMENTS
High School

Does this work interest you? If so, you should prepare for it by taking plenty of math and science courses in high school. Take algebra, geometry, and trigonometry to become comfortable making different calculations. Earth science, chemistry, and physics classes should also be helpful. Geography will help you learn about different locations, their characteristics, and cartography. Benefits from taking mechanical drawing and other drafting classes include an increased ability to visualize abstractions, exposure to detailed work, and an understanding of perspectives. Taking computer science classes will prepare you for working with technical surveying equipment.

Postsecondary Training

It has become the industry standard for surveyors to earn a bachelor's degree in surveying or engineering combined with on-the-job training. Other entry options include obtaining more job experience combined with a one- to three-year program in surveying and surveying technology offered by community colleges, technical institutes, and vocational schools.

Certification or Licensing

All 50 states require that surveyors making property and boundary surveys be licensed or registered. The requirements for licensure vary, but most require a degree in surveying or a related field, a certain number of years of experience, and passing of examinations in land surveying. Generally, the higher the degree obtained, the less experience required. Those with bachelor's degrees may need only two to four years of on-the-job experience, while those with a lesser degree may need up to 12 years of prior experience to obtain a license. Information on specific requirements can be obtained by contacting the licensure department of the state in which you plan to work. If you are seeking employment in the federal government, you must take a civil service examination and meet the educational, experience, and other specified requirements for the position.

Other Requirements

The ability to work with numbers and perform mathematical computations accurately and quickly is very important. Other helpful qualities are the ability to visualize and understand objects in two and three dimensions (spatial relationships) and the ability to discriminate between and compare shapes, sizes, lines, shadings, and other forms (form perception).

Surveyors walk a great deal and carry equipment over all types of terrain, so endurance and coordination are important physical assets. In addition, surveyors direct and supervise the work of their team, so you should be good at working with other people and demonstrate leadership abilities.

EXPLORING

While you are in high school, begin to familiarize yourself with terms, projects, and tools used in this profes-

sion by reading books and magazines on the topic. One magazine that is available online is *Professional Surveyor Magazine* at http://www.profsurv.com. One of the best opportunities for experience is a summer job with a construction outfit or company that requires survey work. Even if the job does not involve direct contact with survey crews, it will offer an opportunity to observe surveyors and talk with them about their work.

Some colleges have work-study programs that offer on-the-job experience. These opportunities, like summer or part-time jobs, provide helpful contacts in the field that may lead to future full-time employment. If your college does not offer a work-study program and you can't find a paying summer job, consider volunteering at an appropriate government agency. The U.S. Geological Survey and the Bureau of Land Management usually have volunteer opportunities in select areas.

EMPLOYERS

Approximately 50,360 surveyors work in the United States. Almost two-thirds of surveying workers are employed in engineering, architectural, and surveying firms, according to the Department of Labor. Federal, state, and local government agencies are the next largest employers of surveying workers, and the majority of the remaining surveyors work for construction firms, oil and gas extraction companies, and public utilities. Only a small number of surveyors are self-employed.

STARTING OUT

Apprentices with a high school education can enter the field as equipment operators or surveying assistants. Those who have postsecondary education can enter the field more easily, beginning as surveying and mapping technicians.

College graduates can learn about job openings through their schools' career services offices or through potential employers that may visit their campus. Many cities have employment agencies that specialize in seeking out workers for positions in surveying and related fields. Check your local newspaper or the Internet to see if such recruiting firms exist in your area.

ADVANCEMENT

With experience, workers advance through the leadership ranks within a surveying team. Workers begin as assistants and then can move into positions such as senior technician, party chief, and, finally, licensed surveyor. Because surveying work is closely related to other fields, surveyors can move into electrical, mechanical, or chemical engineering or specialize in drafting.

EARNINGS

In 2009, surveyors earned a median annual salary of $54,180. According to the U.S. Department of Labor, the middle 50 percent earned between $39,400 and $72,140 a year. The lowest paid 10 percent were paid less than $30,130, and the highest paid 10 percent earned over $89,120 a year. In general, the federal government paid the highest wages to its surveyors, $82,110 a year in 2009.

Most positions with the federal, state, and local governments and with private firms provide life and medical insurance, pension, vacation, and holiday benefits.

WORK ENVIRONMENT

Surveyors work 40-hour weeks except when overtime is necessary to meet a project deadline. The peak work period is during the summer months when weather conditions are most favorable. However, it is not uncommon for the surveyor to be exposed to adverse weather conditions.

Some survey projects may involve hazardous conditions, depending on the region and climate as well as the plant and animal life. Survey crews may encounter snakes, poison ivy, and other hazardous plant and animal life, and may suffer heat exhaustion, sunburn, and frostbite while in the field. Survey projects, particularly those near construction projects or busy highways, may impose dangers of injury from heavy traffic, flying objects, and other accidental hazards. Unless the surveyor is employed only for office assignments, the work location most likely will change from survey to survey. Some assignments may require the surveyor to be away from home for periods of time.

OUTLOOK

The U.S. Department of Labor predicts the employment of surveyors to grow faster than the average for all occupation through 2018. The outlook is best for surveyors who have college degrees and advanced field experience. The widespread use of technology, such as the Global Positioning System and Geographic Information Systems, will provide jobs to surveyors with strong technical and computer skills.

Growth in urban and suburban areas (with the need for new streets, homes, shopping centers, schools, gas and water lines) will provide employment opportunities. State and federal highway improvement programs and local urban redevelopment programs also will provide jobs for surveyors. The expansion of industrial and business firms and the relocation of some firms to large undeveloped tracts will also create job openings. However, construction projects are closely tied to the state of the economy, so employment may fluctuate from year to year.

FOR MORE INFORMATION

For information on awards and recommended books to read, contact or check out the following Web sites:

American Association for Geodetic Surveying
6 Montgomery Village Avenue, Suite 403
Gaithersburg, MD 20879-3546
Tel: 240-632-9716
http://www.aagsmo.org

National Society of Professional Surveyors
6 Montgomery Village Avenue, Suite 403
Gaithersburg, MD 20879-3456
Tel: 240-632-9716
http://www.nspsmo.org

For information on state affiliates and colleges and universities offering land surveying programs, contact

American Congress on Surveying and Mapping
6 Montgomery Village Avenue, Suite 403
Gaithersburg, MD 20879-3546
Tel: 240-632-9716
http://www.acsm.net

For information on photogrammetry and careers in the field, contact

American Society for Photogrammetry and Remote Sensing
5410 Grosvenor Lane, Suite 210
Bethesda, MD 20814-2160
Tel: 301-493-0290
E-mail: asprs@asprs.org
http://www.asprs.org

For information on volunteer opportunities with the federal government, contact

Bureau of Land Management
1849 C Street, NW, Room 5665
Washington, DC 20240-0001
Tel: 202-208-3801
http://www.blm.gov

U.S. Geological Survey
12201 Sunrise Valley Drive

Mail Stop 205P
Reston, VA 20192-0002
Tel: 888-275-8747
http://www.usgs.gov

TECHNICAL WRITERS AND EDITORS

SCHOOL SUBJECTS
Business, English

PERSONAL SKILLS
Communication/ideas, Technical/scientific

MINIMUM EDUCATION LEVEL
Bachelor's degree

CERTIFICATION OR LICENSING
None available

WORK ENVIRONMENT
Primarily indoors, Primarily one location

OVERVIEW

Technical writers, sometimes called *technical communicators*, express technical and scientific ideas in easy-to-understand language. *Technical editors* revise written text to correct any errors and make it read smoothly and clearly. They also may coordinate the activities of technical writers, technical illustrators, and other staff in preparing material for publication and oversee the document development and production processes. Technical writers hold about 46,270 jobs, and editors, including technical editors, hold about 105,040 jobs in the United States.

THE JOB

Technical writers and editors prepare a wide variety of documents and materials. The most common types of documents they produce are manuals, technical reports, specifications, and proposals. Some technical writers also write scripts for videos and audiovisual presentations and text for multimedia programs. Technical writers and editors prepare manuals that give instructions and detailed information on how to install, assemble, use, service, or repair a product or equipment. They may write and edit manuals as simple as a two-page leaflet that gives instructions on how to assemble a bicycle or as complex as a 500-page document that tells service technicians how to repair machinery, medical equipment, or a climate-control system. One of the most common types of manuals is the computer software manual, which informs users on how to load software on their computers, explains how to use the program, and gives information on different features.

Technical writers and editors also prepare technical reports on a multitude of subjects. These reports include documents that give the results of research and laboratory tests and documents that describe the prog-ress of a project. They also write and edit sales proposals, product specifications, quality standards, journal articles, in-house style manuals, and newsletters.

The work of a technical writer begins when he or she is assigned to prepare a document. The writer meets with members of an account or technical team to learn the requirements for the document, the intended purpose or objectives, and the audience. During the planning stage, the writer learns when the document needs to be completed, approximately how long it should be, whether artwork or illustrations are to be included, who the other team members are, and any other production or printing requirements. A schedule is created that defines the different stages of development and determines when the writer needs to have certain parts of the document ready.

The next step in document development is the research, or information gathering, phase. During this stage, technical writers gather all the available information about the product or subject, read and review it, and determine what other information is needed. They may research the topic by reading technical publications, but in most cases they will need to gather information directly from the people working on the product. Writers meet with and interview people who are sources of information, such as scientists, engineers, software developers, computer programmers, managers, and project managers. They ask questions, listen, and take notes or tape record interviews. They gather any available notes, drawings, or diagrams that may be useful.

After writers gather all the necessary information, they sort it out and organize it. They plan how they are going to present the information and prepare an outline for the document. They may decide how the document will look and prepare the design, format, and layout of the pages. In some cases, this may be done by an editor rather than the writer. If illustrations, diagrams, or photographs are going to be included, either the editor or writer makes arrangements for an illustrator, photographer, or art researcher to produce or obtain them.

Then, the writer starts writing and prepares a rough draft of the document. If the document is very large, a writer may prepare it in segments. Once the rough draft is completed, it is submitted to a designated person or group for technical review. Copies of the draft are distributed to managers, engineers, or other experts who can easily determine if any technical information is inaccurate or missing. These reviewers read the document and suggest changes.

The rough draft is also given to technical editors for review of a variety of factors. The editors check that the material is organized well, that each section flows with the section before and after it, and that the language is appropriate for the intended audience. They also check for correct use of grammar, spelling, and punctuation. They ensure that names of parts or objects are consistent throughout the document and that references are accurate. They also check the labeling of graphs and captions for accuracy. Technical editors use special symbols, called proofreader's marks, to indicate the types of changes needed.

The editor and reviewers return their copies of the document to the technical writer. The writer incorporates the appropriate suggestions and revisions and prepares the final draft. The final draft is once again submitted to a designated reviewer or team of reviewers. In some cases, the technical reviewer may do a quick check to make sure that the requested changes were made. In other cases, the technical reviewer may examine the document in depth to ensure technical accuracy and correctness. A walkthrough, or test of the document, may be done for certain types of documents. For example, a walkthrough may be done for a document that explains how to assemble a product. A tester assembles the product by following the instructions given in the document. The tester makes a note of all sections that are unclear or inaccurate, and the document is returned to the writer for any necessary revisions.

For some types of documents, a legal review may also be necessary. For example, a pharmaceutical company that is preparing a training manual to teach its sales representatives about a newly released drug needs to ensure that all materials are in compliance with Food and Drug Administration (FDA) requirements. A member of the legal department who is familiar with these requirements will review the document to make sure that all information in the document conforms to FDA rules.

Once the final draft has been approved, the document is submitted to the technical editor, who makes a comprehensive check of the document. In addition to checking that the language is clear and reads smoothly, the editor ensures that the table of contents matches the different sections or chapters of a document, all illustrations and diagrams are correctly placed, all captions are matched to the correct picture, consistent terminology is used, and correct references are used in the bibliography and text.

The editor returns the document to either the *writer* or a *word processor*, who makes any necessary corrections. This copy is then checked by a *proofreader*. The proofreader compares the final copy against the editor's marked-up copy and makes sure that all changes were made. The document is then prepared for printing. In some cases, the writer is responsible for preparing camera-ready copy or electronic files for printing purposes, and in other cases, a print production coordinator prepares all material to submit to a printer.

Some technical writers specialize in a specific type of material. For example, *technical marketing writers* create promotional and marketing materials for technological products. They may write the copy for an advertisement for a technical product, such as a computer workstation or software, or they may write press releases about the product. They also write sales literature, product flyers, Web pages, and multimedia presentations.

Other technical writers prepare scripts for videos and films about technical subjects. These writers, called *scriptwriters*, need to have an understanding of film and video production techniques.

Some technical writers and editors prepare articles for scientific, medical, computer, or engineering trade journals. These articles may report the results of research conducted by doctors, scientists, or engineers or report on technological advances in a particular field. Some technical writers and editors also develop textbooks. They may receive articles written by engineers or scientists and edit and revise them to make them more suitable for the intended audience.

Technical writers and editors may create documents for a variety of media. Electronic media, such as compact discs and online services, are increasingly being used in place of books and paper documents. Technical writers may create materials that are accessed through the Internet, or they may create computer-based resources, such as help menus on computer programs. They also create interactive, multimedia documents that are distributed on compact discs or memory sticks. Some of these media require knowledge of special computer programs that allow material to be hyperlinked, or electronically cross-referenced.

REQUIREMENTS

High School

In high school, you should take composition, grammar, literature, creative writing, journalism, social studies, math, statistics, engineering, computer science, and as many science classes as possible. Business courses are also useful as they explain the organizational structure of companies and how they operate.

Postsecondary Training

Most employers prefer to hire technical writers and editors who have a bachelor's or advanced degree. Many technical editors graduate with degrees in the humanities, especially English or journalism. Technical writers typically need to have a strong foundation in engineering, computers, or science. Many technical writers graduate with a degree in engineering or science and take classes in technical writing.

Many different types of college programs are available that prepare people to become technical writers and editors. A growing number of colleges are offering degrees in technical writing. Schools without a technical writing program may offer degrees in journalism or English. Programs are offered through English, communications, and journalism departments. Classes vary based on the type of program. In general, classes for technical writers include a core curriculum in writing and classes in algebra, statistics, logic, science, engineering, and computer programming languages. Useful classes for editors include technical writing, project management, grammar, proofreading, copyediting, and print production.

Many technical writers and editors earn a master's degree. In these programs, they study technical writing in depth and may specialize in a certain area, such as scriptwriting, instructional design, or multimedia applications. In addition, many nondegree writing programs are offered to technical writers and editors to hone their skills. Offered as extension courses or continuing educa-

tion courses, these programs include courses on indexing, editing medical materials, writing for trade journals, and other related subjects.

Technical writers, and occasionally technical editors, are often asked to present samples of their work. College students should build a portfolio during their college years in which they collect their best samples from work that they may have done for a literary magazine, newsletter, or yearbook.

Technical writers and editors should be willing to pursue learning throughout their careers. As technology changes, technical writers and editors may need to take classes to update their knowledge. Changes in electronic printing and computer technology will also change the way technical writers and editors do their jobs, and writers and editors may need to take courses to learn new skills or new technologies.

Certification or Licensing

There are no specific certification or licensing requirements for technical writers and editors.

Other Requirements

Technical writers need to have good communication skills, science and technical aptitudes, and the ability to think analytically. Technical editors also need to have good communications skills, and judgment, as well as the ability to identify and correct errors in written material. They need to be diplomatic, assertive, and able to explain tactfully what needs to be corrected to writers, engineers, and other people involved with a document. Technical editors should be able to understand technical information easily, but they need less scientific and technical background than writers. Both technical writers and editors need to be able to work as part of a team and collaborate with others on a project. They need to be highly self-motivated, well organized, and able to work under pressure.

EXPLORING

If you enjoy writing and are considering a career in technical writing or editing, you should make writing a daily activity. Writing is a skill that develops over time and through practice. You can keep journals, join writing clubs, and practice different types of writing, such as scriptwriting and informative reports. Sharing writing with others and asking them to critique it is especially helpful. Comments from readers on what they enjoyed about a piece of writing or difficulty they had in understanding certain sections provides valuable feedback that helps to improve your writing style.

Reading a variety of materials is also helpful. Reading exposes you to both good and bad writing styles and techniques, and helps you to identify why one approach works better than another.

You may also gain experience by working on a literary magazine, student newspaper, or yearbook (or starting one of your own if one is not available). Both writing and editing articles and managing production give you the opportunity to learn new skills and to see what is involved in preparing documents and other materials.

Students may also be able to get internships, cooperative education assignments, or summer or part-time jobs as proofreaders or editorial assistants that may include writing responsibilities.

EMPLOYERS

There are approximately 46,270 technical writers currently employed in the United States. Editors of all types (including technical editors) hold 105,040 jobs.

Employment may be found in many different types of places, such as in the fields of aerospace, computers, engineering, pharmaceuticals, and research and development, or with the nuclear industry, medical publishers, government agencies or contractors, and colleges and universities. The aerospace, engineering, medical, and computer industries hire significant numbers of technical writers and editors. The federal government, particularly the Departments of Defense and Agriculture, the National Aeronautics and Space Administration (NASA), and the Atomic Energy Commission, also hires many writers and editors with technical knowledge.

STARTING OUT

Many technical writers start their careers as scientists, engineers, technicians, or research assistants and move into writing after several years of experience in those positions. Technical writers with a bachelor's degree in a technical subject such as engineering may be able to find work as a technical writer immediately upon graduating from college, but many employers prefer to hire writers with some work experience.

Technical editors who graduate with a bachelor's degree in English or journalism may find entry-level work as *editorial assistants, copy editors*, or *proofreaders*. From these positions they are able to move into technical editing positions. Or, beginning workers may find jobs

as technical editors in small companies or those with a small technical communications department.

If you plan to work for the federal government, you need to pass an examination. Information about examinations and job openings is available at federal employment centers.

You may learn about job openings through your college's career services office and want ads in newspapers and professional magazines. You may also research companies that hire technical writers and editors and apply directly to them. Many libraries provide useful job resource guides and directories that provide information about companies that hire in specific areas.

ADVANCEMENT

As technical writers and editors gain experience, they move into more challenging and responsible positions. At first, they may work on simple documents or are assigned to work on sections of a document. As they demonstrate their proficiency and skills, they are given more complex assignments and are responsible for more activities.

Technical writers and editors with several years of experience may move into project management positions. As project managers, they are responsible for the entire document development and production processes. They schedule and budget resources and assign writers, editors, illustrators, and other workers to a project. They monitor the schedule, supervise workers, and ensure that costs remain in budget.

Technical writers and editors who show good project management skills, leadership abilities, and good interpersonal skills may become supervisors or managers. Both technical writers and editors can move into senior writer and senior editor positions. These positions involve increased responsibilities and may include supervising other workers.

Many technical writers and editors seek to develop and perfect their skills rather than move into management or supervisory positions. As they gain a reputation for their quality of work, they may be able to select choice assignments. They may learn new skills as a means of being able to work in new areas. For example, a technical writer may learn a new software application in order to become more proficient in page design and layout. Or, a technical writer may learn a hypermedia or hypertext computer program in order to be able to create a multimedia program. Technical writers and editors who broaden their skill base and capabilities can move to higher-paying positions within their own company or at another company. They also may work as freelancers or set up their own communications companies.

EARNINGS

Median annual earnings for salaried technical writers were $62,730 in 2009, according to the Bureau of Labor Statistics. Salaries ranged from less than $37,070 to more than $100,020. Editors of all types earned a median salary of $50,800 in 2009. The lowest paid 10 percent earned $28,430 or less and the highest paid 10 percent earned $97,360 or more.

The Society for Technical Communication reports that the median salary of technical writers across all industries was $61,620 in 2008. The highest paid reported earnings of $97,460 or more annually.

PayScale.com reported that technical writers earned salaries that ranged from $42,458 to $70,745 in early 2011.

Most companies offer benefits that include paid holidays and vacations, medical insurance, and 401(k) plans. They may also offer profit sharing, pension plans, and tuition assistance programs.

WORK ENVIRONMENT

Technical writers and editors usually work in an office environment, with well-lit and quiet surroundings. They may have their own offices or share workspace with other writers and editors. Most writers and editors have computers. They may be able to utilize the services of support staff who can word process revisions, run off copies, scan documents and create PDFs, and perform other administrative functions, or they may have to perform all of these tasks themselves.

Some technical writers and editors work out of home offices and use computer modems and networks to send and receive materials electronically. They may go into the office only on occasion for meetings and gathering information. Freelancers and contract workers may work at a company's premises or at home.

Although the standard workweek is 40 hours, many technical writers and editors frequently work 50 or 60 hours a week. Job interruptions, meetings, and conferences can prevent writers from having long periods of time to write. Therefore, many writers work after hours or bring work home. Both writers and editors frequently work in the evening or on weekends in order to meet a deadline.

In many companies there is pressure to produce documents as quickly as possible. Both technical writers and editors may feel at times that they are compromising the quality of their work due to the need to conform to time and budget constraints. In some companies, technical writers and editors may have increased workloads due to company reorganizations or downsizing. They may need to do the work that was formerly done by more than one person. Technical writers and editors also are increasingly assuming roles and responsibilities formerly performed by other people and this can increase work pressures and stress.

Despite these pressures, most technical writers and editors gain immense satisfaction from their work and the roles that they perform in producing technical communications.

OUTLOOK

The writing and editing field is generally very competitive. Each year, there are more people trying to enter this field than there are available openings. The field of technical writing and editing, though, offers more opportunities than other areas of writing and editing, such as book publishing or journalism. Employment opportunities for technical writers are expected to grow faster than the average for all occupations through 2018. Employment opportunities for editors are expected to grow as fast at the average during this period. Demand is growing for technical writers who can produce well-written computer manuals. In addition to the computer industry, the pharmaceutical industry is showing an increased need for technical writers. Rapid growth in the high-technology and electronics industries and the Internet will create a continuing demand for people to write users' guides, instruction manuals, and training materials. Technical writers will be needed to produce copy that describes developments and discoveries in law, science, and technology for a more general audience.

Writers may find positions that include duties in addition to writing. A growing trend is for companies to use writers to run a department, supervise other writers, and manage freelance writers and outside contractors. In addition, many writers are acquiring responsibilities that include desktop publishing and print production coordination.

The demand for technical writers and editors is significantly affected by the economy. During recessionary times, technical writers and editors are often among the first to be laid off. Many companies today are continuing to downsize or reduce their number of employees and are reluctant to keep writers on staff. Such companies prefer to hire writers and editors on a temporary contractual basis, using them only as long as it takes to complete an assigned document. Technical writers and editors who work on a temporary or freelance basis need to market their services and continually look for new assignments. They also do not have the security or benefits offered by full-time employment.

FOR MORE INFORMATION

For information on writing and editing careers in the field of communications, contact

National Association of Science Writers
PO Box 7905
Berkeley, CA 94707-0905
Tel: 510-647-9500
http://www.nasw.org

For information on careers, contact

Society for Technical Communication
9401 Lee Highway, Suite 300
Fairfax, VA 22031-1803
Tel: 703-522-4114
E-mail: stc@stc.org
http://www.stc.org

❑ URBAN AND REGIONAL PLANNERS

OVERVIEW

Urban and regional planners assist in the development and redevelopment of a city, metropolitan area, or region. They work to preserve historical buildings, protect the environment, and help manage a community's growth and change. Planners evaluate individual buildings and city blocks, and are also involved in the design of new subdivisions, neighborhoods, and even entire towns. There are approximately 38,950 urban and regional planners working in the United States.

THE JOB

Urban and regional planners assist in the development or maintenance of carefully designed communities. Working for a government agency or as a consultant, planners are involved in integrating new buildings, houses, sites, and subdivisions into an overall city plan. Their plans must coordinate streets, traffic, public facilities, water and sewage, transportation, safety, and ecological factors such as wildlife habitats, wetlands, and floodplains. Planners are also involved in renovating and preserving historic buildings. They work with a variety of professionals, including architects, artists, computer programmers, engineers, economists, landscape architects, land developers, lawyers, writers, and environmental and other special interest groups.

Urban and regional planners also work with unused or undeveloped land. They may help design the layout for a proposed building, keeping in mind traffic circulation, parking, and the use of open space. Planners are also responsible for suggesting ways to implement these programs or proposals, considering their costs and how to raise funds for them.

Schools, churches, recreational areas, and residential tracts are studied to determine how they will fit into designs for optimal usefulness and beauty. As with other factors, specifications for the nature and kinds of buildings must be considered. Zoning codes, which regulate the specific use of land and buildings, must be adhered to during construction. Planners need to be knowledgeable of these regulations and other legal matters and communicate them to builders and developers.

Some urban and regional planners teach in colleges and schools of planning, and many do consulting work. Planners today are concerned not only with city codes, but also with environmental problems of water pollution, solid waste disposal, water treatment plants, and public housing.

Planners work in older cities or design new ones. Columbia, Maryland, and Reston, Virginia, both built

SCHOOL SUBJECTS
Business, English, Government

PERSONAL SKILLS
Communication/ideas, Leadership/management

MINIMUM EDUCATION LEVEL
Master's degree

CERTIFICATION OR LICENSING
Voluntary

WORK ENVIRONMENT
Primarily indoors, Primarily multiple locations

in the 1960s, are examples of planned communities. Before plans for such communities can be developed, planners must prepare detailed maps and charts showing the proposed use of land for housing, business, and community needs. These studies provide information on the types of industries in the area, the locations of housing developments and businesses, and the plans for providing basic needs such as water, sewage treatment, and transportation. After maps and charts have been analyzed, planners design the layout to present to land developers, city officials, housing experts, architects, and construction firms.

The following short descriptions list the wide variety of planners within the field.

Human services planners develop health and social service programs to upgrade living standards for those lacking opportunities or resources. These planners frequently work for private health care organizations and government agencies.

Historic preservation planners use their knowledge of the law and economics to help preserve historic buildings, sites, and neighborhoods. They are frequently employed by state agencies, local governments, and the National Park Service.

Transportation planners, working mainly for government agencies, oversee the transportation infrastructure of a community, keeping in mind local priorities such as economic development and environmental concerns.

Housing and community development planners analyze housing needs to identify potential opportunities and problems that may affect a neighborhood and its surrounding communities. Such planners are usually employed by private real estate and financial firms, local governments, and community development organizations.

Economic development planners, usually employed by local governments or chambers of commerce, focus on attracting and retaining industry to a specific community. They communicate with industry leaders who select sites for new plants, warehouses, and other major projects.

Environmental planners advocate the integration of environmental issues into building construction, land use, and other community objectives. They work at all levels of government and for some nonprofit organizations.

Urban design planners work to design and locate public facilities, such as churches, libraries, and parks, to best serve the larger community. Employers include large-scale developers, private consulting firms, and local governments.

International development planners specialize in strategies for transportation, rural development, modernization, and urbanization. They are frequently employed by international agencies, such as the United Nations, and by national governments in less developed countries.

REQUIREMENTS

High School

You should take courses in government and social studies to learn about past and present organizational structures of cities and counties. You need good communication skills for working with people in a variety of professions, so take courses in speech and English composition. Drafting, architecture, and art classes will familiarize you with the basics of design. Become active on your student council so that you can be involved in implementing changes for the school community.

Postsecondary Training

A master's degree is the minimum requirement for most trainee jobs with federal, state, or local government boards and agencies. Typical courses include geography, public administration, political science, law, engineering, architecture, landscape architecture, real estate, finance, and management. Computer courses and training in statistical techniques and GIS (geographic information system) are also essential. Most master's programs last a minimum of two years and require students to participate in internships with city planning departments.

When considering schools, check with the American Planning Association (APA) for a list of accredited undergraduate and graduate planning programs. The APA can also direct you to scholarship and fellowship programs available to students enrolled in planning programs.

Certification or Licensing

In 2009, New Jersey was the only state that required planners to be licensed and Michigan required registration to use the title community planner. Although generally not a requirement, obtaining certification in urban and regional planning can lead to more challenging, better-paying positions. The American Institute of Certified Planners, a division of the APA, grants certification to planners who meet certain academic and professional requirements and successfully complete an examination. The exam tests for knowledge of the history and future of planning, research methods, plan implementation, and other relevant topics.

Other Requirements

In addition to being interested in planning, you should have design skills and a good understanding of spatial relationships. Good analytical skills will help you in evaluating projects. Planners must be able to visualize the relationships between streets, buildings, parks, and other developed spaces and anticipate potential planning problems. As a result, logic and problem-solving abilities are also important.

EXPLORING

Research the origins of your city by visiting your county courthouse and local library. Check out early photographs and maps of your area to give you an idea of what went into the planning of your community. Visit local historic areas to learn about the development and history behind old buildings. You may also consider getting involved in efforts to preserve local buildings and areas that are threatened.

With the help of a teacher or academic adviser, arrange to interview a professional urban planner to gain details of his or her job. Another good way to see what planners do is to attend a meeting of a local planning commission, which by law is open to the public. Interested students can find out details about upcoming meetings through their local paper or planning office.

EMPLOYERS

There are approximately 38,950 urban and regional planners working in the United States. About 66 percent of planners work for local governments; others work for state agencies, the federal government, and in the private sector.

Many planners are hired for full-time work where they intern. Others choose to seek opportunities in state and federal governments and nonprofit organizations. Planners work for government agencies that focus on particular areas of city research and development, such as transportation, the environment, and housing. Urban and regional planners are also sought by colleges, law firms, the United Nations, and even foreign governments of rapidly modernizing countries.

STARTING OUT

With a bachelor's degree, there may be employment opportunities as an assistant at an architectural firm or construction office or working as city planning aides in regional or urban offices. New planners research projects, conduct interviews, survey the field, and write reports on their findings. Those with a master's degree enter the profession at a higher level, working for federal, state, and local agencies.

Previous work experience in a planning office or with an architectural or engineering firm is useful before applying for a job with city, county, or regional planning agencies. Membership in a professional organization is also helpful in locating job opportunities. These include the American Planning Association, the American Institute of Architects, the American Society of Civil Engineers, and the International City/County Management Association. Most of these organizations host student chapters that provide information on internship opportunities and professional publications. (See the end of this article for contact information.)

Because many planning staffs are small, directors are usually eager to fill positions quickly. As a result, job availability can be highly variable. Students are advised to apply for jobs before they complete their degree requirements. Most colleges have placement offices to assist students in finding job leads.

ADVANCEMENT

Beginning assistants can advance within the planning board or department to eventually become planners. The positions of *senior planner* and *planning director* are successive steps in some agencies. Frequently, experienced planners advance by moving to a larger city or county planning board, where they become responsible for larger and more complicated projects, make policy decisions, or become responsible for funding new developments. Other planners may become *consultants* to communities that cannot afford a full-time planner. Some planners also serve as *city managers, cabinet secretaries,* and *presidents of consulting firms.*

EARNINGS

Earnings vary based on position, work experience, and the population of the city or town the planner serves. According to the Bureau of Labor Statistics, median annual earnings of urban and regional planners were $61,820 in 2009. The lowest paid 10 percent earned less than $39,460, and the highest paid 10 percent earned more than $94,800. Median annual earnings in local government, the industry employing the largest numbers of urban and regional planners, were around $62,170. In

2009, planners who worked for the federal government earned an average of $88,230 per year.

Because many planners work for government agencies, they usually have sick leave and vacation privileges and are covered by retirement and health plans. Many planners also have access to a city-owned automobile.

Planners who work as consultants are generally paid on a fee basis. Their earnings are often high and vary greatly according to their reputations and work experience. Their earnings will depend on the number of consulting jobs they accept.

WORK ENVIRONMENT

Planners spend a considerable amount of time in an office setting. However, in order to gather data about the areas they develop, planners also spend much of their time outdoors examining the surrounding land, structures, and traffic. Most planners work standard 40-hour weeks, but they may also attend evening or weekend council meetings or public forums to share upcoming development proposals.

Planners work alone and with land developers, public officials, civic leaders, and citizens' groups. Occasionally, they may face opposition from interest groups or local citizens against certain development proposals and, as a result, they must have the patience needed to work with disparate groups. The job can be stressful when trying to keep tight deadlines or when defending proposals in both the public and private sectors.

OUTLOOK

The U.S. Department of Labor expects the overall demand for urban and regional planners to grow faster than the average for all occupations through 2018. Communities turn to professional planners for help in meeting demands resulting from urbanization and the growth in population. Urban and regional planners are needed to zone and plan land use for undeveloped and rural areas as well as commercial development in rapidly growing suburban areas. There will be jobs available with nongovernmental agencies that deal with historic preservation and redevelopment. Opportunities also exist in maintaining existing bridges, highways, and sewers, and in preserving and restoring historic sites and buildings.

Factors that may affect job growth include government regulation regarding the environment, housing, transportation, and land use. The continuing redevelopment of inner-city areas and the expansion of suburban areas will serve to provide many jobs for planners.

However, when communities face budgetary constraints, planning departments may be reduced before other services, such as police forces or education. Planners with master's degrees and GIS and mapping experience will have more employment opportunities.

FOR MORE INFORMATION

For more information on careers, contact
American Institute of Architects
1735 New York Avenue, NW
Washington, DC 20006-5292
Tel: 800-242-3837
E-mail: infocentral@aia.org
http://www.aia.org

For more information on careers, certification, and accredited planning programs, contact
American Planning Association
205 North Michigan Avenue, Suite 1200
Chicago, IL 60601-3009
Tel: 312-431-9100
E-mail: customerservice@planning.org
http://www.planning.org

For career guidance and information on student chapters as well as a list of colleges that offer civil engineering programs, contact
American Society of Civil Engineers
1801 Alexander Bell Drive
Reston, VA 20191-4400
Tel: 800-548-2723
http://www.asce.org

To learn about city management and the issues affecting today's cities, visit this Web site or contact
International City/County Management Association
777 North Capitol Street, NE, Suite 500
Washington, DC 20002-4201
Tel: 202-289-4262
http://www.icma.org

VETERINARIANS

OVERVIEW

The *veterinarian*, or *doctor of veterinary medicine*, diagnoses and controls animal diseases, treats sick and injured animals medically and surgically, prevents

SCHOOL SUBJECTS
Biology, Chemistry

PERSONAL SKILLS
Helping/teaching, Technical/scientific

MINIMUM EDUCATION LEVEL
Medical degree

CERTIFICATION OR LICENSING
Required

WORK ENVIRONMENT
Primarily indoors, Primarily one location

transmission of animal diseases, and advises owners on proper care of pets and livestock. Veterinarians are dedicated to the protection of the health and welfare of all animals and to society as a whole. There are about 54,130 veterinarians in the United States.

THE JOB

Veterinarians ensure a safe food supply by maintaining the health of food animals. They also protect the public from residues of herbicides, pesticides, and antibiotics in food. Veterinarians may be involved in wildlife preservation and conservation and use their knowledge to increase food production through genetics, animal feed production, and preventive medicine.

In the United States, about 80 percent of veterinarians are in private practice. Although some veterinarians treat all kinds of animals, more than half limit their practice to companion animals such as dogs, cats, and birds. A smaller number of veterinarians work mainly with horses, cattle, pigs, sheep, goats, and poultry. Today, a veterinarian may be treating llamas, catfish, or ostriches as well. Others are employed by wildlife management groups, zoos, aquariums, ranches, feed lots, fish farms, and animal shelters.

Veterinarians in private practice diagnose and treat animal health problems. During yearly checkups, the veterinarian records the animal's temperature and weight; inspects its mouth, eyes, and ears; inspects the skin or coat for any signs of abnormalities; observes any peculiarities in the animal's behavior; and discusses the animals eating, sleeping, and exercise habits at length with the owner. The veterinarian will also check the

animal's vaccination records and administer inoculations for rabies, distemper, and other diseases if necessary. If the veterinarian or owner notes any special concerns, or if the animal is taken to the veterinarian for a specific procedure, such as spaying or neutering, dental cleaning, or setting broken bones, the animal may stay at the veterinarian's office for one or several days for surgery, observation, or extended treatments. If a sick or wounded animal is beyond medical help, the veterinarian may, with the consent of the owner, have to euthanize (humanely kill) the animal.

During office visits and surgery, veterinarians use traditional medical instruments, such as stethoscopes, thermometers, and surgical instruments, and standard tests, such as X-rays and diagnostic medical sonography, to evaluate the animal's health. Veterinarians may also prescribe drugs for the animal, which the owner purchases at the veterinarian's office.

Some veterinarians work in public and corporate sectors. Many are employed by city, county, state, provincial, or federal government agencies that investigate, test for, and control diseases in companion animals, livestock, and poultry that affect both animal and human health. Veterinarians also play an important public health role. For example, veterinarians played an important part in conquering diseases such as malaria and yellow fever.

Pharmaceutical and biomedical research firms hire veterinarians to develop, test, and supervise the production of drugs, chemicals, and biological products such as antibiotics and vaccines that are designed for human and animal use. Some veterinarians are employed in management, technical sales and services, and marketing in agribusiness, pet food companies, and pharmaceutical companies. Still other veterinarians are engaged in research and teaching at veterinary medical schools, working with racetracks or animal-related enterprises, or working within the military, public health corps, and space agencies.

Veterinarians in private clinical practice become specialists in surgery, anesthesiology, dentistry, internal medicine, ophthalmology, or radiology. Many veterinarians also pursue advanced degrees in the basic sciences, such as anatomy, microbiology, and physiology.

The U.S. Department of Agriculture has opportunities for veterinarians in the food safety inspection service and the animal and plant health inspection service, notably in the areas of food hygiene and safety, animal welfare, animal disease control, and research. Agencies in the U.S. Department of Agriculture utilize veterinarians in positions related to research on diseases transmissible from animals to human beings and on the acceptance and use of drugs for treatment or prevention of diseases. Veterinarians also are employed by the Environmental Protection Agency to deal with public health and environmental risks to the human population.

Veterinarians are often assisted by *veterinary technicians*, who may conduct basic tests, record an animal's medical history for the veterinarian's review, and assist the veterinarian in surgical procedures. (See "Veterinary Technicians.")

REQUIREMENTS

High School

For the high school student who is interested in admission to a school of veterinary medicine, a college preparatory course is a wise choice. A strong emphasis on science classes such as biology, chemistry, and anatomy is highly recommended.

Postsecondary Training

The doctor of veterinary medicine (D.V.M.) degree requires a minimum of four years of study at an accredited college of veterinary medicine. Although many of these colleges do not require a bachelor's degree for admission, most require applicants to have completed 45–90 hours of undergraduate study. It is possible to obtain preveterinary training at a junior college, but since admission to colleges of veterinary medicine is an extremely competitive process, most students receive degrees from four-year colleges before applying. In addition to academic instruction, veterinary education includes clinical experience in diagnosing disease and treating animals, performing surgery, and performing laboratory work in anatomy, biochemistry, and other scientific and medical subjects.

There are 28 colleges of veterinary medicine in the United States that are accredited by the Council of Veterinary Medicine of the American Veterinary Medical Association. Each college of veterinary medicine has its own preveterinary requirements, which typically include basic language arts, social sciences, humanities, mathematics, chemistry, and biological and physical sciences.

Applicants to schools of veterinary medicine usually must have grades of "B" or better, especially in the sciences. Applicants must take the Veterinary Aptitude Test, Medical College Admission Test, or the Graduate Record Examination. Fewer than half of the applicants

to schools of veterinary medicine may be admitted, due to small class sizes and limited facilities. Most colleges give preference to candidates with animal- or veterinary-related experience. Colleges usually give preference to in-state applicants because most colleges of veterinary medicine are state-supported. There are regional agreements in which states without veterinary schools send students to designated regional schools.

Certification or Licensing

All states and the District of Columbia require that veterinarians be licensed to practice private clinical medicine. To obtain a license, applicants must have a D.V.M. degree from an accredited or approved college of veterinary medicine. They must also pass one or more national examinations and an examination in the state in which they plan to practice.

Few states issue licenses to veterinarians already licensed by another state. Thus, if a veterinarian moves from one state to another, he or she will probably have to go through the licensing process again. Approximately half of the states require veterinarians to attend continuing education courses in order to maintain their licenses. Veterinarians may be employed by a government agency (such as the U.S. Department of Agriculture) or at some academic institution without having a state license.

Veterinarians who seek specialty board certification in one of 20 specialty fields must complete a two- to five-year residency program and must pass an additional examination. Some veterinarians combine their degree in veterinary medicine with a degree in business (M.B.A.) or law (J.D.).

Other Requirements

Individuals who are interested in veterinary medicine should have an inquiring mind and keen powers of observation. Aptitude and interest in the biological sciences are important. Veterinarians need a lifelong interest in scientific learning as well as a liking and understanding of animals. Veterinarians should be able to meet, talk, and work well with a variety of people. An ability to communicate with the animal owner is as important in a veterinarian as diagnostic skills.

Veterinarians use state-of-the-art medical equipment, such as electron microscopes, laser surgery, radiation therapy, and ultrasound, to diagnose animal diseases and to treat sick or injured animals. Although manual dexterity and physical stamina are often required, especially for farm vets, important roles in veterinary medicine can be adapted for those with disabilities.

Interaction with animal owners is a very important part of being a veterinarian. The discussions between vet and owner are critical to the veterinarian's diagnosis, so he or she must be able to communicate effectively and get along with a wide variety of personalities. Veterinarians may have to euthanize an animal that is very sick or severely injured and cannot get well. When a beloved pet dies, the veterinarian must deal with the owner's grief and loss.

EXPLORING

High school students interested in becoming veterinarians may find part-time or volunteer work on farms, in small-animal clinics, or in pet shops, animal shelters, or research laboratories. Participation in extracurricular activities such as with 4-H are good ways to learn about the care of animals. Such experience is important because, as already noted, many schools of veterinary medicine have established experience with animals as a criterion for admission to their programs.

EMPLOYERS

There are 54,130 veterinarians in the United States. Veterinarians may be employed or contracted by the government, schools and universities, wildlife management groups, zoos, aquariums, ranches, feed lots, fish farms, or pet food or pharmaceutical companies. The vast majority, however, are employed by veterinary clinical practices or hospitals. Many successful veterinarians in private practice are self-employed and may even employ other veterinarians. An increase in the demand for veterinarians is anticipated, particularly for those who specialize in areas related to public health issues such as food safety and disease control. Cities and large metropolitan areas will probably provide the bulk of new jobs for these specialists, while jobs for veterinarians who specialize in large animals will be focused in remote, rural areas.

STARTING OUT

The only way to become a veterinarian is through the prescribed degree program, and vet schools are set up to assist their graduates in finding employment. Veterinarians who wish to enter private clinical practice must have a license to practice in their particular state before opening an office. Licenses are obtained by passing the state's examination.

ADVANCEMENT

New graduate veterinarians may enter private clinical practice, usually as employees in an established practice, or become employees of the U.S. government as meat and poultry inspectors, disease control workers, and commissioned officers in the U.S. Public Health Service or the military. New graduates may also enter internships and residencies at veterinary colleges and large private and public veterinary practices or become employed by industrial firms.

The veterinarian who is employed by a government agency may advance in grade and salary after accumulating time and experience on the job. For the veterinarian in private clinical practice, advancement usually consists of an expanding practice and the higher income that will result from it or becoming an owner of several practices.

Those who teach or do research may obtain a doctorate and move from the rank of instructor to that of full professor, or they may advance to an administrative position.

EARNINGS

The U.S. Department of Labor reports that median annual earnings of veterinarians were $80,510 in 2009. Salaries ranged from less than $47,670 to more than $142,910. The average annual salary for veterinarians working for the federal government was $84,200 in 2009. Those who worked for medical and diagnostic laboratories averaged $114,590 per year.

According to a 2010 survey by the American Veterinary Medical Association, the average starting salary for veterinary medical college graduates who worked exclusively with small animals was $71,462 in 2009. Those who worked exclusively with large animals earned an average of $68,826. Equine veterinarians earned an average of $38,468 to start.

WORK ENVIRONMENT

Veterinarians usually treat companion and food animals in hospitals and clinics. Those in large animal practice also work out of well-equipped trucks or cars and may drive considerable distances to farms and ranches. They may work outdoors in all kinds of weather. The chief risk for veterinarians is injury by animals; however, modern tranquilizers and technology have made it much easier to work on all types of animals.

Most veterinarians work long hours, often 50 or more hours a week. Although those in private clinical practice may work nights and weekends, the increased number of emergency clinics has reduced the amount of time private practitioners have to be on call. Large animal practitioners tend to work more irregular hours than those in small animal practice, industry, or government. Veterinarians who are just starting a practice tend to work longer hours.

OUTLOOK

Employment of veterinarians is expected to grow much faster than the average for all occupations through 2018. The number of pets is expected to increase slightly because of rising incomes and an increase in the number of people aged 34 to 59, among whom pet ownership has historically been the highest. Recent trends also show that more people are interested in having cats, in particular, as pets, which will lead to increased demand for feline medicine and veterinary services. Many single adults and senior citizens have come to appreciate animal ownership. Pet owners also may be willing to pay for more elective and intensive care than in the past, as indicated by the rise in pet insurance purchases. In addition, emphasis on scientific methods of breeding and raising livestock, poultry, and fish and continued support for public health and disease control programs will contribute to the demand for veterinarians. The number of jobs stemming from the need to replace workers will be equal to new job growth.

The outlook is good for veterinarians with specialty training. Demand for specialists in toxicology, laboratory animal medicine, and pathology is expected to increase. Most jobs for specialists will be in metropolitan areas. Prospects for veterinarians who concentrate on environmental and public health issues, aquaculture, and food animal practice appear to be excellent because of perceived increased need in these areas. Positions in small animal specialties will be competitive. Opportunities in farm animal specialties will be better, since most such positions are located in remote, rural areas.

Despite the availability of additional jobs, competition among veterinarians is likely to be stiff. First-year enrollments in veterinary schools have increased slightly, and the number of students in graduate-degree and board-certification programs has risen dramatically.

FOR MORE INFORMATION

For more information on careers, schools, and resources, contact

American Veterinary Medical Association
1931 North Meacham Road, Suite 100
Schaumburg, IL 60173-4360
Tel: 800-248-2862
http://www.avma.org

For information on veterinary opportunities in the federal government, contact

Animal and Plant Health Inspection Service
4700 River Road, Unit 114
Riverdale, MD 20737-1228
http://www.aphis.usda.gov

The following Web site offers links to educational and career resources for veterinarians:

NetVet
http://netvet.wustl.edu/vet.htm

VETERINARY TECHNICIANS

OVERVIEW

Veterinary technicians provide support and assistance to veterinarians. (See "Veterinarians.") They work in a variety of environments, including zoos, animal hospitals, clinics, private practices, kennels, and laboratories. Their work may involve large or small animals or both. Although most veterinary technicians work with domestic animals, some professional settings may require treating exotic or endangered species. There are approximately 79,200 veterinary technicians and technologists employed in the United States.

THE JOB

Many pet owners depend on veterinarians to maintain the health and well-being of their pets. Veterinary clinics and private practices are the primary settings for animal care. In assisting veterinarians, veterinary technicians play an integral role in the care of animals within this particular environment.

A veterinary technician is the person who performs much of the laboratory testing procedures commonly associated with veterinary care. In fact, approximately 50 percent of a veterinary technician's duties involve laboratory testing. Laboratory assignments usually include taking and developing X-rays, performing parasitology tests, and examining various samples taken from the animal's body, such as blood and stool. A vet-

SCHOOL SUBJECTS
Biology, Chemistry

PERSONAL SKILLS
Helping/teaching, Technical/scientific

MINIMUM EDUCATION LEVEL
Associate's degree

CERTIFICATION OR LICENSING
Required by certain states

WORK ENVIRONMENT
Primarily indoors, Primarily one location

erinary technician may also assist the veterinarian with necropsies in an effort to determine the cause of an animal's death.

In a clinic or private practice, a veterinary technician assists the veterinarian with surgical procedures. This generally entails preparing the animal for surgery by shaving the incision area and applying a topical antibacterial agent. Surgical anesthesia is administered and controlled by the veterinary technician. Throughout the surgical process, the technician tracks the surgical instruments and monitors the animal's vital signs. If an animal is very ill and has no chance for survival, or an overcrowded animal shelter is unable to find a home for a donated or stray animal, the veterinary technician may be required to assist in euthanizing it.

During routine examinations and checkups, veterinary technicians will help restrain the animals. They may perform ear cleaning and nail clipping procedures as part of regular animal care. Outside the examination and surgery rooms, veterinary technicians perform additional duties. In most settings, they record, replenish, and maintain pharmaceutical equipment and other supplies.

Veterinary technicians also may work in a zoo. Here, job duties, such as laboratory testing, are quite similar, but practices are more specialized. Unlike in private practice, the *zoo veterinary technician* is not required to explain treatment to pet owners; however, he or she may have to discuss an animal's treatment or progress with zoo veterinarians, zoo curators, and other zoo professionals. A zoo veterinary technician's work also may differ from private practice in that it

may be necessary for the technician to observe the animal in its habitat, which could require working outdoors. Additionally, zoo veterinary technicians usually work with exotic or endangered species. This is a very competitive and highly desired area of practice in the veterinary technician field. There are only a few zoos in each state; thus, a limited number of job opportunities exist within these zoos. To break into this area of practice, veterinary technicians must be among the best in the field.

Veterinary technicians also work in research. Most research opportunities for veterinary technicians are in academic environments with veterinary medicine or medical science programs. Again, laboratory testing may account for many of the duties; however, the veterinary technicians participate in very important animal research projects from start to finish.

Technicians are also needed in rural areas. Farmers require veterinary services for the care of farm animals such as pigs, cows, horses, dogs, cats, sheep, mules, and chickens. It is often essential for the veterinarian and technician to drive to the farmer's residence because animals are usually treated on-site.

Another area in which veterinary technicians work is that of animal training, such as at an obedience school or with show business animals being trained for the circus or movies. Veterinary technicians may also be employed in information systems technology, where information on animals is compiled and provided to the public via the Internet.

No matter what the setting, a veterinary technician must be an effective communicator and proficient in basic computer applications. In clinical or private practice, it is usually the veterinary technician who conveys and explains treatment and subsequent animal care to the animal's owner. In research and laboratory work, the veterinary technician must record and discuss results among colleagues. In most practical veterinary settings, the veterinary technician must record various information on a computer.

REQUIREMENTS

High School

Veterinary technicians must have a high school diploma. High school students who excel at math and science have a strong foundation on which to build. Those who have had pets or who simply love animals and would like to work with them also fit the profile of a veterinary technician.

Postsecondary Training

The main requirement is the completion of a two- to four-year college-based accredited program. Upon graduation, the student receives an associate's or bachelor's degree. Currently, there are about 160 accredited programs in the United States. A few states do their own accrediting, using the American Veterinary Medical Association (AVMA) and associated programs as benchmarks.

Most accredited programs offer thorough course work and preparatory learning opportunities to the aspiring veterinary technician. Typical courses include mathematics, chemistry, humanities, biological science, communications, microbiology, liberal arts, ethics/jurisprudence, and basic computers.

Once the students complete this framework, they move on to more specialized courses. Students take advanced classes in animal nutrition, animal care and management, species/breed identification, veterinary anatomy/physiology, medical terminology, radiography and other clinical procedure courses, animal husbandry, parasitology, laboratory animal care, and large/small animal nursing.

Veterinary technicians must be prepared to assist in surgical procedures. In consideration of this, accredited programs offer surgical nursing courses. In these courses, a student learns to identify and use surgical instruments, administer anesthesia, and monitor animals during and after surgery.

In addition to classroom study, accredited programs offer practical courses. Hands-on education and training are commonly achieved through a clinical practicum, or internship, where the student has the opportunity to work in a clinical veterinary setting. During this period, a student is continuously evaluated by the participating veterinarian and encouraged to apply the knowledge and skills learned.

Certification or Licensing

Although the AVMA determines the majority of the national codes for veterinary technicians, state codes and laws vary. Most states offer registration or certification, and the majority of these states require graduation from an AVMA-accredited program as a prerequisite for taking the examination. Most colleges and universities assist graduates with registration and certification arrangements. To keep abreast of new technology and applications in the field, practicing veterinary technicians may be required to complete a determined number of annual continuing education courses. The American Association for Laboratory Animal Science (AALAS) offers three levels of certification for research facility technicians in three principal areas: animal husbandry, facility management, and animal health and welfare.

Other Requirements

As a veterinarian technician, you should be able to meet, talk, and work well with a variety of people. An ability to communicate with the animal owner is as important as diagnostic skills.

In clinical or private practice, it is usually the veterinary technician who conveys and explains treatment and subsequent animal care to the animal's owner. Technicians may have to help euthanize (humanely kill) an animal that is very sick or severely injured and cannot get well. As a result, they must be emotionally stable and help pet owners deal with their grief and loss.

EXPLORING

High school students can acquire exposure to the veterinary field by working with animals in related settings. For example, a high school student may be able to work as a part-time animal attendant or receptionist in a private veterinary practice. Paid or volunteer positions may be available at kennels, animal shelters, and training schools. However, direct work with animals in a zoo is unlikely for high school students.

EMPLOYERS

There are 79,200 veterinary technicians and technologist employed in the United States. Veterinary technicians are employed by veterinary clinics, animal hospitals, zoos, schools, universities, and animal training programs. They also work in boarding kennels, animal shelters, and rescue leagues. In rural areas, farmers hire veterinary technicians as well as veterinarians. Jobs for veterinary technicians in zoos are relatively few, since there are only a certain number of zoos across the country. Those veterinary technicians with an interest in research should seek positions at schools with academic programs for medical science or veterinary medicine. The majority of veterinary technicians find employment in animal hospitals or private veterinary practices, which exist all over the country. However, there are more job opportunities for veterinary technicians in more densely populated areas.

STARTING OUT

Veterinary technicians who complete an accredited program and become certified or registered by the state in which they plan to practice are often able to receive assistance in finding a job through their college's career services office. Students who have completed internships may receive job offers from the place where they interned.

Veterinary technician graduates may also learn of clinic openings through classified ads in newspapers. Opportunities in zoos and research facilities are usually listed in specific industry periodicals such as *Veterinary Technician* and *AZVT News*, a newsletter published by the Association of Zoo Veterinary Technicians.

ADVANCEMENT

Where a career as a veterinary technician leads is entirely up to the individual. Opportunities are unlimited. With continued education, veterinary technicians can move into allied fields such as veterinary medicine, nursing, medical technology, radiology, and pharmacology. By completing two more years of college and receiving a bachelor's degree, a *veterinary technician* can become a *veterinary technologist*. Advanced degrees can open the doors to a variety of specialized fields. There are currently efforts to standardize requirements for veterinary technicians. A national standard would broaden the scope of educational programs and may create more opportunities in instruction for veterinary professionals with advanced degrees.

EARNINGS

Earnings are generally low for veterinary technicians in private practices and clinics, but pay scales are steadily climbing due to the increasing demand. Better-paying jobs are in zoos and in research. Those fields of practice are very competitive (especially zoos) and only a small percentage of highly qualified veterinary technicians are employed in them.

Most veterinary technicians are employed in private or clinical practice and research. The U.S. Department of Labor reports that the median annual salary for veterinary technicians and technologists was $29,280 in 2009. The lowest paid 10 percent made less than $20,180 annually, and the highest paid 10 percent made more than $43,080 annually. Earnings vary depending on practice setting, geographic location, level of education, and years of experience. Benefits vary and depend on each employer's policies.

WORK ENVIRONMENT

Veterinary technicians generally work 40-hour weeks, which may include a few long weekdays and alternated or rotated Saturdays. Hours may fluctuate, as veterinary technicians may need to have their schedules adjusted to accommodate emergency work.

A veterinary technician must be prepared for emergencies. In field or farm work, they often have to overcome weather conditions in treating the animal. Injured animals can be very dangerous, and veterinary technicians have to exercise extreme caution when caring for them. A veterinary technician also handles animals that are diseased or infested with parasites. Some of these conditions, such as ringworm, are contagious, so the veterinary technician must understand how these conditions are transferred to humans and take precautions to prevent the spread of diseases.

People who become veterinary technicians care about animals. For this reason, maintaining an animal's well-being or helping to cure an ill animal is very rewarding work. In private practice, technicians get to know the animals they care for. This provides the opportunity to actually see the animals' progress. In other areas, such as zoo work, veterinary technicians work with very interesting, sometimes endangered, species. This work can be challenging and rewarding in the sense that they are helping to save a species and continuing efforts to educate people about these animals. Veterinary technicians who work in research gain satisfaction from knowing their work contributes to promoting both animal and human health.

OUTLOOK

Employment for veterinary technicians will grow much faster than the average for all other occupations through 2018, according to the U.S. Department of Labor. Veterinary medicine is a field that is not adversely affected by the economy, so it does offer stability. Also, the availability of advanced veterinary services, such as preventative dental care and surgical procedures, will increase the demand for technicians that specialize in these areas. The public's love for pets coupled with higher disposable incomes will encourage continued demand for workers in this occupation.

FOR MORE INFORMATION

For information about certification in the research facility field, contact

American Association for Laboratory Animal Science
9190 Crestwyn Hills Drive

Memphis, TN 38125-8538
Tel: 901-754-8620
E-mail: info@aalas.org
http://www.aalas.org

For more information on careers, schools, certification, and other resources, contact the following organizations:

American Veterinary Medical Association
1931 North Meacham Road, Suite 100
Schaumburg, IL 60173-4360
Tel: 800-248-2862
http://www.avma.org

Association of Zoo Veterinary Technicians
http://www.azvt.org

National Association of Veterinary Technicians in America
1666 K Street, NW, Suite 260
Washington, DC 20006-1260
Tel: 888-996-2882
http://www.navta.net

For information on veterinary careers in Canada, contact
Canadian Veterinary Medical Association
339 Booth Street
Ottawa, ON K1R 7K1 Canada
Tel: 613-236-1162
E-mail: admin@cvma-acmv.org
http://www.canadianveterinarians.net

❑ WASTEWATER TREATMENT PLANT OPERATORS AND TECHNICIANS

OVERVIEW

Wastewater treatment plant operators control, monitor, and maintain the equipment and treatment processes in wastewater (sewage) treatment plants. They remove or neutralize the chemicals, solid materials, and organisms in wastewater so that the water is not polluted when it is returned to the environment. There are approximately 109,090 water and liquid waste treatment plant operators currently working in the United States.

Wastewater treatment plant technicians work under the supervision of wastewater treatment plant operators. Technicians take samples and monitor treatment to ensure treated water is safe for its intended use. Depending on the level of treatment, water is used for human consumption or for nonconsumptive purposes, such as field irrigation or discharge into natural water sources. Some technicians also work in labs, where they collect and analyze water samples and maintain lab equipment.

THE JOB

Wastewater from homes, public buildings, and industrial plants is transported through sewer pipes to treatment plants. The wastes include both organic and inorganic substances, some of which may be highly toxic, such as lead and mercury. Wastewater treatment plant operators and technicians regulate the flow of incoming wastewater by adjusting pumps, valves, and other equipment, either manually or through remote controls. They keep track of the various meters and gauges that monitor the purification processes and indicate how the equipment is operating. Using the information from these instruments, they control the pumps, engines, and generators that move the untreated water through the processes of filtration, settling, aeration, and sludge digestion. They also oper-

SCHOOL SUBJECTS
Chemistry, Mathematics

PERSONAL SKILLS
Mechanical/manipulative, Technical/scientific

MINIMUM EDUCATION LEVEL
Some postsecondary training

CERTIFICATION OR LICENSING
Required

WORK ENVIRONMENT
Indoors and outdoors, Primarily one location

ate chemical-feeding devices, collect water samples, and perform laboratory tests, so that the proper level of chemicals, such as chlorine, is maintained in the wastewater. Technicians may record instrument readings and other information in logs of plant operations. These logs are supervised and monitored by operators. Computers are commonly used to monitor and regulate wastewater treatment equipment and processes. Specialized software allows operators to store and analyze data, which is particularly useful when something in the system malfunctions.

The duties of operators and technicians vary somewhat with the size and type of plant where they work. In small plants, one person per shift may be able to do all the necessary routine tasks. But in larger plants, there may be a number of operators, each specializing in just a few activities and working as part of a team that includes engineers, chemists, technicians, mechanics, helpers, and other employees. Some facilities are equipped to handle both wastewater treatment and treatment of the clean water supplied to municipal water systems, and plant operators may be involved with both functions.

Other routine tasks that plant operators and technicians perform include maintenance and minor repairs on equipment such as valves and pumps. They may use common hand tools such as wrenches and pliers and special tools adapted specifically for the equipment. In large facilities, they also direct attendants and helpers who take care of some routine tasks and maintenance work. The accumulated residues of wastes from the water must be removed from the plant, and operators may dispose of these materials. Some of this final product, or sludge, can be reclaimed for uses such as soil conditioners or fuel for the production of electricity.

Technicians may also survey streams and study basin areas to determine water availability. To assist the engineers they work with, technicians prepare graphs, tables, sketches, and diagrams to illustrate survey data. They file plans and documents, answer public inquiries, help train new personnel, and perform various other support duties.

Plant operators and technicians sometimes have to work under emergency conditions, such as when heavy rains flood the sewer pipes, straining the treatment plant's capacity, or when there is a chlorine gas leak or oxygen deficiency in the treatment tanks. When a serious problem arises, they must work quickly and effectively to solve it as soon as possible.

REQUIREMENTS
High School

A high school diploma or its equivalent is required for a job as a wastewater treatment plant operator or technician, and additional specialized technical training is generally preferred for both positions. A desirable background for this work includes high school courses in chemistry, biology, mathematics, and computers; welding or electrical training may be helpful as well. Other characteristics that employers look for include mechanical aptitude and the ability to perform mathematical computations easily. You should be able to work basic algebra and statistics problems. Future technicians may be required to prepare reports containing statistics and other scientific documentation. Communications, statistics, and algebra are useful for this career path. Such courses enable the technician to prepare graphs, tables, sketches, and diagrams to illustrate surveys for the operators and engineers they support.

Postsecondary Training

As treatment plants become more technologically complex, workers who have previous training in the field are increasingly at an advantage. Employers generally prefer to hire candidates with specialized education in wastewater technology available in two-year programs that lead to an associate's degree and one-year programs that lead to a certificate. Such programs, which are offered at some community and junior colleges and vocational-technical institutes, provide a good general knowledge of water pollution control and will prepare you to become an operator or technician. Beginners must still learn the details of operations at the plant where they work, but their specialized training increases their chances for better positions and later promotions.

Many operators and technicians acquire the skills they need during a period of on-the-job training. Newly hired workers often begin as attendants or operators-in-training. Working under the supervision of experienced operators, they pick up knowledge and skills by observing other workers and by doing routine tasks such as recording meter readings, collecting samples, and general cleaning and plant maintenance. In larger plants, trainees may study supplementary written material provided at the plant, or they may attend classes in which they learn plant operations.

Wastewater treatment plant operators and technicians often have various opportunities to continue learning about their field. Most state water pollution control agencies offer training courses for people employed in the field. Subjects covered by these training courses include principles of treatment processes and process control, odors and their control, safety, chlorination, sedimentation, biological oxidation, sludge treatment and disposal, and flow measurements. Correspondence courses on related subject areas also are available. Some employers help pay tuition for workers who take related college-level courses in science or engineering.

Certification or Licensing

Workers who control operations at wastewater treatment plants must be certified by the state in which they are employed. To obtain certification, operators must pass an examination given by the state. There is no nationwide standard, so different states administer different tests. Many states issue several classes of certification, depending on the size of the plant the worker is qualified to control. While some states may recognize certification from other states, operators who relocate may have to re-certify in the new state.

Other Requirements

Operators and technicians must be familiar with the provisions of the Federal Clean Water Act and various state and local regulations that apply to their work. Whenever they become responsible for more complex processes and equipment, they must become acquainted with a wider scope of guidelines and regulations. In larger cities and towns especially, job applicants may have to take a civil service exam or other tests that assess their aptitudes and abilities.

EXPLORING

It may be possible to arrange to visit a wastewater treatment plant to observe its operations. It can also be helpful to investigate courses and requirements of any programs in wastewater technology or environmental resources programs offered by a local technical school or college. Part-time or summer employment as a helper in a wastewater treatment plant could be a very helpful experience, but such a job may be hard to find. A job in any kind of machine shop can still provide you with an opportunity to become familiar with handling machinery and common tools.

Ask wastewater plant operators or technicians in your city if you can interview them about their jobs. Learning about water conservation and water quality in general can be useful. Government agencies or citizen groups dedicated to improving water quality or conserving water can educate you about water quality and supply in your area.

EMPLOYERS

More than three-quarters of the approximately 109,090 wastewater treatment plant operators in the United States are employed by local governments; others work for water, sewage, and other systems utility companies, the federal government, or private sanitary services that operate under contracts with local governments. Jobs are located throughout the country, with the greatest numbers found in areas with high populations.

Wastewater treatment plant operators and technicians can find jobs with state or federal water pollution control agencies, where they monitor plants and provide technical assistance. Examples of such agencies are the Army Corps of Engineers and the Environmental Protection Agency. These jobs normally require vocational/technical school or community college training. Other experienced wastewater workers find employment with industrial wastewater treatment plants, companies that sell wastewater treatment equipment and chemicals, large utilities, consulting firms, or as instructors at vocational/technical schools.

STARTING OUT

Graduates of most postsecondary technical programs and some high schools can get help in locating job openings from the career services office of the school they attended. Another source of information is the local office of the state employment service. Job seekers may also directly contact state and local water pollution control agencies and the personnel offices of wastewater treatment facilities in desired locations.

In some plants, a person must first work as a wastewater treatment plant technician before becoming an operator or working in a supervisory position. Wastewater treatment plant technicians have many of the same duties as a plant operator but less responsibility. They inspect, study, and sample existing water treatment systems and evaluate new structures for efficacy and safety. Support work and instrumentation reading make up the bulk of the technician's day.

The Internet has become a useful resource for finding job leads. Professional associations, such as the Water Environment Federation (http://www.wef.org), offer job listings in the wastewater field as part of their Web site. Such sites are a good place for someone getting started in the field, as they also list internship or trainee positions available. Also, an Internet search using the words "wastewater treatment plant operator or technician" will generate a list of Web sites that may contain job postings and internship opportunities.

ADVANCEMENT

As operators gain skills and experience, they are assigned tasks that involve more responsibility for more complex activities. Some technicians advance to become operators. Some operators advance to become *plant supervisors* or *plant superintendents*. The qualifications that superintendents need are related to the size and complexity of the plant. In smaller plants, experienced operators with some postsecondary training may be promoted to superintendent positions. In larger plants, educational requirements are increasing along with the sophistication and complexity of their systems, and superintendents usually have bachelor's degrees in engineering or science.

Some operators and technicians advance by transferring to a related job. Such jobs may require additional schooling or training to specialize in water pollution control, commercial wastewater equipment sales, or teaching wastewater treatment in a vocational or technical school.

EARNINGS

Salaries of wastewater treatment plant operators and technicians vary depending on factors such as the size of the plant, the workers' job responsibilities, and their level of certification. According to the U.S. Department of Labor, water and liquid waste treatment plant operators earned median annual salaries of $39,850 in 2009. The lowest paid 10 percent earned $24,580 or less, while the highest paid 10 percent earned $62,200 or more a year. In local government, plant operators earned a median salary of $41,330 in 2008.

In addition to their pay, most operators and technicians receive benefits such as life and health insurance, a pension plan, and reimbursement for education and training related to their job.

WORK ENVIRONMENT

In small towns, plant operators may only work part time or may handle other duties as well as wastewater treatment. The size and type of plant also determine the range of duties. In larger plants with many employees, operators and technicians usually perform more specialized functions. In some cases, they may be responsible for monitoring only a single process. In smaller plants, workers will likely have a broader range of responsibilities. Wastewater treatment plants operate 24 hours a day, every day of the year. Operators and technicians usually work one of three eight-hour shifts, often on a rotating basis so that employees share the evening and night work. Overtime is often required during emergencies.

The work takes operators and technicians both indoors and outdoors. They must contend with noisy machinery and may have to tolerate unpleasant odors, despite the use of chlorine and other chemicals to control odors. The job involves moving about, stooping, reaching, and climbing. Operators and technicians often get their clothes dirty. Slippery sidewalks, dangerous gases, and malfunctioning equipment are potential hazards on the job, but by following safety guidelines, workers can minimize their risk of injury.

OUTLOOK

Employment in this field is expected to grow much faster than the average for all occupations through 2018. The number of job applicants in this field is generally low due to the unclean and physically demanding nature of the work. However, this relative lack of competition means that you can enter the field with ease, given you have adequate experience. The growth in demand for wastewater treatment will be related to the overall growth of the nation's population and economy. New treatment plants will probably be built, and existing ones will be upgraded, requiring additional trained personnel to manage their operations. Other openings will arise when experienced workers retire or transfer to new occupations. Operators and technicians with formal training will have the best chances for new positions and promotions.

Workers in wastewater treatment plants are rarely laid off, even during a recession, because wastewater treatment is essential to public health and welfare. In the future, more wastewater professionals will probably be employed by private companies that contract to manage treatment plants for local governments.

FOR MORE INFORMATION

For current information on the field of wastewater management, contact

American Water Works Association
6666 West Quincy Avenue
Denver, CO 80235-3098
Tel: 800-926-7337
http://www.awwa.org

For information on education and training, contact
Environmental Careers Organization
Tel: 480-515-2525
E-mail: admin@eco.org
http://www.eco.org

National Environmental, Safety and Health Training Association
PO Box 10321
Phoenix, AZ 85064-0321
Tel: 602-956-6099
E-mail: neshta@neshta.org
http://www.neshta.org

For career information, contact or visit the following Web site:
Water Environment Federation
601 Wythe Street
Alexandria, VA 22314-1994
Tel: 800-666-0206
http://www.wef.org